Black Spark, White Fire

Did African Explorers Civilize Ancient Europe?

RICHARD POE

Guardian
(888) 482-7342

Prima Publishing

1 888 482-7352

Published by Prima Publishing, Roseville, California. Member of the Crown Publishing Group, a division of Random House, Inc.

PRIMA PUBLISHING and colophon are trademarks of Random House, Inc., registered with the United States Patent and Trademark Office.

Cover illustration by Richard Neave (facial reconstruction) and Russ Adams (color and clothing). Cover design by The Salmon Studio.

Library of Congress Cataloging-in-Publication Data

Poe, Richard.
  Black spark, white fire : did African explorers civilize ancient Europe? / Richard Poe.
    p. cm.
  Includes bibliographical information and index.
  ISBN 0-7615-0758-2
  ISBN 0-7615-2163-1 (pbk.)
    1. Europe—Discovery and exploration—Egyptian. I. Title.
D62.P63   1997
936—dc21   97-27713
                                                            CIP

02 03 04 05 HH 10 9 8 7 6 5 4 3
Printed in the United States of America
First Paperback Edition

Visit us online at www.primapublishing.com

To my wife, Marie

ABOUT THE COVER ILLUSTRATION

The face on the cover of this book is a forensic reconstruction made from the skull of an Egyptian priest named Natsef-Amun, who died around 1100 B.C. Created by forensic artist Richard Neave at the University of Manchester in 1989, it reproduces the features of Natsef-Amun with sufficient accuracy that his friends and relatives would probably have been able to recognize him from it.

Neave's original sculpture was unpainted. It was also bald, since Natsef-Amun had the shaven head typical of Egyptian priests. For *Black Spark, White Fire,* illustrator Russ Adams added color and clothing. The wig and collar are composites of typical Egyptian apparel. The headdress is copied from Natsef-Amun's mummy case. The skin color is hypothetical.

Because of Natsef-Amun's Negroid features, Neave believes that he was Nubian, and therefore painted him with dark brown skin in his final version of the sculpture (see Figure 1). However, bioanthropologists point out that Natsef-Amun was just as likely to have been a native Egyptian. His skin color could have ranged from very light to very dark. For a full discussion of Natsef-Amun, see chapter 71.

CONTENTS

v

FOREWORD

THE LAST TIME I VISITED EGYPT, I STOOD IN THE GREAT HYPOSTYLE Hall at the Karnak Temple—a sanctuary to the god Amun that is considered to be the most massive religious site in the world. There, I struck up a conversation with an Australian tourist who was visiting the temple for the second time in twenty years.

"You wouldn't believe how ignorant I was of the antiquity of Africa when I first visited this temple, twenty years ago," he confided to me.

"What struck you about this temple then?" I asked.

"I remember thinking to myself how much older the Parthenon must be than Karnak," he admitted.

In fact, the Karnak Temple was already more than a thousand years in the making, by the time the Parthenon was constructed, in the fifth century B.C. It had seen the faces of Thutmose III, Ramesses II, Amenhotep III, Akhnaton, and Hatshepsut. As I listened to the Australian visitor, I knew exactly what was coming next, because I had heard so many similar stories, and witnessed so many similar revelations in the minds of people, awed by their first confrontation with Africa's antiquity.

"It is unfortunate," said the Australian tourist, "that the world knows so little about the classical civilizations of Africa." Indeed it is. I assured my companion that one of the principal missions of my own life, as an author and scholar, has been to present those civilizations in their true light, so that others would appreciate the age and grandeur of those cultures that I have named "classical Africa."

As an educator, I am constantly searching for reliable and accurate books that will help my students comprehend Africa's enormous impact on the development of Western civilization. Such texts are, unfortunately, few and far between. But, when the manuscript of Richard Poe's *Black Spark, White Fire* first came across my desk, in the summer of 1997, I knew that I had struck gold.

In *Black Spark, White Fire*, Poe has provided an overwhelming and convincing case for rethinking European history in the light of its long relationship with Africa. Much of the evidence he cites has long been familiar to readers of Afrocentric literature. We find, for example, the story of Count Constantin de Volney, who traveled to Egypt in the eighteenth century and was moved, by his examination of the ruins of "classical Africa," to conclude that Europe owed all of its arts and sciences to what he called a "black race of men."

We find also a thorough discussion of the debt which Greek philosophy owed to African learning, as admitted by the Greek writers themselves. We hear, for instance, how Herodotos, writing in the fifth century B.C., attributed to Egypt the invention of astronomy, religion, medicine, art, geometry, and the making of solemn processions. We read of the long list of Greek scholars and sages who studied in Africa, such as Thales, Eudoxos, Solon, Democritos, and Plato—a list that includes Pythagoras, the first Greek to call himself a *philosophos* or "philosopher."

We also read, in *Black Spark, White Fire*, of the Greek legends concerning Egyptian explorers who colonized Greece, in ancient times—an old theory recently resurrected by Martin Bernal in *Black Athena.*

All of this material is familiar, in one form or another, to serious students of "classical Africa," and has been available for generations. Poe is neither the first to present it, nor will he be the last. But Poe's work is unique in many respects.

Others have focused on these issues in very specific ways. But *Black Spark, White Fire* covers all the ground simultaneously. Through its great breadth, the book pulls together all the different strands of information, to provide an unusually holistic picture of classical Africa's impact on the West. It is also highly readable. The writing is crisp and clean, the arguments fresh and captivating, filled with new interpretations of data.

Black Spark, White Fire is truly a wonderful book. In some respects, Poe has achieved what others only tried to achieve. What emerges is a brilliant, thoroughgoing narrative of cultural and historical fact. It repositions the discourse on the interaction between ancient Africa and ancient Europe in a remarkably intelligent way.

Poe has produced a classic volume that will stun some but will be discussed by popular and specialized audiences for many years to come. It is a book splendid in its conception, and powerful in its execution—a major work.

The title of *Black Spark, White Fire* provides an appropriate metaphor for the impact of Africa on Europe. For centuries, the testimony of ancient authors, such as Herodotos and Diodoros—who attributed much of Greek civilization to African influence—was accepted as true. But following the enslavement and colonization process that began in the fifteenth century, Africans were reduced to inferior status. It became unthinkable that Africa could have given any "sparks" to Europe.

In recent years, the tide has begun to turn back to the view that prevailed in the ancient world. Many serious scholars, including Cheikh Anta Diop, Theophile Obenga, and Martin Bernal have concluded, not only that the Nile Valley Civilizations were central to the rise of Western culture, but that the people who created those civilizations were black. In *Black Spark, White Fire*, Richard Poe has summarized the new thinking in terms that are easily grasped by the popular reader.

Poe has ventured into the realm of the taboo. He has dared to ask, "How African is Europe?" Some of the evidence he presents is provocative. But all of it is based on a thorough examination of the data available so far. With great critical acumen and a broad knowledge of prehistory and the ancient world, Poe has created an engaging and plausible picture of the role of blacks in bringing civilization to Europe.

— DR. MOLEFI KETE ASANTE
PROFESSOR OF AFRICAN-AMERICAN STUDIES,
TEMPLE UNIVERSITY, AND AUTHOR OF
THE AFROCENTRIC IDEA AND *CLASSICAL AFRICA*

ACKNOWLEDGMENTS

MY FATHER, ALFRED POE, PASSED AWAY IN FEBRUARY, 1997. HE did not live to see this book completed, but every page of it bears his imprint. Words cannot express my gratitude toward him, nor can they capture the beauty of his wise and gentle soul. My father taught me to love history and to respect all people. He was the finest man I ever knew.

Special thanks go to my wife, Marie, who has been my tireless collaborator in the *Black Spark, White Fire* film project, through six long years, during which it often seemed that we were the only two people in the world who believed in it. I am indebted also to Jennifer Basye Sander, the acquisition editor at Prima Publishing who first recognized the value of *Black Spark*. Thanks also to Ben Dominitz, who took a big chance on this book, and to Susan Silva, who carried the project through to completion, after Jennifer departed.

The beautiful cover I owe principally to Mary Beth Salmon, who so brilliantly designed it, as well as to Richard Neave, for kindly granting us the use of his forensic reconstruction. Thanks also to illustrator Russ Adams, for the excellent job he did colorizing and clothing Neave's reconstruction, and to Jim Long and Victor Kongkadee, for their technical assistance in this monumental, and often thankless, task.

I would like to thank project editor Brenda Nichols and copy editor Joan Pendleton for a superb performance under great pressure, as well as all the other people—too numerous to name—in sales, publicity, and other departments, who have helped make *Black Spark, White Fire* a success.

The enormous research required for this project compelled me to hire a small army of assistants. Special thanks go to researcher Veronica Kalas for her massive efforts at the library, as well as to researcher Marcus Boon and translator Kim Gladman for their small, but critical contributions. Thanks also to all the other researchers and translators who contributed to this book but prefer to remain anonymous.

A number of scholars have been tremendously supportive, offering freely of their time and knowledge, and, in some cases, critiquing some or all of the manuscript. I give special thanks to Shomarka Keita, Martin Bernal, and Frank Yurco. Also helpful have been Joseph Greenberg, Bruce Williams, Theodore Spyropoulos, and Frank Snowden, Jr. To all of these scholars—and to many more, too numerous to mention—I am indebted for whatever information I may have gotten right, in this book. Only I am responsible, however, for the errors it may contain.

This is especially true in the case of Frank Snowden, who very graciously answered questions and provided background material, but who strongly disagrees with the fundamental premise of *Black Spark, White Fire*—and perhaps also with my specific interpretations of his work. Since Snowden, regrettably, did not have the opportunity to review the chapters pertaining to his work (due to my time constraints), I feel particularly responsible for any errors I may have made in presenting his ideas.

In our six-year struggle to win academic and financial support for *Black Spark, White Fire,* many doors were slammed in our faces. But others were opened wide. Our earliest supporters have won a special place in our hearts. Among them are Martin Bernal, Shomarka Keita, Frank Yurco, Molefi Kete Asante, John Peradotto, Molly Levine, Phillip Aaron, Fran Pappas, Apostolos D. Fliakos, Armstrong Williams, Paul Zane Pilzer, Dean Williamson, Evelyn B. Kalibala at the New York City Board of Education, Susan Fox at WNET-TV, and Arthur Polk and Katie LaMar Coles of the National Black Republican Council. Special thanks go to Robert Catell and Charles Inniss of Brooklyn Union Gas, who authorized the first and only corporate grant that we have ever managed to raise for *Black Spark, White Fire.*

These acknowledgments would not be complete without mentioning my mother, Lillian Poe, who probably did more than anyone else, through the years, to encourage my interest in Egypt and other ancient civilizations. If I ever finish the "Egyptian novel" that I began at the age of 12, it will be as much her triumph as mine.

INTRODUCTION

IN PITCHING *BLACK SPARK, WHITE FIRE* TO PUBLISHERS AND LITERARY agents, I was challenged, again and again, to explain why a mere journalist should presume to write about a subject as specialized as Bronze Age archaeology. After all, I did not possess a Ph.D. in the subject. Of what value was my opinion?

In fact, a journalist has many key advantages over a scholar, when it comes to writing about ancient history. One of these advantages is the freedom to write or think whatever he wishes—a freedom that scholars do not possess. Each time scholars put pen to paper, their opinions are scrutinized by older and better-established colleagues, ready to savage them at a moment's notice, should they stray too far from the approved paths.

In the course of researching this book, I read many academic papers. Time and again, I was shocked to see how readily mature and influential scholars will attack their younger and more vulnerable colleagues—often in the most mean-spirited and personal fashion—for no other reason than the fact that the younger scholar had the audacity to disagree with them.

Such attacks can cost a young scholar far more than hurt feelings. If they come from a sufficiently influential source, they can cost jobs, grants, and reputation. For that reason, scholars learn early to observe a Byzantine code of etiquette, that invariably dictates which areas are open to speculation, and which are considered off limits.

The power of orthodox opinion over scholars can clearly be seen in the writings of Mary Lefkowitz, a professor of classics at Wellesley College. Lefkowitz has made something of a career, in recent years, of debunking Afrocentrism. In her 1996 book *Not Out of Africa,* she explained some of the reasons for her intense opposition to Afrocentric ideas. Lefkowitz wrote:

To respond to the kinds of allegations that are now being made [by Afrocentrists] requires us in effect to start from the beginning, to explain the nature of the ancient evidence, and to discuss what has long been known and established as if it were now subject to serious question. In short, we are being put on the defensive. . . . Worst of all, making this sort of defense keeps us from going on to discover new material and bring our attention to bear on real interpretative problems. Instead of getting on with our work, we must rehearse what has long been known.[1]

In Professor Lefkowitz's view, "what has long been known and established" is evidently sacrosanct. It should not be questioned, and scholars should not have to waste their time rethinking or defending it. Instead, they should be left alone to focus on "real" problems—by which she apparently means problems that do not challenge orthodox opinion in any fundamental way.

The very fact that a scholar of Lefkowitz's standing could feel justified in making such a pronouncement shows how far our universities have drifted from the Greek ideal—the very ideal that Lefkowitz purports to defend.

It was precisely those things that had "long been known and established" that Sokrates found to be in the greatest need of questioning. Nothing was sacrosanct or above question, in Sokrates' view, not even the very stories of the gods. When confronted by a new idea—no matter how rash or youthful its author, and no matter how wild the idea itself—Sokrates always responded with the same eager curiosity. "Instruct me," he would say. "Enlighten me, in my ignorance." Only by presuming ourselves to be ignorant, and by constantly questioning our most basic assumptions, Sokrates taught, can we even begin to approach the truth.

Of course, it would hardly be fair or realistic to ask scholars to suddenly shed their fear, open their minds and start behaving like Sokrates. This is not a good strategy for people who have bills to pay, mouths to feed, and retirements to plan. In Sokrates' case, it earned him only a death sentence.

But that is where journalists come in. We have the peculiar privilege of being able to flit from one expert to another, asking whatever questions we wish, and drawing whatever conclusions seem reasonable. We can balance the opinions of conventional experts against those of dissident experts. We can conduct our own research, to try to discern which expert seems closer to the truth. Most important of all, should we find that the dissident's story seems more believable than the official story, we may offer this opinion bluntly, with little fear of professional persecution.

Journalists, in short, are the voice of common sense. We are ordinary people, not experts. We bring no wealth of specialized knowledge to a story. But we bring naiveté—an asset that, in many ways, proves far more important, in seeking the truth. Thomas Jefferson once wrote:

> Men by their constitution are naturally divided into two parties.
> 1. Those who fear and distrust the people, and wish to draw all powers from them into the hands of the higher classes. 2dly those who identify themselves with the people, have confidence in them, cherish and consider them as the most honest and safe, although not the most wise depository of the public interests.[2]

The first of these two factions Jefferson called "aristocrats." The second he called "democrats." We find representatives of these opposing factions duking it out over Afrocentrism, just as we find them battling over every other important issue in society. The indignant tone with which Lefkowitz complains of unauthorized questioning from the masses, clearly marks her as an aristocrat.

In *Black Spark, White Fire* we will try to explore the question of Afrocentrism more as Sokrates would have done—with a humble and open mind. Jefferson admitted that we ordinary folk are not always "wise" in our thinking. But we have the advantage of being "honest"—a virtue that, in Jefferson's view, makes us far more likely, in the long run, to choose the right path. I sincerely believe that only a journalist's peculiar blend of naiveté, common sense— and, of course, perennial suspicion—could even begin to untangle the mass of contradictions that experts have managed to weave around the Afrocentric issue.

All of these are good reasons for writing *Black Spark, White Fire.* But, of course, they are not my only reasons. In many respects, this book has been forming inside me since childhood. It began with a small gift from my mother—a little plastic model of "King Tut," that she had bought in a museum gift shop. "King Tut" was fitted with magnets, so that when you shook his sarcophagus, in a certain way, the opposing magnetic fields would cause him to jump or "rise from his tomb."

For some reason, King Tut immediately became my favorite toy. From the moment he was given to me, I could not bear to be separated from him. Every night, for years, I slept with King Tut clenched tightly in my hand, much as other children clutch their stuffed animals. I must confess that he sits on my desk, to this day.

As I grew older, of course, I outgrew my attachment to "King Tut," the toy. But I never lost the conviction that Tutankhamun—the real-life pharaoh, whom "King Tut" represented—was, in some way, my personal property. As I began reading books about Egypt, and learning about the country's ancient history, Tutankhamun predictably became my favorite Egyptian monarch.

I was not yet able to read—and therefore could not have been older than five, or so—when my mother pointed out to me, one day, that one of the photographs in a set of books we had, called *Lands and Peoples*, was of King Tutankhamun. It portrayed one of the painted funerary statues found in Tut's tomb. As anyone who has seen these statues knows, they show the king with coal-black skin. I now know that experts—whether rightly or wrongly—consider this color to be symbolic and conventional, and not at all representative of Tut's actual appearance. As a four- or five-year-old child, however, I had not yet encountered this explanation.

"Why is he black?" I asked my mother.

Mama studied the picture, for a moment, and shrugged. "I don't know," she finally said. "Maybe the Egyptians were black."

I distinctly remember that this answer did not seem right to me, at the time. My childish sense of consistency simply could not reconcile a black Tutankhamun with the reddish-brown Egyptians I had seen, in other pictures. In the end, I put the issue aside. It would be many years before I would think again about the racial identity of the ancient Egyptians.

About the Egyptians, in general, however—and about King Tut, in particular—I continued to think a great deal. In the first grade, I embarrassed my parents by laboriously copying and coloring a panel of Egyptian hieroglyphs from a book, and then telling my class, during show-and-tell, that I had copied them directly from an Egyptian tomb, while on holiday in Egypt with my parents. My teacher, Miss Goodman, believed me. But the deception came unraveled when she asked my parents, at a PTA meeting, about their nonexistent trip to Egypt.

At the age of 12, I conceived the idea of writing a historical novel about Egypt. My continuing enthusiasm for the "boy pharaoh," Tutankhamun, left no question, in my mind, that the novel would have to be set in the late Eighteenth Dynasty, and that one of its principal characters would have to be Tut.

I envisioned the novel as a grand, Micheneresque saga of the Egyptian royal family, that would follow its fortunes from the glory days of Amenhotep III, through the decline of the Empire, under Akhnaton, and end with the dynasty's final collapse, upon the death of Tutankhamun.

For more than a year, I worked fanatically on the project, spending every Saturday afternoon in the public library, where I buried my nose in great, dusty volumes by James Henry Breasted and Gaston Maspero until my eyes ached from the strain. Much to the disgust of my brother Dennis, who slept in the bunk bed above me, the floor beside my bed became cluttered with grocery boxes filled with books and notes pertaining to my "Egyptian novel." All this research proved futile, however, when I finally set out to start writing.

I had not written more than a chapter or two, before it became painfully apparent that I simply did not know how to create adult characters convincingly. I was, after all, just a kid. I didn't even know what made modern adults tick, much less adults 3,500 years in the past. With a heavy heart, I resigned myself to the conclusion that I was simply not old enough, yet, to write the book, and I put the project aside until some future date, when time and maturity would hopefully have healed this deficiency.

To this day, it remains my ambition to bring Eighteenth Dynasty Egypt to life, in fiction, as convincingly as Mary Renault resurrected Mycenaean Greece or Henryk Sienkiewicz Nero's Rome. As I approach midlife, I have almost reached the point where I understand what makes adults tick. In many ways, *Black Spark, White Fire* is an expression of my growing readiness to take up the literary torch that I dropped so many years ago.

In writing this book, I realized how little my priorities had changed, since those long-ago years when I sat in the Syracuse Public Library, plotting my Egyptian epic. Then, as now, I found myself acting as advocate and apologist for my beloved Egypt, attempting to prove to an indifferent world that the Egyptians were every bit as wonderful and accomplished as the Greeks or Romans.

The images of Rome's imperial power, evoked in such movies as *Ben-Hur, Quo Vadis,* and *The Robe,* aroused my admiration as a boy and contributed greatly to my decision in high school to study Latin, rather than some more "useful" language. But I longed to see Egypt portrayed, in Hollywood, with a similar emphasis on its imperial might.

During the research for my abortive novel, I had been deeply impressed to learn that Egypt, in the Eighteenth Dynasty, was a real empire, with extensive conquests in Nubia and Syria–Palestine. In my novel, it was Egypt's role as world conqueror that I wished to convey more than anything else. What a strangely familiar feeling it was, then, to find myself writing away at the section of *Black Spark, White Fire* entitled, "When Egypt Ruled the Waves."

In the most concrete sense, *Black Spark, White Fire* got underway in January 1992. My wife Marie and I had just taken the rather reckless step of getting married and leaving our respective jobs, both at the same time. Vowing that we would never return to the 9-to-5 corporate life, we sought to pool our talents—mine as a writer and Marie's as a television producer—in some worthwhile project that we could pursue together.

I had followed the growing controversy, in the press, over Martin Bernal's *Black Athena*—a book that presents evidence that Egyptians and Phoenicians may have colonized Greece in ancient times. The book was highly technical and, after reading the first volume, it seemed to me that a television documentary translating Bernal's theories into plain English would find a wide and enthusiastic audience.

Later, I realized that tying the project too closely to Bernal's book might prove limiting, since there were many points (minor ones, mostly) on which I disagreed with Bernal, and many other ideas that I wished to emphasize—such as the alleged "blackness" of the Egyptians—that received only passing mention in *Black Athena*. Thus was born *Black Spark, White Fire*—a television documentary which would be written by me, produced by my wife, and, hopefully, aired on some national network.

For nearly three years, we beat the bushes, trying to raise money for the production. Virtually every door was slammed in our faces. Potential grantors turned us down, by the droves. In promoting and researching the project, we spent over $10,000 out of our pockets, at a time when we often did not know how we would come up with the next month's rent.

By 1994, we realized that, if the film was ever going to be made, we would have to pay for it ourselves. It was then that I undertook to write *Black Spark, White Fire* as a book. If it sold well, we calculated, the income from the book could finance the documentary. Getting the book published, however, turned out to be almost as difficult as finding sponsors for the film. The biggest challenge turned out to be finding a literary agent who would represent it.

"Blacks don't read," said some of the agents. "This subject has already been done to death," opined others. "You're not a scholar," objected a few. "There's no market for this," declared most of them. And then there was my favorite objection of all, raised by nearly all the agents to whom I pitched the book: "You're not black. A book like this should be written by a black author." In short, the excuses were many and varied, but the decision was almost always the same: No thanks.

Not all the agents offered excuses or evasions. Some were quite blunt in stating their personal opposition to the book's subject matter. "I'm sure you'll find someone to publish it, and I'm sure you'll sell a lot of books," one agent told me. "But, personally, I'm not interested. I just don't believe that the Egyptians were black."

"People don't want to hear this kind of thing nowadays," declared another agent, her eyes darkening with anger. "People are fed up with black rage. What people want now is black conservatism." The woman thereupon began to tell me about her elderly mother, who lived in a black neighborhood and risked getting mugged every time she went to the grocery store. The woman's point was clear: Any race of people who made life so miserable for her poor old mother did not deserve to be credited with building Egyptian civilization—even if they really did build it.

The unusual candor with which this woman revealed her political motivation was commendable. Less admirable was the unthinking ease with which she assumed that it was perfectly all right to suppress archaeological facts that happened to clash with her political opinions.

Accusations of a "political agenda" have become part of the standard repertoire of criticisms leveled against Afrocentrists. Yet, it is seldom pointed out that the critics of Afrocentrism often proceed from equally tainted motivations.

It has been my goal, in writing *Black Spark, White Fire,* to offer a discussion of the Afrocentric question that is as free as possible from ethnic, racial, and political partisanship. Toward this end, I find myself equipped with certain special advantages.

Because I believe in the inalienable and God-given right of all people to life, liberty, and the pursuit of happiness, I think I am on safe ground calling myself a liberal—at least, in the classical, eighteenth-century sense of that word. At the same time, the sort of "white guilt" that seems to pervade and define liberalism today is as foreign to me as the planet Neptune. I make no apology for my admiration of European civilization. Were I to rank the world's greatest works of literature, according to my personal taste, Homer's *Iliad* and *Odyssey* would undoubtedly appear at the top. I am not quite sure that I would bother filling in the other spaces.

I declare myself equally innocent of any attachment to the sort of fashionable "multiculturalism" that encourages people to place ethnic and racial loyalty above their common identity as Americans. Although my father was the son of Russian Jews and my mother the daughter of Mexican immigrants, both regarded themselves as Americans, pure and simple, and raised their children accordingly. Ethnic pride was not only ignored, in our household, but actively discouraged. The older I grow, the more grateful I have become for the gift of uncluttered and unhyphenated Americanism that my parents bestowed upon us.

It is in the area of ethnic pride that I, perhaps, differ most sharply from my wife. Marie is a Greek-American and proud of it. We live in a Greek neighborhood, celebrate Greek holidays, eat traditional Greek food, and every few weeks, it seems, attend some Greek family get-together, replete with bazouki music and zembekiko dancing.

Marie comes from the sort of people who insist that their kids march down Fifth Avenue, every year, in the Greek Independence Day parade. They are the sort of people who make sure that every paper coffee cup in their diners comes stamped with an image of the Parthenon. Neither Marie, nor her family, nor her multitudinous social and professional contacts in the Greek community, have any sympathy at all for the brand of Afrocentrism that seeks to disparage Greece and its remarkable ancient heritage.

In short, if I wish to live to see my next birthday, I have been obliged to refrain from allowing any hint of such anti-Hellenic sentiment to find its way into this book. Of course, this was never a danger, in any case. My personal admiration for Greece has been with me nearly as long as my enthusiasm for ancient Egypt.

I remember, with great vividness, the blackout of 1965, when electrical power was wiped out across much of the northeastern United States. With no television to entertain us, we sat around the table in our dark kitchen—I and my brothers and sisters—and listened while my father told us the story of the Trojan War.

He must have told us other stories, as well. The blackout lasted for most of the night. Yet, only the Trojan War has survived in my memory. I can still see the candlelight flickering across my father's face, as he told us of the rivalry between the goddesses Hera, Athena, and Aphrodite, of their ill-fated beauty contest, of Paris' reckless choice, of the kidnapping of Helen, and the war-fleet of Agamemnon.

The love that my father felt for classical antiquity was as tangible, that night, as the smell of candle wax, and far more contagious. Its impact has never left me. Years later, when I was nearly thirteen—and already heavily involved in researching my "Egyptian novel"—it emerged again, when I read *The King Must Die* by Mary Renault.

My mind filled with Renault's images of Bronze Age Greece, I remember gazing out my bedroom window, contemplating the bland expanse of suburban houses that stretched to every horizon. The sky was streaked, that evening, with rosy light, exactly like the light that must have appeared, I thought, in the sunset skies over Mycenaean Greece. No words can describe the nostalgia that filled me, in that moment, as I cursed my fate for placing me in 1971 America, rather than where I thought I really belonged, roaming the hills of prehistoric Attika, with Theseus and his warriors.

In writing *Black Spark, White Fire*, I have approached both Greece and Egypt as I would approach two old and dearly loved friends. Whether Greece or Egypt was "greater" is a matter of such supreme indifference to me that I cannot even comprehend the question. From childhood on, both peoples have enriched my life a thousandfold. I take pride in them equally. A lifetime of study and imagination has transformed them both into "my" people, in a way more intimate than any tie of blood.

Did I, in the final analysis, have a goal or ulterior motive in writing this book? If I did, it can only be this: that some reader, sometime, may draw from these pages the same enchantment that moved me that night in 1965, when my father's story brought me momentarily closer to the gods and heroes of ancient times. If I could touch but one reader with such a feeling, then this book will not have been written in vain.

— RICHARD POE

PART ONE

DARKEST
EUROPE

CHAPTER 1

"LIKE FROGS AROUND A POND"

W HEN JULIUS CAESAR MARCHED WITH HIS LEGIONS INTO Germany in 55 B.C., he entered a world nearly as alien and forbidding as the one that confronted Daniel Boone beyond the Cumberland Gap. Germania—as the Romans called it— was a tractless expanse of dense and misty forest, peopled by wild men. By night, the owls hooted and the virgin oaks dripped with mistletoe, casting gloomy shadows in the moonlight. Every creaking twig beyond the campfire might signal the stealthy advance of a bloodthirsty German war party, their yellow hair long and braided, their spears ready, their blue eyes staring like ice from the foliage.

There were no maps of Germany in Roman days. No explorer or geographer had ever penetrated its depths. According to Caesar, even the Germans themselves did not know the extent of their vast forest. He wrote, "There is no man in Germany we know who can say that he has reached the edge of that forest, though he may have gone forward a sixty days' journey, or who has learnt in what place it begins. It is known that many kinds of wild beasts not seen in any other places breed therein."[1]

Among the "wild beasts" unique to the German forest was one Caesar called the urus. "In size," he wrote, "these are somewhat

smaller than elephants; in appearance, color, and shape they are as
bulls. Great is their strength and great their speed, and they spare
neither man nor beast once sighted." Caesar described how the Germans would trap these fearsome brutes in pits, taking their great
horns and dressing them in silver to use as drinking cups at their
banquets.[2]

Modern readers stumbling upon this passage might easily conclude that Caesar was imagining things. Like the unicorn, the grif-
fin, the dragon, and the centaur, Caesar's urus seems, at first sight,
just one more fabulous creature from the menagerie of ancient
myth. Yet paleontologists are inclined to believe Caesar on this
point. He seems to have been describing a real animal, known as the
aurochs or *bos primigenius*—an enormous wild ox that roamed Europe in prehistoric times but is now extinct.[3] In the dense northern
woods of 55 B.C., this mighty denizen of the Ice Age seems to have
found a last refuge.

What other wonders that forest may once have contained, we
will never know, for the trees have long since been felled and the animals slain. Germany today is one of the most densely populated
and heavily industrialized countries on earth. Where once the
ground thundered to the aurochs' angry hoofs, now only the rush of
Volkswagens slices the air along superhighways lined with bill-
boards, charming towns, and gleaming industrial parks. Germany
has become the model for the new, integrated Europe. With all eyes
turning to Europe today as the wellspring of science, culture, commerce, and industry, it is easy to imagine that this neat and well-
ordered continent always lay at the center of civilized life, just as it
does now. But that is not the case.

For the Greeks and Romans, inland Europe was about as far from
the "center" as you could possibly get. Europe was the frontier, the
wilderness, the periphery. The only "center" recognized by the
Greeks and Romans lay smack in the middle of the Mediterranean
Sea—whose name in Latin means "the sea in the middle of the
world." Civilizations had huddled around the Mediterranean for
thousands of years, like shivering campers around a warm fire. Dependent on its fish and trade routes for their very life, the cultured
peoples whom the Mediterranean nurtured never wandered far from
its shores. "We live around a sea," said Sokrates, "like frogs around
a pond."[4]

But not all the frogs who lived around that pond evolved at an equal pace. Some Mediterranean peoples acquired civilization much faster than others. Recent excavations suggest that Beirut, for example—the capital of modern Lebanon—may have been founded around 3000 B.C.[5] Egypt was already a flourishing kingdom with great royal palaces and a rudimentary writing system at least 150 years before that.[6] Archaeologists have even discovered that a city surrounded by stone walls twenty feet high and nine feet thick, and equipped with at least one thirty-foot watchtower, stood on the site of biblical Jericho—now located in the state of Israel—as early as 8300 B.C.[7]

During all those busy centuries when the other nations of the Mediterranean "pond" were rushing to make their mark on the world, poor Europe seems to have been left behind.[8] The Egyptian pharaohs had been sitting on their thrones for at least two thousand years by the time Europe experienced its first major historical event—the Trojan War—sometime around 1250 B.C. As for the Romans, they arrived on the scene only yesterday. Rome had been founded a mere seven centuries before Caesar marched into Germany in 55 B.C.

Throughout the whole period of ancient history, the light of civilization shone very fitfully in Europe. In most parts of the continent, it did not shine at all. From the Golden Age of Athens in the fifth century B.C. to the fall of Rome in A.D. 476, the bulk of Europe's lands slept on beneath their forest canopy, as wild and mysterious as the deepest reaches of the Amazon.

The Greeks and Romans of classical times thought nothing of sailing the friendly Mediterranean. Wealthy Romans would book passage to Egypt or Palestine as casually as we might buy a plane ticket to London today. But to travel into Europe's dark interior was another matter. Nobody knew where such a journey might lead. And no one dared to find out. "The boundaries of Europe are quite unknown," wrote the Greek historian Herodotos (Herodotus) around 450 B.C., "and there is not a man who can say whether any sea girds it round either on the north or on the east."[9]

If the cultivated Mediterranean peoples feared Europe's interior, it seems that they had good reason, for its foggy woods held danger from man and beast alike. When, for example, the Persian king Xerxes invaded Greece in 480 B.C., lions attacked his baggage camels as he marched through Thrace and Macedonia. "That whole region is full of lions and wild bulls with gigantic horns," Herodotos commented.[10]

Wolves posed an even greater threat. Today, these predators are rare in Europe and protected by law. But, in times past, they roamed the land in droves. As recently as 1439, the city of Paris was besieged by wolf packs that emerged from the forest en masse, seizing and devouring innocent wayfarers at the very gates of the city.[11] In antiquity, the situation was far worse. The hills of Attika were so infested with these ravenous canines that, according to one Greek legend, marauding wolf packs once rampaged through the streets of Athens itself. Only the intervention of the god Apollo saved the frightened Athenians from the grisliest of deaths.[12]

For all that, Europe's most dangerous predators were not animals, but men. Greek and Roman writers such as Tacitus, Strabo, Polybios, and Julius Caesar have left us a vivid picture of Europe's feral inhabitants, a picture that leaves little doubt as to why most Greeks and Romans steered clear of the northern forests.

Perhaps the fiercest barbarians were the Celts. In battle, they made a hideous spectacle, stripping themselves naked and howling like beasts. Their hair, soaked with lime, stood back on their heads like horses' manes. Their bodies were painted blue with woad. The Celts would carry back the heads of their victims dangling from their saddles, embalm them in cedar oil and hang them outside their houses or display them to guests. Sometimes the Celts used captured heads as footballs.[13]

The peacetime habits of the Celts were hardly more congenial. According to Diodoros, they were "exceedingly addicted to the use of wine...and since they partake of this drink without moderation ...when they are drunken they fall into a stupor or a state of madness."[14]

Drunk or sober, a Celt was a dangerous companion. "It is their custom," wrote Diodoros, "even during the course of the meal, to seize upon any trivial matter as an occasion for disputation and then to challenge one another to single combat, without any regard for their lives."[15] Celtic table manners may have been appalling, but their sex lives were more frightful still. As late as the twelfth century A.D., the kings of one Irish clan still celebrated their coronations by engaging in ritual sexual intercourse with a horse.[16]

The Gauls of France were great enthusiasts of human sacrifice, which was carried out by holy men called Druids. To slay their victims more efficiently, the Gauls would sometimes construct huge hollow figures woven out of twigs, fill them with human beings, and set the whole contraption ablaze. "They believe that the execution of those who have been caught in the act of theft or robbery or some crime is more pleasing to the immortal gods," Caesar remarked, "but when the supply of such fails they resort to the execution even of the innocent."[17]

Nearly as disagreeable as the Celts were the Scythians, who roamed the vast grasslands of southern Russia. They were expert horsemen who lived and fought from their saddles. Herodotos—who traveled extensively in Scythia—saw the nomadic rootlessness of these people as a key to their military success. He wrote:

> A people without fortified towns, living, as the Scythians do, in waggons which they take with them wherever they go, accustomed, one and all, to fight on horseback with bows and arrows, and dependent for their food not upon agriculture but upon their cattle: how can such a people fail to defeat the attempt of an invader not only to subdue them, but even to make contact with them?[18]

Warlike peoples are often called bloodthirsty. But rarely is the term so literally accurate as when applied to the Scythians, who customarily drank the blood of the first man they slew in battle. In addition, the Scythians took scalps from their victims, softening these trophies by rubbing them between their hands and using them as napkins. "The Scyth is proud of these scalps and hangs them from his bridle-rein," Herodotos wrote. "The greater the number of such napkins that a man can show, the more highly is he esteemed among them."[19]

Some Scythian warriors would sew scalps together to make cloaks. Others would fashion quivers from the skin of their enemies' right arms.[20] For their most hated foes, they reserved a special humiliation. They would turn their enemies' skulls into drinking cups. More prosperous Scyths would line the interior of such skull-cups with gold. Herodotos observed, "They treat the skulls of their kinsmen in the same way, in cases where quarrels have occurred. ... When important visitors arrive, these skulls are passed round and the host tells the story of them: how they were once his relatives and made war against him, and how he defeated them—all of which passes for a proof of courage."[21]

Europeans of the nineteenth century often portrayed "Darkest Africa" as a land of ferocious beasts, impassable jungles, hungry cannibals, and malevolent witch doctors. But, in ancient times, Europe itself must have seemed every bit as perilous to wayfarers from afar. In those days, the term "Darkest Europe" would not have seemed out of place to cultivated travelers from more amicable southern climes.

How did it happen that two such refined peoples as the Greeks and Romans came to be clinging to Europe's Mediterranean coast? Compared to their head-hunting and blood-drinking neighbors, they seem almost like strangers on the continent. The Romans would certainly have agreed with this observation. They never doubted that civilization was foreign to their shores. Indeed, the Romans would have been the first to admit that they had acquired civilized ways from the Greeks, who colonized southern Italy around 750 B.C. From these Greek colonists, the Romans had acquired art, literature, stately buildings, and the worship of new gods. The experience transformed them from a rude, rustic people to the masters of a great empire.

But how had the *Greeks* acquired such polish? At a time when barbarism engulfed all of Europe, Greece alone rose to take its place among the literate and industrious nations of the Mediterranean "pond." For a thousand years, the Greeks alone knew the use of books, mathematics, architecture, and stonemasonry, while the rest of Europe slept. Whatever we mean when we speak of "European civilization," we find its first and purest expression in Greece.

Did the Greeks create this remarkable edifice all on their own? Or did they—like the Romans—have outside help? That is the question we will seek to answer in this book.

CHAPTER 2

WHO DISCOVERED
EUROPE?

MANY CLAIM NOWADAYS THAT CHRISTOPHER COLUMBUS DID not really "discover" America. After all, say the Columbus-bashers, the Indians knew it was here all along. More-over, the Vikings got here first, around A.D. 1000, and—according to a growing number of pre-Columbiana buffs—so did St. Brendan of Ireland in the sixth century, Prince Madoc of Wales in the twelfth, some anonymous Japanese fishermen around 3000 B.C., the Chinese monk Hui-Shen in about A.D. 629, and so on.

All of these arguments, while interesting, miss the point. Accord-ing to *Webster's Collegiate Dictionary,* tenth edition, a thing is "dis-covered" when it is made "known" or "visible." Columbus's achievement lay in the fact that he made America and its inhabi-tants known and visible to everyone else in the world—something neither the Indians nor the various pre-Columbian explorers, real or imaginary, had managed to accomplish.

In a similar way, someone must have discovered Europe once. Europe, as we have seen, was the last of the great Mediterranean regions to acquire civilization. At some time—long, long ago—

someone must have first revealed Europe's existence as a continent to its older and more sophisticated neighbors.

It probably did not happen suddenly and dramatically, as in 1492. Europe, after all, was not as far away as America, and it was connected to the civilized world by land. Its discovery was no doubt a gradual process. As trading expeditions from Egypt or the Near East inched their way slowly westward along Europe's southern shore, generations—perhaps centuries—may have passed before the traders realized the magnitude of this vast new frontier.

Of all regions in Europe, Greece was closest, geographically, to the civilized world, and so the early explorers would likely have found and colonized it first. In fact, Greek legends suggest that this is exactly what happened. The Greeks believed that foreigners came from across the sea, in archaic times, founded cities, established kingly dynasties, and taught the primitive Greeks the arts of reading, writing, building, and much more. The colonists even brought new gods.

A number of different stories in this vein circulated quite widely in ancient Greece. One set of legends told of Egyptian colonists who arrived with a fleet of ships and settled on the Peloponnesian peninsula. Their leader, Danaos, brought his fifty daughters with him from Egypt and made himself king of Argos. His dynasty later gave rise to such well-known heroes as Perseus and Herakles (Hercules). After alluding to the Danaos story in his *History*, Herodotos declares, "How it happened that Egyptians came to the Peloponnese and what they did to make themselves kings in that part of Greece, has been chronicled by other writers; I will add nothing therefore, but proceed to mention some points which no one else has yet touched upon."[1]

Unfortunately, the works of most of those "other writers" did not survive antiquity. We are left only with Herodotos's vague and tantalizing reference to Egyptian colonists—and with a keen regret that he did not continue his digression on the subject for just a few paragraphs longer!

Other legends speak of a second group of colonists, who came to Greece from Phoenicia, a cluster of city-states located on what is now the Lebanese coast. The most famous of these colonists was Kadmos, the traditional founder of Thebes in central Greece. Legend held that Kadmos was a Phoenician prince from the city of Tyre (or

Sidon, in some versions). Among other gifts, he brought to the Greeks the art of writing. Herodotos wrote, "The Phoenicians who came with Kadmos . . . introduced into Greece, after their settlement in the country, a number of accomplishments, of which the most important was writing, an art till then, I think, unknown to the Greeks."[2]

Nor was Greece the only part of Europe touched by these legendary explorers. According to Herodotos, an Egyptian pharaoh named Sesostris once led an army up through Turkey into the Caucasus, marched westward across southern Russia, and fought his way down through Romania and Bulgaria until he reached Thrace. On the way back home, Sesostris planted a colony on the eastern shore of the Black Sea. Herodotos claimed that he had seen the dark-skinned descendants of those Egyptian colonists, still living in the Caucasus after all those centuries.

Of course, the tales of Danaos, Kadmos, and Sesostris are only legends. Many Greeks in Herodotos's day questioned whether such men had ever really existed. These stories belonged to a time so long ago that the Greeks could conceive of it only in terms of fairy tales, complete with gods, giants, monsters, and heroes. They called this period the Heroic Age and thought of it much as we regard the time of King Arthur and his Round Table. To the Greeks, the Heroic Age was a time when men were bolder, stronger, taller, and more virtuous. It was the age of Jason and the Argonauts, of Herakles' Twelve Labors, of the magical voyages of Odysseus (Ulysses), and of Agamemnon's war against Troy.

As fanciful as these stories may seem, scholars have determined that at least some of them correspond to real history. The Trojan War, for example, most likely did occur. Archaeologists have found the remains of King Priam's fabled city on the Turkish coast, destroyed by fire sometime between 1250 and 1240 B.C.[3] This and other evidence has led scholars to conclude that the Greek legends of the Heroic Age are, in many cases, based on real events, most of which can be placed during a period that archaeologists have named the Bronze Age—roughly 3200 to 1200 B.C., in the eastern Mediterranean. If there ever existed any real-life counterparts to Kadmos, Sesostris, and Danaos, it is during these years that we must search for them.

CHAPTER 3

GOLD AND GLORY

WHAT WAS EUROPE LIKE DURING THE BRONZE AGE? WE HAVE already considered the barbarous habits that prevailed in much of Europe during the Greco-Roman period (roughly 776 B.C. to A.D. 476). How, then, should we imagine the continent two thousand years *earlier*—in a time when even the Greeks had barely emerged from the forests?

It was a far different Europe from any we are used to imagining. Most of the peoples familiar to us from classical antiquity—the Gauls, Britons, Germans, Scythians, Greeks, and Romans—would have been present, in some ancestral form, though possibly under different names. Many of these tribes would not have lived where we would expect to find them. The Celts, for example, had not yet invaded western Europe; and all the lands they would later make famous, such as Gaul, Britain, and Ireland, were then occupied by other peoples.

The late Marija Gimbutas—a renowned archaeologist of prehistoric times—described Bronze Age Europe as a "marble cake" of two great cultures.[1] The first culture she called Old European. Its people were the continent's original inhabitants. The Old Europeans, according to Gimbutas, raised the trilithons of Stonehenge and assembled the passage graves, standing stones, dolmens, and other prehistoric stoneworks whose massive, silent, and unexplained presence has long imparted to European landscapes an air of primitive mystery. Many of these people—such as the Basques of Spain and southern France—seem to have been direct descendants of the Stone Age Cro-Magnon race.[2] All of them appear to have followed the universal Stone Age religion, in that they worshiped the Great Goddess of the Earth as their chief deity.

Old Europe came to an end between 4400 and 3000 B.C.,[3] when the second great culture, the so-called Kurgan people, left their homeland in South Russia and came pouring into central and western Europe. For two thousand years, wave after wave of these eastern marauders descended on the defenseless farming settlements of Old Europe. Named by Gimbutas for their characteristic burial mounds (which the Russians call *kurgáni*), these invaders ranged across the continent as far as Britain and Ireland, burning, raping, and murdering with a fiendish abandon unmatched in later centuries until the depredations of Attila the Hun. Their weapons were the bow, the spear, and the battle-ax.[4] Like their Scythian kinsmen, the Kurgan people fought from horseback—a terrifying sight to the Old Europeans, who had never tamed the horse and possibly had never seen one.[5]

All over Europe, the archaeologist's spade turns up signs of the Kurgan people's typical calling cards, such as mass graves filled with men, women, and children, their skulls pierced with axes and spears.[6] However, they did not totally exterminate the Old Europeans. Isolated pockets of Old Europe survived intact in parts of Greece, Spain, Italy, and Scotland and in the Mediterranean islands, such as Sardinia, Crete, and Thera. In other places, Kurgan people and Old Europeans coexisted and intermarried, thus giving rise to the hodgepodge of tribes and cultures that Gimbutas called a marble cake.

This, then, was Bronze Age Europe. It was a restless young land, aboil with warlike spirit. But it was also a haunted land, where witches still called on the Great Goddess in the dead of night and the sacred bonfires blazed on Midsummer's Day. Untroubled by the galloping horses and clanging bronze forges of the new regime, the old standing stones still frowned over the landscape, a silent testament to Old Europe's bloody demise. This was the continent our explorers would have found—with all its blood-lust, turmoil, and ancient mystery—when they made their first landfall in Heroic Age Europe.

Many of those explorers probably met with less than friendly receptions. Cannibalism appears to have been widespread in Darkest Europe. Herodotos tells, for example, of the man-eating Androphagi of the eastern steppes. He also notes that the Issedones—another eastern group—devoured their own fathers when they died.[7]

The Greek geographer Strabo, writing in about 7 B.C., ascribes similar habits to the Celts of Ireland. "Concerning this island, I have nothing further to tell," he writes, "except that its inhabitants are more savage than the Britons, since they are man-eaters. . . . They count it an honourable thing, when their fathers die, to devour them, and openly to have intercourse with their mothers and sisters."[8]

Mythical accounts of Greece's Heroic Age frequently mention cannibalism. Consider, for example, the tale of Lykaon, a legendary king of Arkadia who was fond of butchering and eating his houseguests. Zeus punished Lykaon for his uncordial behavior by changing him into a wolf. From that time on, Lykaon's metamorphosis was celebrated, each year, in secret rites atop Mount Lykaion in Arkadia.[9]

The Greeks regarded this festival as extremely ancient, introduced by a legendary people reputed to be "older than the moon."[10] As such, it probably gives an accurate reflection of the sort of tribal rituals that prevailed in Darkest Europe during the Bronze Age.

At this festival, the Arkadians would kill, dismember, and devour a child. All who partook were reputedly turned into wolves, becoming people again only after they refrained, for nine years, from eating human flesh.[11] As late as Roman times, the Arkadians still observed this ghastly ritual. "I was reluctant to pry into the details of this sacrifice," remarked the Greek travel-writer Pausanias after visiting Mount Lykaion around A.D. 150. "Let them be as they are and were from the beginning."[12]

Even less hospitable than King Lykaon were the man-eating Laestrygonians who greeted Odysseus and his fleet in Homer's *Odyssey*. Although Homer probably composed the *Odyssey* sometime around 800 B.C., the events it describes were supposed to have occurred some 450 years earlier, just after the Trojan War. In that respect, they provide a rare glimpse of Bronze Age Europe, when memory of it was still fresh in Greek minds.

In 1985, Irish explorer Tim Severin traveled Odysseus's route in a replica of a twenty-oared Bronze Age galley. Based on Homer's description, Severin concluded that the harbor where the Laestrygonians attacked Odysseus must have been on the Mani peninsula, a desolate rocky waste that juts out from the southwestern tip of Greece. As Homer describes it, no sooner had the Greeks taken shelter in the harbor, than the Laestrygonians raised the alarm:

> Antiphates [the king of the Laestrygonians] raised a hue and cry throughout the place, which brought the Laestrygonians running up from every side in their thousands—huge fellows, more like giants than men. Standing at the top of the cliffs they began pelting my flotilla with lumps of rock such as a man could scarcely lift; and the din that now rose from the ships, where the groans of dying men could be heard above the splintering of timbers, was appalling. One by one they harpooned their prey like fish and so carried them off to make their loathsome meal.[13]

Of Odysseus's eleven ships, only one escaped the Laestrygonians' wrath. It is not hard to imagine that Bronze Age explorers from Egypt and Phoenicia might have sought shelter in similar coves. Those who wandered, like Odysseus, into the *wrong* harbor would likely have met a similar fate.

Far from home and heavily outnumbered, our hypothetical mariners must have blanched many a time at such sights as flaming wicker giants filled with human victims, naked headhunters smeared with blue paint, and clifftops abroil with rock-hurling cannibals. Their memories ablaze with such spectacles, our intrepid seafarers can only have regarded each new landfall in Darkest Europe with the profoundest unease.

Yet, if Bronze Age Europe was a dangerous place for outsiders, it was also an alluring one—a land of rich trade and fabulous natural wealth. It is easy to imagine why travelers from across the sea would have risked their lives to go there. Gold and silver abounded in Europe, as did copper and tin—the chief ingredients for making bronze. When the Phoenicians began trading in Spain—perhaps around the tenth century B.C.—they found silver so plentiful and cheap that they used it to cast anchor stones.[14] The Laurion mines near Athens were being exploited for silver and lead as early as 2500 B.C. Large quantities of Greek silver have turned up in Egyptian treasuries of the Eleventh and Twelfth Dynasties—roughly 2040–1674 B.C.[15]

On the cold shores of the North and Baltic Seas, precious amber was so abundant that it could be picked up off the beaches like so many pebbles. It was hauled, by land and river, all the way from Denmark down to Greece, along a prehistoric thoroughfare that archaeologists have named the Amber Route. Baltic amber has been found in the holds of 3,300-year-old sunken ships off the coast of Turkey and unearthed in places as far away as Crete and Egypt.[16]

Caravans of oxcarts and riverboats laden with amber nuggets would have enjoyed a grand tour of Bronze Age Europe as they made their way slowly southward. The caravans would have started in the far north, where Scandinavian tribesmen lived in villages of sod huts, trading their amber and furs for bronzeware, Egyptian trinkets, and other scarce but cherished items from the outside world. Then the traders would have moved south through Germany and Switzerland, passing through the territory of a multitude of petty warlords in timber-built towns, grown rich from the tolls they exacted from passing merchants.[17] In Switzerland, they would have passed stockaded villages with log roads built on stilts beside shimmering Alpine lakes.[18] In the mountains of northern Italy, they would have seen cliffs decorated with giant rock carvings.[19] Finally, they would have reached the sea, proceeding ever southward down the Adriatic coast until at last they came to Greece, the gateway to the world, with its many thriving ports.

Other trade routes proceeded entirely by water. The port city of Troy stood on the Turkish coast, overlooking the Dardanelles—as it appears to have done ever since 3000 B.C.[20] Secure behind its towering walls, the city of Priam taxed every ship that passed between the Black Sea and the Aegean.

In many ways, it is shocking how little we really know of Europe between the years 3200 and 1200 B.C. Egyptologists can rattle off the names of nearly every pharaoh who reigned during this time, with the approximate years of his accession and death. Likewise, the histories of Sumer, Babylon, Assyria, and many other Near Eastern states of this period are thoroughly documented, with copious written records.

Not so Europe. Except for a few hundred clay tablets from Greece—most of which appear to be accounting and inventory lists, and none of which seem to be older than about 1400 B.C.—no writings at all have come down to us from Europe's Bronze Age. Its gods, kings, and wars—even the very names of its peoples and tribes—are lost. What little we know must be pieced together from the rotting remains of timber villages buried in the dirt, from the silent dolmens and megalithic graves, from nameless skeletons, broken pots, corroded bronze knives, and clay figurines. It must be gleaned from a few sparse and puzzling references in the chronicles of Egypt and the Near East and reconstructed from vague and fanciful European legends, which may or may not preserve some tangled threads of truth.

Today, the trail is so cold that many scholars have despaired of ever following it. Many question whether Kadmos, Sesostris, or Danaos ever existed. And who knows? Perhaps they never did. But imagine the irony if their stories are true! In Homer's *Iliad*, Achilles faces a dreadful choice. If he flees the battlefield, the gods will grant him a long—but obscure—life. If he stays and fights, he is guaranteed certain death—and everlasting fame. Achilles chooses fame. He dies a young man before the walls of Troy, but his name lives on forever.

The explorers and colonists who came to Europe during the Bronze Age must have been very like Achilles. They left behind a safe but obscure life at home and instead embraced danger. They gambled their lives on the slim hope of achieving lasting glory. Greatness they may have found. But fame, in the end, has eluded them. Statues of Columbus grace city squares on both sides of the Atlantic. But the men who discovered Europe live only in myth and obscurity. Who will speak for them now? Who will argue their case? Who will claim for them the laurels their deeds have earned them?

Fortunately, a new generation of scholars has emerged who appears determined to do just that. More and more researchers today are putting aside old prejudices and beginning to look with new respect at those hoary old legends. Much has been lost, and many facts will never be known. But where scattered evidence remains in the dust, patient scholars have spent lifetimes piecing it together. Thanks to their efforts, the story of that long-ago Age of Exploration is at last beginning to emerge—an amazing saga of seafaring adventure that ended 3,000 years before Columbus was born.

PART TWO

RIDDLE

OF THE

SPHINX

CHAPTER 4

"A BLACK RACE
OF MEN"

B Y 1783, THE BALANCE OF POWER IN THE MEDITERRANEAN HAD shifted quite radically from Bronze Age times. In the endless seesaw of rising and falling empires that we call history, Europe had now gained the upper hand. A visitor from the Bronze Age would have stared aghast at the finely clothed and well-fed inhabitants and neatly manicured landscapes of eighteenth-century Europe. The primeval forests had been cleared for farmland. The lions and aurochs had been hunted to extinction, and the wolves were well on their way to joining them. In Europe's glittering capitals, people enjoyed a level of prosperity, security, and intellectual culture unmatched in human memory.

"A philosopher," wrote English historian Edward Gibbon in the eighteenth century, "may consider Europe as a great republic, whose various inhabitants have attained almost the same level of politeness and cultivation."[1]

No longer did Europeans look within the borders of their own continent for the barbarous and the exotic. The frontier had moved elsewhere. Ironically, Egypt had now acquired a prominent place among those dark and menacing regions where the genteel European feared to tread.

There were, in fact, good reasons for the eighteenth-century European to fear traveling in the Muslim world. At the very least, a voyage to Egypt meant sailing through waters infested with Barbary corsairs, always on the prowl for Christian ships to plunder and Christian slaves to peddle in the bazaars of Tunis and Algiers. If you were lucky enough to make it as far as Egypt, you entrusted your safety to the whims of feuding Mamluk warlords, whose soldiers murdered, raped, and kidnapped with impunity, contemptuous of any law.

In Roman times, Egypt had been the breadbasket of the empire, exporting grain, linen, and papyrus by the ton to every port in Europe. Its library at Alexandria had drawn scholars from every corner of the world. But ever since the Arab horsemen of Amr Ibn el-As had thundered into the Nile Valley in A.D. 639—bringing with them the new religion of Islam—Egypt had been all but closed to the "infidel" West.

Of course, things had loosened up quite a bit by 1783. The bloody Crusades had long since passed, and an uneasy peace had been established between Muslim and Christian. But it was still only the most daring of Europeans who braved Egypt's dangerous shores—traders and mercenaries, for the most part, whose thirst for wealth and adventure overpowered their fear.

Count Constantin de Volney was neither trader nor mercenary. But an adventurer he surely was. Born of a noble French family, Volney came into a substantial inheritance at the age of twenty-four. Like many young nobles, he decided to spend his money on travel. But Volney had little interest in the gaming tables, bordellos, and fancy balls that lured so many of his aristocratic peers to the capitals of Europe. With the mind of a scholar and the heart of an explorer, Volney sought knowledge, rather than pleasure, from his travels. He was determined to go where others had not gone and to learn what others had not yet learned.

"My own country and the neighboring nations," Volney later wrote, "seemed to me to be either too well known or too easy of access. The rising States of America and the savages were not without their temptations; but other considerations determined me in favor of . . . Syria . . . and Egypt."[2]

Volney could not have selected a less comfortable itinerary for his tour. At that time, Egypt and Syria languished under the yoke of

Turkish pashas, who paid for their harems and opulent palaces through ruinous taxation. Poverty, rebellions, and bloody civil wars racked the Arab world with dreadful regularity. But Volney was unconcerned with such political turmoil. It was the rich past of these Eastern realms that captured his imagination, not their tumultuous present. From his avid reading of Greek and Latin classics, Volney had learned that civilization first arose in the dusty lands of the Near East.

"Those are the countries," Volney reflected, in his book *Travels in Syria and Egypt* (1787), "in which the greater part of the opinions that govern us at this day have had their origin."[3] By observing their people, customs, climate, and politics in his own day, Volney hoped to achieve some insight into their ancient past. He was, in fact, destined to achieve exactly such an insight, but in a way that he could hardly have anticipated beforehand.

Nowadays, five-star hotels with golf courses and swimming pools have risen in the very shadow of the Great Pyramid, while tourists arrive by bus and chauffeured car service. But in 1783 the only way to reach the pyramids was on the back of a camel or donkey.

In his writings, Volney left us few details of his first trip to Giza, where the pyramids and the Great Sphinx are located. We can only imagine a long, bumpy ride across the desert west of Cairo, the native guides chattering in Arabic over the braying of the camels. By the time he reached the pyramids, Volney was probably drenched in sweat, his hind parts aching from the ride. He was no doubt relieved at the chance to climb down from the camel and stretch his legs in the hot Sahara sand.

Towering 200 feet above the desert, the Great Pyramid undoubtedly would have seized Volney's attention first. Not only was it the largest of the three Giza pyramids, but it was also by far the most famous. Volney would have read about this pyramid in the pages of his beloved Herodotos. "The pyramids too are astonishing structures," Herodotos wrote in the fifth century B.C., "each one of them equal to many of the most ambitious works of Greece."[4]

What thoughts formed in Volney's mind as he gazed upon these greatest of all human monuments, we do not know, for he did not record them. But we know it could not have been long before Volney turned his attention to a much smaller, but equally intriguing, monument that lay just a few hundred yards north of the Giza pyramids. We know that Volney turned his attention to it, because it was about this smaller monument that he wrote what are perhaps his most famous and oft-quoted words. That monument was the Great Sphinx of Giza, and Volney's thoughts about it form the first piece of a grand historical puzzle, whose solution we will be seeking in the pages of this book.

Soon after arriving in Egypt, Volney had encountered what he called an "enigma"—the physical appearance of the Egyptians themselves. From his reading of history, Volney was well aware that Egypt had suffered many conquests over the centuries, subjugated, at different times, by Persians, Greeks, Romans, Arabs, and Turks, among others. All these conquerors had left their stamp upon the faces of Egypt's people.

But Volney was intrigued by certain features that did not seem to derive from any of Egypt's known conquerors. He was drawn, in particular, to the Copts—a population of native Christians who had resisted Arab assimilation and whom Volney regarded as the most direct descendants of the ancient Egyptians. He wrote, "We shall find them all characterized by a sort of yellowish dusky complexion, which is neither Grecian nor Arabian; they have all a puffed visage, swollen eyes, flat noses and thick lips—in short, the exact countenance of a Mulatto."[5]

The word *mulatto* has passed out of fashionable use in our society, but it is defined in *Webster's Collegiate Dictionary*, ninth edition, as "a person of mixed Caucasian and Negro ancestry." In calling the Copts mulattoes, Volney implied that they traced their ancestry, at least partially, to black Africans. From whence did these modern Egyptians get their "mulatto" appearance? This was the enigma confronting Volney. Not until that hot, dusty day on the plain of Giza, as he stood gazing at the Great Sphinx, did a possible answer present itself.

"When I visited the Sphinx," wrote Volney, "I could not help thinking the figure of that monster furnished the true solution of the enigma."[6]

The Sphinx that Volney saw was little more than a giant head protruding from the sand. Its great paws and body had been buried beneath the dunes for centuries, and no one in Volney's era had ever seen them. Moreover, the head itself was badly damaged. A fanatical Sufi monk named Mohammed Sa'im al-Dahr had broken off the nose of this "pagan" idol in A.D. 1378, in an attempt to "remedy some of the religious errors" of the past, as fourteenth-century Arab historian El-Makrizi put it.[7] Still, enough of the original face remained for Volney to conclude that its stony features "were precisely those of a negro" and that the ancient Egyptians themselves must have been "real negroes, of the same species with all the natives of Africa."[8]

As for the modern Egyptians, with their "yellowish dusky complexion" and "mulatto" appearance, Volney concluded that "after mixing for so many ages with the Greeks and Romans, they have lost the intensity of their first colour, yet they still retain strong marks of their original conformation."[9]

How long Volney stood before the Sphinx, rapt in these obscure reflections, we shall never know. But his writings leave no doubt that the revelation he experienced on the sands of Giza penetrated deep into his soul. Volney was a child of the Enlightenment—that fervent conviction that swept through Europe in the seventeenth and eighteenth centuries that every injustice and evil could be wiped away through science and reason. During his student days in Paris, Volney had frequented the salons of the famous Madame Helvétius,where writers, poets, and philosophers gathered to debate new ideas like "liberty" and the "rights of man." Volney had personally known Benjamin Franklin in Paris and had, no doubt, listened, mesmerized, to every scrap of news from the far-off battlefields of the American Revolution.[10]

Like so many earnest young partisans of the Enlightenment, Volney had also brooded deeply about the trans-Atlantic slave trade, which was reaching its peak just at the time he traveled to Egypt. By then, it is estimated that some 80,000 African captives were being transported to the Americas each year[11]—many of them to the very land of liberty that Volney and his generation had come to idolize.

It was this paradox of black slavery thriving among the very champions of liberty that moved Volney to his greatest epiphany. As he stood that day in the hot sun before the Sphinx, unmindful of the bored, uncomprehending gaze of his Egyptian guides, Volney felt the weight of 5,000 years of history pressing down about his shoulders. All that he had learned and believed about the rise of human civilization seemed upended and reversed in that moment. He later wrote:

> How are we astonished . . . when we reflect that to the race of negroes, at present our slaves, and the objects of our extreme contempt, we owe our arts, sciences, and even the very use of speech; and when we

recollect that, in the midst of those nations who call themselves the
friends of liberty and humanity, the most barbarous of slaveries is justified; and that it is even a problem whether the understanding of negroes be of the same species with that of white men![12]

Years later, inspired, in part, by the revolution that shook France
in 1789, Volney wrote his most famous work, entitled *The Ruins: or
a Survey of the Revolution of Empires*. In it, Volney sought to determine the cause for the rise and fall of civilizations throughout history. He filled the pages with many fine words about the role of
liberty, equality, and natural law in the building of nations. But
most of Volney's insights had already been expressed—and far more
concisely—in the American Declaration of Independence.[13]

If there was a flash of real genius in Volney's magnum opus, it lay
in a brief passage that was little noticed in his day but that may, in
time, come to be recognized as a crucial milestone in Western historiography. For it was there, in the pages of *The Ruins*, that Volney
firmly concluded that civilization had been first conceived "on the
borders of the Upper Nile, among a black race of men."[14]

It is clear enough that Volney was moved to philosophical rap-
tures by his observation of the Sphinx. But were his observations
correct? Did the African features that Volney discerned, both in the
Sphinx and among the modern Egyptians, really exist? Or were they
merely the figment of an overactive imagination?

Much depends on our answer to this question. If Volney's observations were accurate, then Western civilization may indeed owe
its existence largely to black Africans. If his observations were mistaken, we can simply dismiss his whole reverie about "negro" Egyptians as a silly mistake. In fact, many scholars today would point
out that Volney wrote in a time before archaeology and anthropology became proper sciences. He was not trained in modern methods
of analysis. Perhaps his theory is just one more in a long list of eccentric ideas spawned by amateur antiquarians in those cruder and
simpler days, ideas that, for the most part, no longer merit the serious consideration of scholars.

Perhaps.

In the next chapter, we will take up the question of just how reliable Volney's methods were and how seriously we should regard his
opinions.

CHAPTER 5

WERE THE
EGYPTIANS BLACK?

N A VISIT TO AMERICA IN 1912, THE SWISS PSYCHOLOGIST CARL
Jung found himself in Buffalo, New York, standing outside a
factory at quitting time. As the workers filed out, Jung was
fascinated to discover that many of them seemed to exhibit the facial characteristics of American Indians.

"I should never have thought there was such a high percentage of
Indian blood," he muttered to his American companion.

The American laughed. These workers were of purely European
stock, he assured Jung. Not one of them possessed so much as "a
drop" of Indian blood. Perplexed by this response, Jung pondered the
problem. He concluded, at length, that the factory workers must
have acquired Indian-like features in response to certain peculiarities
of the North American climate![1]

Jung's theory was certainly provocative. But he had overlooked a
much more plausible explanation. Jung had failed to consider that
the "Indian" features he had observed in the factory workers might
be nothing more than a figment of his imagination. Like most people, Jung tended to see *what he wanted or expected to see*. All his
life, Jung was obsessed by the idea of race and by the spiritual and

physical unity he believed each race enjoyed with its native soil. Because he envisioned America as a land mystically and biologically bound to the American Indian, Jung expected, from the moment he stepped off the boat in America, to see evidence of the Indian race wherever he turned. And what he expected to see, Jung's potent imagination dutifully conjured up.

Such tricks of the mind have played an equally mischievous role in Egyptology. Many learned commentators have tried, over the years, to discern the race of the ancient Egyptians by studying their statues and paintings. Unfortunately, most of these observers—like Dr. Jung—tended to see exactly what they wished or expected. If two researchers examined the same painting, one would see a "black" Egyptian and the other a "white" one, in accordance with their preconceptions.

Thus, the Senegalese scholar Cheikh Anta Diop—a passionate African nationalist—deduced, from his study of Egyptian artwork, that "the Egyptians perceived themselves as Blacks, and represented themselves as such without possible confusion."[2]

A statue of Pharaoh Mentuhotep I portrayed, in Diop's opinion, "a typical Negro"[3]; a Fourth Dynasty statue of Khufu, the legendary builder of the Great Pyramid, looked to Diop like "a Black man resembling the present-day Cameroonian type,"[4] while "the slender bodies and rhythmic movements" of Egyptian fishermen in a Twelfth Dynasty tomb painting struck Diop as reminiscent "of any work scene in Black Africa today."[5]

Adolf Erman, a nineteenth-century German Egyptologist, also tended to emphasize Egypt's African affinities—though for different reasons than Diop's—and his observations of both ancient and modern Egyptians were shaded accordingly. In 1886, he wrote:

Nothing exists in the physical structure of the ancient Egyptian to distinguish him from the native African. . . . from the Egyptian to the negro population of tropical Africa, a series of links exist which do not admit of a break. The Egyptians . . . cannot be separated . . . from the Kelowi or the Tibbu, nor these again from the inhabitants around Lake Tsad; all form one race.[6]

Conversely, those who prefer *not* to emphasize Egypt's African character have drawn very different conclusions, often from the same evidence. Notable among these is the French Egyptologist

Gaston Maspero, a contemporary of Erman's, who pontificated on the race of the ancient Egyptians in tones every bit as dogmatic and self-assured as those of Diop—but in support of the opposite point of view:

> On examining innumerable reproductions of statues and bas-reliefs, we recognized at once that the people represented on the monuments, instead of presenting peculiarities and the general appearance of the Negro, really resembled the fine white races of Europe and Western Asia.[7]

In much the same vein, the American Egyptologist David O'Connor had this to say, in an article published in *Expedition* magazine in 1971:

> Thousands of sculpted and painted representations from Egypt and hundreds of well-preserved bodies from its cemeteries show that the typical physical type was neither Negroid nor Negro.[8]

O'Connor's quote, in particular, has been cited frequently, in recent years, by those who would view the Egyptians as white. But an observation from Egyptologist Frank Yurco, published in 1989, offers a different perspective on the same evidence. He writes:

> The mummies and skeletons of ancient Egyptians indicate they were Africans. . . . No doubt, many darker-colored Egyptians would be called black in our modern, race-conscious terminology. . . . Some modern Afro-Americans, particularly those with mixed racial ancestry, will find that they look like some ancient (and modern) Egyptians.[9]

Such seemingly contradictory conclusions are not confined only to general impressions of the Egyptians. They plague even the discussion of specific details, such as the texture of the Egyptians' hair. Thus, Jacques Joseph Champollion-Figeac observed in 1839: "Except for the color of the skin, blackened by the hot climate, [the Egyptians] are the same men as those of Europe and western Asia; frizzy, woolly hair is the true characteristic of the Negro race; the Egyptians, however, had long hair, identical with that of the white race of the West."[10]

In reply to this, Diop countered: "Even when the hair of the Egyptian is less woolly than that of other Blacks, it is so thick and black as to rule out any possible comparison with the thin, light hair of Westerners."[11]

And so on. Such examples could be extended to fill an entire volume. And no matter how many we amassed, they would bring us no closer to determining whether Volney, Diop, Erman, Yurco, Maspero, or O'Connor was correct in his observations. The only thing these contradictions clearly *do* demonstrate is that there are many different ways of looking at the same evidence, even among highly trained specialists.

You would be hard put to find any scholar today willing to speak as frankly about race as did Maspero and Erman. However, scholars continue to bicker just as passionately—albeit far more abstrusely— over whether the Egyptians should be considered "black," "white," or something in between. And they have drawn no closer to a consensus than did experts in the days of Volney and Champollion-Figeac. Clearly this question will never be decided by the casual eyeballing of Egyptian paintings, statues, and mummies. If there is to be any resolution, it must come from methods far more objective and scientific. Fortunately, such methods are available. And they have already shed some intriguing new light on Volney's assessment of the Great Sphinx.

Chapter 6

THE TELL-TALE
SPHINX

Does the Great Sphinx really look as "black" as Volney thought it did? The answer depends on which expert you ask. Most Egyptologists today are convinced that the Great Sphinx represents the pharaoh Khafre, who reigned during the Fourth Dynasty, between about 2558 and 2532 B.C. If we look at the very realistic diorite statue of Khafre on display in the Cairo Museum, we can see that Khafre does not seem to have obvious Negroid features. This implies that the Sphinx should not look particularly Negroid either.

However, some experts doubt that the Sphinx really does portray Khafre. In fact, the only real evidence that Khafre built the Sphinx is the single syllable *Khaf*—a fragment of the name *Khafre*—which appears on a severely weathered inscription on a granite stela placed between the statue's paws. Enough of the inscription remains to tell us that the pharaoh Thutmose IV (1401–1391 B.C.) erected this stela to commemorate his restoration work on the statue. But the portion mentioning *Khaf* is so damaged that we really don't know what it says about "Khaf" at all. It might say that Khafre had simply done some previous restoration work on the Sphinx. Or the syllable *Khaf* might have no connection whatsoever with the name *Khafre*. We just don't know.

"Excepting for the mutilated line on the granite stela of Thoth-mosis IV, which proves nothing," wrote Egyptologist Selim Hassan in 1949, "there is not a single ancient inscription which connects the Sphinx with Khafre."[1]

In 1978, Professor Mark Lehner of Chicago University's Oriental Institute undertook to reconstruct the original appearance of the Great Sphinx using state-of-the-art computer technology. Lehner began by photographing the Sphinx, from the front and side. Using these photos, he created a digitized three-dimensional wireframe model. He then plotted 2.6 million surface points on the wireframe and used them as references to superimpose a digital "skin" on the Sphinx. Finally, Lehner took digital images of other known sphinxes and pharaohs and tried to fit them onto the Great Sphinx. In the end, Lehner settled on the face of Khafre from the diorite statue in the Cairo Museum.

"With the face of Khafre," Lehner wrote, "the Sphinx came alive."[2]

Lehner's reconstructed Sphinx became a scholarly sensation. He published major articles in *National Geographic*, *Archaeology* magazine, and the *Cambridge Archaeological Journal*. His digital reconstruction appeared on the *Archaeology* television series on The Learning Channel and on Leonard Nimoy's *Ancient Mysteries* and was featured in Time-Life's popular *Lost Civilizations* series of books.

Lehner had, by all appearances, solved the riddle of the Sphinx. In writing that "the Sphinx came alive" when he superimposed Khafre's face, Lehner seemed to imply that the head of Khafre fit more naturally on the Sphinx than did the heads of other pharaohs he tried. If true, this was a stunning vindication of scholarly theories that the Sphinx actually represented Khafre.

But did it really?

Some critics quietly grumbled. They pointed out that the digital technology he used made it easy to fit just about any head you wished on the Sphinx. Did Khafre's face really fit better than the others? Or had Lehner simply *made* it fit, through skillful use of computer graphics? The fact was that Lehner had never been trained for the job at hand. He was a fine Egyptologist. But Egyptologists are not instructed in the highly technical procedures used in making accurate comparisons between two human faces.

Experts on this subject are easily found, however, in the police departments of any major city. The police are constantly called upon to identify victims and suspects, through comparative studies of photos and bodies. In some cases, they might have to prove that a mug shot taken twenty years ago portrays the same individual seen in a blurry Polaroid snapshot taken last week. Or they might have to establish that a corpse whose face is burned beyond recognition bears some critical resemblance to a smiling family portrait. Over the years, police forensic specialists have learned to produce findings sufficiently accurate to be used as evidence in a court of law—a standard that Mark Lehner's digital reconstruction would probably fail to meet.

Frank Domingo is one of the country's leading experts on face identification. For fifteen years, he served as a forensic specialist for the New York Police Department, retiring in 1993 to start his own consulting practice. Domingo wrote the standard manual used by police around the country for making composite portraits of crime suspects. Over the years, he has frequently been called upon by clients outside of law enforcement for special jobs. In one case, for example, Domingo determined that a faded daguerreotype, believed to be the earliest photograph of Abraham Lincoln, did not, in fact, portray Lincoln at all, but only a close look-alike.

In 1993, Domingo was approached by a team of investigators who were preparing an NBC television documentary entitled *Mystery of the Sphinx*. The leader of the team, an amateur Egyptologist named John Anthony West, believed that the Sphinx was far older than the Fourth Dynasty. If West's theory were true, the Sphinx could not possibly have been built by Khafre. West asked Domingo to conduct an independent investigation to determine whether the face on the Sphinx really represented Khafre.

In conducting facial comparisons, Domingo knew that the difference between a match and a mismatch can often hinge on the tiniest discrepancy—a nuance of the hairline, a skewing of the ears, a crookedness of the teeth. Yet, to Domingo's surprise, the differences between the Sphinx and the statue of Khafre proved to be quite glaring.

Domingo noticed, right away, that the Sphinx had a square-shaped face, while that of Khafre was oval. The Sphinx's eyes were larger than Khafre's, its mouth wider, and its lips thicker. All these differences were significant. But the most telling discrepancy of all was yet to come. Only after Domingo had made detailed measurements of the two faces did the full magnitude of their dissimilarity become clear.

Prognathism is the term anthropologists use to describe the jutting forward of the lower part of the face, a feature prevalent among many (but not all) black Africans. Indeed, back in the nineteenth century, prognathism was one of the key indicators that anatomists hit upon for distinguishing "whites" from "blacks," since black Africans often have a considerable degree of prognathism, while Europeans have little or none.

The linchpin of Domingo's investigation was a comparison of angles between different facial features of the Sphinx and the Khafre statue. Domingo was able to identify three reference points on the Sphinx's face that had not been damaged by the Sufi vandal Mohammed Sa'im al-Dahr. They were the chin, the outer portion of the eye, and the brow ridge. Domingo then compared the angular relation of these three points to the corresponding angles between those same three points on the Khafre statue. The results were startling.

The Sphinx showed dramatically greater prognathism—determined by drawing a line between the outer corner of the eye and the tip of the chin and measuring that line's angle of deviation from the vertical. In the Sphinx, this angle turned out to be a full eighteen degrees wider than the corresponding angle on the Khafre statue. Such a profound discrepancy clearly indicated that the two statues portrayed different individuals (assuming, of course, that Egyptian artists made accurate representations of people's features). More to the point, it also revealed that the Sphinx had a degree of prognathism typical of black Africans. Domingo observed, "The features that I saw, especially in the profile, of the Sphinx, are consistent with those types of features found in Negroids. The features, especially in the profile, of the statue of Chephren [Khafre], are consistent with those types of measurements that are found in Caucasoids."[3]

For the NBC documentary, Domingo was also asked to create a restored image of the Sphinx as it had probably appeared before it was damaged. This did not turn out to be difficult, since many of the Sphinx's important features were still intact. Domingo could easily determine, for example, the original appearance of the mouth, the chin, and the eyes. His biggest challenge turned out to be restoring the nose, which had been largely obliterated.

Domingo took a conservative approach. He could vaguely discern from the Sphinx's broken face the approximate width of the nose at the top and the bottom. What he didn't know was its shape. Working from the available measurements, Domingo constructed a nose that seemed an "average" of other Egyptian noses he had observed on statues and tomb paintings.

The crease or indentation where the flange of the nostrils meets the face was, luckily, still visible on the Sphinx. Domingo knew that most people's noses flare out, to a certain extent, on either side of that crease. His instinct told him that the Sphinx's nose ought to flare out very widely. Nevertheless, since he had no sure proof that the Sphinx's nose was shaped that way, Domingo played it safe and gave his Sphinx a nose that was much narrower than he really thought appropriate.

Today, Domingo regrets his decision. He believes that his initial hunch was correct and that a wider, more African-looking nose would have blended more naturally with the rest of the Sphinx's features. Nevertheless, even with its compromises, the face that Domingo drew seems strikingly African in character (see Figure 3).

Domingo's work on the Sphinx ignited a storm of controversy. John Anthony West wrote an op-ed piece in the *New York Times* in which he praised Domingo's Sphinx and dismissed Mark Lehner's, charging that Lehner's technique could just as easily have been used to prove that "the Sphinx was Elvis Presley."[4] In their 1996 book, *The Message of the Sphinx,* Graham Hancock and Robert Bauval observed that "the mere fact that Mark Lehner is able to graft an image of Khafre onto the battered visage of the Sphinx by means of the 'ARL (Advanced Research Logic) Computer and the AutoCad (release 10) graphics application' proves nothing more than that with good computer graphics you can make anyone's face look like anyone else's face."[5]

None of these criticisms, however, came from Egyptologists, and so they were not regarded as important. Like most specialists, Egyptologists stubbornly resist criticism from outsiders. *The Mystery of the Sphinx,* featuring Frank Domingo's findings, was aired on NBC in 1993, to an audience of 33 million viewers.[6] But, to this day, Mark Lehner's computerized reconstruction remains in favor, at least among orthodox scholars. It seems highly unlikely that Egyptologists will ever accept the conclusions of a policeman over those of one of their own. But that is of no concern to our present discussion.

Whether Khafre built the Sphinx or not, it is clear from Domingo's measurements and facial reconstruction that the statue has certain features that are distinctly African. The press has shown little interest in this aspect of Domingo's work. But its implications may prove far more consequential than any speculations about which particular pharaoh the Sphinx portrays.

During his weeklong trip to Egypt, Domingo spent time wandering the streets of Cairo, taking in the sights. Not surprisingly, considering his profession, Domingo often found himself studying the faces in the crowds with more than a casual attentiveness. As a native New Yorker, Domingo had walked all his life through streets thronging with Puerto Ricans, Dominicans, and other Caribbean peoples, whose European and African forebears had thoroughly mingled over the centuries. In Puerto Rico, for example, it is usually safe to assume that just about anyone you meet has at least a touch of black ancestry, no matter how white they may look on the surface. In Egypt, Domingo observed a range of physical types that reminded him strongly of such multiracial Caribbean populations.

"There's a certain look that you see in the Caribbean, as a result of all the races being mixed together, and it's a very similar look in Egypt," says Domingo. "If you were to look at a street scene of Egyptians, and forget the clothes, you could be in Puerto Rico."[7]

Of course, subjective impressions such as these are of only limited value in determining the genetic character of a people. As we will see in later chapters, modern techniques, such as DNA testing and computerized analyses of skull measurements, are far more effective for this purpose. Nevertheless, if Domingo's work proves nothing else, it proves at least that Count Constantin de Volney was not just seeing things. There are indeed very clear and objective reasons for thinking that the Great Sphinx portrayed a black African. And if the Sphinx was black, then so may have been the people who carved it.

PART THREE

SESOSTRIS
THE GREAT

CHAPTER 7

"BLACK SKIN" AND "WOOLLY HAIR"

SK MOST PEOPLE TO LOCATE THE ANCIENT LAND OF COLCHIS on a map, and you will get puzzled stares. Hardly anyone will know which continent to search. Poor Colchis never achieved the fame of such flashier contemporaries as Egypt, Greece, and Babylon. It left behind no soaring monuments or classic literature. It spawned no Alexanders or Nebuchadnezzars. Today its name fires imaginations only among that tiny circle of mostly Georgian and Russian archaeologists who dig in the muddy soil of the Black Sea's eastern coastline.

Yet, for all its obscurity, Colchis figures prominently in some of the oldest and most important legends of the ancient world. It is to Colchis, for example, that Jason and the Argonauts sailed in their quest for the Golden Fleece. When the Titan Prometheus stole fire from the gods and gave it to man, Zeus punished him by chaining him to Mount Elbrus in the Caucasus Mountains, overlooking Colchis.

Located on the humid, rain-sodden shores of what is now the former Soviet republic of Georgia, ancient Colchis was about as far from Egypt as you could get. Yet, here, in this rude backwater of

Western civilization, we find one of the most important clues in our quest for the racial affinity of the ancient Nile-dwellers.

Sometime around 450 B.C., a ship approached the Colchian shore. We don't know exactly where it put in. The ship could have landed at any number of bustling Colchian settlements or Greek colonies along the coast. As they leaned over the railings, the passengers would have beheld a sight of surpassing strangeness and beauty. Off in the distance, they would have seen the snow-capped peaks of the Caucasus Mountains. Closer to shore, they would have viewed a dark expanse of virgin pines towering to the sky, while all around them in the harbor bobbed the stubby little eight-oared boats of the Colchians.

In the shadow of the pine forests lay marshes, shrouded with mist and thick with ducks and pheasant. The Colchians themselves lived right on the marshes. They built their houses on little hillocks above the water. Instead of streets, they had canals, through which they paddled dugout canoes. Accustomed to cities of marble and tile, the Greek passengers would have marveled at this Colchian town, constructed entirely of wood. There were log towers, log palisades, log cabins with roofs of reed thatch. In this timber-rich land, the Colchian warriors even made their helmets out of wood.

Despite the rudeness of the town, the Colchians who thronged its streets and canals were no paupers. Many wore golden pendants about their necks and iron swords at their belts. Their watery marketplaces teemed with traders from every part of the world, converging on the Colchian shore in quest of gold, metals, gemstones, linen, timber, and slaves. From time immemorial, Colchis had been linked in Greek minds with fabulous wealth. Many were the Greeks who braved the Black Sea's stormy waters to seek their fortunes among Colchis's dark and rain-soaked forests.

On this particular day, one man on the boat stood out from the rest. In the midst of what was probably a rough crowd of sailors and frontier traders, this man would have evinced, with every glance and gesture, a subtle and educated mind. Indeed, he would later win renown as one of history's great geniuses. Called the Father of History by future generations, he would long be remembered as the first known practitioner of modern historical writing.

His name was Herodotos. At the time he visited Colchis, he was probably in his mid-thirties. What business he had in that far-off land, we will never know. But that has not stopped scholars from speculating.

For the Greeks, the chief attraction of the Black Sea region lay not so much in Colchis, but on the Black Sea's northern shoreline, in that part of the world scholars call southern Russia, but which prefers nowadays to call itself the Republic of Ukraine. In Herodotos's day, it was called Scythia. This vast, fertile plain contained more good farmland than the Greeks had ever seen in Europe. Salmon and sturgeon packed Scythian rivers during spawning season, and the Black Sea offered swarms of mackerel and anchovies so dense that, according to some ancient writers, they could be pulled from the water with one's bare hands.

Small wonder that the Black Sea coastline had, for the last hundred years, grown thick with Greek colonies. By the time Herodotos traveled there, Athens was already turning a covetous eye to those colonies and their enormous trade in fish and grain.

Scholars have often wondered why Herodotos wrote so much about Scythia in his *History*. He wrote almost as much about this obscure and barbarous land as he did about Egypt! Russian archaeologist Anatol Ilyich Kudrenko thinks he has an explanation. Kudrenko suggests that Herodotos may actually have been *hired* to write about Scythia. In Kudrenko's view, Herodotos was an agent and paid propagandist for the Athenian leader Perikles.

As Kudrenko points out, it may be only a coincidence that, shortly after Herodotos returned to Athens and published his *History*, Perikles led a naval expedition into the Black Sea, established a protectorate over many Greek colonies there, and placed their lucrative wheat trade under Athenian control. It may also be a coincidence that the Athenian state chose to honor Herodotos with a gift of ten talents for writing his *History*—a sum of money equivalent to two lifetimes' worth of full-time wages. All this may be a coincidence. But Kudrenko, with a typically Russian flair for sniffing out political intrigue, thinks otherwise. He believes that Herodotos's *History* may have been exactly the spark Perikles needed to fire his fellow Athenians with enthusiasm for adventuring in the distant and little-known lands of the Black Sea.[1]

Kudrenko's theory is plausible but speculative. The fact is, we really don't know why Herodotos visited the Black Sea region. And we know even less why he continued eastward on his journey as far as Colchis. Evidently, the land of Prometheus and the Golden Fleece was not a major focus of Herodotos's attention. He devoted no more than a few paragraphs to the Colchian portion of his voyage. Nevertheless, that small digression turned out to hold one of the most provocative passages in Herodotos's entire opus, teasing and perplexing historians for over 2,500 years.

The critical passage concerns the physical appearance of the Colchians. Herodotos describes them only briefly and in passing. But he clearly states that the Colchians he met were "black-skinned" *(melagchroes)* and "woolly-haired" *(oulotriches).*

This statement has presented modern scholars with a vexing problem. One has only to visit modern Georgia to see that the inhabitants of that country are clearly not black. Indeed, most Georgians closely resemble Greeks, Sicilians, and other Mediterranean peoples. The Soviet dictator Joseph Stalin—who was pure Georgian—typified the appearance of his countrymen, with his olive complexion, black hair, and sweeping mustache.

This seeming contradiction has led many scholars to question whether Herodotos has been properly translated. Some scholars— led by classicist Frank Snowden—have insisted that the word *melagchroes* really ought to be translated "dark-skinned," rather than "black-skinned." They also insist that *oulotriches*, while it does refer to woolly hair, may not necessarily refer to hair that is *quite* as kinky as the hair of subtropical Africans.[2]

All this hairsplitting over *melagchroes* and *oulotriches* is interesting enough, from a linguistic standpoint. But it is somewhat beside the point. If the Colchians Herodotos saw were no more dark-skinned or curly-haired than, say, the Greeks themselves, then surely Herodotos would never have bothered to remark on their appearance at all. Even if we agree with Professor Snowden that the Colchians were not *quite* as dark as the tropical Africans and their hair not *quite* as woolly, the fact remains that Herodotos evidently saw the Colchians as *darker than Greeks*, with noticeably coarser hair.

And that leaves us with the same problem as before. For such a description does not tally with the appearance of modern Georgians, who are virtually indistinguishable from Greeks. Shall we assume, then, that the Georgians were darker in past years than they are today? Or did Herodotos simply get his facts wrong? Upon this question hangs one of the most enduring mysteries of antiquity.

CHAPTER 8

FATHER OF
HISTORY? OR
FATHER OF LIES?

THE FIELDS OF SOUTH RUSSIA—OR UKRAINE, AS MOST OF THE region is now called—are studded with large, artificial hills called *kurgáni*. These are the burial sites of the Scythians and other ancient peoples who have roamed this area since at least 4500 B.C.—the same *kurgáni*, by the way, for which Marija Gimbutas named her notorious "Kurgan people," discussed in chapter 3. Since time immemorial, every peasant in the region has known that golden treasures can often be found buried in *kurgáni*. Many thousands of Scythian graves have consequently been looted over the centuries, their precious goldwork melted down and sold to unscrupulous jewelers. Nevertheless, enough *kurgáni* remained intact in the eighteenth century to supply the first generation of Russian archaeologists with ample material for study.

Thanks to Herodotos and other ancient writers, these early Russian excavators began their work with a great deal of knowledge about the Scythians and the other tribes of South Russian antiquity. Before they overturned their first spadeful of earth, they knew that the Scythians were a fair-skinned people with long, yellow hair, who roamed the steppes on horseback, their families and possessions stowed in great wagons. They also knew, from Herodotos and other ancient writers, that the Scythians were fierce and bloodthirsty fighters who made cloaks from their enemies' hides and drinking cups from their skulls.

Nevertheless, despite Herodotos's usefulness as a source, scholars found many of his tales hard to swallow. They were particularly skeptical of the Amazons—female warriors who fought from horseback, just like men, and who supposedly inhabited certain parts of Scythia. According to Herodotos, the Scythians called them *oiorpata*, or "man-slayers."

The story goes that the Amazons migrated to southern Russia after being defeated in battle by the Greeks in Asia Minor. No sooner had they landed in Russia than they acquired horses and began raiding Scythian camps. A party of Scythian warriors rode off in pursuit of the Amazons. But after fighting one battle, the Scythian men suddenly realized that the warriors they had been fighting were women!

Filled with admiration for these mettlesome maidens, the Scythian braves conceived a "strong desire to obtain children from so notable a race," as Herodotos put it, and they soon persuaded the Amazons to accept them as husbands. The women, however, placed one condition on the marriage:

> But the Amazons said, "We could not live with your women—our customs are quite different from theirs. To draw the bow, to hurl the javelin, to bestride the horse, these are our arts—of womanly employments we know nothing. Your women, on the contrary, do none of these things; but stay at home in their waggons, engaged in womanish tasks, and never go out to hunt, or to do anything. We should never agree together. But if you truly wish to keep us as your wives, and would conduct yourselves with strict justice towards us, go you home to your parents, bid them give you your inheritance, and then come back to us, and let us and you live together by ourselves."[1]

Thus, the Amazons and their new husbands went off to live in the lands beyond the Tanais River—a region known in Herodotos's day as Sarmatia, the land of the Sauromatae, where they lived freely and happily ever after, in the Amazon manner. Herodotos wrote,

"The women of the Sauromatae have continued from that day to the present to observe their ancient customs, frequently hunting on horseback with their husbands . . . in war taking the field, and wearing the very same dress as men. . . . Their marriage-law lays it down that no girl shall wed till she has killed a man in battle."[2]

Needless to say, many scholars in the eighteenth and nineteenth centuries tended to look askance at Herodotos's account of the Amazons. They knew that Greek mythology was filled with lore about Amazon warriors, and they assumed that Herodotos was simply indulging in one more retelling of the same tired old yarn. But it was disappointing to see a historian of Herodotos's caliber wasting precious ink on such silliness. Did Herodotos really expect anyone to take such stories seriously?

Maybe not. Herodotos, after all, never claimed that his stories were always true. He simply reported what he heard during his travels and let the reader believe as he chose. For example, he wrote of the Neurians, "It seems that these people are conjurers: for both the Scythians and the Greeks who dwell in Scythia say that every Neurian once a year becomes a wolf for a few days, at the end of which time he is restored to his proper shape. Not that I believe this, but they constantly affirm it to be true, and are even ready to back their assertion with an oath."[3]

After recounting a story that he heard in Egypt, concerning a legendary king who descended into the Underworld and played at dice with the goddess Isis, Herodotos admonished his readers in these words: "Anyone may believe these Egyptian tales, if he is sufficiently credulous: as for myself, I keep to the general plan of this book, which is to record the traditions of the various nations just as I heard them related to me."[4]

And that is exactly what Herodotos did. He traveled the world more widely than anyone else we know of during the fifth century B.C. Although there is some dispute over his actual itinerary, most scholars agree that Herodotos probably visited Syria, Babylon, Persia, Arabia, Asia Minor, Italy, Egypt, Scythia, and Colchis, just as he claimed in his book; and he may have reached Libya and Sicily as well. From each of these places, he brought back legends and lore, presenting them always with the same healthy grain of salt.

But not all of Herodotos's reports were based on hearsay and legend. Some included his own eyewitness accounts. Herodotos was very clear in distinguishing between those things he saw with his own eyes and those he heard about only secondhand. Thus, after touring the Egyptian Labyrinth, he wrote:

> The upper chambers I myself passed through and saw, and what I say concerning them is from my own observation; of the underground chambers I can only speak from report: for the keepers of the building could not be got to show them, since they contained (as they said) the sepulchres of the kings who built the Labyrinth, and also those of the sacred crocodiles. Thus it is from hearsay only that I can speak of the lower chambers. The upper chambers, however, I saw with my own eyes, and found them to excel all other human productions.[5]

This scrupulous honesty earned Herodotos the title of Father of History, bestowed upon him by Cicero in the first century B.C. Unfortunately, not everyone shared Cicero's admiration. Plutarch struck back about 150 years later, naming Herodotos the Father of Lies. Thus began a long tradition of Herodotos-bashing that continues to the present day—most of it every bit as unfair as that with which Plutarch started the campaign.

In the next chapter, we will take a moment to explore the question of Herodotos's veracity. If he was a "liar," then we need not concern ourselves with his reports of dark-skinned and woolly-haired Colchians. Indeed, many scholars today do not concern themselves with the Colchians for precisely that reason. If, on the other hand, Herodotos was telling the truth, and the Colchians were indeed dark-skinned and woolly-haired, then we have a vital clue in our hands for tracking down one of the lost Egyptian colonies of Bronze Age Europe.

CHAPTER 9

THE HERODOTOS-
BASHERS

"IT IS HARD TO UNDERSTAND HOW HERODOTOS COULD HAVE BE-
lieved that the Colchians were Negroes if he really went to
Colchis," writes classicist O. Kimball Armayor. "Herodotos's Colchian Negroes make it all the easier to doubt that he
ever went to the Black Sea at all."[1]

These words—from a 1978 article entitled "Did Herodotus Ever
Go to the Black Sea?"—nicely encapsulate the style of argument favored by Herodotos-bashers through the ages. For Armayor, the
mere fact that Herodotos mentioned black Colchians is *prima facie*
evidence of his mendacity. Armayor's three-step reasoning goes like
this: (1) Herodotos said the Colchians were black; (2) the Colchians
were not black; (3) Herodotos must therefore have been lying.

"Whatever the context," Armayor concluded in another article,
from 1980, "Herodotus does not really know what the Colchians
looked like or he would not call them black and woolly-haired. He
would know if he really went to Colchis."[2]

But how does Armayor *know* that the Colchians were not black
and woolly-haired in Herodotos's day? Simple. He quotes Hippokrates. In the classic work *Airs, Waters, Places,* the Greek physician

described the Colchians who lived near the river Phasis: "the Phasians have an appearance different from that of other men. As to size, they are large and corpulent in body. Neither joint nor vein is evident. They have a yellow flesh, as if victims of jaundice. Their voices are deeper than other men's."[3]

Curiously, Hippokrates' description of the Colchians is very nearly as eccentric as that of Herodotos. Neither one seems to bear much resemblance to Georgia's modern-day inhabitants. But Armayor finds Hippokrates more believable. After all, "Hippocrates' yellow may be the color of Mongol nomads," he suggests helpfully.[4]

But why should we believe in Hippokrates' yellow Colchians while rejecting Herodotos's black ones? Simple. According to Armayor, we should automatically doubt *anything* that Herodotos says, because the man was a habitual liar. And here's the proof:

Exhibit A: Herodotos made gross errors in his measurements of the length and width of the Black Sea.

Therefore, Armayor concludes, Herodotos probably never sailed on the Black Sea.[5] If he had actually sailed there, he would have made accurate measurements, would he not? Well, maybe. But, on the other hand, take a look at some of the early sixteenth-century maps of the New World. Many of them misrepresented the size, shape, and orientation of the American continents far more egregiously than Herodotos did the Black Sea. Shall we assume that Columbus, Vespucci, and Cabral were also liars?

Exhibit B: Herodotos seems to have exaggerated the size of a certain Scythian bronze cauldron, which he claims to have seen with his own eyes.

Judging by Herodotos's description, the vessel must have weighed at least 22.5 tons—more than twice as much as London's Big Ben. Impossible, says Armayor. No archaeologist has ever found a bronze cauldron even close to that size in Scythia, and there is no evidence that the Scythians had the technology to make one.[6]

Here Armayor employs the "argument from silence." Because no giant bronze vessels have been found in Scythia, the archaeological record is said to be "silent" on such artifacts. Armayor deduces from this silence that no such vessels ever existed. But, of course, this is a pure guess. There is no way of predicting what might lie buried in the ground or what might turn up in an excavation tomorrow. Archaeologists are constantly finding things—sometimes entire lost civilizations—whose prior existence no one ever suspected. For that reason, experienced archaeologists admonish their students that "absence of evidence is not evidence of absence." Armayor, however, chose to ignore this conventional advice. Instead, based on nothing more than the arguments cited above, he concluded that Herodotos must have been lying about his entire journey to the Black Sea:

> If he sailed the Pontus [the Black Sea], he almost certainly did not measure it. If he went to Exampaios and found a great bronze there, it almost certainly was not the bronze he says it was. If he reached Colchis, it almost certainly was not inhabited by circumcised Egyptian Negroes. . . . we cannot go on treating his stories as serious evidence of the fifth-century Black Sea.[7]

Astute readers can no doubt judge for themselves the worthiness of Armayor's evidence—and, by extension, that of myriad other Herodotos-bashers throughout history. Fortunately, hard-liners such as Armayor are on the retreat nowadays. A stunning series of archaeological discoveries in recent years has virtually compelled scholars to take a second—and far more respectful—look at Herodotos.

Few anecdotes found in Herodotos have aroused more ridicule than has his account of the Sauromatian Amazons, recounted in the last chapter. Yet, in the mid-nineteenth century, a Russian nobleman and amateur antiquarian named Count Bobrinskoy began to notice that the bones in many of the warrior graves he was excavating had a distinctly female form. The more he excavated, the more he found that these burials of women warriors tended to be concentrated northeast of the Don River—the ancient land of the Sauromatae! In the years since Count Bobrinskoy's discovery, weapons have been found in about one-fifth of all female graves in Sarmatia, dating from the fifth and sixth centuries B.C. Weapons have also been found in the graves of many Scythian women.[8]

Some Russian researchers have suggested that weapons were placed in female graves for ritual purposes only. But archaeologist Jeannine Davis-Kimball counters that "the bones tell a different story. The bowed legs of one 13- or 14-year-old girl attest a life on horseback. . . . A bent arrowhead was found in the body cavity of another woman, suggesting that she had been killed in battle."[9] In Davis-Kimball's view, the conclusion is inescapable: "These finds suggest that Greek tales of Amazon warriors may have had some basis in fact."[10]

Further illustrations abound of Herodotos's newly proven veracity. In the 1950s, researchers unearthed a burial site perfectly preserved in the frozen permafrost at a place called Pazryk, in the Altai Mountains, north of China. This was the easternmost reach of the traditional Scythian lands. The excavators found frozen bodies still stuffed with chopped cypress, frankincense, parsley seed, and anise seed, exactly as Herodotos had described in his account of Scythian funeral customs.[11]

They also found a fur bag containing *cannabis sativa*—otherwise known as hemp or marijuana. This too confirmed Herodotos's account of Scythian "vapor baths" in which the Scythians burned hemp on red-hot stones, allowing their tents to fill with the soothing vapors. "The Scythians enjoy it so much that they howl with pleasure," Herodotos had written.[12]

At a place called Belsk, archaeologists discovered a Scythian workshop where drinking cups were fashioned from human skulls; at other sites, researchers have found royal burials, complete with human sacrifices and great numbers of horses encircling the buried king—all described by Herodotos 2,400 years ago.[13] If it is true, as Armayor contends, that Herodotos never visited Scythia, then the "Father of Lies" must have plagiarized his information from some extraordinarily reliable sources.

Of course, hard-line skeptics will never change. They will never cease bashing Herodotos. No amount of archaeological corroboration will ever quiet their contentious souls, for their battle with Herodotos ultimately transcends facts and evidence. It is a war between rival faiths.

Herodotos represents the voice of ancient tradition. He is the spiritual descendant of those illiterate bards who once preserved in their heads the myths, epics, and genealogies of barbarian kings. For all his many faults and frailties, Herodotos is the memory of the people, the last vital link between modern and legendary times. The skeptics, however, do not see it that way. Ancient tradition does not move them, for they are acolytes, one and all, of the cult of *Besserwissen*.

This obscure doctrine first arose in the eighteenth century, among a clique of German philologists. At the peak of the Enlightenment, these scholars embraced science and reason as their guiding principles. In practice, this meant rejecting anything that could not be proved "scientifically." The Bible was one of their first victims. Once regarded as infallible sacred writ, the scriptures were now scrutinized beneath the cold new lamp of "rational" analysis and pronounced to be nothing more than a collection of pious fairy tales, having no basis in historical fact.

The age of *Besserwissen* had dawned—German for "knowing better." According to this new philosophy, modern scholars automatically assumed that they knew better than the ignorant, superstitious scribblers who wrote the old histories. Virtually anything written in the past was considered suspect.[14] In this new atmosphere, one of the easiest ways for scholars to prove that they were smart, daring, and up-to-date was to poke fun at Herodotos, calling him the Father of Lies and dismissing all that he said. By Victorian times, teachers in every classroom of the Western world were urging their pupils to snicker at the "old liar."

But *Besserwissen* had its limitations. Despite its claims to be scientific, it often led scholars to absurd conclusions. During the eighteenth century, for example, a world-renowned Scottish historian named Dr. William Robertson blandly declared that there had never been any such civilizations as those of the Aztecs, the Mayas, and the Incas. The conquistadors had just made it all up! Of course, Bernal Diaz del Castillo, an eyewitness to Cortés's conquest of Mexico, had described in detail the wondrous cities and temples of the Aztecs in his *True History of the Conquest of New Spain*. But that made no difference. Diaz, after all, was not a trained scientific observer like Dr. Robertson. Dr. Robertson "knew better."

"The Indian temples were merely mounds of earth covered with shrubs, without steps or facings of cut stone," Robertson wrote in his *History of America*. "There is not, in all that vast expanse, a single monument or vestige of any building more ancient than the conquest."[15]

Of course, Dr. Robertson was wrong. Thousands of tourists today can offer Polaroid snapshots of the Pyramid of the Sun and the lost cities of Tikal and Machu Picchu to refute Robertson's "expert" testimony. Nevertheless, he was widely believed in his day, and the memory of America's lost civilizations faded for over a hundred years.

Besserwissen was still alive and well in 1863, when a man named Heinrich Schliemann set out to find the lost city of Troy. Schliemann, a German self-made millionaire who had struck it rich in the import-export business, lacked academic credentials. He knew nothing about *Besserwissen*. Had he studied ancient history at the university, he would have been taught that Homer's *Iliad* was a work of pure fantasy and that, if Troy existed at all, it would certainly not be found where Homer said it would.

Fortunately, Schliemann applied common sense rather than *Besserwissen*. He studied Homer closely, seeking clues to the precise location of the legendary city. Using landmarks in the *Iliad* as a guide, Schliemann proceeded to excavate some 325,000 cubic yards of earth from the hill of Hissarlik in northwestern Turkey. He discovered Homer's "mythical" city of Troy in the exact location where Homer said it would be, complete with a remarkable hoard of gold. Three years later, Schliemann followed another Greek writer, Pausanias, to a second great treasure trove at the Greek site of Mycenae. In a few short years, Schliemann had accumulated a mass of treasure and artifacts that were the envy of every "expert" in the field. "All the museums of the world taken together," Schliemann gloated, "do not have one fifth as much."[16]

Schliemann's finds dealt a stunning blow to *Besserwissen*. Nonetheless, this spiritless philosophy continues to haunt scholarship today. It lingers with particular intensity in the discussions surrounding Herodotos's account of Colchis. Herodotos had a number of fascinating things to say, not only about the physical appearance of the Colchians, but also about legends that tie their civilization closely to ancient Egypt. Yet, few scholars today would risk their reputations by taking these stories too seriously and trying to find out what lies behind them.

More than a hundred years after Schliemann, too many scholars have yet to learn their lesson. They are still too quick to dismiss ancient writings as inherently unreliable. In the succeeding chapters, we will work from a different assumption. We will cast aside the spirit of *Besserwissen* and approach Herodotos with respect. Just as Heinrich Schliemann followed Homer, we will follow Herodotos and other ancient writers wherever the trail leads us. Perhaps, like Schliemann, we too will unearth an unexpected treasure trove of knowledge and wonder.

CHAPTER 10

EGYPTIANS
IN RUSSIA

HERODOTOS HAD AN INTERESTING THEORY TO EXPLAIN WHY THE Colchians of his day had black skin and woolly hair. He suggested that they might be descendants of Egyptian colonists. Herodotos wrote:

> But it is undoubtedly a fact that the Colchians are of Egyptian descent. I noticed this myself before I heard anyone else mention it. . . .
> My own idea on the subject was based first on the fact that they have black skins and woolly hair . . . and secondly, and more especially, on the fact that the Colchians, the Egyptians and the Ethiopians are the only races which from ancient times have practised circumcision.[1]

Herodotos says that the Colchians physically resembled Egyptians and also practiced circumcision like the Egyptians. He further observes that the Colchians wove a form of linen identical to that woven in Egypt. This was the famous Colchian *sardonikos*, whose manufacture and export was a major source of wealth for that country in Herodotos's day. Archaeologists have confirmed that Colchian linen—like the Egyptian variety—was woven on a vertical, two-beam loom, whose distinctive pyramid-shaped weights have been found in abundance in Georgian archaeological sites. Some scholars have suggested that the Colchians acquired this invention from

Greece. But David Braund, a British expert on ancient Colchis, emphatically disagrees. He writes, "The notion that this loom came from Greece . . . is without any foundation. There is no evidence that the vertical two-beam loom was in use in ancient Greece: it was certainly not of Greek origin, but from the Levant and in regular use in Egypt."[2]

But what would Egyptian colonists have been doing in Colchis—over a thousand miles from Egypt, as the crow flies? Again Herodotos had an explanation. Egyptian priests had told him the story of a pharaoh named Sesostris, who once led an army northward through Syria and Turkey all the way to Colchis, westward across southern Russia, and then south again through Romania, until he reached Bulgaria and the eastern part of Greece (which were then collectively referred to as Thrace). According to Herodotos, Sesostris then returned home the same way he had come, leaving colonists behind at the Colchian river Phasis. Here is the story in Herodotos's own words:

> In this way he traversed the whole continent of Asia, whence he passed on into Europe, and made himself master of Scythia and of Thrace, beyond which countries I do not think that his army extended its march. . . . Returning to Egypt from Thrace, he came, on his way, to the banks of the river Phasis. Here I cannot say with any certainty what took place. Either he of his own accord detached a body of troops from his main army and left them to colonise the country, or else a certain number of his soldiers, wearied with their long wanderings, deserted, and established themselves on the banks of this stream.[3]

With his usual concern for accuracy, Herodotos went out of his way to caution the reader that much of the story came to him secondhand from Egyptian priests. He prefaced the tale with this disclaimer: "Up to this point I have confined what I have written to the results of my own observation and research, and the views I have formed from them; but from now on the basis of my story will be the accounts given to me by the Egyptians themselves—though here, too, I shall put in one or two things which I have seen with my own eyes."[4]

Hearsay though it was, Herodotos seemed inclined to believe the story. In support of it, he observed that the Colchians themselves told legends of a long-ago colonization from Egypt, an event that they remembered far more vividly than did the Egyptians. He wrote, "I asked some questions both in Colchis and in Egypt, and found that the Colchians remembered the Egyptians more distinctly than the Egyptians remembered them. The Egyptians did, however, say that they thought the original Colchians were men from Sesostris's army."[5]

The question is, should *we* believe the story? Let us suppose, for a moment, that Herodotos's account is true and that a pharaoh named Sesostris really did leave colonists on the Colchian shores. Where are the descendants of those colonists today? Why do modern visitors to the Republic of Georgia find no black-skinned and woolly-haired people to match Herodotos's description?

Perhaps they are not looking in the right place.

The Caucasus region, which includes Georgia, has some of the oldest human populations in the world. In that remote and mountainous region, there has been little movement or migration since prehistoric times. Ancient peoples have lingered for millennia in secluded valleys, isolated from their neighbors, speaking discrete languages and following unique customs.

In such a setting, it is not unusual for "fossil" populations to exist for generations, unknown to the outside world. So it was that one day, in 1912, a Russian naturalist named V. P. Vradii stumbled upon just such a lost culture while visiting the area of Batumi, on the southwestern coast of Georgia.

Vradii discovered a small colony of about twenty to thirty black people who claimed to have been living in the area since time immemorial. None could tell Vradii exactly how they had come to be there. They spoke only the Abkhazian language. Most followed the Muslim faith. Vradii noticed that many were quite black in complexion, with strongly African features, while others seemed to be a mixture of African and local ancestry.

Vradii published his discovery in 1913, in a newspaper called *Kavkaz*. In response to his article, entitled "Negroes of the Batumi District," the newspaper was flooded with letters reporting other black populations along the Black Sea coast, some numbering in the hundreds. Later researchers reported colonies of blacks as far afield as Azerbaijan (which lies southeast of Georgia, on the border of Iran) and the Crimea.[6] These mysterious black people seemed to be most numerous, however, in the area of Abkhazia—an obscure, ethnic enclave on Georgia's northwestern coast. In response to Vradii's article, one E. Markov wrote:

Passing for the first time through the Abkhazian community of Adzhiubzha . . . I was struck by the purely tropical landscape: Against the background of a bright green primeval jungle there stood huts and sheds built of wood and covered with reeds; curly-headed Negro children played on the ground and a Negro woman passed by grandly carrying a bundle on her head. Black-skinned people wearing white clothes in the bright sun resembled a picture of some African scene.[7]

Thus began decades of scholarly speculation on the origin of these Georgian and Abkhazian blacks. It turned out that many of them had arrived in the region quite recently. In interviews with researchers and journalists, many recounted family legends of having been brought to the region as slaves by Turkish and Abkhazian noblemen. Other families told different tales. In 1925, one village elder told the visiting black American Communist Otto Hall that he and others in the community had been Sudanese mercenaries who settled in Abkhazia after deserting the Turkish army in the late nineteenth century.

It seems evident that many, perhaps most, of today's "Black Sea Negro" populations arrived in recent times, especially from the sixteenth to eighteenth centuries A.D., when Abkhazia was under Turkish rule. Yet, as Martin Bernal has pointed out, stories of black Colchians go back many thousands of years. Long before Herodotos wrote his *Histories,* a Greek poet named Pindar—who lived around 522–443 B.C.—described the Colchians whom Jason and the Argonauts fought as being "dark-skinned."[8] Eight hundred years later, the Church Fathers St. Jerome and Sophronius, writing in the late fourth century, referred to Colchis as the "second Ethiopia" because of its black population.[9]

Today's black Abkhazians—or at least most of them—may indeed have arrived only recently. But the writings of Pindar, Herodotos, and others suggest that black people have been at home in the Caucasus for millennia. This is corroborated by Abkhazian folklore. The so-called Nart Epic—believed to be thousands of years old—tells of 100 black-skinned horsemen who visited the Caucasus and liked it so much that some of them stayed and made their homes there.[10]

Perhaps Africans have been arriving in the Caucasus in a slow, steady trickle since the dawn of time, enticed by its warm climate and lush forests. But if they came in small numbers, they would have made little impact on the population, existing only in small, isolated enclaves like the black Abkhazians of today. The Colchis of Herodotos and other Greco-Roman writers, however, is a country *saturated* with dark-skinned people—a situation that would more likely have arisen if a great many blacks had arrived all at once—say, under the command of the pharaoh Sesostris. Such an army would have made a profound impact on the country, darkening Colchian complexions for centuries to come.

Why, then, do we find no trace of them today? Why do we find only tiny pockets of black Abkhazians, most of whom seem to have arrived during the period of Turkish rule? Perhaps during the 2,500 years that have passed since Herodotos, the black Colchians have simply blended into the general population.

Such an event would hardly be unique. History offers many examples of black communities that have disappeared through intermarriage—and in a much shorter period than 2,500 years. Sociologists have called this process "whitening out." The black people of Argentina, for example, who in 1852 constituted over 14 percent of the country's population—34 percent in Buenos Aires alone—have been thoroughly "whitened out" through intermarriage. There is virtually no trace of them today as a recognizable social group.[11]

Scientists have predicted that a similar process would occur in the United States if people suddenly started choosing their mates in a mathematically random fashion, without regard to color. Once the process was complete, some people would still be left with mildly dark skin, but researchers say that even they would most likely have few Negroid features.[12]

Suppose such a process occurred in ancient Colchis. It is not hard to imagine why some observers, such as Herodotos—arriving on the scene some 1,500 years after it began—would have seen people with dark skin and woolly hair, while other observers, such as Hippokrates, would have seen people with yellow skin. Depending on which part of the country Herodotos and Hippokrates visited, either of these physical types—or a hundred variations in between—might easily have presented themselves. Later, as the centuries advanced, the descendants of Sesostris's army would have been slowly "whitened out."

Generations of Abkhazians have embraced the tale of Sesostris as a source of national pride. Their tiny land has struggled for centuries to preserve its individuality against Georgian and Russian domination. What better way to assert one's uniqueness than to claim descent from an army of Egyptian conquerors?

Dmitri Gulia (1874–1960) was neither the first nor the last propagandist to appropriate the legend of Sesostris for Abkhazia's greater glory. But he was surely the most ambitious. A gifted linguist, ethnographer, and historian—as well as Abkhazia's greatest poet—Gulia brought all his many talents to bear in 1925, when he published his epic *History of Abkhazia*.

There he argued that the Abkhazians were an "Abyssino-Egyptian" people. To prove his point, Gulia amassed an impressive hoard of words and names that were similar in the Egyptian, Abkhazian, and Ethiopian languages. There were family names, names of rivers and mountains, names of pre-Christian deities, and much more. He also noted various customs and folk beliefs that Abkhazia seemed to share with Egypt and Ethiopia. All of these, Gulia proposed, had been brought to the Caucasus by Sesostris and his troops.

In the end, Gulia failed to persuade his fellow scholars. His evidence was judged to be weak, and his theory was soon forgotten. But the strength of Gulia's convictions lives after him. A fierce patriot, Gulia labored all his life to bring the history and scholarship of his native Abkhazia to the attention of an indifferent world. To the day he died, Gulia remained convinced that the mountains and forests of his native land held secrets that would one day lead scholars "to the resolution of a whole range of problems concerning the past not only of the Caucasus but of the whole of Near Asia."[13]

As more and more scholars begin taking seriously Herodotos's enigmatic writings on the black-skinned and woolly-haired Colchians, Dmitri Gulia's heartfelt prophecy may at last come to fulfillment.

CHAPTER 11

NEFERTI'S
PROPHECY

Was there really an Egyptian pharaoh named Sesostris? Or did Herodotos just make him up? Egyptologists do, in fact, believe that Sesostris existed. They do *not*, however, believe that he ever invaded Europe or founded colonies on the Black Sea. Most assume that this part of the story was nothing more than patriotic boasting on the part of the Egyptian priests who recounted it to Herodotos. But was it?

Sesostris seems to be the Greek version of an Egyptian name meaning man of the goddess Wosret—*Senwosret*. Three pharaohs bore that name, all in the Twelfth Dynasty. Significantly, the Egyptian historian Manetho also places the legendary Sesostris in the Twelfth Dynasty. Could one of the three Senwosrets actually have been the conquering Sesostris of legend? And, if so, which one?

Manetho, an Egyptian priest, had access to the temple libraries and the hieroglyphic chronicles of the old pharaohs. Because Egypt was then under Greek rule, Manetho recorded Egypt's history in a massive book called the *Aegyptiaca*, written entirely in Greek and giving the names of the pharaohs in Hellenized forms. Manetho's history was so accurate that his scheme of dividing Egyptian history into thirty royal dynasties is still followed by Egyptologists today, with only minor changes.

According to Manetho, a pharaoh whom he called by the Hellenized name of Sesostris had ruled Egypt during the Twelfth Dynasty and had "subdued the whole of Asia and Europe as far as Thrace" in a period of nine years.[1] This was undoubtedly the same Sesostris of whom Herodotos had written. However, after scholars deciphered Egyptian hieroglyphs in 1824 and began reading the Egyptian king-lists for themselves, they found a discrepancy in Manetho's account.

Manetho says that the first four kings of the Twelfth Dynasty were:[2]

Amenemes I
Sesonchosis
Amenemes II
Sesostris

The original hieroglyphic records, however—in which Amenemes is called "Amenemhat" and Sesostris "Senwosret"—give a slightly different account:

Amenemhat I Sehetepibra (1991–1962 B.C.)
Senwosret I Kheperkara (1962–1928 B.C.)
Amenemhat II Nubkaura (1928–1895 B.C.)
Senwosret II Khakheperra (1895–1878 B.C.)
Senwosret III Khakaura (1878–1842 B.C.)

Thus, Manetho lists only one Sesostris, while the original Egyptian chronicles list no less than three Senwosrets. Which Senwosret shall we equate with the legendary world conqueror? Most Egyptologists believe that features of *all three* Senwosrets may have been combined in Manetho's Sesostris.[3] For example, both Senwosret I and Senwosret III led military expeditions into Nubia, just as the legendary Sesostris did. Senwosret II engaged in large-scale irrigation projects, much as Herodotos records Sesostris to have done.[4] And more than one Senwosret appears to have led armies into Asia.[5]

However, no conventional Egyptologist admits that *any* of these three Senwosrets ever conquered Colchis, Scythia, Thrace, or any other land in Europe. If none of the Senwosrets ever reached the Black Sea, then none could have left "dark-skinned" and "woolly-

x

haired" colonists there. We would then have to assume that not only Herodotos, but also every other Greco-Roman writer who ever spoke of Sesostris—such as Diodoros, Plutarch, Strabo, and Josephus—must have been wrong.

This, in fact, has been the scholarly consensus for at least two hundred years. No self-respecting classicist or Egyptologist today would ever consider the possibility that an Egyptian army marched through southern Russia in the twentieth century B.C.—or at any other time, for that matter. Sesostris's legendary feats would long ago have been dismissed as fairy tales were it not for the determined efforts of a single man.

Martin Gardiner Bernal has often been accused of taking an old-fashioned approach to scholarship. By that, his critics mean that Bernal places too much faith in ancient traditions, such as those recorded by Herodotos. In this regard, the critics are right. Bernal follows in the footsteps of Heinrich Schliemann, who discovered Troy by placing his faith in Homer's account.

Like Schliemann, Bernal is neither a classicist nor an Egyptologist. A professor of Government and Near Eastern studies at Cornell University, Bernal has spent most of his career studying China and the Far East, and he is trained primarily as a political scientist. Nevertheless, like Schliemann before him, Bernal has succeeded in upstaging the specialists. He has followed the ancient traditions with an attentive and open mind, and they have led him to a remarkable series of discoveries—many of which will be discussed in later chapters.

Perhaps Bernal's most audacious theory concerns the story of Sesostris. In 1991, Bernal flouted Egyptological convention by announcing that he believed there was considerable evidence to support Herodotos's story of the world-conquering pharaoh. Herodotos and other ancient writers might have gotten some details wrong, Bernal admitted. It seemed unlikely, for example, that Sesostris had ever conquered India, as Diodoros had written. Nevertheless, Bernal claimed, the evidence for Sesostris's conquests in Colchis and Asia Minor was quite strong and that even his invasion of Scythia and Thrace was not out of the question.

Bernal's theory is profoundly controversial. In effect, it postulates that highly civilized Africans once colonized a primitive Europe still seething with headhunters and cannibals. It is a "world turned upside down," in the disapproving words of classicist Emily T. Vermeule.[6]

Was Sesostris black? Later chapters will explore more thoroughly the ongoing controversy over the race of the ancient Egyptians. Experts remain divided on this question, and many argue that the Egyptian population was a mixture of blacks and whites. In the case of Sesostris, however, there is no need to withhold judgment on the question of his "blackness." Even the most conventional Egyptologists acknowledge that the Twelfth Dynasty—the royal family from which Sesostris sprang—was one of the blackest to ever rule Egypt. Since ancient times, travelers in Egypt have noted that the southern Egyptians have darker skin and more Negroid features than the northern Egyptians. In the extreme south, near the island of Elephantine at Aswan—the traditional border between Egypt and Nubia—the Egyptians on one side of the border are virtually indistinguishable from the exceedingly dark Nubians on the other side.

It is precisely from this border region that the Twelfth Dynasty hailed. The founder of this dynasty, Amenemhat I, was the son of a priest named Senwosret—who apparently came from southern Egypt—and a woman named Nofret from *Ta-Seti*—a name the Egyptians applied both to northern Nubia and the southernmost province of Egypt.[7] That many of the Twelfth Dynasty pharaohs had markedly Negroid features is confirmed by their statues and portraits.

"As expected, strong Nubian features and dark coloring are seen in their sculpture and relief work," comments Egyptologist Frank J. Yurco. Of a limestone relief of Senwosret I found at Karnak, Yurco observes that it "displays such Nubian traits as thick lips and a broad nose with flaring nostrils."[8]

There is an enthralling bit of Egyptian folklore connected with this dynasty. A papyrus now in the Museum of St. Petersburg in Russia tells how King Snofru, a pharaoh of the Fourth Dynasty, once sought to entertain himself by commanding a priest named Neferti to foretell the future. Unfortunately, Neferti's prophecy proved less than amusing. He foretold a time when Egypt would be plunged into chaos, bloodshed, and unrest. In the end, however, a savior would arise to restore Egypt to her greatness. Neferti declared: "A king shall come belonging to the South, Ameny by name, the son of a woman of Ta-Seti, a child of Khen-nekhen. He shall receive the White Crown, he shall wear the Red Crown.... The people of his time shall rejoice, the 'son of Someone' [man of good birth] shall make his name for ever and ever."[9]

Neferti's prophecy came to pass, for Egypt was indeed torn by civil strife from about 2181 to 2055 B.C. Egyptologists call this episode the First Intermediate Period. Egypt's Old Kingdom, which built the mighty pyramids of Giza, came to an end during this time. All major building projects ceased, and Egypt broke up into a multitude of petty princedoms. Manetho wrote that there were "seventy kings in seventy days," so unstable had the royal succession become.[10]

"See now, things are done that never were done before," lamented Ipuwer, a scribe who wrote during this troubled period. "The King has been robbed by beggars. . . . What the pyramid hid is empty. See now, the land is deprived of kingship by a few people who ignore custom."[11]

Egypt was reunified after 2055 B.C. But not until Amenemhat I— the "Ameny" of Neferti's prophecy—mounted the throne in 1991 B.C. did Egypt begin to recover some semblance of its lost glory. Just as Neferti had predicted, Egypt "rejoiced" at the accession of this new dynasty, whose pharaohs vanquished Egypt's foes, filled its treasure houses with plunder, reared great temples and pyramids, and caused the desert to bloom with grand new irrigation projects. "This dynasty ranks as among the greatest," writes Egyptologist Frank Yurco, "whose fame far outlived its actual tenure on the throne."[12]

Just as Neferti foretold, the names of the Twelfth Dynasty kings were indeed remembered "forever and ever" in the annals of Western history. For, if Martin Bernal's theory is correct, these black pharaohs left their mark on Europe every bit as deeply as on their native Egypt.

CHAPTER 12

THE SESOSTRIS
ENIGMA

SESOSTRIS OR NO SESOSTRIS, EGYPTIANS FOR MANY CENTURIES looked back on the Twelfth Dynasty as a golden age. The dynasty founder, Amenemhat I, became such a popular figure in Egyptian folklore that stories about him grew into a thriving literary genre. "More personal details are known about the founder of the new dynasty than about any other Pharaoh," observed Egyptologist Sir Alan Gardiner in 1961.[1]

Nor was the fame of the Twelfth Dynasty confined only to Egypt. More than five hundred years after his death, Senwosret III was worshiped as a god in Nubia. His son, Amenemhat III, may figure prominently in the Hebrew Bible. According to a controversial new theory put forth by Egyptologist David M. Rohl, Amenemhat III may have been the pharaoh whom the Bible says appointed Joseph vizier of Egypt and invited the Hebrews to settle in the land of Goshen.[2]

"The time of Ammenemes and Sesostris was certainly the classical period of Egypt's history," comments Nicolas Grimal, a leading historian of ancient Egypt. As long as the pharaohs reigned, Egypt's scribes and sages looked back to this period for models of perfection in literature and the arts.[3] If we are to believe Herodotos, Diodoros, and the other Greco-Roman writers, the Egyptians were still bragging about their Twelfth Dynasty kings more than a thousand years after the dynasty ended.

What was all the hoopla about? What made this dynasty so much grander than all others, before or after? One answer seems to lie in its cosmopolitanism. The Twelfth Dynasty pharaohs were keenly interested in the outside world. They carried on trade and diplomacy with many foreign nations. They sent out explorers and prospectors to scout for new markets and natural resources. And when they found something they wanted—such as the gold mines and gem deposits of Nubia—they were not averse to sending in the troops.[4]

During the reign of Senwosret I, some offering tables made of precious materials were dedicated to the god Mont in a new temple, near the modern town of El-Tod. An inscription in the temple states that the tables were "twice as beautiful and twice as numerous as all one was accustomed to see in this country before, and representing what foreigners and *explorers, who travel across the lands,* have delivered."[5]

Who were these "explorers who travel across the lands?" How far did they wander in their quest to enrich the pharaoh's coffers? Archaeological evidence suggests that their missions extended to the ends of the known world. During the Middle Kingdom period (Eleventh to Fourteenth Dynasties), gems and precious metals began pouring into Egypt from all over eastern Europe. A special form of the alloy electrum—consisting of 30 percent silver and 70 percent gold—which can only be mined naturally in Transylvania's Apusini Mountains, appeared in Egypt at this time, as did a clear, red and yellow jasper unique to Romania. Amethyst, carnelian, chalcedony, and other semiprecious stones of probable Balkan origin have also turned up at Egyptian sites from this period.[6]

In 1936, an archaeologist named Bisson de la Roque discovered four chests filled with treasure in Senwosret's temple at El-Tod.[7] Every chest was inscribed with the name of Senwosret's son, Amenemhat II. The Tod Treasure, as it was called, contained a mass of gold and silver objects, bracelets, gold ingots and chains, 153 silver bowls, a silver lion, and many precious gems, all brought from distant countries. There were cylinder seals from Mesopotamia, carved in semiprecious stone. Many bowls bore designs typical of North Syria, Crete, and Turkey.[8] There was lapis lazuli that probably came from Afghanistan.[9] And experts have determined that at least some of the silver in the hoard came from Greece—in particular, from the famous Laurion mines near Athens.[10]

Was this booty taken in war? Did it come as diplomatic gifts from friendly monarchs? Or as tribute exacted from subservient vassals? Nobody knows. But the Tod Treasure makes clear that Twelfth Dynasty Egypt—whether through war, diplomacy, or trade—was drawing in wealth from every corner of the world.

Scholars disagree over the extent of the Twelfth Dynasty's imperial conquests. But on some points there can be no dispute. Egypt certainly conquered large portions of Nubia during this time. By the reign of Senwosret III, Egypt had subdued the entire country up to the Second Cataract—a stretch of rough water on the Nile located near the modern Sudanese border. Here, Senwosret III completed a series of ten enormous forts begun by Senwosret I to guard the southern boundary of Egypt's empire.[11] Nubia expert William Y. Adams has called these fortresses "the mightiest fortifications ever erected in the ancient world." He continues:

> Four thousand years after their building, and three thousand years after their final abandonment, the mud walls of these gargantuan relics still rose in places forty feet above the desert sand. . . . Buhen staggers the imagination not only by its size but by the complexity of its defenses. Bastions, loopholes, fosse, drawbridge, glacis—virtually all of the classic elements of medieval fortification are present in this structure. . . . To a greater or lesser degree, the same features are incorporated in most of the other Middle Kingdom fortresses.[12]

As Bernal pointed out, any nation that could bring to bear such massive military force in the south would likely present just as great a threat to the north.[13] There was certainly no lack of motivation for the Egyptians to turn covetous eyes toward Europe and the Levantine coast. Treasures like those found at El-Tod would only have whetted the appetites of Twelfth Dynasty pharaohs for easier access to the gold, silver, and other precious goods of the north.

Yet, generations of Egyptologists have denied that this ever happened. It was long an article of faith among scholars that Egypt never held an empire in Asia until the conquests of Thutmose I (1504–1492 B.C.) in the Eighteenth Dynasty. Before that, the pharaohs supposedly made only brief forays into Palestine, to intimidate the Asiatic tribes. This argument has been applied most frequently to the Twelfth Dynasty, in an attempt to explain away copious evidence of Egyptian military activity in Asia.

It is known, for example, that Senwosret III captured the town of Sekmem in Palestine (probably biblical Shechem) and that a general named Nesmont fought against Asiatic nomads during the period when Amenemhat I and his son Senwosret I shared the throne.[14] Moreover, a fictional story from the Twelfth Dynasty entitled *The Tale of Sinuhe* says that Senwosret I was "created to smite the Bedouin and to crush the sandfarers" and describes him as "the one who severs the neck of those who are among the Asiatics."[15] These words hardly describe a stay-at-home. Of course, scholars generally dismiss such hints of Twelfth-Dynasty expeditions into Asia as referring to mere raids or skirmishes. The purpose of these raids was to intimidate, not conquer, they say. Yet, other references clearly imply that the Egyptians maintained a permanent colonial administration in Asia during the Twelfth Dynasty.

The narrator of the *Tale of Sinuhe*, for example, describes himself as "governor of the domains of the sovereign in the lands of the Asiatics"—a title that would have little meaning if Egypt possessed no Asiatic domains.[16] At another point in the story, the narrator, Sinuhe, advises the Syrians to respect the pharaoh's power.

"Be loyal to him [Senwosret], and he will reward you richly," says Sinuhe. "Be disloyal and you'll risk his implacable wrath."[17] This is advice for a vassal, not an equal. It suggests that the Syrian tribes were subservient to the pharaoh. This impression is reinforced by many references in *The Tale of Sinuhe* to Egyptian messengers or couriers who travel the length and breadth of Syria and Palestine on the pharaoh's business.[18]

Perhaps the richest city on the Levantine coast, at this time, was Byblos, a thriving Phoenician port grown rich from its sea trade. By the Twelfth Dynasty, the rulers of Byblos were so Egyptianized that they commonly gave themselves Egyptian titles, wrote in Egyptian hieroglyphs, and surrounded themselves with Egyptian luxuries.[19] Farther south, near the copper mines of Sinai, more Egyptian monuments have been found from the Twelfth Dynasty than from all other dynasties combined.[20]

Another clue to Egypt's elusive Twelfth Dynasty empire is provided by the so-called Execration Texts. The Egyptians would curse their enemies by writing their names on pots or figurines and then

breaking the objects in a magical ritual.[21] By reassembling the pieces
and studying the texts, archaeologists can determine toward which
countries Egypt directed its hostility during a particular period.
During the Twelfth Dynasty, many cities and peoples in Asia were
singled out for execration, among them Sekmem, Ashkelon, Byblos,
and Jerusalem.[22] This could well mean that these cities were attacked and conquered during that period.

Over the years, many scholars have been persuaded by such evidence that the Twelfth Dynasty pharaohs did indeed control wide
swaths of territory in Asia. As archaeologist William Foxwell Albright put it, in 1960: "Western Palestine, Phoenicia and parts of
Syria were dominated by Egyptian power and material culture.
. . . The Execration Texts [from the Twelfth Dynasty] even enable us
to draw the boundary of the direct sphere of Egyptian control across
central Syria north of Damascus to the Eleutherus Valley in central
Phoenicia."[23]

Yet, until recently, many archaeologists stubbornly refused to accept the idea of Twelfth Dynasty conquests in Asia. Egypt might
have had trade relations with Syria and Phoenicia, they admitted,
perhaps even a sphere of influence, but not a real empire. To build
such an empire would require large-scale wars of conquest, and no
inscriptions had been found describing such wars. Twelfth Dynasty
pharaohs may have fought wars of conquest in the *south*, said the
skeptics, but certainly not in the north. By implication, Sesostris
could never have invaded Europe, the skeptics claimed. After all,
none of the three pharaohs who bore Sesostris's name had ever
marched farther north than Sekmem in Palestine!

The argument from silence had spoken. Or so it seemed. Little
did the skeptics realize that the silence on which their argument depended was about to be suddenly and resoundingly broken.

CHAPTER 13

EGYPTIANS
AT TROY

SCHOLARS WHO RELY A GREAT DEAL ON THE ARGUMENT FROM silence often speak as if important evidence from past ages can always be counted on to survive. If you can't find the evidence, they imply, then it probably never existed. Of course, this is not the way things really work. Artifacts from thousands of years ago are rare and fragile. Nowhere is this more clearly demonstrated than in Egypt, where generations of pharaohs systematically destroyed, defaced, and usurped the monuments of their predecessors in order to enhance their own glory.

One of the greatest usurpers of all was Ramesses II (1290–1224 B.C.), whose name has been gouged in stone from one end of Egypt to the other—often right over the names of previous pharaohs whose monuments Ramesses claimed for himself. It is partly thanks to Ramesses' vanity that the hard evidence of Sesostris's northern conquests lay hidden for so long from archaeologists.

During Egypt's Twelfth Dynasty, a large and important inscription had been erected before the Temple of Ptah at Memphis—an ancient Egyptian city located near the village of Mit Rahina. It stood undisturbed for over six hundred years. Then, one day, Ramesses II decided to rebuild the Temple of Ptah in a way more flattering to himself. In the process, his workmen broke the great inscription into several pieces, the largest of which ended up buried beneath a colossal statue of Ramesses that now stood before the temple. There the fallen inscription lay hidden and forgotten for more than 3,000 years.

A small fragment of it was discovered by British Egyptologist Flinders Petrie in 1909. But there was not enough writing on the piece to make any sense of it. Only in 1974 did archaeologist Sami Farag finally recover the main slab from beneath Ramesses' statue, and then the two pieces were reunited. Some pieces are still missing, but enough of the text has been assembled to begin decipherment. Farag and Belgian Egyptologist Georges Posener studied the stone and published their results in 1980. Their findings have quite simply overturned conventional thinking about Egypt's Twelfth Dynasty.

"The Mit Rahina inscription," wrote Martin Bernal in 1991, "supports what is generally thought to be the most absurd set of stories told by Herodotos and Hellenistic Greek writers."[1] Bernal was referring, of course, to the story of Sesostris and his conquests in eastern Europe.

Of course, the inscription did not come right out and say, "Sesostris invaded Europe and left colonists at Colchis." But, if Bernal's interpretation is correct, it did make assertions almost as stunning. First and foremost, it linked at least one of the three Senwosrets with military campaigns far to the north, in areas that no Egyptian conqueror, even as late as the Eighteenth Dynasty, had ever been known to reach. It specifically mentions Senwosret I and his son Amenemhat II and speaks of military expeditions in Africa and Asia. Some of the conquered lands it mentions are already familiar to Egyptologists. Sinai is listed, as well as Lebanon, and the inscription says that the pharaoh himself (it is not clear which pharaoh) led an invasion of Stt—a word that often refers generically to Asia,[2] but may, in this case, signify northern Syria or Mesopotamia.[3]

All of this evidence would have been sufficiently disturbing to the status quo, even had there been nothing else written on the stone. It confirmed beyond doubt that Egyptian armies had marched deep into Asia during the Twelfth Dynasty.[4] But the stone held even greater wonders. Three of the conquered lands it listed had never appeared in any other Egyptian document. Experts could only guess at their identity. In Egyptian hieroglyphs, these mystery countries were spelled: *Irsi, Iwri,* and *Tmprw* (or alternately—since the "r" sign sometimes indicated an "l" in foreign names—*Ilsi, Iwli,* and *Tmplw*). Bernal thought that *Ilsi* most likely referred to the island of Cyprus, which the Egyptians in later times had called Alasia. Cyprus was rich in copper—the prime ingredient for making bronze—and the Mit Rahina inscription noted knives, daggers, and axes of bronze among the booty taken from Ilsi.[5] As for the name *Iwli,* it reminded Bernal strongly of *W'iwly* (or *W'iwry*) —a word appearing in an Eighteenth Dynasty inscription, which many scholars believed was the Egyptian name for Troy.[6] Had Sesostris stormed the walls of Ilium 650 years before Agamemnon? Had the Egyptians played out their own forgotten *Iliad* on the Troad's windy shores? If Bernal's interpretation was correct, it would seem that they had.

Of all the mystery nations listed on the Mit Rahina stone, none was more provocative than the one spelled *Tmplw*. A conservative interpretation might link Tmplw with the Syrian town of Tunip. However, the inscription noted that one of the products the Egyptian conquerors took from Tmplw was lead, and Syria was never a lead-producing region. Could it be, Bernal wondered, that *Tmplw* was actually an Egyptian spelling for the fabled land of Tubal or Tabalu, mentioned both in the Bible and in certain Assyrian texts?[7]

According to the Bible, Tubal-Cain was the great-great-great-great-grandson of Cain, the evil offspring of Adam and Eve who slew his own brother, Abel.[8] *Cain,* or *qayin,* means "smith" in Hebrew, and *tubal-qayin* means "Tubal the Smith"—regarded by Jewish tradition as the first metalsmith.

"Zillah also had a son, Tubal-Cain," says Genesis 4:22, "who forged all kinds of tools out of bronze and iron."

The biblical land of Tubal is actually named after a different Tubal, who is listed as one of Japheth's sons in Genesis 10:2. Nevertheless, this land has also been linked traditionally with Tubal-Cain and has always been known as a land of metalsmiths.[9] Tubal is mentioned in Ezekiel 27:13, for example, as a country that brought "slaves and articles of bronze" to trade with the Phoenicians of Tyre.

Where was Tubal? Martin Bernal believes that it lay somewhere in central or northeastern Anatolia (Turkey)—a good guess, since archaeologists believe that this region is one of the oldest metal-working centers in the world. Anatolian smiths discovered the secret of iron smelting some 2,000 years before the Iron Age dawned in other areas.[10] Moreover, there is independent evidence that Egyptians had reached Anatolia by the Twelfth Dynasty, for archaeologists have found traces of a cult of the Egyptian pharaoh Snofru not far from the modern Turkish capital of Ankara.[11]

However, there is another possibility for Tubal's location that fits the legend of Sesostris even better. An ancient Jewish tradition places Tubal on the eastern shore of the Black Sea—the land of *Colchis!*[12] Like Anatolia, Colchis has long been renowned for its metalsmithy and appears to have mastered the secrets of bronze-working well in advance of most other countries. Distinguished scholars, such as Henri Frankfort and V. Gordon Childe, have long regarded the Caucasus as one of the world's oldest cradles of metallurgy, rivaling Anatolia.[13]

"Not for nothing is Tubal-Cain . . . often associated with the legendary ancestors of the Georgian and Caucasian peoples," comments David Marshall Lang in *The Georgians.*[14]

In the end, it matters little whether *Tmplw* refers to a place in Anatolia or in the Caucasus. Both countries lay far outside the boundaries of any previously known Egyptian conquest. If Bernal had interpreted the name correctly, it meant that Egypt's empire had reached its greatest extent precisely during the era of the legendary Sesostris.

This new evidence gave formidable support to Herodotos's tale. But it also raised a troubling question. In the past, scholars had always believed that Egypt made its greatest conquests during the Eighteenth Dynasty, when bellicose pharaohs such as Thutmose I and Thutmose III rampaged across Palestine and Syria. Not only were these conquests confirmed by a wealth of inscriptions and archaeological evidence, but they also made sense, from a military point of view. After all, it was only during the Eighteenth Dynasty that the Egyptians acquired such basic weapons as the horse-drawn chariot and the bronze short sword. Before that, they fought on foot, armed only with spear and mace.

Possessing neither chariots, swords, nor horses, why would the pharaohs of the Twelfth Dynasty have succeeded where their better-armed successors in the Eighteenth Dynasty failed? How could

Sesostris's primitive infantry have advanced all the way to the Black Sea, while the gleaming chariots of Thutmose III stopped dead in their tracks at Syria's northern frontier? On the surface, this question would seem to punch a hole in Bernal's theory. It remains an insuperable stumbling block to skeptical Egyptologists to this day.

Yet, there is no great mystery to Sesostris's victories. As ill-equipped as his armies might seem, those he opposed were in far worse straits. For Sesostris brought to the battlefield something none of his foes could emulate—the massive force of an orderly, civilized state.

CHAPTER 14

THE BELT OF
DESTRUCTION

FOR MANY SCHOLARS, THE IMAGE OF AN EGYPTIAN ARMY MARCHING to the Black Sea seems as bizarre and unnatural as the thought of alien beings from the Pleiades building pyramids or carving sphinxes. Indeed, some skeptics express their scorn for the Sesostris story in tones every bit as contemptuous as those normally reserved for the "ancient astronaut" theories of Erich von Daniken.

Yet, there is nothing at all improbable about an Egyptian conquest of the Black Sea region. Southern Russia and the Caucasus do not lie on the opposite ends of the world from Egypt, nor are they separated from it by any great ocean. They lie well within the natural sphere of influence that any strong Egyptian state might acquire—provided no *equally* powerful force stood in its way.

This was amply demonstrated by Ptolemy I Soter, founder of the dynasty of Greek kings who ruled Egypt from 305 B.C. to 30 B.C. When Ptolemy mounted the throne, the world was in chaos. The empire of Alexander the Great had broken up, and its former territories lay available for the taking. Ptolemy lost no time in gobbling up Cyprus, the Aegean islands, and parts of mainland Greece.

"His influence extended right up to the kingdom of the Cimmerian (Crimean) Bosphorus on the northern shores of the Black Sea," writes classical historian Michael Grant.[1] The Ptolemies held on to Cyprus for the next 250 years.

The only reason Thutmose III failed to achieve similar feats in the Eighteenth Dynasty is that his natural route of attack was blocked by an immovable force—the Hittite Empire. This mighty nation dominated Asia Minor from about 1750 B.C. to 1180 B.C., obstructing Egypt's advance to the north and challenging Egypt continually for control of Syria. For later Egyptian conquerors, such as Thutmose III and Ramesses II, the Hittite borders were an impenetrable iron curtain.

Not so for Sesostris. In his day, Asia Minor was a quarreling mass of independent city-states.[2] The Hittites had not yet organized themselves into a nation. Egypt, on the other hand, had been a unified kingdom for at least 1,200 years. The very antiquity of its civilization gave it a decisive advantage. With its large, organized army, Egypt would have had little difficulty overrunning the petty princedoms of Asia Minor. And indeed, that is just what Bernal believes Sesostris did.

Sometime around 1900 B.C., a disaster of major proportions swept through Anatolia, Armenia, and Bulgaria. In Armenia, for example, there was a mass flight of people from the lowlands to the mountains.[3] Bernal claims that the wide band of burnt, plundered, and deserted cities throughout these regions—a "belt of destructions," as he calls it—constitutes hard evidence of Sesostris's passage.[4]

Even in areas where few signs of war can be found, massive disruption is evident. The city of Troy, for example, was not burnt at this time. Nevertheless, the 300-year-old culture that archaeologists have named Troy V came to an abrupt end, replaced by a very different culture.[5] The same thing occurred in Scythia, Romania, Yugoslavia, and other places in the Balkans, where cultural change was so dramatic that archaeologists have marked this period as the end of the Stone or Copper Age in those regions.[6]

Bernal believes he has found traces of Sesostris lingering in the folk memories of various peoples Sesostris conquered. In the Levant, during the eighteenth and seventeenth centuries B.C., figures of the Near Eastern gods Baal, Tessub, Tarkhun, and Reshef are portrayed wearing what appear to be Egyptian crowns, as they raise aloft a hammer or an axe. Bernal suggests that this image of a "godlike destructive pharaoh" was inspired by real memories of Sesostris's rampages.[7]

Although none of the Greco-Roman writers claim that Sesostris conquered Greece, his influence would likely have been felt there as well. Bernal finds a hint of such a folk memory in the name of Kekrops, the legendary founder of Athens. To the Greeks, Kekrops was a supernatural being with the head and torso of a man on a snake's body. Diodoros of Sicily, however, recorded an Egyptian tradition that Kekrops came from Egypt and founded Athens as a colony.[8]

Could *Kekrops* be a Hellenized form of an Egyptian name? In addition to their regular names, Egyptian pharaohs took official "throne names" at the time of their coronation. Bernal points out the intriguing resemblance *Kekrops* bears to *Kheper-ka-Re, Kha-kheper-Re,* and *Kha-kau-Re,* the throne names of Senwosret I, II, and III, respectively.[9]

Perhaps the clearest memory of Sesostris in local folklore was recorded by Herodotos. According to the Father of History, Sesostris raised distinctive monuments in all the lands he conquered:

> Whenever he encountered a courageous enemy who fought valiantly for freedom, he erected pillars on the spot inscribed with his own name and country, and a sentence to indicate that by the might of his armed forces he had won the victory; if, however, a town fell easily into his hands without a struggle, he made an addition to the inscription on the pillar—for not only did he record upon it the same facts as before, but added the picture of a woman's genitals, meaning to show that the people of that town were no braver than women. . . .
>
> Most of the memorial pillars which King Sesostris erected in conquered countries have disappeared, but I have seen some myself in Palestine, with the inscription I mentioned and the drawing of a woman's genitals. In Ionia also there are two images of Sesostris cut on rock, one on the road from Ephesus to Phocaea, the other between Sardis and Smyrna; in each case, the carved figure is nearly seven feet high and represents a man with a spear in his right hand and a bow in his left, and the rest of his equipment to match—partly Egyptian partly Ethiopian. Across the breast from shoulder to shoulder runs an inscription, cut in the Egyptian sacred script: *by the strength of my shoulders I won this land.*[10]

Monuments have indeed been found in Turkey, in locations similar to those Herodotos described. However, they are Hittite, not Egyptian, and they make no reference to Sesostris.[11] Because of this error, Herodotos-basher O. Kimball Armayor drew his usual conclusion that the Father of History must have been lying.[12] However, it seems much more likely—as Bernal points out—that Herodotos was faithfully repeating some local folklore he had heard about these monuments—folklore that happened to be mistaken.[13]

Why would people in Turkey have invented such a story, in Herodotos's day, to explain the existence of a Hittite monument? In all probability, they would have done so only if they already possessed some prior folk memory of an Egyptian pharaoh who had indeed marched through their country at one time. Perhaps they had heard stories about some *other* monuments that Sesostris had raised—monuments that have since disappeared—and incorrectly identified these with the Hittite rock carvings.

Even if Sesostris's "memorial pillars" no longer exist, there are compelling reasons to believe that they once did. One such clue is Herodotos's reference to the "picture of a woman's genitals" carved on some monuments. One of the Egyptian words for woman does, in fact, include a symbol representing female genitalia. The same symbol appears in an Egyptian word meaning "coward." The Egyptians frequently referred to their enemies as cowards, and Senwosret III is known to have carved the word in at least one stela that he raised in Nubia.[14]

Since Herodotos did not read Egyptian hieroglyphs, he could not have been aware of this peculiarity of Egyptian spelling, nor would he have recognized the stylized symbol as representing female genitals unless someone had first explained it to him. All of this suggests that whoever originally told Herodotos the story of Sesostris's monuments also passed on to him the highly accurate information about the use of genitalia in Egyptian hieroglyphs.

Herodotos's source for the story must have been very well informed and reliable. Indeed, the story of the memorial pillars probably forms one of the most convincing parts of the Sesostris folklore Herodotos gathered during his travels.

At this point, we can only guess which of the three Senwosrets was the Sesostris of Herodotos, Manetho, and Diodoros. It seems likely, as Egyptologists have long suspected, that the legendary Sesostris may have been an amalgam of many different Twelfth

Dynasty kings. But whoever or *whatever* Sesostris may have been, his role in Western history appears to have been considerable.

Even if we could prove beyond a doubt that Sesostris invaded Europe and colonized the Black Sea, some might still argue that it doesn't matter. His invasion would still be nothing more than a historical curiosity, on a par with the Viking landings in America over a thousand years ago. True, the Vikings came first, defenders of Columbus will admit, but the Viking colonies did not survive long enough to make any real impact on America.

Likewise, some may argue that Sesostris made no lasting mark on Europe. Even Bernal recognizes that Sesostris, if he ever reached Europe, probably did not build a lasting empire there. More likely, he plundered Europe for what it was worth and then went home, leaving, at most, a single small colony in Colchis. Nevertheless, if Bernal's theory is correct, Sesostris achieved, during that brief moment of glory, far more than many of Europe's greatest monarchs and conquerors. For it was Sesostris, Bernal proposes, who initiated the Bronze Age in large portions of eastern and central Europe.

Before Sesostris marched, Europeans used stone or copper to make tools and weapons. Bronze-smithy was known to only a few Europeans in certain parts of the Caucasus and Bulgaria.[15] After the invasion, however (if we assume the invasion really happened around 1900 B.C.), bronze-working suddenly spread across Scythia and all through the Balkans.[16]

Egypt too made a great leap forward during this time. Technically, the Egyptians had been living in the Bronze Age since at least 2700 B.C., when the first bronze vessels appear there. But the new alloy was not widely used. Bronze is made from mixing copper with about 4 percent tin. The Egyptians had plenty of copper, from their mines in Sinai, Nubia, and the eastern desert. But tin was a rare and precious metal that had to be imported from far-off places like Afghanistan, Mesopotamia, Turkey, Cyprus, and the Caucasus—perhaps even Bohemia and Cornwall. Not until after the invasions of Sesostris did bronze suddenly become the metal of choice in Egypt.[17] For the first time, during the Twelfth Dynasty, Egyptian armies were equipped with a wealth of bronze weapons, including daggers, axes, and sickle swords.[18]

By invading Europe and Asia Minor, it appears that Sesostris gained more than just access to tin mines. He may have plundered Anatolia and the Caucasus for their metalworkers as well. Archaeologists have found evidence that smiths from the Caucasus were living and working in Byblos during the Twelfth Dynasty—a Phoenician city that was likely already under Egyptian rule at this time.[19]

Perhaps these wandering smiths were refugees from the northern war zones. Or maybe they were brought south as captives, for the deliberate purpose of exploiting their skills. Whatever the impetus of their migration it is clear that Anatolian and Caucasian metalsmiths came south, in great numbers. A similar migration throughout central and eastern Europe may help explain the sudden spread of bronze-smithy in those regions, as well.

While the rest of the world enjoyed the benefit of Caucasian and Anatolian metallurgy, it is curious to note that the one region that actually seemed to move *backwards* in metal technology was Anatolia!

"It is a fact," wrote archaeologist Claude Schaeffer in 1948, "that the countries of Asia Minor . . . were, at the beginning of the 2nd millennium, dispossessed of their monopoly and deprived of their best artisans. The absolute poverty of metal types in Asia Minor between 2000 and 1500 B.C. has always struck archaeologists and it is even more remarkable in that it contrasts with the richness of production in the surrounding countries."[20]

How did this turnabout occur? Bernal suggests that, by carrying off the best smiths from conquered Anatolia, Sesostris may have doomed Asia Minor to technological stagnation.[21]

Bernal's theory is fascinating, but tentative. Until more evidence is found, the contribution of Sesostris to Western civilization will remain a matter of guesswork and speculation. Nevertheless, Bernal's work has established one thing beyond doubt: there is far more to the story of Sesostris's march on Europe than mere legend. Thanks to Bernal, it is slowly becoming possible for scholars to at least talk about Sesostris without giggles or sarcasm.

Perhaps, one day soon, archaeologists may actually feel emboldened to explore the question of Sesostris in an active way. Once that occurs, it may not be long before some open-minded young researcher startles the world by unearthing new evidence that confirms the achievements of this most celebrated but elusive of all Bronze Age explorers.

"The notion that there was any truth to the tradition [of Sesostris] has been literally unthinkable to the 19th and most of the 20th century," writes Bernal. "It is now time to reassess it."[22]

PART FOUR

THE
EGYPTIAN
MYSTERIES

CHAPTER 15

MYSTICS AND MADMEN

T HE VIDEO OPENED WITH AN EERIE MONTAGE OF WHIRLING SAND and hoary sculptures from Egyptian antiquity. A solemn colossus of Ramesses II emerged for a moment from out of the sandstorm. Then it melted away before the graceful bust of Queen Nefertiti, the screen shimmering and twisting in a phantasmagoria of forms, redolent, to the trained eye, of state-of-the-art morphing technology from Hollywood's most expensive digital effects studios.

At last, the screen congealed into a scene of breathtaking splendor—the throne room of pharaoh Ramesses II and his beauteous queen Nefertari. Sumptuously resurrected in a faux Egyptian temple on Soundstage 36 of the Universal Pictures lot, the throne room thronged with guards and courtiers, their oiled flesh and resplendent dress evoking Cecil B. DeMille at his finest. To the casual observer, it might have looked as if the days of *The Ten Commandments* and *Land of the Pharaohs* were making a comeback in Tinseltown. But this was no Hollywood epic. All these magnificent sets, costumes, and special effects had been assembled to produce a single, nine-minute rock video. It would be an understatement to say that nothing quite like it had ever been seen on MTV before. The year was 1992. The video was Michael Jackson's "Remember the Time." Jackson had pulled out all the stops. He had hired black director John Singleton, the legendary *wunderkind* whose *Boyz N the Hood* won him an Oscar nomination at the age of twenty-three. The cast was studded with African American celebrities, among them Eddie Murphy and Magic Johnson.

"Remember the Time" won instant fame on its release, mainly because it featured Michael Jackson's first onscreen kiss—planted on the exotic lips of Somali model Iman. However, the video was significant for a more important reason. It portrayed ancient Egyptians with an all-black cast. As the dancers jerked and glided through steps borrowed from the rigid postures of 4,000-year-old tomb paintings, their skin shone bronze, gold, and ebony, a range of complexions not unlike that you might have seen at the court of the real pharaohs.

For seventy years, Hollywood had portrayed Egyptians with white actors, such as Anne Baxter in *The Ten Commandments* and Jack Hawkins in *Land of the Pharaohs*. When blacks appeared in these epics, they usually played Nubian slaves hoisting some royal palanquin. Now all of that had changed in an instant. With "Remember the Time," Michael Jackson and John Singleton had reinvented Egypt for the silver screen. "A kind of *Ebony* magazine version of ancient Egypt," observed one writer in the *New Republic*.[1]

The day the video was released, a New York television station did street interviews with young Manhattanites. A succession of black teenagers gushed their enthusiasm before the camera, striking hieroglyphic poses with their arms and hands.

"It was really cool, especially the kiss," said one young African American lady into the microphone.

Then came a pudgy white kid with freckles.

"I guess it was all right," he said, squinting his eyes in puzzlement, "but I don't get all this Egyptian stuff. What's all that Egyptian stuff about?"

With his innocent question, the boy had given voice to what was fast becoming a groundswell of public opinion. By 1992, millions of white Americans were beginning to ask the same question: Just what *was* all this Egyptian stuff about?

It was, of course, a black thing. Any black American watching "Remember the Time" would have understood instantly the message behind the video—a message almost entirely overlooked by its mainstream reviewers. Since the early nineteenth century, African American writers had been exhorting their people to remember their rich heritage—a heritage that they insisted included the "black" civilization of ancient Egypt.

Count Constantin de Volney's *Travels in Syria and Egypt* had become an international best-seller by the early nineteenth century. The book was to be found "in all libraries"—as one critic, Champollion-Figeac, lamented—and many educated readers were familiar with Volney's claim that the Great Sphinx portrayed a black man.[2] Such speculations made a deep impression on the growing number of educated blacks in the United States. In 1854, the abolitionist and ex-slave Frederick Douglas joined his voice to the rising chorus of black Americans urging educators to devote more attention to the study of ancient Egypt. Douglas declared: "The ancient Egyptians were not white people, but were, undoubtedly, just about as dark in complexion as many in this country who are considered genuine Negroes: and that is not all, their hair was far from being of that graceful lankness which adorns the fair Anglo-Saxon head."[3]

Upon viewing the pyramids of Egypt in 1866, Edward Wilmot Blyden, a black writer from the Caribbean island of St. Thomas, wrote: "Feelings came over me far different from those I have ever felt when looking at the mighty works of European genius. I felt that I had a peculiar heritage in the Great Pyramid built . . . by the enterprising sons of Ham, from which I descended."[4]

By the twentieth century, black writers had grown even bolder. No longer content to pride themselves on the pyramids, some began casting covetous eyes at the entire edifice of classical civilization, seeking, between the lines of Plato, some hidden evidence of African influence. Perhaps the most audacious of the new generation was George G. M. James, a teacher of Greek at Arkansas A&M University.

"The term Greek philosophy, to begin with, is a misnomer," wrote James in his 1954 book, *Stolen Legacy*, "for there is no such philosophy in existence. . . . Greek philosophy is stolen Egyptian philosophy."[5]

James claimed that Sokrates, Plato, and nearly every other learned Greek were initiates in a mystical order from which they had learned—and subsequently pilfered—the secret wisdom of Egypt's priests. This wisdom included philosophy, science, trigonometry, architecture—virtually all the knowledge normally attributed to Greek genius.

"In this way, the Greeks stole the Legacy of the African Continent and called it their own," lamented James. ". . . the result of this dishonesty has been the creation of an erroneous world opinion; that the African continent has made no contribution to civilization, because her people are backward and low in intelligence and culture."[6]

Although James was a scholar, his book was not written with scholarly detachment. Every page burned with a messianic fervor born of James's passionate faith in the rites and doctrines of Freemasonry. Ever since the secret society of the Masons had publicly announced its existence in 1717, its acolytes had insisted that their rituals had been handed down, in a chain unbroken for thousands of years, from the temples of ancient Egypt. James believed literally in the Freemasonic tradition of a worldwide system of lodges and mystery schools, existing since the dawn of time, through which Egyptian priests had dispensed their wisdom to a barbarous world. In one typical passage, he stated:

> There were mystery schools or what we would commonly call lodges in Greece and other lands, outside of Egypt, whose work was carried on according to the Osiriaca, the Grand Lodge of Egypt. . . . Consequently we make a mistake when we suppose that the so-called Greek philosophers formulated new doctrines of their own: for their philosophy had been handed down by the great Egyptian Hierophants through the Mysteries."[7]

James filled his book with learned references to Aristotle and other classical sages. But his theory of Egyptian lodges and mystery schools arose, for the most part, from far less conventional sources. He drew much of it from a 1909 book called *The Ancient Mysteries and Modern Masonry*, penned by a self-proclaimed thirty-second-degree Mason named Charles H. Vail.[8] James cited Vail as an authority on ancient Egypt, taking it for granted that readers would embrace Vail's metaphysical doctrines as unquestioningly as James himself had done.

In this regard, James was more preacher than scholar. The ease with which he confounded facts and mystical dogma brings to mind certain fundamentalist Christians of today who muster impressive scientific data to debunk the theory of evolution or to prove that the earth was created in seven days. In a similar way, James's outlook resembles that of those serene Mormon pedants who never seem to lose hope that archaeologists will someday stumble upon the lost cities of the Nephites and Jaredites, ancient North American civilizations whose putative existence was revealed to Joseph Smith of Palmyra, New York, during a visitation by the angel Moroni in 1827.[9]

Like so many religious writers, James wrote for the faithful, not for the skeptic. Those already converted to James's creed found his book scintillating. To the unconverted, it was laughable. Needless to say, Stolen Legacy made little impact on mainstream scholars over the years, except to provoke their occasional jeers.

Even so, it is precisely from such febrile screeds as Stolen Legacy that flashes of unexpected genius sometimes arise. Creationist critics have, now and then, uncovered real flaws in Darwin's theory of evolution. Archaeologists, in recent years, have realized that the Mississippi Basin does indeed hide a multitude of lost cities, whose now-crumbling earthen pyramids once rivaled those of Egypt in size.[10] The Mound Builders who reared the thousand-year-old ruins at Cahokia, Illinois, do not seem so far removed from the Lamanites of Mormon legend.[11]

In all fairness, we must admit that George G. M. James was neither the first nor the last student of ancient Egypt to harbor unusual beliefs. Sir Flinders Petrie, generally regarded as the father of scientific Egyptology, got his start in 1880 making detailed measurements of the Great Pyramid in an attempt to test the mystical theories of Scottish astronomer Piazzi Smyth, who claimed that the British were the ten lost tribes of Israel and that the dimensions of the Great Pyramid contained coded messages about the Second Coming of Christ.[12]

Much more recently, Mark Lehner, one of today's most respected Egyptologists, based his early research on the prophecies of Edgar Cayce, who claimed, among other things, that Egyptian civilization was founded by colonists from Atlantis.[13] No one would deny that both Petrie and Lehner have contributed significantly to our knowledge of ancient Egypt. And, indeed, both men abandoned their esoteric theories soon after beginning their serious research. All the same, their eccentric evolution as scholars should give pause to anyone who would dismiss too quickly a George G. M. James simply because he reads C. H. Vail.

"Invention is not the product of logical thought," Albert Einstein once observed, "even though the final product is tied to a logical structure."[14] What Einstein meant is that ingenious insights generally arise through what seem, at the time, to be irrational bursts of intuition. His own work illustrated this principle perfectly.

At the age of sixteen, Einstein suddenly asked himself one day, "What would it be like to run beside a light beam at the speed of light?" As he pondered this question, in a deep reverie, Einstein stumbled on some of the key insights that would later form his theory of relativity. But what young Einstein grasped instinctively, he did not yet know how to express. Ten years would pass before Einstein figured out how to quantify those insights into a "logical structure"—a mathematical formula through which he could share his revelation with other scientists.[15]

George G. M. James appears to have experienced a similar epiphany. Unlike Einstein, he failed, in the end, to crystallize his insight into a sufficiently "logical structure" to convince other scholars. Yet, beneath its bluster and bombast, its overstatement, its hocus-pocus, and its tortured facts, *Stolen Legacy* reverberates with a freshness and grandeur undiminished after four decades. James truly was a kind of mad genius. With few facts to go on, he leapt boldly into the darkness. And, as with Einstein, he landed on his feet.

Few scholars today have anything good to say about this strange, inspired man. But, whether they like it or not, James's ideas and obsessions have suddenly resurfaced, forty years after his death, at the core of a vital academic controversy.

CHAPTER 16

IMHOTEP'S
LEGACY

MOUNTED ON A FIFTY-TON STONE PEDESTAL, IN A GRASSY clearing not far from the Metropolitan Museum of Art in Central Park, stands one of New York City's more curious attractions. It is an Egyptian obelisk—a tall, four-sided column of solid granite that comes to a pyramid-shaped point at the top. Thousands of New Yorkers file past it every day. Yet very few know the story of how or why this 3,500-year-old monument to the Egyptian sun god was brought into their midst.

It arrived by ship in New York Harbor in July 1880 and was dedicated with great fanfare on October 9. Marching bands paraded through the streets. A man named Jesse Anthony made an impassioned speech in which he declared that Egypt was the wellspring of all science, literature, astronomy, and art. Watching over the ceremonies was millionaire William J. Vanderbilt, who had funded the whole undertaking.

What was it all about? What strange Egyptomania compelled these otherwise sober-minded New Yorkers to haul a 220-ton chunk of granite across the Atlantic Ocean?[1] What common cause had brought together such personalities as business baron William J.

Vanderbilt, editor William Hulbert, U.S. Navy lieutenant commander Henry Gorringe, and sundry other prominent New Yorkers who
took part? The answer, as British journalist Martin Short revealed in
his 1989 book *Inside the Brotherhood,* is that all of these men were
Freemasons.

Virtually every Main Street in America boasts its Masonic Temple, generally a bland-looking structure where local Boy Scout
troops hold their annual pancake breakfasts and businessmen
gather on weekends to crack open a Budweiser. Few would ever suspect that behind this prosaic exterior lies a secret tradition that, by
some accounts, extends all the way back to pharaonic Egypt.

At the 1880 dedication ceremony of Cleopatra's Needle—the
name given to the obelisk in Central Park—the Jesse Anthony who
spoke so passionately about Egypt's glorious past was none other
than the Grand Master of New York Masons.

"There can be no question," Anthony told the crowd that day,
"but that in the secret societies of Egypt are to be found some elements now embraced in the principles or symbolism of Masonry."[2]

Even as Anthony spoke, obelisk fever was sweeping America. In
Washington, D.C., workmen were putting the finishing touches on
a 555-foot obelisk, made from 81,000 tons of marble blocks. It was
the Washington Monument—the world's largest imitation of an
Egyptian obelisk. The monument's dedication on February 21, 1885,
featured a thoroughly Masonic ceremony. One orator took advantage of the opportunity to declare that the Masons were "enlightened with divine love, their hearts radiant with discovering the joy
of pure love, their souls cherishing—like the ancient Egyptian worshippers of Osiris—the hope of immortality."[3]

George Washington would have been pleased with the ceremony.
He himself was a "Brother" in Alexandria Lodge No. 22.[4] When the
cornerstone was laid for the Capitol building, the Grand Lodge of
Maryland organized the ceremony, which featured Masonic chant-
ing. For the occasion, Washington wore the traditional apron and
sash of his lodge and performed various rituals involving the Masonic emblems of the gavel, the silver trowel, the square, and the
level.

The city of Washington itself was planned as the perfect Masonic
metropolis. Washington and fellow Mason Thomas Jefferson are
said to have personally altered the plan of architect Pierre l'Enfant

to incorporate elements of "sacred geometry," causing the streets of the new capital to form esoteric patterns drawn from Masonic lore.[5] Not surprisingly, George Washington's funeral in 1799 featured many exotic rituals, including the draping of his coffin with a Masonic apron and the presentation by several attending Brethren of sprigs of acacia—a tree native to Egypt—symbolizing the resurrection of Osiris.[6]

Freemasonry did not vanish from the U.S. government with the Founding Fathers. Its continuing vigor through the years is attested to by the thirteen-stepped pyramid topped by an eye in a triangle that graces our dollar bill.[7] This frankly Masonic emblem was officially adopted as the reverse side of the Great Seal of the United States in 1782.[8] President Franklin Roosevelt—himself reputed to be a Mason—ordered the pyramid emblem placed on the dollar bill in 1934, seeing in its accompanying Latin motto, *Novus Ordo Seclorum* ("New Order of the Ages"), an apt metaphor for his New Deal.[9]

America's Founding Fathers clearly saw themselves as inheritors of an Egyptian tradition. But were they *legitimate* heirs or merely pretenders? Did their Freemasonic rituals and lore contain real Egyptian wisdom, or were they simply concoctions of imaginative European occultists in the eighteenth century?

No clear historical record of Freemasonry exists before 1717. As a result, many skeptics have concluded that its "ancient" rites and doctrines must have been fabricated around that time. Masonic tradition, however, claims that the Brotherhood existed in secret for many centuries before, its presence unrecorded because of the vow of silence all Masons were required to swear.[10]

Masonic initiates traditionally swore never to betray or set into writing the secrets of their "Craft," sealing their vows by placing themselves, "under no less penalty... than that of having my throat cut across, my tongue torn out by the root, and buried in the sand of the sea at low water mark." More advanced second-degree initiates bound themselves to the additional penalties of "having my left breast laid open, my heart torn therefrom, and given to the ravenous birds of the air, or devouring beasts of the field as prey."[11] These vows were routinely administered right up until 1986.

During the long centuries when such penalties were, presumably, literally enforced, it is not surprising that Freemasons declined to publish information about their society. As a consequence, we will probably never know how far back the Craft actually extends into antiquity. Nevertheless, some enticing clues suggest that Freemasonic claims to an Egyptian origin should not be dismissed as pure fantasy.

At the root of Masonic legend is the belief that the Craft was born among ancient guilds of stonemasons, whose handiwork includes such famous structures as the temples and pyramids of Egypt, the Tower of Babel, the Temple of Solomon, the great edifices of Greek and Roman antiquity, and the Gothic cathedrals of the Middle Ages. In the view of these stonemasons, God was the Great Architect of the Universe and geometry—because of its importance to builders— was considered the most sacred of all sciences.

In fact, the ancient Egyptians did worship a certain Great Architect as a god. His name was Imhotep. Five thousand years ago, the earliest pharaohs were buried in box-like, mud-brick tombs called "mastabas." But, one day—around 2660 B.C. by most estimates—a pharaoh named Djoser instructed his court architect, Imhotep, to build him a royal tomb like no other.

Imhotep stacked up six mastabas, like a layered cake, with the largest on the bottom and the smallest at the top. When he was done, 850,000 tons of limestone blocks were piled 200 feet into the air. It was the world's first pyramid. Never before had anyone reared such a massive edifice in stone. In building the Step Pyramid of Djoser—as the tomb was later named—Imhotep had effectively improvised a new science of monumental stonemasonry. In the words of the Egyptian historian Manetho, "Imuthes [Imhotep] . . . was the inventor of the art of building with hewn stone."[12]

Imhotep was still remembered in Egypt two thousand years after his death, and was worshiped as a god, with his principal shrine at Sakkara. He was honored not only as an architect and a sage, but also as the founder and patron of all medical arts, for which reason the Greeks identified Imhotep with their god of medicine, Asklepios, and called his temple the Asklepion.[13]

If Imhotep's cult was still going strong in Greco-Roman Egypt, 2,600 years after the great architect's death, is it really so farfetched to imagine that it might have survived, in some form, for an additional 2,000 years? Anyone who has stood before the pyramids or walked within Karnak's Hypostyle Hall has felt the power of Egypt's architectural achievement. How much more would Greek and Roman artisans have felt it in the days when the Great Pyramid still bore its polished limestone sheath and the paint on the temple walls shone fresh and bright? European stonemasons would undoubtedly have gone to great lengths to appease and propitiate the gods who made such wonders possible.

We do not know and perhaps never will know whether the guilds of medieval builders paid secret homage to Imhotep. But we do know that all through the Middles Ages and the Renaissance, alchemists, magicians, sages, and philosophers pored over Egyptian mystical texts purporting to offer the teachings of the Egyptian gods Imhotep and Thoth—usually identified in these manuscripts by the Greek names of *Asklepios* (or *Imouthes*) and *Hermes*, respectively.

In these so-called Hermetic treatises—generally believed to have been written in Roman-occupied Egypt between 100 and 300 A.D. (though some experts think they are much older)[14]—Imhotep appears much as he did in centuries' worth of Egyptian papyri from previous ages—as a figure of awesome wisdom and magical power. One papyrus from the second century A.D., found near the Egyptian town of Oxyrynchus, describes a dream in which "Asklepios" (Imhotep) appears to the author of the papyrus as "someone whose height was more than human, clothed in shining raiment and carrying in his left hand a book."[15] The legend of the Great Architect is, without a doubt, one of the oldest and most enduring in human history. It is also one of the most provocative clues we possess that George G. M. James may not have been quite so far off the mark after all.

In his superhuman mastery of medicine, stonemasonry, necromancy, and other arts, Imhotep personified that strange brew of science and sorcery that constituted Egypt's principal gift to the ancient world. It is from this unlikely mixture that James would have us believe Greek philosophy descended. "Preposterous!" cry the modern defenders of Greek culture. What could the lofty speculations of Plato or the equations of Archimedes possibly have in common with the mumbo-jumbo of Egyptian priests?

Yet, improbable as it seems, the Greeks themselves—not George G. M. James—first suggested that philosophy was born on the banks of the Nile. Greek historians recorded that virtually all of their legendary wise men, from Pythagoras to Plato, had studied in the temples of Egypt. We could, of course, simply ignore these traditions. In the spirit of *Besserwissen*, we could assume that the Greeks just dreamed it all up, much as Dr. William Robertson once assumed that the conquistadors had fabricated their tales of great cities and pyramids in the New World.

And, in fact, that is precisely what many classicists do today. They suggest that the Greeks may have simply invented these accounts of philosophers studying in Egypt in order to gild their intellectual pedigree with a veneer of antique wisdom. But if we claim to admire Greek learning, should we not listen a bit more respectfully to Greek writers? Should we not, at least, consider the possibility that, when the old philosophers called Egypt their teacher, perhaps they knew what they were talking about? In the next few chapters, we will consider the question of philosophy's origins, not from the vantage point of modern-day know-it-alls, but from the *Greek* point of view.

CHAPTER 17

THE FIRST
PHILOSOPHER

WHEN THE STOIC PHILOSOPHER DIO CHRYSOSTOM ARRIVED AT Olbia in 95 A.D., the city was a shambles. Long ago, Olbia had been the largest and wealthiest Greek colony on the Black Sea. But its glory came to an end in 63 B.C., when hordes of savage Dacians and Getae sacked the city. Now only a few rugged frontiersmen remained, scratching out a squalid living among the ruins. These colonists had been dwelling so long among barbarians that they had begun to dress in Scythian clothes and could speak Greek only poorly.

In one respect, however, the Olbians clung tenaciously to their Greek nature. They never lost their taste for learning. Dio discovered that most of them could recite Homer by heart, and many had read Plato. Upon hearing that Dio was a Greek philosopher, the Olbians crowded around him, begging Dio to engage them in a philosophical discussion. So enthralled were the Olbians by their guest that, when an alarm flag suddenly went up on the city walls, warning of an impending Scythian raid, the Olbians paid it no heed. Only when Dio insisted did they grudgingly escort him back inside the city gates and out of harm's way.

Safe behind the walls, Dio at last honored his hosts with a wide-ranging lecture, in which he held forth on such subjects as Plato's vision of the perfect city, the Chariot of Zeus, the movement of the stars, the teachings of the Zoroastrian Magi, and much more. The Olbians were delighted. Cut off for a hundred years from civilization, shivering from the cold of Scythian winters, starved for food, harassed by bandits, they had never lost that most essential of Greek qualities—the hunger for learning.[1]

"Egypt and Phoenicia love money," wrote Plato. "The special characteristic of our part of the world is the love of knowledge."[2]

Love of wisdom—or *philosophia*—seems to us quintessentially Greek. But were the Greeks always such highbrows? Apparently not. Strip the *Iliad* of its lofty rhetoric, and what remains? Two tribal warlords, brawling over who gets to sleep with a female captive through 15,693 verses of dactylic hexameter. Early Greeks, such as Achilles and Agamemnon, would not have known what to do with a Platonic dialogue if it slapped them in the face.

How, then, did the Greeks become philosophers? It seems to have happened during the sixth century B.C. The first Greek ever to call himself a *philosophos* was Pythagoras, born sometime around 570 B.C. As a youth, Pythagoras was renowned for his piety, intellect, and temperate demeanor. He soon became a student of Thales of Miletus, a great thinker of the time, best known for being the first person to correctly predict a solar eclipse (the first person that we know of, that is). Thales was so impressed by Pythagoras's aptitude that he urged the young man to travel to Egypt and study with the priests there. The philosopher Iamblichus recorded the exchange in his *Life of Pythagoras*, written in the third century A.D.:

> Thales, laying stress on his advanced age and the infirmities of his body, advised him to go to Egypt to get in touch with the priests of Memphis and Zeus. Thales confessed that the instruction of these priests was the source of his own reputation for wisdom, while neither his own endowments nor achievements equaled those which were so evident in Pythagoras. Thales insisted that, in view of all this, if Pythagoras should study with those priests, he was certain of becoming the wisest and most divine of men.[3]

Why Egypt? The ancient Greeks looked up to Egypt as an older and wiser culture. They strongly believed that Egyptian priests possessed great stores of ancient wisdom, both mystical and scientific. In his novel *Aithiopika*, written around A.D. 230, Heliodoros alluded to this Greek admiration for all things Egyptian. An Egyptian priest in the story named Calasiris tells of a visit he made to Delphi, during which he was besieged by questioners. Calasiris remarks:

> [The Greeks] plied me with questions on various matters. One would ask how we Egyptians worship our country's gods, while another wished to know how it came about that different animals were adored by different sections of our people, and what was the reason for each cult. Some wished to know about the construction of the pyramids, others about the subterranean mazes. In brief, they omitted not a single point of interest in their enquiries concerning Egypt; for listening to any account of Egypt is what appeals most strongly to Greek ears.[4]

Herodotos exemplifies the respect that Greeks felt for Egypt. He attributes to the Egyptians the invention of geometry, the solar calendar, stone carving, medicine, and astronomy—and indeed, the Egyptians seem to have been early experts in all these areas. Surviving papyri have shown that the Egyptian mathematicians knew how to calculate the area of circles, triangles, and trapezoids, as well as the volume of cylinders, pyramids, and other solids, centuries before these skills were known in Greece.[5] Medical texts from Egypt show that its surgeons were skilled at setting bones, removing tumors, and stitching wounds.[6] And, just as Herodotos said, it was indeed Egyptian astronomers who first devised the 365-day calendar, divided into twelve months of thirty days each, with the days and nights demarcated into twelve hours apiece—the system that we still use today, with minor adjustments.[7]

Being a practical people, the Greeks admired the Egyptians for their science. But the Greeks were also exceedingly superstitious. They never went into battle without first consulting oracles and diviners. When things went wrong, the Greeks exerted far more energy trying to figure out which god had been offended than they did analyzing the problem logically. That is why, in praising the Egyptians for their wisdom, Herodotos reserved his greatest admiration for their piety and religious lore. Such practical Egyptian feats as the invention of the solar calendar merited only passing mention from Herodotos, for these were "mere human matters," as he put it.[8]

Many Greeks believed that the Egyptians worshiped the gods under their true or original names and served them with rites and sacrifices far older and purer than those of other peoples. Greek religion was seen as little more than a pale imitation of the Egyptian ideal, imported into Greece in archaic times. Herodotos reinforced this view when he wrote:

> [The Egyptian priests] also told me that the Egyptians first brought into use the names of the twelve gods, which the Greeks took over from them, and were the first to assign altars and images and temples to the gods, and to carve figures in stone. . . . The names of nearly all the gods came to Greece from Egypt. I know from the inquiries I have made that they came from abroad, and it seems most likely that it was from Egypt, for the names of all the gods have been known in Egypt from the beginning of time. . . . I have the authority of the Egyptians themselves for this.[9]

Herodotos does not explain how the names of Egyptian gods found their way to Greece. But he says it happened long ago, when Greece was still inhabited by an ancient people called the Pelasgians. These Pelasgians sacrificed to the gods and prayed to them but did not call them by any particular names.

"After a long lapse of time the names of the gods came to Greece from Egypt, and the Pelasgi learnt them," Herodotos recounts. Uncertain whether it was proper to use these foreign names, the Pelasgians consulted their oracle at Dodona—the only oracle in the country at the time. The Dodonaean priestesses approved of the new names and recommended their use. "Thenceforth in their sacrifices the Pelasgi made use of the names of the gods," Herodotos concludes, "and from them the names passed afterwards to the Greeks."[10]

Herodotos heard this legend from the priestesses of Dodona, whose oracle was traditionally regarded as the oldest in Greece. It should not be surprising that the Dodonaean oracle approved of Egyptian gods, for according to Herodotos, the oracle itself was founded by an Egyptian priestess.

The three priestesses at Dodona told Herodotos that, long ago, two black doves had flown off from the city of Thebes in Egypt. One had flown to Libya and the other to Dodona. The dove that landed at Dodona had then spoken in a human voice to the Dodonaeans, instructing them to build a shrine on the spot where she alighted. They obeyed, and the oracle of Dodona was born.

Herodotos heard a different version of this tale from the priests of Amun in Thebes. The Egyptians related that two of their priestesses had long ago been kidnapped from Thebes by Phoenicians. One was sold into slavery in Libya and the other in Greece. The priestess in Libya later founded the famous oracle of Ammon (the Libyan version of Amun), while the priestess in Greece founded the oracle of Dodona. Rationalist that he was, Herodotos found the Egyptian version more believable. He concluded that the oracle of Dodona must really have been founded by an Egyptian priestess. Somehow, the Dodonaeans had managed to garble the story, through centuries of telling and retelling, transforming the Egyptian women into magical black doves. Herodotos explained the distortion in this way:

> The story which the people of Dodona tell about the doves came, I should say, from the fact that the women were foreigners, whose language sounded to them like the twittering of birds; later on the dove spoke with a human voice, because by that time the woman stopped twittering and learned to talk intelligibly. That, at least, is how I should explain the obvious impossibility of a dove using the language of men. As to the bird being black, they merely signify by this that the woman was an Egyptian.[11]

This last sentence is often cited as evidence that the Greeks perceived the Egyptians as black. If the Egyptians were not black, the argument goes, then why would the Dodonaeans have called the dove black to indicate that she was Egyptian? The point is well worth considering. However, the passage is far more interesting for another reason. It shows that the oldest oracle on the Greek mainland claimed to have originated in Egypt—and that the Egyptians themselves offered corroboration for the story.

If religious cults could travel from Egypt to Greece, why not philosophy too? Certainly, the Greeks believed that Egypt was the birthplace of philosophy. In his book *Bousiris*, the Athenian orator Isokrates of the fourth century B.C. makes one of the earliest mentions of the word *philosophia* in any Greek text.[12] He states that *philosophia* could only have arisen in Egypt, where priests were given leisure to lead the life of the "contemplative man."[13] Aristotle expressed a similar belief when he wrote, "in Egypt mathematical sciences first commenced, for there the nation of priests had leisure."[14]

Of course, none of this proves that science, religion, or philosophy came to Greece from Egypt. It proves only that the Greeks *believed* that they did. And who knows? Maybe the Greeks were wrong. But since we are examining this question from the Greek point of view, we would do well to follow Pythagoras on his legendary journey to Egypt. Following Thales' advice, the promising young student did indeed present himself to the priests of Memphis and Thebes. And it was under their instruction, according to tradition, that Pythagoras was transformed into history's very first Greek philosopher.

CHAPTER 18

SECRETS OF
THE TEMPLE

IN PYTHAGORAS'S DAY, TRAVEL AROUND THE MEDITERRANEAN
world was relatively easy and routine. Nowhere is this better
illustrated than in Pythagoras's own life. He was born in the
Phoenician city of Sidon, where his Greek father, Mnesarchus, was
engaged in trade. Pythagoras spent his childhood on the Greek island of Samos and, according to his biographer, Iamblichus, later
resided in Egypt, Phoenicia, Babylon, and Italy. Of all the places
Pythagoras visited, none made a deeper impression than Egypt.
Iamblichus describes Pythagoras's years among the Egyptian priests
in these words:

> Here in Egypt he frequented all the temples with the greatest
> diligence, and most studious research, during which time he won the
> esteem and admiration of all the priests and prophets with whom he
> associated. . . . He thus passed twenty-two years in the sanctuaries of
> temples, studying astronomy and geometry, and being initiated in no
> casual or superficial manner in all the mysteries of the Gods.[1]

What sorts of lessons might have been offered in Egypt's temple
schools in Pythagoras's day? One hint comes from Clement of
Alexandria, a Christian philosopher of the early third century A.D.

According to him, "the whole philosophy of the Egyptians" was contained in forty-two books attributed to the god Thoth and stored in the temple libraries. Priests would master those particular books of Thoth that related to their field of expertise. Among the topics covered were: hymns to the gods; the king's life; astrology; cosmography and geography; the construction, provision, and utensils of the temples; the practice of medicine; the laws; the gods; the training of priests; and sacrifices, prayers, processions, and feasts.[2]

In fact, nearly all useful knowledge in Egypt was monopolized by the temples. To learn to read, one had to attend a *Per Ankh*, or "House of Life," run by priests. Books were stored in temple libraries, while priestly historians chronicled the triumphs of Egypt's kings. Physician-priests dispensed medical care. Astronomer-priests watched the heavens and kept the calendar on track, while other priests tended to the Nilometers that measured the height of the Nile's annual flooding.[3]

In Egypt, temples were big business. The various cults owned great herds of cattle and large tracts of farmland, as well as gold mines and other enterprises, their vast wealth tabulated by priestly accountants.[4] According to the Papyrus Harris, the Temple of Amun at Karnak owned more than 2,000 square kilometers of land and employed over 80,000 people during the reign of Ramesses III.[5] Its staff would have included painters, sculptors, architects, farmers, craftsmen, butchers, bakers, confectioners, guards, florists, housekeepers, clerks, and many others, all supervised by specially trained priests.[6]

We can assume that Pythagoras would have acquired a great deal of practical, scientific knowledge in Egypt. However, the Egyptians, like all people in the ancient world, did not draw a sharp line between science and religion. Iamblichus makes clear that Pythagoras was trained in mystical matters at least as thoroughly as in scientific ones, having been, in Iamblichus's words, "initiated in no casual or superficial manner in all the mysteries of the Gods."

The Greek word for mysteries—*mysterion*—means "initiation."[7] Iamblichus seems to imply that Pythagoras was inducted into the secret rites of Egypt's temple cults. This would have been a high honor indeed, normally reserved for priests alone. In Egypt, there were many different grades or degrees of priests, from the lowly *waab*, or "purified," priest to the First Prophet, who attended directly on the image of the god. Each grade of priest was permitted access only to certain limited parts of the temple and was taught only certain spells, rites, incantations, and secret doctrines, in accordance with his rank. If Pythagoras was indeed initiated into "all the mysteries of the gods," he must have risen very far in the priestly hierarchy.

Secrecy was the heart and soul of the Egyptian faith. Sacred doctrines were guarded ferociously from the profane. One of the horrors that the scribe Ipuwer recounted, in order to demonstrate the degree of social breakdown during the First Intermediate Period, was the wholesale divulging of temple secrets to the unworthy: "Behold the hidden chamber, its books are stolen. The secrets in it are revealed. Behold, magical spells are revealed. Incantations are made rough by being repeated."[8]

In the Egyptian faith, secret knowledge conveyed power. The mere possession of spells, formulae, and secret names enabled a magician to command the very gods to do his will. In the Turin Papyrus, for example, the goddess Isis gains control over the sun god Ra by tricking him into revealing his true, or secret, name.[9] Any mortal could do the same if he possessed the same forbidden knowledge. Indeed, it was not by accident that the most dreaded of all Egyptian gods was Amun, who was called the Hidden One and "mysterious of form."[10] Neither god nor man could command him, for his true name was unknowable.

Secret wisdom also provided the key to eternal life. This is evident in the so-called Egyptian *Book of the Dead*—more properly called *The Book of the Coming Forth by Day*—which instructs a departed soul on how to find his way through the treacherous underworld and reach the Field of Rushes, or Egyptian heaven. At every step of the way, the soul would find his way blocked by divine gatekeepers, who would admit him to the next step only if he knew the correct spells, passwords, and secret names of the gods.

For example, when seeking to enter the Hall of the Two Truths, the departed soul is confronted by the dog-headed god, Anubis.

"Do you know the name of this gateway?" asks Anubis.

"'You-Dispel-Light' is the name of this gate," replies the soul.

"Do you know the names of the upper and lower portions of the door?" Anubis counters.

"'Lord of Truth, Master of his Two Legs' is the name of the upper portion,'" says the soul. "'Lord of Strength, the One who Commands the Cattle' is the name of the lower.'"

"Pass you on then," declares Anubis, "for you know."[11]

And so on. By correctly repeating all the passwords and secret formulae, the departed soul proves that he is a god, a risen "Osiris"
who is "true of voice" and qualified to take his place among the
other gods. Some of the formulae are considered more secret than
others. Chapter 137a of the *Book of the Dead*, for example, opens
with these cautionary words:

> Beware greatly lest you do this before anyone except yourself, with
> your father or your son, because it is a great secret of the West, a
> secret of the Netherworld. . . .[12]

> What is done is a secret of the Underworld belonging to the Mysteries
> of the Underworld, a secret image in the God's Domain.[13]

The obscure and puzzling nature of such writings has led Egyptologist Ogden Goelet of the Department of Near Eastern Studies at
New York University to entertain the possibility that Egyptian funerary texts may have a "hidden meaning, perhaps only known to a
few initiates among the priesthood." He continues: "One of the
most frequently encountered themes in all Egyptian mortuary literature is the deceased's assertion of belonging to a select group in the
afterlife. This gives rise to a feeling that one had to be *initiated* into
the world of the dead, as if one were becoming a member of a secret
society in the cosmic sphere."[14]

Some scholars have gone even further than Goelet, suggesting
that the secret society to which he alludes may have existed in the
worldly sphere as well as the cosmic one. According to these scholars, the back-and-forth, question-and-answer format of the *Book of
the Dead* may, in fact, have been modeled after actual initiation ceremonies by which Egyptian priests gained admittance to higher levels of temple secrecy.[15]

If this is true, it tends to support the claim of Freemasons that
their rites descended from the Egyptian Mysteries. A recruit to a
Masonic lodge undergoes a ceremony in which he is ritually
"killed" and "resurrected," just like the Egyptian god Osiris or the
departed soul in the *Book of the Dead*. The Masonic initiate must
also answer a series of cryptic questions with equally cryptic answers, in a manner eerily reminiscent of Egyptian funerary texts.
Like the Egyptian priests, Masons rise, over the years, through a se-

ries of ever higher degrees of initiation, with correspondingly greater access to secret doctrines.

Did Pythagoras partake in such rituals in Egypt? Was he required to "die" and "rise again" before gaining access to the secret teachings of the priests? We have only the word of Iamblichus and other ancient biographers on this point, and their information may not be trustworthy. But it is interesting to note that, after returning to Greece, one of the first things Pythagoras did was to found a secret society called the Cenobites, or *Pythagorikoi* (Pythagoreans), a group whose teachings were widely reputed to be of Egyptian origin.

Was Pythagoras a missionary for the Egyptian Mysteries? Was the Cenobite cult a "lodge" of ancient Freemasonry? Nobody knows. What is beyond dispute, however, is that, to a great extent, all subsequent Greek philosophy traces its roots directly to Pythagoras and his disciples.

CHAPTER 19

"SOMETHING LIKE A FREEMASONRY"

The safest general characterization of the European philosophical tradition is that it consists of a series of footnotes to Plato.

— ALFRED NORTH WHITEHEAD[1]

PYTHAGORAS RETURNED FROM HIS TRAVELS, EAGER TO TEACH the Greeks all that he had learned in Egypt and the countries of the East. But he found the people of Samos indifferent to his teachings. Physical training was much more to their liking. Thus, Pythagoras won his first disciple by going to the local gymnasium, selecting a promising youth, and offering to pay him three *oboli* for every math problem he mastered. Once the youth was hooked on learning, Pythagoras stopped paying him, and the boy went on to become a lifelong devotee of philosophy. Cheered by this small success, Pythagoras was nonetheless "disgusted at the Samians' scorn for education," as Iamblichus put it, and soon left the island forever.[2]

Pythagoras achieved his greatest success in the Greek colony of Croton, in Italy. Soon after arriving, he won 2,000 disciples with a single lecture. The *Pythagorikoi* worshiped their master as a god and refused to call him by his name, which they considered too holy to be pronounced. Instead, they referred to Pythagoras as Himself. Before long, the Pythagoreans became so numerous and powerful that their political influence made itself felt throughout the Greek colonies of Sicily and southern Italy.

"With their secret doctrines and sworn loyalty to each other and to the Master," writes classicist A. R. Burn, ". . . they formed something like a freemasonry."[3] In the end, political rivals drove Pythagoras into exile in the Italian city of Metapontum, where he later died. The Pythagorean sect scattered to the winds, and most of its secret doctrines were lost. But those few scraps that survived were enough to inspire generations of Greek philosophers. Iamblichus wrote:

> Pythagoras is said to have been the first to call himself a philosopher.
> . . . [He taught that] the purest and most genuine character is that of the man who devotes himself to the contemplation of the most beautiful things, and he may properly be called a philosopher. . . . He was the first to give a name to philosophy, describing it as a desire for and love of wisdom, which later he defined as the science of objectified truth.[4]

In Pythagoras's view, truth and beauty were one and the same. The truth could never be ugly, and beauty could not be false. Over a century later, this principle formed the basis of Plato's theory of ideal forms. Indeed, many of Plato's key ideas can be traced directly to Pythagorean doctrine and to the Egyptian theology that underlay it.

After Plato's beloved teacher, Sokrates, was put to death by the Athenians, Plato struggled to make sense of the tragedy. What was the point of pursuing a good life, Plato asked himself, if your ultimate reward was to be condemned like a common criminal? This question haunted Plato for twenty years. He finally resolved it in the *Republic*, written sometime between 380 and 370 B.C. and widely regarded as Plato's masterpiece.

In that book, the character of Sokrates asks Glaukon why a man should bother to pursue truth and virtue when it is the evildoers who seem to prosper in this world. They wrestle with the question through the entire book. In the end, Sokrates concludes that men should pursue good because it is pleasing to the gods and because, after death, the gods will punish or reward us according to our deeds.

To modern Christians, the notion of reward or punishment after death seems familiar and obvious. But it was not so for the Greeks of Plato's day. Death held only despair for the Greeks. Heroes and villains alike ended their days in the shadowy underworld called Hades, their ghosts "clangorously whirling like wild birds this way and that in bewildered fear," as Homer put it.[5]

In *The Odyssey*, Odysseus employs sorcery to conjure up the soul of his dead friend Achilles. At the sight of Achilles' ghost, Odysseus cries, "How I envy your lot, Achilles . . . here I find you a Prince among the dead. To you, Achilles, death can be no grief at all."[6]

But the ghost disagrees. "Better be a hired man on a poor farm on earth," he moans, "than king over all the strengthless dead."[7]

This dismal view of the hereafter was shared by most ancient peoples. The Sumerians, for example, believed that dead souls wandered in darkness, feeding on dust.[8] The biblical Hebrews expected that, after death, they would descend into Sheol, an underground realm not unlike the Greek Hades. Ecclesiastes 9:4–5 portrays the Hebrew afterlife in words that Achilles himself might have uttered: "Even a live dog is better off than a dead lion! For the living know that they will die, but the dead know nothing; they have no further reward, and even the memory of them is forgotten."

Of all the peoples who lived around the Mediterranean "pond," only the Egyptians held a happy view of death. For them alone, death offered the chance for eternal bliss—at least, if you were wise and virtuous. Departed souls went before the gods in the Hall of the Two Truths to be judged. A dead man's heart was placed on one side of a great scale; a feather symbolizing *ma'at,* or "truth," was placed on the other side. Thus each man's heart was weighed, after death, against the standard of absolute truth. If the dead man's heart was found to be false, the she-monster Ammut devoured it. But if his heart was true, his soul won eternal life, as a glorified, heavenly being.

In his devotion to truth as the highest ideal and his belief in heavenly reward, Plato was far closer to Pythagoras and Egyptian theology than to any native doctrine of the Greeks. Indeed, admiration for Egypt informs all of Plato's work. In his *Republic,* for example, Plato rejected Greek democracy and proposed, instead, that the perfect state should be ruled by a caste of Guardians, trained in philosophy and dedicated to the moral improvement of society.

Many Greeks recognized Plato's Guardians as a thinly disguised version of the Egyptian priesthood.

"Plato's contemporaries mocked him," observed the Greek philosopher Krantor, around 300 B.C., "saying that he was not the inventor of his republic, but that he had copied Egyptian institutions."[9]

Where would Plato have encountered such Egyptian ideas? He might have acquired them from Archytas, a Pythagorean philosopher whom Plato befriended when he traveled to Italy around 388 B.C. But several ancient writers claim that Plato received his Egyptian learning straight from the proverbial horse's mouth.

Plato is said to have journeyed to Egypt after Sokrates' death and, by one account, to have remained there for thirteen years. "Plato does not deny importing from abroad the best parts into his philosophy," observed Clement of Alexandria, "and admits a visit to Egypt."[10] Clement also wrote that Plato became the disciple of an Egyptian priest named Sechnuphis of Heliopolis.[11] When the geographer Strabo toured Egypt in the first century B.C., he was shown the places where Plato and the Greek mathematician Eudoxos had supposedly lived and studied while under the tutelage of Egyptian priests. Strabo wrote:

> At Heliopolis, the houses of the priests and the schools of Plato and Eudoxus were pointed out to us; for Eudoxus went up to that place with Plato, and they both passed thirteen years with the priests, as is stated by some writers; for since these priests excelled in their knowledge of the heavenly bodies, albeit secretive and slow to impart it, Plato and Eudoxus prevailed upon them in time and by courting their favor to let them learn some of the principles of their doctrines; but the barbarians concealed most things.[12]

Perhaps it was in Heliopolis that Plato first heard the fable about the Egyptian gods Thoth and Amun, which he retells in his book *Phaedros*. The character Sokrates, in that dialogue, describes Thoth—whom he calls "Theuth"—as the inventor of writing, mathematics, astronomy, and other arts. Plato writes:

> I have heard, then, that at Naucratis, in Egypt, was one of the ancient gods of that country, the one whose sacred bird is called the ibis, and

the name of the god himself was Theuth. He it was who invented numbers and arithmetic and geometry and astronomy, also draughts and dice, and most important of all, letters.[13]

For both Plato and Pythagoras, the teachings of Thoth—in particular "numbers and arithmetic and geometry"—formed an integral part of their philosophy, just as they evidently formed an integral part of the curriculum in Egypt's temple schools. When Plato founded his famous Academy in 387 B.C., he hung a sign over the door saying, "Let no one ignorant of geometry enter here."[14] Plato also urged the Greeks to adopt Egyptian styles of art and music, which he found superior to those of Greece.[15]

One of the most puzzling of Plato's doctrines was his belief in metempsychosis, or the transmigration of souls. In the closing lines of the *Republic*, he recounts the near-death experience of a warrior named Er, who claimed to have seen multitudes of departed souls being reborn in human and animal form. Apparently, the souls had some power to choose the forms they would take in their next lives. Those who lacked wisdom chose poorly, finding themselves reborn as bloodthirsty tyrants or brutish beasts. Only those trained in philosophy, said Plato, were able to make wise choices.

Reincarnation was alien to Greek religion, but it was taught by two Greek sects, the Pythagoreans and the Orphics. Like Pythagoras, the legendary Orpheus was reputed to have derived his doctrines from Egypt. The Greeks, in general, looked upon reincarnation as an Egyptian belief. Thus Herodotos wrote:

> The Egyptians . . . were also the first people to put forward the doctrine of the immortality of the soul, and to maintain that after death it enters another creature at the moment of that creature's birth. . . . This theory has been adopted by certain Greek writers, some earlier, some later, who have put it forward as their own. Their names are known to me, but I refrain from mentioning them.[16]

Conventional scholars deny that the Egyptians believed in reincarnation, but, as is so often the case, the only evidence they can offer is the "argument from silence." No one has yet found an Egyptian manuscript entitled "The Doctrine of Metempsychosis," so these scholars assume that no such doctrine ever existed. If we followed such reasoning consistently, however, we would also be forced to conclude that the Egyptians never married. No document, after all, has ever been found alluding to an Egyptian wedding ceremony.[17]

Most readers will probably have little trouble opening their minds to the possibility that the Egyptians probably did have formal marriage rituals—even though we cannot yet prove that they did. By the same token, we should not be too hasty in rejecting the possibility that metempsychosis was known to the Egyptians, even though the definitive proof has yet to turn up.

In fact, some scholars have already claimed to have found evidence for such a belief in Egyptian texts. In 1911, Sir E. A. Wallis Budge called attention to certain spells in the *Book of the Dead* that empowered the dead soul to take on the form of various animals, gods, and spiritual beings:

> The Egyptians believed in the transmigration of souls. . . . A soul could become a golden hawk, a divine hawk, a *tchatcha* chief, a god of light, a lily, the god Ptah, a Bennu bird, a heron, a "living soul," a swallow, a serpent, and a crocodile. It could remain in each of these so long as it pleased, presumably without losing its identity, and it could pass from one form to another at pleasure.[18]

The Book of the Dead does indeed contain verses that seem to hint at metempsychosis. "I am a long-lived snake . . ." it says, "I am a crocodile immersed in dread . . . I have flown up as a falcon, I have cackled as a goose . . . I have grown as a plant, I have clad myself as a tortoise, I am the essence of every god . . ."[19]

All of this discussion, however, is highly controversial. The Egyptian documents that have come down to us are simply too few and too obscure to allow any firm conclusions on the matter of metempsychosis. As Dr. Ogden Goelet admits, "Much of the *Book of the Dead* is frankly incomprehensible, even for experts. No amount of exegesis can explain many passages."[20]

Oceans of ink have been expended, over the centuries, by scholars and occultists alike, seeking to pinpoint those elements of Platonic and Pythagorean thought that are undeniably Egyptian. No definitive answers will probably ever be found to this question. But there can be no doubt that, in one form or another, the shadow of Egypt loomed large over Greek philosophy. And wherever that shadow appeared, it invariably came dressed in such typically Masonic trappings as secrecy, geometry, initiatory rituals, and doctrines of resurrection.

The existence of secret societies in Greece is undeniable. Their connection with Egypt is strongly attested by legend, as is their role in philosophy's birth. But how far back in the mists of antiquity should we look for the origin of these sects? How long have Greek sages been studying in Egypt, and how long have Egyptian cults thrived on Greek soil? Once again, it is the irascible George G. M. James who provides a bizarre but compelling clue to this mystery.

CHAPTER 20

THE GRAND MASTER

A CCORDING TO DIODOROS OF SICILY, THE EGYPTIANS THEMSELVES possessed records in their temple libraries suggesting that Greek sages and artists had been studying in Egypt as far back as the Heroic Age. Diodoros wrote:

> For the priests of Egypt recount from the records of their sacred books that they were visited in early times by Orpheus, Musaeus, Melampus, and Daedalus, also by the poet Homer and Lycurgus of Sparta, later by Solon of Athens and the philosopher Plato, and that there also came Pythagoras of Samos and the mathematician Eudoxus, as well as Democritus of Abdera and Oenopides of Chios.... Also of the ancient sculptors, the most renowned sojourned among them, namely, Telecles and Theodorus.[1]

Many experts would say that such legendary figures as Orpheus, Melampus, and Daidalos (Daedalus) never existed. But since we are studying the question from a Greek point of view, let us assume, like Diodoros, that they were real people. These ancient heroes and sages would have lived roughly in the time of Herakles and Jason. That would put them deep in the Bronze Age, a time when Greece was taking its first halting steps toward civilization.

Were those first steps guided and inspired by Egyptian cults? Were Orpheus, Daidalos, and Melampus acolytes in an ancient Freemasonry, whose lodges were already thriving on Greek soil hundreds of years before the Trojan War? For George G. M. James, there could be no doubt in the matter. Not only did marginal cults, such as those of the Orphics and Pythagoreans, derive from Egypt, according to James, but so did some of Greece's most venerable and respected shrines and oracles, dating back to heroic times. In James's view, many leading Greek temples were little more than provincial chapters of Egypt's Grand Lodge of the Ancient Mysteries in Thebes.

James pointed, in particular, to the temple of Apollo at Delphi, undoubtedly the holiest shrine in Greece and also one of the oldest. Herakles himself is said to have visited the oracle in archaic times. It was there that a priestess called the Pythia answered questions put to her by visitors, while suspended in a sacred trance. Her words were thought to come directly from Apollo. No Greek ruler would have dreamed of going to war, sending out a colony, or embarking on any other great enterprise without first consulting the Pythia.

For that reason, it was a disaster for Greece when an accidental fire destroyed the temple of Delphi in 548 B.C. The Delphians had to raise the huge sum of 300 silver talents to rebuild it. Messengers were dispatched all over Greece, begging every city for contributions. Strangely, it turned out to be a foreigner—the Egyptian pharaoh Amasis—who gave one of the most generous donations. "From few other places did they obtain so much," Herodotos commented.[2] For his great generosity, the Greeks named Amasis "Philhellene"—"lover of Greece."

But was it really out of love that Amasis contributed? Or was it something else? George G. M. James thought he knew the answer. "Clearly," he wrote, "the Temple of Delphi was a branch of the Egyptian Mystery System, projected in Greece." Indeed, James asserted that the shrine at Delphi was a "foreign institution," directly run by the Egyptian Grand Lodge. By helping out the "brethren" in Greece, King Amasis was only doing his duty as Grand Master of the Osiriaca.[3] James offered little evidence for this claim, beyond his own ebullient faith. Nevertheless, there remain some curious facts about the pharaoh Amasis that make it difficult to dismiss James's theory out of hand.

His real name was Ahmose II; *Amasis* is the Greek version. Not only Amasis himself, but also the entire Twenty-sixth Dynasty, to which he belonged, maintained unusually close ties with Greece. It was during the Twenty-sixth Dynasty, for example, that the Egyptian army filled with Greek mercenaries for the first time and that permanent colonies of Greek traders were established in Egypt.

"Amasis favored the Greeks and granted them a number of privileges," wrote Herodotos.[4] Indeed, of all the Twenty-sixth Dynasty pharaohs, none was more Greek-loving than Ahmose II. Among other favors and concessions, Herodotos says that Amasis set aside the city of Naukratis as a residence for Greeks living and trading in Egypt. He also granted lands for the building of Greek temples and shrines and took a Greek woman named Ladicé for his wife.

According to legend, it was only due to the personal intervention of Amasis that Pythagoras was allowed to study in Egypt. The Egyptians, in general, despised foreigners and normally did not admit them to their temple schools. Pythagoras, however, asked Polykrates, the tyrant of Samos, to write a letter on his behalf to the pharaoh Amasis, seeking permission for Pythagoras to be initiated in the Egyptian temples. Out of friendship for Polykrates, Amasis graciously agreed to provide letters recommending Pythagoras to the priests. But, even armed with these royal letters, Pythagoras still got the runaround. The philosopher Porphyry (233–305 A.D.) described what happened next in his *Life of Pythagoras*.

First, the priests at Heliopolis turned Pythagoras away, sending him on to Memphis. Then the priests at Memphis sent him to Thebes. At last, the Theban priests took Pythagoras in, "from fear of the King," as Porphyry put it. But they did everything in their power to make his road as rocky as possible:

> Thinking that he would desist from his purpose as a result of great difficulties, they enjoined on him very hard precepts. . . . These he performed so readily that he won their admiration, and they permitted him to sacrifice to the Gods, and to acquaint himself with all their sciences, a favor never previously granted to a foreigner.[5]

Why was Amasis so friendly toward the Greeks? The answer seems to lie in his city of origin. Amasis, like all the other pharaohs of the Twenty-sixth Dynasty, came from the city of Sais, located in the Western Delta of Egypt. In 664 B.C., a Saite prince named

Psamtek rose up against the Assyrian and Kushite conquerors, who at that time ruled the northern and southern portions of Egypt, respectively. Largely with the help of Greek mercenaries, Psamtek freed Egypt from foreign domination. For the next 139 years, Egypt was ruled by one Saite pharaoh after another, for which reason the Twenty-sixth Dynasty is often called the Saite Dynasty.

The reliance of the Saite pharaohs on Greek mercenaries doubtless encouraged their cordiality toward Greece. But the bond between Greek and Saite predated Psamtek by many centuries. When Diodoros of Sicily visited Egypt sometime between 60 and 56 B.C., the priests there told him that Athens had originally been founded as a colony of Sais. Its first king, Kekrops, had been an Egyptian, they said, as had many other Athenian kings over the years. Diodoros wrote:

> Now the Egyptians say that also after these events a great number of colonies were spread from Egypt over all the inhabited world. ...Even the Athenians, they say, are colonists from Sais in Egypt. ... Moreover, certain rulers of Athens were originally Egyptians, they say. Petes, for instance, the father of the Menestheus who took part in the expedition against Troy, having clearly been an Egyptian. ... Erechtheus, also, who was by birth an Egyptian, became king of Athens.[6]

Diodoros was skeptical of these boasts, suspecting that the Egyptians were simply trying to claim Athens as a colony "because of the fame of that city."[7] Nevertheless, the priests offered many convincing proofs, which Diodoros felt compelled to repeat. They recounted, first of all, an Egyptian tradition that Erechtheus, during a worldwide drought, had exploited his kinship with Egypt to obtain a vast quantity of Egyptian grain, thus saving Greece from famine. Afterwards, said the priests, Erechtheus established the Mysteries of Demeter at Eleusis—secret rites ostensibly modeled after the Egyptian Mysteries of Isis and Osiris.[8]

Greek legend had recorded these same events, said the priests, though in garbled form. Had not the Greeks long maintained that it was during the reign of Erechtheus that the goddess Demeter had saved them from famine with a gift of grain? And was it not during Erechtheus's reign that the Greeks traditionally believed the Eleusinian Mysteries to have been founded?[9]

In addition, the Egyptian priests claimed that two noble Athenian families, the Eumolpidae and the Ceryces, were descended from priestly orders of Egypt. These families were traditionally charged with administering the sacred rites of Athens. As the priests put it:

> And their sacrifices as well as their ancient ceremonies are observed by the Athenians in the same way as the Egyptians; for the Eumolpidae were derived from the priests of Egypt and the Ceryces from the *pastophoroi* [special priests who carry shrines of the gods in Egyptian processions]. They are also the only Greeks who swear by Isis, and they closely resemble the Egyptians in both their appearance and manners.[10]

Diodoros did not dispute these arguments. But neither did he accept the Egyptians' claim that Athens was their colony. On this point, modern scholars agree with Diodoros. They echo his opinion that the tales of Egyptian kings in Athens were nothing more than the invention of boastful priests. And so the story has remained, for centuries, submerged beneath a swamp of scholarly apathy.

But it has recently resurfaced. One modern scholar has approached the problem from a fresh point of view. He has detected a pattern of long-forgotten links between Sais and Athens enfolded in the legends of Kekrops and Erechtheus—links that would scandalize Diodoros but would no doubt bring only a smile of satisfaction from the newly vindicated George G. M. James.

CHAPTER 21

THE EGYPTIAN
ATHENA

W HAT FIRST CAUGHT MARTIN BERNAL'S ATTENTION WAS NOT
the title or subject of the book, but rather the salmon-
pink brightness of its cover. Only when he drew closer
to the shelf did Bernal see that the book was Cerny's *Coptic Etymological Dictionary.* The year was 1979 and the place Heffers Bookshop in Cambridge, England.

As a scholar of Chinese history and politics, Bernal had no professional involvement whatever with Coptic etymology. But he was a
compulsive language junkie. Many of his happiest hours were
passed in university language labs, listening for hours to tapes of
Welsh and other obscure tongues or gazing lovingly at extinct and
unfamiliar scripts in books that he could not read. Over the years,
Bernal had mastered French, Chinese, Japanese, Vietnamese, and an
African tongue called Chichewa. Now he was deeply absorbed in a
new project—the study of Hebrew and ancient Greek. It was
Bernal's growing knowledge of Greek that sparked his interest in
Cerny's dictionary.

Coptic was the language spoken in Egypt during the early Christian period. After the Arab conquest of 641 A.D., Coptic gradually died out, disappearing completely as a spoken language by the seventeenth century. Nevertheless, preserved in old manuscripts and in the liturgies of Egypt's Coptic Christian church, the Coptic language provides scholars with a priceless window into the speech of the pharaohs, from which it is directly descended.

Coptic was written not with hieroglyphs—which passed out of use around 400 A.D.— but with a modified Greek alphabet. For that reason, Bernal knew that he would be able to sound out the words in the dictionary, using his knowledge of Greek. His only intention, when he opened the book, was to enjoy a few quiet moments, flipping through the pages and mouthing under his breath the strange, archaic syllables of a dead language. But fate was stalking Bernal that day. From the moment he opened that salmon-pink tome, neither his life nor the study of classical history would ever again be the same.

Bernal expected to encounter words in the dictionary that were unlike those of any European language. After all, European tongues had supposedly evolved in complete isolation from those of Africa and the Near East. There would be no reason to find any similarity between them. Yet, Bernal's first brief glance through the dictionary revealed a multitude of Egyptian words that bore a strange resemblance to *Greek* words. It was not just that they were written in the Greek alphabet. The words themselves were actually similar in form and meaning. Two Egyptian towns, for example, were called *Psabet* and *Sobt*, which means "the fortress," in Coptic. These names clearly resemble *Psophis*, a name borne by at least two Greek cities.

Intrigued by this mystery, Bernal purchased the book and took it home. Once again, fate took a hand. Immersed in the care of his newborn son, Bernal found himself in a perfect psychological state for taking a fresh look at an old problem. By day, he studied the dictionary. By night, he tossed sleeplessly, waiting for his son's next outcry. Bernal learned to get by with little or no sleep. Day and night, he walked like a zombie, his eyes red and bleary, his brain swimming with hallucinatory images of soiled diapers and splatters of half-digested milk.

In order to relieve his wife, Bernal often sat, rocking his child through the wee hours of the morning. At such times, his mental inhibitions seemed to melt away. Bernal's sleep-deprived brain would fill with a crazy brew of Greek and Coptic words, coalescing in strange and unexpected ways. In the morning, he would review his revelations of the night, discarding some but recording the more likely candidates in his notebook. In this manner, Bernal's hoard of Greek and Coptic look-alikes grew, day by day.[1]

Later, Bernal went on to study Egyptian hieroglyphs so that he could make correspondences directly between Greek and pharaonic Egyptian. Over the years, he found hundreds of Greek words that seemed to have derived from Egyptian roots. Indeed, Bernal eventually concluded that as much as *20–25 percent* of the ancient Greek vocabulary might have come from Egypt—including the names of many important rivers, mountains, and cities in Greece.

This was far too great a proportion to have been caused by fleeting contact with Egyptian merchants. It suggested massive and prolonged interaction between Greeks and Egyptians in early times—perhaps even colonization. If Bernal's etymologies were correct, historians of the ancient world would have a lot of rewriting to do.

Bernal published his findings in 1987. Needless to say, the academic world was shocked by his claims. The thought of 25 percent of the Greek vocabulary coming from Egypt was sufficiently provocative in itself. But even more disturbing to many scholars was Bernal's insistence on the Egyptian origin of one *particular* Greek word. That word was *Athena*—the name of the patron goddess of Athens.

In the eyes of many scholars, Athena was the heart and soul of classical Greece. It was she who led the Greeks to victory in Homer's *Iliad*. It was her city of Athens that gave birth to Greek learning and democracy. It was Athena to whom the Greeks raised their finest temple, the Parthenon, and it was her colossal statue that brought fame to Greece's greatest sculptor, Phidias. Athena seemed to embody all that was best and loveliest in Greek civilization. If she really came from Egypt, then a large part of Greece's soul was a gift of the Nile.

As unwelcome as many classicists found this possibility, the evidence for an Egyptian Athena was quite strong. Even before he probed into the etymology, Bernal had been aware of the legends linking Athens and the Egyptian city of Sais. He also knew that

Athena—the patron goddess of Athens—was widely regarded, in the ancient world, as identical with Neit, the patron goddess of Sais.

"In the Delta of Egypt . . ." wrote Plato in the *Timaeus*, "there is a certain district called the Saitic. The chief city in this district is Sais . . . the founder of which, they say, is a goddess whose Egyptian name is Neith, and in Greek, as they assert, Athena."[2]

The Egyptians too seem to have treated Athena and Neit as one and the same. Like the other Twenty-sixth Dynasty pharaohs, Amasis poured money into the temple of Neit.[3] But he was not satisfied with promoting her cult in Egypt alone. Amasis also gave generously to a temple of Athena at Rhodes. Herodotos goes out of his way to make clear that it was the Egyptian origin of this temple that inspired Amasis's gift, for legend had it that the temple had been founded by the Danaids, legendary colonists who came from Egypt to settle the Argolid in Greece. Herodotos wrote, "Amasis further showed his goodwill to Greece by sending presents to be dedicated in Greek temples. . . . the gifts to Lindos in Rhodes were not the expression of any personal feeling, but were given because of the tradition that the temple of Athene there was founded by the daughters of Danaus, who touched at the island during their flight from the sons of Aegyptus."[4]

In general, Bernal was struck by the rampant Athena-mania that seemed to rage across the eastern Mediterranean during Amasis's reign. It seemed more than a coincidence, he thought, that Athena worship reached its highest peak in Greece at exactly the same time that Amasis was promoting Neit in Egypt.[5]

But why did Greeks and Egyptians equate these two goddesses in the first place? Bernal noted that they shared many common traits. Athena was a goddess of war, wisdom, and weaving, who was always portrayed in full armor, brandishing a spear and shield. Curiously, Neit was also depicted as a warrior, bearing a shield and crossed arrows. She too was a goddess of war, wisdom, and weaving.[6]

But the names of the two goddesses did not seem at all similar—at least, not on the surface. When Bernal started looking *beneath* the surface, however, he made a crucial discovery. In Egyptian hieroglyphs, the name Neit would be spelled *Nt*. Another name for the city of Sais was *Ht Nt*—"the Temple or House of Neit." As discussed in previous chapters, the Egyptian writing system did not use vowels. However, Bernal deduced from Egyptian words transliterated into Greek or Coptic that the word *Ht*—meaning "House of" or "Temple of"—may actually have been pronounced *At* or *Ath*.

Could it be, Bernal proposed, that the Egyptian name for Sais was actually pronounced *Athanait?* Indeed, since the letter *t* was often dropped from the end of words in Late Egyptian, Bernal guessed that Sais may even have been called something like *Athanai*. This was very close to the Greek *Athenai*—meaning the city of Athens—and to *Athene*—the name of the goddess Athena. Further evidence in favor of Bernal's theory was the fact that the Greek writer Charax of Pergamon had actually written, in the second century A.D., that "the Saitians called their city Athenai."[7]

Ingenious as it was, scholars did not rush to embrace Bernal's radical new etymology. Egyptologists continued to insist that *Ht-Nt* was probably pronounced more like *Hat-neyit* or perhaps *Hawat-Nirati*, rather than *Athanait*.[8] But such hypothetical pronunciations are little more than educated guesses and no more authoritative than Bernal's. The question remains open to this day.

None of this proves, of course, that King Amasis really financed the Delphic Oracle out of proprietary concern for an "Egyptian" shrine. The temple of Apollo at Delphi may or may not have been founded by Egyptians, and George G. M. James failed to offer compelling evidence one way or the other. What is clear, however, is that James's overall view of the relationship between Greek cults and Egyptian pharaohs was not so farfetched after all.

The pharaohs did indeed hold the title of high priest (or Grand Master, if you will) of every temple cult in Egypt. There were indeed religious cults in Greece that claimed to derive from Egypt. And the Egyptians did, in some cases, acknowledge this ancestral connection and even gave money on the strength of it, as seen in Amasis's donation to the temple of Athena in Rhodes. In this matter, as in so many others, James got the broad strokes right, if not always the details.

If Athena really was an Egyptian goddess, then Egypt's cults had been thriving on the Greek mainland for a very long time. Greek legend traced the founding of Athens back to the sixteenth century B.C.[9]—the dawn of the Late Bronze Age, over a thousand years before Plato and Pythagoras. It was then, said the legends, that Athena won her battle against Poseidon for possession of Attika and gave her blessing to Kekrops, the first king of Athens.

What does archaeology tell us about those legendary days? Is there, in fact, any tangible evidence that Egyptians visited Greece during the Late Bronze Age? Indeed, there is. Not only does such evidence exist, but it is also specifically during the period of Athens's legendary Egyptian kings that it abounds most plentifully.

PART FIVE

WHEN EGYPT RULED THE WAVES

CHAPTER 22

THE *PAX*
AEGYPTIACA

A
CCORDING TO GREEK LEGEND, ERECHTHEUS WAS THE FOURTH
king of Athens. He was the king who saved the city from
famine by obtaining a large shipment of Egyptian grain. Or
so claimed certain Egyptian priests. Diodoros of Sicily recorded
their testimony as follows:

> Erechtheus . . . was by birth an Egyptian. . . . Once when there was a
> great drought . . . which extended over practically all the inhabited
> earth except Egypt . . . Erechtheus, through his racial connection with
> Egypt, brought from there to Athens a great supply of grain, and in re-
> turn those who had enjoyed this aid made their benefactor king. After
> he had secured the throne he instituted the initiatory rites of Demeter
> in Eleusis and established the mysteries, transferring their ritual from
> Egypt. . . . And the Athenians on their part agree that it was in the
> reign of Erechtheus, when a lack of rain had wiped out the crops, that
> Demeter came to them with the gift of grain.[1]

How closely does this legend fit the facts we know about Greece
during the Late Bronze Age? Quite closely, in fact. There is no question that Greece imported large quantities of Egyptian grain during

classical times. The evidence is very good that they also did the same in earlier days, when Erechtheus lived.

If we can trust the dates given on the Parian Marble—a broken marble stela, originally set up on the Greek island of Paros around 263 B.C., that gives a history of Greece since legendary times— Erechtheus reigned sometime around 1408 B.C., during the so-called Mycenaean period of Greece (1575–1200 B.C.).[2] Like their descendants in classical times, the Mycenaeans appear to have devoted most of their farmland to olives and grapes, and relatively little to wheat. It is therefore almost inevitable that they would have suffered periodically from the same sort of grain shortages that plagued classical Greece.[3]

We know that the classical Greeks paid for Egyptian grain with silver from their mines. The Mycenaeans also mined silver, and archaeologists have found large quantities of Greek silver in Egypt, going all the way back to the Eleventh Dynasty (2040–1991 B.C.).[4]

Curiously, the Greek word for wheat, *sitos*, does not appear to be European in origin. Scholars have tried to trace its derivation to Assyria or Mesopotamia, but Bernal suggests that it more likely derived from the Egyptian *swt*, meaning "grain."[5] This would put *sitos* in the same class as other well-known Egyptian words that entered the Greek language to describe trade goods from Egypt—words such as *papyros* (papyrus), *ebenos* (ebony), *kommi* (gum), *kiki* (castor oil), *sindon* (fine tissue), *annes* (anise), and so on.[6]

If Diodoros's account is correct, Erechtheus must have been a man of some influence in Athens even before he became king. Why would such a prominent Egyptian have been living in Greece at that time? It may have been for the same reason that upper-class Englishmen lived in nineteenth-century India. If Erechtheus did live around the traditional date of 1408 B.C., that would place him smack in the middle of a period that Martin Bernal has called the *Pax Aegyptiaca*—"the Egyptian Peace"—a time when Egypt seems to have exerted political control over the Aegean world.[7]

The *Pax Aegyptiaca* was a hundred-year period from about 1475 to 1375 B.C. when Egypt appears to have enjoyed unrivaled military and economic supremacy in the eastern Mediterranean.[8] Scholars continue to argue over whether Egypt really possessed an Asian empire during the Twelfth Dynasty (see chapter 13). But for the period of the *Pax Aegyptiaca*, there is no argument at all. Overwhelming evidence confirms that Egypt then presided over what was undeniably the greatest empire in the world.

Egypt's imperial epoch began with the conquests of Thutmose I (1504–1492 B.C.), who subdued large parts of Nubia and marched as far north as the river Euphrates in northern Mesopotamia. His grandson Thutmose III finished the job, crushing all remaining traces of rebellion in Syria-Palestine in the decisive Battle of Megiddo, recounted in the Hall of the Annals in the Karnak temple.

At that point, the Egyptian Empire is believed to have stretched from Syria all the way down to the Fourth Cataract of the Nile, deep in Nubia. Every one of the Phoenician or Canaanite seaports along the Levantine coast was reduced to vassalage. Many letters have survived, written by Canaanite kings to the Egyptian pharaoh during this period. Their cringing subservience testifies to the firmness of Egypt's imperial control.

"At the feet of my king, my lord, my pantheon, my sun-god, seven times I fall," wrote Yapahu, king of Gezer, to Akhnaton, the great-great-grandson of Thutmose III. "Everything which the king, my lord, said to me I have heard most attentively.... Now I have heard the breath of the king, and it goes out to me, and my heart is very serene."[9]

But not only the Canaanites paid homage to Pharaoh. Egypt's power made itself felt even in those far-off lands that lay beyond the *Wadj Wer*—"the Great Green Sea," as the Egyptians called the Mediterranean. An inscription from the reign of Thutmose III shows that the viceroy he installed to rule over Syria also had authority over the Isles in the Midst of the Great Green Sea—a phrase that seems to refer to the islands of the Aegean.[10] A painting in the tomb of Rekhmira, the Grand Vizier of Thutmose III, shows men from Keftiu—the Egyptian name for Crete—bringing tribute to the pharaoh. The accompanying inscription explains: "When they [the princes of Keftiu] hear of his victories over all the countries, they bring their gifts on their backs in order to obtain the breath of life in order to submit to his majesty [Thutmose III] in order that his power could protect them."[11]

Several Egyptian pharaohs claimed suzerainty over a place called Haunebut—"Behind the Islands." Some Egyptologists have theorized that this term referred to the Greek mainland, which lies "behind" the Aegean isles from the Egyptians' perspective. The best

evidence that *Haunebut* really means "Greece" comes from the
Rosetta Stone—an inscription by the Greek pharaoh Ptolemy V
from 196 B.C., written in both Greek and Egyptian. In the Rosetta
Stone, the phrase *Haunebu*—meaning "the people of Haunebut"—
is used as a direct translation of the word for *Greek* whenever that
word appears in the Greek portion of the text.[12]

Ahmose I (1552–1526 B.C.) called the Haunebu his servants in a
stela erected in the temple of Amun at Karnak. In the same stela, he
also gave to his mother, Queen Ahhotep, the title of Mistress of the
Shores of the *Haunebut*.[13] More than fifty years later, the great conqueror Thutmose III also claimed to have brought the *Haunebu* to
heel. In an inscription found at Jebel Barkal in Nubia, he boasted
that he had "trussed the Nine Bows, the Isles in the Midst of the
Great Green Sea, the Haunebut and the rebel foreign countries." He
further declared: "I came and I made you strike those who are in the
Isles and those that live in the Midst of the Great Green Sea. Hearing your war cry, I made them see your majesty like the millstone
pressing on the back of its victims."[14]

Even as late as the Nineteenth Dynasty (1295–1188 B.C.), Egyptian pharaohs were still running roughshod over the poor Aegean islanders—at least in their inscriptions. One monument of the great
conqueror Ramesses II (1279–1212 B.C.) boasted: "Ramesses II, your
prestige has crossed the Great Green Sea and the islands in its midst
are in fear and the envoys of her chiefs come to him for fear governs
their hearts."[15]

Egypt's influence over Greece appears to have been strongest during the reign of Amenhotep III (1390–1352 B.C.). Bronze Age sites in
Greece have yielded a multitude of Egyptian artifacts inscribed with
the names of Amenhotep III and his queen, Tiy.[16] The most impressive of these are a number of faience foundation deposit plaques
found at Mycenae. Such plaques were typically buried under the
corners of temples and other official buildings in Egypt. According
to Bernal, their presence in Mycenae suggests that an Egyptian temple may have been built, or at least planned, in that Greek city during the reign of Amenhotep III.[17]

The same Amenhotep seems to have claimed lordship over
Greece in certain of his inscriptions. Five statue bases that once
held images of Amenhotep III were found in his funerary temple
near Luxor in Egypt. The bases were inscribed with long lists of

cities and countries, each labeled with a picture of a bound prisoner, as if to suggest that it had been conquered by Egypt.

One of the statue bases lists a number of cities under the labels *Keftiu* and *Tanaya*—"Crete" and "Greece." The Egyptian word *Tanaya* is widely understood to refer to the *Danaoi*, or Danaans, an old name for the Greeks used by Homer.[18] Many of the places listed under *Keftiu* and *Tanaya* are obscure, but experts more or less agree that the Egyptian names *Amnisha, Kútunaya, Mukánu, Nupirayy, Kútíra, Kúnúsha, Mishane,* and *Rikatá* refer respectively to the Greek and Cretan cities of Amnissos, Kydonia, Mycenae, Nauplia, Kythera, Knossos, Messenia, and Lyktos. Some believe that the name *W'iwly* (or *W'iwry*) may refer to Troy (Ilios).[19]

Skeptics argue that these lists do not necessarily indicate countries conquered by Egypt, since the lists also include Hatti, Mitanni, Assyria, Babylonia, and other lands that Egypt clearly never ruled.[20] Nevertheless, from the Egyptian perspective, these latter countries may have been considered beaten or subdued simply because they were obliged to make peace with Egypt during the *Pax Aegyptiaca*.

Mitanni, in particular, had been a ferocious enemy of Egypt until it was pacified by Thutmose III. In his final campaign against the Mitannians, Thutmose III led an army across the Euphrates, threatening not only Mitanni, but also all the other states of Asia Minor and Mesopotamia. As a result, says Egyptologist Nicolas Grimal, "In the thirty-third year of his reign he received tribute from Retjenu, as well as from Babylon, Assur and the Hittites: all areas that had been theoretically incorporated into the Egyptian empire by crossing the Euphrates."[21]

One can argue such points *ad infinitum*. Scholars continue to disagree over the extent of Egypt's power during the *Pax Aegyptiaca*. What cannot be denied, however, is that four different Egyptian pharaohs recorded in stone their claim of lordship over the Aegean.

Conventional Egyptologists dismiss such claims as empty boasts. But, if we accord these Egyptian accounts the same respect that we have applied, in previous chapters, to Greek writings, we are left with no choice but to seriously entertain the possibility that Crete and Greece formed part of Egypt's empire. They may not have been under direct Egyptian control, as were Nubia and Syria-Palestine. But, at the very least, their relationship to Egypt appears to have been extremely subservient. From all the preceding evidence—most of which was presented in his book *Black Athena, Volume II*—Martin Bernal felt safe in concluding that "the century 1475–1375 B.C. seems to have been one of Egyptian suzerainty over the Aegean."[22]

If true, this leaves us with a bit of a mystery. How did Egypt manage to project its power across the Mediterranean Sea? During the Eighteenth and Nineteenth Dynasties, when these claims were made, Egypt's enemy, the powerful Hittite Empire, was firmly in control of Asia Minor. The days when a Sesostris could march a land army into Europe were long gone. And, in any case, neither Crete nor the other Isles in the Midst of the Great Green Sea were ever vulnerable to attack by land.

Clearly, the only way Egypt could have "trussed" the Haunebu and "struck" the Islanders (as Thutmose III claimed to have done) or put them "in fear" (as Ramesses II supposedly did) would have been to threaten the Aegean with a powerful navy. Is there, in fact, any evidence that Egypt possessed such a fleet? Indeed there is.

CHAPTER 23

THE WAR FLEET

IN THE EIGHTH YEAR OF THE REIGN OF RAMESSES III—APPROXIMATELY 1178 B.C.—Egypt came face to face with disaster. The enemy confronting her seemed invincible. Already, this adversary had destroyed much of the civilized world. The Hittites, Amorites, and Cypriots had crumbled with hardly a fight. Egypt alone remained unconquered. And now the enemy was massing for the attack.

To this day, we do not know who the invaders were or where they came from. We do know, however, that they possessed one crucial advantage over their victims—sea power. Their mighty armada descended without warning on one defenseless coastline after another. They could attack and withdraw at will, for their huge numbers, fast ships, and nautical skills had given them command of the seas. For that reason, the Egyptians called them Peoples of the Sea.

"No country has been able to withstand their might," says an Egyptian inscription of the time. "The land[s] of the Hittites, Kode, Carchemish, . . . and Cyprus have been destroyed at one stroke. . . . They have crushed their peoples, and their lands are as if they had never been. They marched against Egypt. . . . They laid hands on every land to the farthest ends of the earth. Their hearts were high and their confidence in themselves was supreme."[1]

The only hints we have as to the identity of these people are a few puzzling syllables recorded on the enclosure walls of Ramesses III's funerary temple at Medinet Habu. The inscription tells us that they were not one people, but many, banded together in a conspiracy: "as for the foreign countries, they made a conspiracy in their islands. All at once the lands were on the move, scattered in war . . . a camp was set up in Amur [Syria]. . . . Their league was Prst, Tkr, Shklsh, Dnn and Wshsh."[2]

Prst, Tkr, Shklsh, Dnn, and *Wshsh.* These are the names of the Sea Peoples. But they might as well be written in code. As usual, we are confounded by the vowel-less enigma of Egyptian spelling. We can plug in e's and a's here and there, to render these names at least pronounceable. But the result will be what Egyptologist David M. Rohl calls "Egypto-speak"—not real Egyptian.

The shortcomings of Egypto-speak become embarrassingly apparent whenever scholars stumble across an Egyptian word that happens to have been transliterated into a foreign tongue. Thus, scholars have discovered that the name of the pharaoh we call "Usermaatre Ramesses" in Egypto-speak was actually pronounced *Washmuaria Riamashesha* by the ancient Hittites.[3] The Egypto-speak names of *Amenhotep, Nebmaatre,* and *Neferkheperure* are pronounced *Amanhatpi, Nibmuaria,* and *Naphurria,* respectively, in the cuneiform script of Mesopotamia.[4] How the Egyptians actually spoke these names, we do not know, but it seems a fair bet that *Riamashesha* is a lot closer to the mark than *Ramesses.*

What, then, shall we make of *Prst, Tkr, Shklsh, Dnn,* and *Wshsh?* A good Egypto-speak rendition of *Prst* would give *Peleset* (since "l" and "r" are frequently interchangeable in Egyptian). Some have suggested that the *Peleset* are identical with the Philistines of the Bible. Then there are the Shekelesh, who may be one and the same with the Sikels of Sicily. The Dnn—that's *Denen* in Egypto-speak—may have been the Danaans of Homeric Greece. And so on.[5]

It is all speculation. We know for certain only that the invaders came from many different lands and attacked by sea. Their attack was sufficiently traumatic that it plunged the Mediterranean world into a 300-year dark age. The Hittite Empire never rose again. The citadels of Mycenaean Greece vanished from history. But Egypt survived. Of all the great powers lining the Mediterranean "pond" at the close of the Bronze Age, it appears that Egypt alone possessed the one weapon necessary for fending off the Sea Peoples—a powerful war fleet.

When the invaders descended on Egypt, they came by land and sea simultaneously. One army marched down from Syria, while another sailed right into the mouth of the Nile with a mighty fleet. According to the inscriptions, Ramesses III turned his attention first to the land invaders, crushing the enemy beneath his chariots. Then he prepared for the final showdown—the battle with the enemy ships. Ramesses III reported, "I turned the river mouths into a strong defensive wall, with warships, galleys and coastal vessels . . . fully manned from stem to stern with brave warriors armed to the teeth. They were as ready for battle as lions roaring on the mountains."[6]

The enclosure walls at Medinet Habu portray the titanic battle between the Egyptian fleet and the Peoples of the Sea. In the relief, the foreigners can be seen on their ships, wearing long skirts and peculiar, cockaded headdresses strapped to their chins.[7] The Egyptians attack with their twenty-oared war galleys. Egyptian archers rain down arrows on the enemy decks, while Egyptian sailors disable the Sea Peoples' ships with grappling irons. Meanwhile, Egyptian infantrymen stand by, capturing survivors as they swim ashore. In the end, thousands of Sea People are marched away into slavery. Egypt has won a tremendous victory.

Whoever these Sea Peoples were, they had grossly miscalculated. Drunk with victory after their easy conquest of Cyprus, Asia Minor, and Syria, they had momentarily convinced themselves that they, not Egypt, ruled the waves. Ramesses III and his war fleet lost little time in disabusing the Sea Peoples of this delusion.

What is perhaps most remarkable about this battle is that it was fought during the Twentieth Dynasty (1188–1069 B.C.)—a period of weakness and decline for Egypt. If the Egyptians could bring such sea power to bear in the autumn of their empire, what sort of navy might they have floated 200 years before, at the height of the *Pax Aegyptiaca*?

We can only guess. As is often the case in Egyptian history, the surviving records are so scanty that they raise more questions than they provide answers. We know that the pharaohs used warships from the earliest times. A rock carving at Gebel Sheikh Suleiman, for example, shows Nubian captives lashed to the prows of Egyptian war galleys in the aftermath of a battle that probably took place sometime before 3000 B.C.[8] A painting in the tomb of the Eleventh Dynasty pharaoh Intef shows three heavily armed fighting ships, bristling with archers and mace-men.[9]

The conquering pharaoh Thutmose III made effective use of naval power in his invasion of Syria-Palestine. Thutmose's first move when he marched into the region was to seize the harbors and equip them for heavy military traffic. "Every port town of His Majesty was supplied with every good thing . . ." says an inscription of the time, "with ships of cedar loaded with columns and beams as well as large timbers."[10]

Thutmose immediately put these harbors to work. In at least thirteen successive campaigns against Syria-Palestine, Thutmose brought in his armies by sea—thus eliminating the need for a long overland march. "Thutmose carried it all out so rapidly and successfully," says Lionel Casson, a leading authority on ancient seafaring, "that his military victories may have come about more from the quickness and ease with which he got his soldiers to the theater of combat than to their prowess."[11] Thutmose III also used a fleet of prefabricated riverboats to carry his army across the Euphrates.[12]

But did the Egyptians possess a real navy? Certain documents suggest that they did. A "crew commander" named Ahmose, for example, left an autobiography on the walls of his tomb, in which he portrays a naval career as a fast track to advancement. Starting off as a lowly seaman, Ahmose served on a number of vessels, with names such as *The Wild Bull, Northern,* and *Rising in Memphis.* His big break came when he sailed south with Thutmose I on his Nubian campaign. There, Ahmose distinguished himself by his courage in navigating the Nile's dangerous rapids: "Then I conveyed King Aakheperkare [Thutmose I], the justified, when he sailed south to Khent-hen-nefer, to crush rebellion throughout the lands, to repel the intruders from the desert region. I was brave in his presence in the bad water, in the towing of the ship over the cataract. Thereupon I was made crew commander."[13]

Unfortunately, such scraps as this constitute all the information we possess about the elusive Egyptian navy. No clear records remain of large-scale naval engagements, beyond the single relief at Medinet Habu portraying the battle against the Sea Peoples. Based on the "silence" of Egyptian records, some experts have gone so far as to conclude that Egypt never was a real maritime power at all. To the extent that she even had a navy, say the skeptics, it was used only for fighting on the river and not on the high seas. Indeed, the conventional view has long been that the Egyptians feared the open sea. Egyptologists Ian Shaw and Paul Nicholson write:

> The importance of water transport [in ancient Egypt] . . . arose inevitably from the existence of the river Nile . . . as the principal artery of communication. . . . However, when sailing outside the Nile Valley, on the Mediterranean or Red Sea, the ships seem to have stayed close to the shore. Unlike the Greeks, the Egyptians were evidently not enthusiastic seafarers.[14]

The idea that the Egyptians were coast-hugging landlubbers remains standard among scholars to this day. But the theory has its problems. For one thing, it is based on a double standard. Evidence for seafaring ability is evaluated in two totally different ways, depending on whether it is found in Egypt or in the Aegean. In general, scholars tend to assume that the Greeks and Cretans were great seafarers during the Bronze Age, even when there is very little evidence to prove this. Thus, in the book *Prehistory and Protohistory*, edited by George A. Christopoulos and John C. Bastias in 1974, we find the following statement regarding seafaring among the Bronze Age Cretans:

> Although seafaring was unquestionably very highly developed, there is unfortunately very little positive evidence available about it. Our only sources of information about the ships are a few illustrations, most of them on tiny sealstones. . . . In the circumstances, it is easy to see how the Minoans [Cretans] came to enjoy the virtually unchallenged supremacy of the seas.[15]

In this passage—as in scholarship generally—the lack of positive evidence proves no obstacle to a firm conclusion that the Cretans enjoyed unchallenged supremacy of the seas. In the same book, however, these scholars draw an opposite conclusion about Egypt, when faced with a similar lack of evidence. "The Egyptians seldom ventured out of the Nile," they write, "and, when they did, they stuck to the coasts, since their vessels were not very suitable for the open sea."[16]

This leads to the second, and perhaps more serious, problem with the "landlubber" theory. If the Egyptians were so inept on the water, then how did they manage to beat the Sea Peoples? We are asked to believe that the Egyptians somehow succeeded in building a war fleet and defeating the most awesome naval force ever assembled in the Bronze Age world, with little or no training or prior experience. By this reasoning, the victory over the Sea Peoples was nothing more than a lucky fluke. "Although presumably not used to fighting maritime battles," write Shaw and Nicholson, "the Egyptian navy managed to destroy the Sea Peoples' fleet."[17]

Shall we too presume that the Egyptians were unused to naval combat? Shall we assume that they only "managed" to defeat the Sea Peoples by a stroke of beginner's luck? That they avoided the open sea? That the claims of four different pharaohs to suzerainty over the Aegean were nothing more than braggadocio? Perhaps we should. But before we eliminate Egypt entirely from maritime history, we may wish to consider some additional evidence.

CHAPTER 24

LAND OF
THE GODS

THE OLDEST NAUTICAL YARN IN HISTORY COMES TO US FROM ancient Egypt. More than 3,000 years before the wily Scheherazade lulled King Shahriyar of Persia with her *History of Sinbad the Sailor,* and over a thousand years before Homer wrote his *Odyssey,* Egyptian audiences thrilled to a story of high-seas adventure called *The Tale of the Shipwrecked Sailor.*

Nobody knows when the story was first told. It was copied by a scribe named Imenaa, sometime during the Middle Kingdom period (2040–1674 B.C.), but may well have existed for centuries before then.[1] *The Tale of the Shipwrecked Sailor* recounts the adventures of a luckless mariner marooned on a magical island. As the story opens, the hero sets out on a ship with "one hundred and twenty sailors of the very pick of Egypt." The text continues: "They scanned the sky, they looked at the land. Their hearts were braver than lions, and they could foretell a storm before it arose and a tempest before it came into being."[2]

According to the papyrus, the ship was bound for the mines of Sinai, which means that it must have put forth from one of Egypt's Red Sea ports. The ship is soon lost in a storm, the crew drowned, and our hero washed ashore on an enchanted isle. After befriending a giant serpent-god, from whom he receives many gifts, the sailor is finally rescued by a passing Egyptian vessel. The magical island vanishes, and the marooned sailor goes home to a joyful reunion with his king and family.

Some scholars have suggested that this nameless Egyptian hero is an ancient prototype of Odysseus and Sinbad. That may or may not be true. What is certain, however, is that the culture that created this tale and the audience who enjoyed it—like those who created and enjoyed *Sinbad* and *The Odyssey*—were intimately familiar with high-seas navigation.

Like *Sinbad* and *The Odyssey*, *The Tale of the Shipwrecked Sailor* anchors its fantastic adventures to a framework of real oceans, real sea routes, and real ports of call. The hero sets out from a harbor on the Red Sea. He is stranded on an island far to the south, a two months' sail from the pharaoh's royal residence. Finally, the giant serpent who rules the island describes himself as the Lord of *Pwnt*—a word that can be rendered as either *Punt* or *Pwenet* in Egypto-speak.

Punt was a real country that experts believe lay one to two months' sail due south of Egypt. When the marooned sailor bows down to the serpent king and offers to send him "ships loaded with all the treasures of Egypt," including incense and precious oils, the snake-man laughs and counters: "You are not rich in myrrh and all kinds of incense. But I am the lord of Punt and myrrh is my very own. That *hknw*-oil you spoke of sending, it abounds on this island."

Egyptian audiences would have recognized as perfectly realistic this portrayal of Punt as a land of oils and incense. Much of the myrrh and frankincense offered in Egyptian temples came from Punt. Indeed, the "odors of Punt" are described as a sign of divine presence in Egyptian texts[3] and are likened to the odors of the god Amun.[4]

There is no question that the Egyptians viewed Punt as a holy and enchanted place. Some scholars believe that it was Punt's abundance of fragrant spices and resins that earned the country its mystical reputation. Others have speculated that the Egyptians revered Punt as their ancestral homeland. Whatever the reason, the Egyptians invariably referred to Punt as the Land of the Gods.

Thus, in an Eighteenth Dynasty inscription, the god Amun says to Queen Hatshepsut, who dispatched a large expedition to Punt around 1469 B.C.:

> I have assigned to you the whole of Punt, as far as the lands of the gods, God's lands. It had been heard of . . . in the reports of the ancestors. The marvels that were brought thence under your royal forefathers had been brought . . . from time immemorial. . . . But I will cause your expedition to reach it. . . .[5]
>
> I shall guide the expedition on water and on land to bring back marvels from God's Land . . . opening for them the difficult ways.[6]

The way to Punt does indeed seem to have been difficult. The theme of danger runs through every Egyptian account of a Punt expedition. The scribes never fail to applaud the safe return of the ships from successful missions. On the walls of Queen Hatshepsut's funerary temple at Deir el-Bahri, for example, a fleet of thirty-oared galleys is shown arriving in Punt, accompanied by these words: "Sailing on the sea, and making a good start for God's land. Making landfall safely at the terrain of Punt."

A stela from the reign of Amenemhat II praises the gods for the safe return of an official named Khentykhetywer, the King's Sealbearer, who "had returned safely from Punt, his expedition with him, safe and sound, and his ships resting at Sa'waw [an Egyptian harbor on the Red Sea]."[7] A papyrus from the Twentieth Dynasty tells us that an expedition of Ramesses III "reached the land of Punt, unaffected by any misfortune, safe and respected."[8] Concern for safety is equally evident in a monument raised by the vizier Intefoqer. Instructed by Senwosret I, around 1920 B.C., to organize an expedition of 500 men to sail to Punt, he wrote: "His Majesty commanded the Vizier Intefoqer to construct this fleet at the Koptos dockyards, for travelling and reaching the mining-region of Punt, both to go safely and return safely, all their construction being . . . good and sound beyond anything done in this land formerly."[9]

At least eight pharaohs left monuments celebrating (or implying) the safe return of Punt expeditions. Of course, the Egyptians were far less diligent in commemorating their failures, so we can only guess how many fleets may have been lost. Despite the risks, the rewards of reaching Punt were apparently irresistible. Egyptian texts speak repeatedly of the "marvels of God's Land." In fact, these "marvelous" products give us our best clue as to the location of the mysterious Punt.

Sometime around 2450 B.C., the pharaoh Sahura received 80,000 measures of myrrh and 6,000 bars of electrum from Punt.[10] Other expeditions brought back gold, ivory, spices, resins, monkeys, baboons, leopard-skins, pygmies, and a dark wood that the Egyptians called *hbnyw* or *hbny*—the origin of our modern word *ebony*, though it referred to a wood different from that we call ebony today. All of this suggests a location somewhere in tropical Africa.

Even more telling are the pictures of Punt appearing on the walls of Hatshepsut's funerary temple. They show African scenes of giraffes, rhinos, and hamadryas baboons cavorting among incense trees and *dom* palm trees.[11] They also show houses on stilts—a traditional mode of construction still used in East Africa today.[12]

Pictures of the Puntites themselves, unfortunately, have proved less revealing. Egyptian artists portrayed the Puntites much as they portrayed themselves. These ambiguous depictions have allowed generations of scholars to "blacken" or "whiten" the Puntites, according to their personal taste. Egyptologist K. A. Kitchen tried to stake out a middle ground between "black" and "white" Puntites in a 1993 paper:

> The main Puntite population was mixed. Besides the so-called "Hamitic" type (like Parahu), not very different from the Egyptians in appearance, others represented were clearly of negro stock, in hues of brown and near-black. Parahu [a chief of Punt portrayed in Hatshepsut's relief] wore a continuous series of rings entirely encasing his right leg, as in some parts of the Sudan to modern times.[13]

Whether we choose to regard the Puntites as black, white, or something in between, there can be no question that Punt lay somewhere in East Africa. Egyptian records clearly indicate the route. We know, for example, that several Punt expeditions left from Sa'waw[14]—a harbor on the Red Sea whose remains archaeologists have uncovered at Mersa Gawasis.[15] A papyrus of Ramesses III tells us that Punt was reached by sailing on the "great sea of inverted water"—an apparent reference to the fact that the Red Sea currents flow from north to south during the summer, the exact opposite of the Nile currents.[16]

Finally, we know from *The Tale of the Shipwrecked Sailor* that Punt lay to the south of Egypt, about two months' sail. Such a southerly voyage down the Red Sea could lead to only one of two places: the east coast of Africa or southern Arabia. Since there are no giraffes, rhinos, or pygmies in Arabia, we can safely rule out the latter.

The final clue to Punt's location comes from an inscription of the Twenty-sixth Dynasty that mentions "rainfall upon the mountain of Punt" causing the Nile to flood out of season. The only place in the world where unseasonable rains would produce such an effect would be in the western Ethiopian highlands, where the floodwaters would drain into the Nile through the river Atbara and the Blue Nile.[17]

Over the years, scholars have tried to place Punt in such far-flung regions as Somalia, Sudan, southern Arabia, or even India. But, for all the reasons stated above, most experts today agree that Punt must have lain somewhere in Eritrea or northern Ethiopia. And indeed, certain peoples of that region still recall legends of a snake-king, strangely reminiscent of the serpentine Lord of Punt who appears in *The Tale of the Shipwrecked Sailor*.[18] "Before the Christian religion was known in Ethiopia," says an old Ethiopian manuscript called *A History and Genealogy of the Ancient Kings*, "half the inhabitants . . . were worshippers of Sando the dragon."[19]

K. A. Kitchen estimates that an Egyptian galley would have made thirty miles per day sailing south on the Red Sea, and perhaps half that much on the way north, rowing against the wind. By this reckoning, if Punt really had been located in Ethiopia, the journey there might have taken four to six weeks, and the return trip as much as two months—exactly the time it took the Shipwrecked Sailor to return from his enchanted island.[20] And indeed, the Red Sea waters off Eritrea are thick with islands, any one of which could have provided a real-life model for the magical serpent's kingdom.

So what does all this have to do with the possibility of Egyptian colonies in Greece? Quite a lot. It shows, for one thing, that the Egyptians were indeed "enthusiastic seafarers," contrary to conventional opinion. They undertook massive and costly exploratory missions to the ends of the known world, dispatching hundreds of men at a time, in fleets of thirty-oared galleys, 70 to 100 feet in length.[21]

We also know, from surviving documents, that Egyptian ships sailed the Mediterranean, making routine commercial runs to

Byblos, 250 miles from Egypt.[22] So common were these Mediterranean voyages that the Egyptians built special ships for them,
called *kebenwe* (Byblites) and *keftiu* (Cretans)—vessels that were
specially adapted for sailing to Byblos and Crete, much as East
Indiamen and China Clippers of later centuries were adapted and
named for their characteristic voyages.[23]

If the Egyptians would sail 250 miles to buy pine wood in Byblos,
and 900 miles to obtain gold, incense, and exotic beasts from
Ethiopia, why would they not have sailed 560 miles to Greece, in
whose markets all the riches of Europe could be found? Scholars
have never provided a satisfactory answer to this question. They
have simply asserted, without any good reason, that Egyptian navi-
gators were too timid or inept to cross the Mediterranean Sea.

Orthodox opinion is obviously mistaken on this last point. Egypt's
1,200-year history of trade with Punt and Byblos demonstrates beyond a doubt that she had the ships, the skills, and the motivation for
making long sea voyages. We cannot yet prove that Egyptian fleets
ever sailed to Greece, but in comparison with the Punt expeditions,
such voyages would have been milk runs.

No one alive today is better qualified to speculate on the capabilities
of Egyptian seafarers than Norwegian explorer Thor Heyerdahl, who in
1969 and 1970 crossed the Atlantic Ocean in replicas of Egyptian boats
made from papyrus reeds (see chapter 39). When interviewed recently
for this book, Heyerdahl opined, "They [the Egyptians] could very
easily have sailed from Egypt to Greece. . . . The duration of a reed-boat
crossing . . . would entirely depend on the wind at the time, and the
number of oars available. Probably about a week on average."[24]

All of this, however, may be entirely beside the point. For Egyptians could have reached Greece without ever having had to use
their own ships or crews. Indeed, the ability of Egypt, during the *Pax
Aegyptiaca*, to scout out distant seas *by proxy* may constitute the
ultimate key to the mystery of Bronze Age exploration.

We know for a fact that Egypt commissioned Phoenician fleets
for some exploratory missions. Indeed, Phoenicia's subservience to
Egypt during the Late Bronze Age would have left the Phoenicians
with little choice but to cooperate with Egypt's imperial aims. We
may never know for sure whether Egyptian vessels called on European ports during the Bronze Age. But *Phoenician* vessels certainly
did. And where the Phoenicians went, so, in all likelihood, went
their Egyptian masters.

CHAPTER 25

EXPLORERS
FOR HIRE

MOST OF US LEARNED IN SCHOOL THAT THE PORTUGUESE mariner Vasco da Gama was the first explorer to circumnavigate Africa. Between 1497 and 1499, he sailed all the way from Portugal to India and back again, by rounding the Cape of Good Hope. Da Gama's feat was impressive. But he may not have been the first to accomplish it. Two thousand years before, Phoenician mariners may very well have beaten da Gama to the punch.

The expedition was commissioned by an Egyptian pharaoh named Nekau II Wehemibra—or Necho, as the Greeks called him (610–595 B.C.). For years, Necho struggled to overcome one of the most troublesome obstacles facing Egyptian navigation—the isthmus of Suez. Only about 100 miles wide, this narrow strip of land made an impassable barrier, cutting off Egypt's Nile harbors from the Red Sea and preventing the Egyptians, for centuries, from fully exploiting their trade with the East.

Each time they sailed to Punt, the Egyptians had to dismantle an entire fleet of ships on the Nile, carry the pieces by donkey all the way to the Red Sea, and then reassemble them for the trip to Punt. It was a costly undertaking. One inscription from the reign of Senwosret I describes how 3,756 men—including sailors, scribes, royal retainers, and "citizen-militia"—were required to transport a fleet of new ships from the dockyards of Koptos, on the Nile, to the Red Sea port of Sa'waw for a single voyage to Punt.[1] The entire operation must presumably have been repeated, in reverse, when the ships returned from Punt.

Nobody knows when the idea first occurred to the Egyptians to circumvent this monstrous procedure by digging a canal directly from the Nile to the Red Sea. A relief from the Nineteenth Dynasty shows pharaoh Seti I (1294–1279 B.C.) crossing a canal as he leads his army home from a campaign in Palestine.[2] Some scholars think this canal may have joined the Nile to the Gulf of Suez. But nobody knows for sure. If such a canal did exist in the Nineteenth Dynasty, it apparently fell out of use during the long centuries of war, foreign occupation, and political chaos that followed. By the time of Necho II (610–595 B.C.), the Nile was once again completely cut off from the sea routes to the East.

Necho tried manfully to overcome this problem by digging a canal from the Pelusiac branch of the Nile straight through to the Red Sea. He spared no expense. Over 12,000 workmen were assigned to the job. An entire new city, called Per-Temu Tjeku, was built as a way station for traders near the canal's Red Sea outlet, not far from the modern town of Ismailia.[3] Then, for reasons unknown, Necho suddenly stopped work.

According to Herodotos, an oracle warned the pharaoh that only foreigners would reap the benefit of his canal. This prophecy turned out to be true, for it was the Persians—who conquered Egypt seventy years later—who eventually finished the project.[4] After its completion, the canal remained in use until A.D. 775, when the Caliph Abu Jaafer Abdullah al-Mansur destroyed it, out of fear that rebels might use the waterway to attack Mecca.

Did Necho really abandon work on his canal because of an oracle? Or did he simply run out of money? Nobody knows. We do know, however, that after failing to complete the canal, Necho sought an alternative—and perhaps less expensive—means of connecting the Nile with the Red Sea: by sailing all the way around Africa. Herodotos writes:

The Egyptian king Neco . . . after calling off the construction of the canal between the Nile and the Arabian gulf, sent out a fleet manned by a Phoenician crew with orders to sail round and return to Egypt and the Mediterranean by the Pillars of Heracles. The Phoenicians sailed from the Red Sea into the southern ocean . . . and after two full years rounded the Pillars of Heracles in the course of the third, and returned to Egypt.[5]

So there you have it: history's first recorded circumnavigation of Africa. If the story is true, the voyage likely took place between 609 and 601 B.C.—some 2,100 years before Vasco da Gama. Each reader will have to decide for himself whether to believe the story of Necho's Phoenician explorers. Beyond these few lines from Herodotos, we have no evidence that the voyage ever took place. Indeed, Herodotos himself was skeptical about certain details of the story:

These men [the Phoenicians] made a statement which I do not myself believe, though others may, to the effect that as they sailed on a westerly course round the southern end of Libya [the Greek name for Africa], they had the sun on their right—to northward of them.[6]

This claim seemed incredible to Herodotos because he knew that, if you face in the same direction that the sun moves—that is, toward the west—the sun always appears slightly to your left. Herodotos apparently did not realize that exactly the opposite is true in the Southern Hemisphere. There, a mariner facing west will always see the sun on his *right*. Rather than proving that they were liars, as Herodotos thought, this single observation provides strong confirmation that Necho's Phoenicians did manage to sail at least *somewhere* south of the equator. On the strength of this and other telling details in the story, many scholars today are inclined to believe that the Phoenicians did circumnavigate Africa, exactly as they claimed.

And perhaps they did. We may never know for sure. However, the mere fact that they *tried*—and that they did so on a direct order from an Egyptian pharaoh—is an important clue in our quest. Herodotos's story gives us a rare and telling glimpse into the nuts and bolts of Egypt's imperial *modus operandi*. It shows that the pharaohs sometimes used Phoenician explorers to execute Egyptian missions.

Why would the Phoenicians have performed such a dangerous and difficult service for Necho? No doubt, they were well paid. But it is also likely that they had no choice in the matter. Only a year after mounting the throne, Necho reconquered Egypt's lost territories of Syria, Palestine, and Phoenicia, which had been under Assyrian rule since 742 B.C. Phoenicia was, once again, an Egyptian province and in no position to refuse a pharaonic request.

How often, in the past, had other pharaohs used their prerogative as conquerors to compel Phoenician cooperation? What services did the Phoenicians perform for the mighty pharaohs of old, back in the days of the Twelfth Dynasty or the *Pax Aegyptiaca*? The evidence suggests that these services may have been considerable. Indeed, they may have included nothing less than the exploration and colonization of Europe.

CHAPTER 26

THE PHOENICIANS

W HO EXACTLY *WERE* THE PHOENICIANS? THE SHORT ANSWER IS that they were an ancient people who lived on the Lebanese coast. For some unknown reason, they also happen to have developed into the most brilliant mariners of their age. Nobody knows the full story of why the Phoenicians became such masterful sailors. But at least some of their success can be traced to a certain species of tree, known to botanists as *Cedrus libani.*

The mountains of Lebanon are largely barren today. But, in antiquity, they grew thick with pine forests that towered more than a hundred feet in the air. Prized for their oil and wood, the "cedars of Lebanon" were more than a natural resource. Their piney aroma was holy to the gods. Their oil embalmed the dead. Their proverbial grandeur was a metaphor of power for biblical scribes, such as the prophet Ezekiel (31:3–8): "Behold, the Assyrian was a cedar in Lebanon . . . his height was exalted above all the trees of the field . . . so that all the trees of Eden, that were in the garden of God, envied him."

It is no accident that the string of prosperous city-states that we call Phoenicia grew up in the shade of these mighty forests. From the beginning, it was the Lebanese pines that provided the Phoenicians with both lumber for their ships and a valuable export for their overseas markets. Indeed, the very name *Phoenician* may have derived from an Egyptian word, *Fenekhu*, which some Egyptologists have suggested means "wood-chopper."[1]

In *The Tale of Sinuhe,* a popular Egyptian story from the Twelfth Dynasty (1991–1785 B.C.), the Fenekhu appear as a people living near the city of Byblos, on the Lebanese coast. This is the first mention of Fenekhu in an Egyptian text. But the Phoenicians were certainly known to Egypt long before. Lebanese cedar was already being imported into Egypt during the First Dynasty (3150–2925 B.C.),[2] and the Phoenician city of Byblos was a familiar port of call to Egyptian mariners of the Old Kingdom (2700–2190 B.C.). Indeed, when trade with Byblos was temporarily cut off by the chaos of the First Intermediate Period (2200–2040 B.C.), the scribe Ipuwer bemoaned the loss as a national tragedy: "No one goes down to Byblos today. What shall we do for the coffins imported for our mummies in which the priests are buried and the oil with which [kings] are embalmed as far away as the country of Kaftu [Crete]?"[3]

Egypt depended on Byblos for far more than coffins and cedar oil. Byblos was the key to Egyptian sea power. The best Egyptian ships were always built of Lebanese timber, which was superior to Egypt's native acacia and sycamore wood.[4] During the Fifth Dynasty, for example, the pharaoh Snofru transported "forty shiploads of cedarwood" from Lebanon, much of which he used to build ships.[5]

Nobody knows at what point the Phoenicians themselves first took to the seas, but it must have been early. Archaeologists have found evidence that Byblos was already trading with the island of Cyprus by 3000 B.C.[6] By the Twentieth Dynasty, the Phoenician cities of Byblos and Sidon are clearly portrayed in Egyptian documents as maritime powers. In *The Report of Wenamun,* an Egyptian official describes his voyage to Byblos to buy lumber for shipbuilding, sometime around 1090–1080 B.C. Tjekerbaal, the king of Byblos, boasts to Wenamun: "Are there not twenty ships here in my harbor that do business with Smendes [ruler of Lower Egypt]? As for Sidon, that other place you passed, are there not another fifty ships there that do business with Werekter?"[7]

Clay tablets found at the Phoenician city of Ugarit testify to its colossal sea power, as early as the twelfth and thirteenth centuries

B.C. In one document, dating from the time of the Sea Peoples' invasion (roughly 1207–1178 B.C.), a naval officer petitions the king of Ugarit to equip a flotilla of 150 ships. As Semitist Michael Astour has pointed out, no Greek city-state was able to deploy a fleet of that size until 500 B.C.[8]

The ships of Ugarit were not only numerous, but also often of staggering size. In a letter dating from the late twelfth century B.C., the Hittite king asked the king of Ugarit to provide a cargo ship capable of transporting 2,000 measures of grain in one or two trips. Assuming that the measure used in this letter is the standard *kor* of 300 liters, the proposed cargo must have been about 500 tons. To transport that much grain in one trip, the king of Ugarit would have had to provide a ship more than twice the size of Christopher Columbus's 233-ton *Santa Maria*.[9]

According to the Bible, King Solomon—who is believed to have ruled Israel around 970–930 B.C.—hired ships and crews from the Phoenician king Hiram of Tyre to sail to Ophir, a mysterious land that some scholars have equated with Punt. Like Punt, it was reached by sailing down the Red Sea, from Solomon's harbor at Ezion-Geber:

> And Hiram sent him ships commanded by his own officers, men who knew the sea. These, with Solomon's men, sailed to Ophir and brought back four hundred and fifty talents of gold.[10]

> And from there they brought great cargoes of almugwood and precious stones. . . . So much almugwood has never been imported or seen since that day.[11]

The Phoenicians make their first appearance in Greek literature in the pages of Homer. He calls them *polydaidaloi*—"of many skills"—a people renowned for their talents as jewelers, goldsmiths, and silversmiths.[12] But they were also *polypaipaloi*—"of many tricks"—wily merchants who would lie, cheat, and steal for a profit.[13] In *The Odyssey*, Homer's Phoenicians sail about the Aegean from one Greek city to the next, hawking their trinkets, seducing women, kidnapping children, and stealing precious heirlooms from their unwary hosts.

Homer's negative view of the Phoenicians may have arisen partly from envy. The Greeks too were seafarers, but their Phoenician rivals always seemed to get the jump on them. By the time the Greeks started exploring and colonizing the western Mediterranean, for example—around 750 B.C.—they found that the Phoenicians had arrived there first.[14] Thukydides wrote: "Before any Greeks came to Sicily . . . there were Phoenicians settled all around that island occupying headlands and adjacent islets for trade with the native Sicels. But when the Greeks began to arrive in considerable numbers by sea, the Phoenicians abandoned most of these posts and retired to Motya, Soloeis and Panormos."[15]

The Phoenicians, however, did not always retreat so quietly before their competitors. In the far west, they held out against Greek pressure for a full 600 years. Indeed, their impregnable strongholds in Spain and North Africa barred the way to any Greek ship trying to enter the Atlantic Ocean. Through the whole span of Greece's classical history, the Atlantic was off-limits to Greek shipping. Most Greeks were not even sure that such an ocean really existed.

"About the far west of Europe I have no definite information . . ." Herodotos admitted, "and . . . in spite of my efforts to do so, I have never found anyone who could give me first-hand information of the existence of a sea beyond Europe to the north and west."[16]

Only once did a Greek mariner manage to slip through the Phoenician blockade, around 325 B.C. Pytheas of Massalia returned from his adventure with the first accurate descriptions of the British Isles and the outer coasts of Europe. But no one believed him. For nearly two centuries, learned Greeks denounced Pytheas as a liar and charlatan. The words of Greek historian Polybios, written around 168–146 B.C., were typical: "Pytheas asserts that he explored in person the whole northern region of Europe as far as the ends of the world—an assertion no man would believe, not even if Hermes made it."[17]

Only after the Romans destroyed Carthage—the last independent Phoenician colony in the Mediterranean—in 146 B.C. did the Atlantic finally become accessible to Greek and Roman shipping.[18] Then and only then did the skeptics begin to realize that Pytheas had been telling the truth. The Phoenicians, of course, could have vindicated Pytheas all along. They had been sailing the Atlantic for centuries and knew that his account was accurate. But Phoenician mariners would rather have died—quite literally—than divulge such commercial secrets to Greeks or Romans.

The Greek geographer Strabo tells how a Roman ship once tried to follow a Phoenician vessel to the Cassiterides, or "Tin Islands"— a legendary land in the Atlantic where it was rumored the Phoenicians obtained their tin. To prevent the Romans from learning the route, the Phoenician captain deliberately sailed into a foggy, shoal-ridden area where both his ship and the Roman vessel were dashed against the rocks. The Phoenician captain managed to escape only by clinging to a piece of flotsam. In the eyes of the Phoenician authorities, he had performed his duty well. They compensated the man in full for his loss.[19]

Thanks in large part to the Phoenicians' obsessive secrecy, the full extent of their achievements remains a mystery to this day. We can only attempt to reconstruct their feats from the few scraps of information left to us. Diodoros tells us that, after planting "many colonies throughout Libya and . . . in the western parts of Europe . . . they amassed great wealth and essayed to voyage beyond the Pillars of Heracles into the sea which men call the ocean."[20] By this, Diodoros meant the Atlantic. But where the Phoenicians sailed on that vast ocean, we can only guess.

Some believe the Phoenicians made regular trips to the Cornish tin mines in Britain. One Carthaginian explorer named Hanno claimed to have settled 30,000 colonists on the west coast of Africa around 425 B.C.[21] Phoenician artifacts have been found in the Cape Verde Islands off the African coast and even in the Azores—a thousand miles due west of Gibraltar and fully one-third of the way across the Atlantic Ocean.[22] Indeed, there are scholars today who seriously speculate that the Phoenicians may have sailed all the way to America.[23]

By now, it should be obvious why Necho and other Egyptian pharaohs retained the Phoenicians as explorers-for-hire. Their qualifications for the job hardly need further embellishment. But the details of what they actually accomplished for the pharaohs remain obscure.

According to legend, the Phoenicians first colonized Greece in 1519 B.C. Those were the days when Egypt ruled the waves. Unfortunately, those were also the days when the stream of surviving documents concerning Phoenician seafaring—feeble enough in classical times—dried up to an abysmal trickle. Only a confusion of legends remains to tell us what happened.

Yet, behind those legends lurks a stubborn streak of truth. There is, in fact, good reason to believe that Phoenician fleets were cruising the Aegean at just about the time the Greek legends say they were. If the Haunebu and the Isles in the Midst of the Great Green Sea really trembled before Pharaoh—as so many Egyptian records claim—then the warships that compelled that respect may very well have been Phoenician.

CHAPTER 27

KADMOS

OF THEBES

TODAY, THE REMAINS OF ANCIENT BYBLOS LIE BENEATH A SLEEPY little harbor town called Jebeil, about twenty miles north of Beirut. Here, in 1860, a French scholar named Ernest Renan made the first attempt to formally excavate a Phoenician city. Neither Renan nor anyone else at that time had ever seen a Phoenician town, and scholars had only the vaguest notion of how to recognize Phoenician art or artifacts. They hoped the excavation might clear up some of the mystery. But, in some ways, it only deepened the confusion. Rather than a distinctive Phoenician style, the artifacts found at Byblos revealed a cultural identity crisis.

Renan's first major discovery was a group of stone slabs inscribed with Egyptian hieroglyphs. Next, he found a large bas-relief portraying what appeared to be the Egyptian goddess Hathor, her head adorned with cow's horns and sun disk, exactly as she appeared in Egyptian reliefs.[1] Later excavators at Byblos turned up more in the same vein—Egyptian-style obelisks, a multitude of vessels bearing the insignia of Egyptian pharaohs, a magnificent temple of Hathor dating from the third millennium B.C. Indeed, everywhere archaeologists turned in Phoenicia, they seemed to stumble across the specter of Egypt.

Phoenicia had far more to offer, of course, than ersatz Aegyptiaca. An ancient and industrious people, with their own language, gods, and customs, the Phoenicians had built a vibrant civilization, rooted in the Canaanite culture of Syria-Palestine. But their Canaanite soul dearly loved to adorn itself in Egyptian garb, and archaeologists were often hard put to distinguish where one ended and the other began.

The bas-relief of "Hathor," for example, that Renan discovered in Byblos later turned out not to represent Hathor at all, but rather a Phoenician goddess named Gebal-Baalat—"the Lady of Byblos." It turned out that the Phoenicians identified Gebal-Baalat with Hathor and portrayed their native goddess with all the standard Egyptian iconography typical of Hathor's cult. In this regard, Byblos's patron goddess perfectly symbolized her city's predicament, suspended in a cultural limbo between Egypt and Canaan.

We should not be surprised to find Byblos so Egyptianized. The city had spent much of its early history under Egypt's imperial thumb. At least as early as the Twelfth Dynasty, according to Egyptologist David O'Connor, Byblos "functioned to some degree as a vassal state" of Egypt. It remained sporadically under Egypt's influence for the next 1,000 years.[2]

But the Phoenicians were hardly pushovers. More than once, Phoenician rebels succeeded in breaking loose from Egypt, and, for one brief period, a dynasty of Phoenician kings actually seized and ruled part of Egypt's territory. This happened during the Second Intermediate Period (1674–1553 B.C.), when a league of Asiatic peoples invaded the Nile Valley and conquered northern Egypt.

The Egyptian historian Manetho called the invaders Hyksos, a term that he translated into Greek as "Shepherd Kings." Most Egyptologists believe that *Hyksos* is simply a garbled version of *Hekaw Khasut*—Egyptian for "Rulers of Foreign Lands." While the invaders seem to have been a hodgepodge of various Asiatic tribes, Manetho clearly states that the first wave were led by Phoenician kings: "The Fifteenth Dynasty consisted of Shepherd Kings. There were six foreign kings from Phoenicia, who seized Memphis: in the Sethroite nome they founded a town, from which as a base they subdued Egypt."[3]

Even in defeat, however, Egyptian culture lost none of its hold on the Phoenician soul. The Hyksos rulers honored Egyptian gods, built Egyptian temples, portrayed themselves with Egyptian-style sculpture, and adopted Egyptian royal titles.[4] Rather than Phoenicianizing Egypt, the Phoenicians' brief triumph served only to accelerate their own deepening Egyptianization.

By 1536 B.C., Egypt was back in the saddle. The pharaoh Ahmose expelled the last of the Hyksos from Egypt, and, thirty years later, Thutmose I completed Egypt's revenge, conquering Phoenicia so thoroughly that it remained under Egyptian rule till the end of the *Pax Aegyptiaca*. During this period Egypt exerted its strictest and most systematic control over the country.

No corner of Phoenician life was left untouched. Royal princes were taken as hostages, to be educated at the pharaoh's court and imbued with Egyptian culture. They returned as adults, dressed in Egyptian clothes, decorating their homes with Egyptian art, and burying their dead in man-shaped "anthropoid" coffins, just like those used in Egypt.

Aided by a full-scale colonial administration of "royal messengers" and a network of garrisoned fortresses, an Egyptian viceroy watched over the Asian provinces with the keenness of a hungry vulture. His job was to keep the annual levy of gold, silver, horses, slaves, livestock, oil, incense, wine, and other precious "tribute" flowing ceaselessly back to Egypt. Every province gave according to its means, and wealthy Phoenicia was therefore taxed with particular gusto. Not surprisingly, its tribute was paid largely in cedarwood. An inscription of Thutmose III boasts: "Every year, real cedars of Lebanon are felled for me and brought to my court. . . . When my army returns, they bring as tribute the cedars of my victory, which I have won. . . . I have left none for the Asiatics."[5]

Letters from Phoenician rulers of this period, such as Rib-Addi of Byblos, Zimridi of Sidon, and Abimilki of Tyre, have been discovered in Egypt's royal archives. Their servile tone leaves little doubt that the Hyksos had been thoroughly cured of their past arrogance. Where once Egypt's princes had bowed low before the kings from Phoenicia, now Phoenician rulers petitioned their pharaoh in the fawning language of slaves: "To the lord my king, the sun of the countries, Rib-Addi, your servant, your footstool. At the feet of the sun, my lord, seven and seven times I bow down."[6]

This, then, was Phoenicia during the Late Bronze Age, a land that grew ever more Egyptian with each passing generation. It was from Phoenicia's profoundly Egyptianized nobility that Kadmos, the legendary founder of Thebes, arose. Greek tradition tells us that Kadmos was the son of Agenor, king of the Phoenician city of Tyre. Yet, according to Diodoros, Kadmos was also "a citizen of Egyptian Thebes," which implies that he lived in Egypt and perhaps grew up there.[7]

Diodoros does not explain how a Phoenician prince came to be living in Thebes. If the traditional dates are correct, the Hyksos had already been expelled from Egypt by Kadmos's time, and, in any case, Thebes had never fallen to the Hyksos in the first place. Perhaps Kadmos came from a Hyksos family that was friendly to Egypt and moved down to Thebes after the expulsion. We can only guess.

Greek legend states that Zeus kidnapped Kadmos's sister, Europa, whereupon Kadmos set sail with his brother Phoinix and a party of armed men to search for her. The search party landed in Greece, where Kadmos and Phoinix consulted the Delphic Oracle. Instead of telling them where to find Europa, however, the oracle advised the two brothers to abandon their quest and settle in Greece.

Wisely accepting this divine command, the brothers journeyed to the region of Boiotia, in central Greece. There, they founded the city of Thebes, and Kadmos became its first king. The natives resisted at first. But they were easily defeated, as the Greek writer Pausanias described in his *Guide to Greece,* written during the second century A.D.: "When Kadmos marched in with a Phoenician army and they [the Hyantes and the Aones] lost a battle, the Hyantes ran away the very next night, but the Aones made a ritual supplication so that Kadmos let them stay and intermarry with his Phoenicians."[8]

Nobody knows exactly who the Aones and Hyantes were, but Martin Bernal suggests that the names of both of these peoples may have derived from the Egyptian word *Iwntyw,* which means "bowmen" or "barbarians." Perhaps this was a generic term that Kadmos and his settlers applied to the native Greeks, much as Columbus named the Caribbean islanders "Indians." If this is true, then Kadmos's settlers must have been very Egyptianized indeed. Bernal's etymology implies that they spoke Egyptian at least as readily as they did Phoenician.[9]

Why Kadmos named the new city Thebes is a mystery. The name does not appear to mean anything in Greek. It is tempting to think that Kadmos named it after the Egyptian city of Thebes, where Diodoros says he once lived. However, the Egyptians did not call their city Thebes. Only the Greeks called it by that name. To the Egyptians, it was Wast (or Waset), or sometimes Nu-Amun—"City of Amun."[10]

One popular theory suggests that the Greeks called the Egyptian city Thebes because of a misunderstanding. The Egyptian Thebes had a great temple of Amun called ipet resyt ("southern harem"), which some Egyptologists believe was nicknamed T'ipet—"the harem." When the first Greeks came to Egypt, they may have thought that T'ipet was the name for the whole city. Because it sounded to them like Thebai, they called the Egyptian city Thebai, after their own Thebai in Boiotia.[11]

Maybe so. But it could just as easily have happened the other way around. Perhaps Kadmos actually named his colony T'ipet after the famous temple in the City of Amun. The Greeks would then have mispronounced the name of Kadmos's city as Thebai. Later, when Greeks began traveling to Egypt, they remembered a tradition that the city of Kadmos and the City of Amun were historically related, so they called the Egyptian city Thebai, just like its Greek counterpart. It is all speculation, of course. But if Kadmos really did hail from Egyptian Thebes, as Diodoros claimed, it would have been natural for him to name his colony after a major temple in his hometown.

Unfortunately, most scholars take a dim view of such speculation. To speak of Kadmos as if he really existed is considered naive. In the eyes of modern scholars, Kadmos was only a myth, and Diodoros's writings on Kadmos a myth built upon a myth. Yet, the ancient Greeks never doubted that Kadmos was real. They even claimed to know the precise date when he founded Thebes. According to the Parian Marble, it happened in 1519 B.C.[12]

Conventional scholars, of course, do not take this date seriously. In their eyes, the date is as mythical as Kadmos himself. After all, they argue, it was probably derived by counting backwards through generations of legendary kings, most of whom never existed. How can you find a real date by counting generations of imaginary people?

Obviously, you can't. But those old family trees may not be as fanciful as many experts assume. When Herodotos set out to calculate the date of the Trojan War, traditional genealogy was the only tool he had. Herodotos counted backwards through the lists of Spartan kings until he reached Menelaos, the cuckolded husband of Helen of Troy. Like Kadmos, Menelaos supposedly never existed. But the date Herodotos settled on—about 1250 B.C.—exactly corresponds to the era when most archaeologists agree that the *real* Trojan War took place.[13]

At worst, the date on the Parian Marble represents an ancient—and possibly mistaken—tradition. But, at best, it gives us an accurate reference point for bringing the legendary Kadmos back into the realm of real history. If we proceed on the assumption that the Greek tradition was true—as, indeed, we have resolved to do consistently through this book—then we must consider the possibility that the year 1519 B.C. represents a turning point in history, comparable to the landing at Plymouth Rock in 1620.

CHAPTER 28

THE PHARAOH'S
TRIBUTE

SUPPOSE A PHOENICIAN PRINCE NAMED KADMOS REALLY DID COLO-
nize Greece in 1519 B.C. What role might Egypt have played in
such an operation? In the early stages, possibly none. The
Greek legends say that Kadmos sailed from Tyre. But Thutmose I
did not conquer Tyre until about fifteen years later. If we accept all
these dates and events as literally true, it would appear that Egypt
had no involvement with the expedition, at least in the beginning.

That might have changed later. About fifteen years after founding
Thebes, Kadmos would have received word from home that the king
of Tyre was once again an Egyptian vassal. How might this have altered the status of his colony? Perhaps not at all. In the ancient
world, colonies often enjoyed a political freedom from the mother
country that would have been unthinkable in modern times.

Diodoros records, for example, that after Tyre founded Carthage
around 814 B.C., the Carthaginians used to send a tenth of the city's
revenues to Tyre each year. "But later," he writes, "when they had
acquired great wealth and were receiving more considerable revenues, they sent very little indeed."[1] When Tyre subsequently fell to

Assyrian, Babylonian, Persian, and Greek conquerors, Carthage never felt any obligation to pay allegiance to Tyre's new masters.

An analogous situation might have prevailed in Tyre's hypothetical colony of Thebes a thousand years earlier. But it is also possible that Kadmos's colony might have been drawn, by one means or another, into Egypt's growing sphere of influence. Indeed, Egyptian documents seem to favor the latter possibility. The viceroy of the Asiatic provinces appointed by Thutmose III, for example, did claim authority over the Isles in the Midst of the Great Green Sea, as mentioned earlier.[2] That would have made him responsible for collecting tribute from at least some parts of Greece.

In a single year, Thutmose III claimed to have collected 36,692 *deben* of gold in tribute—the equivalent of three metric tons. Of that amount, 27,000 kilos is specifically said to have come from the Asian provinces and the Isles in the Midst of the Great Green Sea.[3] If we follow the traditional dates, Kadmos's city would have been over forty years old at the time of this levy. Such a thriving Phoenician colony would hardly have escaped the viceroy's notice. If the Aegean isles were being taxed, the mainland, too, may have come under some pressure to pay tribute.

Of course, the pharaoh required more from his Phoenician vassals than mere tribute. He expected *service*—in particular, military service. Throughout its long history, Phoenicia's fleet served many masters. When the Assyrian king Sennacherib marched into Lebanon in about 700 B.C., he assembled a fleet of sixty Phoenician warships to sail against Tyre. Later, Phoenician "prisoners" from Tyre and Sidon manned the fleet that Sennacherib sent down the Euphrates to attack the Babylonians.[4]

The Persian conqueror Cambyses made heavy use of Phoenician auxiliaries. Herodotos observed that "his whole naval power was dependent on them."[5] As for the "Persian" fleet that faced the Athenians at Salamis, it was really a Phoenician fleet. Xerxes and his Persian troops watched the battle from shore.[6] Later, when Alexander the Great captured Phoenicia in 332 B.C., the Phoenicians switched sides once again, serving their Greek masters as faithfully as they had the Assyrians and Persians before them.

The Phoenicians evidently served Egypt in much the same way that they served all their other masters. Egyptian documents make clear that Phoenician vassals were expected to fight for their pharaoh. When, for example, an Amorite warlord named Abdi-Ashirta rebelled against Egypt sometime between 1352 and 1338 B.C., Phoenician rulers such as Rib-Addi of Byblos and Abimilki of Tyre fought valiantly to quell the uprising.

"So long as I am in the city," vowed Rib-Addi, in a letter to the pharaoh Akhnaton, "I guard it for my Lord, and my heart is right toward the Lord my king, so that I will not betray the city to the sons of Abdi-Ashirta."[7]

We have less information, however, regarding the pharaohs' use of Phoenician sea power. It is certain that Phoenician mercenaries served in the navy of the Saite pharaoh Amasis, from about 570 to 526 B.C. But this was very late in Egypt's history. Did Phoenicians also sail for Egypt 900 years earlier, during the *Pax Aegyptiaca?* It appears that they did. A vivid picture of Phoenician naval activity emerges from the so-called Amarna Letters—diplomatic correspondence from the archives of pharaoh Akhnaton (1352–1338 B.C.). The letters reveal that, as Akhnaton's reign wore on, a number of Phoenician cities joined the rebellion of the Amorite king Abdi-Ashirta. At one point, the loyal Rib-Addi of Byblos found himself under attack by ships from three of his fellow Phoenician cities: Beirut, Tyre, and Sidon.

"Put one of your men in each of these cities," Rib-Addi begged the pharaoh, "and prevent them from using their ships against me."[8] Evidently, Rib-Addi's plea fell on deaf ears, for the rebels soon blockaded the neighboring port of Simyra, assisted now by ships from yet another Phoenician city, Arvad.

"As a bird in the fowler's net, so is Simyra," Rib-Addi lamented. "Night and day, the sons of Abdi-Ashirta are against it by land and the men of Arvad by sea."[9] In addition to naval blockades, Rib-Addi also reported ship-to-ship battles. "Two of my ships have been taken," he wrote in one letter. "[The enemy] has seized one of my ships and has actually sailed forth on the sea to capture my other ships."

These letters reveal that Phoenicians already specialized in sea fighting as early as the Late Bronze Age. In this particular case, the rebels used their seapower *against* Egypt. But loyal Phoenicians, such as Rib-Addi, deployed theirs just as effectively on Egypt's behalf. We can only speculate as to what use the pharaohs might have put Phoenician seapower in the days when their grip on the country was more secure. The mere fact that Phoenicia's fleets remained in Egyptian hands throughout the *Pax Aegyptiaca* allows us to draw certain conclusions about this little-known epoch of history.

Scholars today generally insist that Crete and Greece were independent maritime powers during the Late Bronze Age. Although various pharaohs claim to have collected tribute from these countries, scholars contend that the Greek and Cretan emissaries mentioned in Egyptian documents were bringing not tribute, but diplomatic gifts—tokens of friendship, rather than of submission. By this interpretation, the Greek and Cretan kings were equals of the pharaoh, not his vassals.

This theory is hard to square, however, with the military realities of the Late Bronze Age. By conquering Phoenicia, Egypt had monopolized every major port in the eastern Mediterranean. The Greeks and Cretans could sail to their heart's content—but without the pharaoh's permission, their ships had nowhere to land, and no one with whom to trade. It is hard to imagine how the Greeks and Cretans could have stayed in business under these circumstances—unless, of course, they submitted to Egypt.

Perhaps that is what Thutmose III meant when he boasted that he had "trussed . . . the Isles in the Midst of the Great Green Sea."[10] Perhaps that is why, after hearing of Thutmose III's "victories over all the countries," the princes of Keftiu came bearing "gifts on their backs . . . in order to submit to his majesty," as the tomb inscriptions of Rekhmira assert.[11] Submission, under these circumstances, would have been not only a necessary move for the Keftiu and the Haunebu, but perhaps even a shrewd one.

In the ancient world, timely acts of ritual self-effacement saved many a nation from enslavement and destruction. Sometimes they even opened the doors to profitable business relationships. When the Assyrian king Assurnasirpal II advanced on Phoenicia in 877 B.C., for example, the Phoenicians were smart enough to recognize that resistance was futile. They sent delegates bearing gifts to the Assyrian camp. "I received the tribute of the sea coast," Assurnasirpal gloated, "of the inhabitants of Tyre, Sidon, Byblos . . . and Aradus [Arvad] . . . and they kissed my feet."[12]

For the price of this small humiliation, the Phoenicians gained not only their lives but also a valuable customer. Assurnasirpal soon contracted with the Phoenicians to obtain a vast quantity of cedarwood for his new palace at Kalakh, on the upper Tigris. When the palace was finished, he held a great banquet, inviting Phoenician delegates from Tyre and Sidon to join the festivities. "For ten days I entertained the happy men from all these countries," bragged Assurnasirpal in the royal chronicles. "I gave them wine, I let them bathe, I anointed them with oil and did them honour. Then I sent them back to their countries in peace and goodwill."[13]

The moral of the story is that it sometimes pays to be a tributary. Favored vassals, in the ancient world, often *received* gifts from their masters, as well as gave them. Faced with a choice between a disastrous trade war with Egypt and a harmless ritual obeisance, the Greeks and Cretans may well have judged it expedient to swallow their pride and submit—just as the Egyptian documents claim that they did.

Symbolic as that obeisance may have been, it would nonetheless have brought upon the Aegean nations certain inescapable obligations. Tribute, after all, is "protection money." It is a bribe paid to a potential enemy in order to dissuade him from attacking you. By agreeing to pay, you buy safety. But you also surrender part of your freedom. The United States learned this lesson the hard way when it agreed, in 1795, to pay an annual tribute of $21,600 to the Dey Ali Hassan of Algiers in return for his promise to stop seizing American ships and enslaving their crews.[14]

Five years later, a new Dey of Algiers named Bobba Mustapha decided to commandeer the U.S. frigate *George Washington*, which just happened to be in his harbor at a time when he needed an extra ship. The American captain protested, but the Dey snapped back: "You pay me tribute. By that you become my slaves." Unable to dispute Bobba Mustapha's logic, the American captain meekly surrendered his vessel.[15]

Egyptian pharaohs tended to view diplomatic relations in much the same terms as did the Dey of Algiers. Like Bobba Mustapha, the pharaohs would, from time to time, have requested services from their vassals above and beyond the normal payment of tribute. And like the Dey, the pharaohs would not have accepted "no" as an answer.

What these services might have been, we can only guess. They may have included requests for troops to bolster the occasional punitive campaign. A papyrus from Egypt's Amarna period (1348–1338

B.C.) shows what appear to be Greek soldiers serving in the Egyptian army.[16] In the case of the Phoenicians, however, the pharaohs must have made other requests, of a special nature, relating to their peculiar talents and skills.

When rebellion erupted in the territories across the Great Green Sea, who else but the Phoenicians could the pharaohs have dispatched to restore order? When vague reports trickled in of gold, silver, and tin deposits somewhere beyond the limits of the known world, who but the Phoenicians could the pharaohs have appointed to investigate and secure those resources?

For all our painstaking analysis, Kadmos remains a shadowy figure. We cannot prove that he ever existed, nor that he founded Thebes, either in 1519 B.C. or in any other year. But his story does seem to fit into the world of the *Pax Aegyptiaca*. No part of it is inherently implausible. Carving out a city in the wilds of Boiotia, battling for survival against hostile tribes of Aones and Hyantes, Kadmos epitomized the adventuresome spirit of the Bronze Age explorers.

He also epitomized their ties to Egypt. Kadmos's colony, if it really existed, could easily have ended up as an outpost for Egypt's empire. At the very least, it would have served as a vanguard of Egyptian trade and culture. Phoenicia's debt to Egypt was such, during the Bronze Age, that the crafts, gods, and learning Kadmos brought to Europe must have been every bit as Egyptian as they were Phoenician.

It is in the religious sphere, particularly, that Egypt and Phoenicia seem to have shared their deepest unity. Compelling evidence suggests that the cults they served in common may have provided an early prototype for the international "Mystery System" envisioned by George G. M. James. We will examine evidence for this theory in the following section. In the process, we will take up once more the elusive trail of the Egyptian Mysteries, whose lore, doctrines, and hierarchical structure may well have constituted the earliest ancestor of modern Freemasonry.

PART SIX

SECRETS OF
THE MASONS

CHAPTER 29

THE SONS OF
DAIDALOS

G EORGE G. M. JAMES MADE MANY UNLIKELY CLAIMS IN *STOLEN*
Legacy. But perhaps none seems so baseless to the casual
reader as his insistence that Sokrates—the greatest of Greek
philosophers—was an initiate in a Masonic lodge. James offers no
hard evidence for this claim. In the case of Pythagoras and Plato,
James at least had the testimony of ancient authors who confirmed
that these men had studied in Egypt. But, in Sokrates' case, no such
claims were ever made. Plato, in fact, clearly stated that Sokrates
never in his life set foot outside of Greece.[1] Why, then, should we
connect him with the Egyptian Mysteries at all?

James had an answer. He argued that the very lack of evidence
concerning Sokrates' youth and education pointed to the possibility
that he might have been trained in some secret order:

> Very little is known about his early years. . . . Up to the age of 40, his
> life appears to be a complete blank. . . . These circumstances point to
> secrecy in training, and . . . coincide with the requirements for the
> Mystery System of Egypt, and her secret schools, whether in the land
> of Egypt or abroad. . . . All aspirants of the Mysteries had to receive

secret training and preparation, and Sokrates was no exception. He alone of the three Athenian philosophers deserves the appellation of a true Master Mason.[2]

By the phrase "whether in the land of Egypt or abroad," James seems to imply that Sokrates could have acquired his Masonic training outside Egypt—perhaps in Greece. His sedentary life would therefore not have barred Sokrates from "initiation"—at least not by James's interpretation of the Mystery System. But why should we believe James at all? Why should we even consider the possibility that Sokrates was a Mason or that any such thing as Freemasonry even existed in the fifth century B.C.? If this single passage from *Stolen Legacy* were the only evidence at our disposal, we would have no choice but to dismiss all talk of Sokrates' Masonic connection as a figment of James's overeager imagination.

But we *do* have more evidence. You won't find it in the pages of *Stolen Legacy*. James was evidently not even aware that this additional evidence existed. Yet, some angel seems to have watched over *Stolen Legacy* as James wrote. Time after time, his reckless but uncanny intuition guided him down fruitful paths, even when the evidence wore so thin that a single breath might have scattered it like cobwebs. Nowhere was James's intuition taxed more heavily than in his wild surmises about Sokrates. Yet nowhere has it been so powerfully and unexpectedly vindicated.

The crucial clue lies in the words of Sokrates himself, recorded by Plato in *Euthyphro*. There, Sokrates mentions offhandedly that he is descended from Daidalos (Daedalus), the legendary architect, sculptor, and inventor: "Your statements, Euthyphro, are like works of my ancestor Daedalus, and if I were the one who made or advanced them, you might laugh at me and say that on account of my relationship to him my works in words run away and won't stay where they are put."[3]

Sokrates was here making a joke of the fact that Euthyphro's philosophical position never seemed to stay in one place—much like the statues of Daidalos, which were said to be so lifelike that they sometimes got up and walked right off their pedestals. The joke is not important. What concerns us is the fact that Sokrates explicitly called Daidalos his ancestor.

Who was Daidalos? The short answer is that he was a kind of Bronze Age Leonardo da Vinci, a master sculptor, architect, engineer, and all-around genius. According to Diodoros of Sicily, Daidalos was the great-grandson of Erechtheus, the fourth king of Athens. As we saw in chapter 22, Erechtheus was an Egyptian (according to certain Egyptian priests) who became king of Athens after saving the city from famine with a large shipment of grain from Egypt, around 1408 B.C. King Erechtheus also brought the Eleusinian Mysteries to Greece from Egypt, according to the same priests. Daidalos's membership in the Erechtheid family would thus have made him at least partially Egyptian. Sokrates, too, would have been part Egyptian, if he had really been descended from Erechtheus.

Whether there really was a Daidalos and whether he really was Erechtheus's great-grandson is, of course, open to question. It is equally open to question whether Erechtheus was really Egyptian. But Daidalos's alleged connections with Egypt and with its secret wisdom are woven so thickly through every story about him that it seems hard to deny their concrete basis. If ever a real Daidalos lurked behind the smoke screen of myth, his artistic and technical prowess seem likely to have derived from some genuine Egyptian influence.

"In natural ability," wrote Diodoros, "he towered far above all other men and cultivated the building art, the making of statues, and the working of stone. He was also the inventor of many devices which contributed to the advancement of his art and built works in many regions of the inhabited world which arouse the wonder of men."[4]

Diodoros goes on to relate that Daidalos, while still in Athens, took his young nephew Talos as an apprentice. To Daidalos's dismay, the boy proved more talented than his uncle, inventing such tools as the compass, the saw, and the potter's wheel. After watching Talos cut through a stick with a snake's jawbone—the first primitive saw—Daidalos was consumed with envy and promptly hurled Talos to his death from the top of the Acropolis. He was caught, tried for murder, and condemned. But Daidalos managed to flee the country before the sentence was carried out.[5]

According to Diodoros, Daidalos then traveled to Egypt, where he studied sculpture and architecture, winning "great fame because of his genius" and receiving "divine honors" from the Egyptians.[6] One of Daidalos's legendary achievements in Egypt was his design of a magnificent pylon, or gateway, for the "temple of Hephaistos" in Memphis—Diodoros's Hellenized name for the Temple of Ptah.[7]

Later, Daidalos journeyed to Crete, where he was welcomed at the court of King Minos. There he built his most famous creation— the Labyrinth—a gigantic maze so intricate that no one who wandered into it could ever find his way out. Diodoros says that Daidalos "copied" his Labyrinth from an original that he had seen in Egypt, also called the Labyrinth.[8] Scholars still argue over whether there really was an Egyptian Labyrinth, but Herodotos claimed to have seen it with his own eyes: "I have seen this building and it is beyond my power to describe; it must have cost more in labour and money than all the walls and public works of the Greeks put together. . . . The pyramids, too, are astonishing structures . . . but the Labyrinth surpasses them."[9]

Some Egyptologists have identified this edifice with the Twelfth Dynasty mortuary temple of Amenemhat III at Hawara,[10] though others argue that the real Labyrinth has not yet been found, and some claim that it never existed. Real or imaginary, it is this legendary Egyptian building that reputedly provided the model for Daidalos's much better known Cretan Labyrinth.

While he is most famous for his architecture, Daidalos was also credited, in ancient times, with inventing Greek sculpture. Many cities in Greece, Crete, and Sicily claimed to possess statues carved by Daidalos himself.[11] These statues were characterized by their crudeness—a sign of their great antiquity. After viewing a number of such "Daidalic" sculptures in the second century A.D., Pausanias commented, "They are somewhat odd in appearance, but something divine stands out in them."[12]

Having traveled extensively in Egypt, Diodoros recognized the "odd" appearance of Daidalos's statues for what it was—the mark of Egyptian influence. "The proportions of the ancient statues of Egypt," he wrote, "are the same as in those made by Daedalus among the Greeks."[13] Diodoros observed the same Egyptian influence in other Greek sculptors of early times, such as the brothers Telekles and Theodoros, who had also reputedly studied in Egypt. Referring to a famous wooden statue of Apollo carved by the brothers in Samos, Diodoros wrote, "And they say that this statue is for the most part rather similar to those of Egypt, as having the arms stretched stiffly down the sides and the legs separated in a stride."[14] Whether the wooden Apollo at Samos really looked this way, we do not know, for it has long since vanished. The description Diodoros gives, however, faithfully represents the conventions of Egyptian sculpture, which did indeed require artists to portray their subjects with arms stretched stiffly down the sides and left leg stepping forward. Daidalos appears to have followed the same convention. This stepping motion may, in fact, have contributed to the folklore about Daidalos's statues coming to life, as one ancient commentator on Plato's Meno remarked: "Daidalos the Athenian was foremost among the sculptors of that time. He was also first to design a statue with legs apart, the images before that time having their limbs worked together. From that time derives the account current among many, of statues moving and walking around."[15]

If this ancient theory is correct, then Greek sculpture may owe its first inspiration to Egypt. Accustomed as he was to the sophisticated art of Greco-Roman times, Pausanias found the Egyptian rigidity of Daidalos's statues "somewhat odd." But back in the Bronze Age, when Daidalos lived, the techniques he learned in Egypt would have been state-of-the-art. The simple innovation of separating the legs and putting one foot forward may very well have caused Daidalos's statues to appear magically lifelike to the primitive Greeks.

There is another explanation for the legend of Daidalos's statues coming to life that is even more suggestive of Egyptian influence. When Egyptian sculptors carved an image of a god, the statue was believed to be dead until brought to life by a priest. This was accomplished through a ceremony called the Opening of the Mouth, during which the priest would touch the eyes, nose, and mouth of the statue with craftsmen's tools, such as an adze or a chisel. The newly "opened" organs would then be able to see, breathe, and speak, with the divine presence of the god.[16] If the early Greeks really did learn to sculpt from Egyptian teachers, the Opening of the Mouth ceremony would surely have formed part of the curriculum.

Art historians have long recognized that early Greek sculptors, from about 630 to 480 B.C., often rendered human figures in the so-called kouros pose—arms stiffly at the sides and left leg extended, exactly according to Egyptian convention.[17] Greek statues of this period also frequently portray people wearing Egyptian-style wigs.[18] Such Egyptianesque artwork was most popular during Greece's so-called Archaic Period—several centuries too late to have been carved by Daidalos himself. Still, this Archaic Age fad may have echoed a much older Daidalic tradition.

By now, the reasons for alleging a connection between Daidalos and Freemasonry should be plain to most readers. That he studied and worked in Egypt and was moreover granted divine honors there surely implies that Daidalos was inducted into the Egyptian Mysteries. That he worked as an architect and stonemason is even more telling, for it is through these specific professions and the guilds that represented them that Freemasonry was supposedly handed down through the centuries.

This brings us back to Sokrates. It happens that Sokrates, like Daidalos, was a stoneworker by trade. Like his father, Sophroniskos, Sokrates worked as a marble-cutter, which made him, quite literally, a Master Mason. The connection Sokrates claimed with his "ancestor" Daidalos was, therefore, as much professional as genetic. This convergence of craft and blood was probably more than coincidental. In the ancient world, professions were handed down from father to son, through many generations. Daidalos's son Ikaros, for example, was a craftsman, just like his father.[19] The guild of craftsmen, in ancient Athens, would therefore have been bound not only by common interest, but also by common ancestry.

Stonecutters, like all Greek craftsmen, held Daidalos in the greatest reverence. At Athens, they honored Daidalos in a special shrine called the Daidaleion. The rites of the Daidaleion evidently lay at the heart of an Athenian craftsmen's guild, which scholars believe called itself the *Daidalidai*—the "Sons of Daidalos."[20] Sokrates would certainly have been a member of this order, as would his father before him. Membership in the Daidalic guild may therefore have passed, in an unbroken chain, from Sokrates all the way back to Daidalos himself.

Scholars still argue over what Sokrates really meant when he called Daidalos his ancestor. Some say that he claimed literal descent from Daidalos's family—the most obvious interpretation.[21] Others insist that Sokrates called Daidalos his ancestor only figuratively, as the mythical founder of Sokrates' trade and guild.[22] Both theories are probably correct. In fifth-century Athens, the difference

between Daidalos's real and cultic "descendants" was probably neb-
ulous to the point of irrelevancy. His literal descendants would
most likely have formed the core of the Daidalic guild. And those
guild members who were *not* descended from Daidalos probably
claimed that they were anyway.

George G. M. James does not seem to have known about the Sons
of Daidalos. At least, he never mentioned them in *Stolen Legacy.*
But when he called Sokrates a Master Mason, he could hardly have
spoken with better authority. To the extent that we can prove that
anything like Freemasonry existed in the ancient world, Sokrates
does appear to have had a direct link to it. For it is in the mysterious
rites and traditions of the Daidalidai that we find the best evidence
for the seeds of archaic Freemasonry.

CHAPTER 30

THE DEMIURGE

IN 1600, JOHN BOSWELL, LAIRD OF AUCHINLECH, A SCOTTISH NOBLE-
man, joined the local stonemason's guild in Edinburgh. He was
not trained as a stonemason, nor did he work in that trade. Why
he sought to join such a guild and why he was accepted into it was
never recorded.[1] Boswell was not alone in his peculiar hobby, however. Some years later, an Englishman named Elias Ashmole likewise joined a mason's lodge in England. Ashmole had no training in
stonemasonry, either, but he was a notorious alchemist, astrologer,
and all-around occultist.[2] These qualifications evidently satisfied
the guildsmen who approved Ashmole's admission in 1646.[3]

The migration of non-masons into masonic lodges reached epi-
demic proportions in the seventeenth century. A membership list
from 1670 shows that only ten out of forty-nine members of a lodge
in Aberdeen were actually masons. The list included three noblemen, an attorney, a customs official, a professor of mathematics,
and two surgeons.[4] The lodge that Elias Ashmole joined had no
working masons at all. And, in 1658, a man named John Mylne,
calling himself Master of the Lodge at Scone in Scotland, recorded
that he had, "at his Majesty's own desire, entered James VI [the Stu-
art king of Scotland, who later became James I of England] as free-
man, mason and fellow craft."[5]

Kings, scholars, royal officials, noblemen—what drew all these people to enlist in a craftsmen's guild? Rumors flew wildly during the seventeenth century. Many whispered that the masons' lodges were more than guilds; they were repositories of a secret, mystical tradition handed down since ancient times.[6] But no one could prove it. The vow of secrecy sworn by masonic guildsmen barred them from divulging not only the history and purpose of their lodges, but sometimes even their very existence.

All of that changed in 1717. It was then that a group of Englishmen calling themselves the Ancient Fraternity of Free and Accepted Masons gathered at the Apple-Tree Tavern in London and announced that they were merging their four separate lodges into a single Grand Lodge of England.[7]

The group made no pretense of being engaged in what they called "operative," or working, masonry. Despite their name, they were not a craftsmen's guild, nor were their members stonemasons. Instead, they called themselves "speculative" Masons, disciples of an ancient Craft, or spiritual discipline, inherited from the sages of old. Its purpose was not to build stone edifices on earth, but to craft the perfect temple of the human soul. They were, in short, the first group of true Freemasons to publicly announce their existence in the modern world.

Many Masons were horrified. To them, the public announcement of the Grand Lodge seemed a betrayal. Its members were denounced as "oath-breakers" who had violated their pledge of secrecy.[8] But the dissenters were outnumbered. Other lodges soon followed the lead of the "oath-breakers" and came out of hiding. By 1723, fifty-two lodges were registered with the Grand Lodge of England, at least twenty-six of which had operated under cover since well before 1717.[9] The secret order was no longer secret. For the first time, the Craft was exposed, for all to see.

It was an odd group, to say the least. The Freemasons of the eighteenth century claimed no overt connection with the builders' trade. Yet, their society retained many of the trappings of a real craftsmen's guild. While purporting to offer spiritual enlightenment, the Craft veiled its teachings behind elaborate rituals, incorporating the tools and technical vocabulary of architects and stonemasons.

New members were called entered apprentices and were likened, in Masonic doctrine, to a rough, unfinished building stone that needed to be dressed and polished to perfection. As members progressed in their spiritual growth, they were promoted to Fellow Craft and finally to Master Mason, much as real stonemasons advanced through the ranks of apprentice, journeyman, and master.

For their ceremonies, Freemasons dressed in leather aprons and symbolically wielded all the traditional tools of the stonecutter's art, such as hammer, chisel, level, square, compass, and plumb line. These commonplace objects were imbued by the Masons with profound metaphorical significance. Even God Almighty was subjected to a peculiarly Masonic metamorphosis. The Brethren referred to him as the Great Architect of the Universe or sometimes the Grand Geometrican—geometry being a sacred discipline to the Masons, just as it was an indispensable tool of the working architect.

What did it all mean? How and where did this strange brew of craftsmanship and mysticism first arise? In fact, the doctrines of "speculative" Freemasonry, as they first appeared in the seventeenth and eighteenth centuries, were not so different from the beliefs of ordinary working masons from centuries past. Most working masons of the Middle Ages, in fact, would have recognized these beliefs and probably would have agreed with them. Indeed, the "speculative" lodges of the eighteenth century may have grown naturally out of the working lodges of medieval times, just as Masonic folklore claims.

The Dark Ages that followed Rome's fall were a time of ignorance and barbarism. Literacy nearly vanished in Europe. Universities closed. Books became rarities. Living standards plummeted. One of the few places where learning survived was within the small brotherhood of architects and stonemasons who reared the great castles and cathedrals. The emperor Charlemagne—who reigned from A.D. 768 to 814—was illiterate. But the architects and masons who designed and built Charlemagne's great cathedral at Aachen could not afford to emulate their master's ignorance. To do their jobs, they not only had to read and calculate, but also had to design with a fine sense of beauty and proportion. They were artists, mathematicians, engineers, and scholars, all in one.

They were also mystics. During the Middle Ages, architecture was looked upon as a sacred science. God and Christ were often portrayed in the illuminations of medieval Bibles as compass-wielding Divine Architects—an image that directly foreshadows the Masonic notion of the Great Architect of the Universe.[10] Just as God was thought to have designed the universe in accord with architectural principles, so cathedrals and churches were expected to conform, in their proportions and orientation, to ancient mystical requirements. Altars, for example, always had to face east, just like the altars of Roman temples. Churches were generally built on the sites of old pagan shrines, not only because these locations symbolized Christianity's triumph over heathenism, but also because they were thought peculiarly propitious for worship. Astronomical alignments were also taken into account. For example, at Chartres Cathedral, completed in 1134, the stained-glass window of Saint Apollinaire contains a pane of clear glass, so aligned as to cause a beam of light to strike a specific mark on the floor at high noon every Midsummer's Day.[11]

Medieval folklore abounds with stories emphasizing God's concern for the proper orientation of churches. When, for example, the stones of a new church in Sussex were found magically rearranged each morning, builders concluded that they had laid the foundation in the "wrong" place. They searched for an omen to show them the "right" location and ultimately found four oxen lying in a field, back-to-back, in a cross formation. There, they rebuilt the church, in the shape of a cross. Another story tells of a Sussex church that was wrenched out of its east-west alignment by the devil. Saint Dunstan and his workmen managed to return the church to its proper orientation, but only after considerable demonic harassment.[12]

The Middle Ages was a time, in the words of medieval scholar Pauline M. Matarasso, "when things were rarely what they seemed, when the outward appearance was merely a garment in which to dress some inward truth."[13] Just as every verse of medieval literature was charged with religious allegory, so every angle, measurement, and proportion in a church's construction was imbued with theological import. The architect's job involved, in part, modulating and directing those messages through the application of sacred geometry. Sometimes the symbolism was overt, as in the case of circular or cross-shaped churches. Of these popular medieval designs, Honorius of Autun wrote, in 1330: "Churches made in the form of a cross show how people of the church are crucified by this world; those made round in the form of a circle show that the church is built throughout the circuit of the globe to become the circle of the crown of eternity through love."[14]

More often, however, the "sacred geometry" was incorporated so subtly into a building's design as to be indiscernible to the untrained eye. If an architect wished, for example, to emphasize a cathedral's dedication to the Holy Trinity, he might lay out the ground plan *ad triangulum*—by the triangle. Such a ground plan did not mean that the building itself would be triangular or that any obvious triangles would appear within it. Quite the contrary.

To the ordinary parishioner, a cathedral built *ad triangulum* would look much like any other cathedral. But unbeknownst to the faithful, the placement of every wall, vault, and chantry would have been determined by means of a grid composed of pairs of equilateral triangles superimposed over each other to form Stars of David. The floor plan was then fitted into this Star of David grid. By this means, the architect ensured that every proportion in the building derived, in some way, from triangular geometry. Yet the triangles themselves would remain visible only to God.

The invisibility of sacred geometry did not make it any less important to the masons and architects of the Middle Ages. Determining the underlying geometry of a new cathedral was considered a grave and momentous responsibility. The building of the Milan Cathedral, for example, was delayed for years when rival factions of masons quarreled, around 1400, over whether to build the church *ad triangulum* or *ad quadratum* (by the square). The feud was finally resolved through a compromise—the floor plan was to be *ad quadratum* and the elevation *ad triangulum*.[15]

Medieval builders encoded secret messages in their work as well by spelling out pious phrases, letter-by-letter, using *gematria*—a cipher employed by Jewish mystics whereby numbers are substituted for each letter of the alphabet. The design of King's College Chapel in Cambridge, for example—built between 1446 and 1515—features a relentless repetition of the number 26. The church has 26 stained-glass windows and 26 structural uprights; each pair of fans in the vaulting contains exactly 26 ribs. And so on.[16]

As any good occultist knows, 26 is the number representing the Holy Tetragrammaton—the unspeakable four-letter name of God in the Old Testament, which is spelled *YHVH*—for *Yahweh*—in the Hebrew alphabet. In the *gematria* cipher, *Y* is given the value of 10,

H the value of 5, and *V* the value of 6. The letters *Y* + *H* + *V* + *H* would therefore equal 10 + 5 + 6 + 5, which is 26. As if to punctuate the point, a seventeenth-century wood carving placed over the western door of King's College Chapel actually contains the Tetragrammaton, spelled out in Hebrew letters.[17]

All of this seems rather farfetched to our modern sensibility. But in medieval times, such mystical schemes were not only common elements of church architecture, but also widely recognized and accepted as such, even by people who did not possess the occult training to decipher them. Thus William of Malmesbury, after viewing the St. Mary Chapel at Glastonbury in the twelfth century, commented: "In the pavement may be seen on every side stones, designedly inlaid in triangles and squares, and figured with lead, under which, if I believe some sacred enigma to be contained, I do no injustice to religion."[18]

In their obsession with the mystical properties of measure, proportion, and orientation, the medieval architects were only following in the footsteps of their Roman predecessors. Supernatural concerns permeate the writings of the Roman architect Vitruvius, whose book *On Architecture*, written in the first century B.C., was widely read by architects right up through the Renaissance.

Vitruvius recommended that building sites be selected, at least partly, through divination and the reading of omens.[19] When building temples, Vitruvius commanded, "Let the altars look to the east."[20] But perhaps his most lasting contribution was his vision of the architect as a kind of perfect philosopher. It was the Vitruvian architect—scholar, scientist, mystic, and craftsman, all rolled into one—whose image haunted the profession all through the Middle Ages and found its ultimate expression in modern Freemasonry.

Pythagoras taught that spiritual perfection was attained through the four cardinal disciplines of arithmetic, geometry, music, and astronomy.[21] In each of these areas, Pythagoras noted, beauty emerged from the symmetry of mathematical relationships. By mastering the underlying arithmetic of beauty, the philosopher attained harmony with the *kosmos*—the "universal order"—and harmony with himself.

Vitruvius applied this same principle to architecture. In order to make a beautiful building, Vitruvius taught, the architect must first apprehend beauty itself. This was accomplished, first, through the study of geometry, which imparted the secrets of "proportion and symmetry."[22] In addition, wrote Vitruvius, the architect, "should be . . . a mathematician . . . a diligent student of philosophy, acquainted with music . . . familiar with astrology."[23]

The curriculum Vitruvius recommended was frankly Pythagorean. But it was probably from Plato that he learned it. Following Pythagoras, Plato's Academy in Athens also based its teachings on the four cardinal disciplines of music, arithmetic, astronomy, and, especially, geometry.[24] "Let no one ignorant of geometry enter here," warned the sign over the Academy door. [25] In Plato's view, geometry expressed the inmost secrets of the universe, and God himself was the ultimate geometrician.[26] "Geometry is the knowledge of the eternally existent," Plato declared in his *Republic*.[27]

It should hardly come as a surprise, then, to learn that Plato's writings contain one of the earliest known references to God as a Great Architect of the Universe. The term Plato uses is *Demiourgos*. Literally, it means "one who works for the people"—a "public worker," as opposed to a farmer, a slave, or an aristocrat. In common speech, the word usually referred to craftsmen, such as metalsmiths, potters, and masons; and it is in this sense that Plato employs it. In the *Timaeus*, Plato speaks of the Demiourgos as a Divine Craftsman who, in the beginning of time, used *geometry* to bring forth order from chaos.[28]

"He constructed this present universe," wrote Plato. "And he himself acts as the Constructor [Demiourgos] of things divine."[29] In describing the Creation, Plato constantly employs the terminology of building and masonry. The standard Loeb Classics translation of the *Timaeus* generally renders *Demiourgos* as "Constructor" or "Artificer." At one point, Plato even explicitly calls the Demiourgos an "Architect"—*Tektainomenos*.[30]

This passage from the *Timaeus* later inspired the Gnostic sages of Roman-occupied Egypt to name their Creator-God "Demiourgos"—the Demiurge. Surely it is Plato's Demiurge who also provided the model for those compass-wielding Gods and Christs so favored by medieval illustrators. When Vitruvius spoke of the architect as sage and philosopher, it was Plato's vision of a divine Artificer that inspired him. And on who else but Plato's Demiourgos could the Freemasons have based their Great Architect of the Universe?

Should we, then, look to Plato alone for the ultimate origin of Freemasonry? Was it Plato who first charged the builder's art with an aura of divinity? The evidence suggests otherwise. Like the Freemasons themselves, and like their predecessor Vitruvius, Plato seems only to have been repeating a tradition that was already hoary with age by the time he adopted it. If we would seek the Divine Architect in his original form, we should look not to eighteenth-century London, nor to Rome of the first century B.C., nor even to Athens four hundred years earlier. Our quest must take us to a very remote time indeed, no later than 3150 B.C., and to a land far removed from the cheery camaraderie of London's Apple-Tree Tavern. That land is ancient Egypt.

CHAPTER 31

THE SHABAKA STONE

THE MOST LIKELY CANDIDATE FOR THE EGYPTIAN DEMIOURGOS WAS a god named Ptah. He was the patron of all who worked in metal, wood, or stone and was himself a craftsman, with his own heavenly workshop.[1] All arts were sacred to Ptah, including those of architecture and stonemasonry. For this reason the great architect Imhotep—the inventor of the pyramid, discussed in chapter 16—was deified, after his death, as the "son of Ptah."[2] If anything like Freemasonry existed in ancient Egypt, it is surely in the cult of Ptah that we should seek it.

A strong suggestion of Masonic hierarchy lies in the traditional title held by the high priest of Ptah. He was called *wer kherep hemw*—"Supreme Leader of Craftsmen."[3] If the high priest wielded the kind of administrative authority his title implies, then the cult of Ptah must have played a vital role in Egyptian industry. It may even have functioned as a kind of state-sponsored craftsmen's guild, not unlike the Sons of Daidalos in Athens.

Nobody knows when Ptah was first worshiped. His cult appears on the stage of history at the same time as Egypt herself. Tradition holds that Egypt was founded by the legendary king Menes. According to legend, he united Upper and Lower Egypt, founded the First Dynasty, and established Memphis as the capital of the newly uni-

184

fied kingdom. Experts have identified the legendary Menes with a real pharaoh named Narmer, whose inscriptions suggest that he did indeed unify Egypt, sometime between 3150 and 3125 B.C. Menes—or Narmer, if you prefer—was evidently a great builder. Herodotos records an Egyptian tradition that Menes (whom he calls Min) built the city of Memphis, after draining the site through a massive diversion of the Nile waters:

> The priests told me that it was Min, the first king of Egypt, who raised the dam which created Memphis. The river used to flow along the base of the sandy hills on the Libyan border, and this monarch, by damming it up . . . drained the original channel and diverted it to a new one. . . . To this day, [the dam] . . . is most carefully watched by the Persians, who strengthen the dam every year; for should the river burst it, Memphis might be completely overwhelmed.[4]

A pharaoh so devoted to building and engineering projects must have valued his artisans highly. He showed this by honoring their god. From the very beginning, Ptah appears to have been the patron deity of Memphis. Herodotos says that Menes built the fabulous Temple of Ptah, Memphis's chief attraction. As elsewhere in his writings, Herodotos identifies Ptah in this passage with Hephaistos, the Greek god of crafts: "On the land which had been drained by the diversion of the river, King Min built the city which is now called Memphis. . . . In addition to this the priests told me that he built there the large and very remarkable temple of Hephaistos."[5]

For the rest of Egypt's history, Memphis remained the seat of Ptah's cult. So central did Ptah become to Egypt's identity that most scholars believe the very word Egypt derived from him. The Egyptians called Memphis Hwt-ka-Ptah—"the House of Ptah." It is thought that the Greeks mispronounced this name as Aiguptos—whence we get our modern word Egypt.[6]

The reason for Ptah's enduring power in Egypt is not hard to find. After Menes, the Egyptian pharaohs continued to build on a grand scale, rearing some of the most remarkable structures ever seen. Herodotos declared that "more monuments that beggar description are to be found" in Egypt "than anywhere else in the world."[7] Ptah provided the driving force behind these achievements.

Did he also provide the seeds of sacred geometry? That is harder to determine. Occultists through the ages have tried, with great ingenuity, to prove that Egypt's temples and pyramids incorporated secret messages in their measurements and proportions. If true, this would suggest a direct—and distinctly Freemasonic—link between Egyptian and Gothic architecture. But evidence has, so far, been scarce.

That the Egyptians were accomplished geometricians is beyond doubt. According to Herodotos, they first used geometry to redraw property boundaries that had been altered by the Nile's annual flood:

> Any man whose holding was damaged by the encroachment of the river would go and declare his loss before the king, who would send inspectors to measure the extent of the loss, in order that he might pay in future a fair proportion of the tax at which his property had been assessed. I think this was the way in which geometry was invented, and passed afterwards into Greece.[8]

Herodotos may be right. The Greek word *geometry* actually means "measuring the earth," and it is quite likely that the Egyptians invented the discipline originally for this purpose. But geometry soon evolved into a full-fledged science. The Rhind Mathematical Papyrus, for example, includes a diagram showing what appears to be a sophisticated geometric proof of the value of π— written by an Egyptian scribe over 1,300 years before Euclid's *Elements*. If modern scholars have interpreted this diagram correctly, then "there are depths in Egyptian geometry which have sometimes gone unrecognized," admits scientific historian Robert Palter.[9]

Egyptian papyri also give accurate formulae for calculating the area of trapezoids, triangles, cylinders, circles—even truncated pyramids.[10] Defenders of Hellenic culture are often quick to point out that such calculations would have been child's play for Greek mathematicians. Of course, this is true. But comparing the science of classical Greece with that of Bronze Age Egypt is a bit like comparing modern brain surgery with medieval leeching. The comparison is unfair because the time difference is so vast.

When Egyptian geometricians first worked out the value of π, classical Greece did not even exist. The Rhind Mathematical Papyrus was written in 1650 B.C. but copied from an original that was 200 years older, from about 1850 B.C.[11] By contrast, the earliest Greek mathematicians, such as Thales and Anaximander, did not appear until the sixth century B.C.—some 1,300 years later.[12] That is more than the time span separating 1990s America from the reign of Charlemagne. The Egyptians may not have been the greatest geometricians of antiquity, but they were surely the first—and that by a long shot.

Egypt's early achievements in mathematics were not always clearly remembered or acknowledged by the later Greeks. Archimedes, for example, claimed that Eudoxos of Cnidus—a Greek mathematician who lived during the fourth century B.C.—was the first to calculate the volume of a four-sided pyramid. Yet the Moscow Mathematical Papyrus, written in 1850 B.C., shows that the Egyptians knew this formula at least 1,500 years earlier.[13] Since Diodoros records that Eudoxos studied in Egypt, we can reasonably suspect that Eudoxos may have learned the formula there and simply passed it on to the Greeks.[14] But Archimedes seems not to have realized this.

From the entire 2,500-year span of Egypt's pre-Greek history, only about a dozen crumbling scrolls have survived on the subject of mathematics.[15] Based on such paltry evidence, it is impossible to say how much the Egyptians really knew. But the evidence we do have in hand suggests that a great deal of what we now call "Greek" mathematics may really have come from Egypt.

Did some of Egypt's lost teachings include the principles of sacred geometry? We have no sure proof that they did. Yet, it is evident that Egyptian builders attributed mystical significance to at least certain elements of their work. The concern that the Egyptians lavished on their temple floor-plans, for example, seems to have gone far beyond the practical. One text from the reign of Thutmose III claims that the pharaoh rebuilt a temple using a blueprint dating from the legendary era when Egypt was ruled by spirits and demigods. "The great plan was found in Denderah," says the text, "in old delineations written upon leather of animal skin of the time of the Followers of Horus."[16]

One of the sacred books listed in the catalog of an Egyptian temple library at Edfu, dating from about 140–124 B.C., is called *Book of the Plan of the Temple.*[17] This may have been one of the 42 Books of Thoth mentioned by Clement of Alexandria, one of which is supposed to have covered the construction of temples.[18]

We can only guess what was written in this book. But it seems a safe bet that astronomical lore formed part of its subject matter.

Egyptian temples are renowned for the accuracy of their alignment with heavenly reference points. The great temple of Ramesses II, which was carved into the cliffs at Abu Simbel, for example, was laid out in such a way that, twice a year, during February and October, the rising sun would penetrate all the way to its deepest recesses, bathing the statues of Ramesses and the sun gods Ra-Harakhty and Amun-Ra in light.[19]

As early as the Second Dynasty, Egyptian architects aligned the foundations of new temples to the four points of the compass, in a ceremony known as *pedj shes*—"stretching the cord." A priest would use a sighting device and a kind of astrolabe called a *merkhet*, or "instrument of knowing," to line up the foundation with certain constellations, such as Orion and the Great Bear, marking the crucial reference points with pegs and cords. This ritual, first shown in an inscription from the reign of Khasekhemwy, around 2686 B.C., enabled architects to align temples and pyramids with great accuracy, to within half a degree of the true north-south axis.[20]

We can only guess what sorts of beliefs prompted the Egyptians to fuss so compulsively over the celestial alignment of their buildings. But there is no guesswork involved in noting the resemblance between these Egyptian practices and the preoccupation with astronomy that also haunted Greek, Roman, and medieval builders. It is hard not to wonder whether such mystical notions were transmitted to Europe from Egypt.

If so, they would not have been transmitted alone. Other architectural ideas are known to have crossed the Mediterranean in very early times. The most dramatic example would be the fluted column. Every art historian knows that the Doric, Ionic, and Corinthian columns that graced Greek and Roman temples found an early ancestor in the fluted colonnade of the mortuary temple built by pharaoh Djoser at Sakkara, sometime between 2667 and 2648 B.C. It was probably Imhotep who designed this temple, and possibly he who first conceived the idea of decorating stone columns with the fluted pattern of a papyrus bundle.

How Imhotep's invention made its way to Greece we can only guess. But there can be no disputing that it did, sometime around the seventh century B.C., when the first "Doric" temples appeared.[21] Was this the only innovation that Europeans ever adopted from the followers of Ptah? Or were there more? Many Masons would argue, along with George G. M. James, that Freemasonry itself was among these cultural borrowings. Seldom can they offer any proof for this contention beyond the whisperings of occult folklore. Nevertheless, they may be correct.

The clearest evidence we have that Masonry came from Egypt can be found in the so-called Shabaka Stone, an inscribed slab of black basalt that the Earl Spencer, a noted antiquities collector, donated to the British Museum in 1805. Spencer had acquired the piece in Egypt, where farmers had punched a hole in it and used it for a millstone, grinding away most of the text through years of heavy use.

Enough of the writing remained, however, for later Egyptologists to conclude that the Shabaka Stone contained one of the most important religious texts ever to come out of Egypt. Inscribed by the Nubian pharaoh Shabaka in about 710 B.C., the stone is actually a copy of a much older text, called the Memphite Theology. Shabaka explains, in the inscription, that he decided to preserve the Memphite Theology in stone when it was discovered that the older scroll had been damaged by worms. The archaic language of this Memphite Theology suggests to Egyptologists that it must have been written during the Old Kingdom period (2700–2190 B.C.).[22]

When the stone was first translated, it created a stir among scholars, for it presented the god Ptah in an unexpected new role—as Creator of the universe. According to the stone, Ptah brought all the other gods into being by conceiving them in his heart and speaking them with his tongue:

For the very great one is Ptah, who gave [life] to all the gods... through this heart and through this tongue... Thus all the gods were born... For every word of the god came about through what the heart devised and the tongue commanded... Thus it is said of Ptah: "He who made all and created the gods." ... Thus Ptah was satisfied after he had made all things.[23]

In plain English, what this means is that the Egyptians revered Ptah—a divine architect—as the creator of "all things." The Shabaka Stone therefore presents us with the first known reference to a heavenly being exactly matching the description of Plato's

Demiourgos. This does not exactly prove that Freemasonry was born in the temple of Ptah. But the Shabaka Stone leaves little doubt that the Masons' most distinctive totem—the Great Architect of the Universe—found his earliest home in Egypt.

CHAPTER 32

SOLOMON'S TEMPLE

IN FREEMASONRY, EVERY INITIATE TO THE RANK OF MASTER MASON must undergo a peculiar ceremony. The initiate is required to play the role of "Hiram Abiff"—a Phoenician craftsman who was allegedly murdered during the building of Solomon's Temple. During the course of the drama, the initiate is blindfolded, ritually "killed," wrapped in a blanket, and "buried" by three brethren of the lodge, who play the role of Hiram's murderers. At the end of the ceremony, the Worshipful Master of the lodge—playing the role of King Solomon—"resurrects" the initiate by gripping his hand in the secret Lion's Paw handshake of a Master Mason, whispering in his ear the secret Mason's word, and removing the blindfold.[1]

Nobody knows how long the Freemasons have been using this story in their initiation rite. There is evidence that Hiram Abiff was honored by medieval masons as early as 1410, when the so-called Cooke Manuscript—a legendary history of the mason's craft—portrayed a certain "king's son of Tyre" (presumably Hiram) as the inheritor of a mysterious "science" passed down since the days before Noah's Flood.[2] The story may or may not have been used in Masonic rituals at the time this manuscript was written. But the Cooke document certainly confirms that working masons, at least as far back as the fifteenth century, viewed the Phoenicians—and

Hiram Abiff in particular—as important figures in the history of their trade.

Why the Phoenicians? If the Masonic tradition began in the Temple of Ptah, we would expect Egypt to play the central role in Masonry's rites and legends. Yet the Phoenicians appear to have usurped Egypt's place. To this day, Masons look to the Temple of Solomon—not to any Egyptian temple—as the ultimate repository of divine wisdom. They regard its measurements and proportions as embodying the most guarded secrets of sacred geometry. Masons attribute the perfection of Solomon's Temple not so much to the genius of Solomon or the Hebrews, but to the occult wisdom of the Phoenician Master Masons who allegedly built it—in particular, to King Hiram of Tyre and the craftsman Hiram Abiff, both called Grand Masters in Masonic folklore.

Scholars have shown that the legend of the Phoenician Grand Masters contains at least some element of truth. The Hebrew kings depended heavily on Phoenician expertise in building their public edifices. King David, for example, contracted with King Hiram I— who ruled the Phoenician city of Tyre between 986 and 935 B.C.— to build a palace in Jerusalem. "Now Hiram, king of Tyre, sent messengers to David," says the Book of Samuel, "along with cedar logs and carpenters and stonemasons, and they built a palace for David."[3] Most experts agree that David's palace, like other buildings contracted from the Phoenicians, probably adhered to the conventions of Phoenician style and would have resembled the public buildings of any Phoenician city.[4]

According to the Bible, Solomon followed his father's example. When it came time to build the temple of the Lord, he turned again to Phoenicia—and, in particular, to an old family friend, King Hiram I of Tyre. "So give orders that cedars of Lebanon be cut for me," wrote Solomon to Hiram, in the Book of Kings. "My men will work with yours, and I will pay you for your men whatever wages you set."[5]

Great logs of cedar were felled in Lebanon and floated down on rafts. Stones were quarried and cut to such perfection that, once they arrived at the building site, they had only to be fitted together, with no need for further chiseling or hammering. "In building the temple," says the Book of Kings, "only blocks dressed at the quarry were used, and no hammer, chisel or any other iron tool was heard at the temple site while it was being built."[6]

The outer walls of the temple were built of stone, the ceiling and interior entirely of cedar. When it came time to decorate the temple, King Hiram sent to Solomon a craftsman who was also named Hiram or Huram (the spelling varies in different books of the Bible). In 2 Chronicles 2:13, he is called Huram-abi—"Huram is my father"—the form that the Masons later transmuted into Hiram Abiff. The Book of Chronicles describes Hiram in this way:

> Solomon gave orders to build a temple for the Name of the Lord and a royal palace for himself. . . . Solomon sent this message to Hiram king of Tyre. . . . "Send me . . . a man skilled to work in gold and silver, bronze and iron, and in purple, crimson and blue yarn, and experienced in the art of engraving to work in Judah and Jerusalem with my skilled men. . . ." Hiram king of Tyre replied . . . "I am sending you Huram-abi, a man of great skill, whose mother was from Dan and whose father was from Tyre. He is trained to work in gold and silver, bronze and iron, stone and wood, and with purple and blue. He is experienced in all kinds of engraving and can execute any design given to him."[7]

Contrary to Masonic legend, the Bible does not say that Hiram— or Huram or Huram-abi—was the son of King Hiram (though his name does mean "Hiram is his father"). In fact, Huram is described in I Kings 7:13–14 as the son of "a widow from the tribe of Naphtali." The Bible also fails to confirm that Hiram was Master of the Work, in charge of the entire building project, as Masonic legend claims. Instead, it portrays Hiram mainly as a smith, responsible for forging and crafting the metallic decorations, such as the two bronze pillars, named Jakin and Boaz, that stood before the temple.

Perhaps the greatest difference between the biblical and Masonic accounts is that Hiram is not murdered in the Bible. Masonic legend holds not only that Hiram was murdered, but also that his death prevented the temple's completion. The Bible, on the other hand, says that Hiram "finished all the work he had undertaken for King Solomon in the Temple of God."[8]

How do we account for these discrepancies? Many experts have concluded that the Masonic legend is simply wrong and that it represents nothing more than a fictional retelling of the biblical tale, spiced up with a few mystical flourishes. This is an easy way to dismiss the story, but probably not accurate. There is strong evidence that the Masonic legend of Hiram Abiff is based on a real oral tradition—one that is possibly more ancient than the biblical account of

Huram-abi. In fact, the Hiram Abiff legend is probably a hybrid, in which two or more different stories have been grafted together—a theory that we will explore in more detail in chapter 35.

One thing the Hiram Abiff legend tells us, without any ambiguity, is that the Freemasons regard Phoenicia as an important transmitter of their ancient tradition. Masonic legend holds that Hiram and the other Phoenician artisans who worked on Solomon's Temple were Freemasons. Indeed, it was supposedly because Hiram refused to divulge the secret Mason's word that the three murderers killed him. Masonic folklore also alleges that it was the Phoenician Masons who initiated King Solomon himself into the Brotherhood, appointing him Israel's first Grand Master.[9]

None of this can be proven, of course. But the biblical tale does confirm that Phoenician artisans were highly regarded during the period when Solomon's Temple was built—about 958 to 951 B.C. Homer echoed this impression, about a hundred years later, when he called the Phoenicians *polydaidaloi*—"many-skilled"—and portrayed them as gifted craftsmen, especially in silver and gold work.[10]

How did the Phoenicians acquire these skills? Evidently, from Egypt. Phoenician artisans, from the earliest times, looked to Egypt for their models. Early Phoenician sites yield a multitude of enthusiastic but crude attempts to imitate far more sophisticated Egyptian wares. Even architectural motifs, such as the obelisk, were borrowed from Egypt, as mentioned in chapter 27. During the long years that Egypt dominated Phoenicia, it seems almost certain that Phoenician masons, architects, painters, and smiths would have apprenticed themselves to Egyptian masters, on a large scale.

By this means, they would have acquired not only the skills of Egyptian craftsmen but also a reverence for their special god, Ptah. Such a massive transmission of Ptah's cult to Phoenicia could easily have given rise to Masonic legends concerning the Tyrian Grand Lodge.

Of course, we have no Egyptian documents describing the foundation, in Phoenicia, of a cult of Ptah. But we have something almost as provocative. An Egyptian story called *The Report of Wenamun* explicitly portrays the power that Egyptian cults wielded in Phoenicia generations after the last Egyptian troops had withdrawn from the country. While *The Report of Wenamun* concerns itself mainly with the cult of Amun, we can assume that our hypothetical cult of Ptah would have found itself in a similar relationship with Phoenicia.

In the story—which most experts believe is based on real events—an Egyptian envoy named Wenamun is dispatched to Byblos to buy cedarwood to build a sacred bark for the god Amun.[11] Two hundred years before, an Egyptian envoy would have been greeted like a king in Byblos. But by 1090–1080 B.C., the approximate time of Wenamun's journey, Egypt's empire was a shambles, its power broken and its envoys despised. In the story, the only thing Wenamun has going for him is that he represents an ancient and respected Egyptian cult—an advantage that he exploits to the hilt.

From the moment he leaves Egypt, Wenamun meets nothing but poor treatment. In the port of Dor, he is robbed of all his money, and the king turns a deaf ear to his complaints. Wenamun has to steal thirty *deben* of silver to continue his journey. Arriving in Byblos, Wenamun is then scorned by the prince. For each of the next twenty-nine days, a messenger arrives from Tjekerbaal, the prince of Byblos, commanding Wenamun: "Leave my harbor!" Wenamun is right on the brink of sailing back to Egypt in despair when a summons from the prince finally arrives.

It seems that, while Tjekerbaal was making offerings in the temple, a certain young man in his party was seized by a sacred trance and began to prophesy, warning the prince to receive the Egyptian messenger. "It is Amun who sent him!" the young man cried. At this, Tjekerbaal finally relented and sent for Wenamun. He does not fear Egypt, but evidently Tjekerbaal still fears Egypt's gods.

When Wenamun finally stands before the prince, Tjekerbaal treats him at first with contempt. "I am not your servant," the prince declares when Wenamun asks him for cedarwood, "and I am not the servant of him who sent you either." Only for money, says Tjekerbaal—and lots of it—will he even think of complying with Wenamun's request. But suddenly, the prince seems to reconsider. He reminds himself that the timber is for the god Amun, and this seems to give him pause. Tjekerbaal then indulges in a brief soliloquy, which provides a rare glimpse into the way Phoenicians viewed their cultural subservience to Egypt. The prince reflects: "Amun has founded all the lands. He founded them after having first founded the land of Egypt from which you have come. Thus craftsmanship came from it in order to reach the place where I am! Thus learning came from it in order to reach the place where I am!"[12]

All at once, Tjekerbaal has adopted a conciliatory—if not a downright submissive—posture. He extols the Egyptian god Amun as the founder of every land—including his own, we presume. He admits that it is from Egypt that the Phoenicians acquired learning and craftsmanship. Here the prince of Byblos finally shows his true face. The twenty-nine days of humiliation to which he subjected Wenamun were evidently no more than a bargaining ploy, designed to keep the Egyptian envoy off balance. In the end, Tjekerbaal cannot help but acknowledge Egypt's cultural preeminence, and we see that he does not really wish to provoke Amun's wrath.

Sensing his advantage, Wenamun goes on the attack. He accuses Tjekerbaal of having insulted the small image of the god that Wenamun brought with him from Egypt. "But look, you have let this great god spend these twenty-nine days moored in your harbor," he says ominously. "Did you not know that he was here? . . . You are prepared to haggle over the Lebanon with Amun, its lord?"[13] Thereupon, Wenamun launches into a soliloquy of his own, this one on the power and glory of Amun.

> There is no ship on the river that does not belong to Amun. His is the sea and his the Lebanon of which you say, "It is mine." . . . He was the lord of your fathers! They passed their lifetimes offering to Amun. You too, are the servant of Amun! If you . . . carry out his business, you will live, you will prosper, you will be healthy; you will be beneficent to your whole land and your people.[14]

Surprisingly, considering Tjekerbaal's previous belligerence, this little speech seems to do the trick. Tjekerbaal agrees to do business with Wenamun: his workmen fetch the cedarwood, payment soon arrives from Egypt, and Wenamun's mission is accomplished. In the lawless world of the eleventh century B.C., the wily Wenamun has managed to get what he wanted, without troops, without threats, and with relatively little money—Tjekerbaal grumbles until the end that the pharaohs of old would have paid a much higher price.

How did Wenamun do it? It seems that the linchpin of his negotiating strategy was to assert Egypt's *religious authority* over Phoenicia—an authority that Tjekerbaal could not deny. If there is a moral to this tale, it seems to be that *the cult is mightier than the sword*. Long after the cities of the Levantine coast ceased to fear Egypt's arms, they evidently still honored its gods. The uneasy banter between Wenamun and Tjekerbaal foreshadows, in many ways, the diplomacy between medieval kings and their church. Even the most Catholic monarchs would attempt, from time to time, to bully or outmaneuver the pope. But they would seldom push matters so far as to risk excommunication.

For Tjekerbaal, Egypt represents more than just a spiritual authority. He also calls Egypt the source of learning and craftsmanship. In the ancient world—and particularly in ancient Egypt, as we have seen—little distinction was made between the practical and the mystical. Egyptian physicians, for example, were just as likely to prescribe spells, amulets, and magical chants as they were medication. In fact, surviving medical papyri from Egypt suggest that they generally prescribed both, just to be on the safe side.[15]

In the same way, Egyptian craftsmen would have mingled their practical work with magic and mysticism. They would never have dared to lay a foundation, dress a building stone, or forge a bronze idol without muttering the proper incantation, appeasing the relevant spirits, and observing the appropriate taboos. Egyptian craftsmen no doubt imparted these superstitions to their Phoenician apprentices as diligently as they taught the principles of design, construction, and metalsmithy. Precisely this amalgam of science and sorcery seems to have given birth to the earliest Masonic doctrine.

Did Egyptian artisans, in fact, bring Freemasonry to Phoenicia? Did they induct Phoenician craftsmen into the Mysteries of Ptah? It appears likely that they did. We may never prove that "Hiram Abiff" was really the Grand Master of a Tyrian Lodge or that he ever initiated Solomon into its rites. But, in the next chapter, we will examine compelling evidence that the Egyptian god Ptah ruled over the arts and crafts of Phoenicia as firmly as Amun ruled over Tjekerbaal of Byblos.

CHAPTER 33

THE CRAFTY ONE

"A MONG THE NATIONS IN TOUCH WITH THE GREEKS," WROTE THE Jewish historian Josephus, in the first century A.D., "it was the Phoenicians who made the largest use of writing both for the ordinary affairs of life and for the commemoration of public events. Of this I think I need say nothing, as the facts are universally admitted."[1]

Scholars puzzled over this statement by Josephus for hundreds of years. It seemed incredible to them that Josephus would single out the Phoenicians, of all people, as the nation that "made the largest use of writing." Virtually nothing was left of their literature. Beyond a few weathered inscriptions, the only pieces of Phoenician writing that anyone had ever seen were excerpts of the so-called *Phoenician History* of Sanchuniathon, quoted by Bishop Eusebius of Caesarea in A.D. 314. Sanchuniathon, a Phoenician priest, had allegedly copied the myths and legends of his country from inscribed columns in the Temple of Melkart in Tyre, after the temple was ruined by an earthquake. Scholars believe that he lived in the sixth or seventh century B.C. (though some have placed him as early as the second millennium B.C.).[2] But no one knew for certain if Sanchuniathon had ever really existed.

The last great Phoenician library had disappeared in 146 B.C. when the Romans captured Carthage. Before burning the city and demolishing

THE CRAFTY ONE   199

its buildings, the Roman general Scipio gave its entire library to the Numidians—an African people who had been allies and vassals of the Carthaginians.³ At that point, the books vanish from history. Their fate remains one of the mysteries of archaeology.

Bereft of written documents, scholars of ancient Phoenicia were forced, for many years, to rely mainly on guesswork, supplemented with a few scanty references in the Bible and in Greco-Roman literature. All of that changed, however, in 1928. A farmer, ploughing his field at a place called Ras Shamra, on the Syrian coast, accidentally stumbled upon an underground passageway leading to a vaulted tomb.⁴ He had discovered the lost city of Ugarit—a once-mighty port that had been destroyed by the Sea Peoples around 1200 B.C. and never rebuilt.

Ugarit was a little too far north to be considered Phoenician in the strictest sense. Scholars have traditionally applied the word *Phoenician* only to the coastal cities of ancient Lebanon, such as Byblos, Tyre, Sidon, and Arvad.⁵ However, many experts now believe that the Greeks—who gave us the word *Phoenician*—would probably not have made so fine a distinction. They would probably have seen no difference between the people of Ugarit and those along the Lebanese coast and would have called both of them Phoinikes.⁶ Ugarit was, after all, just as much a seafaring power as the Phoenician cities. Moreover, its culture and religion were so close to those of Phoenicia as to be indistinguishable.

It was the cultural similarity between Phoenicia and Ugarit that made the find so exciting. For Ugarit yielded one thing that no Phoenician site ever had—writing. And lots of it. Archaeologists found a huge store of clay tablets from the late Bronze Age, most of them inscribed in a Semitic language called Ugaritic, very similar to the Phoenician tongue. The tablets included not only administrative records, but also long sagas of the gods, goddesses, and heroes of Ugarit—most of whom were identical with the gods and heroes of the Phoenicians. For the first time, scholars had found a window into the Phoenician soul.

Chief among the Ugaritic—and Phoenician—gods was Baal. Readers of the Bible would have recognized his name instantly. It was the worship of Baal, the cruel and sensuous god of the Canaanites, that provided the greatest temptation to the Israelites, who were constantly forsaking the true God of Abraham for Baal's seductive—and often highly sexual—rituals: "Then the Israelites did evil in the eyes of the Lord and served the Baals. They forsook the Lord, the God of their fathers, who had brought them out of Egypt. . . . They provoked the Lord to anger, because they forsook him and served Baal."[7]

Needless to say, the texts of Ugarit presented Baal in a considerably more favorable light—as the lord of earth, sky, thunder, and fertility. His saga is among the most important of the great epic poems of Ugarit. It begins with a great battle between Baal and Yam, the god of the sea. Baal wins the battle, just as the earliest Phoenician seafarers long ago won their first battles against the waves. Having achieved this victory, Baal suddenly realizes that he still lacks one thing—a palace worthy of his new greatness.

"Lo, Baal has no house like the gods," he complains to El and Asherath, the king and queen of heaven, "no court like the sons of Athirat."[8] After gaining permission to build a new palace, Baal seeks the help of a god named Kothar-wa-Hasis—whose name means "skillful and wise."[9] He is the Ugaritic patron of arts and crafts—a metalsmith, sculptor, and architect. It was Kothar-wa-Hasis who made the two magic clubs with which Baal vanquished the sea god Yam.[10] Now Kothar-wa-Hasis uses his skills to build a home of surpassing beauty for Baal, "a palace of silver and gold, a palace of pure lapis lazuli," in the words of the Ugaritic text.[11]

Who is Kothar-wa-Hasis? Often called simply Kothar in the texts, he seems to be the Ugaritic version of a divine craftsman worshiped all over Syria-Palestine.[12] The Canaanites of Ebla called him Kasharu.[13] The Phoenicians called him Khousor.[14] But, everywhere, his name appears to have had a similar meaning—"skillful," "clever," "crafty," the "crafty one."

An intriguing hint as to the real identity of this "skillful" god can be found in the tablets of Ugarit. In praising Kothar, one epic declares, "His seat is at Memphis, his throne is at Kaphtor."[15] Memphis, of course, is a city in Egypt, and Kaphtor is the place that the Egyptians called Keftiu—the island of Crete. Clearly, the text implies that Kothar is more than just a god of the Canaanites. His power is international in scope. The point is made even more clearly in the saga of the hero Danel, where Kothar is twice described as the "Lord of all divine Memphis."[16]

As previously discussed, Memphis was the capital of Egypt during the Old and Middle Kingdoms. The only "Lord of Memphis" recognized by the Egyptians was the craftsman god Ptah, whose temple cult dominated that city. In granting the title Lord of Memphis to Kothar-wa-Hasis, the Ugaritic tablets unmistakably imply that Ptah and Kothar are one and the same god. Not surprisingly, the Phoenician god Khousor was also identified with Ptah in ancient times. Archaeologist Sarah P. Morris acknowledges that there was a "cult connection" between Kothar, Khousor, and the Egyptian Lord of Memphis.[17]

It is this cult connection that will most likely lead us to the roots of ancient Freemasonry. When the Phoenicians first learned about Ptah from their Egyptian teachers, they appear to have named him Khousor—the "crafty one." Perhaps *Khousor* was not even a real name, originally, but simply a respectful title applied to the god Ptah, much as the Israelites sometimes referred to their god, Yahweh, as El-Shaddai, the "Almighty," or El-Elyon, the "All-Highest."

As such, the title *Kothar,* or *Khousor,* bears a strong resemblance to the Greek name *Daidalos,* which also means "skillful" or "crafty" in Greek. Daidalos, the legendary sculptor, architect, and inventor is, thus, the "skillful one," just like Kothar. Does this mean that Daidalos is the Greek version of Ptah? Well, no, not exactly. That honor probably goes to the god Hephaistos. As previously noted, Greek writers routinely used the name *Hephaistos* when referring to the Egyptian god Ptah, as when Herodotos observed that it was the pharaoh Min who built the "large and very remarkable temple of Hephaistos" in Memphis.[18]

Like Ptah, Hephaistos is a god of fire and the patron of all arts and crafts. Like Ptah, Hephaistos had his own workshop or smithy, where he forged such wonders as the shield of Achilles. To the Greeks, Hephaistos was the bringer of civilization. A Homeric hymn, probably written in the sixth or seventh century B.C., states that before Hephaistos taught people to build houses, they lived in caves "like beasts":

> He who taught, along with gray-eyed Athena,
> shining gifts for mortal men, they who used to live
> in caves in the mountains, like beasts,
> But now, having learned arts through Hephaistos, famous in crafts,
> easily they dwell all the year round in their own homes.[19]

Experts have failed to find any convincing etymology for the name *Hephaistos,* either in Greek or in any other European language. They do not know what the name means or where it came from.[20] But Egypt seems a likely source. The earliest reference to Hephaistos was found inscribed on a tablet on the island of Crete. It was written in the so-called Linear B script used by the Mycenaean Greeks during the Late Bronze Age, from about 1400 to 1100 B.C. The word found by archaeologists was *a-pa-i-ti-jo*—apparently, a very old version of *Hephaistios*, which could refer to either a person, a festival, or a month named after the god Hephaistos.

Working backwards from *apaitijo*, linguists have deduced that the actual name of the god Hephaistos, in Mycenaean times, was probably *A-pa-i-to*.[21] This is, in fact, very close to *Ptah*. The only real difference lies in the vowels, whose placement and pronunciation, as we have seen, are largely a matter of guesswork in Egyptian. Ptah's name, for all we know, may really have sounded a lot like *Apaito* in Egyptian. And, indeed, Martin Bernal believes that the name "Hephaistos" very likely derived from that of the Egyptian god Ptah. [22]

The fact that the earliest reference to Hephaistos has turned up on the island of Crete reminds us of the Ugaritic formula, "His seat is at Memphis, his throne is at Kaphtor." Is it only a coincidence that Hephaistos is first mentioned on Kaphtor, the very island where Kothar-wa-Hasis is said to have his "throne"? If so, then the coincidence goes even deeper. For it is also on the island of Crete that we find the first hint of a cult of Daidalos—the same cult that later grew into the craftsmen's guild called the Sons of Daidalos.

Tablets have been found at the ancient Cretan site of Knossos, also from the Late Bronze Age and also inscribed in Linear B, in which offerings of oil are dedicated to a shrine called *da-da-re-jo*. Sarah Morris believes that this word is an early form of *Daidaleion*—the "Shrine of Daidalos."[23] If Morris is correct, this could indicate that Daidalos—the legendary Athenian sculptor and architect—was already worshiped as a god in Crete during the Late Bronze Age. But another possibility is also likely.

During this early period, the term *daidalos* may actually have referred to Ptah himself. The best evidence for this is a poem by Pindar—who was born about 518 B.C.—in which a knife made by Hephaistos is called a knife "of Daidalos." Obviously, the knife could not have been made by both Hephaistos and Daidalos at the same time. One scholar has therefore proposed that Pindar really meant to say that the knife was made by Hephaistos daidalos—

"Hephaistos the skillful"—and that Pindar abbreviated the name simply as *daidalos*—"the skillful one."[24]

If true, this would make *Daidalos* a direct parallel of the Ugaritic name *Kothar* or the Phoenician *Khousor*—both of which also appear to mean "the skillful one" and also apparently refer to the Egyptian god Ptah. The Shrine of Daidalos in Bronze Age Crete might therefore have really been a shrine to "Hephaistos the skillful," rather than a shrine to the sculptor Daidalos. The Athenian sculptor may have ended up with the name *Daidalos* for much the same reason that one Ugaritic silversmith named himself *Ktrmlk*—"Kothar is king."[25]

If Daidalos really named himself after Hephaistos, this would explain why the two often seem to exchange roles in Greek mythology, almost as if the ancient Greeks were not quite sure which was which. Thus, when Theseus escapes from the Labyrinth, some versions of the story say that it is Daidalos who helps him, while others put Hephaistos in this role. One scholar has even called Daidalos a *doppelgänger*, or "double," of Hephaistos.[26] As such, Daidalos would play a role in the Greek cult of Hephaistos strangely similar to that played by Imhotep in the cult of Ptah.

We introduced Imhotep, in chapter 16, as the man who designed the first pyramid for the pharaoh Djoser. Thus, Imhotep, like Daidalos, was both an architect and an inventor. But the parallel goes further. An inscription from the reign of Djoser indicates that Imhotep was also known as a carpenter and a *sculptor*—just like Daidalos. The inscription honors Imhotep with these titles: "Seal-bearer of the King of Lower Egypt, one who is near the head of the King, Director of the Great Mansion, Royal representative, High Priest of Heliopolis, Imhotep, the carpenter and the sculptor."[27]

After his death, Imhotep was named the "son of Ptah" and given his own cult. The same thing happened to Daidalos. In the traditional genealogies of Athens, Daidalos was listed as a direct descendant of the god Hephaistos and was given his own special shrine, the Daidaleion.

This is not to imply that Daidalos and Imhotep were one and the same. Imhotep was unquestionably a real person, born in Egypt, and it is quite likely that Daidalos too was a man of flesh and blood, born in Athens. If these two men really lived, they could not possibly have been identical. However, it is just possible that their *legends* became entwined, long after their deaths.

Many scholars have pointed out that the story of Daidalos's sojourn in Egypt does not occur in most versions of the tale. The usual version has Daidalos traveling directly to Crete after fleeing Athens and never visiting Egypt at all. When Diodoros claimed that Daidalos won "great fame because of his genius" in Egypt and received "divine honors" from the Egyptians, he may have been confusing part of Imhotep's legend with the story of Daidalos.[28] On this, we can only speculate.

It requires little speculation, however, to conclude that both Daidalos and Imhotep were devotees of a single religion—the cult of Ptah. This is strongly suggested by the extensive connections between the cults of Ptah, Hephaistos, Kothar, and Khousor, so dramatically documented in Sarah Morris's 1992 book, *Daidalos and the Origins of Greek Art*. To the extent that anything resembling Freemasonry existed in the Bronze Age world, Daidalos and Imhotep were clearly two of its leading avatars.

At this point, we have come very far toward proving that Sokrates was a follower of the Egyptian god Ptah. By calling himself a descendant of Daidalos and by taking part in the craftsmen's guild called the Sons of Daidalos, Sokrates claimed a lineage that stretched back to the foundation of Egypt, circa 3125 B.C. It was Ptah whom the Greeks extolled for bringing them out of the caves and into fine houses. It was Ptah's international cult that inspired and taught Greek craftsmen. In view of these facts, it would seem reasonable to suggest that it was Sokrates—the stonemason-turned-philosopher—who first instructed Plato in the mysteries of the Demiourgos: the Great Architect of the Universe.

Of course, none of this justifies George G. M. James's extravagant assertion that Sokrates was a Master Mason. We have succeeded only in showing that Sokrates' family and guild may have traced their lineage back to the Egyptian cult of Ptah. To prove George G. M. James completely correct, we would have to go much further. We would have to demonstrate a direct connection between the cult of Daidalos and modern Freemasonry—in particular, a connection with the British lodges that announced themselves to the world in 1717. At first glance, bridging such a 2,000-year gap would seem an impossible task. Yet, surprisingly, the evidence for such a connection has turned out to be quite strong.

CHAPTER 34

THE GRAIL KNIGHTS

ON A LONELY SEASIDE PROMONTORY, SOME MILES SOUTH OF THE Israeli port of Haifa, stand the ruins of a Crusader castle called Athlit. It was built in 1218 by an order of knights who called themselves the Poor Fellow-Soldiers of Christ and the Temple of Solomon. Understandably, the group seldom used its full name. Sometimes it called itself the Knights of the Temple of Solomon, other times just the Order of the Temple. But its favorite abbreviation—and the one by which history knows it best—was the Knights Templar.[1]

The castle of Athlit was excavated by archaeologists in 1932. On its grounds they found a cemetery with nearly a hundred graves, most of them long since worn smooth of any inscriptions. But some still bore a few markings. Of these, two graves were found carved with what could only be called Masonic insignia, such as the square, hammer, and plumb stone. The Masonic nature of these emblems was confirmed by the fact that one of the tombstones bearing them evidently belonged to a man holding the title of Master of the Templar Masons.

Other Templar graves have been found, mostly in Europe, bearing similar emblems. But the tombstones at Athlit—a castle occupied by the Templars only from 1218 to 1261—clearly constitute what British writers Michael Baigent and Richard Leigh have called "the earliest known incidence of gravestones bearing Masonic devices."[2] Just who were the Knights Templar, and what did they have to do with Freemasonry?

The Templars were an order of warrior monks, sworn to poverty, chastity, and obedience. Their official mission was to protect the hordes of Christian pilgrims who had descended on the Holy Land following Jerusalem's capture by the Crusaders in 1099. But some researchers have concluded that the real purpose of the Templars was quite different from their official one. When the first nine Templars arrived in Jerusalem in 1119, they completely ignored the pilgrims. Instead, they set up their headquarters in the Al-Aqsa Mosque, right next to the ancient site of Solomon's Temple, and started *digging.*

The enthusiasm with which the Templars burrowed into the Temple Mount led British researcher Graham Hancock to speculate that they might have been searching for some treasure or relic reputed to have been buried beneath Solomon's Temple. The southern end of the Temple Mount, where the knights lived, was honeycombed with subterranean chambers, carved out of the rock by King Herod the Great during the Roman era. The Templars greatly enlarged these catacombs, fitting them with elaborate arches, vaults, and roofs.[3] They also dug new shafts deep into the living rock.[4]

Nobody knows if the Knights Templar ever found what they were seeking. They stayed in Jerusalem only until 1187, when the Muslim king Saladin recaptured the city. By 1291, the Muslims had driven the Templars from Palestine altogether, and by 1312, their order was officially dissolved. Nevertheless, the Templar legacy lives on. To this day, rumors and legends abound that the Knights Templar acquired some kind of secret, mystical knowledge during their 172 years in Palestine.

The Templars may not have found anything beneath the rock of Jerusalem's Temple Mount. But they do seem to have gained some uncanny store of wisdom. In the brief 194 years of their existence, the tiny band of nine French knights grew to become one of the largest, wealthiest, and most powerful religious orders in Europe.

Thanks to their glamorous reputation as defenders of the Holy Land, every king in Christendom competed to shower the Templars with riches and estates. In 1131, the king of Aragon actually bequeathed a third of his kingdom to the Templars.[5] Before long, the Order of the Temple held lands and castles all over Europe and Palestine. It soon branched into business, acquiring its own fleet of ships and making a fortune in trade.[6] The uniform of the Templars— a brilliant white mantle, decorated with a red *patté* cross—became a familiar sight in every royal court, harbor, and counting house of Europe.

Popular belief holds that Jewish moneylenders were the chief financiers of medieval Europe. But, in fact, the Templars did a far brisker business. They operated a full-scale international banking system, taking deposits, issuing letters of credit, and lending money at interest rates that could soar as high as 60 percent for late payments. Henry III of England once found himself so deeply in debt to the Templars that he had to turn over the crown jewels as collateral.[7]

The greatest and most lasting glory of the Templars, however, lay in neither their military prowess nor their fabulous wealth. It lay in their skill as *architects*. Some of the finest churches and castles of the Middle Ages were built by Templars. Everywhere they settled, they left their distinctive round churches—modeled after the circular Church of the Holy Sepulchre that stands over Christ's tomb in Jerusalem.[8] The archaeologist C. N. Johns, after excavating the Templar castle of Athlit, remarked on the "exceptional" skill of its builders, which far exceeded ordinary medieval standards.[9]

In his 1992 book, *The Sign and the Seal,* Graham Hancock suggests that the Templars' prowess in building stemmed from a secret architectural tradition, inherited from ancient times, to which the Templars had somehow become privy. One likely source of that tradition may have been the Cistercian abbot Bernard of Clairvaux—later to become Saint Bernard. Hancock points out that the Templars owed their very existence to this powerful cleric, who interceded with Pope Honarius II to gain approval for the new order.

Bernard was known as a leading proponent of sacred geometry and Gothic architecture. During the building of Chartres Cathedral, Bernard was constantly behind the scenes, plying the Bishop of Chartres with his aesthetic advice and meeting frequently with the masons and architects.[10] To Bernard, the geometry of a church was everything. "There must be no decoration," he once declared, "only proportion." On another occasion, Bernard cryptically remarked, "What is God? He is length, width, height and depth."[11]

Where Bernard managed to acquire these mystical notions, we can only guess. But their influence on medieval Europe was profound. Graham Hancock goes so far as to suggest that Bernard—and his protégés, the Templars—were largely responsible for the explosion in Gothic building that erupted during the mid-twelfth century.[12] The Templars not only formed their own guilds of masons and craftsmen, but also sponsored other existing guilds.[13] Their influence over the building trade became every bit as pervasive as their hold on banking and finance.

Shortly after the founding of the Templar order a new craze swept Europe—chivalry. Most people associate the Middle Ages with the kind of high honor and courtly love that prevails in Hollywood romances of King Arthur's court. But, before the Templars, such chivalry was virtually unknown. The real King Arthur—who is believed to have been a British warlord of the fifth century A.D.—would likely have been a crude and violent man, prone to brigandage and rape. Early Celtic legends offer a far less appealing portrait of Arthur than does the Hollywood screen.

In one of these stories, a young couple approaches Arthur for help while he and his knights, Kai and Bedwyr, are playing dice on a hilltop. The woman, Gwladys, pleads with Arthur to defend her. She has just eloped with her lover Gwynnlwy, and her father is riding in pursuit of them, determined to kill Gwynnlwy and take Gwladys back home. But if Gwladys wants help, she has clearly come to the wrong place. The story relates that Arthur is so smitten by Gwladys's beauty that he considers killing Gwynnlwy himself and taking Gwladys for his wife.

Fortunately, Kai knows his master well enough to guess what is on his mind. "Are you not ashamed to think such thoughts," Kai scolds him, "when you have always promised to help those who need protection?" Sheepishly, Arthur admits that Kai is right. After frightening off the girl's father, Arthur allows the couple to go in peace. We can only guess what might have happened, though, had Kai not been around to prod his master's sluggish conscience.[14]

Another early legend portrays Arthur as a thief. It tells how he sneaked up one day on a saintly hermit named Padern while the man was asleep, intent on stealing a valuable tunic that Padern had received from the patriarch of Jerusalem. As soon as Arthur grabbed the tunic, however, the ground yawned beneath him, swallowing Arthur up to his chin. Padern set him free only after Arthur humbly begged his forgiveness.[15]

Such was knightly honor at the dawn of the Middle Ages. The real Arthur may not have been quite as loutish as he appears in early British folklore. But, clearly, the audience who enjoyed these tales regarded such behavior as normal. Cruelty and lawlessness were endemic among medieval knights. Their poor example was emulated at every level of society. As late as the mid-eleventh century, Bishop Burchard of Worms decried the condition of one parish in these terms: "The subjects of St. Peter's Cathedral are murdering each other like wild beasts. They will suddenly arise and attack people for no reason, simply because they happen to be drunk or want to show off. . . . Moreover, the murderers are not only unrepentant but they go about, boasting of their deeds."[16]

By the twelfth century, however, change was in the air. A new breed of knight had arisen, eager to win renown as a defender of the innocent, a champion of noble ladies, and a model of Christian piety. What sparked this amazing metamorphosis was a sudden proliferation of verse—in particular, a spate of lengthy poems glorifying, of all people, King Arthur! This was not, however, the old King Arthur of Celtic legend. The barbarian warlord had undergone a literary rehabilitation. Arthur had been transformed by twelfth-century poets into a wise and godly ruler whose knights of the Round Table aspired to the highest standards of honor, justice, and religious devotion.

Like so many other advances in medieval civilization, the taming of King Arthur seems, in large part, to have been engineered by the Templars. It was accomplished through the Templars' sponsorship of a popular new literary genre called the Grail Romance—epic poems that recounted Arthur's legendary quest for the Holy Grail.

The first of these romances, entitled *Le Conte du Graal*—"The Story of the Grail"—was penned by Chrétien de Troyes around 1182. It may have been only a coincidence that Chrétien was sponsored by the Count of Champagne—who also happened to be a key sponsor of the Knights Templar.[17] But there was no mistaking the

Templar involvement in the German Grail epic, *Parzival*. Its author, Wolfram von Eschenbach, claimed to have learned the Grail story from a certain "Kyot de Provence"—whom scholars later identified as a Templar scribe named Guiot de Provins.[18]

Not surprisingly, considering their provenance, the Grail Romances tended to paint the Templars in heroic colors. The Knights of the Temple appear in many of the poems as keepers of the Grail—the magical, life-giving cup from which Christ drank at the Last Supper. Medieval readers of *The Perlesvaus*, for example, would have instantly recognized the Grail Knights as Templars by their white mantles, imprinted with a large red cross. In *Parzival*, Wolfram von Eschenbach made the point even more plainly, stating explicitly that the "guardians of the Grail" were "Templars."[19]

What did it all mean? What was this Holy Grail that the Templars claimed—or at least were rumored—to possess? By most accounts, the Grail was the cup of Christ. In *Parzival*, however, it was a stone—perhaps linked with the fabled Philosopher's Stone of the alchemists, reputed to have the power of changing base metal into gold. Recent best-sellers have speculated that the Grail might represent anything from the lost Ark of the Covenant to the royal blood of Israel's House of David, allegedly restored through the Merovingian dynasty of France.

In short, nobody really knows. But of one thing we can be certain. The legend of the Grail—and the mysterious knightly order that appears to have promulgated that legend—wrought extraordinary changes in medieval society. There can be no doubt that the Knights Templar left Europe more beautiful, more orderly, and more *civilized* than they had found it. In that respect, they proved faithful heirs to an ancient tradition, of which Daidalos, Imhotep, and Sokrates were leading exemplars.

Long ago, the Sons of Daidalos also brought beauty and order to a barbarous Europe. Like the Knights Templar, they too were architects, craftsmen, and stonemasons, masters of technical skills, yet at the same time poets and dreamers, who saw in their craft a transcendent metaphor for the highest of human yearnings.

The similarity between these two groups may have been coincidental. But it probably wasn't. Compelling evidence suggests that the Knights Templar knew all about the Sons of Daidalos and consciously sought to emulate them. Indeed, as we shall see in the following chapter, their inheritance from the Daidalidai may well have passed in an unbroken chain, handed down from mason to mason, across the incredible span of more than 1,500 years.

CHAPTER 35

THE MURDERED
APPRENTICE

FREEMASONS HAVE LONG REGARDED THE TEMPLARS AS A CRUCIAL source of their occult doctrines. Many historians would agree. In case after case, the most cherished rites, symbols, and traditions of the Masons have been traced directly to some Templar forerunner. The appearance of Masonic emblems on 600-year-old Templar tombstones at Athlit is only one of many such instances. Yet, even if we accept the Templar origin of Freemasonry, we are still left with a nagging question: Where did the Templars acquire their secret doctrines in the first place?

One possible answer lies in a remote Scottish church named Rosslyn Chapel. The church overlooks the wild and wooded canyon of the North Esk River, a few miles south of Edinburgh. Built in the fifteenth century, Rosslyn Chapel is best known for its elaborate and mysterious carvings, many devoted to pagan and magical motifs. Figures such as the Green Man—a Celtic fertility god—peer out from every nook and cranny, hinting at secrets from some darker, more primitive past.[1]

Perhaps the most haunting of Rosslyn Chapel's carvings appears over the western door—the face of a young man with a large gash on his right forehead. According to legend, he is the Murdered Apprentice. The woman who appears on his right is called his Widowed Mother. Legend holds that a master mason working on Rosslyn Chapel left for Rome one day, leaving a certain column unfinished. The master returned to find that his apprentice had completed the job for him. Seeing that his apprentice had done the work more beautifully than he ever could, the envious mason killed his protégé with a blow to the head.[2] To this day, the wondrously carved "Apprentice Pillar" stands at the eastern end of Rosslyn Chapel.[3]

Some readers may have noticed that this tale bears a strong resemblance to another story of a "murdered apprentice"—the legend of Daidalos and his nephew Talos, recounted in chapter 29. Like the master mason of Rosslyn Chapel, Daidalos murdered his apprentice when he saw that the boy's talents surpassed his own. The Greek myth also relates that upon hearing news of Talos's death, his mother, Perdix—Daidalos's sister—hanged herself in despair.[4] Both Talos and Perdix were subsequently worshiped as gods, immortalized in shrines on the Athenian Acropolis[5]—just as the Murdered Apprentice and his Widowed Mother were commemorated in stone at Rosslyn Chapel.

There seems little doubt that the legend of the Murdered Apprentice served some ritual purpose in the minds of whoever built Rosslyn Chapel. Equally certain is that the builders of the chapel based this tale on the story of Daidalos and Talos. But why? What interest did anyone up in the wilds of fifteenth-century Scotland have in an obscure Greek myth about a craftsman who killed his apprentice? Until recently, there was no sure answer to this question.

A possible answer has emerged, however, from the investigations of two British researchers. In 1978, Michael Baigent and Richard Leigh made a stunning discovery. While in Scotland to research a television documentary on the Templars, they stumbled on a curious graveyard in the village of Kilmartin, in Argyll. It contained some eighty tombstones, dating from the fourteenth to eighteenth centuries, all marked with Templar or Masonic emblems.[6] Subsequent research disclosed that the Kilmartin churchyard was only one of sixteen Templar burial grounds in Argyll.[7] Baigent and Leigh had found compelling proof that a colony of Templars lived in Scotland generations after the Order had supposedly been disbanded.

The fate of the Templar Order has long been cloaked in mystery. On Friday, October 13, 1307, all Europe was shocked when King Philippe IV of France suddenly arrested every Templar in his domain. Within a few weeks, hundreds had confessed to a shocking list of crimes, ranging from the worship of pagan idols to the practice of obscene sexual rites and the denial of Christ.

Since these confessions were extracted under torture, it is hard to know how much of them to believe. That the Templars held unorthodox beliefs seems evident from the mystical allegories permeating the Grail Romances. Nevertheless, most historians agree that Philippe IV's attack on the Templars probably owed more to his greed for Templar properties than to any sudden attack of religious zeal on his part.

Rightly or wrongly, the pope was soon persuaded to withdraw his support from the Templar Order. On November 22, 1307, he called on all Christian kings to hunt down and arrest the Templars wherever they might be found. Hundreds were burned at the stake. But many more disappeared into thin air. Indeed, the entire Templar fleet and all the treasures of the Order vanished without a trace. Rumors circulated for years about where the fugitive Templars might have fled.

Scotland was often mentioned as a possible destination. One English Templar had actually confessed to his interrogators that some of his brethren had fled there.[8] Moreover, Scotland seemed a likely hideout, since it lay outside the pope's jurisdiction. The Scottish king, Robert the Bruce, had been excommunicated since 1306, when he murdered his rival, John Comyn, in a church.[9] Moreover, Bruce was engaged in a savage war against England and could not afford to be choosy about his allies. He would undoubtedly have welcomed such highly trained warriors as the Templars, no matter what accusations had been made against them. Indeed, persistent rumors have suggested, over the centuries, that it was a charge of Templar cavalry that won the day for Bruce in 1314 at the battle of Bannockburn, where Scotland finally gained its independence.[10]

The Templar cemeteries discovered by Baigent and Leigh provided strong evidence that the legend was true. It seemed that a large contingent of Templars had indeed found refuge in Scotland. In their 1989 book, *The Temple and the Lodge*, Baigent and Leigh further revealed that the Templar fugitives had intermarried with the

Scottish clans through the years, passing on their architectural and occult traditions to succeeding generations. One of the clans most heavily saturated with Templar lore, according to Baigent and Leigh, was that of the Sinclairs. Of this ancient dynasty, a cryptic seventeenth-century letter states: "The Lairds of Roslin have been great architects and patrons of building for many generations. They are obliged to receive the Mason's word which is a secret signal masons have throughout the world to know one another by."[11]

In 1441 King James II of Scotland appointed one of these Lairds of Roslin—Sir William Sinclair—as "Patron and protector of Scottish Masons."[12] The title was hereditary, meant to remain in the Sinclair family forever. Why they merited such an honor is unknown. But it is clear that William Sinclair was a special man. Not only was he trained as an architect—unusual in itself for a Scottish lord—but he was evidently privy to whatever secret architectural tradition the Templars had brought with them to Scotland. Sinclair sought to immortalize that tradition in the carvings and sacred proportions of Rosslyn Chapel.

Sinclair undertook the building of Rosslyn Chapel in 1446.[13] It was finished forty years later by his son Oliver. If the Sinclairs were as crucial in the formation of modern Freemasonry as Baigent and Leigh assert, then the arcane messages inscribed on the walls of Rosslyn Chapel provide an unusually clear window into Masonic thinking more than 200 years before the brotherhood went public. Judging by those carvings alone, we would have to conclude that the tale of the Murdered Apprentice was of central importance to Masons in the fifteenth century.

It seems a fair bet that the Daidalos story—and the ritual it represented—was directly inherited from the Knights Templar who took refuge in Scotland after 1307. But where had the Templars learned of this myth? And what did it mean to them?

One hint comes from Etruscan artifacts found in Italy. The Etruscans dominated Italy's northwestern coast from about 900 to 300 B.C. They were a wealthy, seafaring people, who also happened to have been great architects and engineers. The Etruscans taught the Romans to build roads, aqueducts, and even the so-called Roman arch—which should more accurately be called the Etruscan arch. Like the Romans, the Etruscans owed much of their civilization to Greece. They wrote with Greek letters, made Grecian art, and worshiped Greek gods. It was probably from the Greeks that the Etruscans learned to build.

Several Etruscan artifacts have been found featuring what appear to be early Masonic emblems—all associated with carvings or statues of Daidalos and his craftsman son Ikaros.[14] The oldest of these is a gold seal, from about 470 B.C.,[15] on which the embossed figures of Daidalos and Ikaros are clearly labeled with the Etruscan forms of their names. Both wear the traditional short *chiton* of the Greek artisan. In his hands, Daidalos carries a saw and an adze, Ikaros a double axe and a T-square.[16]

It is provocative to find the cult of Daidalos thriving in Italy at the very moment in history when architecture and civil engineering took root in that country. Even more provocative, however, is the fact that these early followers of Daidalos appear to have used craftsmen's tools as cult emblems—a practice they shared with the Knights Templar and the Freemasons. The use of such emblems, as we have seen, has been a distinguishing hallmark of Masonic groups throughout history. There is evidence that it goes all the way back to Egypt.

The Egyptian Opening of the Mouth ceremony, discussed in chapter 29, employed craftsmen's tools—specifically the adze and the chisel—for ritual purposes. In that ceremony, a priest, playing the role of Ptah, would touch the mouth of the statue with a chisel, to impart the gift of speech. A priest playing the god Anubis would then touch it with an adze.[17]

Craftsmen's tools may also have inspired the forms of many Egyptian hieroglyphs, if we can believe the folklore handed down by Diodoros. In his description of the Egyptian writing system, he notes, "Now it is found that the forms of their letters take the shape of animals of every kind, and of the members of the human body, and of implements and *especially carpenters' tools.*"[18]

All of this suggests that the ritual significance assigned to tools and implements by the Etruscan worshipers of Daidalos may have had its origin in Egyptian cults. We have already seen how this tradition might have been passed from the Egyptians to the Greeks, and then to the Etruscans. But how would it have made the leap from the Etruscans to the Templars? In fact, the route is fairly direct.

The Etruscan tradition lived on in Italy through the *collegia* or guilds of Roman masons and architects. It was mainly from these

Roman *collegia* that medieval builders later inherited their architectural know-how. It is also from these *collegia* that Masons claim to have inherited at least some of their esoteric doctrines. If this is true, we can reasonably suppose that the Greek cult of Daidalos was one of those inherited doctrines. The Romans, after all, revered Daidalos just as highly as had the Greeks and Etruscans. And the wall reliefs at Rosslyn Chapel suggest that the Templars too held Daidalos in high esteem. In fact, the cult of Daidalos appears to represent one of the clearest examples of an unbroken Masonic tradition, stretching from Bronze Age Greece to at least the fifteenth century A.D.

But why Daidalos? And why Talos? What did the legend of the Murdered Apprentice really mean to builders and masons? What power did it hold to compel its faithful preservation nearly fifteen centuries into the Christian era? To answer this question, we must look beyond the story itself. We must uncover its hidden meaning, coming face to face, in the process, with an old and terrible secret—a legacy of shame inherited from the very birth of human civilization.

CHAPTER 36

THE CURSE OF CAIN

ACCORDING TO THE BIBLE, ADAM AND EVE HAD TWO SONS, NAMED Cain and Abel. Cain became a farmer and Abel a herdsman. One day, the brothers went before the Lord to offer the fruits of their labors. Abel brought "fat portions from the firstborn of his flock." Cain, on the other hand, being a farmer, brought "the fruits of the soil." For some reason that the Bible does not explain, God accepted Abel's sacrifice but rejected that of his brother, Cain. Burning with resentment, Cain lured his brother into a field and slew him.

"Your brother's blood cries out to you from the ground," said the Lord. "Now you are under a curse. . . . When you work the ground, it will no longer yield its crops for you. You will be a restless wanderer on the earth."[1]

Just as God predicted, Cain left his homeland and wandered the earth, finally coming to a place called Nod. There a curious thing happened. Despite the curse, Cain and his family prospered. In fact, Cain built a city in Nod—the very first city in the world—and named it Enoch, after his son. Cain's descendants went on to win renown as the founders of nations and the inventors of many arts.

His great-great-great-great-grandson Jabal, for example, became "the father of those who live in tents and raise livestock." Jabal's brother Jubal became "the father of all who play the harp and flute."

As for their half-brother Tubal-Cain, he became the world's first metalsmith. The book of Genesis says that he "forged all kinds of tools out of bronze and iron."[2]

Some curse! Judging from the biblical account, it would seem that Cain and his "accursed" brood were chosen by God for no less a task than civilizing the earth. From Cain and his family arose farming, herding, building, music, and metalsmithy—virtually every civilized art that separates man from beast. Why would God have bestowed such an honor on a sinner who murdered his own brother?

Some modern scholars have suggested a startling answer to this question. They have theorized that Cain and his children achieved all these technological breakthroughs not in *spite* of Cain's crime, but as a direct result of it. According to this theory, the murder—or rather the *sacrifice*—of Abel actually transformed Cain from a simple farmer into a builder of cities.

"The primal homicide," writes Patrick Tierney in his 1989 book, *The Highest Altar: The Story of Human Sacrifice*, "was originally the salvific event which secured urban life, metallurgy, music and animal husbandry for humanity. A seemingly senseless homicide paved the way for civilization. Progress was bought for a price. Part of the price was Abel's death."[3]

As a journalist, Tierney spent six years in the Andes Mountains of South America, researching the cult of human sacrifice that prevails to this day among descendants of the Incas and other Indian communities. In his attempt to explain the phenomenon, Tierney drew upon the work of scholars such as Walter Burkert and Hiam Maccoby, who have concluded that blood sacrifice—and particularly *human* sacrifice—was the spark that lit the first fires of civilization.

"Through solidarity and cooperative organization," writes classicist Walter Burkert, "the sacrificial ritual gave society its form."[4] Indeed, so indispensable was the blood sacrifice to civilized life, in Burkert's view, that he proposed renaming the human species *Homo necans*—"man the killer." In the same vein, a British rabbinical scholar named Hiam Maccoby suggested that Cain was really the first "sacred executioner"—a specially sanctified priest whose job it is to perform the "necessary" but unpleasant task of sacrificing people.[5]

In many societies around the world, both ancient and modern, such sacred executioners are ostracized from the community as punishment for their bloody deeds. But they are also honored, feared, and believed to possess magical powers. Thus, Cain was banished from his homeland. But God also granted him special favor and protection: "But the Lord said to him, 'If anyone kills Cain, he will suffer vengeance seven times over.' Then the Lord put a mark on Cain so that no one who found him would kill him."[6]

In short, Cain seems to walk a fine line between God's favor and condemnation—a predicament familiar to farmers, craftsmen, miners, and other wielders of technology in every primitive society. Deep in every human soul lurks the suspicion, inherited since prehistoric days, that technology is wicked. Those who use it risk God's wrath. Perhaps the most eloquent expression of this Stone Age attitude came from a man named Smohalla, a prophet of the Umatilla Indian tribe: "You ask me to plough the ground? Shall I take a knife and tear my mother's bosom? . . . You ask me to dig for stone? Shall I dig under her skin for her bones? . . . You ask me to cut grass and make hay and sell it, and be rich like white men! But how dare I cut off my mother's hair?"[7]

In Smohalla's view, farming and mining were offensive to Mother Earth. Societies all over the world have shared similar beliefs. When the Greek titan Prometheus first gave fire to man, an enraged Zeus punished Prometheus by chaining him to Mount Elbrus in the Caucasus and sending an eagle to devour his liver every day. Clearly, the gods of Olympus did not wish men to stay warm at night or to cook their food. Similarly, the God of the Bible reacted with dismay when he saw how effectively work proceeded on the Tower of Babel.

But the Lord came down to see the city and the tower that the men were building. The Lord said, "If . . . they have begun to do this, then nothing they plan to do will be impossible for them. Come, let us go down and confuse their language so they will not understand each other." So the Lord scattered them from there over all the earth, and they stopped building the city.[8]

The Jewish *Book of Enoch* actually attributes technology to the intervention of the demon Azazel. This prophetic book was never included in the Bible. However, it was sufficiently well respected by the biblical scribes that it was quoted in the Epistle of Jude 14–15.[9] For 1,500 years, the *Book of Enoch* was lost to Europeans. But, in 1773, the Scottish explorer James Bruce rediscovered the book in Ethiopia.

It may be only a coincidence that Bruce happened to have been a Freemason.[10] But probably it was more than that. The Masons, after all, had long revered the prophet Enoch, whom they identified with the Egyptian god Thoth. According to the *Royal Masonic Cyclopedia*, Enoch was the one who first "taught men the art of building."[11] And it has long been rumored that Bruce's real purpose in visiting Ethiopia was not to search for the source of the Nile, as he claimed, but to recover lost manuscripts.[12]

Bruce never did find the source of the Nile, but he found manuscripts in abundance. Among these were several copies of the *Book of Enoch*, translated from the original Aramaic or Hebrew into an Ethiopian language called Ge'ez. Bruce brought them back to Europe. When the *Book of Enoch* was finally translated into English in 1821, it revealed, for the first time in 1,500 years, many previously unknown details about the corruption of man by wicked angels in the days before the Flood. One of these stories told how the demon Azazel had taught men the use of metal, stone, paint, and mirrors:

> Moreover, Azazel taught men to make swords, knives, shields, breast-plates, the fabrication of mirrors, and the workmanship of bracelets and ornaments, the use of paint, the beautifying of the eyebrows, the use of stones of every valuable and select kind, and of all sorts of dyes, so that the world became altered. Impiety increased: fornication multiplied; and they transgressed and corrupted all their ways.[13]

In the *Book of Enoch*, as in the sacred legends of countless other religions, technology is viewed as a rebellion against God. Farmers, miners, builders, and metalsmiths labor under a curse, their struggle for self-betterment dogged by jealous deities, ever eager to shrivel man's crops and undermine his buildings. In the end, only a bribe of human blood will keep the gods at bay. Only under the spell of this gruesome ritual did our forebears gain the courage to use their crafts and skills. Thus did they earn the title of *Homo necans*—"man the killer."

Of course, many anthropologists still dispute this theory. But the evidence for *Homo necans* seems hard to deny. Is it only a coincidence that the most advanced peoples of the New World—the Aztecs, Mayas, and Incas—were also the very peoples most addicted to human sacrifice? And is it only by chance that such missionaries of technology as the Masons, Templars, and Daidalidai virtually defined themselves by the story of an innocent boy's cold-blooded murder?

Preserved, through countless ages, through the rites and traditions of craftsmen's guilds, the tale of Daidalos and his Murdered Apprentice calls out to us across the centuries. It reminds us of our debt to the murderer Cain. But it reminds us too of our freedom from that ancient horror. We cannot forget that *Homo necans* wrought his first wonders amid the stench of human blood. But, in the end, it was the *renunciation* of human sacrifice that elevated man to the full measure of civilization. It is this last and greatest leap forward that the cult of Daidalos appears to have commemorated. And it seems to have been in Egypt that man took this leap, for the very first time.

CHAPTER 37

OSIRIS THE
CIVILIZER

E VERY SOCIETY HAS ITS OWN STORIES ABOUT GODS AND HEROES who, long ago, introduced farming, metallurgy, architecture, and other civilized arts to mankind. Among the Egyptians, the earliest "civilizing god" appears to have been Ptah. Manetho called him the "first man"—implying that Ptah was originally a human being. The fact that Ptah was always portrayed as a mummy with a distinctly human head—rather than an animal head—seems to confirm that the Egyptians viewed Ptah as a real human ancestor, an earthly king who became a god only after his death. Manetho wrote, "The first man or god in Egypt is Hephaistos [Ptah], who is also renowned . . . as the discoverer of fire. . . . Hephaistos reigned in Egypt for 680 years."[1]

Ptah was clearly the founder of Egyptian civilization. Yet he never attained the popularity of Osiris—widely considered to be Egypt's preeminent civilizing hero. Ptah may have been first, but he was far from the favorite. One reason for Osiris's greater renown may lie in the hidden dynamics of the "curse of Cain." If the theory of *Homo necans* is correct, then Ptah would have brought the curse of Cain upon Egypt from the first moment he harnessed fire and introduced craftsmanship. Ptah would have been remembered with respect, but also with fear, as the bringer of ritual bloodshed to mankind.

On the other hand, Osiris—Ptah's great-great-grandson, according to Manetho—appears to have taken the first step toward *lifting* the curse of Cain and ending the practice of human sacrifice. If the theory of *Homo necans* is correct, then we should hardly be surprised to find that the Egyptians remembered Osiris's achievement with far more warmth and gratitude than they did the bloodier exploits of his great-great-grandfather.

The Egyptians believed that Osiris, like Ptah, had been a mortal man who ruled over an earthly kingdom. Diodoros portrays the mortal King Osiris—not the god he later became—as Egypt's greatest civilizer. Diodoros writes:

> Special esteem at the court of Osiris and Isis was also accorded to those who should invent any of the arts or devise any useful process; consequently, since copper and gold mines had been discovered . . . they fashioned implements with which they killed the wild beasts and worked the soil, and thus in eager rivalry brought the country under cultivation, and they made images of the gods and magnificent golden chapels for their worship. . . . [Osiris] was the first to drink wine and taught mankind at large the culture of the vine and the use of wine. . . . The one most highly honoured by him was Hermes [Thoth], who was endowed with unusual ingenuity for devising things capable of improving the social life of man.[2]

Perhaps the greatest of Osiris's achievements, however, is the one that seems least relevant to us today. "Osiris was the first," writes Diodoros, "to make mankind give up cannibalism."[3] Modern readers can hardly appreciate the importance of this innovation. For us, cannibalism seems too distant a threat to arouse our concern. But for the early Egyptians, the threat was immediate and overpowering.

Inscribed on the walls of Pharaoh Wenis's pyramid, sometime between 2375 and 2345 B.C., is an incantation that Egyptologists have named the "cannibal hymn."[4] In the inscription, Wenis is described as "he who eats men, feeds on gods." He is also called the "divine hawk" who "devours whole" those he "finds on his way." The hymn continues:

It is Shesmu who carves them up for Wenis,
Cooks meals of them for him in his dinner-pots.
Wenis eats their magic, swallows their spirits . . .
And the pots are scraped for him with their women's legs. . . .
Wenis feeds on the lungs of the wise,
Likes to live on their hearts and their magic. . . .
Lo, their power is in Wenis' belly.[5]

No one knows whether Wenis actually partook of such grisly meals as he boasts. These references to cannibalism may have been ritual expressions, left over from earlier and more barbarous days. But the cannibal hymn leaves little doubt that there was a time—however remote—in Egypt's past when human flesh was indeed cooked and eaten. Such rites evidently served as a magical exercise through which the king could acquire the power and wisdom of the people he consumed.

Cannibalism is the oldest and most fundamental form of human sacrifice. In fact, the two practices are nearly inseparable. The Aztecs, for example, habitually devoured the flesh of their sacrificial victims, often served up with maize and chili peppers.[6] According to Pausanias, when the Greeks of Arkadia sacrificed a child, each year, at a secret festival atop Mount Lykaion, they also ate the child's body.[7] It is a thin line that separates *Homo necans* from *Homo edens*—"man the eater"—a line so thin, in fact, that it hardly exists.

By forbidding cannibalism, Osiris set a moral chain reaction into motion. He forced people to question whether it was right to look upon other human beings as a mere source of nutrition—whether magical or culinary. Once that doubt had been planted, it was only a matter of time before all other forms of human sacrifice were brought into question. And, indeed, archaeologists have found clear evidence that ritual murder of all kinds went into a steep decline as the cult of Osiris gained power.

Like Cain and his enterprising brood, the earliest Egyptians seem to have built their civilization on blood. Right up through the First Dynasty (3150–2925 B.C.), the death of any Egyptian king would be followed by a wholesale slaughter of servants and retainers, their bodies buried around the king's tomb so that they could serve their master in the afterlife.[8]

By the dawn of the Old Kingdom (2700–2190 B.C.), however, a new spirit was in the air. Inspired, perhaps, by the teachings of Osiris, the Egyptians seem to have acquired a new respect for human life. No longer did they butcher legions of servants at the death of a king. Instead, the dead king had to make do with small statues of servants, called *shabti* or *ushabti*, which were placed in his tomb and inscribed with magical formulae ensuring that they would—in the words of the inscriptions—"do any work which has to be done in the realm of the dead."[9]

To the early pharaohs, the first *ushabti* must have seemed a poor substitute for flesh-and-blood attendants. But imagine the sigh of relief that arose from the servants' quarters! The use of *ushabti* constituted what anthropologists call a "substitution sacrifice"—the replacement of a real sacrifice with a purely symbolic one. While the *Ushabti* Revolution was hardly man's first attempt to "cheat" the gods of their sacrificial blood, it was probably the most decisive. Never before had such a powerful civilization renounced its bloody habits on such a massive scale.

Another probable example of a substitution sacrifice in Egypt is the so-called "foundation deposit." These were small pits, filled with ritual offerings, placed in strategic points of public buildings, such as under the corners or beneath the gateway. The apparent purpose of these foundation deposits was to curry divine favor for the building so that the gods would permit it to stand forever. The Egyptians would fill the pits with amulets, scarabs, small models of tools, samples of building materials, and commemorative plaques. They would also place food offerings in the pits, including wine, bread, and portions of sacrificed animals, such as oxen.[10]

Was there ever a time when these foundation deposits contained human victims or body parts? There probably was. The notion that a human being must be sacrificed and buried beneath any new building is extremely old and can be found all over the world. Hindu scriptures, for example, specifically call for a human sacrifice at the erection of a new building.[11] German folk tales frequently tell of children buried alive in the masonry of castles and churches, in order to strengthen the walls.[12]

Journalist Patrick Tierney found evidence that such rites may continue to this day in some Indian communities of the Andean highlands. One Peruvian engineer told Tierney that every pillar of a certain stone bridge across the Ilave River was believed by the locals to contain the body of a child who had been sacrificed. "The people think that sacrificing and burying a child inside makes the bridge strong," the engineer explained, "so the river won't carry it away."[13]

Anthropologists call such offerings foundation sacrifices because the victim is usually buried in the building's foundation. By means of such bloodletting, the builders bribe the envious gods into allowing the new building to stand. Moreover, the sacrificial victim is believed to haunt the building ever after, serving as its guardian spirit.

Foundation sacrifices were common in the ancient Near East. The Bible says that when Hiel of Bethel rebuilt the city of Jericho, during the time of King Ahab, "He laid its foundations at the cost of his firstborn son Abiram, and he set up its gates at the cost of his youngest son Segub."[14] Many scholars interpret this passage to mean that Hiel sacrificed his sons and buried them beneath the new city—a Canaanite ritual all too familiar to archaeologists of Syria-Palestine.[15] Ancient buildings in this region are often found with the skeletons of sacrificial victims—usually infants—buried in their foundations.[16]

The foundation deposits placed in Egyptian buildings strongly suggest that, at one time, Egyptian masons too may have protected their handiwork with an offering of human life. By the Old Kingdom period, however, these hypothetical human victims had already been completely replaced with bread, wine, and oxen. The substitution of food and drink for human victims—if indeed, that is what the foundation deposits signify—may well have been yet another ripple in the chain reaction of compassion initiated by Osiris.

Human sacrifice is an addiction. Societies practice it not because they wish to, but because they believe that they have no choice. If they stop killing, the gods will punish them, they believe. Everything they have gained through their bloodletting—their cities, houses, and farms—will then be taken away, and they will revert to savagery. At least, that is their fear. The logic of human sacrifice falls apart, however, when the "addicts" come in contact with another society that has succeeded in "kicking the habit"—without suffering any dire consequences.

A large part of the reason for Mexico's rapid conversion to Catholicism in the sixteenth century seems to have been the awe—

and envy—felt by many native Mexicans at the Conquistadors' freedom from human sacrifice. When Cortés first proposed to Montezuma, for example, that he stop the ritual bloodletting, the Aztec emperor was horrified. "How can you want us to lose the whole city?" he asked in disbelief. "Our gods are very annoyed with us, and I don't know if they would even stop at your lives were we to do as you ask."[17]

Later, however, the Spaniards demonstrated that the Aztecs had nothing to fear. First, they smashed the idols atop the Great Pyramid of Tenochtitlan and replaced them with images of the Virgin Mary and Christian saints. Next, they held a solemn mass. The Aztecs waited for disaster. But, instead, a much-needed rain watered their fields the very next day. From that moment on, according to Cortés, all human sacrifices ceased in the Aztec capital.[18]

Egypt offered a similarly bloodless alternative to the peoples of the Bronze Age Mediterranean. At Osiris's prodding, the Egyptians had boldly denied the gods their quota of blood. Yet the fields of Egypt still sprouted, its cities still stood, and its pyramids still rose from the sand. Osiris had proved that *Homo necans* can thrive without killing and eating his fellow man.

The legend goes that, after successfully civilizing Egypt, Osiris then turned his attention to the rest of the world. Diodoros writes:

> Of Osiris they say that, being of a beneficent turn of mind, and eager for glory, he gathered together a great army, with the intention of visiting all the inhabited earth and teaching the race of men how to cultivate the vine and sow wheat and barley; for he supposed that if he made men give up their savagery and adopt a gentle manner of life he would receive immortal honors.[19]

And so he did. According to Diodoros, Osiris marched with his army through Ethiopia, Arabia, India, and Greece. Wherever he went, Osiris founded cities, dammed rivers, and taught the natives to farm and make wine.[20] In the end, Osiris won the "immortal honors" he coveted. He was worshiped as a god, not only in Egypt, but in every country of the Mediterranean world, right up until the dawn of Christianity.

No one knows for sure whether King Osiris really existed or whether he accomplished even half of what the legends ascribe to him. Many theories have been put forth to explain the tale of

Osiris's missionary exploits. Martin Bernal thinks that the story may describe the conquests of Sesostris in garbled form.[21] The Greeks, on the other hand, equated Osiris with their god Dionysos, who taught the Greeks to make wine and who was believed to have come from Thrace—following the same route described by Diodoros for Osiris's march.

Many Egyptologists are willing to concede that a real Osiris may have ruled part of Egypt in some remote period. It seems unlikely, however, that such a prehistoric king could have physically marched through all the countries listed by Diodoros. More likely, the story symbolizes the spread throughout the world of an *idea*—the peculiarly Egyptian notion that men can achieve a "gentle manner of life," that they can build, farm, forge metals, and dam rivers without lubricating their every move in a torrent of human blood.

The story may also symbolize the spread of a cult—in particular, the cult of primitive Freemasonry. For it was precisely Osiris's "gentle manner of life" that the Sons of Daidalos appear to have championed. And it seems to be Osiris's victory over human sacrifice that we find enshrined in the ritual of the Murdered Apprentice.

CHAPTER 38

SON OF
THE WIDOW

W HEN AGATHOKLES, THE GREEK TYRANT OF SYRACUSE, marched on Carthage in 310 B.C., the Carthaginians flew into a panic. How could their enemy have gotten so close to the city? Why had the gods permitted it? In the end, the Carthaginians concluded that they were being punished for their sins. They had grown lax in their religious devotions. In the past, the Carthaginians had sacrificed their firstborn sons to the god Baal. But now many of them held out, secretly substituting the children of slaves for their real offspring. Diodoros described what happened next:

> When . . . they saw their enemy encamped before the walls, they were
> filled with superstitious dread, for they believed that they had ne-
> glected the honours of the gods. . . . In their zeal to make amends . . .
> they selected two hundred of the noblest children and sacrificed them
> publicly; and others who were under suspicion sacrificed themselves
> voluntarily, in number not less than three hundred. There was in their
> city a bronze image of Kronos [Baal] extending its hands, palms up and
> sloping toward the ground, so that each of the children when placed
> thereon rolled down and fell into a sort of gaping pit filled with fire.[1]

From this story and others like it the Phoenicians acquired their ugly reputation as child-killers. Of course, they were hardly the only ancient people guilty of such horrors. Greek legend abounds with tales of ritual filicide. Agamemnon, for example, sacrificed his daughter Iphigenia to the goddess Artemis in exchange for fair winds to carry his fleet to Troy. The Cretan hero Idomeneus vowed that he would sacrifice to the sea god Poseidon the first living creature he met when he returned safely from Troy. Unfortunately, it turned out to be his son. But Idomeneus kept his vow.[2]

The Phoenicians, however—and the other Canaanites, as well—clearly surpassed their neighbors in the scale and cruelty of their sacrifices. A cemetery of slain children—called a *tophet,* or "place of fire"—found at Carthage contained around 20,000 graves. Some graves contained animals, but the vast majority bore human remains, making the site "the largest cemetery of sacrificed humans ever discovered," according to archaeologists Lawrence Stager and Samuel Wolff.[3]

The Phoenician penchant for human sacrifice has led some experts to speculate whether the Masonic legend of Hiram Abiff may actually refer to a foundation sacrifice, enacted during the building of Solomon's Temple. The temple was, after all, built largely by Phoenicians. Would its builders not have sought to "protect" their handiwork in the traditional Phoenician manner—with a human victim buried in the foundation?

They might. However, the Bible says that Hiram "finished all the work he had undertaken for King Solomon in the Temple of God."[4] He was not killed before the work was completed, as the Masons say. How, then, could he have served as a foundation sacrifice? The easy way out of this dilemma would be to simply dismiss the Masonic legend—or even the biblical account—as empty myth. But to do so would violate our consistent policy, followed throughout this book, of treating ancient traditions with respect. Let us proceed on the assumption that both biblical and Masonic accounts reflect true events. Our task, then, becomes to find some way to reconcile the contradictions between the two.

In fact, the reconciliation turns out to be surprisingly easy. The simplest answer is the most straightforward and literal. If we interpret the Masonic ritual of Hiram Abiff as an exact and literal replay of what actually occurred during the building of Solomon's Temple, we are led to a surprising conclusion—that Hiram was never killed at all! The crucial detail is that the initiates who *play* Hiram in the ceremony are never really killed. They simply go through the *motions* of being killed. Could it be that the real Hiram also participated in just such a mock sacrifice?

There are good reasons for thinking that he did. For one thing, the Jewish religion strictly prohibited human sacrifice. Solomon would never have permitted his temple to be defiled with human blood, no matter what the Phoenicians wished. A mock sacrifice, on the other hand, might well have been permitted as a compromise. In fact, mock sacrifices are a common form of substitution, well known to anthropologists. The rite of Hiram Abiff would thus be a substitution sacrifice in the tradition of the Egyptian *ushabti* and foundation deposits.

Such a substitution would have been very much in the spirit of Solomon's Temple, which itself functioned as a kind of giant *ushabti*. Long ago, God commanded Abraham to sacrifice his son Isaac. Tradition says that Abraham took Isaac to the top of Mount Moriah—the very site where Solomon later built his temple—in order to perform the ritual. On top of the mountain was a great rock called *Even Ha-Shettiya*—"the Rock of the Foundation"—believed by the Jews to lie at the very center of the world. It was on this rock that Abraham bound Isaac and prepared him for sacrifice.

Just as Abraham raised the knife to deal the fatal blow, God stopped him and told him to sacrifice a ram instead of Isaac. This event, known in Jewish tradition as the *Akedah*, or the "binding of Isaac," was a classic substitution sacrifice. God had let it be known that a ram was an acceptable substitute for a firstborn son. From that moment on, Abraham and his descendants were freed from the obligation of human sacrifice.

Solomon surely had this story in mind when he selected the *Shettiya* as the foundation stone of his temple. In fact, Solomon built the whole temple around this sacrificial rock. The *Shettiya* formed the actual floor of its Holy of Holies, and the Ark of the Covenant was placed right on top of the unhewn stone. If there ever was a foundation sacrifice at Solomon's Temple, it was the "sacrifice" of Isaac, symbolized by the *Shettiya*.

In all likelihood, the *Shettiya* had been a blood-drenched Canaanite altar since prehistoric times, and Mount Moriah a regular scene of pagan worship. By sanctifying this grisly arena of death as a House of the Lord, Solomon not only ended the slaughter forever, but also made his temple a living emblem of man's freedom from human sacrifice. The temple is long gone, destroyed by the Babylonians in 587 B.C. But its message lives on in the legend of Hiram Abiff. Today, the Shettiya still rests atop Mount Moriah, sheltered now by a Muslim shrine called the Dome of the Rock. But long centuries have passed since the rock was fed with human blood. Great cities of glass and steel rise from every continent. Satellites and space stations wheel about the earth. But no longer do we pay the price of Cain for these achievements.

Like the Egyptian *ushabti*, the binding of Isaac, the raising of Solomon's Temple, and the crucifixion of Christ, the Masonic ceremony of Hiram Abiff marks our transformation from *Homo necans* to *Homo creans:* "man the creator." It reminds us of a nightmare from which we awakened long ago. It reassures us that we are free now to build, plan, and prosper.

A similar message comes to us from an old British folktale, first recorded around A.D. 1136 by Geoffrey of Monmouth in his *History of the Kings of Britain.* It tells how a British king named Vortigern once tried to build a fortress in Snowdonia to defend Wales against the invading Anglo-Saxons, sometime during the fifth century A.D. But Vortigern's workmen could not make any headway because their building materials kept disappearing. Vortigern's wise men told the king that the only way to complete the fortress would be to find *a boy without a father,* slay him, and sprinkle his blood over the foundation.

After searching the kingdom far and wide, the king's men came up with a boy named Merlin—the same Merlin who later became King Arthur's chief counselor. The boy had no father, because his mother had been impregnated by a spirit. But unknown to the king and his men, young Merlin was a powerful magician. The story tells how Merlin staved off his imminent sacrifice by using his prophetic powers to reveal that two dragons lay buried alive beneath the fortress foundation. These dragons had been causing all the troubles, Merlin told the king. The dragons were duly dug up and released from their underground prison. No further problems plagued the builders, who completed the fortress—with no need for a child sacrifice![5]

What is interesting about this story is its reference to a traditional belief that sacrificial victims must be *fatherless*. Patrick Tierney observed a similar custom among the Andean Indians, who
specifically seek out orphans for their sacrifices in order to avoid
dealing with the nuisance of protective parents.[6] Such considerations would have been paramount in the ancient world, where the
law of the blood-feud required a man to avenge his son's murder.
What better way to avoid such vendettas than to target only those
victims who lacked male protection?

Here we encounter the final clue in our quest to link Sokrates
with the Freemasons. Before proceeding, let us review the evidence.
We have seen, in previous chapters, that the Egyptians believed civilization was born in their country and was spread throughout the
world by a king named Osiris. We have established that the Egyptian cult of Ptah was a likely instrument for spreading civilization,
since Ptah was the patron of all arts and crafts and since he was worshiped throughout the Mediterranean world, in Phoenicia, Crete,
and Greece.

We have seen that the cult of Ptah manifested itself in Greece
through a craftsmen's guild called the Sons of Daidalos—and that
Sokrates was apparently a member of this guild. We have seen that
the Divine Craftsman worshiped by the Daidalidai has similar attributes to the Egyptian Ptah, Plato's Demiurge, and the Masons'
Great Architect of the Universe. We have also seen that the cult of
Daidalos used craftsmen's tools as sacred emblems—a practice they
shared with the Knights Templar, the Freemasons, and the priests of
Egypt.

Finally, we have noted that a somewhat garbled, but still recognizable, version of the story of Daidalos and Talos was carved on the
walls of Rosslyn Chapel in Scotland—one of the earliest Masonic
shrines in Europe. This is the clearest evidence yet of a direct cultic
connection between the Sons of Daidalos and modern Freemasonry.
It shows that the sacred story of Daidalos and Talos was also sacred
to the early Masons.

But why? Evidently, the early Masons honored Talos, the Murdered Apprentice, for the same reason that they honored Hiram
Abiff, the murdered Grand Master: both symbolized sacrificial victims. And both, it seems, were used in rituals of mock sacrifice.

At the moment Solomon first sees the dead body of Hiram Abiff in the Masonic initiation rite, he cries, "Oh, Lord my God, is there no help for the widow's son?"[7] Solomon is referring, of course, to Hiram, whose mother is described in the Book of Kings as "a widow from the tribe of Naphtali."[8] Hiram is, in fact, fatherless. And he is persistently described as the Son of the Widow in Masonic lore and ritual.

But so is the Murdered Apprentice! The grieving woman carved into the walls of Rosslyn Chapel is traditionally called the "Widowed Mother." Like Hiram Abiff, the Murdered Apprentice is therefore a Son of the Widow. It may be that the phrase "son of the widow" was once widely understood to refer to a sacrificial victim. In their quest for fatherless boys, the ancient priests would not have encountered many victims like Merlin, whose mothers had conveniently slept with disembodied spirits. Most of the time they would have had to make do with boys whose fathers had died. We may therefore speculate, with some confidence, that the curious phrase "son of the widow"—applied to both Hiram and the Murdered Apprentice—descends from a time when fatherless waifs were singled out for sacrifice.

The story of Daidalos and Talos thus appears to echo the primal murder—the sacrifice of Abel by Cain. Daidalos stole his nephew's talent by killing him. He also reenacted the original human sacrifice through which arts and crafts entered the world.

In ritualistic terms, it seems likely that the tale of the Murdered Apprentice served a similar purpose to that of the Hiram legend. Both were probably acted out in sacred dramas. Both may have served as mock sacrifices. If our analogy between Hiram and Talos holds true, it is also likely that the drama of the Murdered Apprentice served, in ancient Greece, as a rite of initiation, just as the Hiram drama serves today. The reenactment of Talos's murder may even have formed the very ceremony by which young men were welcomed into the Sons of Daidalos.

Did Sokrates himself participate in such a rite? Did he play the role of Talos, just as modern initiates play Hiram Abiff? We can only guess. But, in one way or another, we can be sure that the Sons of Daidalos would have imparted to Sokrates the chief elements of the Talos story, as well as its secret cultic meaning. He would, in short, have learned about the "curse of Cain"—though by another name, of course—and he would have learned of man's struggle to break that curse. Perhaps he would even have learned how King Osiris of Egypt abolished cannibalism and sought to institute a more "gentle manner of life" throughout the world.

How these doctrines may have inspired and influenced Sokrates' philosophy is a subject too large for this book. But there seems little question that the cult of Ptah left its mark on Sokrates' most brilliant pupil, Plato, whose Demiurge peers out at us so plainly from the worn hieroglyphs of the Shabaka Stone.

"It is evident that Sokrates taught nothing new," wrote George G. M. James, "because his doctrines . . . have been traced to the teachings of the Egyptian Mystery System."[9] As usual, the cantankerous James has overstated his case. To say that Sokrates learned everything he knew from the Sons of Daidalos is clearly going too far. Yet, it does appear that the Egyptian Mysteries thrived in fifth-century Athens and that Sokrates partook of them. Conventional history has yet to make room in its textbooks for the role of secret societies and esoteric cults. But only when it does will we truly begin to understand where we came from and where we are going.

PART SEVEN

THE GREAT
GREEN SEA

CHAPTER 39

VOYAGE OF
THE *RA*

A S WE HAVE SEEN, ANCIENT LEGENDS CLEARLY STATE THAT EGYP-
tian and Phoenician vessels made regular voyages to Greece
during the Bronze Age. Yet, generations of scholars have argued that such travel was impossible. According to these scholars,
neither the Egyptians nor the Phoenicians had the skill or ambition
to launch such expeditions at that early date. Their boats were too
small and flimsy, said the scholars. In fact, the prevailing view was
that Egyptian and Phoenician mariners were hardly more capable of
crossing the Mediterranean Sea during the Bronze Age than we are
of flying to Alpha Centauri today.

But were the ancient mariners really so inept? Scholars today are
not so sure. In the past, theories about ancient seafaring tended to
come from deskbound landlubbers, whose only knowledge of the sea
came from textbooks. But since the 1940s, a new wave of researchers
have insisted on testing such theories firsthand. By building exact
replicas of ancient ships and sailing them on the open sea, scholars
have been able to assess the actual capabilities of these vessels. The
results have been startling. Each new expedition adds further weight
to the view that ancient mariners sailed farther, faster, and more
skillfully than any of the landlubbing "experts" ever suspected.

Perhaps none of the ancient mariners have been maligned more unfairly than the Egyptians. After studying old paintings of Egyptian ships, experts long ago concluded that these vessels were poorly designed for ocean travel. Their fragile hulls would snap like matchsticks in a gale, and their flat bottoms would slip and slide uncontrollably in rough seas. Such vessels were suitable only for river traffic, the experts concluded. On the open sea, they were doomed.

Even today, this view remains popular among some Egyptologists. Yet, as early as 1954, a Norwegian explorer named Thor Heyerdahl already had his doubts. That year, archaeologists discovered a 4,600-year-old Egyptian barge buried in a pit near the Great Pyramid of Giza. It was 142 feet in length—the largest Egyptian ship ever recovered intact. Certain telltale features of this ancient vessel convinced Heyerdahl that the Egyptians must have known a good deal more about shipbuilding and high-seas navigation than scholars had previously acknowledged.

Heyerdahl was already famous for sailing 4,300 miles across the Pacific in a balsa raft called *Kon-Tiki*. By this means, he had sought to prove that the Incas—who built similar rafts—might have crossed the Pacific Ocean and colonized Easter Island in ancient times. Scholars still doubt that such a prehistoric expedition ever took place. But, thanks to Heyerdahl's 1947 voyage, they can no longer claim that it was impossible.

Now Heyerdahl had begun to wonder whether the Egyptians might have accomplished similar feats. In 1954, he examined the buried ship from Giza with great interest. It was a fragile vessel, built of thin cedarwood planks, obviously suited only for ceremonial processions on the Nile. Yet, despite its delicate construction, Heyerdahl sensed that the ship had been designed in imitation of sturdier ocean-going craft.

"The exquisite lines of the ship were specialized to perfection for true ocean voyaging," wrote Heyerdahl. "Its gracefully curved hull with elegantly upthrust and extremely high bow and stern had all the characteristic features found only in seagoing vessels, specially shaped to ride breakers and towering waves."[1]

In fact, the ship from Giza was of a *papyriform* design, Heyerdahl realized. Though made of wood, it was shaped to resemble a much older type of vessel, built from bundles of papyrus reeds. Egyptian tombs abounded with paintings and models of these reed boats, lashed together at both ends, with bow and stern arching high into the air.

"All the other large wooden ships depicted from Pharaonic times in Egypt were also papyriform," Heyerdahl noted. "They all had the older papyrus boat as their direct model. It was precisely this model, built of papyrus, which had all the seagoing ship's characteristics, with prow and stern soaring upward, higher than a Viking ship."[2]

Had the Egyptians of early times used such reed boats for sailing the high seas? The experts said no. Reed boats were supposedly too flimsy for this purpose. But Heyerdahl's curiosity had been aroused. He wrote:

> I wanted to find out if the Egyptians had originally been able boat-builders and seafarers . . . I wanted to find out if a reed boat could withstand a sea voyage of 250 miles, the distance from Egypt to Lebanon. I wanted to find out if a reed boat would be able to sail even farther, even from one continent to another.[3]

Heyerdahl believed that the ancient Egyptians were accomplished seamen. But he needed proof. He was sufficiently confident in his theory that, in 1969, he staked his life on it. He resolved to cross the Atlantic Ocean in a replica of an Egyptian reed boat.

Wild papyrus had been extinct in Egypt for centuries, and the art of weaving great bundles of papyrus into seaworthy craft was consequently forgotten. So Heyerdahl scoured the upper reaches of the Nile, deep in the heart of Chad and Ethiopia, in the hope of finding traditional craftsmen who might still remember the ancient technique.

One night, while staying as the guest of a Laki chieftain near Lake Zwai in Ethiopia, Heyerdahl slept in a bed of strangely familiar design. It was, he remarked, "of the same type as the ancient Pharaoh's beds in Cairo Museum: a wooden frame on legs, holding an open net of interwoven strips of leather."[4] Whether the Laki had learned to make such beds from the ancient Egyptians, or the other way around, Heyerdahl could not say. But these Ethiopian tribesmen clearly shared a common heritage with Egypt. All over northeastern Africa, Heyerdahl encountered similar echoes of Egyptian culture. He found many traditional craftsmen, in both Chad and

Ethiopia, whose forefathers had taught them to weave papyrus boats nearly identical to those painted on Egyptian tombs.

With papyrus from Lake Zwai and boatbuilders from Chad, Heyerdahl set up his shipyard in the Egyptian desert, at the very foot of Khufu's Great Pyramid. Even by ancient standards, the *Ra*—as Heyerdahl dubbed the new craft—was a pitiful tub. The giant cargo vessel described in the story of the Shipwrecked Sailor was said to have been 120 cubits long—about 206 feet—with a crew of 120 sailors.[5] By contrast, the *Ra* was only about 36 feet from stem to stern, with barely enough room for its 7 crewmen to stretch their legs. Moreover, unlike the great cedar ships that had plied the seaways to the land of Punt, the *Ra* was built only of fragile reeds.

Yet, it was known that such papyrus boats had made long ocean voyages in ancient times. The prophet Isaiah observed that the Ethiopians, or "Cushites," visited foreign lands in such vessels. "Woe to the land of whirring wings, along the rivers of Cush," declared Isaiah, "which sends envoys by sea in papyrus boats over the water."[6] According to Eratosthenes (285–194 B.C.), director of the Library of Alexandria in Egypt, "papyrus ships with the same sails and rigging as on the Nile" commonly sailed to India and Ceylon in Hellenistic times.[7] If reed boats could cross the Indian Ocean, why not the Atlantic?

Heyerdahl set sail from the Moroccan port of Safi on May 25, 1969. In the two-month voyage that lay ahead, the *Ra* proved its mettle many times, even in the grip of ferocious gales and 15-foot waves. The papyrus swelled like a sponge, becoming sturdier and harder as it soaked up seawater. The most punishing seas only caused the *Ra* to flex like a spring, absorbing the violence of the waves. *Ra* covered 557 nautical miles in the first eleven days, at a respectable average speed of 2.5 knots.

The worst problem of the voyage turned out to be caused by the boatbuilders' single deviation from traditional Egyptian design. The ancient tomb paintings clearly showed that the high, curved stern was supposed to be fastened to the deck with a heavy cable. But Heyerdahl's team had left out this feature, thinking it unnecessary. As a result, the stern sank slowly into the ocean as the voyage progressed, reducing their speed and causing the ship to yaw wildly off course. In the end, the adventurers were forced to abandon the floundering *Ra* only days from safe harbor in Barbados. They had traveled over 3,000 miles.

Heyerdahl tried again in 1970. This time, he learned from his previous mistakes. The *Ra II* was built exactly according to Egyptian specifications. After fifty-seven days, Heyerdahl sailed triumphantly into Bridgetown Harbor in Barbados, ending an epic journey of 3,270 nautical miles. He had not proved that the ancient Egyptians ever crossed the Atlantic. But he had shown, beyond question, that they were fully capable of such a voyage. Contrary to expert opinion, neither the alleged flimsiness of the boat nor its flat bottom had proved to be a problem.

If Heyerdahl had used a cedarwood galley, such as those the Egyptians sailed to Punt, he might have completed the trip even faster. The *Ra* was not streamlined for speed. But the great wooden galleys were. After viewing the Egyptian barge unearthed at Giza in 1954, Heyerdahl had remarked that it was "so perfectly streamlined and elegant that the Vikings had not built anything more graceful. . . ." Indeed, Heyerdahl saw little functional difference between the design of the Egyptian vessel and that of the Viking longships.[8] He suspected that their performance in the water would be similar.

If so, then the Egyptian galleys would have been very fast indeed. No one has yet tested a full-scale replica of an Egyptian "Punt" ship, but the performance of Viking longships has been exhaustively documented.

In 1964 and 1969, marine archaeologist Robert Marx made two attempts to cross the Atlantic in replicas of Viking war cruisers. Adverse weather prevented Marx from reaching America both times, but he sailed the longships for a total of more than 7,000 miles. In the process, Marx smashed many conventional theories about Viking navigation.

Before Marx's voyages, most historians had estimated that Viking ships might have sailed at a speed of 4 to 6 knots—allowing them to cover 100 to 150 miles per day.[9] Marx, however, had averaged 11 to 12 knots on his best days—a speed that theoretically could have taken him across the Atlantic Ocean in only two weeks.[10] The great discrepancy Marx revealed between the scholarly estimates and the actual performance of Viking ships may apply to Egyptian vessels as well. As discussed in chapter 24, K. A. Kitchen guessed that Egyptian galleys covered only 30 miles per day on their way to Punt.[11] We can only wonder how this theory might stand up to the actual test of a Robert Marx or a Thor Heyerdahl.

Another misconception long held by scholars is that ancient ships were unable to tack, or sail against the wind, because they used only a single square sail. According to this theory, ancient mariners could use their sails only on those rare occasions when the wind was blowing in exactly the direction they wished to travel. But this too appears to be a myth. On his Viking voyages, Marx found that, when the winds were light, he could sail as much as 70 degrees into a contrary wind.[12] Archaeologists have noted that pictures of Egyptian ships, from at least as early as the Eighteenth Dynasty, show sails equipped with brails, enabling Egyptian mariners to fold them, like Venetian blinds, for tacking against the wind.[13]

Scholars have also underestimated the muscle power of ancient rowers. It was long an article of faith among Bronze Age historians that Jason and the Argonauts could never have rowed their galley through the Bosphorus Straits and into the Black Sea, as legend claimed. Bronze Age galleys supposedly lacked enough oars to buck the fierce currents that constantly poured through the straits. Only in the eighth century B.C., said the "experts," did Mediterranean sailors gain regular access to the Black Sea, after Greek shipwrights figured out how to stack fifty oarsmen, in two layers, on a single galley.[14] Irish explorer Tim Severin, however, ignored the experts and successfully duplicated Jason's feat in 1984, in a replica of a Bronze Age galley equipped with only twenty oars.[15]

Perhaps the greatest—and most groundless—objection scholars have raised to the legendary accounts of Bronze Age seafaring is the supposed reluctance of early mariners to brave the open sea. This argument fails on two counts. First, neither the Phoenicians nor the Egyptians needed to cross the open sea to reach Greece. They could have hopped from port to port all the way around the Levantine and Turkish coasts until they reached the Aegean. But, what is more important, Egyptian and other ancient mariners were probably nowhere near as fearful of the deep as modern experts have assumed.

Contrary to the belief of landlubbers, "shore-hugging" is far more treacherous than deepwater sailing. Experienced mariners head for the open sea the moment they see a storm rising. Out at sea, a ship can ride even the largest swells. But, close to shore, the waves rear up into deadly breakers. Even in calm weather, coastal waters swirl with trick currents that can dash a boat to pieces against the rocks without warning.

On the first *Ra* expedition, Thor Heyerdahl brought along Santiago Genoves, a Mexican anthropologist. After barely surviving a barrage of storms off the African coast, the *Ra* finally reached the safety of the open sea. "I thought the sea got worse the farther out one came, but it's the other way around," Genoves admitted to Heyerdahl. "Among anthropologists we often speak about how primitive sailors might have traveled to this or that place, as long as they keep close inshore, but that's the worst place of all!"[16]

Ancient seafarers undoubtedly learned the same lesson, and probably quite early. At least 60,000 years ago (and maybe three times as long ago, by some estimates), Stone Age tribes crossed from Southeast Asia to Australia by boat or raft.[17] Depending on the sea level at the time of their crossing, they would have had to traverse anywhere from 40 to 100 miles of ocean, far from sight of any land. Clearly, the ancestors of today's Australian aborigines were no strangers to deepwater sailing. Why, then, should we assume that Egyptians and Phoenicians during the Bronze Age were any less capable?

The small size of Bronze Age ships has often been cited as an impediment to long ocean voyages. But, as we have seen, these ships were not always small. As long ago as 2600 B.C., the Egyptians were building 142-foot barges, such as the one excavated at Giza in 1954. Ugaritic documents from the late twelfth century B.C. refer to cargo ships more than twice the size of Columbus's *Santa Maria*, as we noted in chapter 26.[18]

In any case, experienced mariners understand that size has little effect on a vessel's seaworthiness. Modern sportsmen have crossed the Atlantic in boats as small as 6 feet and, in one celebrated case in the late 1980s, on a Windsurfer. A Japanese Boy Scout sailed from Japan to San Francisco in a 19-foot sloop, in only 93 days. "Over the past century," Robert Marx observes, "there have been more than 120 intentional solo or two-man extended ocean voyages in small sailing craft less than twenty feet long."[19]

Clearly, the study of early seafaring remains in its infancy. Only in the last fifty years have the Heyerdahls, Marxes, and Severins begun taking to the seas in their primitive rigs. And only since the 1960s have scuba-diving archaeologists begun to excavate ancient shipwrecks in a systematic fashion. What little we have learned, in this short time, has already shattered most conventional notions about the limits and skills of ancient seafarers. But further surprises may lie ahead. The evidence, in fact, is fast taking shape that the years of the Late Bronze Age—otherwise known as the *Pax Aegypti-aca*—may have seen a surge of oceangoing exploration on a scale that would not be duplicated until the age of Christopher Columbus and Henry the Navigator.

CHAPTER 40

THE METAL
OF KINGS

I N THE YEAR 1868, TWO AMATEUR ARCHAEOLOGISTS NAMED AUGUSTE Salzmann and Alfred Biliotti were digging for Greek statues on the island of Rhodes. In the process, they discovered some curious domed chambers buried in the earth and lined with massive stones. Neither Salzmann nor Biliotti had ever seen anything quite like them.

Inside these gloomy structures, Salzmann and Biliotti felt that they had entered a different world. Nothing looked familiar. Here were crude, faceless statues, carved in rigid postures, that bore no resemblance at all to the graceful figures of classical Greek sculpture. Here were rough ornaments of gold, glass, carnelian, and rock-crystal, graven with strange emblems. Most perplexing of all, Salzmann and Biliotti found tools and weapons that were fashioned not from iron or steel—the usual materials employed by classical Greeks—but from bronze.

Who would make swords out of bronze? In classical Greece, this relatively soft alloy was used for sculpture and jewelry, but never weapons. Clearly, the men who had built these dome-shaped tombs had been a breed far different from the ordinary Greeks. The crudeness and strangeness of the artifacts persuaded the excavators that they must have discovered tombs from an older, more primitive era of Greek history.

In this, they were correct. However, Salzmann and Biliotti seriously underestimated just how old these tombs really were. The excavators guessed that they might have dated from about the sixth century B.C. But they were off by more than 700 years. The best estimates today date the Ialysos tombs to sometime between 1400 and 1200 B.C.[1] Unwittingly, Salzmann and Biliotti had stumbled right into the heart of the Greek Bronze Age.

It would be another eight years before Heinrich Schliemann's excavations at Troy and Mycenae would finally compel scholars to acknowledge the existence of Mycenaean civilization—the name eventually given to this older, cruder Greek culture. But they ought to have known about it sooner. Certainly, there had been no shortage of clues. Scholars had been reading accounts of the Greek Bronze Age for centuries, in Homer and other ancient writers. But they had never taken these stories seriously.

In his poem *Works and Days*, Hesiod had written of a time, long ago, when "armor was of bronze and tools were of bronze, for black iron was not yet." Hesiod himself had probably never, in his life, seen a sword made of bronze. He lived around 725 B.C., when tools and weapons were made exclusively from iron and had been for over four centuries. Yet the memory of the Bronze Age remained fresh enough, in Hesiod's day, to survive in legends and folktales. Homer too lived during the Iron Age, probably around 800 B.C. But his poems were set some 450 years earlier, during the time of the Trojan War. Faithful to the old legends, Homer invariably dressed his heroes in bronze armor and put swords of bronze in their hands.

"The Trojans came on," wrote Homer, "like lines of waves on the sea, line behind line, flashing in bronze." Every battle of *The Iliad*, in fact, resounds with "the clash of men in bronze breastplates," with shields "plated in bronze," and with "the flashing of bronze."[2] That such gear was utterly unknown in Homer's day testifies to the poet's remarkable care for historical accuracy.

To the Greek storytellers, bronze weapons went hand in hand with magic, marvels, and high adventure. It was with a bronze sword that Perseus beheaded Medusa. It was in bronze war gear that the Argonauts fitted themselves in their quest for the Golden Fleece. The Greeks remembered the Bronze Age as a time of miracles, an era when all things were possible. The very gods had walked the earth in those days. Satyrs, centaurs, nymphs, and gorgons had haunted every forest. It was an age of kings and heroes, of voyages to enchanted isles, of gleaming palaces and hoards of gold.

Gold especially seems to typify Homer's Bronze Age. In *The Odyssey*, Telemachos marvels at the riches of Menelaos's palace, declaring, "See what a blaze of polished copper and gold and electrum and silver and ivory goes through this echoing hall. . . . I am awed by the very sight of it."[3] In *The Iliad*, Homer seldom alludes to the cities of Orchomenos, Troy, and Mycenae without noting that they are "rich in gold." When King Priam of Troy seeks to ransom the body of his son Hector, he dips into the city's vast treasury and extracts "ten talents of gold . . . two shining tripods, four caldrons and a very lovely cup" without a second thought.[4]

The fabulous wealth of Bronze Age kings was confirmed when Heinrich Schliemann excavated Troy and Mycenae in the 1870s. Schliemann discovered a hoard of bronze weapons, silver ingots, vessels of gold, silver, and electrum, and a cache of gold jewelry, including rings, bracelets, headdresses, and earrings buried at Troy, which he dubbed the Jewels of Helen. Schliemann proved equally lucky at Mycenae, where, in 1876, he excavated the graves of Bronze Age rulers whose bodies lay covered in golden death masks and breastplates of gold. The women of Mycenae went to their graves adorned with gold diadems in their hair and gold toilet boxes at their side. Schliemann even found two children wrapped, from head to foot, in sheets of gold.[5]

In the years since Schliemann's windfall, archaeologists have learned that such lavish displays typify Bronze Age sites, not only in Greece, but in Egypt and Syria-Palestine as well. Bronze Age cities are distinguished by their resplendent palaces, brimming treasuries, and abundance of imported goods. The wave of prosperity that clothed Mycenae's chieftains in gold brushed every shore of the Bronze Age world with the same Midas touch.

Thus, when Achilles refused Agamemnon's bribes, he evoked the wealth of Egypt as a metaphor for opulence. "Not if he gave me ten times as much . . ." Achilles cried, "or gave all . . . that is brought into Thebes of Egypt, where the greatest possessions lie up in the houses . . . not even so would Agamemnon have his way with my spirit."[6] The treasures of Tutankhamun that so stunned the world when they were unearthed in 1922 represented but a token of Egypt's fabled wealth during the Bronze Age. In this respect—as in so many others—Greek legend spoke truly.

The Bronze Age was, above all, a cosmopolitan era, a time when every port bustled with merchants and travelers from a dozen different countries. Homer hints at the era's international temper when he describes the wanderings of Menelaos after the fall of Troy. "I wandered through Cyprus and Phoenicia and Egypt," Menelaos declares. "I have seen Ethiopians and Sidonians and the Erembi in their native haunts: even Libya, where the ewes bring forth their lambs with horns."[7]

As Stanley Burstein, an ancient historian at California State University, has noted, Homer does not present Menelaos's itinerary as being, in any way, extraordinary. Menelaos does not visit strange and magical isles in unknown waters, like Odysseus, but simply tours the familiar, civilized world.[8] His journey encompasses the commercial and diplomatic sphere that would have been accessible to any Bronze Age king—a sizable sphere indeed, stretching as far east as Phoenicia, south to Ethiopia, and west to Africa's Libyan coast.

But all this travel, trade, and wondrous prosperity came to an abrupt end around 1200 B.C. The world plunged into a massive economic depression. International trade collapsed. Cities were destroyed, burned, and permanently abandoned. The Sea Peoples ravaged every coast. Piracy and war replaced peaceful trade, and the Mediterranean world sank into a three-hundred-year dark age.

Is it only a coincidence that 1200 B.C.—the approximate year in which these disasters began—also happens to be the very year that scholars have designated as the dawn of the Iron Age? Is it purely by chance that the world collapsed into chaos at the very moment that metalsmiths learned to forge weapons and tools from the new black metal? Probably not. Many scholars see a direct relationship between the fall of the bronze industry and the decline of the magnificent civilization that thrived on it.

Bronze represented far more to the ancient kings than just a raw material for making swords. It was a gift of the gods. It was the spirit of the age. Its magic brought peace and plenty to every realm and filled royal coffers with gold. It was, above all, the forging and selling of bronze—and the quest for its raw components—that drove men to their ships to explore the limits of the known world. And it was that same quest that lured them, from time to time, to venture far beyond those limits.

CHAPTER 41

THE BRONZE
LORDS

NOBODY KNOWS WHO INVENTED BRONZE. BUT MOST ARCHAE-ologists agree that it was probably sometime during the fourth millennium B.C. when early metalsmiths first tried mixing copper with 2 to 15 percent tin. The result was a new metal that was far easier to work than copper because it melted at lower temperatures. Once it cooled, however, the new alloy proved harder and stronger than either of its two components. The Bronze Age was born. Never again would the world be the same.

It was probably in western Asia—perhaps Mesopotamia—that bronze first came into vogue. By 3200 B.C., the Bronze Age was in full swing throughout the Near East. Mesopotamian kings armed their soldiers with the finest bronze weapons. The new metal must have conveyed a sense of invincibility to its wielders. But the gods proved fickle. No sooner had they offered this new gift to mankind than, just as suddenly, they chose to revoke it.

The problem with bronze is that its crucial ingredient, tin, is very scarce. Sometime during the third millennium B.C., the tin supplies appear to have run out. Archaeologists have determined that when the Babylonian conqueror Sargon the Great marched his armies from the Persian Gulf to the Mediterranean Sea, between 2251 and 2196 B.C., many of his troops were compelled to fight with copper weapons. There was simply not enough bronze to go around.[1]

The tin crisis of the third millennium B.C. appears to have jolted eastern rulers into action. They responded with a surge of trade and exploration. Within a short time, tin was again pouring into the foundries of the Near East. But much of it now came from mines as far away as Spain and central Europe. Copper weapons were never again seen in the civilized world. But the looming fear of tin depletion—and the frenetic quest to avoid it—would drive the engines of history for a thousand years to come.

It was precisely this thousand-year period that caught the attention of Norwegian scholar A. W. Brøgger in 1936. He called it "the great millennium of seafaring."[2] In his presidential address to the 1936 Second International Conference of Archaeologists in Oslo, Brøgger proposed a radical revision of seafaring history. Contrary to popular opinion, Brøgger declared, Columbus and the other fifteenth- and sixteenth-century explorers had not been the first to open up trade and travel on the high seas. Their so-called Age of Exploration was only one of a long series of seafaring epochs that had flourished and receded in cyclical fashion since prehistoric times.

It was during the Bronze Age, said Brøgger, that the greatest outburst of pre-Columbian seafaring had occurred. "Distance was no object" to Bronze Age mariners, said Brøgger. They "knew no frontiers, needed no passport or identity papers or tickets. The earth was free, the world lay open, and they wandered across it as though a thousand miles was nothing but a joyous adventure."[3]

Joyous, it may have been. But the great "adventure" of Bronze Age seafaring was driven by more than wanderlust. The quest for tin lured mariners ever farther into unknown waters. "It is inherent in the whole idea of the bronze industry," Brøgger noted, "that it encouraged seafaring and communications to an incomparably greater degree than the raw-material production of the Stone Age."[4]

Brøgger observed that tin supplies often had to be shipped from mines that were hundreds, even thousands, of miles away from the corresponding sources of copper. To bring these two components together at centralized smelting and manufacturing sites was a task as complex and formidable as that faced by any multinational oil company today. The knowledge and resources required for such a project could "only be supplied," said Brøgger, "by big businesses with a grasp both of production possibilities and of the market."[5]

Brøgger's "big business" theory implies a class of bronze moguls—veritable Rockefellers and Carnegies of the ancient world—presiding over industrial empires as vast and intricate as U.S. Steel. Who were these bronze lords? Where did they live? What language did they speak? Brøgger does not say. But it seems likely that whatever nation controlled the seas would also have dominated the bronze trade. During the *Pax Aegyptiaca*, at least, that nation may well have been Egypt.

Whoever they were, these bronze lords made exploration their top priority. Their quest for new trade routes, markets, and tin mines never ceased. As a result, Brogger claimed, Bronze Age mariners ventured into seas that would not be rediscovered until the fifteenth century A.D. They "had a clear picture of the geographical outlines of the Atlantic coasts of western Europe and the lands of the North Sea," said Brøgger. "The Azores and Madeira and the other Atlantic islands were also at this period discovered and known. Large parts of Africa were visited regularly, and it is probable that Africa had been circumnavigated."[6]

Brøgger's vision of the great millennium of seafaring remains controversial to this day. But no one can dismiss Brøgger as a mere "crackpot." He was a distinguished scholar, well respected for his work in Scandinavian archaeology. As director of the Norwegian museum in Oslo, Brøgger did groundbreaking work on the Viking longships unearthed at Gokstad and Oseberg.[7] His impeccable credentials compel us to take seriously even Brøgger's most fanciful speculations.

And some of those speculations were quite daring indeed. In the same 1936 paper in which Brøgger put forth his theory of a great millennium of seafaring, he boldly suggested that Bronze Age mariners might also have crossed the Atlantic Ocean. Indeed, Brøgger argued that such a crossing was virtually inevitable in view of climatic conditions on the North Atlantic. "The prevailing winds and currents," he argued, "almost compel the discovery of Central America from Spanish and Portuguese harbors, when once open-sea voyages are begun."[8]

Brøgger was referring to the trade winds and currents that sweep constantly from the vicinity of the Canary Islands all the way to the Caribbean. Any ship that ventures into that part of the Atlantic Ocean must fight very hard *not* to be pulled straight to America. This was clearly demonstrated by Thor Heyerdahl during his first *Ra* voyage in 1969. Only one day after leaving the port of Safi, in Morocco, disaster struck. Both steering oars of the *Ra* snapped in two. The boat was now helpless. It could not be steered or controlled in any way.

For fifty-five days, the *Ra* drifted, at the mercy of wind and current. But it never strayed far off course. By the time the crew finally abandoned their sinking vessel, they had drifted to within a few days' sail of Barbados, just off the South American coast. "Just beyond Safi," wrote Heyerdahl, "the ocean current and the trade wind seize anything that floats and send it to America."[9]

The same weather systems led to the accidental discovery of Brazil in 1500. When Pedro Álvares Cabral set out from Portugal with a fleet of thirteen ships, he thought he was bound for India. Cabral's plan was to sweep far to the west, where he could catch the trade winds that would carry him around Africa's Cape of Good Hope into the Indian Ocean. But the winds failed Cabral at the crucial moment. Becalmed in the Atlantic Ocean, Cabral was swept by the currents straight west, in the direction exactly opposite to the one he wanted to go. He landed on the coast of a strange new land, far to the west, which he named Brazil.

If Bronze Age shipping was as extensive as Brøgger surmised, how many merchant vessels, bound for ports in Africa, Spain, or Britain, might have found themselves pulled, completely by accident, to the shores of America? And how many of them, like Cabral's wandering fleet, might eventually have found their way home to tell others of their discovery? We can only guess.

To this day, most scholars still reject the possibility that ancient mariners could have crossed the Atlantic Ocean. But a growing body of archaeological evidence has quietly begun winning converts to this controversial theory. In the next chapter, we will review some of this evidence and allow readers to judge for themselves.

CHAPTER 42

THE COCAINE
MUMMIES

"THE FIRST POSITIVE RESULTS WERE A SHOCK," REMEMBERS SVETLA Balabanova, a toxicologist at Munich University. "I was absolutely sure it was a mistake."[1]
The year was 1992. As part of a study on ancient drug use, Balabanova had analyzed hair and tissue samples from nine mummies in Munich's Egyptian Museum, ranging in date from 1070 B.C. to A.D. 395. To Balabanova's surprise, all nine mummies tested positive for cocaine and hashish, while eight revealed high levels of nicotine.[2] The hashish was only mildly surprising. Experts had long known that the ancient Egyptians had used lotus, opium, and marijuana as intoxicants.[3] But how could the Egyptians have obtained coca and tobacco—plants that were supposedly unknown outside the Americas before 1492?

Most experts refused to believe Balabanova's results. The tests must have been mistaken, they said. Or perhaps the mummies had been inadvertently contaminated by pipe-smoking archaeologists or even coke-snorting lab technicians. These arguments, however, were not plausible. Balabanova's lab had a sterling reputation for accuracy. Moreover, Balabanova had found nicotine *inside* the mummies' hair shafts—where it would have shown up only after being metabolized by the body.

Even so, experts chose to ignore the "Cocaine Mummies"—as the press later dubbed them—hoping the issue would just go away. It didn't. In 1996, British researchers announced that hair and tissue samples taken from Egyptian mummies in the Manchester Museum had also tested positive for nicotine. The tests, run at two laboratories in London, provided independent confirmation of Balabanova's findings.

What does it all mean? Now that the tests themselves have been at least partly vindicated, scholars find themselves confronted with a difficult choice. It is conceivable that the Egyptians might have ingested certain Old-World plants that contain small quantities of nicotine. But cocaine is another matter. Either the Egyptians had access to some unknown and now-extinct plants in the Old World, bearing high concentrations of cocaine, or they must have had trade contact with America. Neither explanation seems very probable. But scholars must now take both very seriously.

Rosalie David, Keeper of Egyptology at the Manchester Museum, told the London *Sunday Times* in 1996 that the new results obligated scholars to take a fresh look at the possibility of ancient contact between Egypt and America. "We have always said there is no evidence," she admitted. "But there is never any evidence until it appears, so now we have to look at everything."[4]

The Cocaine Mummies do not prove that ancient Egypt traded with America. But they compel us to look at such claims with new respect. Almost since the day Columbus landed at Guanahani Island, Europeans have speculated whether Romans, Egyptians, Phoenicians, and other ancient peoples might have gotten there first. A surprising quantity of evidence has emerged over the years to support such claims. Yet only a few scholars have dared to explore these issues with an open mind.

Perhaps the best known of these is Thor Heyerdahl himself. No researcher has done more to demonstrate the sheer plausibility of long ocean voyages in ancient times. Heyerdahl has argued that peoples on many continents learned the arts of civilization from prehistoric seafarers who visited their shores—a point that he presses not only by testing primitive craft on the high seas, but also by conducting formal, archaeological digs in places like northern Peru and Easter Island.

"Many orthodox members of our profession have pooh-poohed Heyerdahl without adequate justification," observes Richard P. Schaedel, an expert on Andean civilization at the University of Texas. "But others, including myself, think that his procedures have been scientifically satisfactory and his contributions substantial."[5]

Another researcher who has suffered more than his share of "pooh-poohing" is Harvard marine biologist Barry Fell. In studying the effect of ocean currents on the dispersal of peoples, plants, and animals throughout the world, Fell concluded that early seafaring must have been far more extensive than scholars ordinarily imagine. He found support for his theory in mysterious stoneworks that litter the New England countryside. Many are of immense size. The sprawl of ruins at Mystery Hill (now open to tourists, under the name "America's Stonehenge"), in North Salem, New Hampshire, for example, covers twenty acres. Roof stones spanning a ten-foot-wide rock-slab chamber at South Woodstock, Vermont, weigh about three tons each.

Archaeologists have long dismissed such ruins as "colonial root cellars." But Fell and other researchers have pointed out that New England's massive dolmens, standing stones, post-and-lintel arches, and cyclopean chambers seem far more at home among the megalithic monuments of Europe, found at such prehistoric sites as Stonehenge, than they do among the churches and farmhouses of seventeenth-century Puritans. Radiocarbon analysis of charcoal found at Mystery Hill has, in fact, shown that the site was occupied as early as the second millennium B.C.—the height of the Bronze Age[6]

In his 1976 book, *America B.C.*, Fell claims to have identified inscriptions from Mystery Hill and other sites as examples of the Celtic Ogam and Iberian Punic scripts, suggesting that these megalithic temples may have been used at various times by Celts and Phoenicians. At present, most experts dismiss such alleged inscriptions as random scratches or even forgeries. Interested readers can judge for themselves by the photographs in *America B.C.* whether Fell's inscriptions really look like random scratches or whether his megalithic temples and burial chambers really resemble colonial root cellars. Those lucky enough to live within driving distance of "America's Stonehenge" can satisfy their curiosity in an even more direct manner.

Skeptics are usually quick to point out that neither Heyerdahl nor Fell is an "expert" in the study of ancient history. Fell is a marine biologist, while Heyerdahl holds a doctorate in zoology. Their amateur status provides a convenient excuse for archaeologists and other specialists to ignore their findings. But not every proponent of ancient trans-Atlantic travel is an amateur.

Ivan Van Sertima, for example, a professor of African Studies at Rutgers University, holds degrees in linguistics and anthropology. In 1976, Van Sertima ruffled academic feathers with a book called *They Came Before Columbus: The African Presence in Ancient America.* It examines evidence that West African traders might have crossed the Atlantic centuries before Columbus.

Experts dispute Van Sertima's claim that the famous Olmec heads of Mexico really portray black Africans. Artwork is notoriously subject to personal interpretation, as discussed in chapter 5, and such arguments will no doubt continue *ad infinitum.* But it is harder for scholars to dismiss the multitude of European explorers who left eyewitness accounts of black people living among the Indians at the time of the Spanish conquest.

For instance, during his 1513 march to the Pacific Ocean, Vasco Nuñez de Balboa stumbled on an Indian village where he found a number of black war captives being held. "Balboa asked the Indians where they got them," wrote Lopez de Gomara in his 1554 *Historia de Mexico*, "but they could not tell, nor did they know more than this, that men of this color were living nearby and they were constantly waging war with them. These were the first Negroes that had been seen in the Indies."[7] Peter Martyr d'Anghera, another early historian of the Spanish Conquest, wrote of this same tribe of Central American blacks: "The Spaniards found Negroes in this province. They only live one day's march from Quarequa and they are fierce. . . . It is thought that Negro pirates from Ethiopia established themselves after the wreck of their ships in these mountains. The natives of Quarequa carry on incessant war with these Negroes."[8]

In 1975, two skeletons were unearthed at Hull Bay in the U.S. Virgin Islands, identified by experts as two Negroid men in their thirties. The remains were found in layers dated to about A.D. 1250. One of the men wore a pre-Columbian Indian wristband. Experts refused to draw any conclusions, however, because a modern-looking nail was found near one skeleton and salt water had seeped into the bones, making accurate carbon-dating impossible.[9] Similar skeletons have been found, however, at other pre-Columbian sites. In 1974, the Polish craniologist Andrzej Wiercinski revealed that no fewer than 13.5 percent of the skeletons from the Olmec cemetery of Tlatilco were Negroid.[10]

Perhaps the most dramatic evidence to arise recently of an ancient trans-Atlantic crossing is the alleged Roman ship that marine archaeologist Robert Marx claims to have found submerged off the coast of Brazil. Marx found Roman amphorae, encrusted with centuries of barnacles and other marine growth, littering the sea bottom in Brazil's Bay of Guanabara in 1982. Classicists have identified the jars as third-century Roman amphorae from the ancient port of Zilis on Morocco's Atlantic coast.[11] Unfortunately, bureaucratic obstacles have, so far, prevented Marx from finishing the excavation.

Some readers may find themselves wary of the evidence presented in this chapter, and rightly so. Most of it is quite new, and all of it highly controversial. Keep in mind, however, that there is no longer any controversy over the question of whether Columbus was the first to cross the Atlantic. That claim was refuted beyond doubt in 1963, when Norwegian archaeologists Helge and Anne-Stine Ingstad discovered the remains of a 1,000-year-old Viking village at L'Anse aux Meadows in Newfoundland.[12]

The theory that Vikings might have crossed the Atlantic during the Middle Ages was once just as unproven and controversial as the other proposals in this chapter. But the evidence for such a crossing is now beyond dispute. As Egyptologist Rosalie David observed, "There is never any evidence until it appears."

Is it possible that A. W. Brøgger was right? Could America have formed part of the same Bronze Age world that included Egypt, Phoenicia, Crete, and Greece? Did ships from Mediterranean lands make regular crossings of the Atlantic and trade with the peoples of ancient America? At first glance, it hardly seems possible. If Bronze Age peoples had discovered America, how could they have simply turned around and forgotten about it later?

Yet, implausible as it seems, that is exactly what the Vikings of the Middle Ages did. After a few generations, they abandoned their colonies in Greenland and North America. Thereafter, these lands were remembered only in legend. As we will see in the next chapter, similar legends of colonies beyond the Atlantic Ocean lingered in the classical world. Their haunting testimony warns us of the evanescence of human achievement, which may flourish today, but tomorrow vanish from memory.

CHAPTER 43

LOST
KNOWLEDGE

"THE ANCIENTS WILL BE SHOWN TO HAVE MADE LONGER JOUR-
neys, both by land and by sea," wrote the Greek geographer Strabo in the first century A.D., "than have men of a
later time."[1]

With these words, Strabo gave voice to a widespread belief in the
ancient world—that men of past ages had wandered the earth with a
freedom unknown to their descendants. Just as the bronze-wielding
heroes of old were thought to be taller, stronger, braver, and wealth-
ier than contemporary men, so they were also imagined to have
traveled more widely. It turns out that the legend of a golden age of
travel may have contained more than a glimmer of historical truth.

The Greek pharaoh Ptolemy II Philadelphos (282–246 B.C.), for
example, dispatched ships to explore the Red Sea coast and carry
ambassadors to the fabled "Cinnamon Country"—evidently another name for the Land of Punt. No one seemed to remember that
these coasts had already been thoroughly explored by the Egyptians
at least 2,200 years earlier. It seems that Egypt had lost contact with
Punt during the 900 years that had passed since the last recorded
Egyptian expedition, sent by Ramesses III.[2]

What else had been forgotten during those 900 years? And what trauma could have struck the world during those centuries so all-encompassing as to cause such a massive forgetting? The Norwegian scholar A. W. Brøgger suggested an answer to this question in 1936. In his view, it was the collapse of the bronze industry and the dark age that followed that led directly to the erasing of thousands of years' worth of nautical lore from human memory. Brøgger wrote: "When iron begins in earnest to come into use, the old metal trade . . . enters into a period of depression. The demand for tin and copper declines. The period of large-scale production is past. . . . A long-established business goes into liquidation and disappears. The Maritime Age is over."[3]

As a consequence of this economic collapse, says Brøgger, familiar ports of call, from the west coast of Africa to the shores of America, were gradually abandoned, not to be discovered again for nearly 2,700 years. Seafaring continued, of course. But, without the bronze lords to finance large expeditions, the knowledge of Bronze Age mariners slowly faded. Though celebrated in classical literature, the exploits of Greek and Phoenician explorers in later centuries were, in Brøgger's opinion, but a pitiful remnant of what had gone before.

"The Greek written sources," he writes, "show only the end phase, the period when geography is in transition from the *maritime* world-picture of the Bronze Age to the *continental* one of the Early Iron Age."[4]

Nobody knows exactly why the bronze industry collapsed. The most plausible theory seems to be that, as tin grew scarcer, its rising price forced metalsmiths to invent better methods of smelting iron.[5] Unlike tin, iron is one of the most common elements on the planet, forming 5.8 percent of the total mass of the earth's crust.[6] Once metalsmiths learned to smelt it effectively, they would have found themselves in possession of vast metal reserves right in their own backyard. The quest for distant sources of tin would have faded in importance and the shipping industry with it.

However it happened, there is no question that the bronze trade collapsed, leaving depression and war in its wake. Archaeologists have long noted a dramatic decline in the standard of living as the Iron Age dawned. All over the eastern Mediterranean, the splendor and luxury that typified Bronze Age life gave way to squalor. Archaeologist Jane Waldbaum describes the transformation in her 1978 book, *From Bronze to Iron*: "As one flourishing center after another fell, established diplomatic and commercial patterns were also disrupted and curtailed. Bronze Age cosmopolitanism was followed by increasing isolation, provinciality, and poverty . . . a decrease in what might be considered luxury goods . . . a decrease in craftsmanship."[7]

The change was gradual. The bronze lords probably hung on to their ailing business well into the Iron Age. Waldbaum notes that bronze even made a brief comeback, around 900 B.C.[8] No doubt, tin prospecting continued well after this date on a limited scale. As late as the Roman era, the Phoenicians were still guarding the secret of their tin sources as jealously as they had back in the days when tin really mattered. This is clearly demonstrated by Strabo's famous story of the Phoenician captain who deliberately wrecked his ship on the rocks in order to prevent Roman pursuers from following him and learning the route to the Tin Islands.[9]

Despite such lingering efforts to keep the bronze trade alive, the Iron Age would no doubt have seen a gradual forgetting of many important sea routes. The last remnants of the old seafaring knowledge probably died with the Phoenicians in 146 B.C. when the Romans crushed Carthage. Nevertheless, tantalizing rumors of lands across the Atlantic were preserved in many Greek writings. One of these appears in Plato's *Timaeus*. In describing the location of the legendary Atlantis, Plato states that it lay "in front of the . . . Pillars of Herakles . . ."

> and it was possible for the travelers of that time to cross from [Atlantis] to the other islands, and from the islands to the whole of the continent over against them which encompasses that veritable ocean. . . . For all that we have here, lying within the mouth of [the Mediterranean], is evidently a haven having a narrow entrance; but that yonder is a real ocean, and the land surrounding it may most rightly be called, in the fullest and truest sense, a continent.[10]

Readers may choose for themselves whether to believe the legend of Atlantis. What is important for our purposes is not Atlantis itself, but the vast continent that Plato says lay *beyond* Atlantis, far to the west, "encompassing" the Atlantic Ocean. This could only be America. But how did Plato know about it?

Remember that during the fifth century B.C., when these words were written, Greek ships were barred from entering the Atlantic Ocean by a permanent Phoenician blockade. So complete was the blockade and so impenetrable the Phoenician secrecy that Herodotos was not even sure that the Atlantic Ocean existed. "I have never found anyone who could give me first-hand information of the existence of a sea beyond Europe to the north and west," he confessed.[11]

Plato's tale of a vast western continent obviously could not have come from contemporary Greeks. In fact, Plato attributes the story to Egyptian priests, in the city of Sais, who supposedly told it to the Athenian ruler Solon about two hundred years earlier. The Greek historian Theopompos may have drawn from the same tradition when he wrote, in the fourth century B.C., of a "continent" that was "infinite" in extent, unlike Europe, Asia, and Africa, which were bounded by water.

Krates of Mallos—director of the great Library of Pergamum in the second century B.C.—was even more explicit. Ever since Pythagoras, the Greeks had known that the earth was spherical, but Krates warned that it was nevertheless impossible to reach the Far East by sailing westward. Why? Because two great continents stood in the way—a northern continent called Peroikoi and a southern one called Antipodea.[12]

In the first century B.C., Diodoros wrote of some Phoenician mariners from the city of Carthage who "were driven by strong winds a great distance out into the ocean. And after being storm-tossed for many days, they were carried ashore."[13] The Phoenicians found themselves on a huge island with mountains, plains, and navigable rivers, many days' sail to the west of Africa. The island was inhabited, says Diodoros, by people with fine houses as well as gardens and orchards, well tended and irrigated.

Another version of this tale, recounted in the book *Concerning Marvelous Things Heard*—traditionally attributed to Aristotle, who wrote in the fourth century B.C.—says that so many Carthaginians emigrated to this new land that the authorities back home feared that Carthage might become depopulated and decline in power. Consequently, they imposed a death penalty on anyone emigrating to the new land and massacred all the colonists there to prevent them from divulging the secret of its location.[14] The Carthaginians then resolved to keep the new land secretly available, says Diodoros, in order "to have ready in it a place in which to seek refuge against an incalculable turn of fortune, in case some total disaster should overtake Carthage. For it was their thought that, since they were masters of the sea, they would be able to move, households and all, to an island which was unknown to their conquerors."[15]

Some scholars have suggested that this secret colony may have lain in the Azores, the Canaries, Madeira, or the Cape Verde Islands. However, both Diodoros and Aristotle specifically note that the forbidden island had navigable rivers—a description that would apply only to such places as Haiti, Cuba, or the American mainland.[16]

Many readers will no doubt marvel at the sight of so many clear references to America in Greek writings. Yet these stories probably represent only a fragment of what was lost. Harborside taverns in the ancient Mediterranean no doubt buzzed with such tales, many of them passed down intact from the Bronze Age. But as the years went by, the stories were forgotten. The great age of ancient seafaring receded into myth. And the march of human progress—which we like to imagine as always moving forward—made a temporary, but wholesale, retreat.

"It is just as with the Norwegian voyages to Vinland," concluded A. W. Brøgger wistfully in his 1936 address. "At the end of a seafaring epoch it is no use making 'discoveries': they disappear in the general ruins. . . . There is no steady progress: there are ups and downs, jumps and mutations."[17]

CHAPTER 44

SECRET OF THE
LABYRINTH

"OUT IN THE DARK BLUE SEA THERE LIES A LAND CALLED Crete," wrote Homer, "a rich and lovely land, washed by the waves on every side, densely peopled and boasting ninety cities. . . . One of the ninety towns is a great city called Knossos, and there, for nine years, King Minos ruled and enjoyed the friendship of almighty Zeus."[1]

This famous passage in Homer puzzled people for centuries. No one could deny that Crete was lovely. But great wealth and royal cities seemed out of place there. From classical times to the present, Crete remained a backwater of the Greek world. The narrow, mountainous island, 160 miles long and 35 miles wide, was distinguished mainly by its poverty, isolation, and fierce inhabitants.

Yet the legends told another tale. During the Bronze Age, Homer's Crete had been a powerful empire. Its fabled King Minos ruled what the Greeks called a "thalassocracy"—a kingdom of the sea—that included most of the Greek islands and even collected tribute from the mainland. In Minos's fabulous court at Knossos, the great architect Daidalos built his Labyrinth. The Greeks believed Minos had received the divine laws directly from Zeus, imparting to the Greeks

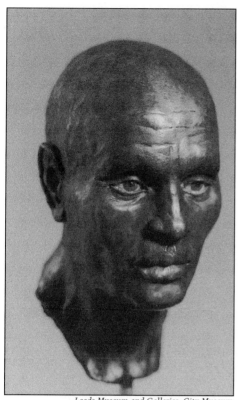

Leeds Museum and Galleries, City Museum

FIGURE 1
A forensic reconstruction made from the skull of Egyptian priest Natsef-Amun. This is the original work upon which the cover illustration is based.

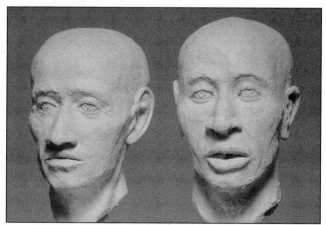

Manchester Museum, University of Manchester

FIGURE 2
Tomb inscriptions indicate that the Two Brothers had the same mother and possibly the same father. Yet one appears Caucasoid and the other Negroid in these forensic reconstructions—aptly illustrating the wide range of physical types that prevailed in ancient Egypt.

Frank Domingo, retired detective, NYPD

FIGURE 3

Forensic artist Frank Domingo reconstructed the damaged face of the Great Sphinx, in 1993. He now believes he should have made the nose broader. Even with the narrow nose, however, the Sphinx's features are, in Domingo's view, "consistent with those . . . found in Negroids."

Frank Domingo, retired detective, NYPD

FIGURE 4

The prognathism of the Sphinx—that is, the degree to which the lower face projects forward—is widely considered a Negroid characteristic.

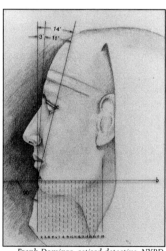

Frank Domingo, retired detective, NYPD

FIGURE 5

Most Egyptologists assume that the Sphinx represents the pharaoh Khafre. But Domingo showed that a well-known statue of Khafre has little or no prognathism.

FIGURE 6
Queen Nefertiti appears quite Caucasoid in this famous portrait. But some of her blood relatives are known to have had kinky hair and Negroid features. Nefertiti's family—like those of many African Americans— appears to have included a wide range of physical types.

FIGURE 7
In this detail from one of her portraits, Nefertiti is shown with Negroid features. Did she really look this way, or was the artist simply following a convention of portraying people as Negroid? Nobody knows.

Ippolito Rosellini Monumenti dell'Egitto e della Nubia,
Monumenti istorici, 1834, plates CLV and CLVI

FIGURE 8

This wall relief from the tomb of Seti I shows the range of human types
known to the Egyptians. Four Egyptians with red-brown skin appear at the
upper left, followed by four Syro-Palestinians, four Nubians, and four Libyans.
The Egyptians distinguished themselves physically from the very dark and
very Negroid Nubians. But they also distinguished themselves from peoples
who were lighter and more Caucasoid than they, such as the Syro-Palestinians
and Libyans. In their physical features, the Egyptians, on average, seem to
have lain somewhere in between.

FIGURE 9

The inscription on this incense burner, dating from about 3300 B.C., portrays an Egyptian-style pharaoh, accompanied by Egyptian royal emblems. Yet, it was not found in Egypt, but at Qustul in Nubia. No inscriptions found in Egypt, from this early period, offer such clear examples of pharaonic symbolism. Did the first pharaohs come from Nubia, in the heart of Africa?

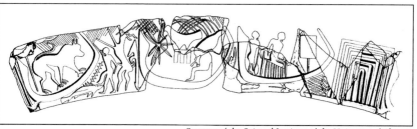

FIGURE 10

A reconstruction of the inscription on the Qustul incense burner. A pharaoh wearing the familiar White Crown rides the center boat. Above, to the left, is the Horus falcon. Further left is the royal rosette. The serekh—a large hieroglyph representing the royal palace—appears at far right.

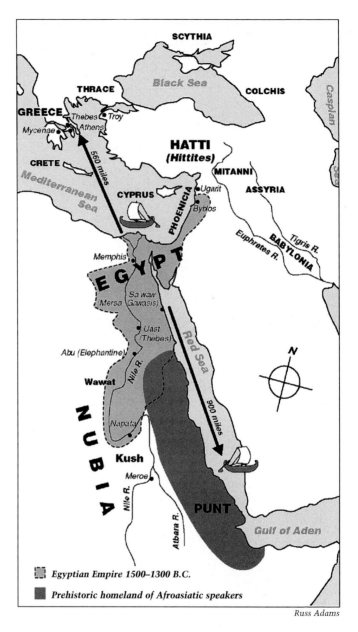

Russ Adams

FIGURE 11

The darkly shaded area represents the hypothetical homeland of the Afroasiatic language family—where the most
distant ancestor of the ancient Egyptian tongue was spoken.
Curiously, this region corresponds to the Land of Punt,
mentioned in Egyptian records. Was Punt the ancestral
homeland of the earliest Egyptians?

FIGURE 12

In 1969 and 1970, Norwegian explorer Thor Heyerdahl crossed the Atlantic Ocean in the *Ra* and the *Ra II* (shown here)—replicas of Egyptian reed boats. These voyages proved that Egyptian vessels were well-designed for navigating the high seas.

FIGURE 13

Egyptian sailors voyage to the Land of Punt, somewhere on the coast of Ethiopia. If the Egyptians could sail 900 miles to Punt, why is it so hard to believe that they could have sailed a mere 560 miles to Greece?

FIGURE 14

These ruins, near the Greek city of Argos, still reveal their original pyramidal shape. According to tradition, Akrisios and Proetos—great-grandsons of the Egyptian king Danaos—built a pyramid near Argos. Archaeologist Theodore Spyropoulos believes that the structure pictured here may be all that remains of their legendary monument. It is one of several Greek pyramids, all built sometime before 2400 B.C.

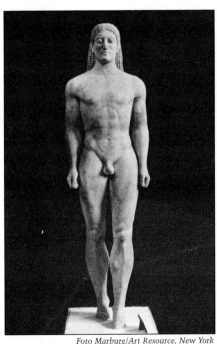

FIGURE 15

The earliest Greek statues—such as this example from the sixth century B.C.—employ rigidly stylized postures borrowed from Egyptian art. Legend holds that the Greeks learned to sculpt from Daidalos—an Athenian artist who studied in Egypt.

the proper manner of worship and sacrifice, the crafting of divine images, and the practice of sacred Mysteries.

"Cretan law codes were among the earliest and most abundant as well as the most admired in the Greek world," writes Sarah Morris in *Daidalos and the Origins of Greek Art*, "such that sages and lawgivers from other states—especially Lykourgos of Sparta—traditionally visited Crete for inspiration."[2]

In addition to laws, Minos also brought peace and prosperity. Thukydides painted him as the civilizer of the Greek world. Before Minos's time, piracy and lawlessness had ruled the Aegean, and every Greek had carried weapons for protection. "To wear arms was as much a part of everyday life," Thukydides wrote, "as with the barbarians."[3] He continued:

> And the first person known to us by tradition as having established a navy is Minos. He made himself master of what is now called the Hellenic sea, and ruled over the Cyclades, into most of which he sent the first colonies. . . . The islanders . . . were great pirates. . . . But as soon as Minos had formed his navy, communication by sea became easier, as he colonized most of the islands, and thus expelled the malefactors. The coast population now began to apply themselves more closely to the acquisition of wealth, and their life became more settled.[4]

Who was this Minos? Until 1900, most scholars thought of him as a myth. All of that changed, however, when a British archaeologist named Arthur Evans began digging on a hill called Kephala—the traditional site of Knossos—just south of the Cretan city of Herakleion. Within a few short months, Evans's workmen had stripped away the hill to reveal one of the great wonders of archaeology.

The massive, multistoried stone edifice sprawled over 3.2 acres. Evans immediately dubbed it the Palace of Minos—though, to this day, there is no definite proof that the building was a palace. One researcher has even argued that it was a giant mortuary temple, housing a cult of the dead.[5] Whatever its original function, the great complex of cubicles, corridors, stairways, colonnades, and storage rooms at Knossos showed that the legends of a great kingdom in Crete had been true. The building was large and intricate enough to qualify as a real-life Labyrinth—just like the one that Daidalos supposedly built for King Minos. Evans declared:

We now know that the old traditions were true. We have before our eyes a wondrous spectacle—the resurgence, namely, of a civilization twice as old as that of Hellas. It is true that on the old Palace site what we see are only the ruins of ruins, but the whole is still inspired with Minos's spirit of order and organization, and the free and natural art of the great architect Daedalus.[6]

If there ever was a real Daidalos, his handiwork could be seen most clearly in Crete. And what lovely handiwork it was! Evans discerned that the lintels of the Labyrinth had once stood atop festive colonnades, painted red, with capitals of cobalt blue. Bright frescoes portraying elegantly garbed ladies and graceful youths with long black tresses adorned its walls. The abundance of gaily painted flowers, dolphins, and other natural scenes on the walls lent an airy, carnival atmosphere to the "palace," redolent of the urbane and carefree life Evans imagined for its builders.

But there was also an air of mystery about the Labyrinth. Its rooms abounded with emblems and talismans, bespeaking long-dead and little-known cults. "Horns of consecration"—like those on the altar of Solomon's Temple—lined its battlements. Sacred bulls, tridents, and snake-wielding goddesses hinted at long-forgotten Cretan Mysteries. Of all the sacred emblems found at Knossos, none was more distinctive or prominent than the so-called double ax—an ax with a cutting edge on both sides.

These axes were found carved on the walls and painted on storage jars called *pithoi*. Bronze axes were placed on poles before special altars, and gold axes left as offerings in sacred grottoes. So prevalent was the double-ax motif at Knossos that Evans concluded that the very name *Labyrinthos* meant "House of the Double Ax"—derived from *labrys*, the word for "double ax" in the Lydian tongue of Asia Minor.

What did it mean, this double ax? At first glance, it seems to be a weapon. But it may have had other uses as well. In chapter 35, we noted that the figures of Daidalos and Ikaros, embossed on an Etruscan gold seal, or "bulla," from about 470 B.C., were shown to be carrying four tools—a saw, an adze, a T-square, and a *double ax*.[7] Apparently, the double ax was regarded, in the ancient world, as one of the basic tools of a carpenter or craftsman. For that reason, it served as a sacred emblem of the cult of Daidalos—and, therefore, of primitive Freemasonry.

Did the double ax symbolize Daidalos's cult as far back as the Bronze Age? If so, then the ubiquity of this symbol in the Palace of Knossos indicates a special reverence for Daidalos in Crete. Other evidence supports this conclusion. As discussed in chapter 33, the very first reference to a shrine of Daidalos was found in Crete, in the form of a Bronze Age offering tablet addressed to Da-da-re-jo— the Daidaleion.[8] Also discussed in chapter 33 is the fact that the name *Daidalos*—"the skillful one"—probably referred, in Bronze Age times, to the god Hephaistos, who was, in turn, identified with the Egyptian god Ptah, the Phoenician god Khousor, and the Ugaritic god Kothar.

"His seat is at Memphis," says the Ugaritic epic, of Kothar. "His throne is at Kaphtor."[9] Kaphtor, as noted earlier, was an ancient name for Crete. The Ugarites evidently believed that the god Kothar (Ptah) was enthroned not only in Egyptian Memphis but also on the island of Crete. This confirms that Ptah—in his Cretan form—did indeed occupy a special seat of honor in Minoan society. The double ax of Knossos may well have been his symbol.

Some scholars have argued that the "cult of the double ax" came to Crete from Asia Minor and, before that, from Mesopotamia. These regions did have a cult of the double ax. But, as Martin Bernal points out, Egypt is much closer to Crete, and it too seems to have used the double ax as a religious emblem.[10] As far back as 1923, Professor Percy Newberry suggested that Egypt was the source of the Minoan double-ax cult. He observed that this symbol was used specifically in the Western Delta—the part of Egypt that lies closest to Crete.[11]

It is also in the Western Delta that we find the city of Sais, whose patron goddess was Neit. Martin Bernal calls this goddess Black Athena because she was the Egyptian version of the Greek goddess Athena, as discussed in chapter 21. Professor Newberry noted that the emblem of Neit—a shield shaped like a figure eight—was also a favorite symbol of the Minoans.[12]

From Sais, wrote Diodoros, Egyptian colonists sailed forth to found Athens—or, at least, so claimed the Egyptian priests.[13] "Indeed," Diodoros continues, "the Egyptians say that their ancestors sent forth numerous colonies to many parts of the inhabited world, by reason of the pre-eminence of their former kings and their excessive population."[14]

Were some of those colonists sent to Crete? And did they bring the cults of Ptah, Neit, and other Egyptian gods along with them? Perhaps. Sir Arthur Evans, the discoverer of Knossos, believed that Egyptian influence had been decisive in Minoan history. Noting the large number of Egyptian artifacts found at early Minoan sites, Evans observed that "the determining cause of this brilliant development of early civilization is . . . traceable to the opening out of communications with the Nile Valley across the Libyan Sea."[15]

Martin Bernal points out the close resemblance between the name of the Cretan king Minos and that of the Egyptian pharaoh Min, or Menes, who unified Upper and Lower Egypt around 3150 to 3125 B.C.[16] As we discussed in chapter 31, Menes built the temple of Ptah in Memphis and instituted massive building and irrigation projects. And according to the Roman historian Aelian, Menes also founded one of Egypt's most important religious institutions—the cult of the Apis bull.[17]

The Apis bull was the holiest of Egypt's sacred animals, specially dedicated to the god Ptah and considered to be Ptah's embodiment on earth.[18] There could be only one Apis bull alive at any one time. When he died, the whole country went into mourning, and the priests scoured the land to find a new Apis bull, who was thought to be conceived by the god and was recognized by twenty-nine distinctive marks on its body.[19]

Once identified, the new Apis bull was taken to live in a special sanctuary near the Temple of Ptah in Memphis. There it was bathed, oiled, and perfumed, fed with honey cakes, and supplied with cows for its sexual pleasure.[20] While it lived, the Apis bull symbolized the strength and virility of Egypt's pharaoh.

An important bull cult also seems to have lain at the root of King Minos's royal power. Excavators found a multitude of bulls portrayed in the frescoes of the Palace of Knossos. They also found a magnificent libation vessel, decorated with gold, rock crystal, and mother-of-pearl, in the form of a bull's head. Bull imagery abounds in Cretan legend. Zeus, for example, took the form of a bull when he kidnapped Europa and conceived Minos.

Another story holds that Minos, while struggling against rivals for the throne, asked the god Poseidon to send him a bull from the sea, which he could sacrifice for victory over his foes. When a bull did emerge from the waves, however, it was so beautiful that Minos decided to keep it. Punishment came swiftly. Poseidon smote Minos's wife, Queen Pasiphae, with lust for the beautiful bull. She coupled with the beast and bore a child with the head of a bull and a human body. The monster was named the Minotaur—"the Bull of Minos." Horrified, King Minos ordered Daidalos to build the Labyrinth as a prison for the Minotaur. There the monster lived, dining on human flesh from sacrificial victims.

We thus see that both Menes and Minos were regarded as founders of a bull cult, founders of a nation, and founders of a tradition of monumental building. Bernal points out that the word *mn*, in Egyptian, can mean "be firm, established." The name of Menes (or Min, as Herodotos calls him) might therefore mean something like "the founder." Perhaps *Minos* too had the same meaning for the Cretans.[21]

Scholars have long suspected that *Minos* is not the name of any particular Cretan king, but rather a traditional title for *all* Minoan sovereigns, much like *pharaoh* in Egypt. If Crete really did import the arts of civilization from Egypt—as Sir Arthur Evans suspected—the ceremonial title of Minos may well have been imported right along with them. So may have the cult of the Apis bull, which would have arrived in Crete by sea just like Poseidon's bull in the legend of the Minotaur. Minos's title may actually proclaim him as the bringer of Ptah's cult to Crete—just as Menes himself was the founder of Ptah's cult in Egypt.

In any case, it is certain that Egypt had already made contact with Crete as far back as Menes's time—and even before then. Archaeologists have found distinctively Egyptian artifacts in Crete dating back to the prehistoric Naqada culture, which flourished in the Nile Valley between 4000 and 3150 B.C.[22]

When civilization finally arrived in Crete, it struck all at once. Around 2000 B.C., the islanders suddenly began rearing magnificent "palaces," like that at Knossos, where before they had built only small towns and villages. Most experts agree that the change was too sudden and dramatic to have evolved from internal forces alone. Some inspiration from abroad clearly sparked this explosion of palace building.[23]

Perhaps it was the memory of such foreign influence that gave rise to the legend, recounted by Diodoros, that Daidalos copied the design for his Cretan Labyrinth from an Egyptian original. Diodoros wrote:

> [The Egyptian king] Mendes . . . did build himself a tomb known as the Labyrinth, which . . . was impossible to imitate in respect of its ingenious design; for a man who enters it cannot easily find his way out, unless he gets a guide who is thoroughly acquainted with the structure. And some say that Daidalos, visiting Egypt and admiring the skill shown in the building, also constructed for Minos, the king of Crete, a labyrinth like the one in Egypt.[24]

Some scholars have even suggested that the word *labyrinth* may be Egyptian rather than Lydian in derivation. The Egyptian word *lapi-ro-hun-t*—which means "temple on the mouth of the sea"—bears at least as close a resemblance to *labyrinthos* as does the Lydian word *labrys*.[25]

Even so, scholars today prefer to emphasize the Near Eastern—rather than the Egyptian—influence over Minoan Crete. They also prefer to attribute that influence to trade, rather than to outright colonization. But whether the building arts were brought to Crete by Egyptians or Phoenicians, by traders or colonists, the result is the same—an island uniquely dedicated to the cult of Ptah and to all his wondrous arts. We have already seen that Ptah established his "throne" in Crete, according to the Ugaritic texts. It is probably no coincidence that we also find on that island the most dramatic evidence yet for the lost era of Bronze Age seafaring.

CHAPTER 45

THE MELTING POT

ONE OF THE OLDEST AND BITTEREST CONTROVERSIES IN AR-chaeology rages between two scholarly factions calling themselves diffusionists and isolationists. Diffusionists believe that civilization spreads like a contagion, "diffusing" from one culture to the next through trade, conquest, and colonization. Isolationists, on the other hand, believe that civilizations grow up on their own, through a process of "independent invention," with little or no help from the outside.

Undoubtedly, Thor Heyerdahl is the world's most famous diffu-sionist. But even Heyerdahl takes second place, in terms of schol-arly prestige, to Cyrus H. Gordon. Now retired as professor of Near Eastern Studies at Brandeis University, Gordon remains an author-ity on ancient Semitic tongues, having written the standard *Ugaritic Grammar.* Gordon's formidable scholarship has long been a stumbling block to those who would like to dismiss his more un-orthodox theories.

Gordon shocked academia in 1970 by publishing a book called *Before Columbus: Links Between the Old World and Ancient America.* As radical as it seemed, the book represented only the log-ical extension of ideas Gordon had been developing for years. In his view, all great civilizations learn from one another. Only by trading ideas with neighboring cultures, Gordon believes, can a people rise from barbarism. He writes:

> Primitive societies may be independent of each other. . . . But all high, technologically developed civilizations are the result of international stimulation so that all of them are connected by what they have learned from each other. . . . This is true just as much today as it was in antiquity. Nobel prizes are awarded to creative spirits whose achievements have been made possible by international stimulation; they are not won by the inhabitants of remote deserts, oases and mountaintops.[1]

Gordon first applied this principle in the area of his specialty—the eastern Mediterranean of ancient times. For Gordon, the region was a fabulous melting pot in which cross-fertilization between many peoples stimulated great achievements. In itself, this was not a radical idea. But Gordon raised academic eyebrows in 1955 when his book *Homer and Bible* pointed out strong parallels between Greek and Semitic folklore—similarities that could be explained only if Greece and Syria-Palestine had been in close contact from early biblical times. Orthodox scholarship did not admit such old and intimate ties between Europe and the Near East. Clearly, Gordon's melting pot was blended a lot more smoothly than the conventional one.

Deeper controversies lay ahead. Gordon next turned his attention to one of archaeology's most nagging puzzles—the decipherment of the Minoan language. Arthur Evans had discovered thousands of clay tablets at Knossos, inscribed in three different writing systems. The oldest he called "Cretan heiroglyphs" (2000–1650 B.C.), the second oldest "Linear A" (1650–1450 B.C.), and the most recent "Linear B" (1450–1250 B.C.).

Linear B was deciphered in 1953 by an ingenious young architect named Michael Ventris. Its language turned out to be an early form of Greek. This did not necessarily prove that the Minoans were Greek. It only suggested that Greek-speaking people might have occupied Crete after 1450 B.C., seizing control from the native Minoan inhabitants.

Most scholars agreed that the older Linear A probably represented the real language of the native Cretans—a language that could not possibly be Greek. Emmett Bennett had already proved, back in the early 1940s—using military code-breaking procedures acquired during his service as a U.S. Air Force cryptographer—that Linear A and Linear B were two different languages. Various Greek authors had also recorded that the Eteocretans, or "true Cretans"— who still lived in eastern Crete during classical times—spoke a non-Greek language. Most experts suspected that these Eteocretans were remnants of the original Minoans.

So what language did they speak? Scholars considered Etruscan, Cypriot, and Hittite. They explored the possibility that the Minoans might have spoken some previously unknown "Aegean" or "Anatolian" tongue.[2] But no one considered what was perhaps the most obvious possibility.

According to Greek legend, Crete was ruled by *Phoenicians*. The royal house of Crete was founded by Europa, a Phoenician princess from the city of Tyre (or Sidon, in some accounts). After changing to a bull and carrying Europa on his back to Crete, Zeus made love to her and conceived a child. That child was Minos, soon to be king of Crete.

Other hints of Phoenician influence had been quietly noted by other scholars. Perhaps the strongest clue lay in the Minoan buildings themselves. The earliest excavators, not only of Knossos but also of the very similar Mycenaean ruins on the mainland, had noted how little resemblance these monuments bore to the stonework of classical Greece. A few went further than this. They suggested that the closest parallels to the art and architecture of the Bronze Age Aegean could be found in Syria-Palestine.

Claude F. A. Schaeffer, for example, on discovering a massive fortress at the Phoenician city of Ugarit in 1948–1950, was struck by its resemblance to the Cyclopean architecture of Mycenae and Troy.[3] The great archaeologist Sir Leonard Woolley had noted that frescoes and construction methods seen at Knossos were strangely similar to those found in the royal palaces of North Syria. "There can be no doubt," he concluded, "but that Crete owes the best of its architecture, and its frescoes, to the Asiatic mainland."[4]

Such clues, however, were usually ignored. Most scholars assumed, at the time, that the Phoenicians did not begin sailing long distances and planting colonies until well into the Iron Age, around 900 or 800 B.C. During the period when Linear A was in use— roughly 1650–1450 B.C.—they were considered barely capable of skimming their own coastlines. If the Bronze Age Phoenicians could not even *reach* Crete, how could they have colonized the island and imposed their language on it? The possibility seemed so farfetched, it was not even considered.

Cyrus Gordon, however, approached the problem more objectively. The sound values of Linear B were already known. Since Linear A used identical symbols, Gordon proceeded on the assumption that they probably represented identical sounds as well. He began sounding out the unknown words from Linear A to see what language they resembled.

While transcribing one tablet, Gordon realized, with great excitement, that the words it used for different types of pots were identical to corresponding words in Semitic languages of the ancient Near East. Subsequently, Gordon found that the syllable *u* meant "and" in Linear A and that *kunnishu* meant "wheat." *U* and *kunnishu* also meant "and" and "wheat" in certain Semitic tongues.[5]

Eventually, Gordon managed to decipher complete phrases in Linear A—phrases that used Northwest Semitic grammar and idioms with perfect accuracy. He even discovered that the mysterious Eteocretan inscriptions, written in the Greek alphabet and dating from about 600 to 300 B.C., appeared to be written in the same Semitic tongue as Linear A.[6] Gordon was sure enough of his ground that when he finally announced his findings in the November 1963 issue of *Natural History*, he boldly entitled his article "The Decipherment of Minoan."[7]

In Gordon's view, the evidence was conclusive: the people of Minoan Crete—or at least some of them—had spoken a Northwest Semitic language in the same family as Phoenician and Ugaritic. This implied that they could have been a Syro-Palestinian people—"Phoenicians" in the broadest sense of the word. Gordon's theory did not prove that all Minoans were Phoenicians. But it did seem to indicate that Phoenicians had dominated the island—at least during the Linear A period of 1650 to 1450 B.C.—just as the legend of Europa implies.

More than thirty-four years after Gordon's findings were published, they are still hotly contested. Scholars have been forced to admit that Linear A and Eteocretan contain Semitic words, but they still deny that the languages themselves might be Semitic.[8] Linear A remains, to this day, officially "undeciphered." And the Bronze

Age Phoenicians are still seen, by many scholars, as having been timid shore-huggers.

In the meantime, Gordon's speculations have only grown bolder, ranging far beyond Crete and the eastern Mediterranean. In 1970, he published *Before Columbus*. Drawing on a wealth of archaeological and literary evidence, Gordon renewed the claim made decades earlier by A. W. Brøgger that America had been a familiar place to Old World mariners, beginning at least as early as the Bronze Age.

In the book, Gordon discussed many controversial and little-known archaeological finds, among them a Roman head, from about A.D. 200, excavated in a Mexican pyramid;[9] the Paraíba Stone, found on a Brazilian plantation in 1872 and inscribed with Phoenician characters;[10] the Bat Creek Inscription, carved in Roman-era Hebrew and unearthed from a burial mound in Tennesee in the 1890s;[11] the Metcalf Stone, found in Fort Benning, Georgia, in 1966 and bearing what appear to be Minoan symbols, including the double ax.[12] Gordon also explored evidence of Egyptian loan words in the Aztec language,[13] and he analyzed Mayan and Aztec legends about visitors from across the sea.

Perhaps most compelling were the variety of Central American sculptures that Gordon presented portraying what appear to be non-Indian faces. There is, for example, the Mediterranean Merchant Prince—a Mayan incense burner carved in the form of a man with a pointed beard, a large "Semitic" nose, and other distinctly Near Eastern features.[14] Then there is the Mixtec Negro Head from Oaxaca, Mexico, of which Gordon writes, "The black color and the features, such as the thick lips, leave no doubt in anyone's mind that the artist has portrayed a Negro."[15]

Limited space forced Gordon to offer only a smattering of these portraits. A far more impressive collection can be found in Alexander von Wuthenau's 1969 *The Art of Terracotta Pottery in Pre-Columbian South and Central America*. Interested readers would do well to consult it.

In Gordon's view, the sheer volume of non-Indian portraits from Central America suggested that, once more, international stimulation had spurred human advancement. Was it only a coincidence that America's highest civilizations were found in the very region where winds and currents would tend to bring wayward mariners from Africa and the Mediterranean? Gordon thought not.

"The Mesoamerican scene was complex," he wrote, "with Caucasians from Eurasia and blacks from Africa. . . . The peoples of pre-Columbian America confront us with great variety racially and linguistically."[16] By 1492, says Gordon, most of these foreign types had been absorbed into the Indian population.[17] But their cultural impact had already stimulated a renaissance. In Gordon's view, it was precisely this trans-oceanic cross-pollination that accounted for the great leap forward taken by such peoples as the Olmecs, Maya, and others from Mesoamerica. He wrote: "Cultural flowering is produced by the creative combination of different peoples, each with something significant to contribute. . . . No people is pure racially or linguistically. Creative peoples, and the languages they speak, are the results of felicitous combinations."[18]

If Gordon's theory is correct, high civilization arose in Europe for much the same reason it did in Central America—through a "felicitous combination" of native and foreign peoples. It will likely be years before scholars reach a consensus on the question of trans-Atlantic travel in ancient times. But, by now, it should be clear to most readers that so small a puddle as the Mediterranean Sea could hardly have presented Bronze Age explorers with an insuperable obstacle. Indeed, as we will see in the next chapter, the new science of underwater archaeology has all but rendered such questions obsolete.

CHAPTER 46

THE PTAH SHIP

O NE OF THE WORLD'S OLDEST GRAVEYARDS OF SUNKEN SHIPS CAN
be found off Turkey's southern coast. Strategically poised
along the route between Europe and the Near East, this
coastline has ambushed unwary travelers since the Stone Age. With
its deadly combination of shallow waters, treacherous reefs, and unpredictable weather, it has devoured ships with the voracity of
Scylla and Charybdis. Untold thousands of vessels have perished
there over the centuries. Until quite recently, they lay undisturbed
at the bottom, as silent and unreachable as lost Atlantis.

But eternal repose was not to be theirs. In the nineteenth century
came Turkish sponge divers equipped with a newfangled invention
called the diving suit. A wondrous spectacle greeted those early pio-
neers of the deep. Ships of every century and nationality lay broken
on the stony sea bottom, bathed in greenish light and crawling with
eels and groupers.

Alongside modern steamships, their bulkheads rusting in the
brine, lay scattered remnants of Greek and Roman galleys—and of
vessels far older than that. As far as the eye could see lay heaps of
pithoi and amphorae—ceramic pots used to store cargo in ancient
times—spilled across the sea bottom from timber hulls that had
long since crumbled from saltwater corrosion and the tunneling of

teredo worms. If any trace still remained of the legendary Bronze
Age seafarers, surely it was here that archaeologists would find it.
The first breakthrough came in 1960. A shipwreck discovered off
Cape Gelidonya in southern Turkey was found to contain Bronze
Age artifacts, making it the oldest wreck ever found. Never before
had anyone attempted to conduct a formal archaeological dig beneath ninety feet of seawater. But a young classical archaeologist
named George Bass took on the challenge, managing to improvise a
set of procedures that continue, to this day, to form the backbone of
marine archaeology.

After conducting a photographic survey of the site and making a
detailed map, the team set to work numbering each object lying on
the seafloor and giving it a plastic tag. Just as in conventional excavations on land, Bass's goal was to preserve a record of the site so
exact that future scholars would know exactly where each artifact
had lain in the original wreck—even generations after the site had
been completely cleared.

The ship appeared to have been a kind of seagoing metalsmithy.
Bass found thirty-four copper ingots—all in the flat "ox-hide" shape
typical of the Bronze Age—as well as quantities of bronze and tin.[1]
Hundreds of bronze tools were also found, including axes, hoes,
picks, spatulas, spear points, and knives—most of them broken. Perhaps a traveling metalsmith had sailed along the Turkish coast, collecting scrap metal in every port, Bass reasoned. From the ingots in
the hold, the smith might have forged new tools to trade for the broken ones. It was an intriguing theory, but impossible to prove.

Most scholars at the time assumed that the ship would turn out to
be Greek. The Mycenaeans, after all, were believed to have held a
virtual monopoly on Bronze Age shipping. But Bass was struck by
the large number of Near Eastern artifacts on the ship, including pottery, weights for scales, various personal objects, and cylinder seals.[2]
Could the wreck be Phoenician, Bass wondered? If so, its cargo might
help explain one of the great mysteries of Bronze Age archaeology.

Greek pottery had been found in abundance at Bronze Age sites
throughout the Mediterranean, but very few Phoenician pots had
been found. This had long been cited as proof that Greeks—not
Phoenicians—dominated the Bronze Age seas. But what if the Phoenicians had traded something that was not carried in pots? What if
they sold *metal*?

In that case, their business would leave behind few clues for the archaeologists. Metal ingots would be melted down and cast into tools or weapons. No trace of their Phoenician origin would remain. As for those famous Greek pots, even they might be evidence of Phoenician seafaring, Bass theorized. Why assume that they had been carried by Greek ships? They might just as well have been loaded onto Phoenician vessels in Greek harbors, filled with olive oil, wine, or other perishables, and transported to distant customers across the sea by the Phoenicians. The Greeks who filled those pots may never have left home.[3]

In the 1960s, the scholarly world was not yet ready to imagine a Bronze Age Mediterranean so alive with Phoenician shipping. Bass's theory was savagely attacked. A new discovery, however, soon silenced the critics. In 1984, an observant sponge diver discovered yet another wreck off Turkey's southern coast, this one near a place called Ulu Burun. The ship was much bigger and older than the one at Cape Gelidonya, which had been dated to about 1220 B.C. Experts later determined that the Ulu Burun wreck probably sank around 1375–1325 B.C. Sailing at the height of the *Pax Aegyptiaca*, its fabulous cargo testified to the splendor of the era. It would change forever our view of Bronze Age seafaring.

Again, it was George Bass who conducted the excavation, this time at the head of his own Institute of Nautical Archaeology (INA), which he had founded at Texas A&M University in 1973. The dig presented fearsome technical obstacles. Pieces of the hull and cargo lay scattered along a steep underwater slope, ranging from 140 to 170 feet deep. At such tremendous depths, divers ran a far greater risk of becoming disoriented from nitrogen narcosis—the dreaded "rapture of the deep"—and of dying from the bends. But after twenty-four years of experience excavating sunken ships around the world, Bass and his team were equal to the task.

From the first inspection, it was evident that Ulu Burun was a site unlike any other, "an archaeologist's dream," in the words of INA president Don Frey.[4] Not only was it the oldest shipwreck ever found, but its cargo was also incredibly rich. Gold, ivory, silver, precious gems, exotic woods, and vessels of fragrant oil lay scattered on the sea floor along with a veritable fortune in metal ingots.

"The insurers took a pounding when this ship sank, I'll tell you that!" quipped INA archaeologist Robin Piercy.[5] At Cape Gelidonya,

Bass had been impressed by the large quantities of copper and bronze recovered. But all the metal raised from that wreck had amounted to no more than a single ton. By contrast, the ship at Ulu Burun had carried six tons of copper ingots and a sizable load of tin. There was enough copper, Bass calculated, to make "300 bronze helmets, 300 bronze corselets, 3,000 spearheads and 3,000 bronze swords."[6]

The large number of Canaanite and other Near Eastern artifacts on-board hinted that the ship might be Phoenician. Bass and his team found weapons, jewelry, and over a hundred amphorae of clearly Canaanite style, as well as large wide-mouthed jars called *pithoi*, similar to those portrayed lashed to the decks of Canaanite ships in one Egyptian tomb painting of the fourteenth century B.C. The team also found cylinder seals of quartz and hematite, bearing distinctly Near Eastern inscriptions that mixed Babylonian, Assyrian, and other Mesopotamian motifs. Someone on the ship must have used those seals for signing contracts and documents, rolling his personal mark onto clay tablets. Whoever that person was, he evidently hailed from the Near East.

But not all the artifacts were Canaanite. Many turned up that were unmistakably Greek. On board was a wide variety of Mycenaean tableware, as well as a gold chalice of characteristic Mycenaean design. Of the two bronze swords found on the ship, one turned out to be Canaanite, while the other was indisputably Greek. "Perhaps," Bass later mused, "the crew of our ancient merchantman was as mixed as those aboard modern tramp steamers."[7]

There were Egyptian artifacts as well. The team found a damaged gold ring inscribed with hieroglyphs and a tortoise shell such as the Egyptians used to make lutes. A gold scarab bearing the name of Queen Nefertiti in Egyptian helped date the ship to the fourteenth century B.C.

In the ship's hold, they found Canaanite amphorae filled with yellow *Pistacia* resin—used by the Egyptians in burial rites—and a cargo of small black logs, which proved upon lab analysis to be *Dalbergia melanoxylon*—a dark-wooded tree that grows south of Egypt and throughout Central Africa. Tutankhamun's famous tomb contained a bed, chair, and stool made from this lovely black wood, which the Egyptians called *hbny*. Although *Dalbergia melanoxylon* is not true ebony, the Egyptian word *hbny*—which many experts believe was borrowed from another African tongue, possibly of the

Congo-Saharan family—is indeed the root of our modern word *ebony.*

Greek swords. Egyptian scarabs. African ebony. Canaanite pottery. The dense skein of trading relationships required to bring all these goods together in one ship was mind-boggling. Here were six tons of copper that likely came from Cyprus. Here were ingots of tin that may have been mined in Turkey or Afghanistan. There were lumps of amber that could only have come from the Baltic coast, on the North Sea. The cargo gave mute testimony to a world far more complex and interconnected than anyone had dreamed would have been possible in that remote area.

If the ship were indeed Phoenician, as Bass suspected, then it was already over three hundred miles from its home port and apparently continuing westward, as Bass deduced from a careful analysis of its cargo.

How much farther would the ship have sailed, had it survived? Farther up the coast of Asia Minor? All the way to Greece? Through the Dardanelles and into the Black Sea? To Crete? To Italy? Even to the far-off isle of Sardinia, 1,100 miles farther to the west? As far as Bass could tell, any one of these destinations would have been equally plausible.

To this day, Bass has drawn no conclusion about the ship's port of origin. The weight of evidence points toward Phoenicia. But the diversity of its crew renders the question nearly moot. Wherever it hailed from, this was an international ship. Its crew, to use A. W. Brøgger's phrase, "knew no frontiers, needed no passport or identity papers or tickets." For them, "The earth was free, the world lay open, and they wandered across it as though a thousand miles was nothing but a joyous adventure."[8]

What bound them together was a common enterprise—the conquest of the sea. It was ships and crews like this one that pushed the limits of the known world ever farther during the Bronze Age. In their quest for new lands and markets, Kadmos and Danaos themselves may have stood on such decks, their holds packed with Canaanite *pithoi.* Such men were united, regardless of nationality, by their love of commerce and adventure. They may also have been united by a common religion.

One of the most intriguing artifacts recovered from the ship at Ulu Burun was a plaque of green stone bearing the hieroglyphic inscription "Ptah, Lord of Truth." When he first saw it, Bass asked himself, "Is it possible that someone on this voyage worshiped Ptah, who was not only an Egyptian creator of the universe, but also the patron god of craftsmen, especially metalsmiths?"[9]

Perhaps it was the wrong question. "Someone" on the ship may well have worshiped Ptah. But it might have been more to the point to ask whether *everyone* on board adhered to this cult.

CHAPTER 47

THE SEA GUILD

E VERYONE KNOWS THAT EUROPE'S GREAT AGE OF EXPLORATION began in the 1430s, when Prince Henry of Portugal—better known as Henry the Navigator—dispatched the first caravels down the African coast in search of gold. What most people probably do not know is that Henry appears to have been inspired in this endeavor largely by the Knights Templar. During the Inquisition's campaign against the Templars, beginning in 1307, one of the few countries that actually cleared them of all charges was Portugal. The Portuguese Templars were allowed to continue much as before, under the new name of the Knights of Christ.[1]

All the energy that they had previously devoted to crusading in the Holy Land was now poured into a new project—the conquest of the sea. The Templars had long been accomplished sailors, crisscrossing the Mediterranean in their merchant fleet. Now, in their new guise as the Knights of Christ, they led the way to the deep ocean. Prince Henry the Navigator was himself a Grand Master of the Order, and Vasco da Gama a Knight of Christ.[2] Christopher Columbus, in 1479, married the daughter of a former Grand Master. When Columbus struck out for America, his sails bore the emblem of the Knights of Christ—the red Templar cross.[3]

There is a distinct possibility that during the Bronze Age the followers of Ptah may have played a role similar to that of the Templars in fifteenth-century Portugal. That both of these groups appear to have shared an interest in seafaring may, in fact, be more than coincidental. We already discussed, in chapters 33 and 34, the possibility that the Templars inherited certain traditions from the cult of Ptah. Their nautical penchant may well have formed part of that same ancient inheritance.

Experts have long noted that seafaring played an unusually large role in the craftsmen's cults of the Bronze Age Mediterranean. Kothar-wa-Hasis, for example—the Ugaritic Ptah—bears the curious title, in some tablets, of "son of the sea."[4] His Phoenician counterpart, Khousor, was believed to have invented the raft and been the first to sail.[5] In Greek tradition, Daidalos invented sailing.[6] Thus, the green plaque found at Ulu Burun bearing the words "Ptah, Lord of Truth" does not seem to have been out of place in its maritime setting.

In fact, the heavy cargoes of copper, tin, and scrap metal found on the sunken ships at Cape Gelidonya and Ulu Burun may help explain why the gods of craftsmanship, metallurgy, and seamanship were so thoroughly intertwined. In Bronze Age times, seafaring and metalworking formed two sides of the same industry. Neither could exist without the other. The bronze lords were, therefore, obliged to function as shipping barons as much as metal tycoons.

Kadmos himself played just such a double role in Greek legend. As an explorer and seafarer, he crossed the Mediterranean, landed in Greece, battled the savage Aones and Hyantes, and founded the city of Thebes. Through all these adventures, however, Kadmos never lost sight of his commercial purpose. Legend also credits him with introducing bronzeworking to Greece and opening the gold mines of Thrace.[7] His mythological career illustrates how the metal trade may have spurred Europe's exploration and settlement.

The tale of Kadmos also hints at the role of mystery cults in Bronze Age seafaring. Diodoros claims that Kadmos, while en route to Greece, stopped off at the island of Samothrace, where he was inducted into the Mysteries of the Kabiri.[8] *Kabir* is a Semitic word meaning "Great One." Worshiped in Phoenicia as well as Greece, these Great Ones were magical dwarfs, believed to operate forges and smithies deep in the earth. Other ancient accounts say that Kadmos not only joined but also actually founded the Kabiric Mysteries in Samothrace.[9]

During the Bronze Age, every island of importance in the eastern Mediterranean boasted some local cult of metalworking gods, such as the Telchines, Daktyls, Kouretes, and Kabiri. Usually these deities were conceived as diminutive, gnomelike creatures. Herodotos explicitly connects the Kabiri with the cult of Ptah. In describing the "temple of the Kabiri" in Egypt, Herodotos notes that the images of the Kabiri "resemble those of Hephaistos [Ptah], and are supposed to be his sons."[10]

With its "seat" in Memphis, its "throne" in Crete, and its followers spread from Greece to Syria-Palestine, the cult of Ptah possessed a uniquely international reach. Such a cosmopolitan faith could well have provided the perfect religious glue to unite such polyglot crews as that of the Ulu Burun ship. The green plaque inscribed to Ptah, Lord of Truth may well have contributed as much to political peace among the crew as to the ship's protection from wind and wave.

The cult of Ptah may, in fact, have provided the religious basis for actual guilds of merchant seamen. Cyrus Gordon argues strongly for the existence of such guilds among Bronze Age mariners: "It is becoming abundantly clear that there was an important element in the fabric of the Bronze Age Mediterranean: an international network of merchant mariners organized in guilds. We know of them from texts such as the Ugaritic tablets (1400–1200 B.C.)."[11]

In Gordon's view, this "international network" served the interests of what he called "thalassocrats," or "Sea Peoples"—maritime powers whose quest for profit transcended national boundaries and tribal loyalties. "The Sea People were not limited to one ethnic or linguistic group," writes Gordon, "though their leadership may have tended to come from a special elite."[12]

The term *Sea Peoples*, of course, was used by the Egyptians to describe the league of seaborne marauders who threatened the Nile Delta around 1200 B.C. (as discussed in chapter 23). Gordon applies the term more broadly to include Minoans, Phoenicians, and all other peoples who made their living through seafaring. In Gordon's view, the Sea Peoples acted almost as stateless cartels, investing in overseas properties as indiscriminately as today's transnational corporate behemoths. "Thalassocrats cannot be pinned down to any special land area," he writes. "They control islands and ports from which they exploit whatever districts are necessary for raw materials."[13]

Archaeology supports the notion that the bronze lords operated from island strongholds. Nearly every major island of the Mediterranean became a center for shipping, mining, and metallurgy during the Bronze Age, as well as a home to mystery cults dedicated to the metal trade. Archaeologist Sarah Morris notes that the Phoenicians typically exploited mines and other mainland resources from staging areas on nearby islands.[14]

From such bases, the bronze lords could visit the mainland briefly for specific missions of trade, mining, or prospecting.[15] In his clash with the Aones and Hyantes, Kadmos learned the hard way that European tribes did not always take kindly to foreigners stealing their land. A strategy of island-hopping, punctuated with brief expeditions to the mainland, was tailor-made to maximize profits while minimizing conflict with the natives.

The bronze lords appear to have followed their island stepping-stones far beyond the familiar waters of the eastern Mediterranean. Metal ingots of the same standard shape as those found on the ships at Ulu Burun and Cape Gelidonya have turned up as far west as Sardinia. "While I believe those ingots were cast from local ore," George Bass comments, "their shape may suggest a Near Eastern presence in the western Mediterranean in the Late Bronze Age."[16]

That the cult of Ptah presided over such explorations seems hard to dispute. As we have seen, foreign versions of Ptah, such as Khousor, Kothar, Hephaistos, and Daidalos, were clearly linked to seafaring in Bronze Age legend, as were the Kabiri, whom Herodotos described as sons of "Hephaistos," or Ptah. The green plaque found at Ulu Burun suggests that at least some crewmen on Phoenician ships even worshiped Ptah by his Egyptian name.

Cyrus Gordon may well be right in supposing that leagues of stateless thalassocrats ruled the Bronze Age seas. But the reverence these Sea Peoples evidently held for the cult of Ptah hints at their subservience toward Egypt. Dating, as it does, from the time of the *Pax Aegyptiaca*, the green plaque found at Ulu Burun testifies to an age when Egypt must have exercised enormous influence—perhaps even control—over the sea guilds.

This was an age when a Phoenician ruler such as Rib-Addi of Byblos could call himself "servant" and "footstool" of the pharaoh,[17] an age when the Egyptian conqueror Thutmose III could boast that he had "trussed . . . the Isles in the Midst of the Great Green Sea" and compelled the Keftiu, or Minoans, to bring "gifts on their back . . . in order to submit to his majesty."[18] It was an age, in short, when Egypt ruled the waves.

The evolution of the phrase *Wadj Wer*—literally, the "Great Green" or "Great Green Sea"—enables us to trace the expansion of Egyptian seafaring over the centuries. Most Egyptologists agree that the Great Green originally meant the swamps of the Nile Delta. During the time of the Old Kingdom, however, it came to mean "sea," particularly the Red Sea—the route to Punt. By the New Kingdom period, however, the phrase "Great Green Sea" clearly referred to the Mediterranean.[19]

It seems clear that Egyptian mariners expanded their horizons over hundreds of years from local African waters to the far-flung sea lanes of the Mediterranean. How far they wandered across the Great Green Sea we can only guess. As we previously discussed, the Egyptians possessed whole classes of seagoing vessels, which they called Byblites (*kbnwt*) and Cretans (*kftiw*).[20] Most experts agree that these terms described types of ships originally designed to sail to the specific parts of the world for which they were named.[21]

If this interpretation is correct, then it is certain that the Egyptians made regular runs at least as far as Crete and Phoenicia. How much farther did they sail? On this question, we must await the verdict of archaeology. As this book goes to press, the eighty-three-year-old Thor Heyerdahl is hard at work excavating the Phoenician port of Lixus, now located on Morocco's Atlantic coast. "Little archaeological work has been done in the city, as generally in this part of Africa," observes field leader Oystein Kock Johansen, director of Oslo's Kon-Tiki Museum. "We are likely to come across Moslem sites, as well as sites from Byzantine, Roman, Greek, pre-Greek, Phoenician and maybe even Egyptian periods."[22]

Excavations such as this may or may not yield evidence, someday, of extensive Egyptian seafaring in the Mediterranean. But, whatever role the Egyptians played—whether as mariners themselves or as sponsors and cult leaders of the metal trade—their impact on Bronze Age exploration appears to have been profound.

Mesmerized by the achievements of Columbus and other European explorers, generations of scholars assumed that Europe must have monopolized the seas since ancient times. They envisioned a Bronze Age Mediterranean dominated by Greek fleets. But modern archaeology has failed to support this theory. A new picture is emerging of a world in which Egyptians, Phoenicians, and Semitic-speaking Cretans jockeyed for influence in a complex and cosmopolitan milieu, of which Europe formed only the most distant and savage periphery.

The very name of Europe provides striking evidence for this theory. If Greeks had explored the Mediterranean first, one would expect its lands to bear Greek names. But this does not appear to be the case. Just as the Italian explorer Amerigo Vespucci bestowed his name on America, so it appears that Bronze Age explorers once chose a name for Europe, rooted in their distinctive language, culture, and religion. And, as we will see in the following chapter, the literary and linguistic evidence strongly suggests that whoever thought up the name *Europe* was probably not European.

CHAPTER 48

WHY IS EUROPE CALLED "EUROPE"?

BY THE FIFTH CENTURY B.C., NO ONE REMEMBERED ANY LONGER how Europe had gotten its name. Herodotos treated the question as an unsolvable riddle. "As for Europe," he wrote, "nobody knows . . . where it got its name from, or who gave it, unless we are to say that it came from Europa, the Tyrian woman, and before that was nameless."[1]

Herodotos is referring here to the familiar story of Europa, the Phoenician princess whom Zeus kidnapped and seduced after he took on the form of a bull. Certainly, the name seems to fit. But Herodotos's theory raises more questions than it answers. As Herodotos himself admits, the legendary Europa never, in her life, set foot on European soil. Moreover, her name seems ill-suited for a major land mass. In Greek, it means something like "broad-faced" or "wide-eyed." Why would anyone give such a name to a continent?

One explanation comes from the Greek lexicographer Hesychios of Alexandria. During the fifth century A.D., Hesychios recorded an ancient tradition that Europa's name meant "dark one" or "land of the sunset."[3] If this is true, then *Europa* is not a Greek word at all. To find a word similar to *Europa* meaning "land of the sunset" or "dark one," we would have to go to the Semitic languages of the Near East.

The Akkadians of Mesopotamia, for example, referred to the sunset as *erebu.*[4] In Ugaritic, the verb used to describe the setting of the sun was *arabu,* and in Phoenician *arob.*[5] Almost every Semitic tongue uses a similar word to signify sunset, darkness, and the west.[6] Many scholars believe that the Greek name *Europé* derives from the Semitic root *'ereb* and its variants. Indeed, Europa herself may be a Hellenized version of a Phoenician goddess of the sunset and the evening star,[7] whose name was spelled *'rb* and might have been pronounced something like *'Arabu.*[8]

If Europa really is a goddess of the sunset, then the name of her brother Kadmos makes all the more sense. For *Kadmos* appears to derive from a Phoenician word, *qadm,* meaning "east" or "easterner."[9] Kadmos and Europa might therefore represent east and west, sunrise and sunset. Perhaps they are even versions of the Ugaritic twins, Shachar and Shalim, "dawn" and "dusk."

Like Kadmos and Europa, Shachar is the brother and Shalim the sister. Shachar rules the east, and Shalim the west. In the Ugaritic tablets, these twins even bear the title *agzrym bn ym*—"islanders, children of the sea"—suggesting that they may have received special reverence from seafarers.[10] It would make sense that Bronze Age explorers, sailing far to the west, might have named their new continent after the sunset—in particular, after the *goddess* of the sunset—just as Hesychios claimed.

If this is true, the name they gave the new continent reveals a great deal about how the early seafarers regarded Europe. Among the ancient peoples of the Mediterranean, the land of the sunset was an enchanted realm, haunted by demons, gods, monsters, and spirits of the dead. It was in the west that the sun "died" each night, leaving the world in shadow. Europe must have seemed a very strange and ominous place indeed to receive such a name from its Bronze Age discoverers.

The belief that dead souls resided in the west seems to have started in Egypt and, from there, spread throughout the eastern Mediterranean. The Egyptians believed that spirits of the dead sailed on the boat of the sun god to a place called Sekhet Hetepet— the "Field of Rushes" in the land of the sunset. There they feasted, hunted, made love, and otherwise enjoyed eternal life. But only the righteous were admitted to Sekhet Hetepet. First, their hearts had to be weighed before the great judge Osiris. Those found wanting were damned. The righteous were declared *maa-kheru*—"true of voice"—and allowed to enter paradise.

The Greeks appear to have borrowed the concept of a western paradise from Egypt. Their word for the blessed dead was *makares*—which many scholars believe is a direct loan from the Egyptian *maa-kheru*.[11] As noted in chapter 19, the Greeks—like most ancient peoples—put little hope in the afterlife. In Homer, even divine heroes such as Achilles ended up in Hades, "clangorously whirling like wild birds this way and that in bewildered fear."[12] Yet, parallel to this belief—and seemingly in contradiction to it—the Greeks also spoke of a land far to the west where the *makares* resided in eternal bliss.

It appears that there were two entirely separate beliefs about the Underworld current in ancient Greece. The grim and frightful Hades of Homer's *Odyssey* clearly dominated Greek imaginations right up until the dawn of the Christian era. Yet many Greeks embraced mystery cults—generally believed to be of foreign origin—which claimed to offer more attractive alternatives.

The most famous of these cults were the so-called Eleusinian Mysteries, or Mysteries of Demeter. As noted in chapter 22, Diodoros recorded a tradition that the Eleusinian Mysteries were brought to Athens by Erechtheus, the fourth king of Athens, who was himself reputed to be an Egyptian. "After he had secured the throne," writes Diodoros, "he instituted the initiatory rites of Demeter in Eleusis and established the mysteries, transferring their ritual from Egypt."[13]

Contrary to traditional Greek belief, the Eleusinian Mysteries offered eternal bliss to initiates—a promise that probably accounted for the cult's great popularity. "Thrice blessed are those among men who, after beholding these rites, go down to Hades," wrote Sophokles of the Mysteries. "Only for them is there life; all the rest will suffer an evil lot."[14]

After death, initiates in the Eleusinian Mysteries became *makares* and journeyed to a land far to the west called the Elysian Fields—reminiscent of the Egyptian Field of Rushes. Sometimes this land was called the Garden of the Hesperides or the Isles of the Blest. By whatever name, the Greeks imagined this paradise on the extreme western edge of the earth, where land gave way to the boundless Okeanos—the Atlantic Ocean. Also in the far west was the entrance to Hades, which Homer called Erebos—a word that most scholars derive from Semitic 'Ereb, or "land of the sunset."

Homer's use of a Near Eastern word like Erebos suggests that the Phoenicians too regarded the west as an abode of the dead. Certainly, many Phoenician gods were thought to dwell in the western islands.[15] Like the Greeks, the Phoenicians may have borrowed from Egypt their belief in a magical, spirit-haunted land of the sunset.

Imbued as they were with Egyptian superstition, Bronze Age explorers of every nationality must have approached the western seas with extreme trepidation. Homer's Odyssey paints a vivid picture of how the west must have appeared to Bronze Age eyes. Each time Odysseus's vessel is blown off course by malevolent fate or an angry god, he and his crew are swept ever westward into seas that grow stranger, deadlier, and more wondrous the closer they veer to the setting sun.

Odysseus and his men battle a one-eyed giant named Polyphemos; they narrowly escape the cannibal Laestrygonians; they are turned into swine by Circe the witch; their ears stopped up with wax, they glide safely past the deadly Sirens, whose seductive song has lured many a sailor to his death. At last, they come to Erebos, "the land of death." Located on the westernmost shore of the earth, Erebos hides the entrance to the Underworld. It is the true "land of the sunset," just as its name implies.

But the name is Semitic, not Greek. Such linguistic and other textual clues have moved scholars, over the years, to speculate that Homer may have compiled his Odyssey from a patchwork of old folklore inherited from the Phoenicians. The French scholar Victor Bérard even argued, in 1902, that Homer's poem was based on a long-lost Phoenician epic and that Odysseus himself was originally a Phoenician hero.[16] Bérard's theory was ridiculed for decades. But in recent years it has won new respect.[17]

Whether they were Egyptian, Phoenician, or Minoan, the earliest Bronze Age explorers must have expected, when they entered western seas, to meet witches, giants, cannibals, and monsters, not unlike those that faced Odysseus. No doubt, Europe's shores offered more than enough real-life terrors to uphold the west's reputation for danger. As their ships hurtled through fog and tempest, the early explorers must have fancied themselves hanging at the very brink of Erebos.

Yet, there must have been quieter moments, too, when the adventurers glided past unknown shores on seas that ran smoother than glass. At such times, the Isles of the Blessed must have seemed very close. A thousand prayers must have risen from sailors' lips over the centuries, giving thanks to Europa, goddess of the west, for safe arrival in her enchanted domain.

So it was that the continent of Europe gained its name—or, at least, so goes the theory. If, indeed, Europe was named after the princess Europa, as Herodotos guessed, and if Hesychios correctly translated *Europa* as "land of the sunset," then the name of that continent speaks to us more powerfully than any artifact dug from the earth. Its very syllables evoke the wonder and terror with which Bronze Age mariners faced the unknown. Even now, after 4,000 years, Europe's name resounds with the spanking of sails and the groan of cedar planks. Even now, it transports us to that long-forgotten era, when the world was fresh, and an uncharted continent stretched, wild and raw, across the Great Green Sea.

PART EIGHT

THE
PYRAMIDS
OF GREECE

CHAPTER 49

THE LEGEND
OF DANAOS

IN PREVIOUS CHAPTERS, WE SPOKE A GREAT DEAL ABOUT KADMOS AND his Phoenician colonists. But it would be wrong to give the impression that Phoenicians were the principal colonizers of Greece. A much larger role seems to have been played by settlers from Egypt. Indeed, one of these settlers, Danaos, appears to have given his name to the entire nation.

Who was Danaos? According to Greek legend, he was a prince of Egypt. Apollodoros, an Athenian scholar of the second century B.C., says that Danaos quarreled with his twin brother, Aigyptos, "concerning the kingdom," which seems to imply that the brothers fought over the throne. Subsequently, Danaos no longer felt safe in Egypt. Apollodoros continues: "As they afterwards quarreled concerning the kingdom, Danaus feared the sons of Egypt [Aigyptos], and by the advice of Athena, he built a ship, being the first to do so, and having put his daughters on board he fled."[1]

Danaos sailed, first, to the island of Rhodes. There, he built a temple to Athena, in gratitude for her advice and protection. Centuries later, the pharaoh Amasis gave generous gifts to this temple

299

because of its legendary connection with Danaos (see chapter 21). After a short stay in Rhodes, the exiles departed for Greece.

Much as New Englanders today preserve the site of Plymouth Rock, the ancient Greeks long remembered the exact place where Danaos and his daughters supposedly first set foot on Greek soil. It was called Apobathmi and was located just south of Argos, on the Peloponnesian peninsula. In his *Description of Greece,* written around A.D. 174, Pausanias noted the site as a point of interest for tourists.[2] The year of Danaos's landing, according to the Parian Marble, was 1511 B.C.[3]

Pausanias mentions that Danaos arrived in Greece with an entire "fleet," which implies that he brought far more people with him than just his family.[4] The intimidating size of this fleet and the number of troops it carried may have contributed greatly to what happened next. Greek tradition holds that Argos was inhabited by Pelasgians at the time Danaos landed. These were the people—discussed in chapter 17—whom legend regarded as the original inhabitants of Greece. Appropriately enough, they were ruled by a king named Pelasgos.

One version of the story holds that King Pelasgos welcomed the Egyptians warmly, inviting Danaos and his daughters to settle in the country as his guests. Apollodoros, on the other hand, says that Pelasgos "surrendered the kingdom to him" and that Danaos "made himself master of the country."[5] Either way, the legends agree that Danaos replaced Pelasgos as king of Argos. It is hard to imagine how Danaos could have accomplished this, unless he had brought a considerable army with him.

However large Danaos's forces may have been, those of his brother Aigyptos were apparently larger. No sooner was Danaos ensconced in his new kingdom than Aigyptos arrived in Greece, demanding that his fifty sons be permitted to marry Danaos's fifty daughters. Some versions of the tale suggest that it was to escape this marriage that Danaos and his daughters had fled Egypt in the first place.

Evidently, Danaos did not have the military strength to resist. He agreed to the marriage, whereupon all fifty of his daughters were wedded to the sons of Aigyptos on a single day. But treachery was afoot. Danaos gave daggers to each of his daughters and ordered them to murder their bridegrooms while they slept. All obeyed, except one. Danaos's eldest daughter, Hypermestra, refused to murder her husband. For this virtuous act, the gods rewarded Hypermestra. Her husband, Lynkeos, succeeded Danaos as king, and it was Hypermestra's descendants who inherited the throne of Argos.

Despite his treachery, Danaos was long remembered as a wise and capable ruler. The dynasty he founded gave rise to some of the greatest heroes in Greek legend, including Perseus and Herakles. His daughters too were remembered, for establishing the secret rites of the Thesmophoria—a festival in which women camped out for three days, away from men, in order to worship Demeter, the Greek goddess usually identified with Isis. "It was the daughters of Danaus," wrote Herodotos, "who brought this ceremony from Egypt and instructed the Pelasgian women in it."[6]

But perhaps the most lasting achievement of Danaos was to give a new name to the Greeks. In the play *Archelaos*, Euripides explains, "Danaos, the father of fifty daughters, on coming to Argos took up his abode in the city of Inachos [Argos] and throughout Greece he laid down the law that all people hitherto named Pelasgians were to be named Danaans."[7]

From that day forth, and for many centuries to come, the Greeks—or at least a large portion of them—were known as Danaoi, or Danaans. In the *Iliad*, Homer never refers to "Greeks" but only to Danaans (whom he also calls Argives and Achaians). Egyptian documents from the New Kingdom also refer to Greece as Tanaya, and to the Greeks as Dene.[8] To the extent that Greece existed as a nation during the Late Bronze Age, it appears to have taken its identity from a single tribe called the Danaans.

The clear implication is that the Greeks who sacked Troy were the direct inheritors of Danaos's kingdom. Their very sense of nationhood derived from Danaos. If there is any truth to the Danaos legend, we must consider the possibility that Greek civilization arose, in the Bronze Age, largely as a result of Egyptian colonization. But how true is the legend?

There is no simple answer to that question. The traditional accounts are filled with contradictions. The Egyptian historian Manetho, for example, says that Danaos was the brother of a pharaoh named Ramesses (also called Sethos or Sethosis). Manetho tells us that Ramesses was a mighty conqueror, "whose power lay in his cavalry and his fleet."[9] When Ramesses set out to conquer

Phoenicia and Cyprus, he left his brother Danaos (whose Egyptian name was Harmais) to rule Egypt in his place. But Danaos betrayed his brother's trust and attempted to seize the throne. Hearing news of the betrayal, Ramesses returned to Egypt with his army and drove Danaos into exile.

So far, Manetho's story seems to resemble the Greek account. The problem arises when we try to assign Manetho's characters to real pharaohs. Most experts agree that "Harmais" could only have been the pharaoh Horemheb, who ruled Egypt from about 1323 to 1295 B.C.[10] But there is no record that Horemheb seized the throne from a brother named Ramesses or Sethos or that he ever fled to Greece. Indeed, Horemheb was buried in Egypt's Valley of the Kings. In addition, Manetho says that Harmais ruled for only four years and one month, while Horemheb had a long reign of twenty-eight years.[11]

The picture grows even murkier when we try to use the Greek accounts to identify Danaos. According to Apollodoros, Danaos's great-grandfather Epaphos was ruler of Egypt and founder of the Egyptian city of Memphis. This would seem to identify Epaphos with Menes, the historical pharaoh who really did found Memphis sometime around 3150–3125 B.C. But very little else in the Greek legend seems to accord with what we know about Menes and his family.

According to the Greeks, Danaos's great-great-grandmother was a mortal woman named Io, who was bedded by the god Zeus. Out of jealousy, Zeus's wife, Hera, changed Io into a cow and sent gadflies to torment her, whereupon Io fled Greece and swam across the sea to Egypt. There, she bore Zeus a son named Epaphos, who became the ruler of Egypt and the great-grandfather of Danaos.

The fact that Io came from Greece, in the legend, has led some experts to speculate that Danaos and his family were really Greek exiles, living in Egypt. By this interpretation, Danaos fled to Greece when he got in trouble because it was his ancestral homeland.[12] His arrival in Greece was therefore a homecoming, not an invasion. The problem with this theory, however, is that it puts a Greek family in the unlikely position of ruling Egypt for at least five generations and even founding the capital city of Memphis. Apollodoros writes:

> [Io] gave birth to a son Epaphus beside the river Nile ... and was married to Telegonus, who then reigned over the Egyptians. ... Reigning over the Egyptians, Epaphus married Memphis, daughter of

Nile, founded and named the city of Memphis after her, and begat a daughter Libya, after whom the region of Libya was called. Libya had by Poseidon twin sons, Agenor and Belus. Agenor departed to Phoenicia and reigned there. But Belus remained in Egypt, reigned over the country, and married Anchinoe, daughter of Nile, by whom he had twin sons, Egyptus and Danaus.[13]

Apollodoros's genealogy leaves little doubt that the Greeks saw Danaos's family as an Egyptian royal dynasty. In fact, the only Greek who appears in the story is Io herself. Not only does she marry an Egyptian king named Telegonos, but her descendants also marry Egyptians, in the guise of "daughters of the Nile." Apollodoros notes that seven of Danaos's daughters even had an Ethiopian mother.[14] Whatever Greek blood Io brought to the mix seems to have become seriously diluted over the years.

In fact, even Io herself may not have been Greek. She seems to have symbolized the Egyptian goddess Isis in the story. Apollodoros, for example, explicitly identifies her with Isis. "And she [Io] set up an image of Demeter, whom the Egyptians call Isis," writes Apollodoros, "and Io likewise they called by the name of Isis."[15] Every Egyptian pharaoh claimed Isis as his mother, and Io too appears as the mother of a pharaoh. Both Isis and Io were said to have taken the form of cows, and both were portrayed by artists in a similar fashion. "The statues of Isis show a female figure with cow's horns," writes Herodotos, "like the Greek representations of Io."[16] It is hard to escape the conclusion that Io is simply a Hellenized version of Isis.

Whether or not we choose to regard Io as Greek, there was certainly no doubt in Herodotos's mind that Danaos and his daughters were Egyptian. In discussing the genealogy of Danae, the great-great-granddaughter of Danaos, Herodotos commented, "If . . . we trace the ancestry of Danae, the daughter of Acrisios, we find that the Dorian chieftains are genuine Egyptians."[17] Herodotos was also referring to the Danaids when he wrote, "How it happened that Egyptians came to the Peloponnese and what they did to make themselves kings in that part of Greece, has been chronicled by other writers."[18]

Even the physical appearance of the Danaids was remembered, in Greek legend, as having been distinctly African. They are described as "black" in the plays of Aischlos (Aeschylus), as are their cousins, the fifty sons of Aigyptos. In *The Suppliants*, the Danaids call themselves "black and smitten by the sun," while, in the same play, Aischylos has Danaos notice that the "black limbs" of his nephews stand out against their white robes.[19]

Plato clearly did not look upon the Danaids as Greek. To him, they were "barbarians." In *Menexenos*, Plato concludes that the cowardice and treachery of certain Greek cities resulted from their having been "contaminated" with foreign blood, while the valor and nobility of his native Athens derived from its pure Greek heritage. Plato writes: "For we are not like many others, descendants of Pelops or Kadmos or Aigyptos or Danaos, who are by nature barbarians . . . but we are pure Hellenes, uncontaminated by any foreign element."[20]

As with so many other Bronze Age legends, the exact dates and details behind the Danaos story may never be known. But its overall message seems clear: *Greece was colonized by Egyptians.* The legend implies, further, that Greece emerged as a nation largely through the leadership of Egyptian kings, who planted royal dynasties and founded Egyptian cults on Greek soil. If the Danaos legend itself were our only evidence for this claim, we might find it hard to swallow. But, as we will see in the following pages, archaeology has provided spectacular and unexpected support for this ancient belief.

CHAPTER 50

MIN, MINOS, AND MENES

PERHAPS THE GREATEST UNANSWERED QUESTION CONCERNING THE Danaos story is, When did it happen? The Parian Marble says that Danaos landed in Greece in 1511 B.C. Apollodoros, on the other hand, says that Danaos's great-grandfather Epaphos founded the city of Memphis, which had to have occurred at least 1,600 years earlier. The Egyptian account has similar discrepancies. Manetho attributes to Aigyptos (whom he also calls Ramesses, Sethos, and Sethosis) military exploits that seem to have been borrowed from the lives of Ramesses II and Sesostris, neither one of whom could possibly have been the brother of "Harmais," or Horemheb.

How do we account for this confusion? The legend itself may offer the best clue. Virtually every one of its important characters appears as the founder or personification of a nation. King Pelasgos, for example, symbolizes the Pelasgians, Danaos the Danaans, and Aigyptos—whose name simply means "Egypt" in Greek—the Egyptians. Manetho even records a tradition that Egypt took its name from Danaos's brother. Manetho relates that after Aigyptos returned with his army and drove Danaos from the country, "the land was named Aigyptos after him."[1]

All of this suggests that the characters in the Danaos legend should be regarded not so much as individuals, but as symbols of entire nations. Aigyptos, Danaos, and Pelasgos clearly represent the Egyptians, Danaans, and Pelasgians. But the interactions among these three peoples described in the story may have taken centuries to unfold. Legends and historical events from a multitude of different eras seem to have been jumbled together in the same story, and the characters themselves appear to be composites whose biographies are spliced together from a wide range of legendary heroes.

The Greeks, for example, may have lumped together more than one Egyptian explorer under the guise of Danaos. This is the same mistake that the Aztecs made in 1519, when Cortés landed in their country. Because the Aztecs had traditional tales of a mariner named Quetzalcoatl landing on their shores centuries before, they imagined that Cortés might be the same person and actually called him Quetzalcoatl. Had the Aztecs remained in power, Mexican historians to this day might still insist that Quetzalcoatl landed in their country in the year 1519.

It seems reasonable to assume that some Egyptian seafarer really did land at Apobathmi in 1511 B.C., as the Greek legends recount. But, although the Greek storytellers remembered this visitor as "Danaos," he may not have been the original Danaos. Another may well have come to Greece centuries before, within a few generations of Egypt's unification—just as the legends imply.

Many clues in the story point to a very early time period for Danaos. Apollodoros, for example, ascribes to Danaos the invention of seafaring—an event that must have occurred during the Stone Age. As noted in the last chapter, Danaos's great-grandfather Epaphos is called the founder of Memphis, which seems to identify him with Menes, who ruled Egypt around 3150–3125 B.C.

Aigyptos too seems to be linked with the founding of Memphis. As discussed in chapter 31, the new city of Memphis was dedicated to the god Ptah and was called *Hwt-ka-Ptah*—"the House of Ptah"—which the Greeks corrupted to *Aigyptos*. If Egypt was really named after Danaos's brother Aigyptos, as Manetho claims, then Aigyptos presents as good a candidate as Epaphos for identification with the legendary King Menes. In any case, both characters seem to link Danaos with Egypt's earliest kings.

What evidence do we have that Egypt was sending out colonists at such an early date? One such clue was already mentioned in chapter 20. The Egyptian priests told Diodoros that many colonists—including Danaos—had gone out from Egypt in the years following the reign of Isis and Osiris. This would put the colonizations at the very dawn of Egypt's history. Diodoros wrote, "Now the Egyptians say that also after these events a great number of colonies were spread from Egypt over all the inhabited world. . . . They also say that those who set forth with Danaus, likewise from Egypt, settled what is practically the oldest city of Greece, Argos . . . Even the Athenians, they say, are colonists from Sais in Egypt."[2]

In fact, some scholars have speculated that just such a migration might have taken place during Egypt's early years. As noted in chapter 44, Sir Arthur Evans pointed to the "opening out of communications with the Nile Valley" as the "determining cause" of Crete's early advancement.[3] Evans theorized that Crete had been colonized by Libyan refugees expelled from Egypt at the start of the Third Dynasty (around 2700–2600 B.C.) as the pharaohs consolidated their hold over the Delta. There is, in fact, considerable archaeological evidence that new people arrived in Crete around this time—people whose culture resembled that of the Libyans.[4]

Other scholars have speculated that Crete might have been settled by an earlier generation of refugees—Lower Egyptians fleeing before Menes's conquering army. These Lower Egyptians may have brought with them the distinctive "figure-eight" shield of the goddess Neit, which subsequently became an important symbol of the Minoans (though archaeologists have not yet found examples of this symbol in Crete, older than about 2000 B.C.)[5] Readers will recall from chapter 21 that Neit—the goddess whom Martin Bernal has called Black Athena—had her cult center in the northern Egyptian city of Sais. It was to this goddess that Danaos and his daughters erected a temple on the island of Rhodes, according to Greek legend.

Whether the alleged colonization took place during Menes's reign or some four or five centuries later, as Evans believed, it seems clear that people were migrating out of Egypt at an early date. Even in

2700 B.C., the memory of King Menes would have been fresh in Egyptian minds, the cults and traditions he established strong. Some of those traditions may well have survived through the legends of the Cretan king Minos.

As discussed in chapter 44, the names Minos and Menes seem closely related. Herodotos calls King Menes "Min," and *Minos* is nothing more than *Min* with the Greek masculine ending *os* affixed to it. Many scholars believe that *Minos* was a royal title in Crete, applied to every king. Similarly, more than one of Egypt's early rulers bore the name *Mn*.

As previously noted, most Egyptologists are confident that the pharaoh Narmer is the legendary Min, or Menes. They draw this conclusion partly from the fact that Narmer left an inscribed plaque that seems to depict him as the conqueror of Lower Egypt. Egyptologists have also noted that jar sealings found at Abydos seem to link Narmer's name with the hieroglyph of a gaming board, which represents the syllable *men*, or *meni*. The same glyph appears in other inscriptions, however, alongside the name of Hor-Aha, the son and successor of Narmer.[6] Did *men* represent an honorary title, of some sort, inherited from father to son? Nobody knows.

What we do know is that the mysterious syllable *mn*, or *min*, plays a prominent role in legends of Greece's early colonization. As noted in chapter 44, Thukydides ascribed to King Minos and his navy the colonization of the Greek islands called the Cyclades. Before Minos, says Thukydides, these islands were held by Phoenicians and also by Carians from Asia Minor. Thukydides wrote, "The islanders too were great pirates. These islanders were Carians and Phoenicians, by whom most of the islands were colonized. . . . But as soon as Minos had formed his navy, communication by sea became easier, as he colonized most of the islands, and thus expelled the malefactors."[7]

Archaeologists agree that the Greek islands do seem to have come under foreign attack during the period between 2800 and 2200 B.C. Some experts link this development to Thukydides' account of Minoan colonization.[8] An even more remarkable transformation occurred on the mainland, however. It was precisely during this period that a mysterious new people appeared in Greece—a civilization of master builders and expert seafarers whose surviving monuments include enormous, pyramid-like burial mounds.

The Greeks called these people Minyai—Minyans. Very little is known about them. But the similarity of their name both to the Cretan King Minos and the Egyptian Menes has been noted by scholars. Who were these people? Some experts believe they may have been Egyptians. Indeed, recent discoveries in archaeology suggest that the arrival of the Minyans in Greece may have been the very event that inspired the legend of Danaos.

CHAPTER 51

THE MARVELOUS
MINYANS

IN 1984, IRISH EXPLORER TIM SEVERIN SET SAIL FROM THE GREEK PORT of Pefkakia. Ahead of him lay a 1,500-mile journey that would take him through the Dardanelles and across the Black Sea, all the way to what was then the Soviet Socialist Republic of Georgia. Severin's vessel, the *Argo,* was an exact replica of the sort of twenty-oared galley that once cruised the Bronze Age Aegean. His purpose was to duplicate the voyage made by Jason and the Argonauts in their legendary quest for the Golden Fleece.

Many scholars said it could not be done. Even with twenty men straining at the oars, the *Argo* would never pack more than 8 horsepower—far too little to buck the currents of 3–4 knots pouring out of the Bosphorus Straits. Indeed, on its first approach to the Straits, the *Argo* floundered in the current like a stick of driftwood, just as the experts had predicted.

Severin used his ingenuity, however. By steering dangerously close to shore, he was able to ride short patches of countercurrent that carried him, stepping-stone fashion, right into the Black Sea.[1] The real Jason might well have used the same trick. After seven weeks at sea, the *Argo* sailed triumphantly into the Georgian port of

Poti—just as the legendary Jason had once entered the harbor of the Colchian king Aeetes. Severin had proved that the voyage of Jason and the Argonauts was at least possible.

But who were the Argonauts? The roster of crewmen on the original *Argo* reads like a Who's Who of legendary heroes, from Herakles, the strongman, to the magical lyre-player Orpheus. The Argonauts seem to have represented the best and bravest from all of Greek mythology. But how many of them were actually Greek?

In the *Argonautica*—an epic poem about Jason's voyage, written by Apollonios Rhodios in the third century B.C.—the Argonauts are always called Minyai, or Minyans. After listing their names, Apollonios observes, "Such and so many were the noblemen who rallied to the aid of Aeson's son [Jason]. The people of the place called them all Minyai, since most of them and all the best could claim descent from the daughters of Minyas. Thus, Jason himself was the son of Alcimede, whose mother was Clymene, one of Minyas' daughters."[2]

According to Apollonios, the Argonauts—or most of them, at any rate—traced their descent to King Minyas, the legendary founder of the Minyan nation. Legend held that Minyas built and ruled one of the wealthiest cities of Bronze Age Greece, called by Homer "Orchomenos, rich in gold." Archaeologists know that the real Orchomenos was burned and abandoned during the mayhem that ended the Bronze Age. But, as late as Roman times, its fabled riches were still remembered. Pausanias wrote, "This Chryses had a son called Minyas, and after him the people over whom he ruled are still called Minyans. The revenues that Minyas received were so great that he surpassed his predecessors in wealth, and he was the first man we know of to build a treasury to receive his riches."[3]

As wealthy as the Minyans were, they evidently yearned for more. Most scholars agree that if there was a real quest for the Golden Fleece, it was probably a prospecting expedition sent to find gold in Colchis.[4] To this day, the Svan mountaineers of the Georgian highlands continue to catch gold dust by placing the fleece of sheep in mountain streams.[5] The Minyans of Greece may have heard of this practice and sent Jason to investigate.

But who were these Minyans? Nobody knows. Legend held that Minyans settled in Iolkos, Thessaly, Pylos, and various Aegean islands, as well as at Orchomenos. Indeed, they appear to have been one of the most prominent peoples occupying Bronze Age Greece.

Yet their origin is obscure. The name *Minyan* appears to have the same root as *Minos*, prompting some scholars to speculate that they were colonists from Crete.[6] But this is only a guess. The word *Minyan* could also be derived from the Egyptian name *Min*, or *Menes*. And, indeed, some experts suggest that Egypt was the Minyan homeland.

One of the strongest clues of an Egyptian origin lies in the Minyans' apparent talent for hydraulic engineering—the building of dams, dikes, and canals. In classical times, a great lake called Kopais covered most of the lands once held by the Minyans of Or-chomenos. But Pausanias recorded a tradition that the lake had not always been there. In Bronze Age times, towns and cities—includ-ing the original Minyan city of Orchomenos—had supposedly stood on what was later to become the lake bottom. These cities were covered by water, wrote Pausanias, when Herakles—in his war against the Minyans—stopped up the channels that drained the lake water into the sea.[7]

In garbled form, this legend records one of the most remarkable engineering feats of the ancient world. Modern archaeology has con-firmed that Lake Kopais was indeed dry during Bronze Age times. But this was not its natural state. The lake was drained by human intervention. Left to their own devices, the rivers Kephissos and Melas flow into the plain of Kopais, forming swamps in the summer and a lake 9 to 15 feet deep in the winter. But, in Bronze Age times, an extraordinary system of dikes and sluices diverted the flood-waters to the sea, exposing over 200 square miles of new farmland.

Excavated in the 1930s by the German archaeologist Siegfried Lauffer, the Kopais drainage system is widely recognized as having been the most ambitious engineering project undertaken in ancient Europe. Lauffer discovered that the lake bed had been surrounded by earthen dikes, up to 150 feet thick, and reinforced at certain places with 6-foot-thick Cyclopean stone walls. Around the outside of this enclosure, the floodwaters of the Kephissos and Melas Rivers flowed in a wide moat, draining into a canal on the eastern side of the lake bed.

Over five miles long and more than 250 feet wide at some points, this canal emptied into the *katavothrai*—natural, underground tun-nels eroded through the limestone base of Mount Ptoon, through which the waters of Lake Kopais drained every spring into the sea. It was because of this natural drainage that Lake Kopais turned into a shallow swamp each spring. But the Minyan engineers improved on nature by widening many of the *katavothrai* and digging an immense underground channel of their own, over a mile in length and more than 200 feet deep in some places. It was an astonishing achievement.

Whether the divine hero Herakles really destroyed the drainage works at Kopais—as Pausanias maintained—is, of course, debatable. But archaeologists agree that the plain of Kopais was indeed reflooded, at the end of the Bronze Age, when the Minyan dike system fell into neglect and disrepair.[8] For centuries, engineers sought, in vain, to revive the Minyan drainage system. Strabo says that a mining engineer named Krates attempted to drain the lake for Alexander the Great but succeeded only partially.[9] The Romans tried under the Emperor Hadrian, and the French in the 1870s. But not until 1889 did British engineers finally succeed in draining Lake Kopais as completely and efficiently as the Minyans had done thousands of years before.

What is most striking about the Minyan drainage works is how old they are. At first, Lauffer believed that they had been built in Late Mycenaean or even Hellenistic times. Subsequent excavations however, changed his mind. As we will see in the next chapter, Lauffer ultimately concluded that the drainage system could not have been built later than the period archaeologists call Early Helladic, sometime between 3000 and 2000 B.C.[10] At that time, Greece was barely crawling out of the Stone Age. How did the Minyans acquire such expertise in such primitive surroundings? One theory is that their engineering skills were imported from abroad.

The oft-noted resemblance between *Minyai* and *Minos* might suggest Crete as a likely source. But the Minoans had little need for irrigation on the scale of Lake Kopais and had never developed such skills.[11] As for the Mesopotamians, they were certainly accomplished irrigators, but they lived far away, separated from Greece by a great expanse of land. Egypt, on the other hand, was close. Nothing stood between Egypt and Greece except a few hundred miles of water.

"It has always been my belief," commented Thor Heyerdahl in a 1997 newspaper interview, "that the ocean was a conveyor of early contact among civilizations and not an element of their isolation."[12]

If we agree, with Heyerdahl, that bodies of water tend to *join* ancient cultures, rather than separate them, then Egypt emerges as the clearest and most likely source of the Minyan hydraulic technology.

Certainly, the Egyptians were renowned for their skill in managing water. Each summer, when rains in the Ethiopian highlands caused the Nile to overflow its banks, the Egyptians would siphon off the floodwaters into an intricate network of canals and basins to even out the spillover. Herodotos told how the Egyptians created Lake Moeris by draining water from the Nile.[13] He also wrote that Sesostris supplied water to desert towns through a system of dikes and canals—a story that has been confirmed by archaeological evidence showing that Senwosret II irrigated vast new farmlands in the Fayum region.[14]

Hydraulic engineering was already well advanced in Egypt by the time Menes united the country. A ceremonial macehead from the reign of "Scorpion"—the name Egyptologists give to Menes's predecessor on the throne of Upper Egypt—shows the king digging a canal, in what appears to be an elaborate ground-breaking ritual. The Scorpion Macehead reveals that irrigation was not only well developed in prehistoric Egypt, but was also considered an important royal duty.[15] Another Egyptian king, Kheti I, left a similar memorial around 2100 B.C. in which he boasted of his irrigational feats. It reads: "I brought a gift for this city . . . a channel of ten cubits. . . . I excavated for it upon the arable land. . . . I made a water supply for this city . . . which had not seen water. . . . I made the elevated land a swamp. I caused the water of the Nile to flood over. . . . Every neighbor was (supplied with) Nile water to his heart's desire."[16]

Menes himself was renowned in legend for his hydraulic feats. As discussed in chapter 31, Herodotos recorded a tradition that Menes diverted the Nile with a great dam to clear land for his new city of Memphis. Needless to say, the Egyptians possessed all the skills necessary for undertaking a project on the scale of draining Lake Kopais. Whether they actually *did* so is another question. In the next chapter, we will examine the wealth of evidence pointing to Egypt's role in the extraordinary achievements of Minyan civilization.

CHAPTER 52

THE EGYPTIAN
HERAKLES

No HERO OF ANCIENT GREECE IS MORE WIDELY KNOWN THAN
Herakles. Under his more familiar name of *Hercules* (given
him by the Romans), the strongman of legend has inspired
comic books, B-movies starring Steve Reeves, the television series
Hercules: The Legendary Journeys, and, most recently, an animated
feature film from Disney. Yet, despite Herakles' enduring popularity,
there are few figures in Greek legend more charged with mystery.

Dressed in a lion skin and armed with a club, Herakles seems a
throwback to some forgotten Stone Age past. Indeed, Walter Burkert, a leading authority on Greek religion, believes that the tale of
Herakles may be as old as 20,000 years.[1] Where did he come from
originally? Many theories have abounded since ancient times. But
none are as puzzling or persistent as the claim made by Herodotos,
Diodoros, and others that the original Herakles was not a *Greek*
hero at all, but an Egyptian god.

"The Egyptians have had a god named Herakles from time immemorial," Herodotos wrote.[2] Originally, this Egyptian Herakles
had been a man, said Diodoros. But, after using his great strength to
clear the earth of wild beasts, Herakles was worshiped as a god by

the grateful Egyptians. The priests with whom Diodoros spoke claimed that their Herakles had lived more than 10,000 years ago. By contrast, the Greek Herakles was a mere whelp, having walked the earth only a generation before the Trojan War.

Diodoros concluded that the Greek hero must have adopted the name of his Egyptian predecessor. In the process, he also appeared to have taken on many of the stories and attributes of the Egyptian Herakles. Noting, for example, that both Greek and Egyptian versions of Herakles were said to have cleared the earth of wild beasts, Diodoros commented that this story seemed far more appropriate for a primitive hero from 10,000 years ago than for a Greek during the time of Jason and Orpheus.

By the time the Greek Herakles lived, said Diodoros, "most parts of the inhabited world had already been reclaimed from their wild state by agriculture and cities and the multitude of men settled everywhere over the land."[3] The slaughtering of wild beasts would no longer have been an urgent priority. Equally out of place for the Greek Heroic Age, in Diodoros's view, were the traditional weapons and wardrobe of the Greek Herakles. Diodoros wrote: "Likewise, both the club and the lion's skin are appropriate to their ancient [Egyptian] Herakles, because in those days arms had not yet been invented, and men defended themselves against their enemies with clubs of wood and used the hides of animals for defensive armor."[4]

Was there, in fact, an Egyptian god named Herakles? At first glance, it seems unlikely. The name *Herakles* appears to be Greek for "glory to Hera." But there are problems with this interpretation. Herakles was, in fact, the object of Hera's hatred, a living reminder to her of Zeus's infidelity with a mortal woman. From the time Herakles was an infant, Hera plotted his death. Why would Herakles have been named after his greatest enemy?

The Greeks often associated Herakles with an Egyptian god named Heryshef, whose name means "he who is upon his lake." They even named the town where Heryshef's temple cult was centered Herakleopolis Magna—"the great city of Herakles." Little is known about this god, however, and it is impossible to say how closely Egyptian beliefs about him fit those described by Herodotos and Diodoros. Martin Bernal has suggested that Herakles' name might actually mean "glory to Horus"—*Haru-kles*.[5] But this is only a guess. The identity of the Egyptian Herakles remains something of a mystery.

To Greek historians such as Herodotos and Diodoros, however, the Egyptian Herakles was a reality. Since these writers had the advantage—which we do not—of being able to converse firsthand with the Egyptian priests, it seems reasonable to accept their judgment. In fact, the Egyptian Herakles was not the only one to be found outside Greece. Many ancient writers commented on the amazing dispersion of Herakles cults throughout the known world.

In addition to the Egyptian, Phoenician, and Greek versions, acknowledged by Herodotos, Diodoros added a Cretan Herakles to the mix. Cicero counted six altogether, including the Roman Hercules. The Roman writer Varro opined that no less than twenty-four versions of Herakles could be found from one end of the Mediterranean to the other.[6] Herodotos was convinced, however, that the Egyptian Herakles was the oldest of them all. He wrote, "It was not the Egyptians who took the name Herakles from the Greeks. The opposite is true: it was the Greeks who took it from the Egyptians. There is plenty of evidence to prove the truth of this, in particular, that both parents of Herakles—Amphitryon and Alkmene—were of Egyptian origin."[7]

Herodotos seems to imply that Herakles' parents would have been more likely to name their son after an Egyptian god, since they themselves were Egyptian. But in what way were Herakles' parents "of Egyptian origin"? Evidently, Herodotos was referring to the fact that they were Danaids—descended from the Egyptian king Danaos. Herakles' parents, Alkmene and Amphitryon, were first cousins. Both were grandchildren of the hero Perseus, who was, in turn, the great-great-great-grandson of Danaos. Of course, this did not make Herakles 100 percent Egyptian. The Danaids, after all, had been intermarrying with Greeks for generations. But it did make Herakles a descendant of Egyptian royalty.

According to legend, Herakles' parents were also part Ethiopian. Apollodoros wrote that the wife of Perseus—Herakles' great-grandmother—was Andromeda, daughter of Cepheus and Cassiopeia, the king and queen of Ethiopia.[8] Greek artists often followed a convention of depicting Andromeda as white.[9] But the Roman poet Ovid clearly described her as *fusca*—"dark." Although she bore the color of her native Ethiopia, Ovid wrote, Andromeda nevertheless entranced Perseus with her beauty.[10] No doubt, the producers of Disney's animated *Hercules* would have thought twice about giving their hero blond hair and blue eyes had they done a bit more research on his family origins.

We, of course, have no way of knowing to what extent the Herakles of legend represents a real person. But even if he does not, his portrayal as an African prince—part Egyptian and part Ethiopian—suggests that the ancient storytellers held a profoundly different view of Bronze Age Greece than that served up by Hollywood scriptwriters.

Rightly or wrongly, ancient tradition places African dynasts at the head of some of Greece's most powerful and prominent cities. It also portrays Herakles as an ambitious hydraulic engineer, responsible for damming rivers and digging canals all over Greece—an occupation peculiarly appropriate for a prince of an Egyptian royal dynasty.

In the fifth of Herakles' Twelve Labors, for example, the hero was compelled to clean up a huge mound of cow manure left by the herds of Augeas.[11] He accomplished this by rerouting the rivers Alpheios and Peneios through the dung heap, sweeping away the malodorous mass in an instant. Herakles was also said to have dammed up the river Strymon with stones and redirected the river Kephissos to create Lake Kopais in Boiotia.[12]

It is hard not to suspect that some real-life engineering feats lay behind all these folktales of damming, channeling, and flooding. In a similar way, the loggers of nineteenth-century America wove yarns of the giant Paul Bunyan, who could clear a whole forest with a sweep of his ax. Bunyan, of course, was only a myth. But the hewing of America's virgin timber was an overwhelming reality, an enterprise so vast that it could be captured only through legend and symbol.

Was Herakles a Paul Bunyan of his time? Do his adventures reflect the achievements of real-life canal diggers and dam builders in early Greece? If so, then the legend implies that those ancient engineers had a strong ancestral link with Africa and particularly with Egypt. It seems more than coincidental that Herakles' great-great-great-great-great-great-grandfather Danaos was also remembered, in legend, for his feats of water engineering.

Apollodoros says that the countryside around Argos was "water-less, because Poseidon had dried up even the springs out of anger."[13] Homer, too, refers to the region as "Argos the thirsty."[14] According to legend, it was Danaos who finally succeeded in bringing water to Argos. How he accomplished this varies from one version of the story to another. An ancient scholiast, or commentator on Homer, simply wrote that Danaos "brought water to the Peloponnese which was without."[15] Hesiod says that Danaos and his daughters dug wells at Argos.[16] According to Apollodoros, the sea god Poseidon re-vealed the spring of Lerna to Danaos's daughter Amymone after he slept with her.[17]

The details differ, but the theme remains the same: Danaos and his daughters were clearly remembered as having brought water to the Argolid. Danaos's name may even reflect this achievement. Martin Bernal suggests that it comes from an Egyptian word spelled *dni*, which means "to allocate or irrigate."[18] Was Danaos, then, the *dniw*—"the irrigator"? It is, at least, possible.

It would certainly have made sense for Danaos, as an Egyptian ruler, to have made irrigation his top priority. Supplying water to his Pelasgian subjects would have been a sacred duty, by Egyptian thinking, as well as a means for Danaos to assert his royal authority. The role of water supplier would have passed to succeeding genera-tions as long as the dynasty lasted.

We may never know for sure whether Danaos or Herakles really existed. And, even if they did, we may never be able to fix precise dates or places to them. Herakles, in particular, seems to have been reborn and embellished in human imagination at least a dozen times since his Stone Age beginnings. If there was a real hero by that name during the Greek Bronze Age, his adventures have long since become hopelessly entwined with those of the twenty-three other Herakleses catalogued by Varro.

Even so, it seems hard to deny that some grain of truth must lie behind the persistent legends of an Egyptian dynasty establishing it-self in Greece. It seems harder still to ignore the strong folk memory linking that dynasty with ambitious works of hydraulic engineer-ing. This connection has grown much stronger in recent years, thanks to the work of a Greek archaeologist named Theodore Spy-ropoulos. His conclusions have shocked many experts—but have largely vindicated the ancient legends.

Spyropoulos's excavations have revealed an early Greece dominated by the fabled Minyans—a nation of builders, irrigators, metallurgists, and seafarers. In their achievements, Spyropoulos sees a real-life model for the legendary engineering feats of Danaos and Herakles. Even more to the point, Spyropoulos sees strong evidence that the most likely homeland of these Minyans was Egypt.

CHAPTER 53

THE PYRAMID
OF AMPHION

IN HIS *DESCRIPTION OF GREECE,* PAUSANIAS NOTES THAT NOT ALL
Greeks accepted the story that Kadmos came from Phoenicia.
Some apparently believed that "the Kadmos who came to the
Theban land was an Egyptian, not a Phoenician."[1] Pausanias disputed this claim, arguing that Kadmos had indeed been a Phoenician. Nevertheless, the mere fact that Pausanias had to make such
an argument shows that there were hidden complexities to the
story of how Thebes was settled.

There is, in fact, good reason to believe that the city of Thebes
was founded *twice.* The first founding may well have been carried
out by Egyptians. Long after that first city was destroyed and abandoned, the site may then have been resettled by Kadmos and his
Phoenicians. It would be natural, under such circumstances, for
later poets and storytellers to confuse Kadmos with the Egyptian
colonists who preceded him. Such confusion may well have given
rise to the belief in an Egyptian Kadmos, cited by Pausanias.

The ambiguity appears first in Homer. He consistently refers to
the Thebans as Kadmeiones—"Kadmeians"—which presupposes
that Kadmos founded the city. Yet Homer explicitly names the twins

Amphion and Zethos as the city's *first* founders. In *The Odyssey,* Homer called them "Amphion and Zethos, first founders of Thebes-with-the-Seven-Gates: its fortifiers too, for not even men of their might could dwell in that open domain except it were walled and towered."[2]

Who were Amphion and Zethos? Legend holds that they were twin brothers, born to Zeus and a mortal woman named Antiope. Zethos turned out to be a hunter and warrior. His brother Amphion, however, became a musician. Pausanias says that after Amphion erected the first altar to Hermes, the god rewarded him with a magic lyre. Wild animals and even stones would follow Amphion when he played. Ancient writers report that when Amphion built the walls of Thebes, the stones moved into place of their own accord, to the music of his lyre.[3]

According to Pherekydes, the attacks of the warlike Phlegyans forced the twins to fortify their new city.[4] Hekataios names a number of other tribes in the area, including the Aones, Hyantes, Temmikes, Leleges, and Pelasgians.[5] The fact that Aones and Hyantes were still present in the region when Amphion and Zethos built their city implies that the twins arrived well before Kadmos. As noted in chapter 27, Kadmos drove off the Hyantes and absorbed the Aones through intermarriage.[6]

According to Pherekydes, the Phlegyans overran and destroyed the city after Amphion and Zethos died. Abandoned for generations, the site returned to life only later, when Kadmos arrived. Very little of the original city built by Amphion and Zethos appears to have survived, though archaeologists may have found some traces of it in the form of several houses and a fortified wall dating from a very early period, around 2900–2400 B.C.

The most prominent structure to have weathered the Phlegyan assault was the so-called Tomb of Amphion and Zethos. Throughout classical antiquity, it remained an important landmark of Thebes. Located just north of the city gates, the tomb rested atop a large, thickly wooded rise that, since ancient times, has been called Amphion Hill.

"The tomb of Amphion and Zethos is a small mound of earth," Pausanias commented when he visited the site in the second century A.D. Actually, it is a tumulus built of mud bricks and stone, as archaeologists later discovered. But, in Pausanias's day, it appears that the tomb was already buried under a mound of earth. According to legend, Amphion and Zethos rested side by side inside the "small mound." Pausanias noted that the people of Thebes held the tomb in special reverence, believing that earth from the burial site had a magical power to grant fertility to their fields. He wrote:

> The tomb shared by Amphion and Zethos is a small mound of earth. The inhabitants of Tithorea in Phocis like to steal earth from it when the sun is passing through the constellation Taurus. For if at that time they take earth from the mound and set it on Antiope's tomb [the mother of Amphion and Zethos], the land of Tithorea will yield a harvest, but that of Thebes be less fertile. For this reason the Thebans at that time keep watch over the tomb.[7]

Although the tomb lay just outside the city gates, archaeologists have ascertained that, for three thousand years, no one dared build in its vicinity. The entire hill on which the tomb stood was evidently considered taboo.[8] Archaeologists now know that there was a good reason for this prohibition. But, in Pausanias's day, no one seems to have remembered what that reason was. The hill had accumulated a thick coat of soil over the years. Shrubs and trees carpeted its slopes. After so many centuries, the Thebans had long forgotten what lay beneath all that earth and greenery.

The hill of Amphion kept its secret until 1971. Then a Greek archaeologist named Theodore Spyropoulos decided to excavate the site. At the time, Amphion Hill looked much as it probably had to Pausanias—a wide, flat hump of earth covered with trees and bushes. At the top was the "small mound of earth" mentioned in Pausanias's book. This had been partially excavated, in 1917, by the Greek archeologist A. Keramopoullos. But Keramopoullos had done only a cursory inspection of the site. It now fell to Spyropoulos to unlock the secret of Amphion Hill.

Soon after he started digging, in 1971, Spyropoulos made a remarkable discovery. Beneath the "small mound of earth" was a tumulus built of sun-dried bricks. If this was indeed a burial site from the Early Bronze Age—as most experts believed—then it was a tomb of exceptionally fine quality, considering its age. Other Greek tumuli from that era were crude affairs of earth and pebbles. But Amphion and Zethos had been laid to rest in a sepulcher of solid brick.

As he continued excavating, Spyropoulos found a stone-lined chamber embedded deep in the tumulus, with two depressions in the floor. Was it only a coincidence that there were spaces for *two* bodies—or was this the actual resting place of Amphion and Zethos? Grave robbers had ransacked the grave centuries ago, but enough fragments of gold jewelry remained to convince Spyropoulos that the tomb had once held a rich store of royal treasure. The jewelry included four gold pendants shaped like lilies and topped with what Spyropoulos called "papyroid" forms—a typical Egyptian motif.[9]

The biggest surprise was yet to come. As Spyropoulous began systematically clearing away the earth and vegetation from the hill, he struck a hard surface underneath. Further investigation showed that the interior of the hill was a solid core of earth and sand, congealed into a hard natural cement. This concrete-like material was very common in the ground near Thebes. It was a natural deposit, not man-made.

Nevertheless, as the excavators slowly stripped the soft earth from the hill's hard interior, Spyropoulos came to a startling realization. The "hill" was not a hill at all! Since at least the time of Pausanias, visitors to the site had assumed that the "small mound of earth" at the top constituted the entire tomb. Covered with earth and overgrown with shrubs and trees, the hill itself seemed no more than a natural part of the landscape. But Spyropoulos now realized that Amphion Hill was an integral part of the ancient monument. Long ago, its cement-like core had been shaped by human hands.

In what must have been a tremendously costly and difficult undertaking, prehistoric builders had sculpted the natural cement of the hill into a vast and deliberate pattern. Erosion had softened its shape over the years, but Spyropoulos could still discern the outlines of an immense, terraced structure with three distinct layers, or steps. The brick tumulus on top formed the fourth, or top, layer of the entire edifice. As he gazed in wonder at the monument, soaring over 100 feet into the air, Spyropoulos could think of only one word to describe it—*pyramis*. The hill of Amphion was a pyramid!

And there was more. After descending down a well at the top of the pyramid, Spyropoulos discovered a vaulted passageway 65 feet down, carved right into the rocky core of the hill, complete with staircases, niches, and a complex floor plan of branching tunnels that Spyropoulos found "quite similar" to the layout of Egyptian tombs.[10] "At a depth of 20 meters (65 feet)," wrote Spyropoulos, ". . . the soft rock and compressed gravel of the hill have . . . such solidity and stability that the carved structures and their components are marvelously preserved and offer a picture of monumental and excellent work."[11]

Unfortunately, Spyropoulos was unable to proceed further. As Commissioner of Antiquities for Thebes, he was under government authority. Spyropoulos was transferred away from Thebes before completing his exploration of the tunnels. To this day, he remains convinced that a royal tomb lies concealed somewhere in the depths of the mound. But, for twenty-five years, he has had no opportunity to find out.

During his student days at the University of Athens, Spyropoulos had taken a keen interest in Egyptology. He knew that the earliest Egyptian pyramids had been built in layers, or steps, not unlike the layered mound he had excavated at Amphion. Beginning with the famous Step Pyramid of Djoser—probably built around 2660 B.C.—the Egyptians continued rearing stepped pyramids for at least three more centuries, even long after the more familiar smooth-sided variety had come into vogue. Spyropoulos could not help wondering whether Egyptian architects might have assisted in the work at Amphion.[12]

With its circular base, the Amphion mound is actually more cone-shaped than pyramidal. Nevertheless, it greatly resembles a stepped pyramid when viewed in profile—almost as if someone had tried to create the impression of an Egyptian pyramid, using the crude materials at hand. In Spyropoulos's view, the intricate tunnels that honeycomb the mound speak even more clearly of Egyptian influence.

The Pyramid of Amphion, as Spyropoulos called it, hinted at a lost civilization far more sophisticated than any thought to have been possible in Early Bronze Age Greece. The carving of the hill had been a colossal undertaking, requiring wealth, discipline, and endless manpower. No impoverished rabble of village farmers or herdsmen could possibly have organized it. The monument's shape may not have fit the classic definition of an Egyptian pyramid in every detail. But it was indisputably foreign in its scale and intricacy. Its very existence in Greece posed a tantalizing riddle that Spyropoulos was determined to solve.

CHAPTER 54

A LOST
CIVILIZATION

THE MOST PUZZLING THING ABOUT THE PYRAMID OF AMPHION WAS its great age. Potsherds found in the tomb showed that it could not have been built later than the period known as Early Helladic II—roughly 2900–2400 B.C.[1] Yet, Greeks did not build magnificent tombs in those days. The typical grave of that era was an urn of funeral ashes, buried beneath a small earthen mound.[2] In general, Greece at the opening of Early Helladic II was a primitive place, its inhabitants still living in mud-brick villages, chipping their tools from flint and obsidian much as they had since the Stone Age. How did such people learn to build pyramids?

In Egypt, archaeologists had been able to trace the gradual evolution of building skills over many centuries. They could see how masons had experimented with larger and larger mud-brick mastaba tombs until finally Imhotep piled six mastabas one on top of the other to make the first pyramid. No such evolution could be seen, however, in Early Helladic Greece. The Theban pyramid might as well have dropped from the sky.[3]

Spyropoulos was sure that the people who built the pyramid had imported their skills from Egypt. He theorized that Amphion and Zethos themselves might have been Egyptian colonists who settled Boiotia during the Early Bronze Age. When Spyropoulos published this opinion, however, in a 1972 article entitled "Egyptian Colonization of Boiotia," his theory was met with scorn and derision.

Undaunted, Spyropoulos has continued to flesh out his theory over the last twenty-five years. As Commissioner of Antiquities, first for Thebes and later for Arkadia, Spyropoulos has conducted innumerable excavations, demonstrating that the Amphion pyramid was no isolated phenomenon. On the contrary, Spyropoulos has linked the pyramid to a mysterious lost civilization that appears to have flourished in Greece between 2800 and 1700 B.C. He identifies that civilization with the Minyans, the same legendary people who ruled "golden Orchomenos" and sailed to Colchis in quest of the Golden Fleece.

Spyropoulos does not contend that all the Minyans were Egyptian. But he believes an Egyptian elite may have dominated Minyan civilization. "The arrival of Egyptian princes in Boiotian Thebes, either by marriage or otherwise, does not belong to the sphere of the impossible," Spyropoulos commented.[4] In southern Greece, as well, in Spyropoulos's view, Egyptian dynasts such as Danaos appear to have played a role in the rise of Minyan power.

Tradition links the family of Danaos to certain pyramid-like structures in southern Greece. One stands near the village of Hellenikon, just outside Argos. It is a true four-sided pyramid, built of limestone (see fig. 14). Spyropoulos believes that Pausanias had this monument in mind when he wrote:

> On the way from Argos to Epidauria there is on the right a building made very like a pyramid. . . . Here took place a fight for the throne between Proetos and Acrisios; the contest, they say, ended in a draw. . . . For those that fell on either side was built here a common tomb.[5]

Legend holds that Proetos and Akrisios were great-grandsons of Danaos, and thus members of an Egyptian royal family. The structure alleged to be their pyramid rests on a hilltop overlooking the Argolic Gulf—Danaos' traditional landing place. Using thermoluminescent analysis, scientists have dated the Hellenikon pyramid to Early Helladic II—just like the Pyramid of Amphion.[6] A similar coincidence of dating has enabled Spyropoulos to connect these Greek pyramids with yet another set of Egyptianesque ruins in prehistoric Greece—the remarkable drainage system at Kopais.

As mentioned in chapter 51, the German archaeologist Siegfried Lauffer had theorized, back in the 1930s, that the drainage works had been built no earlier than the Mycenaean period. Other researchers agreed. Some insisted that Lake Kopais could not have been drained before about 1700 to 1200 B.C.[8] Others argued that Roman or Hellenistic rulers had done the job.[9]

Spyropoulos teamed up with Lauffer in 1978 to settle the question. They focused on the so-called Megali Katavothra (Great Tunnel)—one of the main natural water channels running beneath Mount Ptoon. When the drainage works were built, the Megali Katavothra had been reinforced with stone walls by ancient engineers. Spyropoulos and Lauffer removed some of these stones and dug into the claylike silt behind them. Every one of the potsherds they removed from the silt turned out to date from between 2900 and 2400 B.C.—Early Helladic II.[10]

This was a startling find. It implied that the waterworks dated from the same period as the pyramids of Amphion and the Danaids.[11] Could it be that the same mysterious people who had constructed the drainage system had also built the pyramids? Spyropoulos believed that they had.

A number of other hydraulic projects in Greece have also been dated to Early Helladic II, among them dams and artificially improved *katavothrai* found at various sites, such as Lake Stymphalos, associated with the legendary feats of Herakles.[12] All this damming and irrigating must have created a huge surplus of farmland. Archaeologists have, in fact, found evidence of massive grain storage in Greece, dating once again to Early Helladic II. In 1946, Spyridon Marinatos studied a number of curious, dome-shaped buildings in Boiotia, concluding that they resembled typical Egyptian granaries, of a type commonly depicted on Egyptian tombs. Most scholars, however, rejected Marinatos's theory.

The problem was that it violated two cherished assumptions about prehistoric Greece. It suggested, first, a strong degree of Egyptian influence in early Greece—something that most scholars considered out of the question in 1946. Second, it implied that Greece was far more advanced during the Early Helladic period than anyone had previously suspected.

The large numbers and hefty size of the *Rundbauten*—or "round houses," as German archaeologists had named them—would have provided an immense volume of grain storage. Those in Boiotia measured up to 26 feet in diameter. Marinatos studied the remains of one monstrous brick Round House in the Argolid that had originally stood more than 86 feet tall and about 288 feet wide. If it were really a granary, it would have been large enough to hold the entire grain production of the Argolid region.[13] Only a powerful, well-organized state, controlling large tracts of territory, could have amassed such a surplus. The problem was that no such state was believed to have existed in Early Helladic Greece.

Conventional opinion never accepted Marinatos's theory that the *Rundbauten* were Egyptianesque granaries. To this day, most experts insist that they were houses, or perhaps temples or tombs. If Marinatos was right, however, the size and quantity of these storehouses hint at the fabulous wealth of the Minyan kings.

Spyropoulos has found evidence that Minyan wealth did not rest on agriculture alone. Working with his archaeologist son George, Spyropoulos recently excavated a sprawling metallurgical facility near the Arkadian villages of Steno and Agiorgitika that seems to have been in use between 2500 and 1700 B.C. Consisting of numerous workshops and kilns, the site represents the largest prehistoric metalworking plant ever found.[14]

Scholars have long recognized that Early Helladic II was a period of massive change in Greece. It was precisely during this era that Greece became "civilized." Stone Age farming villages gave way to tiled palaces, stocked with luxury goods from overseas. Flint tools gave way to fine bronze implements. Spyropoulos refers to this explosion of technology and commerce as "the great boom."[15] The change was so dramatic that even the most conventional scholars have entertained the possibility that an advanced people from overseas may have colonized Greece during this period.

The source of these colonies, however, is usually thought to have been Anatolia.[16] Spyropoulos agrees that many immigrants did come from Asia Minor during this time. But he argues that Egyptians too joined the migration. Many of these Early Helladic settlers may have booked passage on Cretan ships, Spyropoulos suggests. Because they arrived with the fleet of King Minos, he argues, the settlers received the name *Minyans*, regardless of their country of origin. Spyropoulos writes, "We have the right to ask whether those Minoans, criss-crossing the Mediterranean region ... transported, with their ships, not only products, but also people—settlers—to Greece and elsewhere ... One such diaspora and migration of Minyans (... Egyptians, in this case), we may find in Boiotia."[17]

Spyropoulos is confident that the years ahead will reveal ever more spectacular remains of the Minyan culture. "This gradual unveiling of a glorious past expands the limits of the cultural tradition of Greece for at least one thousand years beyond the Mycenaean Era," he exults.[18] Equally strong is Spyropoulos's conviction that future excavations will prove the Egyptian origin of many Minyan colonies. Spyropoulos's views, however, remain controversial among archaeologists. Most continue to believe that Greece lay beyond the reach of Egyptian settlers in the Bronze Age. Only time will tell who is right.

Until more evidence appears, we can only gaze upon the Pyramids of Greece and wonder. Could they speak, the pyramids might tell us of mighty fleets, bristling with oars, making their first landfall in Greece. They might weave a saga of Phlegyans, Pelasgians, Aones, and Hyantes battling to defend their land against the newcomers. But the pyramids say nothing. Inscrutable and mysterious, they stand silent over the landscape, hoarding the secrets of Europe's birth as jealously now as they have for the last 4,000 years.

PART NINE

THE MASTER RACE

CHAPTER 55

THE TABOO

It will be seen that when we classify Mankind by color, the only primary race that has not made a creative contribution to any civilization is the Black Race.

— ARNOLD TOYNBEE
A Study of History, 1934

IF THERE IS ONE LESSON THAT THE LAST CENTURY AND A HALF OF archaeology should have taught scholars, it is that the old legends should be taken seriously. Only by studying Homer did Heinrich Schliemann locate the ruins of Troy. Only by probing the legends of King Minos did Sir Arthur Evans find the key to the lost palace of Knossos. "Experience teaches, I believe, that it's always wisest to give the benefit of the doubt to tradition," commented archaeologist Carl Blegen, whose own study of Homer enabled him, in 1939, to excavate what appear to be the remains of King Nestor's palace.[1]

Unfortunately, the experience of Blegen, Schliemann, and Evans has been disregarded by modern scholars. Few are willing to take seriously the legend of Danaos. Dulled imagination has, no doubt, contributed through the years to the systematic neglect of the Danaos legend. But darker motives may also have lent a hand. In his 1987 book, *Black Athena, Volume I*, Cornell University professor Martin Bernal has traced the slow decline of scholarly belief in the legend of Danaos over the last two centuries. He finds that racial prejudice has figured prominently among the reasons for that decline.

Right up until the eighteenth century, Bernal observes, most scholars took for granted that the legend of Danaos was true. Thus, in 1788, the learned French churchman Abbé Barthélemy wrote a popular historical novel entitled *The Voyage of the Young Anarchasis*. In it, he portrayed Greek civilization as the result of a happy fusion between primitive Greek natives and Egyptian colonists. Barthélemy wrote, "Thus the Greeks, emerging from their forests, no longer saw objects under a frightening and sombre veil. Thus the Egyptians in Greece softened bit by bit the severe and proud expressions in their paintings. The two groups, now making a single people, created a language that sparkled with vivid expressions."[2]

In presenting the Egyptians as colonizers of Greece, Barthélemy was only following the conventional wisdom of his day. But that conventional wisdom soon changed. Within a few short years, scholars no longer believed that Greeks and Egyptians had merged to create a single people. Indeed, they rejected entirely the possibility that Egyptians had colonized Greece at all. In 1835, the British scholar Connop Thirlwall confidently declared that "settlers of purely Egyptian blood, crossing the Aegean and founding maritime cities, appears inconsistent with everything we know about national characters."[3]

What was it precisely about the "national character" of the Egyptians—or at least those of "purely Egyptian blood"—that persuaded nineteenth-century scholars to conclude that they were incapable of crossing the sea and founding colonies? Simple. The Egyptians were African. As French Egyptologist Gaston Maspero disparagingly observed in 1893, "Thothmes III and Rameses II resemble Mtesa of Central Africa more than they do Alexander or Caesar."[4]

By the nineteenth century, most Europeans assumed that the "national character" of the African was servile and weak. Even if they had made it to Europe, scholars of the day surmised, African colonists would have failed to subdue the native tribes. Europeans, after all, even in their primitive Bronze Age state, were believed to have possessed greater courage, intellect, nobility, and physical strength than Africans.

Thus was born the theory of the Master Race, a belief—particularly prevalent in England and Germany—that white people were biologically destined to conquer any other people with whom they came into contact. According to this theory, it was scientifically im-

possible for an inferior race, such as that of the Egyptians, to conquer a "master race" such as that of the Greeks.

Bernal argued that scholars over the last two centuries had abandoned the legend of Danaos mainly because it violated the tenets of
the Master Race theory. "To these German and British scholars," he
wrote in *Black Athena, Volume I,* "the stories of Egyptian colonization and civilizing of Greece violated 'racial science' as monstrously
as the legends of sirens and centaurs broke the canons of natural
science."[5]

Of course, most scholars today reject such theories of racial superiority. But they continue, out of sheer habit, to regard the legend of
Danaos as inherently implausible.[6] Even Bernal himself, in the early
stages of his research for *Black Athena,* discovered that he was not
immune to such unconscious prejudices.

A noted scholar of Chinese history and politics, Bernal had
little knowledge of ancient Greece. He started the research for
Black Athena almost by accident. Being partially Jewish in descent,
Bernal decided, in 1975, to study Hebrew as a means of getting
in touch with his Jewish roots. It wasn't long before he noticed
that many of the Hebrew words he was learning bore an eerie
resemblance to Greek words, which had a similar or identical
meaning.

How could that be? As far as Bernal knew, the Hebrews never
came anywhere near Greece, nor had Greeks ever ventured into
Jewish territory before Alexander the Great. As he delved deeper
into the subject, however, Bernal began to find answers. He was
startled to discover that linguists regarded Hebrew and Phoenician
as dialects of the same Canaanite tongue. So close were the languages that, in biblical times, speakers of Hebrew would have been
able to converse freely with Phoenicians.

Perhaps the "Hebrew" words he was finding in his Greek dictionary were really *Phoenician* words, Bernal guessed. Unwittingly,
Bernal had stumbled on a possible solution to what had long been a
nagging linguistic mystery. Experts had long puzzled over the fact
that only about half of all Greek words were indisputably European
in origin. The other 50 percent had no apparent relatives anywhere
on the European continent. Had they come from outside Europe?
Nobody knew.

Years of study and comparison led Bernal to the conclusion that up to 25 percent of Greek words may have derived from Phoenician roots (though he has since lowered this estimate to below 20 percent).[7] This still left another 25 percent to be accounted for, however. Bernal was stumped. He could think of no other people, other than the Phoenicians, who might have come to Greece in sufficient numbers to impress their language on the natives.

In fact, the answer was right under Bernal's proverbial nose. But, like generations of other European scholars, he had been systematically programmed to ignore the evidence. As described in chapter 21, the missing piece of the puzzle finally fell into place for Bernal in 1979 as he was browsing through Heffers Bookshop in Cambridge, England. While leafing through a Coptic dictionary, Bernal was struck by the number of Coptic Egyptian words that resembled Greek words. Was it possible that the mystery component to the Greek language was Egyptian?

Bernal decided that it was. His research convinced him that 20–25 percent of Greek words were very likely derived from Egyptian roots. This was an important breakthrough. But Bernal couldn't understand why it had taken him so long to make the connection. Egypt, after all, was quite close to Greece. There were even Greek legends of Egyptian colonists settling the country under Danaos. Why, then, had it never occurred to Bernal to consider Egypt as a possible source for Greek vocabulary?

With a shock, Bernal realized that he had been hobbled by an unconscious taboo. Years of conventional schooling had conditioned him to believe that Greece and Egypt could never have mixed in ancient times. An invisible line had been drawn in his mind, separating Europe from Africa as profoundly as if they were distant star systems, hovering trillions of miles from each other in interstellar space.

A glance at the map was sufficient to see that no such insuperable barrier lay between Greece and Egypt. Yet the unspoken taboo had prevented Bernal from drawing the obvious conclusions. Had specialists in ancient history been similarly blinded? Did they routinely overlook or misinterpret evidence of Egyptian influence, simply because their worldview included no place for Egyptian colonies in Greece? Bernal suspected that they did.

"It was the breaking of the taboo that really excited my interest in historiography," Bernal recalls. Historiography is the study of history writing. It examines what historians wrote, why they wrote it, and whether they wrote accurately. Bernal now plunged into a full-scale study of everything that had been written since ancient times on the subject of Egyptian and Phoenician colonies in Greece.

He quickly discovered that the dominant opinion among scholars had sharply changed in the early nineteenth century. Before that time, most scholars had accepted what Bernal calls the Ancient Model. This was the view of Greek history formulated by the Greeks themselves, who believed that their country had indeed been colonized and civilized by explorers from across the sea, such as Kadmos and Danaos.

In the nineteenth century, Bernal discovered, the Ancient Model was suddenly replaced by a new view of history that he called the Aryan Model. According to this theory, Greece was civilized not by people from Africa and the Near East, but by a race of blond-haired, blue-eyed "Aryans" from the north—members, that is, of the Master Race.

As far as Bernal could tell, this radical rewriting of history was based on very poor evidence. Its motive appeared to be political rather than scholarly. Those who pushed it tended to be racial ideologues, obsessed with the need to prove that Europeans had created Greece with little or no help from "inferior" races. The Aryan Model was thus "conceived in sin," as Bernal put it, and therefore inherently unreliable. Even so, the Aryan Model continues—in only slightly modified form—to dominate classical scholarship to this day.

In *Black Athena*, Bernal called for the restoration of a slightly updated version of the Ancient Model. He urged scholars to disavow the racially inspired theories of the last 200 years and to look afresh at the legends of Kadmos, Danaos, and Sesostris. *Black Athena* is a massive work. To this day, it remains only half finished. Fifteen years of research preceded the publication of the first two volumes in 1987 and 1991. Two more volumes are promised in the years to come. But, even in its half-completed state, *Black Athena* has already succeeded in sending shock waves through academia.

Many scholars have found the book deeply offensive. Colgate University classicist John E. Rexine declared that *Black Athena* was "dangerous" and "an affront to scholarly civility."[8] Archaeologist Sarah Morris complained that it "bolstered ... an Afrocentrist agenda" and that "Bernal's arguments have only contributed to an avalanche of radical propaganda without basis in fact."[9]

Yet, even the angriest scholars cannot deny the book's importance. In 1989, the American Philological Association felt compelled to devote a special session to debating the pros and cons of *Black Athena*. The news media have collared Bernal repeatedly for television interviews and featured him in national magazines such as *Newsweek*. In an article sharply critical of *Black Athena*, classicist Edith Hall acknowledged that the book had "excited more controversy than almost any other book dealing with Greco-Roman antiquity to have been published in the second half of the twentieth century."[10]

In the following pages, we will attempt to bypass the controversy and examine the issues dispassionately. We will explore the rise of the Master Race theory and assess its curious role in the shaping of modern views about Greece. After weighing the evidence, readers may judge for themselves whether Bernal's accusations ring true.

CHAPTER 56

DUMB BLONDS

I N 1879, ONE-QUARTER OF THE EARTH'S SURFACE WAS UNDER BRITISH rule. Never before in history had any people achieved such power. Understandably, many Englishmen came to believe that their armies were invincible. The British colonists in Natal, South Africa, were even more confident than most. Only one year before, they had easily put down a rebellion by Gaika and Galeka tribesmen, suffering very few casualties.[1] Having watched the Gaika and Galeka flee before their guns, the British concluded that African warriors were cowardly and contemptible.

For that reason, when Lord Frederick Chelmsford led an army into Zululand in the winter of 1879, his worst fear was that the Zulus would be so frightened that they would never come out to fight.[2] But Chelmsford need not have worried. On January 22, an army of Zulu warriors obligingly descended on one of Chelmsford's isolated columns, encamped at a place called Isandlwana.

A Lieutenant Curling, who survived the ensuing battle, later recalled that the British were not concerned at first, even when the Zulus charged them *en masse*. Their experience fighting other African peoples convinced them that a few rounds of massed fire would soon scatter the attackers in a panic. The British "never dreamed," said Curling, that "the Zulus would charge home."[3] But they did. Braving rockets, artillery, and concentrated rifle fire, the Zulus hurled themselves at the British lines, climbing over the bodies of their own dead.

In the end, the British were slaughtered, almost to a man. Over 800 British soldiers, 52 officers, and some 500 of their African allies were massacred and ritually disemboweled—1,300 in all. More British officers were killed that day than in the entire battle of Waterloo.[4]

When news of the massacre reached Britain, it aroused shock and horror. But it had another effect as well. A new tone began to creep into the words of British journalists and politicians, one rarely heard in connection with African warriors. It was a tone of *respect*—a respect that only increased in the coming months as British casualties mounted and tales of Zulu ferocity became dinner-table conversation. "We now have ample proof," the *Times* admitted, "not only of [the Zulus'] valour but also of their skill in strategy."[5]

Many great thinkers have tried, over the years, to explain what causes racial prejudice. Some have claimed that it derives from a primitive fear of strangers, inherited from the days when cave dwellers defended their turf against any and all outsiders. But if British contempt for Africans were motivated by such defensive feelings, then surely those feelings would have intensified, rather than diminished, following the slaughter at Isandlwana. Instead of despising the Zulu more, the British took off their hats to them, elevating the Zulus, temporarily, almost to the status of equals.

The evidence of the Zulu War—and of history, in general—seems to suggest that racial prejudice is a natural by-product of military dominance. It is one of the ways that conquerors express their contempt for the conquered. The easier the conquest, the greater the contempt. Because the Zulus offered fiercer resistance than other Africans, whites tempered their prejudice toward them, according the Zulus higher status than they did other Africans. Later anthropologists even toyed with the idea that the Zulus might be part Caucasian.[6]

Today, it seems almost natural for blacks to be locked in a perpetual struggle to free themselves from white domination. Yet, it is only in the last five hundred years that Europeans have gained the firearms and sea power to subdue and enslave black people on a large scale. For precisely that reason, it is only in the last five centuries that Europeans have begun to express a generalized contempt for Africans. No such attitude appears to have existed in the ancient world. In the years before gunpowder, African archers and spearmen could hold their own against European armies. Consequently, white people harbored no special hostility toward blacks, nor did they preach any doctrine of black inferiority.

This does not mean that people in the ancient world were free of prejudice. The Greeks and Romans clearly regarded themselves as superior to foreign "barbarians." But they do not appear to have singled out black "barbarians" for any special opprobrium. Nor did they attribute their own alleged superiority to membership in a white race. The Greeks and Romans did not divide their world into black and white. In their eyes, the fair-skinned savages of northern Europe were just as alien and barbarous as the coal-black Ethiopians of tropical Africa.

This attitude is clearly expressed in the writings of the Roman architect Vitruvius Pollio. In his book *On Architecture,* Vitruvius distinguished between three basic types of human beings. On the one hand, there were the "races of the north," who Vitruvius said were "characterized by tall stature, fair complexion, straight red hair," and "blue eyes." On the other hand, there were the southern peoples, who had a smaller stature, dark complexion, curly hair and "black eyes."[7] Between these two extremes were Vitruvius's own people, the Romans, who lived neither in the north nor the south, but right in the middle.

Vitruvius then went on to compare the strengths and weaknesses of the different peoples. Northerners were brave in battle, he observed, but somewhat stupid. "Northern peoples, steeped in a thick climate amid reluctant air, are chilled by the damp, and have sluggish minds," he wrote.[8] Southerners, on the other hand, while timid in battle, were keenly intelligent, their "minds rendered acute by the heat."[9] Vitruvius continued, in the same vein:

> Now while the southern peoples are of acute intelligence and infinite resource, they give way when courage is demanded because their strength is drained away by the sun; but those who are born in colder

regions by their fearless courage are better equipped for the clash of arms, yet by their slowness of mind they rush on without reflection, and through lack of tactics are balked of their purpose.[10]

The Romans had the best of both worlds, Vitruvius claimed. Living right in the center, between north and south, they enjoyed the benefits of both climates, while suffering the ill effects of neither. Italy was just cold enough to make the Romans brave, but not so frigid that it would dampen their wits. Vitruvius wrote:

> Italy presents good qualities which are tempered by admixture from either side both north and south, and are consequently unsurpassed. And so, by its policy, it curbs the courage of the northern barbarians; by its strength, the imaginative south. Thus the divine mind has allotted to the Roman state an excellent and temperate region in order to rule the world.[11]

The Greeks appear to have subdivided humanity along lines similar to those of the Romans. They too distinguished themselves sharply from both the fair people of the north and the dark people of the south, seeing themselves as the perfect compromise between the two. It is interesting to note that the Greeks also shared Vitruvius's opinion that fair-haired northerners were not very bright. The stereotype of "dumb blonds" is evidently older than we think! Conversely, the Greeks also appear to have shared the Roman belief that dark skin accompanied high intelligence.

"The races that live in cold regions and those of Europe," wrote Aristotle, "are full of courage and passion but somewhat lacking in skill and brainpower: for this reason, while remaining generally independent, they lack political cohesion and the ability to rule others." Greeks, on the other hand, because they lived in a "midposition geographically," their climate neither too hot nor too cold, were perfectly suited, in Aristotle's opinion, to rule other peoples.[12]

Clearly, both Greeks and Romans viewed themselves as belonging to a kind of Master Race. Both imagined that their peoples were uniquely equipped to rule over "barbarians." Yet, neither looked upon their white skin as a sign of their superiority. On the contrary, they were just as proud of being darker than the northern Europeans as they were of being lighter than the Africans. Their sense of superiority derived explicitly from their claim to be perfectly balanced *between* the two extremes. As we will see in the next chapter, there is even evidence that black Africans enjoyed a status in the ancient world higher than that of the blue-eyed savages.

CHAPTER 57

THE
UNCONQUERABLE
KUSHITES

SOMETIME AROUND 525 B.C., ACCORDING TO HERODOTOS, THE Persian king Cambyses decided to conquer Ethiopia. To spy out the land, Cambyses first sent envoys to the Ethiopian king. They carried rich gifts, such as a robe of Tyrian purple, a golden chain and armlets, a cask of palm wine, and myrrh in an alabaster box.

Sensing treachery, the Ethiopian king received the gifts with scorn. "You have come to get information on my kingdom," he accused the envoys. "Therefore you are liars, and that king of yours is unjust." The king then presented his visitors with a challenge. Handing a great bow to the envoys, he commanded them to take it back to Cambyses with the following message: "When the Persians can draw a bow of this size thus easily, then let him raise an army of superior strength and invade the country of the long-lived Ethiopians. Till then, let him thank the gods for not turning the thoughts of the children of Ethiopia to foreign conquest."[1]

The king's warning was plain. If the Persians were not strong enough to draw the bow, then they were too weak to fight the Ethiopians, who could pull such bows with ease. Enraged by this defiance, Cambyses marched against Ethiopia. But he was forced to withdraw, without a fight, when his supplies ran out and his men resorted to cannibalism. Centuries later, Diodoros of Sicily attributed Cambyses' failure to the intervention of the gods. He wrote, "By reason of their piety . . . [the Ethiopians] manifestly enjoy the favor of the gods . . . and although many and powerful rulers have made war upon them, not one of these has succeeded in his undertaking."[2]

Who were these unconquerable Ethiopians? Literally, *Aithiopes* meant "burnt-faced people" in Greek—people whose skin had been scorched dark by the sun.[3] The Greeks and Romans used this term to refer to a wide range of African peoples. In the story of Cambyses, Herodotos writes specifically about those Ethiopians who lived along the Red Sea coast. Diodoros, however, attributes piety and indomitability equally to all the Ethiopian peoples.

In the eyes of Greek and Roman writers, the heartland of "Ethiopia" was a region south of Egypt along the upper reaches of the Nile, deep in the heart of Nubia. The ancient Egyptians called this land Kush. At the time Herodotos and Diodoros wrote, the Kushites were a highly civilized people who built cities, wrote in hieroglyphs, and buried their kings in pyramids. Just as Diodoros stated, the Persians never did succeed in conquering Kush, nor did the Greeks or Romans who came after them.

The Kushites were, without a doubt, a black people. Their surviving artwork makes this plain, as do innumerable descriptions from Greek and Roman writers. "[The Ethiopians] are black in color," wrote Diodoros, "and have flat noses and woolly hair."[4] Other African tribes were also called "Ethiopian" by the Greeks, apparently because they too had black skin and Negroid features. Most scholars agree that the term *Ethiopian* became a catch-all, among Greeks and Romans, to describe black Africans in general as well as Kushites in particular.

In past years, many scholars have tried to prove that the Greeks and Romans despised "Ethiopians" as thoroughly as have Europeans of the last two centuries. But the evidence does not support this view. In fact, the Greeks and Romans appear to have held the Kushites in high regard, admiring not only their prowess in war, but also their wisdom, their righteousness, their ancient traditions, and their physical beauty.

Perhaps no scholar has done more to rediscover the ancient view of black Africans than has Frank M. Snowden, Jr. In 1944, Snowden became the first African American to earn a doctorate in classics from Harvard University. For nearly forty years, he combed Greco-Roman art and literature for any mention or portrayal of black people. Snowden's findings—presented in such works as *Blacks in Antiquity* (1970) and *Before Color Prejudice* (1983)—have effectively shattered many long-cherished myths.

Chief among these is the assumption that Ethiopians traveled to Greece and Rome mainly as slaves and that they endured from the Greeks and Romans the same sort of mean-spirited ridicule and caricature that has traditionally afflicted blacks in the United States. Scholars, in the past, have cited the large number of Greek and Roman portraits of blacks as evidence for this alleged contempt, seeing in such portraits a Greco-Roman fascination with the "ugly," the "grotesque," and the "comic." "The negro perhaps unfortunately has always appealed to the comic side of the Caucasian," concluded Grace H. Beardsley in her 1929 study, *The Negro in Greek and Roman Civilization.*[5]

Snowden, however, saw little that was either ugly or funny in the Greco-Roman portraits of blacks. "Negro subjects are among some of the finest and most sympathetically executed pieces to have come from the workshops of ancient artists," he later wrote. The "ugly" or "comic" elements scholars perceived in these portraits evidently owed more to modern prejudice, Snowden concluded, than to the intent of the artists.[6]

Snowden's survey of Greek and Roman literature yielded similar results. Far from being objects of revulsion, Ethiopians were often praised for their beauty. "The Ethiopians," wrote Herodotos, "are said to be the tallest and best-looking people in the world."[7] On the death of a famous Ethiopian animal fighter named Olympius, the Roman poet Luxorius wrote, in the sixth century A.D.: "O wonderful, O bold, O swift, O spirited, O always ready! Not at all does your swarthy body harm you because of its blackness. So did nature create black precious ebony . . . so do black Indian incense and pepper give pleasure."[8]

In the same vein, the Greek poet Asklepiades addressed a love poem to a woman named Didyme, in which he wrote, "Gazing at her beauty I melt like wax before the fire. And if she is black, what difference to me? So are coals but when we light them, they shine like rosebuds."[9]

Of course, this praise is somewhat backhanded. The poets are saying that Ethiopians can be beautiful *despite* their blackness. But, as Snowden pointed out, an aesthetic bias toward lighter skin does not imply that Greeks and Romans looked upon blacks as inferior. It simply shows that, like most people, they preferred the familiar over the strange. German women with blond hair and blue eyes also fell short of conventional Roman beauty standards, according to Snowden, which tended to favor brunettes.

"Classical authors," writes Snowden, "frequently stated a preference for 'Mediterranean' complexion and features—a middle point between the extremes of blond, blue-eyed northerners, and black, woolly-haired southerners."[10]

What surprised Snowden was not that Ethiopians failed to meet the conventional standards of Greek and Roman beauty—that much was normal and expected. What surprised him was that so many Greco-Roman artists and poets chose to *defy* convention by extolling the beauty of black people—and did so without embarrassment or hesitation.

Indeed, Roman poets frequently praised the charms of black women at the expense of their own Italian ladies. Martial, for example, declared that he loved a girl who was "blacker than night," even though he was pursued by another whiter than a "washed swan."[11] In the same spirit, other poets defied convention in the opposite manner—by stating their preference for blond barbarian women from the north. "Barbarian!" wrote Ausonius to his German slave girl Bissula. "But you, kid, are ahead of all the Latin girls."[12]

"On the whole," Snowden concluded, "the number of expressed preferences for blackness and whiteness in classical literature is approximately equal."[13]

The frequency with which Ethiopians appeared in Roman artwork and literature suggested to Snowden that there must have been great numbers of them living in Italy. Many, of course, were brought there as slaves. But it appeared that a goodly number had also lived there in freedom. Ethiopians were just as likely to be philosophers, priests, athletes, warriors, or merchants in the Roman world as they were servants.[14]

The Greeks' first brush with Ethiopians *en masse* came not in the slave mart, but on the battlefield. Homer and other ancient writers claim that the legendary king Memnon of Ethiopia brought an army of black soldiers to fight the Greeks at Troy.[15] Centuries later, the Persian king Xerxes invaded Greece with an army that included large numbers of Ethiopian mercenaries.[16]

In general, Ethiopians were major players in the power politics of the Mediterranean world. Around 751 B.C., the Nubian king Piankhi stormed into Egypt and established a dynasty of Ethiopian pharaohs. One of his descendants, Taharqa, led an army into Palestine to support the Israelite king Hezekiah against the Assyrians.[17] For this and other feats, Strabo included Taharqa in a list of history's greatest conquerors.[18] The prophet Isaiah referred to the Kushites as a people "dreaded near and far, a nation strong and proud."[19]

The Romans quickly learned to admire the Ethiopians as foes on the battlefield. After fighting all the way from Italy to Egypt and conquering every nation in between, the Roman juggernaut was finally stopped dead in its tracks by the Ethiopians. From the moment Augustus occupied Egypt in 30 B.C., the Romans had nothing but trouble from their southern frontier. The first Nubian attack came only five years after Augustus seized Egypt.

"The Ethiopians . . . attacked the Thebais," wrote Strabo, "took Syene and Elephantine and Philae, and enslaved the inhabitants, and also pulled down the statues of Caesar."[20] Although the Romans subsequently drove the invaders back, Nubia remained a thorn in Rome's side until the last days of the Empire. Three times, Augustus sent his armies into Nubia, but he never succeeded in reducing Kush to a Roman province.[21]

Three hundred years later, the Nubians were still a problem. The Emperor Diocletian was obliged, at the end of the third century A.D., to pay tribute to two Ethiopian tribes called the Nobatae and Blemmyes in order to stop their raids. These tribes continued collecting Roman tribute for the next two hundred years.[22] Under these circumstances, it is hardly surprising that the Romans looked upon black Africans with respect, if not always with warmth.

For all their fierceness, the Nubians were most renowned in the ancient world not for their military prowess, but for their righteousness. Diodoros said that they enjoyed "the favor of the gods."[23] In the *Iliad*, Homer says that Zeus and the other Olympian gods feasted for twelve days with the "blameless Ethiopians."[24] Of their fabled piety, Diodoros wrote:

> And they say that [the Ethiopians] were the first to be taught to honor the gods and to hold sacrifices and festivals and processions . . . and the other rites by which men honour the deity; and that in consequence their piety has been published abroad among all men, and it is generally held that the sacrifices practised among the Ethiopians are those which are the most pleasing to heaven.[25]

People as proud and self-satisfied as the Greeks and Romans could never bring themselves to regard any foreigner as perfect. But the Ethiopians appear to have come closer than most. Other peoples earned the contempt of Greeks and Romans by knuckling under to their threats. But the unconquerable Kushites never yielded. Living on the far frontiers of civilization, they remained tantalizingly beyond Europe's control. In Homer's words, they were "the farthermost of men," a mysterious race, whose kings and deeds were the stuff of legend.[26]

Even greater respect was accorded, however, to another dark-skinned people—the Egyptians. A great deal of controversy has arisen in recent years as to whether the Egyptians should be regarded as "black." In the next chapter, we will consider what the Greeks and Romans had to say about this question.

CHAPTER 58

BLACK, WHITE, OR REDDISH-BROWN?

HERODOTOS WAS CONVINCED THAT THE COLCHIANS, WHO LIVED on the eastern shore of the Black Sea, were descended from Egyptian colonists. As discussed in chapter 10, one of the strongest proofs Herodotos offered was his claim that the Colchians physically resembled Egyptians. "But it is undoubtedly a fact that the Colchians are of Egyptian descent," he wrote. "My own idea on the subject was based first on the fact that they have black skins and woolly hair."[1]

Herodotos clearly implies, in this passage, that black skin and woolly hair were considered by the Greeks to be Egyptian traits. Does this mean that the Greeks looked upon the Egyptians as "black," in the modern sense of that word? Most scholars say no. Among the most outspoken on this point is none other than Frank Snowden.

Snowden claims that the Greek word *Aithiops*, or *Ethiopian*, should be seen as roughly equivalent to our modern concept of a "black person." Any person who fit the physical description of a black, in Snowden's opinion, would have been designated an Ethiopian in the ancient world. Had the Greeks and Romans seen the Egyptians as black, Snowden reasons, they would have called them Ethiopians. Ancient literature, however, offers no example of the word being applied to an Egyptian. Snowden therefore concludes that the Egyptians could not have been black.

Of course, it is worth pointing out that Snowden does not consider *himself* to be black either. "I don't consider myself anything," he told a reporter for *The Sciences* in 1997. "If they had a 'mixed race' category on the census, I'd mark that off."[2]

Snowden's strong—and somewhat idiosyncratic—views on racial identity raise the question of just what he means when he uses the term "black." In most of his recent articles, Snowden insists that the Greeks and Romans applied the word "Ethiopian" only to those Africans whose skin was the very "blackest" and whose hair was the "wooliest or the curliest of all mankind" (though Snowden himself contradicts this extreme definition in some of his earlier writings. See chapter 65).[3] When he claims, therefore, that the ancient word "Ethiopian" is equivalent to the modern word "black," Snowden clearly implies that the only people, in modern times, whom he considers to be genuinely "black" are those with the very "blackest" skin and "wooliest" hair—a description that rules out millions of light-skinned African Americans.

Among those ruled out by this definition is Snowden himself. He clearly does not fit the extreme definition of an "Ethiopian." Snowden's *café au lait* complexion and relatively Caucasoid features raise the possibility that he—like the Egyptians—might not have been called *Aithiops* in Greco-Roman times. Since Snowden does not look upon himself as black, it seems reasonable to assume that he would not consider the Egyptians to be black either, should they turn out to look anything like Snowden.

One almost gets the impression that Snowden is granting the Egyptians the same courtesy that he wishes the U.S. Census Bureau would do for him. If, indeed, this is so, Snowden's position is not at all unreasonable. But it is somewhat confusing for those who are not privy to his personal views on race.

On one point, Snowden is quite correct. The Greeks and Romans did indeed draw a distinction between Egyptians and Ethiopians. They never called an Egyptian "Ethiopian" and never called an Ethiopian "Egyptian." It is also clear, however, that Greeks and Romans saw physical and cultural *similarities* between the two peoples. The resemblance was, in fact, sufficiently strong to convince

Greco-Roman historians that Egyptians and Ethiopians may have shared a common ancestry.

Diodoros, for example, recorded a tradition that Egypt had originally been founded by colonists from Ethiopia. He wrote:

> Now the Ethiopians, as historians relate, were the first of all men. . . . They say also that the Egyptians are colonists sent out by the Ethiopians, Osiris having been the leader of the colony. . . . And the larger part of the customs of the Egyptians are, they hold, Ethiopian, the colonists still preserving their ancient manners. For instance, the belief that their kings are gods, the very special attention which they pay to their burials, and many other matters of a similar nature are Ethiopian practices, while the shapes of their statues and the forms of their letters are Ethiopian.[4]

The Roman writer Lucian said that the Ethiopians, "being in all else wiser than other men," had invented astrology and taught it to the Egyptians.[5] Herodotos too alleged cultural parallels between Egypt and Ethiopia. Both peoples, he noted, practiced circumcision. While Phoenicians and Syrians also observed this custom, Herodotos noted that they were latecomers, having learned the practice only recently from Egypt. "As between the Egyptians and the Ethiopians," he wrote, "I cannot say which learned from the other, for the custom is evidently a very ancient one."[6]

Perhaps the most obvious similarity between Egyptians and Ethiopians was that both had dark skin. The Roman historian Suetonius mentions a drama that was being rehearsed in Rome at the time of Caligula's death in which spirits of the Underworld were played exclusively by Egyptian and Ethiopian actors.[7] This was typecasting based on skin color. The Greeks and Romans conceived of the Underworld as a dark place, ruled by Hades, or Pluto, a black god. Egyptians and Ethiopians seemed good candidates to play Underworld spirits, because both had skin noticeably darker than that of the Romans.

Herodotos was not the only Greek writer to associate the Egyptians with "black" skin. As noted in chapter 49, Aischylos called the daughters of Danaos "black, and smitten by the sun." In the same play, when the Egyptian fleet is spotted approaching Greece, Danaos comments, "The men on board are plainly seen, their black limbs showing from their white attire." Danaos' daughters respond: "Abominable is the lustful race of Aegyptus . . . they have sailed here, attended by a mighty black host. . ."[8] Epaphos, too, the king of Egypt and the great-grandfather of Danaos, was called "black" by Aischylos.[9]

It is clear that the Greeks and Romans perceived the Egyptians as a dark-skinned people. However, most classical accounts present the Egyptians as having been significantly lighter than their southern neighbors. Thus the Roman poet Manilius wrote:

> The Ethiopians stain the world and depict a race of men steeped in darkness; less sunburnt are the natives of India; the land of Egypt . . . darkens the bodies mildly . . . its moderate climate imparts a medium tone. The Sun-god dries up with dust the tribes of Africans amid their desert lands; the Moors derive their name from their faces, and their identity is proclaimed by the colour of their skins.[10]

Here, Manilius lists five different dark-skinned peoples—Ethiopians, Indians, Egyptians, Sahara-dwelling Africans, and Moors—ranking them by complexion from darkest to lightest. The Ethiopians are the darkest of all, while the Moors, or Mauri, of North Africa are presented as the lightest. The Egyptians were envisioned as being right in the middle, two shades lighter than the Ethiopians, but two shades darker than the Moors.

The picture Manilius paints seems to correspond well with the way that the Egyptians viewed themselves. This can clearly be seen from a painted relief on the wall of Seti I's tomb, in which the four types of people recognized by the Egyptians are depicted (see Figure 8). From left to right, they are labeled Egyptians (Rmt), Syro-Palestinians ('Aamw), Kushites (Nhsyw), and Libyans (Tjhnw) in the hieroglyphic text.

The Egyptians are shown with reddish-brown skin. Next come the Syro-Palestinians, who appear in two different shades, both somewhat lighter than the Egyptians. The Kushites follow, with coal-black complexions and noticeably Negroid features. Last in line are the Libyans, the lightest of all, shown with snow-white skin.

This tomb painting—along with a similar one from the tomb of Ramesses III—is often cited as proof that the Egyptians were not black. The Egyptians, after all, are depicted in these reliefs with skin that is lighter than that of the Nubians and features less Negroid. What is usually overlooked, however, is that, out of five different skin tones (if we count the two different shades of Syro-Palestinian), the reliefs portray Egyptians as only one shade lighter than Nubians, but fully *three* shades darker than the very white Libyans. In the spectrum of human color, the Egyptians clearly ranked themselves on the darker end.[11]

Some scholars have argued that the Egyptians were not really reddish-brown in color but only painted themselves that way as an artistic convention. As proof, they cite the fact that many Egyptian artists portrayed men as reddish-brown, but women as light yellow in complexion. Some have even argued that men were painted darker because they acquired deeper suntans than the women through their performance of manly outdoor labor.

There are two problems with this argument. First, both Libyans and Syro-Palestinians lived in desert lands every bit as sunny as Egypt. Why, then, would the Egyptians have been the only ones to acquire a tan? Second, the convention of painting men and women in two different colors was observed mainly during the Old Kingdom period, from about 2700 to 2190 B.C. After that, the convention became far less popular, and artists began to paint both men and women brown. The New Kingdom pharaoh Tutankhamun and his queen, Ankhesenamun, for example, were both colored the same reddish-brown hue in their famous portraits.[12]

The testimony of Greek and Roman authors makes it plain that the color conventions of Egyptian artists were just that—conventions. No ancient writer who visited Egypt ever observed that Egyptian men were uniformly reddish-brown or their women uniformly yellow. On the contrary, Greek and Roman authors recorded a wide range of skin tones and physical types in Egypt, ranging from very black to very light. The reddish-brown color used to typify Egyptians in paintings appears to have been a kind of "average" complexion, meant to represent all the various shades of Egyptian skin taken as a whole.

Flavius Philostratus observed that the southern borderlands of Egypt were inhabited by people who seemed to be hybrids, darker than Egyptians, yet lighter than Ethiopians.[13] However, even in the extreme north of Egypt, far from the Nubian border, "Ethiopian" features could still be discerned. Achilles Tatius described a Delta herdsman as "dark-skinned, not absolutely black like an Indian, but like a half-breed Ethiopian."[14] The use of expressions such as "half-breed Ethiopian" suggests that Greeks and Romans saw a resemblance between Egyptians and their southern neighbors that went beyond mere skin color.

In later chapters, we will explore the genetic, anthropological, and archaeological evidence for the kinship that some classical authors alleged between Egypt and Ethiopia. For now, what is important to understand is that—contrary to the claim of some experts—Greek and Roman authors offer *no definitive answer* to the question of whether we should call the Egyptians black, in the modern sense of the word.

What they do tell us is that the Egyptians were seen as physically distinct from the Ethiopians—just as the Greeks and Romans distinguished themselves physically from the blond and blue-eyed Germans and Scythians. If we assume, however, from this evidence alone, that the Egyptians were not black—as some experts have done—then we are obliged, for consistency's sake, to likewise assume that the Greeks and Romans were not white. Both conclusions seem overly radical, given the evidence at hand.

The question of Egyptian "blackness" has always resembled that of the proverbial glass of water, which can be seen as either half-full or half-empty, according to the observer's predilection. Much of the evidence cited in this chapter to suggest kinship between the two peoples has been drawn from the work of Frank Snowden, who has used it to prove exactly the opposite point—that the Egyptians were *unlike* the Ethiopians. Readers must ultimately judge for themselves which interpretation they find more compelling.

In any case, the kinship that Greeks and Romans obviously perceived between Egypt and Ethiopia goes a long way toward explaining why Vitruvius and other ancient writers would associate dark skin with high intelligence. To the Greeks and Romans, the "sunburnt" peoples of the south—Egyptians and Ethiopians alike—were nothing less than the founders of civilization. What is truly astonishing is how effectively proponents of the Master Race theory were able to turn this ancient opinion topsy-turvy in the centuries that followed.

CHAPTER 59

THE ARYAN RACE

EUROPE, LIKE AFRICA, HAS HAD ITS SHARE OF UPS AND DOWNS. IN the days of Caesar and Alexander the Great, Europe seemed unbeatable. But its power waned during the Middle Ages. The year 1304, in particular, found Europe in a serious downswing. Anyone who had tried to suggest, in that year, that white people were the world's dominant race would have been laughed into silence.

It was Muslims and Mongols, not Europeans, who held the upper hand in 1304. European Crusaders had been driven from the Holy Land in 1291. Moorish sultans from Africa continued to rule parts of Spain, just as they had since 712. The Mongols held Russia, which they had conquered—along with much of Central Europe—between 1237 and 1242. Now they grew rich selling their white subjects to Muslim slave traders.

During the Middle Ages, Russians and other Slavic peoples became the primary source of slaves for the Mediterranean world. Slavic women filled the harems of Turkish sultans. Slavic men rowed the galleys or worked the fields for Muslim lords, while Slavic children brought a good price in slave auctions from Cairo to Baghdad. The very word *Slav* came to mean "slave" in English and other languages.[1]

Not surprisingly, white people—and particularly Slavs—came to be regarded as an inferior race outside of Europe. "Their temperaments are frigid, their humors raw," wrote the Muslim scholar Sa'id al-Andalusi. "They lack keenness of understanding and clarity of intelligence, and are overcome by ignorance and dullness, lack of discernment, and stupidity."[2] Another Muslim writer, in the tenth century, offered the opinion that Iraqis, not Europeans, were the world's most intelligent and attractive people. He wrote:

The people of Iraq have sound minds . . . a proficiency in every art . . . and a pale brown color, which is the most apt and proper color. . . . They do not come out with something between blond, blanched and leprous coloring, such as the infants dropped from the wombs of the women of the Slavs and others of light complexion; nor are they overdone in the womb until they are burned . . . such as the Ethiopians and other blacks. . . . The Iraqis are neither half-baked dough nor burned crust, but between the two.[3]

Cringing beneath the contempt of their conquerors, many white people resigned themselves to inferior status. One Russian chronicler, lamenting the enslavement of his people by the Mongols, wrote, "The (Mongols) . . . learn warfare from their youth. Therefore, they are stern, fearless and fierce towards us. . . . We cannot oppose them, but humiliate ourselves before them, as Jacob did before Esau."[4]

The tables, however, were about to turn sharply in Europe's favor. Surprisingly, it began with what ought to have been a military breakthrough for the Muslims. Arab craftsmen, not Europeans, succeeded in making the first gun, in 1304.[5] Yet, it turned out to be Europeans, some hundred years later, who put this new invention to work most effectively on the battlefield. By the time Henry the Navigator sent his first caravels down the African coast in the 1430s, his explorers went heavily armed with cannon and muskets.

Europe's rise to world supremacy followed with breathtaking speed. With it came a new self-image for Europeans. Gone were the days when white people bowed low before Asian and Muslim rulers. Now it was the brown, black, red, and yellow people of the world who bowed before them. A new idea arose in European minds. While the Greeks and Romans had claimed superiority only for their fellow Mediterraneans, the new European declared that all white people—northerners and southerners alike—shared a common superiority over nonwhites. The Scottish philosopher David

Hume summed up the new thinking, in 1748: "I am apt to suspect the Negroes, and in general all the other species of men, to be naturally inferior to the whites. There never was any civilized nation of any other complexion than white, nor even any individual eminent in action or speculation."[6]

This was a far cry from the days when Vitruvius linked dark skin with intelligence and fair skin with stupidity. But an even bigger turnaround was yet to come. It started in 1786, when Sir William Jones announced a new discovery in linguistics. An English judge and scholar, Jones spoke many languages. After taking up residence in India, he began studying Sanskrit, the language of ancient Indian scripture.

As Jones's studies progressed, he noticed an odd thing. He found that an extraordinary number of Sanskrit words resembled words in Latin and Greek! There was, for example, the word *father*. In both Greek and Latin, this was *pater*, and in Sanskrit *pitár*.[7] Jones concluded that these resemblances were too strong and too many to be attributed to mere coincidence. Indeed, the three languages seemed so close that Jones concluded "no philologer could examine them all three without believing them to have sprung from some common source, which, perhaps, no longer exists."[8]

It was not long before Jones realized that the same common source that had given rise to Latin, Greek, and Sanskrit had also produced the Celtic, Germanic, and Slavic tongues—virtually every major language family of Europe! How could so many European tongues be related to a language spoken in ancient India? Jones could only guess that offshoots of the same ancient tribe had once settled both India and Europe, bringing their language with them. But who were these people, and where had they come from?

Subsequent scholars provided an answer. They pointed out that Indian scriptures, such as the *Rig Veda*, told of a mysterious race calling themselves the Arya—or "nobly born"—who had come down from the north and conquered India in ancient times. According to one controversial interpretation of the texts, the "Aryans" were fair-skinned and the native Indians, whom they conquered, dark-skinned.[9] The white conquerors—who eventually became the ruling Brahmin caste of India—were alleged to have imposed their Aryan language on the dark-skinned Dravidians.

Many presumed that these Aryans had been the ancestors of modern Europeans.[10] Originating someplace north of India—perhaps in the mountains of Central Asia—the Aryans had allegedly come pouring out of their ancestral homeland during prehistoric times. One group had supposedly invaded India, while the others had turned west and colonized Europe, bringing the Aryan language with them. Scholars named this language Indo-Aryan or Indo-European.

A small clique of German scholars took the Aryan theory even further. In the 1820s, they renamed Europe's ancestral tongue *Indogermanisch,* or Indo-Germanic, on the assumption that the German language was the closest, of all European tongues, to the original speech of the Aryans.[11] In so doing, they planted the seeds of a movement that would later come to be known as "Germanism" or "Indo-Germanism."

As the nineteenth century wore on, the Germanist theory spread from linguistics to anthropology. Its proponents pointed to the wide variety of physical types in Europe and argued that all these peoples could not possibly have descended from the same Aryan race. Clearly, one European "race" must represent the real Aryans. The others were simply natives, conquered and "Aryanized" by the invaders.[12] Germanist scholars gave the name *Herrenvolk*—or "Master Race"—to the original Aryans because they believed these people had mastered all the other races in their path. As we have seen, nineteenth-century Germanists were not the first to think in terms of a Master Race. But they gave the concept its modern name.

Who was this *Herrenvolk?* Which of Europe's peoples had the honor of being the true Aryans? Not surprisingly, German scholars proposed their own people as the best candidates. The Aryans, they declared, had been German. By the term *German,* they meant not only the inhabitants of modern Germany, but all other "Nordic," or northern, peoples who spoke Germanic languages, such as the English, Dutch, and Scandinavians.

Germanic tribes were believed to have been the last to leave the Aryan homeland and thus were held to have the purest Aryan blood of any people in Europe. Some scholars even suggested that the Aryans had not come from Central Asia at all, but had dispersed from a homeland in northern Germany.[13]

Because Germans were typified by blond hair and blue eyes, it was proposed that the original Aryans must have been fair.[14] Thus was born the idea, later made infamous by the Nazis, of a blond Master Race. The German *Herrenvolk* was held to be the strongest, bravest, most intelligent, and most spiritual of all Europe's peoples. For the first time, racial superiority was gauged entirely by complexion—the lighter the skin, the better the people.

Gone was the ancient presumption that dark skin connoted high intelligence. The "dumb blonds" of antiquity had achieved their final revenge. Needless to say, Vitruvius and Aristotle would have been shocked at the notion of blond superiority. But even greater surprises lay ahead. What was about to happen next would have paralyzed the Greeks and Romans with disbelief.

CHAPTER 60

THE DORIAN
DILEMMA

"WHAT SPLENDID BODIES YOU CAN SEE TODAY," DECLARED Adolf Hitler, on seeing a photograph of a sleek woman swimmer. "It is only in our century that young people have once again approached Hellenistic ideals through sports. How the body was neglected in earlier centuries."[1]

This outburst, recounted by Hitler's architect, Albert Speer, revealed a little-known side of the Fuhrer—his great admiration for all things Greek. "Hitler believed that the culture of the Greeks had reached the peak of perfection in every field," Speer observed.[2] Indeed, Hitler's autobiography, *Mein Kampf,* was filled with praise for the glories of ancient Greece. "What makes the Greek ideal of beauty a model," Hitler wrote, "is the wonderful combination of the most magnificent physical beauty with brilliant mind and noblest soul."[3]

Why would Hitler, a staunch proponent of German superiority, concede such status to a Mediterranean people such as the Greeks? The answer is that Hitler did not see the ancient Greeks as Mediterranean. He considered them to be a branch of the German race. Speer explained: "By the Greeks he meant the Dorians. Naturally his view was affected by the theory, fostered by the scientists of the period, that the Dorian tribe which migrated into Greece from the north had been of Germanic origin and that, therefore, its culture had not belonged to the Mediterranean world."[4]

As Speer correctly observed, the notion of Germanic Greeks was not an invention of Hitler's. Like so many of Hitler's key ideas, it was drawn from the conventional scholarship of the day. The "dumb blonds" had achieved their final revenge. No longer were the glories of classical civilization ascribed to swarthy Mediterraneans. Now, it was blond invaders from the north who took the credit.

Germanist theorists hypothesized that both Greece and Italy had been colonized by fair-haired Aryans in prehistoric times. The influence of these Aryans had supposedly sparked the high civilizations of Greece and Rome. But then a strange thing had happened. Accustomed as they were to their cold German homeland, the blond invaders began to wither in the Mediterranean heat. One by one, the blonds died out, leaving the darker Greek and Italian populations intact. That, concluded the Germanists, was why modern Greeks and Italians were darker than the blond invaders who had allegedly built their civilizations.

Even at the time this theory was proposed, many found it absurd. Some of the sharpest criticism came, not surprisingly, from scholars in Mediterranean countries. In his 1901 book, *The Mediterranean Race*, Italian anthropologist Giuseppe Sergi questioned how a race of robust German warriors could be so frail as to shrivel up and die from a climate as gentle as that of Greece and Italy. "I would add that a race cannot even be said to be physically superior if it is unable to resist the mild climate of the Mediterranean," he opined.[5]

Sergi pointed to classical artwork as evidence that the Greeks and Romans had been just as dark in ancient times as they were in Sergi's day. "The types of Greek and Roman statuary," he declared, "do not in the slightest degree recall the features of a northern race . . . in the delicacy of the cranial and facial forms, in smoothness of surface, in the absence of exaggerated frontal bosses and supra-orbital arches, in the harmony of the curves, in the facial oval, in the rather low foreheads, they recall the beautiful and harmonious heads of the brown Mediterranean race."[6]

Germanists countered that Achilles and the god Apollo were called *xanthos,* or "fair," in Greek writings. This implied, they claimed, that the Greeks envisioned their gods and heroes as Nordic blonds. But Sergi observed that the Greeks were prone to use the word *xanthos* in describing any sort of light hair, even chestnut brown.[7] Moreover, the mere fact that Achilles' hair attracted any notice at all from Homer showed that its color was unusual for a Greek.

We have already seen that Greeks and Romans saw their own physical type as falling midway between the fair northerners and the dark Africans. And most scholars today would agree that ancient writings portray the Greeks as predominantly brunet.[8] Yet, the notion of blond Greeks continues to thrive among the general public. The Nordic features of Disney's Hercules seem to provide a case in point. Blond Greeks also turned up in an attack on Martin Bernal's *Black Athena*, published in the conservative *National Review* in 1990. After noting Bernal's claim that ancient Egypt was a black civilization and that Greece was colonized by Egyptians, the writer countered, "There is scant support for this in the historical record. The ancient Egyptians did not depict themselves as black. The mummies are not negroid. Herodotos depicts the ancient Greeks as blond."[9]

Herodotos, of course, did not depict the ancient Greeks as any such thing. But this writer's faith in Nordic Greeks was evidently strong enough to obviate, in his mind, the need for careful fact checking.

The Scottish philosopher David Hume had made a radical break with the past when he declared, in 1748, that "there never was any civilized nation of any other complexion than white."[10] But the Aryanists now went even farther. To them, only blond Nordics were capable of civilization. Greeks and Italians, no matter how "white" their complexion, could never have done it without Nordic leadership.

Unfortunately for the Aryanists, archaeology did not support their claim. On the contrary, all evidence seemed to indicate that wherever "Aryans" actually did appear in prehistoric times, the first impact of their arrival seems to have been to *lower*, rather than raise, the level of civilization. Even V. Gordon Childe—an outspoken advocate of Aryan superiority—was forced to acknowledge that archaeology painted the Aryan invaders of Europe as "disgusting savages," "wreckers," and even cannibals. In 1926, he wrote, "Even in barbarian Europe the material culture of the Nordics was not originally superior to that of the Danubian peasants or the megalith-builders. In Transylvania they appear frankly as wreckers; in the Ancient East and the Aegean they appropriated and for a time impaired older and higher civilizations."[11] Recent work by archaeologist Marija Gimbutas, published in her books *The Language of the Goddess* (1989) and *The Civilization of the Goddess* (1991), has supported the notion that the Aryan invasion of Europe resulted, at least initially, in an overall decline in living standards.

The legendary Dorians, whom Hitler so admired, were even more destructive than most. Thukydides says that they seized the Peloponnese about eighty years after the Trojan War.[12] Archaeologists have, in fact, found evidence of widespread warfare in Greece at that time. The event that Thukydides remembers as the invasion of "the Dorians and the Heraclids" marked the end of Mycenaean civilization and the beginning of Greece's 400-year Dark Age. Carl Blegen described it in these words:

> The Dorian invasion, whatever its source, and however it ran its course, has left a broad gash, like a fire-scar in a mountain forest, cutting through the archaeological panorama of ancient Greece. Many towns and settlements that flourished in the preceding Heroic age were henceforth abandoned or declined to a state of insignificance. Even some of the great and noted strongholds sank into virtual oblivion, and the places where they had stood were lost to the view of man.[13]

It should be noted that most scholars today question whether the destructions of 1200 B.C. were really committed by Dorians or even whether the Dorians existed at all.[14] Moreover, there is no compelling reason to believe that the Dorians were blond or even Germanic. On the contrary, ancient tradition describes them as a wandering branch of the Greek people, speaking their own dialect of Greek.[15]

Yet, even if we accept the Aryanist theory at face value and assume that a race of blond Germanic "Dorians" really invaded Greece around 1200 B.C., the evidence suggests that the principal contribution of these northern supermen to Greek culture was its obliteration.

The undeniable savagery of Europe's northern tribes in antiquity has long been a stumbling block to proponents of the Master Race theory. How could the Germans be called the creators of civilization when the evidence showed that they destroyed civilized life wherever they encountered it? Even Hitler was troubled by this paradox. In *Mein Kampf,* he tried to excuse the barbarism of ancient Germany as a consequence of climatic conditions: "Hence it is an unbelievable offense to represent the Germanic peoples of the pre-Christian era as 'cultureless,' as barbarians. That they never were. Only the harshness of the northern homeland forced them into circumstances which thwarted the development of their creative forces."[16]

Hitler himself must have realized the feebleness of this argument, however, for he generally dealt with the question of Germany's ancient barbarism by scrupulously avoiding it. Albert Speer recalls Hitler's irritation when his SS chief Heinrich Himmler began sponsoring archaeological digs of ancient German settlements. Mortally embarrassed by the whole endeavor, Hitler declared:

> Why do we call the whole world's attention to the fact that we have no past? It isn't enough that the Romans were erecting great buildings when our forefathers were still living in mud huts; now Himmler is starting to dig up these villages of mud huts and enthusing over every potsherd and stone ax he finds. All we prove by that is that we were still throwing stone hatchets and crouching around open fires when Greece and Rome had already reached the highest stage of culture. We really should do our best to keep quiet about this past. Instead, Himmler makes a great fuss about it all. The present-day Romans must be having a laugh at these revelations.[17]

As Hitler's uneasiness so clearly attests, proponents of the Master Race theory have been forced, from the beginning, to accommodate themselves to a nagging contradiction. On the one hand, the ancient Germans were undeniably savage. On the other hand, the doctrine of Aryanism demanded that Germans take credit for civilizing the world.

Somehow, Hitler—like generations of Aryanists before him—managed to balance these assertions in his mind. It was a triumph of "doublethink"—the process, described by George Orwell in his novel *1984*, of believing wholeheartedly in two mutually exclusive facts.

A similar act of doublethink was performed in Egyptology. When the Master Race theory was first brought to the study of Egypt, it faced contradictions even more stupendous than those confronting it in Europe. But the proponents of Aryan superiority proved themselves once again to be masters of doublethink. As we will see, in the next section, it is largely thanks to their supple imaginations that so much confusion still prevails over the race of the ancient Egyptians.

PART TEN

CHILDREN

OF HAM

CHAPTER 61

THE CURSE
OF HAM

SCHOLARS TODAY ARE TRAINED TO GIVE THE SAME AMOUNT OF CRE-
dence to the Bible that they give to other ancient traditions—
practically none. In past centuries, however, the Bible was
still viewed as God's Word. Scholars were then obliged to take very
seriously anything the Bible said regarding who the Egyptians were
and where they came from. For that reason, the story of Ham has acquired an importance far out of proportion to the few lines devoted
to it in the Book of Genesis.

Egypt is called Mizraim in the Bible. According to the Book of
Genesis, Egypt took its name from Mizraim, the son of Ham, who,
in turn, was the son of Noah. Nowhere does the Bible state whether
the descendants of Mizraim were black or white. But the Book of
Genesis does contain a revealing list of Mizraim's brothers. It reads:
"The sons of Noah who came out of the ark were Shem, Ham and
Japheth. . . . These were the three sons of Noah, and from them
came the people who were scattered over the earth. . . . The sons of
Ham: Cush, Mizraim, Put and Canaan."[1]

Cush, Mizraim, Put, and Canaan. These were the "Hamites"—
the descendants of Ham, each one the founder of a nation. Scholars

have long puzzled over this list. The first two nations are easy enough to identify. Cush almost certainly refers to the Nubian kingdom located between the Second and Third Cataracts of the Nile that the Egyptians called Kush and that the Greeks and Romans regarded as the heartland of Ethiopia. Just as obviously, Mizraim is Egypt. The third Hamite nation is a bit more mysterious. Nobody really knows where Put lay, though some scholars in the past have placed it in Libya, while others have identified it with Punt, located on the East African coast.[2] If either of these theories is true, then the first three Hamitic nations in the list were all located in Africa. Does this mean that the Hamites were black?

The Bible does not explicitly say so. Nevertheless, most European scholars, by the year 1600, used the term *Hamite* interchangeably with *black*.[3] The identification of Hamites with blacks comes from a Jewish oral tradition first recorded in the *Babylonian Talmud* in the sixth century A.D. There the story is told that Ham crept up on his father, Noah, and, for some unexplained reason, castrated him while he slept. On awakening, Noah cursed his son, in these words:

> Now I cannot beget the fourth son whose children I would have ordered to serve you and your brothers! Therefore it must be Canaan, your firstborn, whom they enslave. And since you have disabled me . . . doing ugly things in blackness and night, Canaan's children shall be born ugly and black! Moreover, because you twisted your head around to see my nakedness, your grandchildren's hair shall be twisted into kinks, and their eyes red; again because your lips jested at my misfortune, theirs shall swell; and because you neglected my nakedness, they shall go naked, and their male members shall be shamefully elongated! Men of this race are called Negroes.[4]

A different—and somewhat tamer—version of the story can be found in the Bible. The Book of Genesis says only that Ham "saw his father's nakedness" while Noah lay drunk. This seems a far less egregious sin on Ham's part than castrating his father. Even so, Noah still punished it with a curse. The biblical version of the curse makes no mention of blackness. It says:

> Cursed be Canaan! The lowest of slaves will he be to his brothers. . . .
> May Canaan be the slave of Shem. . . . May God extend the territory of Japheth; may Japheth live in the tents of Shem, and may Canaan be his slave.[5]

Thus, Canaan receives two versions of the curse. In the Bible, he is cursed only with slavery. In the *Babylonian Talmud*, he is cursed with both slavery and blackness. From this slender evidence, American slaveowners wove an elaborate theological justification for their enslavement of blacks. Claiming that Noah's curse applied to Ham and all his progeny, American slaveowners interpreted the story as a license to enslave any "Hamites," or black people, anywhere in the world. Neither the Talmud nor the Bible, however, supports this interpretation.

Both texts make clear that Noah placed the curse not on all of Ham's sons, but only on Canaan. In one respect, this makes perfect sense. The Bible tells us that the Canaanites were indeed later conquered by the Hebrews. Thus the sons of Canaan were enslaved by the sons of Shem, exactly as Noah had predicted.

In another respect, however, Noah's curse against Canaan presents a puzzle for scholars. The Canaanites, as previously discussed, were the ancient inhabitants of Syria-Palestine. Most notable among the Canaanite peoples were our old friends, the Phoenicians. No mainstream scholar today envisions the Phoenicians as having been black. Yet, the legend recorded in the *Babylonian Talmud* clearly implies that they were.

Archaeologists have long since established that the Phoenicians spoke a Semitic language, worshiped Semitic gods, and observed Semitic customs, as, indeed, did all Canaanite peoples. This would seem to make the Phoenicians Semites, or "sons of Shem," like the Hebrews. Yet, the Bible clearly states that the Phoenicians were descendants of Ham, not Shem. In 1901, the Italian anthropologist Giuseppe Sergi addressed the problem, in these words:

> With regard to the Phoenicians, we are in some obscurity. Those who, with Petrie and Sayce, rely on the testimony of the homophonies from the Old Testament, or from anthropological types revealed by Egyptian monuments, consider them to be Hamites. . . . It is true that the Egyptians have represented them of a brick-red color, like themselves. . . . On the other hand, there are some who consider that the Phoenicians were Semites. This view is found especially among historians, who chiefly rely on the language.[6]

Nowadays such disputes have receded into the background. The Bible no longer commands the authority it once did among scholars. Most now assume that the Phoenicians were Semites and that the

Bible was simply wrong.[7] If, however, we remain consistent in our policy toward ancient tradition, we must grant to the Bible at least the same respect we have already accorded various Greek legends. This obliges us to at least consider the possibility that the Phoenicians may have shared kinship with the Egyptians and Ethiopians, just as the Bible says.

Such a scenario would not, in fact, require that we deny the Semitic heritage of the Phoenicians. There is no reason why a Hamitic people could not have become "Semitized" over the years, acquiring the language, dress, and culture of the Semites—perhaps even widely intermarrying with Semites—while still retaining some Hamitic traits.

In this regard, it is interesting to note that the tomb painting of Seti I, discussed in chapter 58, seems to show two types of Syro-Palestinian, one with yellow skin, the other painted reddish-brown. Can it be that the artists were trying to depict two distinct physical types—specifically, a dark-skinned Hamitic type and a lighter-skinned Semitic type—intermixed among the Canaanites? We can only guess.

Rightly or wrongly, there is no denying that the *Babylonian Talmud* portrays the Phoenicians as black. Nor can there be any question that another group of Hamites, the Ethiopians, were also black. Traditional scholars long assumed that the remaining Hamites—Egyptians and Put-ites—must also have been black, by analogy. This may or may not be a correct assumption. But if the biblical genealogy makes anything clear, it is that the Jews—like the Greeks—perceived the Egyptians to be closely related to the Ethiopians.

Tradition, however, is only tradition. Right up through the eighteenth century, scholars relied mainly on the ancient writings to resolve such questions as the ancestry of the Egyptians. But new tools became available in the early nineteenth century. The science of anthropology was hailed, at first, for its supposed ability to transcend prejudice and personal opinion. But, in the end, even the most rigorous techniques of physical analysis failed to liberate researchers from the dungeon of their own preconceptions.

Imbued, as so many were, with the Master Race theory, early anthropologists drew from the evidence what they wished and discarded the rest. In so doing, they took the first steps in a radical and far-reaching project that continues to this day—the systematic whitening of the Hamites.

CHAPTER 62

IN SEARCH OF THE "TRUE NEGRO"

F THE HAMITES WERE INDEED BLACK, AS BOTH BIBLICAL GENEALOGY and Jewish oral tradition imply, then scientists ought to have no trouble proving it through analysis of their physical remains. That, at least, has been the assumption among scientists for the last 200 years. Unfortunately, researchers have clouded the issue by bringing to their anatomical investigations as many prejudices as they previously brought to the study of artwork and literature. Even in the face of hard evidence, such as human skulls and mummies, rival interpretations abound.

The first area of disagreement is the definition of race itself. What does it mean, anatomically speaking, for a person to be "black"? The German naturalist Johann Friedrich Blumenbach suggested, in 1795, that a black person (or "Ethiopian," to use his term) was distinguished by black skin, muscular body, thick lips, flat nose, projecting upper jaw, and black, "curly" hair.[1]

This is a clear enough description. The problem is that many people who would ordinarily be considered black fail to fit this description in every detail. The celebrated fashion model Iman, for example, is a native-born African from Somalia. Although she has dark skin and frizzy hair, her lips are no thicker than those of Italian film star Sophia Loren. Iman entirely lacks the flat nose and projecting jaw described by Blumenbach. In fact, her facial features are hardly distinguishable from those of many southern Europeans. In this respect, Iman is not at all exceptional. Millions of Africans—especially in the northeastern part of the continent—share similar features.

It was because of such "in-between" types as Iman that Blumenbach concluded that the boundaries between races were fuzzy. The major races did not end in clear, sharp lines, he observed, but rather blended into each other gradually. Blumenbach wrote, "For although there seems to be so great a difference between widely separate nations . . . yet when the matter is thoroughly considered, you see that all do so run into one another, and that one variety of mankind does so sensibly pass into the other, that you cannot mark out the limits between them."[2]

Because of people like Iman, some early anthropologists went to great lengths to try to separate "true Negroes" from those who appeared to be "mixed" with other races. Ultimately, they concluded that only those Africans having the blackest of skin, the thickest of lips, the woolliest of hair, and the most prominent of projecting jaws should be considered "true Negroes." The rest were assumed to be mixed.

Anthropologists separated these "mixed" types into two categories. Those whose features seemed closer to the "Negro" were called Negroid. Those whose features veered more in a "Caucasian" direction were called Caucasoid. Virtually all of these people, however, whether Negroids, Caucasoids, or "true Negroes," would have been classified as black if they lived in America. This can clearly be seen by the fact that Iman—who would have been described as Caucasoid by anthropologists of the past—is invariably labeled as "black" by the U.S. media.

Nowhere did the ambiguity over Negroids, Caucasoids, and "true Negroes" cause greater confusion than in the study of ancient Egypt. The first scientist to make a thorough study of Egyptian remains was a Philadelphia physician named Samuel Morton. Like most Americans of his day, Morton was a proponent of the Master Race theory. He believed not only that white people were superior to

blacks but also that Germans and Anglo-Saxons—Nordics, that is—
were superior to all other whites.[3] Morton dedicated his life to proving this theory. The tool he used was craniometry—the
measurement of human skulls.

Morton collected skulls of various races and filled them with
mustard seed or lead shot to ascertain the amount of space available
for the brain. In a series of books published in 1839, 1844, and 1849,
Morton announced his conclusion that the brains of Germans and
Anglo-Saxons were the largest of all, those of American Indians considerably smaller, and those of blacks smaller still.[4]

Morton had found the proof he sought. He became a scientific
celebrity in his day. Though a Yankee, Morton found his most ap-
preciative audience in the South, where slaveowners were eager to
find a scientific rationale for black slavery. Upon Morton's death in
1851, the *Charleston Medical Journal* declared: "We of the South
should consider him our benefactor, for aiding most materially in
giving to the negro his true position as an inferior race."[5]

Long after his death, Morton's work was cited as an authoritative
proof of white—and particularly Germanic—superiority. But Harvard paleontologist Stephen Jay Gould decided to take a second look
at Morton's data in 1977. He made a surprising discovery. "In short,
and to put it bluntly," wrote Gould, "Morton's summaries are a
patchwork of fudging and finagling."[6] Morton had, in fact, crudely
weighted the evidence in favor of his Master Race theory.

To prove, for example, that American Indian crania were smaller
than white crania, Morton had exploited the well-known anatomical fact that taller people tend to have larger brain cases than shorter
people. He therefore packed his Indian sample with large numbers
of tiny Peruvian Indians, while keeping the number of tall, large-
brained Iroquois to a minimum. This dramatically lowered the average size for Indian brains as a group. Morton was equally selective
with his white sample, but in the opposite direction. The Hindus—
whom Morton considered an integral part of the Caucasian race—
were all but eliminated from Morton's Caucasian sample, because,
as Morton himself put it, "the skulls of these people are probably
smaller than those of any other existing nation."[7]

Morton's failure to correct for stature is only one of many
methodological errors Gould discovered. Working from Morton's

raw data, Gould made corrections for all the errors he found and re-calculated the average brain size for each race. The glaring differ-ences Morton had claimed between white, black, and American Indian brains shrank to insignificance in Gould's new figures.[8]

In one respect, Gould's efforts were unnecessary. Modern scien-tists had long since recognized that brain size bore little or no rela-tionship to intelligence. Even Morton himself had been troubled by the fact that the tiny-brained Inca built a high civilization, while the large-brained Iroquois did not.[9] By the time Gould came along, mainstream scholars no longer cited Morton's data as proof of white superiority.

Nevertheless, Gould's exercise was important for another reason. It demonstrated how easily "hard" scientific data can be manipu-lated by a researcher's prejudice. Morton's personal commitment to the Master Race theory clearly influenced the "average" sizes of his sample crania. Equally suspect were Morton's observations on the racial identity of the ancient Egyptians.

Morton viewed Egypt almost as an ancient version of the antebel-lum South—a country in which black slaves served white masters. He drew this conclusion partly from studying Egyptian reliefs in which Nubian prisoners of war were shown bound and helpless. Of course, Libyans and Semites—whose skin was much lighter than that of Egyptians—were also portrayed as captives in Egyptian art-work. An unbiased observer might have concluded that black cap-tives were not singled out for enslavement any more than white ones. But Morton saw only what he wanted. "Negroes were numer-ous in Egypt," he concluded in 1844, "but their social position in ancient times was the same that it is now, that of servants and slaves."[10]

Moved by his vision of white masters and black slaves, Morton then went on to make two fateful—but probably incorrect—as-sumptions about ancient Egyptian anatomy. His first assumption, made after examining a large number of Egyptian skulls, was that there were four distinct racial groups in ancient Egypt. The first group, said Morton, was "Caucasian" people whose origin lay either in Europe or Asia. The next two groups were people of supposedly mixed race. One of these groups Morton described as more Negroid in appearance. The other appeared to him more Caucasoid. Both, however, were mulatto, in Morton's view. Finally, there was a group that Morton called "unmixed Negro."[11]

The problem with Morton's first assumption—as bioanthropologist Shomarka Keita has pointed out—was that Morton's criteria for assigning skulls to each of his four groups were subjective and arbitrary.[12] If the Somali model Iman, for example, had died in ancient Egypt and her bones been examined by Morton, there is a possibility that he would have classified her as a Caucasian, based on her facial structure alone. There is no way of telling how many ancient Imans may have ended up among Morton's "white" Egyptians.

The second assumption Morton made was that the "Caucasians" he found represented the "real" Egyptians. He proposed that they had descended from a mysterious white race that had migrated into Africa during prehistoric times and founded Egyptian civilization. These "real" Egyptians had then enslaved the native "Negroes" and interbred with them, giving rise to a mulatto population.

In fact, Morton had no real evidence for assuming that the Caucasian types he found were any more likely to be real Egyptians than the mixed types. Indeed, two of Morton's most faithful disciples disagreed with him on this point. After studying the evidence, Josiah Nott and George Gliddon were forced to conclude, in 1854, that it was the Negroids, not the Caucasians, who represented what they called the "Old Egyptian type."[13]

Neither Nott nor Gliddon was eager to draw this conclusion. Both were champions of white superiority, like Morton, and would no doubt have preferred white Egyptians to Negroid ones. But the evidence seemed to offer little choice. Having accepted that the Old Egyptian type was Negroid, Nott and Gliddon were now faced with a dilemma. If these Negroids were really mulattoes, as Morton believed, then the Old Egyptian type was the product of race mixing. Yet, Nott and Gliddon were firmly convinced that race mixing *destroyed* civilizations, rather than built them.

Nott and Gliddon were both fierce advocates of slavery. A physician from Mobile, Alabama, Nott toured the country, amusing audiences with what he jokingly called his "lectures on niggerology."[14] In these talks, Nott declared that blacks were a separate species from whites and railed against the "insulting and revolting" practice of race mixing, which could only end, he warned, in the white race being "dragged down by adulteration and their civilization destroyed."[15]

Gliddon too lectured widely on black inferiority. A diplomat rather than a scientist, Gliddon sought out specialists such as Morton and Nott whose work he could use to defend slavery. It was Gliddon, as U.S. consul in Cairo, who had procured the Egyptian skulls and mummies used in Morton's landmark study. In his proslavery pamphlets, Gliddon later cited Morton's research as proof that "the Negro races had ever been servants and slaves," even in the far-off days of ancient Egypt.[16]

Given their views, it is easy to see why Nott and Gliddon objected to a "mulatto" origin for Egyptian civilization. They contrived an unusual argument to get around it. In their 1854 book, *Types of Mankind*, Nott and Gliddon admitted that the Old Egyptians had been Negroid. But they refused to accept that the Egyptians had acquired such Negroid traits through the "revolting" practice of actually sleeping with blacks.

Instead, they proposed an entirely different source for these Negroid features. Nott and Gliddon suggested that the Old Egyptians had arisen from a separate and unique African race, one that possessed some black features but shared no actual kinship with "true Negroes."[17] In other words, this mysterious race had a Negroid appearance, but no "Negro" blood.

By this means, Nott and Gliddon managed to save the Old Egyptians from the taint of "Negro" ancestry, while still providing an explanation for the many physical traits they shared with "Negroes." Nott and Gliddon's theory may seem a clumsy contrivance to modern readers. Moreover, it is a contrivance whose political motivation seems obvious. Even so, a version of Nott and Gliddon's theory remains popular among many respected scholars today.

In fact, one of the chief arguments raised nowadays to discredit Afrocentrism is that East Africans—such as Somalis, Ethiopians, and Egyptians—supposedly belong to a race entirely separate from that of West Africans. For that reason, say the critics, the Egyptians and other East Africans should not be lumped together with the "true Negroes" of West Africa and should not be called black. Such arguments preserve the legacy of Nott and Gliddon with unmistakable clarity.

Until the 1840s and 1850s, the tradition of black Hamites had remained largely intact, especially among devout Christians. But now science—in the guise of Morton, Nott, and Gliddon—had challenged the ancient tradition. It suggested that the most prominent of all Hamites, the Egyptians, belonged to a race utterly distinct from the "true Negro."

Whether the Egyptians were closer to Morton's Asiatic Caucasians or to Nott and Gliddon's Old Egyptian type was immaterial. The important point was that science had now freed the Egyptians from any connection with the "true Negro" of West Africa and therefore from any taint of kinship with the despised field hands of Southern plantations. Future generations would push the argument even further, until the word Hamite had utterly reversed its traditional meaning.

CHAPTER 63

WHITE
PHARAOHS

SINCE THE TIME OF HERODOTOS, MOST HISTORIANS HAVE RIGHTLY regarded the pyramids as Egypt's finest achievement. But why did the Egyptians suddenly start building them? In the early twentieth century, proponents of the Master Race theory offered what was perhaps a predictable explanation. They proposed that a *Herrenvolk*, or Master Race, of white people, had invaded Egypt at the dawn of history, conquered the Negroid people who lived there, and made themselves kings. These white pharaohs then set their new subjects to work building pyramids. Because they were credited with founding some of Egypt's earliest royal dynasties, the invaders were called the Dynastic Race.

This theory probably received its strongest support from the work of a British anatomist named Grafton Elliot Smith. While serving as Professor of Anatomy at Cairo Medical School, Smith conducted medical examinations of innumerable Egyptian mummies, beginning in 1901. He was struck by the unusual appearance of mummies from the Fourth Dynasty cemetery surrounding the Great Pyramid at Giza.

Smith saw the mummies found at Giza as being far more Caucasoid than those he had examined from the much older predynastic cemeteries. The difference seemed sharp enough to persuade Smith that he had discovered a race of newcomers, unrelated to the original Egyptians. His associate D. E. Derry later observed: "The unexpected discovery was made that the pyramid builders were a different race from the people whose descendants they had hitherto been supposed to be. . . . Quite definitely, they had not come from the south as the Dynastic people were far removed from any negroid element."[1]

Smith later opined that the newcomers were "Armenoids"— a branch of the white race—who had probably started infiltrating Egypt during the First Dynasty, around 3000 B.C.[2] Smith claimed that the Armenoids were running the country by the Second Dynasty. He found Armenoid features during this period "much more common and pronounced in the aristocracy than in the working classes."[3] Smith described the Armenoid influence in these terms:

> The aristocracy was permeated with the influence of these foreigners. Not only the actual human remains, but also the remarkable portrait statues of the Pyramid Age reveal the profound influence of the newcomers. Without any marked change in stature, or in the colour of the hair or eyes, the Egyptian's physique now becomes much more robust and muscular. The effeminate features of the proto-Egyptian are replaced by the more virile type of the mixed dynastic Egyptian race.[4]

At a time when the Master Race theory was enjoying an extraordinary vogue in academia, Smith's discovery seemed almost too good to be true. Here was scientific proof that white people had built the pyramids! There was only one catch to the theory. Smith's Dynastic Race was haunted by the same unanswerable question that had long plagued proponents of German superiority in Europe.

As discussed in chapter 60, Aryanists had long been troubled by the fact that Germany—the supposed wellspring of civilization— had been practically the last place in Europe to acquire civilized ways. How could barbarians be said to have civilized people who were obviously more advanced than they? It was a question to which Aryanists had never provided a good answer.

Their usual tactic was to invoke racial mysticism. Whatever the Germans lacked in technical skills, Aryanists argued, they more than made up for in bravery, virility, adventurousness, religiosity, and other invisible and mysterious qualities of the Aryan soul. Elliot Smith employed a similar argument in his defense of the Dynastic Race.

Smith could not deny that, at the time his Armenoids arrived, Egypt already possessed one of the oldest and highest civilizations in the world. Centuries before the first pyramid was built, Egypt's kings had been rearing magnificent temples and tombs, decorated with hieroglyphs and wrought in the familiar Egyptian style. What exactly did the Egyptians have to learn from the Armenoids?

Try as he might, Smith could find no answer to this question. Even the pyramids themselves, though grander in scale than what had gone before, were basically extrapolations from older types of Egyptian tombs. If the Armenoids were really the civilizers of Egypt, then where were the signs of their civilization? Smith had no choice but to fall back on the same sorts of quasi-mystical arguments used by the Germanists. He suggested that the gifts brought by the Armenoids had been strictly invisible ones—energy, virility, and the like. Smith wrote:

> It is impossible to detect any material addition to Egyptian culture that can be attributed to the new-comers. All the wonderful developments of the arts and crafts that followed upon their coming were clearly the result of the evolution of the characteristically Egyptian practices and inventions, which can be referred back to a period centuries before the aliens reached Egypt. . . . The fact is definite enough that their influence was exerted almost exclusively in stimulating the further development of the characteristic local culture.[5]

In the end, the impact of Smith's Dynastic Race seemed a bit anticlimactic. The Armenoids had not really changed the country at all. They had simply *invigorated* it. And indeed, Smith admitted that the Dynastic Race itself was soon absorbed into the Egyptian population. "As time went on," wrote D. E. Derry, "the mixture of the two races obscured the outstanding differences so clearly demonstrated in the earlier graves."[6]

Experts remain divided as to what extent Smith's Dynastic Race may have really existed. During the brief time that it supposedly flourished, the signs of Armenoid influence were disturbingly vague. Not only did the invaders fail to leave any distinctive artifacts, but, as Smith observed, the statues and artwork of the period reveal no change in physical features. Hair, skin, eyes, and stature all appear the same. Only Smith's vague impression that statues of this period grew more "robust" testifies to the presence of the alleged newcomers.

Many experts charge that Smith's Dynastic Race was a mirage, based on wishful thinking and tortured interpretation of the evidence.[7] As with the "Caucasians" of Samuel Morton, it is hard to say how many perfectly normal Egyptian skulls might have been labeled "Armenoid" simply because their crania seemed a bit larger, their noses narrower, or their jaw lines more heroic.

Others opine that there may indeed have been a gradual infiltration of people from Syria-Palestine during this period. But, either way, experts see no reason to regard the newcomers as a Master Race. If anything, they appear to have been just one more in a long line of immigrant groups who flocked into Egypt over the years, only to be quickly absorbed by Egypt's older and stronger culture.

How, then, did the influence of these Armenoids come to be so grossly inflated in Smith's mind? As with so many other scholarly assumptions about Egypt, the answer seems to lie in Smith's fervent belief in the Master Race. Smith was an ardent racial theorist. He strongly believed that nations rose and fell in accordance with their racial purity. Egypt presented Smith with what he considered a perfect laboratory in which to prove his theories.

As Smith saw it, white people had been migrating into the Nile Valley from the north since prehistoric times, while black people had been flooding in from the south. The country therefore provided an excellent gauge for measuring the effects of race mixing. In 1916, Smith wrote:

> The peculiar geographical circumstances of Egypt, which regulated the process of admixture, enables us the more easily to study it and appreciate its effects. For the country may be compared to a moderately well-insulated tube into the lower extremity of which negroid people forced their way, while into the upper end the inhabitants of the Mediterranean littoral were percolating.[8]

Originally, Smith believed, both Egypt and Nubia had been inhabited by a dark-skinned people, neither black nor white, whom he called the Brown Race. It was they who had built the remarkable civilization of predynastic Egypt. But sometime around 3000 B.C., Smith believed, both Egypt and Nubia were invaded. "Armenoids" entered Egypt from the north, bringing their unique blend of virility and energy. Meanwhile, an incursion of "negro tribes" from the south brought sensuousness, effeminacy, and a "retarding" influence.[9] The impact of these black tribes was felt most keenly in Nubia, wrote Smith:

> Negro infiltration was a drag and a hindrance.... [Nubia's] culture was definitely degraded as the influence of the dark races of the south made itself more and more felt. The contrast between Egypt and Nubia.... demonstrates in the most striking way the reality of the far-reaching effects of admixture respectively with a stimulating, virile, white race and a retarding and sensuous black race.[10]

As the years went by, even the Egyptians succumbed to black infiltration. The population slowly darkened. "Armenoid traits . . . became to a large extent deleted," Smith lamented.[11] In Smith's view, the degradation of the Egyptian race had continued unabated right up to modern times.

"Even at the present day," Smith observed indignantly, "intermingling with negroid populations of the south is still going on . . . while Egyptian blood is constantly being adulterated with negro."[12] As Smith saw it, the consequences for Egypt were both inevitable and disastrous. He wrote:

> The singular lack of originality, and the slavish devotion to convention, which are the outstanding features of the modern Egyptian, are sure tokens that the former abilities of the race have been affected by fifty centuries of negro admixture, which has more than counterbalanced the infusion of virile northern blood that in some measure helps to explain the greatness of Egypt's achievements in the zenith of her power and influence.[13]

In many ways, Smith faced a dilemma similar to that which had confronted Josiah Nott and George Gliddon more than fifty years before. As an outspoken opponent of race mixing, Smith found himself in the uncomfortable position of trying to explain how the most enthusiastic race mixers of the ancient world—the Egyptians—had managed to build one of history's greatest and most long-lasting civilizations.

Like Nott and Gliddon, Smith accomplished this partly through semantics. He simply redefined the original Egyptians as a Brown Race, distinct and separate from the "true Negro." But Smith went even further. By rewriting Egypt's history as a grand struggle between white civilizers and black destroyers, he effectively transferred the credit for Egypt's greatness to the white portion of its gene pool. In so doing, Smith took a page from Samuel Morton's book. Morton too had acknowledged that Egypt abounded with mulatto and "Negro" types. But it was only the Caucasian Egyptians, according to Morton, who were desended from "the Mizraimites of Scripture, the posterity of Ham" and only they who could truly be called Egyptian.[14]

Had the scribes of the Talmud and Bible been alive to witness all this, they would doubtless have thrown up their hands in despair. What had happened to the sons of Ham? Were they white, black, or brown? The picture seemed to change with each passing generation. By the 1930s, virtually no trace of the ancient tradition remained. The "curse" of blackness had been lifted entirely from the sons of Ham.

In the writings of modern scholars, the Hamites had now come full circle, traversing the spectrum of human complexion from one extreme to the other. When they emerged at last in the twentieth century, not only had the Hamites grown unambiguously white, but they had also assumed the position of Master Race of all Africa.

CHAPTER 64

THE LOST
WHITE TRIBE

ULUGETA SERAW WAS A TWENTY-EIGHT-YEAR-OLD ETHIOPIAN immigrant. He had come to the United States in 1980 with the goal of getting an accounting degree and going back to Ethiopia to help his country. Eight years later, Seraw was still struggling to put himself through school and driving an airport shuttle-bus for a living in Portland, Oregon.

One night in November 1988, two friends dropped Seraw off at his apartment building after a party. All three men were Ethiopian. As Seraw stood on the sidewalk, saying good-night to his friends, a carload of skinheads suddenly pulled up from the rear.

Accounts differ as to what happened next. Morris Dees, a civil rights attorney who later brought suit on behalf of Seraw's family, pieced together the following account from the conflicting testimony. Evidently, the skinheads began honking their horn, demanding that the Ethiopians move their car. Before the Ethiopians had a chance to comply, however, three skinheads suddenly jumped out.

All sported shaved heads and steel-toed Doc Martens work boots. One was an eighteen-year-old "death-metal" rock singer named Kenneth Mieske—better known on the local music scene as Ken Death.

While one skinhead battered Seraw with brass knuckles, Mieske struck him in the back of the head with a baseball bat. "He like buckled..." one skinhead later told police. "Then I saw the bat hit again. He was down on his knees and ... Bam! ... He fell face first."[1]

Mieske evidently struck with all his might. The blows to Seraw's head were so loud that a witness who heard them from a nearby apartment building thought they were gunshots. Seraw lay unconscious on the sidewalk, blood pouring from his cracked skull. He died a few hours later, in the intensive care unit.

Later, at his trial, Mieske proudly admitted to the murder. He had never met Seraw before and had no personal grudge against him. But Mieske was a Nazi skinhead, heavily influenced by the White Aryan Resistance movement. In Mieske's eyes, Seraw deserved to die. Why? Because he was black.[2]

To a Nazi skinhead, the attack made perfect sense. Seraw, after all, was an African immigrant. His brown skin, frizzy hair, and Negroid features marked him as the enemy—a black man. Mieske had summed up the skinhead attitude shortly after the murder when he told a friend, "It's just a ... nigger's dead. That's all it is."[3]

Yet many anthropologists would never have called Seraw black. Like most Ethiopians—and, indeed, like many East Africans, in general—Seraw's skin was only mildly dark. His nose was not flat, his lips were not very thick, and he did not have a dramatically projecting jaw. Seraw was therefore not a "true Negro," in anthropological terms. He was a Hamite.

Ken Death would probably have been very surprised to learn that most anthropologists, by the mid-twentieth century, had concluded that Hamites—such as Mulugeta Seraw—were white. "The Hamites ... are Caucasians," wrote British anthropologist Charles G. Seligman in 1930. "[They] belong to the same great branch of mankind as almost all Europeans."[4]

How, then, did Ken Death manage to mistake a white Caucasian for a black man? The answer is that although Hamites had been officially classified as whites, they did not always *look* white. Indeed, they sometimes looked so black that only an "expert" such as Seligman could tell the difference. Seligman described the Hamites in these terms:

> Among the Eastern Hamites ... the nose is straight ... the lips are often thick ... the hair is often frizzly, but sometimes wavy or almost

straight . . . the colour of the skin varies, it may be yellowish, coppery, red-brown, through every grade of *cafe-au-lait* to black, according to the amount of miscegenation that has taken place.[5]

Thick lips, frizzy hair, black skin . . . but nonetheless Caucasian.
How did such a paradox come about? Like Nott and Gliddon, Seligman and other anthropologists of his day had drawn an arbitrary
line through the peoples of Africa. On one side were the "true Negroes." On the other side were the Egyptians, Ethiopians, Somalis,
and other "Hamites." As with Nott and Gliddon's work, the purpose of this exercise appears to have been to isolate the "true Negroes" of West Africa from any possible connection with the
ancient civilizations of East Africa.

Egypt, Nubia, and Ethiopia all boasted magnificent ancient ruins.
But the racial theories of the day did not allow for the possibility
that black people could have built such monuments on their own.
Assumptions of this nature put a strong pressure on scholars to find
a "non-black" origin for East Africa's high civilizations. Any physical or cultural differences found between East and West Africans
were therefore magnified out of all proportion in an effort to prove
that East Africans were an entirely different race.

The bonds of kinship between African peoples, however, were
not so easily severed. Negroid features could be found in abundance
on both sides of the east–west divide. If Seligman and his colleagues
wished to paint the Egyptians and other East Africans as white, then
they had no choice but to promote millions of very black-looking
Africans—such as Mulugeta Seraw—into the status of honorary
Caucasians.

The physical appearance of East Africans aided considerably in
this effort, for many did indeed appear to be at least partially Caucasian in descent. One of the first Europeans to notice this fact was
the British explorer Sir Richard Burton. In 1854, disguised as an
Arab merchant, Burton became the first European to explore what
was then called Somaliland. He noted that many people in the region appeared to be "half-castes"—a cross between white and black.
Burton described the Somalis in these terms: "The crinal hair is
hard and wiry, growing, like that of a half-caste West Indian. . . . The
eyes are large and well-formed, and the upper features are frequently

handsome and expressive. The jaw, however, is almost invariably prognathous and African; the broad, turned-out lips betray approximation to the Negro."[7]

Observations such as this gave rise to the belief that Caucasian invaders must have penetrated East Africa in early times, intermarrying with the native people and civilizing them. By the 1850s, these mysterious white settlers were already being linked with the biblical Hamites.[8]

Scholars were soon struck with a kind of "Hamitomania." Signs of Hamitic influence were found all over Africa. Virtually any tribe that was thought to be unusually brave, attractive, or technically proficient was promptly assigned to the Hamitic race. By 1930, Hamitomania had reached such a peak that only a few isolated pockets of "true Negroes" were still acknowledged on the continent. In that year, Seligman summed up the prevailing view in his influential book, *Races of Africa*. He wrote:

> The Hamites—who are Caucasians, i.e. belong to the same great branch of mankind as almost all Europeans—are commonly divided into two great branches, Eastern and Northern. . . . The Eastern Hamites comprise the ancient and modern Egyptians . . . the Beja, the . . . Nubians, the Galla, the Somali and Danakil and . . . most Abyssinians [Ethiopians]. The Northern Hamites included the Berbers . . . the Tuareg and Tibu of the Sahara, the Fula of Nigeria and the extinct Guanche of the Canary Islands.[9]

In addition to the Hamites, Seligman described "Half-Hamites," "Nilotes," and Bantu peoples, all of whom he considered to be "hamiticized Negroes"—native Africans with a mixture of Hamite blood.[10] This mixed group included such famous warrior tribes as the Zulu and the Masai. "The noses of the Masai are noticeably finer than those of . . . other tribes," Seligman observed. "In colour, too, the Masai betrays his Caucasian blood, for his skin is described as tinged with reddish brown."[11] Indeed, as Seligman saw it, the vast majority of African peoples were at least partly Hamitic. He wrote: "The true Negro is mainly confined to the neighbourhood of the Guinea Coast, including Nigeria and the French Sudan with some part of the Cameroons and perhaps the Congo. The rest of negro Africa consists of negroes hamiticized to a varying extent."[12]

In Seligman's view, whatever Africa had managed to achieve through the centuries had been due entirely to the influence of the Hamitic invaders. He wrote:

> It would not be very wide of the mark to say that the history of Africa south of the Sahara is no more than the story of the permeation through the ages, in different degrees and at various times, of the Negro and Bushman aborigines by Hamitic blood and culture. The Hamites were, in fact, the great civilizing force of black Africa from a relatively early period. . . . The civilizations of Africa are the civilizations of the Hamites.[12]

Seligman attributed virtually all physical differences between Africans to intermarriage with Hamites. But scientists today have largely rejected this theory. Most consider it far more likely that Africans simply evolved into a number of different forms as an adaptation to local climate.

Even so, the Hamitic hypothesis remains quietly influential among scholars to this day. Many still insist, as an article of faith, that East Africans (like the Egyptians) are completely unrelated to "true Negroes" (like the West African ancestors of black Americans). Such distinctions are, of course, lost on laymen, who tend to see the world in more commonsensical terms. Certainly, Ken Death and his skinhead cronies saw little reason to regard the "Hamitic" Mulugeta Seraw as any different from the black Americans they met every day.

Are the East Africans, in fact, black or white? In the next and final sections of this book, we will examine the latest evidence from genetics, anthropology, linguistics, and archaeology. In determining whether Ken Death or Charles Seligman was closer to the truth, we will also ascertain whether the most famous of all East Africans— the Egyptians—should be considered part of the black race.

PART ELEVEN

THE
FIRST MEN

CHAPTER 65

THE BATTLE LINE

Egypt is to African American culture as Greece is to white culture.

— DR. MOLEFI KETE ASANTE

B Y THE LATE 1980S, ANCIENT EGYPT HAD BECOME ONE OF THE most hotly contested battlefields in America's endless feud between the races. Hardly a single African American could be found who was not thoroughly convinced that the ancient Egyptians had been black. White Americans, on the other hand, believed almost universally that the Egyptians had been Caucasian. A battle raged through America's schools and colleges. Parents, teachers, administrators, and university professors found themselves locked in an angry debate over how Egyptian history ought to be taught.

As the decade wore on, the Afrocentrists seemed to gain a clear advantage. One major school district after another adopted "multicultural" curricula in which Egypt appeared as a black nation. White teachers who did not toe the line increasingly found themselves besieged by classrooms full of angry black students who denounced them as "racists" and accused them of teaching "lies."

To Arthur M. Schlesinger, Jr., it was all perfectly horrifying. The distinguished historian could well remember the days of Senator Joseph McCarthy's anti-Communist crusade, when, as Schlesinger put it, "right-wing students . . . used to haunt the classrooms of liberal Harvard professors (like me) hoping to catch whiffs of Marxism emanating from the podium."[1] Now Schlesinger saw a new witch hunt brewing in the nation's classrooms, this one perpetrated in the name of liberalism. He felt obliged to speak out.

In his 1991 book, *The Disuniting of America,* Schlesinger charged that Afrocentrists were falsifying history. Instead of focusing on the many real achievements of black people, he complained, they invented elaborate myths. Among these, Schlesinger wrote, was their persistent claim that black Americans shared a common heritage with ancient Egypt.

"The Afrocentrist case rests largely on the proposition that ancient Egypt was essentially a black African country," Schlesinger observed.[2] But was it really? Schlesinger seemed to imply otherwise. However, he refrained from offering a clear opinion on the subject, pleading a lack of expertise in Egyptology. Instead, Schlesinger quoted four scholars, two of whom denied that the Egyptians were black and two of whom said that they were a "mixed population"— whatever that meant. Egyptologist Miriam Lichtheim took the hardest line. She said:

> I do not wish to waste my time refuting the errant nonsense which is being propagated in the American black community about the Egyptians being Nubians and the Nubians being black. The Egyptians were not Nubians, and the original Nubians were not black. Nubia gradually became black because black peoples migrated northward out of central Africa. The "Nile Valley School" is obviously an attempt by American blacks to provide themselves with an ancient history linked to that of the high civilisation of ancient Egypt.[3]

What was missing from Lichtheim's quotation—as well as from all the others cited by Schlesinger—was any clear definition of what she meant by the word *black.* In denying, for example, that the Egyptians and the original Nubians had been black, did Lichtheim mean to imply that they had been white? Did she mean, in fact, that they looked like Europeans? Most casual readers of Schlesinger's book would probably have assumed that such was her meaning.

Yet not even the most ardent proponents of the Hamitic hypothesis had ever dared to "whiten" the Egyptians or Nubians to quite that extent. Even Charles Seligman, while claiming that the original Egyptian and Nubian stock was Hamitic (and therefore Caucasian), was still forced to admit, in the same breath, that many of these honorary "Caucasians" had black skin and Negroid features. Lichtheim appeared to be walking the same semantic tightrope.

Between Lichtheim's blanket denial that Egyptians and Nubians had been black and Egyptologist Frank Yurco's more ambiguous assertion that Egyptians could be found in every color of the rainbow, Schlesinger must have found the expert testimony he cited just as confusing as most of his readers probably did. In the end, he drew no conclusion on the question of Egyptian "blackness."

However, it really did not matter what color the Egyptians were, Schlesinger insisted. Whether they were black, brown, or purple with pink polka dots, the Egyptians were still unrelated to African Americans. He wrote, "But any relationship between Egyptians, whatever color they may have been, and black Americans is exceedingly tenuous. Black Americans do not trace their roots to Egypt. The great majority of their ancestors came from West Africa, especially the Guinea coast."[4]

This, then, was the point. Schlesinger refused, on principle, to acknowledge any connection between Egyptians and black Americans—*no matter what color* the Egyptians turned out to be. His position was eerily similar to that espoused by proslavery agitators Josiah Nott and George Gliddon in 1854. But coming, as it did, from a celebrated liberal, Schlesinger's curious attitude went largely unnoticed by reviewers.

It was noticed, however, by Shomarka O. Y. Keita, a bioanthropologist at Howard University, who came across Schlesinger's book in 1992. Although a black American himself, Keita had little interest in Afrocentrism. He shared Schlesinger's concern over the many myths and inaccuracies fostered by some Afrocentric educators. Yet, as Keita leafed through *The Disuniting of America*, he was disturbed to find that Schlesinger seemed to be fostering a few myths of his own.

Chief among these was the long-discredited Hamitic hypothesis, which seemed to loom unspoken behind many of Schlesinger's key assumptions. It showed its face with particular clarity in the quotation Schlesinger had selected from Miriam Lichtheim. What could Lichtheim have meant, Keita wondered, when she said that the original Nubians had not been black? It was a statement that made sense only if you looked upon the earliest Nubians as "Hamites," distinct from the "true Negroes" who allegedly migrated into the country after 3000 B.C.

The original, or "A-Group," Nubians, as far as Keita was aware, were a typical East African people. Past scholars had called them Hamites because their features were felt to be less Negroid than those of West Africans. But if Hamitic features disqualified people from being black, then millions of East Africans—from Iman to the emperor Haile Selassie—would have to be similarly disqualified. Was Lichtheim seriously proposing that Haile Selassie had been white?

Keita concluded that neither Lichtheim nor Schlesinger had thought the problem through with sufficient thoroughness. Accordingly, he sat down and composed a letter to Schlesinger. In it, Keita warned of the pitfalls of trying to separate native-born Africans into black and white categories—an artificial distinction that obscured their common Africanness. Keita never seriously expected a reply from the famous historian, but he was pleasantly surprised when one arrived, dated July 30, 1992. Schlesinger wrote, "You raise interesting anthropological points regarding matters about which this historian can only plead ignorance. In any event, whatever the origins of ancient Egyptians, I do not see that it is especially relevant to black Americans today, most of whom trace their ancestry to West Africa, not to Egypt."[5]

In effect, Schlesinger had simply restated the position in his book. But he had also highlighted the sharp double standard that he applied—however unconsciously—to Europe and Africa. Despite the many obvious differences between European peoples, Schlesinger clearly regarded Europe as a single entity, whose common heritage extended back to Greece and Rome. Schlesinger wrote, for example:

> Whatever the particular crimes of Europe, that continent is also the source—the *unique* source—of those liberating ideas of individual liberty, political democracy, the rule of law, human rights, and cultural freedom that constitute our most precious legacy and to which most of the world today aspires. These are *European* ideas, not Asian, nor African, nor Middle Eastern ideas, except by adoption.[6]

Africans, on the other hand, could not claim membership in such a distinctive continental community, Schlesinger implied. They were far too Balkanized. "Africa contains some 850 distinct ethnic and linguistic groups," he noted. For that reason, the cultural and historical affinities of Africans supposedly went no further than their immediate tribes. Indeed, Schlesinger went so far as to suggest that the only history black Americans shared in common was their history of servitude. "Any homogeneity among slaves derived not from the African tribe but from the American plantation," Schlesinger concluded.[7]

By this reasoning, an Anglo-Saxon descended from wild Germanic tribes could legitimately take pride in his cultural inheritance—however distant and tenuous—from ancient Greece. But a black African must not take pride in ancient Egypt. The double standard did not go unnoticed by Keita. "I am surprised that you would invoke genetics when the issue is culture," he remarked, in a letter of September 26:

> On a genetic level, more Tunisians and Egyptians than Scandinavians have remote Greek ancestors, but the Greco-Roman "heritage" is deemed ancestral to Scandinavia. How many Anglo-Saxons have Greek ancestry? There is no straight natural line of descent from Pericles to George Wallace, Cecil Rhodes or the Gaelic speaking ancestors of John Kennedy . . . The Ukrainian "heritage" is viewed as part of the "European" heritage. The number of Western Europeans with Ukrainian ancestry is not viewed as relevant to the question.[8]

This time, Schlesinger did not respond. But Keita's brief correspondence with him had drawn a clear battle line. Keita's argument was based on *consistency*. If Europeans, with all their warring tribes and cultures, could be regarded as a single people sharing a common heritage, then why should Africans not likewise be entitled to a common cultural identity?

Since the time of Nott and Gliddon, many scholars had tended to split Africa sharply between the civilized Hamites of the east and the savage "Negroes" of the west. But Keita argued that it was inconsistent and arbitrary to bisect Africa in this way, while allowing Europe to stand as an inviolable, cultural monolith.

The Greeks and Romans would have understood Keita's point perfectly. The idea of sharing a common European identity with the northern barbarians would have amused and horrified them. Likewise, they would have been mystified by the modern division of Africans into Hamites and "true Negroes." Of course, the Greeks and Romans were well aware that all Africans did not look alike—just as they knew that all *Europeans* did not look alike. Diodoros, for example, shows an awareness of Africa's diverse physical types in his description of the Ethiopians who lived south of Egypt: "But there are also a great many other tribes of Ethiopians. . . . The majority of them, and especially those who dwell along the river, are black in color and have flat noses and woolly hair."[9]

In saying that a "majority" of Ethiopians had black skin, flat noses, and woolly hair, Diodoros clearly implied that some Ethiopians did *not* possess those features. Yet, all alike were considered Ethiopians.

Frank Snowden notes that the Greeks and Romans used the word *Ethiopian* to refer to at least two different "sub-types of the Negroid race," as he calls them. One of these subtypes Snowden calls the "true . . . African Negro." The other, he describes as "Nilotic" or "Hamitic," distinguished by such features as "less curly to almost straight" hair and "long narrow faces."[10] Despite their differences, both types were called Ethiopian.

Greco-Roman writings offer no hint that the ancient authors viewed East and West Africa as inhabited, respectively, by two distinct races, corresponding to the Hamites and "true Negroes." The inhabitants of both regions were called Ethiopians. In 338 B.C., for example, the Greek geographer pseudo-Scylax described a Phoenician trading colony on the island of Cerne, off the west coast of Africa. He wrote: "At Cerne, the Phoenicians carry on trade. . . . After unloading their goods, they take it over to the mainland in small boats; there live Ethiopians with whom they trade. . . . the Ethiopians wear skins and drink from ivory cups, their women wear ivory necklaces, and even their horses have ivory decorations."[11]

Although its location is disputed, scholars have traditionally identified Cerne with Hern Island, located at the mouth of the Rio de Oro in the Western Sahara, a territory just north of Mauritania, currently held by Morocco.[12] The story places Ethiopians thousands of miles from the traditional Ethiopian heartland, south of Egypt. Yet pseudo-Scylax drew no distinction between these western "Ethiopians" and those in the east.

According to Snowden, the Greeks and Romans applied the term *Ethiopian* very broadly to peoples living in the area "bounded in the east by the Red Sea and on the west by the Atlantic, perhaps as far south along the Atlantic coast as Cameroon."[13] All alike were called *Aithiops* and were evidently regarded as kindred peoples.

Also regarded as kin to the Ethiopians were the ancient Egyptians. As noted in chapter 58, Diodoros cited a tradition that Egypt had been founded by Ethiopian colonists. He wrote:

Now the Ethiopians, as historians relate, were the first of all men. . . .
They say also that the Egyptians are colonists sent out by the Ethiopians, Osiris having been the leader of the colony. . . . And the larger
part of the customs of the Egyptians are, they hold, Ethiopian, the
colonists still preserving their ancient manners. For instance, the belief that their kings are gods, the very special attention which they
pay to their burials, and many other matters of a similar nature are
Ethiopian practices, while the shapes of their statues and the forms of
their letters are Ethiopian.[14]

Was Diodoros correct? Was there, indeed, a fundamental kinship
between Egyptian and Ethiopian? Did Egypt share with "black
Africa" precisely the sort of common cultural heritage that Professor Schlesinger denies? In the ongoing debate over Afrocentric education, much depends on whether we can trust in the accuracy of
Diodoros's account. It is to this question, therefore, that we will devote the remaining pages of this book.

CHAPTER 66

THE MOTHER
TONGUE

IN 1930, WHEN CHARLES SELIGMAN WROTE *RACES OF AFRICA*, NO respectable scholar would have dared to challenge the Hamitic hypothesis. There was simply too much evidence in its favor—or, at least, so it seemed. The evidence of anatomy, culture, and linguistics all seemed to converge to support the theory that a tribe of white invaders had conquered and civilized Africa in ancient times.

The anatomical evidence seemed the strongest. Hamites simply *looked* white. At least, they looked whiter than most Africans. Their light skin, "fine" features, and often smooth hair seemed to speak for itself. In addition, "Hamitic"-looking Africans seemed to share certain cultural characteristics. Experts had long theorized that the original Hamites had been cattle-herding nomads, whose warlike ways enabled them to subdue the peaceful farming tribes of Africa. Was it only a coincidence that some of Africa's greatest warrior peoples, such as the Masai and the Zulu, also happened to be cattle herders—and also appeared to have an admixture of Caucasian blood (at least, in the eyes of some experts)?

The final proof came from linguistics. Scholars in the nineteenth century had recognized that the languages of many Hamitic peoples—such as the Egyptians, Ethiopians, and Somalis—appeared to be distant cousins to Semitic languages such as Hebrew and Arabic. Since the Semitic tongues had mainly been spoken in the Middle East, linguists concluded that the Hamites too must have come from the Middle East.

The picture was now complete. Long ago, in prehistoric times, a tribe of warlike, cattle-herding white people had lived in the Middle East, all speaking the same mother tongue, called Hamito-Semitic. At a certain point, one group of these Hamito-Semites had wandered south into Africa, where they conquered the native black people and founded Hamitic civilization. Their cousins who remained behind in the Near East later evolved into the Semites.

For most experts, the evidence seemed conclusive. Was it not preposterous to imagine that millions of people living in northeastern Africa could have acquired Caucasoid features, cattle-herding cultures, and Hamitic languages all at the same time purely by chance? The only explanation for such a consistent cluster of traits seemed to be that these traits had been inherited from the same ancestral tribe—a tribe of Caucasians, to be exact, speaking a distinctly Middle Eastern tongue.

The cluster, however, was not as consistent as its proponents would have liked to think. Indeed, subsequent events would prove that, for all its popularity, the Hamitic hypothesis was little more than a mirage, composed of two parts wishful thinking and one part fudged data. By the early 1960s, the theory was virtually defunct. Most of the credit for this turnaround goes to a brilliant young linguist named Joseph H. Greenberg.

Fresh out of graduate school in the late 1940s, Greenberg had taken on what most linguists of his day thought an impossible task—the classification of all African languages. More than 800 known languages were spoken in Africa. Greenberg set out to determine exactly how each one of them was related to the others.

To accomplish this, Greenberg employed a simple but effective method that he later called "mass comparison." He wrote out long lists of words from a number of different languages and displayed words of identical meaning side-by-side, in a row, across the page. Whenever Greenberg found two words of identical meaning that also had a similar sound, he would make a note of the match. When enough matches were found between two or more different languages, Greenberg assumed that those matching languages had probably descended from a common ancestor and belonged in the same language family. He would then confirm the relationship by comparing their grammatical structure.

When he started work, debunking the Hamitic hypothesis was the last thing on Greenberg's mind. But flaws in the theory began showing themselves almost immediately. The first breakthrough came when Greenberg attempted to classify the language of the Fulani people. This was a powerful warrior nation, whose empire, by 1810, stretched from the western Sudan across the whole of Nigeria. Their good looks and prowess in battle had attracted the admiration of Europeans.

Charles Seligman had described the Fulani as "the purest representatives of the Hamitic element in Nigeria—straight-haired, straight-nosed, thin-lipped . . . and skin reddish-brown in colour, the women distinguished by their beauty of countenance and graceful carriage." He noted disapprovingly, however, that "free intermarriage and wholesale concubinage with the races whom they had conquered" had resulted in a "general coarsening in build and features and the frequent appearance among them of the frizzly hair and prognathous mouth of the Negro."[1]

Warlike by temperament, cattle herders by tradition, and—most important of all—Caucasoid in appearance, the Fulani seemed the perfect model of a Hamitic people. For that reason, no one had been surprised when the German linguist Karl Meinhof announced his conclusion that the Fulani spoke a Hamitic language.

But did they? When Greenberg examined the Fulani language, he found no evidence to support Meinhof's conclusion. Neither the words nor the grammar of the Fulani tongue bore the slightest resemblance to any other allegedly Hamitic language. On the contrary, it was the Hausa people—conquered subjects of the Fulani—whose language was Hamitic.

The Fulani tongue clearly belonged in an entirely different language family that Greenberg called Niger-Congo. Indeed, the resemblance between Fulani and such Niger-Congo tongues as Wolof and Serer-Sin was so obvious that Greenberg was at a loss to explain how a linguist of Meinhof's skill could have failed to notice it. Greenberg was forced to conclude that Meinhof had simply seen what he wanted to see. The German linguist's well-known enthusiasm for the Master Race theory had caused him to imagine Hamitic languages where none existed.

"Using Meinhof's methods," Greenberg complained, "one could prove that Algonkian [an American Indian language] was Hamitic."[2]

Greenberg soon discovered that entire groups of languages had been similarly misclassified. The Bantus, for example, had long been considered "half-Hamites," mainly because they were perceived as great warriors and cattle herders (the Zulus are Bantu) and because the features of some Bantus appeared slightly Caucasoid to some experts. Meinhof had obligingly concluded that their languages also were half-Hamite. "Bantu is a mixed language," he declared, "descended of a Hamitic father and a Negro mother."[3]

But, once again, Meinhof was wrong. Greenberg easily demonstrated that every one of the Bantu tongues belonged in the Niger-Congo family, just like Fulani. The Hottentot language and the tongues of the Dinka, Shilluk, and Nuer also turned out to have been falsely "Hamiticized." By the time Greenberg was finished, the Hamitic language family had been pared down to a fraction of its original size.

Nevertheless, it was far from dead. A large and undeniably valid language family—which included ancient Egyptian—could still be found clustered in north and northeastern Africa. Moreover, this family showed a clear—albeit distant—relationship to the Semitic tongues. Was this the real Hamito-Semitic family—the linguistic remnant of the great white conquerors from Asia?

Greenberg had his doubts. In fact, he had good reason to suspect that this language family had not come from Asia at all. On the contrary, it appeared to be purely African. Greenberg drew this conclusion partly from the fact that there seemed to be vastly more Hamito-Semitic languages in Africa than in Asia.

Greenberg had identified five different branches of Hamito-Semitic, including Kushitic, Egyptian, Berber, Chadic, and Semitic. Of these five branches, four were found exclusively in Africa. The fifth branch—Semitic—included some languages in the Middle East but also included others in Africa, such as the Amharic, Tigre, and Tigrinya tongues spoken in Ethiopia. "If four out of five groups are entirely in Africa," Greenberg observes, "and the remaining one is partly in Africa, the implication is that they probably began in Africa."[4]

Because the Semitic branch was only one of five—and not even the largest one, by a long shot—Greenberg questioned whether it even made sense to call the whole language family Hamito-Semitic. Why not call it Hamito-Cushitic, Hamito-Berber, Hamito-Egyptian, or Hamito-Chadic? Any one of these would be equally appropriate.

But, then again, why even use the word *Hamitic* at all, Greenberg asked himself. Had any anthropologist ever formulated a satisfactory definition of what a Hamite really was? Before Greenberg's discoveries, people had assumed that the Hamites were a race of cattle-herding Caucasoid warriors who spoke Hamito-Semitic languages. Now it appeared that there was little or no correlation between any of these cultural, anatomical, and linguistic traits.

The breakdown of the Hamitic stereotype was particularly evident in the Chadic group. Through mass comparison, Greenberg had discovered that the Chadic branch contained an astounding 150 African tongues, spread over a vast area of West Africa, including Nigeria and the Cameroons. This made it, by far, the largest of all the Hamito-Semitic branches.

Yet, virtually none of these innumerable Chadic speakers fit the standard Hamitic profile. They were not warlike. They did not breed cattle. And they did not look Caucasoid. By their sheer force of numbers, the Chadic speakers statistically obliterated the formerly neat correspondence between cattle-herding Caucasoid warriors and Hamitic languages.

Was there even such a thing as a distinct Hamitic people, Greenberg wondered. Better to leave such questions to the anthropologists. For his part, Greenberg resolved to avoid confusion by giving the Hamito-Semitic language family a new name, this one devoid of any ill-founded or unproven assumptions about race or culture. The term Greenberg chose was *Afroasiatic.*

It is a testament to the weakness of the Hamitic hypothesis that so few scholars sprang to its defense in the face of Greenberg's assault. Only a few short years after Greenberg announced his results—which he did in a series of papers between 1949 and 1954—the word *Hamite* all but vanished from scholarly discourse (at least, in America). Some European linguists still speak of a Hamito-Semitic language family, but the term *Afroasiatic* has become standard in the United States and in many other countries.

Greenberg did not exactly disprove the Hamites' existence. It still seems reasonable to suppose that the "sons of Ham" mentioned in the Bible may have represented an actual people. But Greenberg's evidence made it clear that, whoever the real Hamites may have been, there was little justification for painting them as a white Master Race from Asia.

In fact, the original homeland of Afroasiatic speakers appears to have been somewhere in Ethiopia. Greenberg deduced this from the fact that the languages of the Cushitic branch, spoken mainly in Ethiopia, were far more divergent from each other than were those of any other branch. Indeed, one group in western Ethiopia—called Omotic because its speakers lived near the Omo River—was so different from the other Cushitic tongues that Greenberg suspected it might be a sixth branch of Afroasiatic.

Such sharp differences suggested that the sub-branches of Cushitic had diverged from each other at a very early date and had been evolving independently for much longer than had the branches of other Afroasiatic sub-families. This implied that the Afroasiatic language family had been evolving longer in Ethiopia than it had in other parts of Africa—strong evidence that Ethiopia was its original homeland.

What all of this meant is that, at some point—perhaps as early as 12,000 to 10,000 B.C., according to recent estimates—a people speaking a hypothetical mother tongue called Afroasiatic had probably migrated out of Ethiopia.[5] Some traveled west, giving rise to the Chadic tongues. Others fanned out across North Africa, where their language evolved into the Berber family. One adventurous group left Africa altogether and settled in the Near East, where its language slowly diverged into such well-known Semitic tongues as Hebrew, Phoenician, Arabic, and Assyrian.

And, of course, one group settled in Egypt. This is the group whose language later evolved into the tongue of the pharaohs and of the hieroglyphs. Could it be that these Afroasiatic speakers were the "first men" of whom Diodoros wrote? Were these the legendary "Ethiopian" colonists who allegedly founded Egypt? Most experts would say no. Even if Afroasiatic colonists had settled Egypt between 12,000 and 10,000 B.C., most experts consider this migration too remote in time to have been preserved in folklore. Mastodons, woolly mammoths, and saber-toothed tigers were still roaming the earth during that period. Ice Age glaciers still covered large portions of the Northern Hemisphere. It seems hard to believe that an event of such extreme antiquity could have been remembered in Diodoros's time.

Yet, what is hard to believe is not necessarily impossible. The parallel between Greenberg's theory and Diodoros's account seems too close to be coincidental. Whether or not the story of the "first men" conveyed a literal account of an Ice-Age migration, it does seem to reflect an awareness of real ancestral relationship between Egypt and Ethiopia. In the next chapter, we will examine Egyptian culture to see just how real that legendary connection with Ethiopia may have been.

CHAPTER 67

OUT OF AFRICA

"**N**OW THE ETHIOPIANS, AS HISTORIANS RELATE, WERE THE FIRST of all men," wrote Diodoros. "They say also that the Egyptians are colonists sent out by the Ethiopians. ... And the larger part of the customs of the Egyptians are, they hold, Ethiopian, the colonists still preserving their ancient manners."[1]

Where did Diodoros come up with such a story? By his own account, he drew most of it from the books of Agatharchides of Cnidus and the geographer Artemidoros of Ephesos, as well as from certain other historians "whose homes were in Egypt." Diodoros corroborated these written accounts, he says, by conversing with Egyptian priests during his stay in Egypt and by consulting "with not a few ambassadors from Ethiopia ... who were then in Egypt." On the strength of these inquiries, Diodoros confidently concluded that Agatharchides, Artemidoros, and the rest had been "accurate in all they have written."[2]

But were they? Modern scholars are not so sure. Many regard Diodoros's story as a fairy tale. Despite their skepticism, however, a surprising amount of evidence has emerged independently from archaeology, anthropology, and linguistics to suggest that key aspects of Egyptian culture were indeed brought up from the south by migrating African colonists.

As discussed in the previous chapter, the mother tongue from which the Egyptian language descended almost certainly came from the south. Joseph Greenberg pointed to Ethiopia as the homeland of this ancestral language. Another linguist, Christopher Ehret of the University of California at Los Angeles, is even more specific. He believes that the earliest Afroasiatic speakers lived on a strip of land stretching along the Red Sea coast all the way from Nubia to northern Somalia (see Figure 11).[3] This territory happens to encompass the fabled Land of Punt, lending support to the theory that Punt was the ancestral homeland of some of the Egyptians' earliest ancestors.

Ehret believes that a group of Afroasiatic speakers left their homeland between 12,000 and 10,000 B.C. and migrated north into Egypt. Archaeologists have confirmed that early settlers from this region brought many of the skills, customs, and beliefs from which Egyptian civilization was built. Foremost among these was cattle herding.

The Egyptians had a love for cattle that bordered on the fanatical. Their favorite goddesses, Isis and Hathor, were portrayed as cows. Their pharaoh was called a "strong bull" and his mother "the cow that hath borne a bull."[4] Pharaohs and wealthy noblemen boasted of the size of their cattle herds. While Jews and Christians liken their God to a shepherd, the Egyptians imagined theirs as a divine cowpoke. "Well tended are men, the cattle of God," wrote one Egyptian scribe.[5]

Whence came this bovine obsession? Earlier generations of anthropologists have noted that many African tribes shared a similar passion for cattle. Among the Ugandans, anthropologist J. Roscoe noted, "Men become warmly attached to their cows; some of them they love like children, pet and talk to them, and weep over their ailments. Should a favorite cow die, their grief is extreme and cases are not wanting in which men have committed suicide through excessive grief at the loss of an animal."[6]

A Ugandan chief would "frequently bemoan the loss of one of his cows with more genuine and heartfelt grief than he would display if he lost a wife or a child," observed Sir Harry Johnston in 1902.[7] Like the pharaohs of Egypt, the king, or *mugabe*, of Ankole was called the "leading bull of the herd."[8] The Dinka and Nuer peoples of the Sudan deformed their cattle's horns for ritual purposes in exactly the same way that the Egyptians deformed theirs, as revealed in Old Kingdom tomb paintings.[9]

Because so many of Africa's great cattle-herding cultures appeared in the Sahara and East Africa, among peoples with allegedly "Hamitic" or "half-Hamitic" looks, earlier anthropologists concluded that cattle herding must have been a Hamitic trait. They proposed, in fact, that domestic cattle had been introduced to Africa in prehistoric times by hordes of Hamitic white conquerors from the Middle East.

But, in fact, just the opposite seems to have occurred. Archaeologists now know that tribes of Afroasiatic and Nilo-Saharan-speaking peoples were herding cattle in the grasslands south of Egypt as far back as 9000 to 8000 B.C. It is they—not white people from Asia—who appear to have brought domestic cattle to Egypt, as early as 6000 B.C. or before.[10] Other cattle-herding peoples seem to have migrated into Egypt from the Sahara, as the great North African grasslands dried up and became desert, between 4000 and 2000 B.C.[11]

Pottery making also appears to have entered Egypt from the south. Some of the oldest pottery in the world was made by the Afroasiatic and Nilo-Saharan-speaking peoples who lived south of Egypt. Pots have been found in that region dating from as far back as 9000 B.C. "Soon thereafter, pots spread to Egyptian sites," notes Ehret.[12]

No institution of ancient Egypt displays more profoundly African roots than its monarchy. Diodoros noted this fact when he wrote: "And the larger part of the customs of the Egyptians are, they hold, Ethiopian. . . . For instance, the belief that their kings are gods, the very special attention which they pay to their burials, and many other matters of a similar nature are Ethiopian practices."[13]

The Egyptians did indeed regard their king as a god. In fact, the pharaoh appears to have filled the role of what anthropologists call a "divine king." In his 1890 classic, The Golden Bough, anthropologist Sir James Frazer put forth the theory that in primitive societies kings were regarded as gods or demigods, with direct power over the forces of nature. If the king was strong and virile, then the land would be fertile and the kingdom prosperous. But if the king grew sick or feeble, likewise the kingdom would suffer. "There is only one way of averting these dangers," wrote Frazer. "The man-god must be killed as soon as he shows symptoms that his powers are beginning to fail."[14]

Anthropologists have found copious evidence that the Egyptian pharaoh was regarded as just such a divine king as Frazer had

410 T H E F I R S T M E N

described. The Roman writer Ammianus Marcellus noted that the Egyptians blamed their king whenever the crops failed.[15] In an instruction to his son, King Amenemhet I took personal credit for the fertility of the fields and the abundant waters of the Nile. He wrote: "I was one who produced barley and loved the corn-god. The Nile respected me . . . None hungered in my years, nor thirsted in them. Men dwelt (in peace) through that which I wrought. . . . All that I commanded was as it should be."[16]

In this respect, the Egyptian pharaohs resembled other African monarchs who were also believed to control the forces of nature. Many African societies would put their kings to death when they showed signs of weakness or old age, since it was believed that the king's infirmity could work its way through the whole community and the natural world.

The king of the Varozwe, for example—a Shona people of Zimbabwe—was strangled to death as soon as his hair began to gray, his teeth to fall out, his sight to fail, or his sexual potency to diminish.[17] A sixteenth-century Portuguese traveler named J. Dos Santos recorded a similar custom among the kings of Sofala. He wrote: "It was formerly the custom of the kings of this land to commit suicide by taking poison when any disaster or natural physical defect fell upon them, such as impotence, infectious disease, the loss of their front teeth, by which they were disfigured, or any other deformity or affliction."[18]

Many experts believe that the pharaohs of prehistoric Egypt were also put to death when they became sick or weak. Although this practice disappeared at the dawn of history, certain Egyptian ceremonies seem to preserve hints of it. On the thirtieth year of their reigns, for example, pharaohs would traditionally hold a *Heb-Sed* or "Sed festival," to reconfirm their claim to the throne. Some experts believe that the *Heb-Sed* was originally a kind of trial or ordeal by which an aging pharaoh proved to the people that he was still vigorous, strong, and sexually potent.

In prehistoric times, a pharaoh who failed the test might have been put to death. Even in later days, aging pharaohs seem to have used the *Heb-Sed* as a means of proving to a doubting populace that they were still qualified to rule. Thus, Ramesses II held twelve different *Sed* festivals in his long reign, staging them ever more frequently as he grew older.[19]

At the high point of the ceremony, the pharaoh would assert his power over the world by shooting an arrow to each of the four directions of the compass.[20] The Kitara people of East Africa have traditionally practiced a similar ritual, which they call "shooting the nations." At his coronation and in each year of his reign, the Kitara king reaffirms his power by firing an arrow to the four cardinal points and declaring, with each arrow he unleashes, "I shoot the nations to overcome them."[21]

Few aspects of Egypt's culture seem more quintessentially "Egyptian" than its cult of the dead. We remember the Egyptians best for their mummies, tombs, and funerary spells, their awesome pyramids and mortuary temples. Yet, Diodoros said that "the very special attention" that the Egyptians paid to their burials was an "Ethiopian" custom.

In fact, many African peoples did mummify their dead, much like the Egyptians. Some would smoke-dry their deceased kings, wrap their bodies in cloth, and keep them at hand, unburied, for years at a time.[22] Often, the internal organs would be removed, as in Egyptian mummies. When Sonni Ali, the emperor of Songhay, died in 1492, for example, his sons gutted his body and filled it with honey.[23]

Ancestor worship provides another cultural link between Egypt and the rest of Africa. Most African peoples impute to the souls of dead ancestors a godlike ability to bring good or bad fortune to the living. Ancestral spirits, for that reason, are placated with rich offerings and elaborate rituals to win their favor. The souls of dead kings, in particular, are revered for their power and wisdom. In Uganda, kings are believed to continue watching over their people long after death. Special temples are built through which their spirits can be consulted for advice.[24]

It is in their peculiar reverence for their ancestors that the Egyptians were at their most African. Every pharaoh became a god upon his death, his cult maintained through his personal mortuary temple. Many of the greatest Egyptian gods, in fact—such as Osiris and Isis—were considered to be the ancestral spirits of real kings and queens who had died and achieved immortality long ago.[25] In the Harvest Festival of Min, portrayed on reliefs of Ramesses II and Ramesses III, statues of the royal ancestors going back to King Menes, the founder of Egypt, were brought before the king in order to "give life" to him.[26]

Humbler Egyptians also became ancestral spirits after death, able to help or harm their descendants as they chose. Archaeologists have found innumerable letters in Egypt written to the ghosts of deceased relatives, imploring their assistance or begging them to cease their attacks.[27] "What harm did I ever do to thee that . . . thou shouldst lay thine hand upon me?" wrote one Egyptian man to his dead wife.[28] The Egyptians also commemorated their departed relatives with small "ancestral busts" that were kept in the home. Many of these busts have been found carved with detailed accounts of the owner's family tree.[29]

Egyptian religion reveals its African roots in many other respects as well. Greek and Roman writers expressed shock at the menagerie of cats, snakes, donkeys, birds, crocodiles, beetles, hippopotami, cattle, and baboons that populated the Egyptian pantheon. Yet, animal gods remain, to this day, a characteristic feature of many African cults.[30] Like so many other Africans, the Egyptians wore masks and animals' tails during religious rites and used hand clapping in their festivals.[31] Egyptian boys and girls were subjected to circumcision, possibly as a rite of passage to adulthood. Male and female circumcision remains, to this day, a widespread practice throughout Africa.[32]

Some art historians have seen, in the rigid poses of Egyptian sculpture, the same sort of conventional postures familiar from the artwork of other African peoples, such as the Yoruba and Edo.[33] This observation reminds us of Diodoros's claim that the Egyptians derived "the shapes of their statues" from the Ethiopians.[34]

We could go on listing cultural parallels between Egypt and the rest of Africa *ad infinitum*. Indeed, were we to catalogue them exhaustively, they would no doubt fill an entire book. With their usual disdain for ancient legends, scholars today continue to disparage Diodoros's account. Yet, the evidence is strong—and growing stronger all the time—that large portions of Egyptian culture can indeed be traced to the heart of Africa, just as Diodoros maintained.

CHAPTER 68

WRETCHED KUSH

IN THE EXTREME SOUTH OF EGYPT, AN IMMENSE GRAY BULGE OF granite surges out from the midst of the river right in the center of downtown Aswan. Because of its elephant-like appearance, the Egyptians named this island Abu—"the Elephant." The Greeks called it Elephantine, and it is by that name that we know it today.

Elephantine is one of the most important landmarks of the ancient world. Since time immemorial, it has marked the southern boundary separating Egypt from Nubia. It also marks the end of smooth sailing on the Nile. Just south of Elephantine, a fearful torrent of rapids—known as the First Cataract—foams and thunders through treacherous granite outcroppings. "It is impossible to proceed further in a boat," writes Herodotos, "on account of the sharp peaks which jut out from the water, and the sunken rocks which abound in that part of the stream."[1]

Here the southbound traveler must disembark, proceeding on foot through a strange and inhospitable land. In these southern climes, the sun burns without mercy. Unlike Egypt, whose shores are lush with black, fertile soil and forested with palm and acacia trees, this country is a barren rock. Heat shimmers upward in waves from its tawny plains. Drought parches the earth. This is Nubia, the land of the "burnt faces," or Aithiopes. Herodotos writes, "South of

Elephantine the country is inhabited by Ethiopians. . . . At this point one must land and travel along the bank of the river for forty days. . . . After the forty days' journey on land one takes another boat and in twelve days reaches a big city named Meroe, said to be the capital city of the Ethiopians."[2]

In Herodotos's day, Meroe was a wonder to behold. Located deep in the heart of Nubia, where the Blue Nile intersected the Fifth Cataract, Meroe was a royal city, built in the lavish Egyptian style. To the east rose the tombs of the Nubian kings, pyramids of brick and stone rising 50 to 100 feet above the desert. Their subterranean burial chambers lay crammed with golden treasure. Sumptuous, two-storied palaces graced the city. Grand temples, their walls adorned with Egyptian hieroglyphs, rose to the sky in honor of such Egyptian deities as Isis and Amun.

Some scholars have suggested that the overwhelming "Egyptian-ness" of Meroe's civilization convinced Diodoros that the Ethiopians must have colonized and civilized Egypt. If indeed Diodoros was moved by such reasoning, then he was mistaken. As the skeptics are quick to point out, the Nubian style, as it appeared during Diodoros's time, was copied from Egypt, rather than the other way around.

We noted, in chapter 57, that the Kushites successfully resisted all attempts by the Greeks, Romans, Persians, or Assyrians to absorb Nubia into their empires. In earlier times, however, the Kushites were more vulnerable. Centuries before the Greeks, Romans, Persians, or Assyrians even existed, one empire did manage to bring the Nubians to heel. That empire was Egypt.

From the earliest times, Nubia's chief attraction for the Egyptians seems to have been its rich gold mines. Some scholars have even suggested that the name *Nubia* derives from *nub*, the Egyptian word for gold.[3]

As early as 3125–3100 B.C., the pharaoh Aha appears to have launched a devastating series of attacks against Ta-Seti—"the Land of the Bow"—one of the ancient names for Nubia. The pharaoh Snofru invaded the country around 2600 B.C., taking 7,000 Nubian captives.

It was not until 2000 B.C., however, that the Egyptians appear to have attempted a permanent colonization of Nubia. After seizing all the Nubian lands as far south as the Second Cataract, the Egyptians erected a string of ten huge fortresses, marking the southern boundary of their new possessions.[4] About 500 years later—motivated perhaps by the discovery of gold in Upper Nubia—the pharaoh Thutmose II stormed south, extending Egypt's holdings in Nubia another 350 miles, all the way to the Fourth Cataract.[5] On his victory stela, Thutmose II boasted: "Then this army of His Majesty arrived at wretched Kush . . . This army of His Majesty overthrew those barbarians . . ."[6]

From that moment, all of Nubia became a full-fledged Egyptian colony. The Egyptians remade the country in their image. Six brand-new Egyptian towns were built, complete with houses, stores, workshops, and temples, all populated with Egyptian settlers. An Egyptian official known as the King's Son of Kush was appointed viceroy over the new province, to rule in the pharaoh's name.

For the next 300 years, a vigorous policy of "Egyptianization" was enforced. Kushite princes were educated in Egypt.[7] Temples to Egyptian gods were built all over Nubia.[8] By the time Egypt lost control of its Nubian colonies in the eleventh century B.C., the Kushite upper classes were hardly distinguishable from Egyptians. They wrote in Egyptian hieroglyphs, worshiped Egyptian gods, dressed in Egyptian clothes, and—from about 730 to 270 B.C.—buried their kings in pyramids.

Thus began Nubia's golden age. The Kushites grew so strong that they even conquered their former Egyptian masters for a brief time, establishing what became known as the Twenty-fifth, or "Nubian," Dynasty. Kushite kings ruled Egypt from about 730 to 656 B.C., until they were chased out by Assyrian invaders. Even after their expulsion, Nubian monarchs continued awarding themselves the title of pharaoh and claimed the status of Egypt's true and rightful rulers.

It was these heavily Egyptianized Nubians whom Diodoros would have encountered in his travels on the Nile. In the eyes of many experts today, the similarities Diodoros observed between Nubian and Egyptian culture were nothing more than the residue of 2,000 years of Egyptian colonialism. Rather than Nubian colonists civilizing Egypt, they say, it was Egyptian colonists who civilized Nubia.

But the story may not be so simple. To understand why, consider how easily an archaeologist of 3,000 years hence, finding Europe overrun with McDonald's restaurants, Euro-Disney theme parks, and U.S. military bases, might conclude that it was the Americans who settled Europe, rather than the other way around. He would be right to interpret these artifacts as evidence of American domination. But he might easily overlook the fact that the direction of cultural influence had dramatically shifted in the 500 years since Columbus. A similar shift might well have occurred between Egypt and Nubia in very remote times.

As we saw in the last two chapters, there is, in fact, considerable evidence to suggest that Egypt derived its civilization from the south. Unfortunately, many scholars today have not yet figured out how to accommodate this new evidence to the older, more conventional theories about Egypt's relationship to Nubia.

According to conventional thinking, Egypt and Nubia were separated by far more than just the island of Elephantine. They were separated by race. The Egyptians are seen as white, the Nubians as black. Viewed in this way, Egypt's domination of Nubia becomes a kind of full-dress rehearsal for Europe's later colonization of Africa. In fact, in an influential 1984 paper by the distinguished Nubiologist William Y. Adams, the ancient Egyptians were explicitly portrayed as a Bronze Age version of Europe's pith-helmeted nineteenth-century colonialists. Adams wrote:

> A century ago the phrases "darkest Africa" and "the dark continent" were encountered often in European and American literature.... African darkness thus contrasted with European and American enlightenment.... Four thousand years earlier, on the same continent, the equivalent of "darkest Africa" was "miserable Kush." The ancient Egyptians seldom referred to their African neighbors in any other terms. They too professed a moral superiority which incidentally provided a cover for more than two thousand years of colonial domination.[9]

Adams implies that the Egyptians who sailed past the island of Elephantine imagined themselves to be descending, like Joseph Conrad's hapless hero, into the "heart of darkness," a world of barbarism, superstition, and exotic savages. He even emphasizes that, like Conrad's jungle-ridden hell, Nubia was populated by *blacks*—a people "racially distinct" from the Egyptians. Adams writes, "They [the Nubians] remain also racially distinct from the Egyptians, exhibiting a stable blend of Caucasian and Negroid strains which apparently goes back to the beginning of history. This hybrid character results in the Nubians usually being designated as 'black' by the Egyptians and other foreign viewers."[10]

Racially black and culturally "miserable," the Nubians suffered the further indignity of being technically primitive. Adams notes that they languished in the Stone Age long after the Egyptians had forged the world's oldest and greatest civilization. He writes, "The people who lived to the south continued to pursue in most respects a Neolithic way of life even while their northern neighbors reared the towering edifice of pharaonic pomp and power. Pharaonic civilization impinged on them . . . but it was an external, alien force."[11]

While Adams goes to some lengths to emphasize what he calls the "racial" distinction between Egypt and Nubia, he never goes so far as to claim that this alleged difference actually caused the conflict between the two countries. Such an implication does appear, however, in the writings of Harvard classicist Emily Vermeule. In her oft-quoted 1992 attack on Martin Bernal's *Black Athena*, Vermeule writes:

> Bernal also believes that Egypt was essentially African, and therefore black. But he does not say what we are to make of the historical accounts of Egyptian pharaohs campaigning against black neighbors to the south, in the Land of Kush, as when Tuthmosis I of Egypt, around 1510 B.C., annihilated a black Kushite army at the Third Cataract and came home with the body of a black Kushite prince hanging upside down from the prow of his ship. Perhaps Bernal thinks of this as African tribal warfare?[12]

Bernal may or may not conceive of Egypt's conflicts with Nubia as "tribal warfare." On that, we can only guess. But Vermeule's heavy sarcasm leaves little doubt as to where she stands on the question. The very savagery of the fighting between Egyptians and Nubians, she seems to imply, proves that they were racially unrelated. Had they belonged to the same race, she implies, they would never have fought so viciously.

Most readers, I trust, are endowed with sufficient common sense to see the fallacy of this argument. We have no trouble believing that, in World War II, the Germans exterminated millions of their fellow Europeans in death camps. Why, then, should we find it hard to accept that one African people, the Egyptians, might see fit to hang the chieftains of another African people, the Nubians, upside down from the prows of its warships? The most charitable thing we can say about Vermeule's argument is that it sheds little light, one way or the other, on the relationship between Egypt and Nubia.

How, then, should we envision that relationship? If Adams and his followers are correct, the Nubians were a scruffy tribe of black primitives, forcibly civilized only through 2,000 years of Egyptian missionary work. If this is true, we would have to assume that Diodoros was mistaken. It hardly seems likely that Egypt could have learned much of any value from Stone Age tribesmen. Nor does it seem likely that the Egyptians shared any ancestral kinship with the Nubians if, indeed, they were as "racially distinct" from the Egyptians as Adams and Vermeule paint them.

Dramatic new evidence, however, has recently cast doubt on this conventional wisdom. Prehistoric Nubia can no longer be dismissed as a primitive backwater. Nor can its culture be separated from Egypt's quite so neatly as it was in the past. Indeed, as we shall see in the next chapter, archaeologists have only begun to reveal Nubia's most surprising secrets.

CHAPTER 69

THE INCENSE
BURNER

FOR HOURS, BRUCE WILLIAMS HAD BEEN STARING AT THE SMALL stone object, turning it this way and that in his hands. It was drum-shaped, with a shallow depression in the top, rather like a heavy ashtray. There was no great mystery about the object's purpose. It was clearly an incense burner. The depression at the top was meant to hold the incense. What were mysterious, however, were the inscriptions on the sides, crude figures and pictographs gouged deep into the stone.

The inscription showed three ships sailing in procession. One of the ships carried a lion—perhaps a deity. That much, at least, was clear. But the contents of the other two ships were hard to make out. Their destination, too, was puzzling. All Williams could tell was that they appeared to be sailing toward an object that looked like a set of square doorways nested one inside the other.

Had the censer come from a grave just a couple of centuries more recent, Williams would have had no hesitation at all in arriving at an interpretation. The symbol of the concentric doorways looked unmistakably like a *serekh*—a common hieroglyphic emblem used by the early Egyptians to represent the façade of the pharaoh's palace. Under ordinary circumstances, Williams would have concluded without a second thought that the three ships were sailing toward the royal palace.

But this piece had been made no later than 3300 B.C., by Williams's reckoning. At that early date, there were not supposed to have been any such things as pharaohs or pharaohs' palaces. Moreover, the piece had not even been found in Egypt. It had come from Qustul, located just north of the Sudanese border. Modern Qustul lay within the political boundaries of the Arab Republic of Egypt. But, in ancient times, the site was nearly two hundred miles deep in the heart of a country the Egyptians had called *Ta-Seti*—"Land of the Bow." The censer, in short, was Nubian.

In 3300 B.C., the experts claimed, Nubia was a barbarous realm ruled by feuding tribal clans. Its neighbor, Egypt, was not much more sophisticated. How, then, could an incense burner from that primitive era—and portraying a pharaoh's royal palace—have turned up in Nubia? As he sat in the basement of Chicago's Oriental Institute that day in 1977, Williams was completely stumped. Little did he suspect that he was on the verge of one of the most explosive discoveries in modern Egyptology.

The censer had been collecting dust in a museum display case for over a decade. It had been found by archaeologist Keith C. Seele in 1964. Seele had gone to Nubia in 1962 to lead an emergency team charged with rescuing as many artifacts as possible from Lake Nasser—a man-made body of water created by the new Aswan High Dam that was scheduled to flood the entire region. It was a tremendous task. The trick was to work fast and to avoid wasting time on less important sites.

Originally, Qustul was judged to be one of the least promising areas. Some team members advised bypassing it altogether. And, indeed, Seele spent most of his time in Nubia excavating other areas. He had a hunch, though, that Qustul might hold a few surprises. Seele's intuition served him well. When he finally turned his attention to Qustul, in his very last digging season in Nubia, in 1964, Seele discovered a cemetery of thirty-three tombs.

Twelve of the tombs were tremendous, each one large enough to have served a predynastic Egyptian king. Grave robbers had plundered the tombs in ancient times. Yet it was clear that they had once contained lavish riches. Even now, beneath the heaps of broken pots and stoneware, Seele's diggers turned up a few items of jewelry that the tomb robbers had missed—a finely crafted bracelet of gold or electrum here, a lovely beaded necklace of carnelian, amethyst, faience, and rock crystal there.[1] It was in one of these graves—coded "L-24" by the excavators—that the mysterious incense burner came to light.

What was really surprising was the age of the tombs. The cemetery clearly dated from the time of the so-called A-Group—a prehistoric people believed to have dominated lower Nubia from about 3800 to 3100 B.C.[2] A-Group remains have long been a familiar sight to archaeologists in Nubia. But before the discovery of Cemetery L— as Seele named the site—no one had ever found remains as rich as these.

Here, in this remote corner of Africa, an elegant and cosmopolitan culture had flourished centuries before the pyramids were built. The mighty lords of the A-Group had availed themselves of trade goods from every corner of the known world. In addition to huge quantities of native pottery, the tombs were filled with bottles, flasks, bowls, and large storage jars from Egypt—many inscribed with hieroglyphs. There were also vessels from Syria-Palestine of a type that had never been found in Egypt and that may have indicated a direct trade link between Nubia and Asia.[3]

Seele speculated that the tombs might be royal, evidence of a long-lost dynasty of Nubian kings. Unfortunately, this theory flew in the face of conventional opinion. Nubia was neither wealthy enough nor sufficiently well organized during the A-Group period to support a monarchy, said the experts. Whoever lay buried in Cemetery L could not, by definition, have been Nubian royalty. And that was that.

Seele's theory was subjected to the worst fate known to academia—the silent treatment. Following his discovery, several major scholarly works were published on Nubia's A-Group culture. But none made even passing reference to the mysterious Cemetery L.[4] The grandees of Nubian studies had spoken. For more than ten years, Cemetery L was ignored as completely as if its treasures lay, still unexcavated, at the bottom of Lake Nasser. Seele died of cancer without ever seeing his theory vindicated.

Only much later, in 1976, was a young research associate named Bruce Williams assigned to catalogue the tremendous quantity of artifacts Seele had brought back from Nubia. There were literally mountains of broken potsherds, stoneware fragments, and other artifacts from more than 2,000 graves. All of these had to be sorted and analyzed, the broken pieces glued back together where possible. Sketches and diagrams had to be made and the whole project written up for publication. It was a Herculean task.

In the midst of this tedious work, Williams found himself sitting, one day in 1977, in the basement of the Oriental Institute, turning the incense burner this way and that. As he studied it, Williams could not shake the feeling that there was something *familiar* about this inscription.

An experienced museum archaeologist, Williams was thoroughly versed in the minutiae of Egyptian iconography. He knew by heart all the formulae, symbols, stock scenes, and artistic motifs likely to turn up on any Egyptian object. Years of training now tugged at Williams's memory, as he studied the censer.

Large chunks of the inscription were missing. But Williams could still make out a number of important details. He was certain that the censer portrayed a procession of three ships sailing toward a *serekh*, or royal palace. It was also plain that one of the ships held an animal, perhaps a lion. The first ship was heavily damaged, but Williams felt confident that it contained a bound prisoner, kneeling on a platform, guarded by a soldier bearing a mace. Only the lower parts of the prisoner and soldier survived, but Williams had seen enough bound and kneeling prisoners in Egyptian artwork to extrapolate the rest.

It was the middle ship that presented the real puzzle. Here, the entire hull of the ship was missing, except for the two high prows. Only the very top of the passengers still showed. Despite the damage, Williams felt certain that he had seen those shapes in the boat before.

The table on which he was working was covered with brown paper to protect the artifacts. Williams took out his pen and started sketching on the paper, letting his mind run free. The longer he sketched, the more certain Williams became that he *knew* what was in that middle boat.

That rounded, conical shape angled off to the right—was it not exactly at the right height and in the right position to be resting on the head of a king seated in the boat? Was it not shaped exactly like the White Crown of Upper Egypt? And that curved shape just to the left of the crown—did it not look exactly like the falcon symbol of the god Horus, with part of its head missing, hovering over the pharaoh? And was that not a rosette in front of the falcon, a symbol of royalty in Egypt's predynastic era?[5]

"Oh, I've got this!" Williams cried suddenly. "This is it!"

As his colleagues in the room gathered round, Williams re-sketched his restoration for them, chattering excitedly as he filled in the missing parts. Everything fit exactly into place, he showed them, just as you would expect, according to the well-known conventions of early Egyptian art. Here was the king, seated in his bark, arrayed in the full regalia of Egyptian royalty. Here was the god Horus, poised overhead, symbolizing the pharaoh's divine majesty.

But wait! This was *not* Egyptian art. This censer had been found, not in Egypt, but nearly 200 miles deep in Nubia. Moreover, for the time the censer was made, archaeologists had found no trace in Egypt of any other inscription showing such a clear use of royal emblems such as the White Crown, the Horus falcon, the *serekh*, and the rosette. If Williams's restoration was correct, this censer had been inscribed with nothing less than the earliest known portrait of a pharaoh ever discovered. Why, then, had it turned up in Nubia, rather than Egypt?

Perhaps, Williams thought, *because the pharaoh portrayed on this censer is Nubian, not Egyptian.* It was a stunning thought. Could the earliest pharaoh have actually been Nubian? Even Keith Seele would have been shocked. Seele had gone to his grave believing that Nubian kings lay buried in Cemetery L. But he had never imagined that those kings might have been pharaohs, arraying themselves in all the formal regalia of an Egyptian monarch. Nor had he imagined that such Nubian pharaohs could have predated the Egyptian ones by generations.

Until now, the pharaohs of Egypt had been the earliest kings known to have ruled anywhere in the world. If it now turned out that Nubian pharaohs had preceded them, then the very institution of Divine Kingship would have to be seen as a Nubian import, carried into Egypt from the south. Nubia, in that case—rather than Egypt—might now qualify as the birthplace of the world's first monarchy. The implications were staggering.

The little incense burner threatened not just a major revision in the history of Egypt, but also a rewriting of man's saga as a species. If Williams was correct, then historians, for the first time in 2,000 years, would be compelled to reopen the pages of Diodoros and consider, with a new humility, whether the "first men"—the founders of civilization—might have come from "Ethiopia" after all.

CHAPTER 70

THE LOST KINGS
OF TA-SETI

GYPTOLOGIST WILLIAM C. HAYES OF NEW YORK'S METROPOLITAN
Museum of Art and illustrator H. M. Herget faced a daunting
task in 1941. They had been assigned by *National
Geographic* magazine to bring ancient Egypt to life, through a
series of lavish illustrations. The plan was to show the Egyptians
living, working and playing in authentic settings, just as they had
really appeared more than 3,000 years ago. But how *did* the
ancient Egyptians look? From Volney's "Negro" Egyptians to
Samuel Morton's "Caucasians," nearly every shade of the human
spectrum had been proposed, at one time or another, for the ancient
Nile-dwellers.

Unwilling to rely on guesswork, Hayes and Herget drew on the
best, most up-to-date anthropological knowledge available. What that
meant, in practice, was that they based their artwork largely on the
Hamitic hypothesis—the prevailing orthodoxy of the day. Gorgeously
executed, the classic edition of *National Geographic*, dated July–
December 1941, stands to this day as a testament to that elusive, long-
sought scholarly dream—an ancient Egypt populated almost entirely
by white people.

Bruce Williams was only eleven years old when he stumbled on the magazine, hidden away among the back issues in his school library. The year was 1954. Already deeply fascinated by the ancient world, young Williams pored over every page, entranced by the beautifully rendered spreads. Today, Williams points to the July–December 1941 *National Geographic* as one of the key factors inspiring him to embark on an Egyptological career. It also played a considerable role in shaping Williams's early—and highly inaccurate—view of who the Egyptians were and how they looked.

In keeping with the Hamitic hypothesis, the *National Geographic*'s illustrators had portrayed the Egyptians as unambiguously Caucasian. "They made ancient Egypt look like Manhattan, circa 1940," Williams recalled in a recent interview. "The people actually look like upper-class New Yorkers in Egyptian garb, with the aristocratic noses, the pallor. They don't look African at all."[1]

The few black people who appeared in the feature were invariably portrayed as servants, slaves, or captives, and often explicitly labelled "Negro" or "Kushite," to distinguish them from Egyptians. It was a vision of ancient Egypt that had changed little since Josiah Nott had toured the antebellum South in the 1850s, amusing crowds with his "lectures on niggerology." Like Nott's colleague and partner, the proslavery pamphleteer George Gliddon, Hayes, Herget, and the editors of the *National Geographic* seemed to agree that "the Negro races had ever been servants and slaves," even as far back as ancient Egypt.[2]

By the time Williams entered graduate school, the Hamitic hypothesis had been largely debunked by Joseph Greenberg and other researchers. Nevertheless, its ghostly influence seemed to haunt every lecture hall, its key assumptions lingering like stale perfume between the pages of each textbook. Years of graduate study left Williams with a vague impression of the Egyptians as a "Mediterranean" or "Near Eastern" people. Like most Egyptologists of his generation, Williams was trained to give little thought to the fact that Egypt happened to be located in Africa.

In the late 1970s, however, Williams found himself, quite unexpectedly, face to face with Egypt's Africanness. Inhaling the dusty aroma of Nubian potsherds day after day in the basement of the Oriental Institute, Williams, for a number of years, had little opportunity to think of anything else but Africa and of its enigmatic relationship to Egypt.

Who exactly were the lost kings of Nubia? Who was buried in those splendid tombs at Qustul? The more Williams pondered these questions, the less confident he felt that conventional explanations would suffice. The easy solution, of course, would be to say that the censer was an import from Egypt. The inscription, after all, looked Egyptian and used Egyptian royal insignia. But there were two problems with this argument.

First, the censer itself, in its form and style, was of a type found only in Nubian A-Group sites. Such censers simply do not appear in Egypt.[3] Moreover, when the Qustul incense burner was subjected to geochemical analysis, it was found to be made from a distinctive mineral typically found at Nubian sites such as Aswan, Kalabsha, and Meroe.[4] Did it seem plausible that Egyptians would have quarried Nubian stone, transported it back to Egypt, carved it into a distinctly Nubian style of incense burner, then exported the censer back to Nubia? Probably not.

The other problem with the "Egyptian import" argument was that no archaeologist had found any evidence that such royal insignia as the serekh and the White Crown were being used in Egypt during this early period. Why assume that the Egyptians would have exported items that—according to the best archaeological data—the Egyptians themselves had not yet invented?

There was some evidence that the Egyptians had used falcons and rosettes to symbolize kingship as early as the Qustul period. However, these Egyptian examples tended to be isolated and ambiguous. No Egyptian inscription of this time had ever brought together so many different royal emblems in such a clear and obvious representation of pharaonic power as had been done on the Qustul censer. The sophisticated combination of symbols on the censer strongly suggested that the Nubians had been the first to develop a full-fledged monarchy, with control over a large and well-ordered territory.

But if the Nubians were organized in a kingdom as early as 3300 B.C., why had no previous evidence been found for this mysterious African state? In fact, it had. Egyptologists had simply failed to grasp the significance of this evidence.[5]

The Nubian desert, for example, abounded with rock drawings from roughly the same period as the Qustul incense burner, many showing distinctly "Egyptian" themes and symbols. Ivory seals from the A-Group period had been found featuring kingly *serekhs*. A mud seal impression found at Siali—also dating from the A-Group period—showed a man saluting a *serekh* surmounted by a falcon.

In the latter inscription, the *serekh* was actually labeled with a bow—the hieroglyphic emblem for Ta-Seti, Land of the Bow—implying that the man was paying homage to a Nubian state. One bowl from Qustul even showed vultures tearing at a fallen enemy who is labeled with the signs for Ta-Shemau—Upper Egypt—possibly indicating that the Nubians had defeated Upper Egypt in battle.[6]

Every one of these inscriptions had been found in Nubia. Yet experts had always assumed that they referred to an Egyptian monarchy, rather than a Nubian one. Williams was no longer so sure. The evidence was clear that a powerful dynasty had indeed ruled Ta-Seti in prehistoric times. A count of the royal tombs at Qustul suggested that as many as twelve generations of kings may have been buried there. Why, then, should experts assume that every recognizable symbol of royal authority found in that country would be of foreign origin?

Williams felt confident that his lost kingdom of Ta-Seti was a reality. In pushing this theory, he was fortunate to receive the wholehearted support of the Oriental Institute and the University of Chicago. Even before Williams had had a chance to publish his findings in scholarly journals, the university sent out press releases to the major media, touting Williams's discovery of what it called the "Lost Pharaohs of Nubia." Publicity reached a crescendo on March 1, 1979, when the *New York Times* ran a front-page story headlined "Ancient Nubian Artifacts Yield Evidence of Earliest Monarchy." The article declared: "Evidence of the oldest recognizable monarchy in human history, preceding the rise of the earliest Egyptian kings by several generations, has been discovered in artifacts from ancient Nubia in Africa. . . . The discovery is expected to stimulate a new appraisal of the origins of civilization in Africa."[7]

Such a blatant assault on conventional opinion could hardly go unchallenged. It came as no surprise to Williams or anyone else when the Old Guard rallied for a counterattack. What did prove surprising, however, was the feebleness of their arguments. Some critics insisted that the Qustul censer must have been an Egyptian import, despite the fact that it was a typically Nubian object made of indisputably Nubian stone. Others charged that the censer had been wrongly dated and that it came from a later period than Williams believed.

One scholar actually resorted to the desperate tactic of claiming that the Qustul censer had not really been found in Tomb L-24 at all! He claimed that the paperwork on the excavation had been sloppy, that the censer had really been found outside the grave, and that its date was therefore unknown. Fortunately, Williams had the documents on hand to prove that this accusation was false. The censer's removal from the tomb had, in fact, been duly recorded on a "grave sheet," dated February 17, 1964, and signed by archaeologist Carl DeVries.[8]

After nearly twenty years, Williams's theory remains controversial. But it also remains conspicuously alive. Some modifications have been necessary in response to new evidence. An impressive royal tomb was excavated, for example, near the Egyptian city of Abydos. The early date of this tomb—which appears to have been roughly contemporary with the Qustul incense burner—increases the probability that Egyptian and Nubian monarchies may have evolved at roughly the same time.[9] Williams has therefore toned down his earlier insistence that Nubia's monarchy came first.

Nevertheless, the Qustul incense burner has proved beyond doubt that Nubian civilization was far more advanced at a far earlier age than anyone ever suspected. It also shows that the earliest Nubians were strikingly "Egyptian" in their art and pictographs. Ta-Seti may or may not have been Egypt's parent. But the fact that both Egypt and Nubia used identical royal insignia as early as 3300 B.C. strongly suggests that the two countries were, at least, siblings.

It is unfortunate that the former kingdom of Ta-Seti now lies underwater. Future excavations will, no doubt, continue to push the date of Egypt's earliest monarchs back ever farther, while comparable excavations in much of Nubia are now impossible. Unless some future generation acquires the technology to conduct archaeological digs at the bottom of Lake Nasser, we may never know for sure whether the first pharaohs appeared in Egypt or Nubia.

Nevertheless, we can make educated guesses. It is well to keep in mind that the overall direction of cultural influence in the prehistoric Nile Valley was, for many centuries, relentlessly *northward*. The so-called Khartoum Mesolithic culture, for instance, which flourished in Nubia around 7000 B.C., is widely recognized as the oldest African civilization.

When settled communities finally started appearing in Egypt around 6000 B.C., the prehistoric Egyptians made pottery, figurines, cosmetic palettes, and other artifacts that looked strangely similar to those found at Khartoum Mesolithic sites.[10] Clearly, Egypt was copying from Nubia in 6000 B.C., not the other way around. Is it so far-fetched to imagine that Egypt might have maintained the same pattern of borrowing right up until the Qustul period?

Williams, at least, finds this proposition eminently reasonable. More than twenty years spent chasing down the "Lost Pharaohs of Nubia" have convinced Williams that the deeper one looks into Africa, the closer one draws to the wellspring of Egyptian culture. The eleven-year-old boy who, in 1954, marveled at scenes of white Egyptians in *National Geographic* has grown up to become one of the most outspoken advocates of Egypt's fundamentally African roots.

"I started out not having any ax to grind about the African connection with Egypt," Williams reflects. "But, over the years, I have gotten more and more interested in that connection, more and more convinced that Egypt's Africanness is not only important for understanding ancient Egypt, but that it may be the most important thing *to* understand. The way of looking at the world to be found in, say, the Hebrew Bible or in Babylonian literature or amongst the Greeks is very different from anything you find in Egypt. And that difference is its Africanness."

CHAPTER 71

FACES OF
THE DEAD

I N THE PRECEDING CHAPTERS, WE HAVE ESTABLISHED THAT THE EGYP-
tians spoke an African language whose origins probably lay in
Ethiopia. We have likewise ascertained that Egypt's religion,
monarchy, and burial customs bore a strange similarity to those
found in other parts of Africa. All of these factors seem to imply
that the Egyptians were an African people, rather than a race of
white "Hamites" from Asia.

But did the Egyptians *look* African? Ever since Count Constantin
de Volney made his controversial pronouncement in 1787 that the
Great Sphinx was a "Negro," scholars have been scrutinizing Egyptian artwork for any indication they could find of the Egyptians'
racial affinities. As we observed in chapter 5, researchers who embark on this course of inquiry inevitably run afoul of their own preconceptions. Those who are convinced, from the beginning, that the
Egyptians were black invariably seem to find "blackness" in every
painting and statue they examine. Those who prefer white Egyptians
show a similar propensity for seeing exactly what they wish to see.

The Egyptian artists themselves are partly to blame for this confusion. In Egyptian artwork, different portraits, even of the same

individual, can often give radically different impressions. For example, the famous bust of Queen Nefertiti found at Tell el-Amarna is often cited as evidence that the Egyptians were white, because of its light skin and Caucasoid features. Yet, many other portraits of the same queen feature the full lips and prognathous jaw of a black African (see Figure 7).

Egyptian art was often extremely stylized—at the expense of realism. This becomes particularly evident when Egyptian artists attempt to distinguish between people of different races or nationalities. Generally, when portraying racial differences, the Egyptians employed the same tactic used by modern cartoonists. They created caricatures based on an "average" type of each racial group. Because Nubians tended, on average, to be darker and more Negroid than Egyptians, they were often drawn with uniformly black skin and pronounced Negroid features. Because Egyptians, on average, tended to be lighter than Nubians, they were often drawn with uniformly brown skin.

Of course, every anthropologist knows that the real Nubians were not uniformly black, nor were the Egyptians uniformly reddish-brown. In fact, Egyptian artists often painted Nubians with skin that was chocolate brown rather than black, and with features that differed little from Egyptian features.[1] The physical distinction between the two peoples—while it certainly existed—seems to have been far more gradual and fuzzy, in real life, than it appears in the caricatures of Egyptian artists.

Fortunately, modern anthropological science has provided a method for discerning the actual appearance of the Egyptians that is more reliable than the casual eyeballing of artwork. In the last thirty years, forensic artists have perfected the technique of facial reconstruction—restoring the approximate appearance of a person's face using only the skull as a reference. This technique is so accurate that it is commonly used by homicide detectives to identify bodies that have decomposed beyond recognition. When done properly, the likeness should be sufficiently close that friends and relatives can identify the deceased from the reconstruction.

Forensic artist Richard Neave, of England's Manchester University, is one of the leaders in the field today. Some 50–60 percent of Neave's reconstructions, over the last twenty-five years, have been positively identified by living relatives. Many of Neave's most important clients, however, are not police detectives, but archaeologists, curious to put a living face on the skulls and mummies they have drawn from the earth.

In 1989, a group of British scientists under the auspices of the Manchester University Museum decided to undertake a complete pathological examination of an Egyptian mummy, using all the latest medical techniques in the fields of radiology, endoscopy, histology, dentistry, and serology. As part of the project, Neave was asked to reconstruct the mummy's face.

Little was known about this particular mummy. In 1823, an Italian antiquities dealer named Giuseppe Passalacqua found the mummy in a wooden coffin while he was digging near the causeway of the funerary temple of Queen Hatshepsut at Deir el Bahri. Inscriptions on the coffin and funeral dressings indicated that the mummy's name was Natsef-Amun and that he had been a priest in the great temple of Amun in Thebes—commonly known as the Temple of Karnak—sometime during the reign of King Ramesses XI (around 1113–1085 B.C.)[2]

The inscriptions also noted that Natsef-Amun was a *waab* priest—a so-called purified priest of secondary rank—whose official titles included Scribe of Accounts of the Cattle of the Estate of Amun; incense bearer; Scribe in the Shrine of Montu, Lord of Thebes; Scribe of the Oblations Made to All the Gods of Upper and Lower Egypt; and so on.

All of this seemed to indicate that Natsef-Amun was a kind of middle manager in the "Cult of Amun, Inc." His duties would have included attending to the daily rituals of the god Amun, writing and copying texts, doing clerical work in the Shrine of Montu, and keeping records of how much grain was offered to the sacred cattle of Amun and how much was eaten by them.

Undoubtedly, Natsef-Amun was an able scribe and accountant. He was probably also a member of a respected family. Priestly rank in Egypt was usually passed on from father to son, and it is known that Natsef-Amun was married to the daughter of a high-ranking priest.[3] Beyond that, however, there seemed nothing extraordinary about Natsef-Amun's life. He was simply an ordinary Egyptian.

In reconstructing Natsef-Amun's face, Neave employed state-of-the-art techniques. First, the mummy's head was photographed, using x-ray computer tomography, and the information stored on digital tape. From these data, scientists at the Department of Medical Physics and Bio-Engineering at University College Hospital, London, reconstructed a three-dimensional digital image of the mummy's skull. A special milling machine then used this digital image as a model to form an exact duplicate of Natsef-Amun's skull out of polystyrene.

Now the actual reconstruction could begin. Neave inserted wooden pegs into twenty-one specific points on the polystyrene skull, each peg representing the average depth of flesh to be expected at that point. Using modeling clay, Neave then began painstakingly building in the muscles of the face, over which he molded the skin, nose, eyelids, lips, ears, and other "soft," or fleshy, features. Prodded by Neave's skillful hands, the soft parts of the face took their shape naturally from the bones underneath.

It was always something of a revelation for Neave, at this point in a reconstruction, to see what sort of face issued from the clay. This particular face, however, was even more surprising than most. Neave had not proceeded very far when he realized that there was something very strange indeed about the way Natsef-Amun was shaping up.

"A face with somewhat negroid features emerged," Neave later wrote, with typically British understatement.[4] In fact, with his wide nose and generous lips, Natsef-Amun would have had little trouble blending into the crowd at 125th Street and St. Nicholas Avenue in Harlem. He was unambiguously and indisputably black. Skeptical readers may judge for themselves, in this matter, for it is Natsef-Amun's face that appears on the cover of this book.

"It was surprising to me," Neave recalled, in a recent interview. "I have to admit to not having seriously thought about the fact that Egypt is part of the continent of Africa."[5]

The Egyptologist in charge of the project, Rosalie David, was equally baffled when she first saw the face taking shape in Neave's studio. After some reflection, however, David decided that Natsef-Amun's appearance was not so hard to explain. After all, he did come from Thebes, she pointed out to Neave, and Thebes was located in southern Egypt, not far from Nubia. Perhaps Natsef-Amun was a Nubian, she suggested, rather than an Egyptian.

It was not a bad guess. In her reasoning, David was simply following a time-honored, Egyptological tradition. Generally, when

Egyptologists encounter any face that appears particularly Negroid in a painting or statue, they tend to assume that it represents a Nubian. However, this assumption is not always correct.

Natsef-Amun, for example, lived in a part of Egypt where, according to anthropologists, the population has *always* included a large number of Negroid-looking people. Even in prehistoric times, Natsef-Amun would not have been out of place in southern Egypt. Why, then, should we assume that he or his family came from Nubia?

Back in the heyday of the Hamitic hypothesis, scholars took for granted that the only "real" Egyptians were the light-skinned Caucasoid variety. But such arbitrary distinctions fail to give an accurate picture of the complex family relationships that actually prevailed in ancient Egypt.

A good example of these relationships emerged at the turn of the century when archaeologists excavated an Egyptian tomb near the town of Rifeh. The tomb contained the mummies of two brothers, Khnum-Nakht and Nekht-Ankh, who had lived during the Middle Kingdom period (2040–1674 B.C.). When the mummies were unwrapped and examined in 1908, experts were surprised by the difference in their appearance.

Dr. John Cameron, who made an anatomical study of the "Two Brothers"—as they were subsequently dubbed—remarked that there was a "remarkable racial difference in the features presented by each. These differences are so pronounced that it is almost impossible to convince oneself that they belong to the same race, far less to the same family."[6]

In short, Khnum-Nakht appeared to be "black," while Nekht-Ankh appeared to be "white"—a distinction that was dramatically confirmed in 1973, when Richard Neave reconstructed the faces of the Two Brothers at Manchester University.[7] (See Figure 2)

Over the years, Egyptologists have offered various explanations for the "racial" difference between the Two Brothers. Predictably, the "black" brother, Khnum-Nakht, was judged to be Nubian. But how did a Nubian come to be the brother of an Egyptian?

In the tomb inscriptions, both brothers were identified as the sons of a woman named Khnum-aa, who was apparently an heiress of a land-owning family. The "black" brother, Khnum-Nakht, was further identified as the son of a local mayor. However, the father of

Nekht-Ankh—the "white" brother—was not specifically mentioned. This led some Egyptologists to speculate that the two brothers might have had two different fathers, only one of whom was a Nubian. Others have suggested that the "black" brother, Khnum-Nakht, may have been adopted.

Only recently has the possibility been seriously considered that Nekht-Ankh and Khnum-Nakht may be exactly what they seem to be—full brothers, with the same mother and father. At the Manchester Museum, where the sarcophagi and reconstructed heads of the Two Brothers are now on exhibit, the display plaque reads: "However, it is accepted nowadays that a child may well inherit a marked similarity to one of his parents while having no resemblance at all to the other. This could well be the case with the two brothers."

What came as a revelation to the learned scientists and scholars who studied the Two Brothers would have been obvious, from the beginning, to any African American. In fact, it is quite common, among mixed populations, for one sibling to come out with distinctly "black" features and another with "white." Bioanthropologist Shomarka Keita suggests that these British researchers may have been hobbled in their scientific thinking by a lack of personal experience observing large and varied black populations.

Until the Two Brothers are finally subjected to the new technique of DNA "fingerprinting," we cannot know their actual relationship for sure. But whether they are foster brothers, half-brothers, or full brothers, the mere fact that they appear in the same family says a great deal about the racial composition of ancient Egypt.

Even if Khnum-Nakht was only the half-brother of Nekht-Ankh, this would still mean that his "Nubian" father would have been mayor of an Egyptian town and husband to a wealthy Egyptian heiress. The allegedly "Nubian" family of Natsef-Amun held a similarly lofty status in the priesthood of Amun. Confronted by the growing roster of distinguished "Nubians" revealed by Neave's work, we are left to wonder just how many "Nubians" managed to infiltrate Egypt's wealthy and elite classes in ancient times.

Judging from Neave's reconstructions, the number appears to have been high. Of the seven Egyptian faces Neave has reconstructed so far, two of them he characterizes as Negroid—nearly 30 percent of the total. Of course, it is risky to draw statistical conclusions from such a small sample. Yet, if the number of Negroid

Egyptians approached anything close to 30 percent, and if any significant proportion held similar status to that of Natsef-Amun and
Khnum-Nakht, then we must seriously question whether it makes
any sense to regard such a large and socially prominent segment of
Egypt's population as foreigners or outsiders.

While still in its infancy, the science of forensic reconstruction
has already raised some provocative questions about ancient Egypt.
How many families in Egypt were like the family of Khnum-Nakht?
How many Caucasoid Egyptians had brothers, sisters, mothers, and
fathers with Negroid features? And, even among the Caucasoid
Egyptians, how many were genuinely Caucasian? Neave notes that
even those Egyptians with very European-looking features may, in
many cases, have had quite dark skin.

The picture emerging from Neave's work bears little resemblance
to the traditional Egypt portrayed in the July–December 1941
National Geographic. We see little evidence that "Nubians" in
Egypt served mainly as slaves attending white masters. Khnum-
Nakht and Natsef-Amun challenge Egyptologists to rethink the old
definitions of *Nubian* and *Egyptian*. In the years ahead, experts will
have to consider whether the line between these two peoples was
ever quite as sharp as they have imagined it.

CHAPTER 72

THE ONE-DROP RULE

"I AM A NEGRO," WROTE WALTER WHITE. "MY SKIN IS WHITE, MY eyes are blue, my hair is blond. The traits of my race are nowhere visible upon me. . . . Why then do I insist that I am a Negro, when nothing compels me to do so but myself?"[1]

When White wrote these words in 1948, racial segregation was still the law in many states. Blacks were compelled to live in separate communities, worship in separate churches, go to separate schools, and marry only among themselves. A person's legal and social status hinged dramatically on the question of whether he was perceived as black or white. For that reason, people such as Walter White—who came from black families but nevertheless had enough Caucasian ancestry to pass as whites—were faced with a hard decision.

They could try to live as whites, thus enjoying a more felicitous legal and social status. But, in return, they would have to renounce family and friends. Having too many black acquaintances could be a liability for someone trying to "pass." Many made this hard choice.

"Many Negroes are judged as whites," wrote Walter White in his 1948 autobiography. "Every year approximately twelve thousand white-skinned Negroes disappear—people whose absence cannot be explained by death or emigration. Nearly every one of the fourteen million discernible Negroes in the United States knows at least one member of his race who is 'passing.' "[2]

White chose to remain "black." Indeed, he became a passionate fighter for civil rights. Time and again, White risked his life, exploiting his Caucasian appearance to infiltrate and spy upon anti-black groups such as the Ku Klux Klan. From 1931 until he died in 1955, White served as executive secretary of the National Association for the Advancement of Colored People.

Yet, despite all his contributions to the black community, White's Caucasian appearance was sometimes a barrier to full acceptance. One morning, as he stood on a Harlem subway platform, White accidentally stepped on the toe of a man behind him. White turned to apologize.

"He was a Negro," White recalls, "and his face as he stared at me was hard and full of the piled-up bitterness of a thousand lynchings and a million nights in shacks and tenements and 'nigger towns.'"

"Why don't you look where you're going?" said the man. "You white folks are always trampling on colored people."[3]

The plight of Walter White and millions like him stems from a unique American tradition known as the one-drop rule. By this principle, anyone possessing so much as one drop of black blood is to be considered fully black. In the days when blacks and whites were segregated by law, many Southern states enshrined the one-drop rule in their legal code. Other states set less rigorous definitions, allowing people to call themselves white if they could prove that their black ancestry was less than, say, one-sixteenth or one-thirty-second of the whole.[4] "African blood is pretty powerful," quipped Booker T. Washington once, to a white Southern audience. "Just one drop and you are counted on my side."[5]

Nowadays, liberal Americans like to speak of the one-drop rule as a relic of a distant and unenlightened past. But we still live today in a society where people are routinely required to identify themselves by race on official forms of all kinds, for the purposes of medical treatment, census reports, affirmative action quotas, anti-discrimination actions, and the like. As the recent controversy over golf champion Tiger Woods indicates, the criteria that we use today for deciding who belongs to which race are little changed from those that prevailed in the Old South.

Woods aroused consternation among many blacks when he told talk-show host Oprah Winfrey that he did not consider himself to be African American. Since his family tree includes Caucasians, blacks, American Indians, and Southeast Asians, Woods quipped that a more appropriate label for him would be "Cablinasian."[6]

Woods thus identified himself with the growing number of Americans of mixed ancestry who wish to call themselves "multiracial" rather than choose between black, white, and some other overly specific category. For many blacks, Woods's position seems a betrayal, a rejection of his black heritage. No matter how fractional his African ancestry, Woods is obliged, in their eyes, to identify himself as wholly African. The one-drop rule remains, for these critics, a valid gauge of who is black and who is not.

Anthropologists estimate that 75 to 90 percent of black Americans possess white ancestry to some degree.[7] Yet, faced with a college application form and asked to choose whether they will be classified "white," "black," "Hispanic," or "other," millions will choose to be black for legal and social reasons, even in cases where a preponderance of their genes come from Europe.

Outside the United States, the one-drop rule is virtually unknown. Even under the apartheid system of South Africa, people of mixed ancestry, such as Tiger Woods, were classified as "colored," rather than "black," and were even permitted to change their legal status to white if their skin was sufficiently fair and their hair straight enough to pass a pencil through.[8] Within our borders, however, the one-drop rule remains strongly in force.

Rare is the American who does not react with puzzlement, even today, when confronted with a person who chooses to call himself "multiracial" or "biracial" because he has one white parent and one black. In our minds, there is simply no such thing as a multiracial person. The one-drop rule does not allow for such a category. It demands that people of mixed background be considered black, and that is exactly how most Americans view them, to this day.

When it comes to ancient Egypt, however, things get more complicated. Many classicists, Egyptologists, and other specialists who implicitly accept the one-drop rule in ordinary life, passionately disavow it in all discussions relating to the racial identity of ancient Egyptians. They will refer automatically, let's say, to a scholarly colleague as black if that colleague happens to possess some visible trace of black ancestry. But they will vehemently deny that the

Egyptians should be called black unless it can be shown that their genes are 100 percent African, their skin very dark, their hair extremely frizzy, and their features profoundly Negroid.

It is in this dramatic divergence between ordinary definitions of black and Egyptological ones that communication between scholar and layman breaks down. It is, in fact, primarily because of this semantic quibble that the question of Egyptian blackness continues to arouse so much controversy today.

In *Black Athena*, Martin Bernal tried very hard to bridge this semantic gap by carefully qualifying his view of Egyptian race. He wrote:

> To what "race," then, did the Ancient Egyptians belong? I am very dubious of the utility of the concept "race" in general because it is impossible to achieve any anatomical precision on the subject. . . . Nevertheless I am convinced that, at least for the last 7,000 years, the population of Egypt has contained African, South-West Asian and Mediterranean types. It is also clear that the further south, or up the Nile, one goes, the blacker and more Negroid the population becomes. . . . I believe that Egyptian civilization was fundamentally African. . . . Furthermore, I am convinced that many of the most powerful Egyptian dynasties which were based in Upper Egypt—the 1st, 11th, 12th and 18th—were made up of pharaohs whom one can usefully call black.[9]

Bernal's statement was, in fact, a reasonable expression of the scholarly consensus. Yet, in the ten years since it was published, Bernal's position on Egyptian blackness has been assailed from all ends of the political and scholarly spectrum.

"We have to go beyond Bernal," declared Leonard Jeffries, in a lecture to his black studies class, filmed in the BBC documentary *Black Athena*. Like most Afrocentrists, Jeffries was delighted with Bernal's book. As he lectured, Jeffries kept a copy of *Black Athena, Volume I*, constantly at hand, patting it lightly and reverently from time to time. Yet, when it came to the critical question of defining the race of the ancient Egyptians, Jeffries clearly let it be known that Bernal had fallen short.

"We have to go beyond Bernal," Jeffries told his students. "See, whiteness *limitates* you. It limits you even when you get into something serious like this [pointing toward the book]. And let's deal with that."

Jeffries "dealt" with the question by explaining that Bernal was still regrettably under the influence of the "value system of the rightness of whiteness." As a result, said Jeffries, "he cannot make a clear statement that the Africans of the Nile were African. He's still holding onto that 'maybe they were kinda *brown* and *mixed.*'"

Bernal's whiteness, Jeffries implied, had blinded him to the obvious: that to be *mixed* with black was the same as *being* black.

"See, when you get into that 'mixture,' mixed with *what?*" Jeffries asked rhetorically, to a chorus of knowing chuckles around the room. "If you mix *anything* with African, you're in trouble. Because African genes are dominant genes. European genes are recessive genes. So any mixture is going to move toward Africa."

Though couched in the jargon of modern genetics, Jeffries's statement was, at root, an expression of the one-drop rule. For Jeffries— as for most Afrocentrists—the ancient Egyptians were black for the same reason that millions of modern Americans are black: because they possessed *some* discernible quantity of African genes.

Most of the criticism of *Black Athena* did not come from Afrocentrists such as Jeffries. It came from the other end of the spectrum, from those who objected that Bernal was *too* definite and *too* explicit in calling the Egyptians black. Caught in the crossfire between opposing viewpoints, *Black Athena* seemed to please no one. But by the very controversy it aroused, and by the sheer number of specialists whom it forced to go public with their views, *Black Athena* succeeded in evicting from the closet one of academia's most embarrassing and well-hidden skeletons.

The first rule of rational debate is to define one's terms. It can serve no purpose to argue whether the Egyptians were black or white when the antagonists in the debate have not yet even agreed on what the terms *black* and *white* really mean. Yet, from the time of Samuel Morton to the present, this is exactly what scholars have done.

Classicists, Egyptologists, and Africanists, in fact, lack the expertise to determine what it really means to be black or white. Such questions are better handled by geneticists and physical anthropologists. It is to these disciplines, then, that we turn in the next chapter. From them, we will seek an answer to the Forbidden Question—the single, most critical question in the entire Afrocentric debate, yet the very one that nobody, on either side of the fence, seems willing to ask.

CHAPTER 73

WHAT DOES
IT MEAN TO
BE "BLACK"?

MOST PEOPLE ASSUME THAT THEY KNOW WHAT A "BLACK" PERson is. Americans, for example, think that anyone with the slightest discernible trace of African ancestry should be called black. South Africans, on the other hand, have traditionally reserved the term *black* only for people of purely African descent. In many other countries, to be black means to have pitch-black skin—not brown, not tan, not yellow, but pitch-black. All of these definitions seem obvious and reasonable to the people who hold them. Yet, all cannot be right at the same time.

We can turn to science for help. But, unfortunately, many scientists seem just as confused as the laymen when it comes to race. Consider a recent paper by physical anthropologist C. Loring Brace. The paper was written in collaboration with five other colleagues, David P. Tracer, Lucia Allen Yaroch, John Robb, Kari Brandt, and A. Russell Nelson. Since Brace was the dominant author, however, we will, for convenience's sake, cite only Brace by name in the following discussion.

In this 1996 paper, Brace sought to prove, among other things, that Martin Bernal, Cheikh Anta Diop, and others were wrong to refer to the ancient Egyptians as black.[1] In Brace's view, this position was "hopelessly simplistic, misleading, and basically wrong."[2] One of the reasons it was wrong, Brace argued, was that to call the Egyptians black implied that they belonged to a black "race." As every practicing bioanthropologist knows, however, it is no longer considered proper to subdivide humanity into races.

Instead, Brace proposes grouping people into "clusters," which he defines as a group of people sharing similar physical traits. He finds eight major clusters in the world, including African, Amerind (American Indian), Asian-Mainland, Australo-Melanesian, Eskimo-Siberian, European, Jomon-Pacific, and South Asian (Indian subcontinent).[3]

Of course, the layman may have trouble discerning the difference between Brace's clusters and the conventional idea of race. A cluster of people sharing similar characteristics is, after all, what most people understand a race to be, anyway. Brace anticipates this problem and addresses it.

"These regional clusters are not simply an attempt to resuscitate the old-fashioned 'race' concept under another name," he assures readers. But why isn't it? Well, because the race concept, says Brace, assumes that each race possesses an "underlying essence," whereas clusters are not based on any such assumption.

What Brace means is that the traditional theory of race presumes that behind every race lies a "pure," or "essential," form of that race, which epitomizes not only the physical traits, thought to be typical of that race, but also certain mental and spiritual characteristics that supposedly go along with the physical ones. Thus, the pure or essential Caucasian would not only be a tall, muscular fellow with blond hair, blue eyes, fair skin, and a big brain, but also exhibit such allegedly Caucasian traits as tremendous courage, a love for freedom, ferocity in battle, high intelligence, and nobility of spirit.

But why did so few white people fit this ideal? "Racial impurity" was the usual explanation. If a white person turned out to be short, flabby, brunet, cowardly, slavish, and stupid, it was presumed that some ancestral mixture with other, less upstanding races had caused the problem.

In the past, many anthropologists believed that the world was once inhabited only by "pure races," unmixed with other races. A pure white race, for example, was thought to have existed somewhere in Scandinavia or the Caucasus, at some point. Likewise, a pure black race was also presumed to have existed, probably in West Africa. The pure black race was thought to have exhibited only the most extreme or exaggerated features of the "true Negro"—pitch-black skin, extremely frizzy hair, dramatically projecting jaw, and so on—as well as various characteristic mental and physical features, among them indolence, dullness, cowardice, servility, sensuality, and the like.

As the races began spreading out from their ancestral homelands, the theory goes, they inevitably encountered each other and inter-married, giving rise to "mixed" offspring, whose physical, mental, and spiritual features were intermediate between the pure black and the pure white ideals. This interbreeding supposedly accounts for the gradation, or *cline*, that is alleged to exist between races in places like East Africa.

But how did all of these pure races *become* pure in the first place? This question had always posed a problem for racial theorists. In the nineteenth century, it proved particularly troublesome, because most people then still assumed that human beings had descended from Adam and Eve. The biblical account seemed to contradict the pure race theory. If all people came from the same ancestors, churchgoers reasoned, then, even if they split off into different races, those races would still be related to each other and, by definition, would not be pure.

In the nineteenth century, racial theorists solved this problem by rejecting the biblical account of creation altogether and proposing the theory of polygenism, or multiple origins. This theory held that the different races came into being independently of each other in different parts of the world and that, originally, there had been no blood relationship between them at all. Some polygenists went so far as to propose that the races were different *species*, as dissimilar from each other as a coyote is from a fox.

Polygenism was fraught with problems, however. For the religious-minded, it seemed to suggest that the Bible was wrong and that God had created man not once, but many times. For advocates of the popular new theory of evolution, polygenism suggested something even more improbable. Presuming that there were three fundamental races—Caucasoid, Negroid, and Mongoloid—it meant that at least three times, in three different parts of the world, random forces of natural selection just happened to create the same species—man. The odds against such a random occurrence happening three times are, of course, astronomical.

For these and other reasons, the theory of polygenism slowly petered out. Its swan song came in 1962 in a controversial book called *The Origin of Races*. In that book, anthropologist Carleton Coon argued once more that the races had all evolved separately. But his message fell on deaf ears. Polygenism died with Coon, and the theory of race succumbed not long after. Without separate origins to explain where races came from, it had simply become too difficult for scientists to argue that there had ever been pure races in the first place.

The problem now was to explain how people around the world had come to look so different from each other. If all had descended from common ancestors, why, then, did they not all look alike?

One explanation was microevolution. The theory goes that people who stay in one place over long periods of time will tend to adapt to the local climate through a series of small physical changes. A hot, sunny climate, for example, will tend to darken the skin. A dry climate will tend to narrow and elongate the nose. And so on. The longer people stay in a certain area, the more they will tend to physically adapt themselves to the climate. Diet also contributes to microevolutionary change.

The second factor contributing to human diversity is what scientists call genetic drift. This is the tendency of human populations, over time, to "drift" in one direction or another for no special reason at all. When you have millions of people intermarrying, it is mathematically impossible for all of their children, year after year, to be born with exactly the same sets of features. Small changes occur virtually at random. As the years go by, some of those changes stick and are passed on to succeeding generations. Thus a breeding population will tend to drift slowly in a certain direction over time, pushed along in its course by nothing more than the random influence of mathematical probability.

The theory goes that, through thousands of years of genetic drift and microevolution, human populations formed into clusters, each one exhibiting different physical traits. For the most part, however, these clusters of people never lost contact with each other. One cluster faded gradually into the next cluster, through what are called *clines*—gradients of physical change. Clusters did not end in sharp borders.

Thus, the clusters never, at any time, could be said to have separated into completely "pure" races. Nor could any particular subcluster—such as the "true Negro" or the blond "Nordic"— be characterized as truer, purer, older, or more authentic than any of the other subclusters.

In practice, this meant that the "true Negro" of the Congo could no longer be considered more authentically "Negro" than, say, the Zulu, with his supposedly half-Hamitic features. Nor could the blond Norwegian be considered any longer to be more genuinely white than the brunet Italian. All the different subtypes in a cluster were now regarded as variations on the same theme, presumed to have arisen within the cluster at roughly the same time.

This is what Brace meant when he said that his clusters did not represent races in the traditional sense of the word. There was no perfect or pure European type, for example, within the European cluster. Brunets were considered just as European as blonds, dunces just as European as geniuses, and cowards just as European as war heroes. The clusters were simply groupings of people with similar physical features, created by the random forces of natural selection and genetic drift.

Because mankind was now separated into clusters rather than races, Brace implied, it no longer made sense to ask whether the ancient Egyptians belonged in the black race. The real question was whether or not they belonged in the African cluster.

In one respect, Brace's argument was out of date. Most of the anthropologists he was arguing against had been dead for anywhere from 50 to 100 years. By 1996, few educated people conceived of a race in terms any different from Brace's clusters. For most people, a race was nothing more than a group of people living in a particular region who shared certain physical traits.

Of course, some people still associated race with inherited mental traits as well—traits such as intelligence. But this idea was in no way challenged by substituting the word *cluster* for *race*. If people in one cluster could inherit darker skin than people in another cluster, why could they not also inherit greater or lesser intelligence? In renouncing the old theory of pure races, Brace had therefore renounced very little that was relevant to the question at hand.

What remained to be answered were the same two questions that had haunted Egyptology since the field began: (1) What does it mean to be black? and (2) Did the ancient Egyptians fit that definition of blackness? To his credit, Brace attempted to wrestle with both of these questions. But, as we shall see in the next chapter, they defeated him in the end. Even with all the new terminology and all the state-of-the-art methods of anatomical and computerized statistical analysis Brace employed, he found himself, ultimately, no better equipped to answer these questions than was Johann Friedrich Blumenbach, who first confronted them back in 1794.

CHAPTER 74

WHERE'S THE BEEF?

THE NOVEMBER 1995 ISSUE OF *THE BARNES REVIEW* WAS TYPICAL. One article argued that censorship in Nazi Germany had not really been so bad. An excerpt from a book by former Waffen SS general Leon Degrelle praised Hitler for restoring order in Germany. Another article quoted Irish American newspapers from the year 1940, claiming that England, not Germany, was the real enemy. And so on.

The pro-Nazi slant of *The Barnes Review* should come as no surprise. Its publisher, Willis Carto, has made something of a career of rewriting twentieth-century history along similar lines. His weekly newspaper, *The Spotlight*, has insisted for years that America fought on the wrong side in World War II, that the death toll in the Holocaust was wildly exaggerated, that Hitler had gotten a bad rap from Allied propagandists, and that Zionist interests are undermining America.

What made this particular issue of *The Barnes Review* special, however, was its cover story, headlined "Ancient Egypt: Were the Pharaohs Blond?" In the article, Phillip Bonner—described as a "multilingual author" who is "a former member of the Ohio Bar" and who "specializes in ancient history"—presented evidence that ancient Egypt had been ruled by a Nordic Master Race. Much of his argument relied on the familiar "eyeballing" method, in which one scrutinizes ancient artwork and mummies and makes subjective judgments about their "race." Bonner wrote, for example: "A book called *Chronicle of the Pharaohs* was recently published showing paintings, sculptures and mummies of 189 pharaohs and leading personalities of Ancient Egypt. Of these, 102 appear European, 13 look black and the rest are hard to classify. All nine mummies look European."[1]

Bonner also cited harder evidence, however. He quoted leading anthropologists, such as Carleton Coon, who, in 1939, opined that the daughter of the pharaoh Khufu had been "a distinct blonde."[2] He also cited Raymond A. Dart, who, in 1940, concluded, from a study of 2,861 Egyptian skulls, that 10 percent had "Nordic" characteristics and that the Nordic race constituted "the Egyptian pharaonic type."[3]

Prominent among the experts cited by Bonner were Loring Brace and his five colleagues, mentioned in the last chapter. Quoting from their article, "Clines and Clusters vs. 'Race': A Test in Ancient Egypt and the Case of a Death on the Nile," published in the 1993 *Yearbook of Physical Anthropology*—which is simply an earlier version of the 1996 article cited in the last chapter—Bonner wrote:

> Anthropological measurements of 25 different groups of skeletons from around the world, from ancient to modern times, were statistically analyzed to see which groups were most similar to ancient Egyptians. In their own words, this is what the researchers concluded: "As a whole, they show ties with the European Neolithic, North Africa, modern Europe, and, more remotely, India, but not at all with sub-Saharan Africa, eastern Asia, Oceania or the New World." The group of skeletons which most closely resembled the ancient Egyptians was that from the French Neolithic.[4]

It is easy to see why Brace's findings proved so welcome to the racial theorists at *The Barnes Review*. For most of his expert opinions, Bonner had been forced to rely on hoary old books dredged up from sixty-year-old library stacks. But Brace had provided a spanking new study, fresh from the lab and exuding state-of-the-art scientific credibility. His study had concluded, in no uncertain terms, that Egypt's closest biological "ties" were with Europe and that Egypt had no ties at all with "sub-Saharan Africa."

Brace himself would, no doubt, have been horrified to see his work used for such a purpose. In his paper, Brace repeatedly stressed his liberal motives and sympathies. He condemned Master Race theorists, past and present. He declared that racial labels "not only prevent us from dealing with human biological variation in an adequate fashion, but they also lend themselves to the perpetuation of social injustice." Brace ended his paper with a frankly political exhortation: "Because it [the race concept] has neither biological nor social justification, we should strive to see that it is eliminated from both public and private usage. Its absence will be missed by no one, and we shall all be better off without it. R.I.P."[5]

Admirable sentiments! But how, then, did the *Barnes Review* writer Phillip Bonner come to so misunderstand Brace's purpose as to cite his work in support of the Master Race theory? The answer is that Bonner was following a time-honored principle of clear thinking, probably best enunciated by steel magnate Andrew Carnegie.

"As I grow older," Carnegie once said, "I pay less attention to what men say. I just watch what they do."[6]

Like Carnegie, Bonner had ignored what Brace *said* about his egalitarian goals. Instead, he had zeroed in on what Brace was actually *doing* through his very pointed—and controversial—interpretation of the evidence. If Brace's article were a sandwich, we might liken its liberal platitudes to the bread. The data and its interpretation were the meat. In true Carnegie fashion, Bonner had simply discarded the bread and gone directly for the beef.

The core of Brace's research involved craniometric data—skull measurements—that had been subjected to computerized statistical analysis. Brace conceded that craniometry had a checkered past. He expressed scorn for racial theorists such as J. Philippe Rushton, who, in a 1989 study, had purported to measure intelligence by "the crude expedient of running a tape measure around the skull and reading off the numbers."[7]

Such abuses, however, did not imply that cranial measurements were useless. On the contrary, Brace wrote, "the increasingly powerful arsenal of methods that are at our disposal" made it possible to learn a great deal from human skulls.[8] Brace put one of these "powerful" new methods to work in his study.

The first step was to make a list of "trivial," or "non-adaptive," traits. These are traits that are believed to play no role in survival.

Dark skin, for example, would be judged "adaptive" because it helps people adapt to a tropical environment by protecting them from sunlight. It is therefore critical to survival. For that reason, two different groups of people living in the tropics might evolve dark skin, as a survival strategy, even if the peoples had no genetic relationship to each other. The fact that both peoples ended up with dark skin would therefore be irrelevant, said Brace, in trying to determine whether they were related.[9]

The trivial, or non-adaptive, traits, however—such as the relative flatness of the face—Brace believed to be a much better sign of genetic relationship. Since facial flatness served no particular survival purpose, two groups of people who turned up with similarly "flat" faces might be presumed to have inherited that flatness from common ancestors.

The odds of finding such ancestral relationships increased when you measured not one, but a whole battery of trivial or non-adaptive traits simultaneously. This is where the computers came in. In Brace's study, twenty-one measurements were taken for each skull, all of them related, in one way or another, to cranial height, nasal projection, and facial flatness. These traits were then compared to the same twenty-one traits in the skulls of other groups.[10]

This is called multivariate analysis—the simultaneous comparison of a whole slew of different variables for each object being studied. Computers enable anthropologists to compare many more variables at the same time than would have been possible in the old days. The computer searches for "clusters" of common features between different groups. The sheer number of different variables whose relationships can now be calculated increases the chances that the clusters the computer identifies may represent real ancestral relationships. At least, so goes the theory.

Brace ran his study using two groups of Egyptian skulls, one from a predynastic cemetery at Naqada and one from a Late Dynastic group in Giza. These were compared to skulls from all over the world to see with which regions they seemed to cluster most closely.

The first time Brace ran the program, it grouped the Egyptian skulls unmistakably with the European cluster. He then ran it again, this time breaking down the European cluster by geographical region and time period—creating such groups, for example, as Continental Europe, Northwest Europe, and Russia Neolithic. This time, a slightly different result was obtained. The Late Dynastic Egyptians now clustered with the French Neolithic, while the predynastic Egyptians clustered with Nubia, India, and Somalia.[11]

The change was of minor interest, though, as far as Brace was concerned. The major point was that *all* of these groups—including Egypt, Nubia, India, and Somalia—had clustered far more closely with Europe than they had with Africa. In other words, Africa appeared in one cluster, while India, Nubia, Somalia, Egypt, North Africa, and Europe all appeared in another, entirely different and unrelated, cluster.

Had Charles Seligman or Karl Meinhof been alive, they would have jumped with glee. Here, at last, was the long-sought scientific proof that the Hamitic hypothesis had been right all along! Not only did Brace's computer show a clear relationship between the traditional "Hamitic" areas of north and northeastern Africa, but it showed, just as clearly, that the people of these Hamitic regions were directly related to Europeans!

Of course, Brace himself did not evoke the long-discredited Hamitic hypothesis. But he summed up his findings in a way that Seligman, Meinhof, and their ilk would certainly have found congenial. He wrote:

> It is obvious that both the Predynastic and the Late Dynastic Egyptians are more closely related to the European cluster than they are to any of the other major regional clusters in the world. . . . Whatever else one can say about the Egyptians, it is clear that their craniofacial morphology has nothing whatsoever in common with Sub-Saharan Africans'. Our data . . . provide no support for the claim that there was a "strong negroid element" in Predynastic Egypt.[12]

The data seemed hard to dispute. These were not the vague personal impressions of Count Constantin de Volney gazing at the Sphinx. On the contrary, these were objective measurements of real skulls, crunched by cutting-edge computer programs and interpreted by, not one, but six leading anthropologists. It would seem that Afrocentrism was dead. Not only Egypt, but also Nubia, Somalia, and North Africa had all been severed decisively from the African continent.

In keeping with his stated goal of avoiding "racial" terminology, Brace refrained from trying to determine whether the Egyptians were either black or white. He suggested, in fact, that they were neither. "Attempts to force the Egyptians into either a 'black' or a 'white' category have no biological justification," he concluded.[13] But the real import of Brace's findings was lost on no one. In his paper, Brace had gone out of his way to state his opposition to Afrocentrism. He wrote, for example:

> Recently, there have been attempts to claim Egypt as a support for pride in a "black" heritage, as, for example, in the statement that "Egyptians belong among the black races" [by Cheikh Anta Diop]. . . . We would have to argue that these statements are hopelessly simplistic, misleading, and basically wrong. Even the categorical labeling of the civilization of ancient Egypt as "fundamentally African" [by Martin Bernal] is misleadingly simplistic.[14]

In Brace's view, his computer had thoroughly debunked Afrocentrism. If the Egyptians were not "negroid," if they were utterly unrelated to the "African" cluster, and if their closest relatives in the world were French, then how could it be said that black people had built the pyramids? Neither *The Barnes Review* nor anyone else who read the article could possibly have failed to grasp its implications: If Brace was correct, then none of the world's renowned civilizations—not even Nubia!—had been built by black people.

But *was* Brace correct? Not everyone was so sure.

CHAPTER 75

THE EXORCIST

SOME READERS MAY BE CONFUSED AT THIS POINT. NOT ONLY HAD Loring Brace and his colleagues grouped the Egyptians with Europeans, but they had grouped the *Nubians* with Europeans as well. Brace had clearly implied that the Nubians were unrelated to tropical Africans. Yet, most readers have already noticed by now that virtually all historians, ancient and modern, have traditionally regarded the Nubians as black.

Dr. Rosalie David provides a case in point. When she got her first glimpse of the Negroid face taking shape in the forensic reconstruction of Natsef-Amun, described in chapter 71, her first and most natural reaction was to suggest that he must have been Nubian. Like most Egyptologists, David used the term *Nubian* almost as a synonym for *black*.

Rare is the scholar who, upon setting out to disprove Afrocentric claims, will not begin his argument by contrasting the Egyptians with the Nubians. He might point out, for example, that the Greeks referred to the Nubians as Ethiopians—"burnt faces"—but did not apply this term to the Egyptians. This demonstrates, the critics claim, that the Nubians were black, but not the Egyptians. Others point to the tomb paintings of Seti I and Ramesses III, noting how the Egyptians painted themselves with reddish-brown skin, as opposed to the jet-black and very Negroid-looking Nubians.

In all such arguments, the point is the same. The Nubians are held up as "real" blacks—an absolute standard to which the poor, brown-skinned Egyptians just don't measure up. In effect, such arguments imply their own definition of "blackness"—that *a black, by definition, is a person who looks like an ancient Nubian or Ethiopian.*

Yet now it appeared that Loring Brace and his colleagues were turning this ancient assumption on its ear. According to Brace's state-of-the-art computer program, the Nubians physically resembled Europeans, but bore *little or no resemblance* to tropical Africans. When Brace's Nubian sample was subjected to a discriminant analysis—a statistical technique that can supposedly tell from which groups a particular sample should be *excluded*—Brace found that "Nubians cannot be excluded from modern Europeans . . ." but that "Nubia . . . comes only a few percentage points from being excluded from Sub-Saharan Africa."[1]

The chameleon-like facility with which the Nubians seem to switch from one race to another, according to scholarly whim, did not begin with Loring Brace. Anthropologist Bruce Trigger notes a long tradition of similar metamorphoses in scholarly portrayals of the ancient Nubians. In one 1978 paper, Trigger wrote:

> These interpretations of Nubian history had the fluidity characteristic of most racist thinking. The rulers of Kush generally were portrayed as "Caucasoid" ("Hamitic") when Kush was being described as a source of civilizing influences for the rest of sub-Saharan Africa, but these same rulers were characterized as Blacks when the region's achievements were considered in relation to those of ancient Egypt.[2]

In other words, the Kushites became white when their achievements were being compared *favorably* to those of the rest of Africa. But when their accomplishments were being compared *unfavorably* to the achievements of ancient Egypt, the Kushites were demoted to the status of blacks.

In his paper, Trigger was writing about racial theorists of the past, such as Elliot Smith. But many contemporary scholars evince an ambiguity toward Nubian "blackness" that would hardly have been out of place in Smith's day. Nubiologist William Y. Adams, for example, offered these curious observations, in his 1977 book, *Nubia: Corridor to Africa:*

I have seldom referred to the Nubians as "black," not out of any racial sensitivity, but because they have only intermittently been "black." By that I do not mean that their skin color and facial features have changed significantly in the historic period; I believe in fact that they have remained pretty much the same since the earliest times. But race is largely in the eye of the beholder. . . . To be technically accurate the Nubians are mostly of a chocolate-brown color; one could and can see them either as "black" or as "white" according to the prejudices of one's time and temperament.[3]

Adams then offered examples of particular periods of Nubian history during which he thought the Nubians might appropriately be called either black or white. During those times when the Nubians "were subject to prejudice and oppression as a result of their skin color," Adams wrote, it would be "sociologically meaningful in today's terms" to call them "black." At other times, however, it was the Nubians who attacked and exploited the "much darker peoples of inner Africa." In referring to these periods, Adams opined, "it would be more sociologically meaningful to call them [the Nubians] 'white.' "[4]

In effect, Adams had defined "black" as "victim" and "white" as "conqueror." As the Nubians flip from one role to the other, through their history, Adams seems to imply that scholars are perfectly justified in changing their racial identity accordingly.

There is no reason to assume that Brace or his colleagues share Adams's peculiar ideas about race. Brace himself is, no doubt, perfectly sincere in his stated opposition to racial thinking. Yet sincerity is no guarantee against error. The Nubians' racial identity remains as "fluid" in Brace's hands as it ever was in the heyday of Elliot Smith. Brace's sentiments may be sterling, but his methods clearly bear further scrutiny. It is impossible not to suspect something very odd about an experiment that finds the Nubians—a people regarded by every ancient writer as "Ethiopian" and portrayed in Egyptian art as pitch-black and Negroid—to be more related to Europeans than to other Africans.

Where does the truth lie in all this? If Brace's methods are flawed, then surely other methods must exist through which we can obtain more accurate results. But what are those methods? It is to this question that Dr. Shomarka O. Y. Keita has devoted a considerable amount of research.

Keita, as readers will recall from chapter 65, was the physical anthropologist who crossed swords with Arthur M. Schlesinger, Jr., over the question of Egypt's kinship with the rest of Africa. He adheres to what anthropologists call the "no-race" theory. Keita believes that it is erroneous to classify people into races. Indeed, it is racial thinking, he charges, that has led scientists repeatedly to false conclusions, especially in their studies of ancient Egypt, and of Africa, in general.

The problem, Keita says, is that many scientists today do not even realize that they are thinking in racial terms. So ingrained and automatic have these assumptions become that many scientists—such as Loring Brace and his colleagues—will pride themselves openly on their allegiance to the no-race school, while, at the same time, conducting research that is heavily compromised by racial concepts. Keita has dedicated himself, in recent years, to identifying and exorcising these lingering ghosts of racial thinking wherever he finds them.

"The concept of race, racial thinking, and approaches using received racial schema are a part of a theoretical world view deemed by most anthropologists to be incorrect and passé," wrote Keita in a lead article for the September 1997 *American Anthropologist*, co-written with Rick A. Kittles. "But . . . racial thinking and the use of racial terms or categories still exist and are seen in the sampling strategies used in studies addressing the origin of modern humans."[5]

What drives Keita, in his mission, is a relentless concern for *method*. Racial thinking fails, in his view, not because it is immoral or mean-spirited, but because it is bad science, leading researchers to set up their inquiries around false assumptions. A doctor, for example, who assumes that sickle-cell anemia is a disease specific to the "black race" will fail to consider sickle-cell as a possibility when examining people from Greece or Italy—even though small numbers of people in these areas have been known to get the disease.

"For people who work in any branch of science," Keita commented, in a recent interview, "the validity of the method is more important than the result. Sometimes you get the same result using methods that are invalid. But one must always use the valid technique."[6]

Keita's love for sound method was with him even in high school. His senior year fell in 1971–1972 shortly after Frank Snowden's

Blacks in Antiquity was released (in 1970). Like so many African Americans at the time, Keita was intrigued by the book. But he was even more captivated by the footnotes that formed nearly a third of the text. Such copious documentation spoke of a thoroughness and attention to detail that Keita resolved to emulate someday in his own work.

Years later, as a fourth-year medical student, Keita learned skeletal anatomy at the Smithsonian Institution from one of the most exacting taskmasters in the field. He still recalls how Larry Angel would force him to measure the same skull over and over until his readings matched Angel's. "You had to practice and practice," says Keita. "It was like learning how to do a surgical operation."

Angel impressed upon Keita the importance of methodological rigor. He taught him to weigh many different explanations for the same phenomenon, rather than just accept the easy or obvious solution. One of the ways Angel demonstrated this principle was by exploring a wide range of unusual explanations for the combination of physical features found among Mediterranean peoples.

Even as late as 1979, when Keita was studying with Angel, the Hamitic hypothesis remained quietly influential among anthropologists, despite the fact that it had been officially debunked. Most tended to view the Mediterranean world, from southern Europe to North Africa, as populated entirely by white people, who were assumed to have colonized the area in prehistoric times.

Angel wondered, however, whether it might not have been the other way around. Perhaps it was the Africans who had done the colonizing. Linguist Joseph Greenberg had already established that the Afroasiatic language family had probably begun in Ethiopia and that the Semitic branch of that family had spread into the Near East from Africa. If the Semitic languages really came from Africa, Angel reasoned, they obviously could not have floated into Asia of their own accord. They had to be carried by large groups of people.

Assuming that the first speakers of proto-Semitic did indeed come from Africa, they would likely have dispersed over wide areas of the Near East. Later they would have blended into the local population, after passing on their language to the natives. But evidence of their presence might still be visible. Angel examined many skulls from the prehistoric Near East and found some that did seem to exhibit African traits. Could these be the remains of the first proto-Semitic colonists?

If they were, then how far had the colonization spread before it petered out? Angel thought that it might have reached as far as Europe. Back in the 1940s, Angel had conducted an investigation of prehistoric Greek skeletons. Skeptical of Nazi claims that the ancient Greeks had been ruled by a blond Master Race, Angel had been trying to see if he could find any trace of Nordic-looking "Dorian" invaders. Not surprisingly, Angel found little evidence to support the Nazi vision of a Greece dominated by Nordics. On the contrary, Angel's research seemed to indicate an unexpectedly wide range of diversity among the ancient Greeks. Some Mycenaean skulls that Angel examined looked as if they had come straight from Egypt.[7] Could these too be the vestiges of an African colonization?

Keita would often look back, in later years, with a kind of quiet astonishment, to his days with Larry Angel. A respected, white scientist, Angel was, in Keita's words, "a classic nineteenth-century-style liberal gentleman scholar." Yet, the theories he espoused often seemed as outrageously Afrocentric as anything Keita had read in the pages of Cheikh Anta Diop.

As he became increasingly familiar with Afrocentric writings, Keita's growing sense of scientific propriety was often offended by the crass chauvinism and looseness with facts that seemed endemic to the genre. Yet, the more Keita learned about Afrocentric claims, the more persistently he was reminded of Angel's work.

All of this seemed to suggest that scientific truth, if pursued with sound methods and an open mind, could lead into stranger—and infinitely more rewarding—realms than the wildest of chauvinist fictions. It was a lesson that Keita would carry with him in future years as he embarked upon his own explorations of the physical anthropology of ancient Egypt.

CHAPTER 76

RETURN OF THE "TRUE NEGRO"

"ATTEMPTS TO FORCE THE ANCIENT EGYPTIANS INTO EITHER A 'black' or a 'white' category have no biological justification," wrote Loring Brace. "[A]ny rational denial that an Egyptian is one thing must also be accompanied by a denial that an Egyptian is the other."[1]

When Keita first encountered these words in Brace's paper, he could find little fault with them. A "no-race" man himself, Keita agreed that it would be wrong to shoehorn the Egyptians into a strict "black" or "white" category. Yet, as he read carefully through the paper, it seemed to Keita that Brace did not always practice what he preached.

Brace's criticism of Martin Bernal, for example, made little sense unless viewed through a racial lens. In his paper, Brace stated that he agreed with Bernal about many things. He conceded, for example, that, out of racial prejudice, past scholars may have downplayed Egypt's contribution to Western civilization. "With this we are in complete sympathy," Brace wrote.[2]

But Brace's sympathy ran out when it came to the word *black*. He did not feel that that word should be applied to the Egyptians. Particularly objectionable was the title of Bernal's book, *Black Athena*.

It gave people the impression, Brace complained, that the Egyptians were part of "Black Africa."[3] But why was that bad?

In Brace's view, it was bad not only because the Egyptians were unrelated to Black Africa, but also because they were arguably not even African at all. "Even [Bernal's] categorical labeling of the civilization of ancient Egypt as 'fundamentally African,' " Brace wrote, "is misleadingly simplistic."[4]

What could Brace have meant by all of this? He had already argued that there was no such thing as race—only clines and clusters. If there were no such thing as a black race, then how could Brace turn around and talk about a "Black Africa"? In addition, Egypt was indisputably located on the African continent. What, then, could Brace mean by implying that Egypt was not "African"?

Fortunately, for confused readers such as Keita, Brace went on to explain exactly what he meant. After noting with approval that Bernal had been "cautiously noncommittal about the 'racial' nature of the ancient Egyptians," Brace complained that, unfortunately, many of Bernal's readers had not followed his example. Brace wrote:

> Others . . . have taken the symbolic import of the words "Black Athena" and the designation of Egyptian civilization as "African" to mean that the ancient Egyptians must have looked like West Africans and their modern "black" descendants in America. . . . Our data and treatment obviously have a bearing on these matters, and we use them here to take issue with the provocative implications in Bernal's title.[5]

Here, then, was the rub. To call the Egyptians either black or African, in Brace's opinion, was to imply that they looked like *West Africans*. It implied, in other words, that they had the extreme characteristics of "true Negroes." Because the Egyptians did not, in fact, look like "true Negroes," Brace implied, it was wrong to describe them as either black or African.

But who ever said that the words *black* and *African* meant "true Negro"? This was certainly not the standard Afrocentric position. As discussed in chapter 72, even the most radical Afrocentrists, such as Leonard Jeffries, tend to define both "blackness" and "Africanness" in terms of the one-drop rule. They regard any mix of African blood, however slight, as making a person both black and African.

Most Afrocentrists freely acknowledge the mixed character of Egypt's ancient population. Ivan Van Sertima, for example, in a discussion of Egypt's relationship with "Black Africa," readily cited figures from a 1905 survey of Egyptian skeletal material which found that, from the predynastic period through the Fifth Dynasty, only "24 percent of the males and 19.5 percent of the females were pure Negro." From the Sixth to the Eighteenth Dynasty, wrote Van Sertima, the number of "pure Negroes" shrank to only 20 percent of the males and 15 percent of the females.

Undaunted by these relatively low figures, Van Sertima wrote, "But the density of the Negro-African racial presence in predynastic and dynastic Egypt is an empty statistic in itself. What should concern us is the contribution of black Africans to the birth of Egyptian civilization, their participation in the growth and development of that civilization."[6]

What this meant was that Van Sertima was perfectly willing to regard as "African" a country in which only 20 percent of the population could be defined as "pure Negroes." Clearly, it was not the Afrocentrists who insisted on making a rigid equation between the terms *black, African,* and *true Negro.*

Loring Brace, on the other hand, evidently did insist on such an equation. He proved this by the peculiar manner in which he labeled his clusters. When Brace ran the program, the African peoples analyzed by his computer split off into two clusters. The first, as previously noted, contained Egyptians, Nubians, Somalis, and North Africans. The second encompassed people from Tanzania, Gabon, and Benin—all areas in which people tend to resemble the stereotypical "true Negro."[7]

This clustering actually proved little, beyond the obvious fact that some Africans look more like "true Negroes" than others. But Brace imbued the finding with artificial significance by labeling the true Negro cluster "African." He thus created the impression that the "true Negro" was more genuinely and authentically African than those who clustered with the other group.

Having implicitly defined Africanness in terms of resemblance to the "true Negro," Brace and his computer had little trouble de-Africanizing the Egyptians. The farther the Egyptians diverged from the "true Negro," in average appearance, the less African Brace considered them to be. Since the Egyptians, on the average, tend to look different from people in Gabon, Benin, and Tanzania, Brace's study naturally concluded that they were unrelated to the African cluster.

Had Brace followed the same logic in analyzing his European samples, he might have concluded that only the "Northwest Europe" cluster (England, Faeroe Island, Norway) was authentically European. Other clusters would then be regarded as more or less "European," to the extent that they resembled that Northwestern group. But Brace did not choose to analyze Europe in this manner. He deemed every sample from Europe to be just as "European" as every other sample.[8]

It would have made sense for Brace to apply the same standard to Africa that he did to Europe. There is, in fact, nothing obvious or natural about his assumption that "true Negroes" are the "real" Africans. One could just as easily designate the Caucasoid-looking African of the northeast as the more authentic variety. In fact, James Cowles Prichard—widely hailed as the father of British anthropology—offered precisely this opinion, in 1843, when he suggested that the Egyptian was the defining African type, while the "true Negro" was simply an "exaggerated and extreme representation" thereof.[9]

Prichard's opinion was, of course, every bit as arbitrary as Brace's. Neither of these men had any special authority or qualification to determine who is African and who is not. But it is revealing to note how differently they interpreted the same body of evidence.

The effects of Brace's highly selective labeling showed themselves with particular intensity in his analysis of the Egyptians of predynastic Naqada. Brace's computer showed, not surprisingly, that the Naqadans bore little resemblance to the "true Negroes" of Tanzania, Gabon, and Benin. "Our data, then, provide no support for the claim that there was a 'strong negroid element' in Predynastic Egypt," Brace concluded.[10]

But had Brace interpreted the evidence correctly? Previous studies on skulls from the very same predynastic cemetery at Naqada had drawn very different conclusions. In 1966, for example, a brilliant young pre-med student named Michael Crichton—the same Michael Crichton, by the way, who later wrote *Jurassic Park*—had studied the Naqada skulls for his senior thesis at Harvard University. Using a computerized, multivariate analysis similar to that employed by Brace, Crichton had found that the Naqada skulls exhibited a distinctly Negroid character.

The difference lay in the sample Crichton had chosen to represent the "Negro." He had used skulls from the Teita tribe of

Kenya—a people who, in certain respects, resemble the Egyptians far more closely than do the "true Negroes" of Tanzania, Gabon, and Benin.[11] Even so, Crichton still worried that the "Negroes" he had chosen for comparison might not have been close *enough* to the Egyptians to accurately reflect the diversity of Negroid types in Africa.

"A study which used other Negro groups, specifically Nubians," Crichton wrote, "might better indicate how the Egyptians stand in relation to the whole range of variation among Negroes."[12]

What Crichton meant was that there were many kinds of "Negroes" in Africa, whose degree of resemblance to the Egyptians varied greatly. Since the Nubians were "Negroes" too, they ought, in theory, to be just as legitimate a standard of "Negro-ness" as the Kenyans. Crichton did not say so explicitly, but using Nubians as a standard of comparison would obviously increase the degree of resemblance between Egyptian and "Negro," as measured by the computer. In the process, Crichton implied, it might yield a more accurate picture of the closeness of Egypt's kinship with the rest of Africa.

Crichton was putting into practice, in his thinking, what Brace only talked about. Brace had claimed that there was no such thing as a "pure" or "true" Negro, but only different types of Africans, none more pure or authentic than any other. Had he really believed this, Brace would never have singled out the "true Negro" cluster as the only one to be labeled African. By doing so, Brace had pointedly excluded from Africa many peoples—such as the Somalis and Nubians—who are regarded as black by most people.

As we have seen, the Nubians and Somalis ended up clustering with the predynastic Egyptians in Brace's study. But since Brace had not labeled these groups "African," the fact that the Egyptians resembled them was not taken as evidence of Egyptian blackness or Africanness. Like the Hamitic theorists of old, Brace was able to sever the Egyptians from Africa only by amputating the whole of northeastern Africa with them!

Brace's computer had, in fact, done little more than confirm what generations of scholars had already known—that Egyptians look a lot more like East Africans than West Africans and that some East Africans, at least in certain facial features, have a resemblance to Europeans. No one had ever disputed this fact. But did it really mean that East Africans should not be considered African?

Clearly, Brace's methods were inadequate. Any experiment that excluded the Nubians, of all people, from Black Africa was playing fast and loose with racial definitions. What, then, was the solution? Was there, in fact, a scientific methodology that could reliably ascertain the degree of kinship Egypt shared with the rest of Africa?

According to Keita, there was. But it must begin, as with all proper scientific inquiries, by asking the right question.

CHAPTER 77

BLACK, WHITE, OR BIOLOGICALLY AFRICAN?

WERE THE EGYPTIANS BLACK? THAT DEPENDS. IF YOU EQUATE the word *black* with "true Negro," then the answer is no. But if you apply the one-drop rule, you can probably make a good case that most Egyptians would have qualified as black. In short, it is a matter of opinion. As long as people define blackness in various ways, there will never be agreement on this subject.

As a scientist, Shomarka Keita is happily exempt from having to address such delicate social questions. The definition of blackness does not fall within the purview of modern bioanthropology (at least, not among those who adhere to the "no-race" school). Instead, Keita focuses on what he believes is a far more important question: *Were the ancient Egyptians biologically African or biologically European?* Or, to put it another way: *Did the Egyptians evolve in Africa, or did they evolve somewhere outside Africa?*

Keita's approach to the question places little weight on how the Egyptians looked. Appearance, after all, can be deceptive. Consider a single blonde, born into a family of brunettes. Is she more related to people in her immediate family or to other blonde "Nordics" around the world?[1] Or consider a white mother with a black child. Is the child more related to other black children in the neighborhood or to his own mother?

The deceptiveness of physical appearance was dramatically demonstrated in Brace's study. Brace's computer, for example, showed that the closest relatives to the "true Negro" were the Australo-Melanesians—a group that includes native New Guineans and Australian aborigines. It is easy to see why Brace's computer would have clustered these groups with Africans. Both "true Negroes" and Australian aborigines have similar noses and other facial characteristics. But does that prove that they are related?

Geneticists say no. In fact, serogenetic and DNA analysis seems to indicate that "true Negroes" and Australians are the two *least* related peoples in the world. If we create a tree of human relations, based on DNA, no two branches appear farther apart than tropical Africans and Australians. Genetically, the Australians and Melanesians seem closest to Southeast Asians, with whom they have little physical resemblance.[2]

Which data should we trust? Should we believe the skull measurements or the DNA? Keita suggests that we trust neither. DNA analysis is far more reliable, according to Keita, but even this method is subject to the same kind of personal interpretation that often obscures the real meaning of skull measurements. A geneticist who decides that a particular sequence of genes represents a Caucasian or a "true Negro" type may have reached this conclusion for reasons just as arbitrary—and just as mistaken—as those of an anatomist drawing similar inferences from a set of skull features. At present, there is no way to eliminate human error from these processes.

We can, however, minimize error, says Keita, by balancing several different types of data against each other. Anatomical, cultural, historical, linguistic, and genetic data should all be assessed in tandem, he says, before any theories are formed about relationships between different peoples.

When we subject ancient Egypt to this kind of across-the-board analysis, the signs seem to point overwhelmingly toward a greater kinship with other Africans than with people outside Africa. We have already noted, for example, that Egypt's language, monarchy, and religion appear to have come from the south. In their physical features, too, the Egyptians show a distinct overlap with Africans from farther south.

Several studies, for example, have found that ancient Egyptians tended to have very long shins and forearms, especially during the predynastic era. Anthropologists recognize this feature as an adaptation to tropical climate. It is, in fact, fairly typical of equatorial Africans. Since Egypt's climate is not tropical, it seems reasonable to suppose that the Egyptians inherited this feature from people who wandered up from the south—a scenario strangely reminiscent of Diodoros's account that Egypt was settled by Ethiopian colonists.[3]

Diodoros also comes to mind when we consider the facial characteristics of the ancient Egyptians. Negroid, or "Ethiopian," traits seem far more prevalent among the earliest predynastic Egyptians— those closest in time to the hypothetical colonization—than they do among later Egyptians. Many experts have observed, for example, that the people of the Badari culture (4400 to 4000 B.C.)—the oldest of Egypt's predynastic civilizations—had markedly Negroid features.[4] Microscopic analysis of Badarian hair has shown it to be semi-frizzy, like that of "mulattoes" and of many East and West African populations.[5]

The Naqadan culture, which arose afterwards, was also distinguished by Negroid-looking people. As mentioned in the last chapter, Michael Crichton's 1966 computer analysis revealed that the predynastic Naqada skulls were similar, in many respects, to skulls from Kenya. Why, then, did Brace's study find so little resemblance between the Naqadans and the "true Negro"?

The answer lies in the particular features Brace chose for testing. Among these were the form of the nose and the "flatness" of the face—areas in which the average East African tends to differ most sharply from the average West African. Even Crichton noted that the "Negro" character of the Naqadans was "relatively slight."[6] But does that mean that the Naqadans were not black?

Not exactly. Features that an expert would consider only "slightly" Negroid will often appear profoundly Negroid to a layman. Consider, for example, the reconstructed face of Natsef-Amun that appears on the cover of this book. Most people would take one look at Natsef-Amun and conclude that he was black. Yet, to an expert, his skull would appear only slightly Negroid.

The reason for this is that Natsef-Amun lacks many features considered essential for the "true Negro." The most important of these is prognathism, or the jutting forward of the lower face. In a recent interview, forensic artist Richard Neave made the following observations about Natsef-Amun's skull: "It doesn't have the classic appearance of the negroid skull. . . . It's a very straight skull . . . There was a certain amount of prognathism, but not as much as one would expect from a full-blown African skull."[7]

A "full-blown African," in Neave's view, would be one that displayed all the characteristic features of the "true Negro." Because Natsef-Amun displayed only some of these features, he was, in Neave's opinion, only "somewhat negroid."[8] Like the predynastic Naqadans, Natsef-Amun was viewed as an "intermediate" type, hovering somewhere between the black and white ideals. Readers must judge for themselves, by studying the picture on the cover, just how closely the "somewhat negroid" Natsef-Amun measures up to their own conception of blackness.

There is, in fact, little reason to conclude that East Africans, such as Iman, Haile Selassie, and Natsef-Amun, are any less "black" than West Africans. Some might argue, of course, that East Africans are black only according to the one-drop rule. Hamitic theorists would say that East Africans look the way they do because they are hybrid descendants of white invaders and black natives. This would make them at least partly white.

But Keita is skeptical of this explanation. He points out that the sheer numbers of white invaders necessary to effect such a massive genetic change would be mind-boggling. A migration of such biblical proportions would have left clear traces for archaeologists to find. Yet, no signs of it have turned up. On the contrary, Keita notes, "there is evidence for movement out of Africa at the very time when some claim in-migration."[9] Far more plausible, in Keita's opinion, is the theory that East Africans have narrow noses, "straight" (rather than prognathous) faces, and the like because they simply evolved these features on their own.

Most scientists agree that modern humans, of the species *Homo sapiens sapiens*, first emerged on the African continent and then spread out to colonize the world around 100,000 years ago. This is the so-called Out of Africa theory. But what did those first colonists look like when they left Africa? Were they black?

Keita suggests that the colonists may have already evolved into a wide range of physical types before they ever left Africa. DNA studies, in fact, seem to indicate that the early human population experienced two great periods of "fissioning," in which it diverged into markedly different groups. The first such "fissioning" appears to have occurred between 150,000 and 115,000 years ago, the second about 70,000 years ago.

Significantly, the first evidence of modern humans in Europe does not appear until 35,000 years later. Before that, Europe appears to have been inhabited only by Neanderthals, who are now believed to have evolved separately from *Homo sapiens*. In other words, the first colonists to arrive in Europe, around 33,000 B.C., were not only "modern" humans, but may even have evolved many characteristically "European" features before they ever left their African homeland.[10]

By this reasoning, the "Hamitic" peoples of North and East Africa may well have been the *ancestors* of Caucasoid people—rather than hybrids created by intermarriage with white invaders. If this is true, then African "Hamites" and European "Caucasians"—while they may indeed share a common ancestry—have been evolving separately for at least 35,000 years. Such a vast period of separation would make their "kinship" hardly any deeper than the common ancestry that presumably unites every other group of people in the world.

If Keita's theory is true, then the Hamites of East and North Africa could well be 100 percent African. Their Caucasoid appearance would have resulted primarily from microevolution and genetic drift rather than intermarriage with whites. In fact, at the time these Caucasoid Africans assumed their present form, white people—in the modern sense of the word—may not even have existed yet!

If Hamites are, indeed, 100 percent biologically African, then it makes little sense to try to gauge their Africanness—as Brace did—by measuring their resemblance to some other randomly selected group of Africans such as the "true Negroes." Both would be African, to the same degree. Both Negroid and Caucasoid looks would be variations on a single African theme.

It will likely be many years before the technology of DNA analysis develops to the point where scientists can offer reliable solutions to these mysteries. Few Egyptian mummies have been tested yet, and preliminary results are sketchy and controversial. One Egyptian mummy from the Twelfth Dynasty was judged to be a hybrid, some of whose genes came from sub-Saharan Africa while others came from unspecified regions outside tropical Africa.[11] Whether his gene sequences make him a genuine hybrid is, however, a matter of opinion, just as it is with skull measurements. We cannot yet interpret such data with assurance.

Were the Egyptians black? That is entirely up to you. But were they *biologically African?* It would seem that they were. After considering the full range of anatomical, linguistic, cultural, archaeological, and genetic evidence, Shomarka Keita feels confident in concluding that the original Egyptians—by which he means the predynastic people of southern Egypt, who founded Egyptian civilization—evolved entirely in Africa. Both culturally and biologically, he says, they were more related to other Africans than they were to non-Africans from Europe or Asia.

Through the years, Keita believes, the Egyptians appear to have blended with many immigrants and invaders, many of whom were lighter-skinned and more Caucasoid in appearance than the original Egyptians. Libyans, Persians, Syro-Palestinians, Assyrians, Greeks, and Romans all left their imprint on the faces of Egypt. But Egyptian civilization remained profoundly African to the very end.

Keita himself rarely resorts to such crudely racial expressions as *black* and *white*. But if we might be forgiven a momentary lapse into everyday speech, it would probably not hurt to conceive of Keita's theory as the polar opposite of the Hamitic hypothesis. Whereas the Hamitic theorists saw Egypt as a nation of white people that was gradually infiltrated by blacks, the biological evidence seems to suggest that it was more like a black nation that was gradually infiltrated by whites.

None of the evidence presented in the thirteen chapters of this section proves conclusively that Diodoros was correct. We cannot say for sure whether Egypt was really founded by colonists from "Ethiopia." Nevertheless, it should be clear by now that the kinship which Greeks, Romans, and Hebrews perceived between Egypt and Ethiopia was hardly a figment of their imagination. As has happened so many times in the history of archaeology, scholars and scientists have been forced to drop their skepticism and to look with new respect at one of the most puzzling, and seemingly fanciful, legends of the ancient world.

PART TWELVE

CONCLUSION

CHAPTER 78

TOWARD A NEW
EGYPTOLOGY

IN THIS BOOK, WE HAVE FOLLOWED A TRAIL OF CLUES THAT HAS LED US from the heart of Africa to the frigid shores of the North Sea. We have listened to the tales of ancient writers and measured their words against the theories of archaeologists, historians, anthropologists, linguists, geneticists, and other experts. In the process, we have encountered a view of history significantly different from the conventional one—a history in which Africa appears as the mother of Western civilization.

In the end, readers must decide for themselves how compelling the evidence really is. As we have observed many times in these pages, the theories we have explored are controversial. They may or may not be true. But, as we have also noted repeatedly, the conventional theories often seem to hang on threads that are no less tenuous.

If I have accomplished anything in this book, I hope it has been to open readers' minds to the sobering—yet wonderful—fact of how little we really know of the distant past and how much more remains to be learned. The greatest discoveries in archaeology—far from ending with Heinrich Schliemann and Sir Arthur Evans—seem, even now, to lie well in the future.

Until quite recently, most Egyptologists did not deign to approach the question of Afrocentrism at all. They harkened to the distant clamor of its agitators no more than did Archimedes to the cries of blood-crazed Roman legionnaires slaughtering their way through the streets of Syracuse. Like Archimedes, the Egyptologists huddled over their diagrams, hoping that the barbarians would go away. But also like Archimedes—who ended his life skewered on a Roman *gladius*—they proved dangerously mistaken in that hope.

Ann Macy Roth is one of the few Egyptologists today who has recognized both the danger and the promise that Afrocentrism poses for her profession. She is also one of the few who has proposed a constructive alternative to the "Archimedean" approach of the past. In a 1995 article entitled "Building Bridges to Afrocentrism: A Letter to My Egyptological Colleagues," published in the *American Research Center in Egypt Newsletter*, Roth wrote:

> The number of African-Americans who are taught this material is growing, and we will increasingly have to deal with its inaccuracies and exaggerations simply in order to teach our students. This gap between our field and the Afrocentric version of it is not going to go away. And by setting ourselves against the whole phenomenon in an adversarial and often condescending way, we make it impossible for the responsible educators involved in the movement (and there are many) to tap our expertise and improve the accuracy of the materials they teach.[1]

Roth came to this conclusion after being appointed in 1993 to teach Egyptology at predominantly black Howard University. Predictably, her African American students proved ferociously inquisitive about any issues surrounding the putative blackness of the Egyptians. Fielding their questions, day in and day out, Roth came to think more deeply than most about the tensions that have traditionally poisoned relations between Egyptologists and Afrocentrists.

Clearly, the two camps were at odds. But whose fault was it? The Afrocentrists certainly deserved part of the blame. Many wove fantastic theories about Egypt, claiming that the Egyptians possessed magical powers, flying machines, and other advanced technology and dismissing as "racist" anyone who challenged their assertions.

One could hardly blame Egyptologists for avoiding such disagreeable arguments. But eccentric theories about the psychic properties of melanin do not constitute mainstream Afrocentrism any more than New Age speculations about extraterrestrial pyramid builders constitute mainstream Egyptology. The problem was that Egyptologists tended to draw little distinction between responsible Afrocentrists and their counterparts on the lunatic fringe. Both were accorded the same icy disdain. Roth wrote: "In most cases, our reaction to Afrocentrism is avoidance: we deal with the issue by dismissing it as nonsense, by disparaging the knowledge of its proponents. . . . It is impossible to build bridges if we discourage discussion."[2]

Just why were Egyptologists so skittish in the face of such perfectly reasonable questions as "What color were the ancient Egyptians?" Afrocentrists and their many young followers generally concluded that "racism" lay behind their discomfort. But the real reasons were more complex. Part of the problem, Roth admitted, was that Egyptologists often had simply not studied the question thoroughly enough to have a ready answer at hand. She wrote:

> "What color were the ancient Egyptians?" This is a question that strikes fear into the hearts of most American Egyptologists. . . . Few of us have devoted much thought or research to the contentions of the Afrocentric movement, so we nervously try to say something reasonable, and hope that the questioner won't persist and that we won't end up looking silly or racist or both.[3]

In addition, Roth pointed out, there were professional implications to such questions that often made Egyptologists reluctant to take a public stand on them. She wrote:

> Egyptology tends not to be taken quite seriously by people who study other parts of the ancient world. Already many noted departments of Near Eastern Studies with extensive faculty in ancient Mesopotamia and the Levant do not feel it necessary to teach or support research in Egyptology at a similar level. We fear, perhaps, that if we endorse the view that ancient Egypt was a "black civilization," we will further cut ourselves off from our colleagues who study other civilizations contemporary with ancient Egypt. At the same time, there is no place for us in African studies departments, which generally tend to address questions related to modern history and current political and social problems.[4]

Finally, Roth observed that there was a tendency among Egyptologists—many of whom spend a great deal of time in Egypt—to be influenced by the racial definitions that prevail among modern Egyptians. Unlike Americans, Egyptians do not divide themselves into rigid categories of black and white. A very light person might be called "white" and a very dark one "black," but someone of an intermediate shade might be called "brown" or "wheat-colored." The Egyptians, in short, distinguish by skin tone, rather than race.

Working among Egyptians, as so many Egyptologists do, they are understandably hesitant to describe the Egyptians' ancestors in terms that modern Egyptians might object to. "This categorization of the modern population is only partly relevant to the question," writes Roth, "although it contributes to the reluctance of Egyptologists working in Egypt to describe the ancient Egyptians as 'black.' "[5]

This issue probably merits a small digression on my part that goes somewhat beyond Roth's argument. Many Egyptologists, it appears, have imbibed, through their anthropological studies, a strong commitment to the doctrine of "cultural relativism"—the conviction that no culture should be considered better than any other culture. On the surface, cultural relativism seems an excellent antidote to its polar opposite, cultural arrogance—the tendency to hold up one's own culture as the standard of perfection. In practice, however, cultural relativism brings its own brand of unique problems.

Practitioners of this philosophy often display a reflexive tendency to assume that a foreign people's customs or attitudes are better, more humane, or more enlightened than one's own—even in cases where they are not. In the wholesale manner with which some Egyptologists—and scholars in other disciplines, as well—rush to embrace the racial definitions current in modern Egypt, we may see an example of cultural relativism in one of its less salutary moments.

Many scholars tend to assume that the Egyptian attitude toward race is more enlightened than the American. It is quite common, for instance, to read, in scholarly attacks on Afrocentrism, approving references to the aversion modern Egyptians seem to feel at having either themselves or their ancient ancestors characterized as black. Why, these critics wonder, can we benighted Americans not follow the Egyptian example?

Often cited in support of such arguments is Abdel-Latif Aboul-Ela, director of the Cultural Office of the Egyptian Embassy in

Washington, D.C. In 1989, Aboul-Ela achieved temporary notoriety when he became ensnared in a racial controversy over a Ramses the Great exhibit at the Texas State Fairgrounds in Dallas. A group calling itself the Blacology Speaking Committee had threatened to boycott the exhibit, charging that the exhibitors had not placed sufficient emphasis on the alleged blackness of Ramesses II. Aboul-Ela's exasperated response became the centerpiece of a *Washington Post* article headlined "Egypt Says Ramses II Wasn't Black." His statement read, in part:

> They should not . . . involve us in this racial problem that I thought was solved and buried a long time ago. We are not in any way related to the original black Africans of the Deep South. Egypt, of course, is a country in Africa, but this doesn't mean it belongs to Africa at large. This is an Egyptian heritage, not an African heritage. . . . We cannot say by any means we are black or white.[6]

As readers of this book should realize by now, Aboul-Ela's vision of an Egypt sharply divorced from the rest of Africa does not mesh with current scientific thinking. Moreover, there are many Egyptians who would disagree with it. An Egyptian-born schoolteacher in Detroit named Mostafa Hefny, for example, fought against an Immigration Department directive that automatically classified him as "white"—along with all other immigrants from Europe, North Africa, and the Middle East. "My complexion is as dark as most Black Americans," he told *Jet* magazine in January 1991. "My features are clearly African. . . . Classification as it is done by the United States government provides whites with legal ground to claim Egypt as a White civilization. . . . We are fools if we allow them to take this legacy from us."[7] Political grandstanding such as Hefny's is unusual, however. Most Egyptians are more than happy to accept their status as what Egyptian scholar Soheir A. Morsy ironically calls "honorary whites."[8]

Unaware of such nuances, many Americans felt that Aboul-Ela had simply taken a commendable stand against Afrocentric silliness, in the flap over the Ramesses II exhibit. His statement was widely quoted in popular and scholarly articles alike.

Classicist John E. Rexine, for example, in a 1992 attack on *Black Athena*, naively implied that Aboul-Ela's opinion on Egyptian blackness should be taken as authoritative—apparently for no other reason than the fact that Aboul-Ela was himself an Egyptian. It would be interesting to see what would happen to the study of prehistoric America if archaeologists acquiesced as readily in the beliefs of American Indians. Many traditional Indians, after all, consider the notion that their ancestors wandered over the Bering Strait from Asia to be a silly—and even blasphemous—lie of the white man.

So far, specialists have not seen fit to abandon the Bering Strait hypothesis in favor of Indian creation myths. Rexine, however, seemed to think it obvious that Aboul-Ela's statement ought to be taken as the definitive resolution of the question of Egyptian blackness. That this had not happened seemed to him frankly incredible. "Still, the Afrocentrists persist," Rexine complained.[9]

Perhaps if Rexine had understood more about the Egyptian attitude toward race, he might have been less eager—and less naive—about citing such opinions in support of his argument. When it comes to the subject of Egypt's relationship to the rest of Africa, modern Egyptians are, in fact, far from objective.

In 1984, Columbia Pictures released a television mini-series on the life of the late Egyptian president Anwar Sadat. The title role was given to the distinguished black actor Louis Gossett, Jr., perhaps best known for his portrayal of Fiddler in the mini-series *Roots*. Gossett was perfect for the part. With makeup and costume, he was a dead ringer for Sadat. But the Egyptians did not see it that way.

The mini-series *Sadat* was banned in Egypt. Indeed, so deeply were the Egyptians offended that *all* films produced or distributed by Columbia Pictures were similarly banned. There were many objections to *Sadat*. Some Egyptians felt that it distorted history. Others thought that it portrayed Muslim customs inaccurately. But prominent among the stated objections was a strong revulsion against the idea of a black actor playing Sadat. The *New York Times* explained: "Throughout his presidency, Mr. Sadat appeared particularly sensitive about his dark complexion, which prompted jokes and ridicule. The portrayal of Mr. Sadat by a black man has revived the issue of race in Egypt, where it is usually deeply submerged."[10]

Deeply submerged or not, color prejudice is a reality in modern Egypt. In her article, Ann Macy Roth candidly acknowledged its presence. She wrote:

There exist terms in modern colloquial Egyptian Arabic to describe skin color, most commonly "white," "wheat-colored," "brown," and "black." In practice, however, these terms are frequently applied inaccurately, so that people are (flatteringly) described as lighter in color than they actually are. The term "black" is viewed almost as a pejorative and is rarely used.[11]

In short, the Egyptians view the word *black* as an insult. It is hardly surprising, then, that they would shrink from the claims of Afrocentrists. Indeed, most modern Egyptians would prefer to think of themselves as white. "I have been told by most of the modern Egyptians with whom I've discussed the question," writes Roth, "that, if they had to use the categories of the modern Western world, they would describe themselves as white. (There are some exceptions, but few would describe themselves as black)."[12]

All of this leaves practitioners of cultural relativism in something of a quandary. The one-drop rule favored by Afrocentrists obviously has its drawbacks. But are we really in a position to pronounce the one-drop rule morally inferior to the definitions favored by modern Egyptians? It is a question well worth pondering.

In her article, Roth touched on these racial questions only in passing. Her main point was that Egyptologists had many complicated reasons for being skittish about the blackness issue. And, of course, she was right.

But Roth went on to do something unusual in her article. Unlike other scholarly writers on the subject, she proposed a solution to the impasse between Afrocentrists and Egyptologists. Even more unusual, Roth's solution did not fall into the usual pattern of placing all the blame on Afrocentrists and calling on blacks to do all the changing. On the contrary, Roth's prescription required action only on the part of Egyptologists themselves.

What Roth recommended was an exercise in positive thinking. Instead of viewing Afrocentrism as a threat, she suggested, why not embrace it as an opportunity? Egyptology departments needed the same thing that every department needed—more students. Egyptology, after all, had always suffered from obscurity. But Afrocentrism—through the intense interest in Egypt that it sparked among black students—had provided a golden opportunity to break into the mainstream. Roth wrote:

The level of interest and enthusiasm about ancient Egypt is amaz-
ingly high in the African-American community. When I first arrived
at Howard University, I was stunned by the enthusiasm I met with,
both from my own students and from students outside of my classes
(not to mention the prevalence of Egyptian-themed clothing and jewelry). At Howard, Egyptology is not a peripheral field in which one
might take an elective as a novelty.... Egyptian culture is seen as
a heritage to be proud of, and something worth learning about.
... there is a real potential for the expansion of our field among these
students.[13]

If more black students enrolled in Egyptology courses, Roth argued, they would become more scholarly in their approach to ancient Egypt and, at the same time, less susceptible to the eccentric
theories of crackpots and demagogues. "A few of these may go on to
become Egyptologists," Roth predicts, "whether with an Afrocentric agenda or not."[14]

Of course, the prospect of a rising young generation of Afrocentrists armed with Ph.D.s in Egyptology will probably not fill every
scholarly heart with glee. But Roth insists that such an infusion of
new blood would enrich the field, not harm it. "Afrocentric scholars
with traditional training can serve as a useful corrective to the European vantage point inherent in traditional Egyptology," she writes,
"by focusing on questions that it might not occur to traditional
Egyptologists to ask. We all ought to help train these scholars."[15]

Roth's vision depends on the ability of Egyptologists to rethink
their curriculum in such a way as to make room for the interests
and concerns of black students. This is not as formidable a task as it
sounds. It simply means acknowledging those areas where the Afrocentrists have been raising legitimate questions all along and treating those questions with the respect that they should have received
in the first place.

With unusual candor, Roth notes the many areas where future research may prove that the Afrocentrists have been closer to the
truth than their mainstream critics:

The nature and extent of Mediterranean connections with ancient
Egypt are worthy of further study, and may offer scope to arguments
more truly Afrocentric than those propounded by Bernal.... In Africa, too, there were certainly connections of some kind with areas
beyond Nubia.... All of these areas have been receiving more atten-

tion in recent years, and it may be that there was more contact between Egypt and the rest of Africa, or between Egypt and Europe, than
our current interpretations allow.[16]

What Roth is calling for amounts to nothing less than a new
Egyptology—though Roth herself would never put it in such ambitious terms. And, as her article makes clear, the fact that Roth's
new Egyptology looks a lot more like Afrocentrism than the old
Egyptology is no mere coincidence. Ignored, debunked—at times,
viciously excoriated—the Afrocentric perspective has nonetheless
stayed in the ring and won its right to be heard.

"I have come to believe," writes Roth, "that the Afrocentric
movement has a great potential to advance or to damage our field.
Which of these directions it takes will depend upon the degree to
which traditionally-trained American Egyptologists can come to
understand and adapt to its existence."[17]

CHAPTER 79

THE NEFERTITI
DOLL

W HEN FRANK YURCO MADE HIS FIRST ARCHAEOLOGICAL EXPE-
dition to Egypt in 1971, his wife, Diane, came with
him. During the day, Frank pursued his work, leaving
Diane with a lot of free time on her hands. She and an Egyptian
friend decided to amuse themselves, one day, by touring one of the
nearby villages.

The two made a striking pair. Diane's friend was a native-born
Egyptian, whose partially French ancestry made her unusually tall
and fair by Egyptian standards. Diane, on the other hand, was
African American. Born on the Caribbean island of Grenada, her
blend of African, Scottish, and English ancestry gave her skin a *café
au lait* complexion that was not unlike the color of many Egyptians.
As the two women strolled through the village, onlookers stared
and exchanged comments in Arabic.

"The short one is definitely Egyptian," opined one villager,
within earshot of the women. "The other one is probably a
khawaja—a foreigner."

In fact, just the opposite was true. Diane was the *khawaja* and
her friend the native Egyptian. Nevertheless, Diane's African blood

made her *look* Egyptian to these vigilant *fellahin*, while her friend's French blood gave her a distinctly foreign appearance.

"Many of the people in Luxor thought Diane was Egyptian," recalls Frank Yurco. "She could pass for an Egyptian very easily. There are many other people I've heard from who have had that experience, African Americans who have traveled in Egypt and have been mistaken for indigenes."[1]

Most scientists today agree that the modern Egyptians look very much like their ancient forebears. Some anthropologists argue, of course, that the Egyptians grew lighter and more Caucasoid in the centuries following the predynastic era. This may or may not be true. But it is generally agreed that later invaders, such as the Persians, Greeks, Romans, Arabs, and Turks, did not settle or intermarry in sufficient numbers to leave much of an impact on the population. As a result, the Egyptians today are believed to look much as their ancestors did in pharaonic times.[2]

For that reason, it was worth noting that an African American, such as Diane Yurco, could blend so easily into the crowds of modern Luxor. Her experience suggested that Diane might have been equally at home in the Egypt of the pharaohs—a possibility that caught the attention of her Egyptologist husband.

As a boy, Yurco had discovered the famous July–December 1941 issue of *National Geographic* while rummaging in a used bookstore. Its images lingered in his mind for many years. Young Yurco could hardly think of the word *Egyptian* without imagining those pallid, European-looking faces brought forth from the imagination of illustrator H. M. Herget. Moreover, all through the 1950s, Yurco had sat transfixed in darkened theaters, watching Jack Hawkins, Charlton Heston, and other white actors preening in Egyptian finery in such Hollywood spectacles as *The Ten Commandments* and *Land of the Pharaohs*—movies in which black people appeared mainly in the role of Nubian slaves.

Egyptological training, of course, corrected many of these early impressions. In his textbooks, Yurco saw photos of the modern Egyptians and knew that they were not white. But it took somewhat longer for pop culture to relax its emotional grip on Yurco's mind. Even when Yurco arrived in Egypt in 1971 to take part in the Oriental Institute's epigraphical survey, he still found himself marveling as he walked down the streets of Luxor, surrounded on every side by brown and bronze-skinned people.

"It made me aware," Yurco reflects, "that there was a big disconnect between the way Egypt was represented in the popular culture and the way it really was on the ground over there."

The seeds that were planted in Yurco's mind in 1971 bore copious fruit in later years. Yurco has emerged as one of the leading champions of an African Egypt. When Ann Macy Roth spun her vision of a New Egyptology, it could have been Yurco that she had in mind as the model for its ideal practitioner.

Yurco himself is white. He is also thoroughly conventional in his views and methods. Yet, long before it became fashionable, Yurco was deeply engaged in productive dialogue with leading Afrocentrists. He has played a major role in bringing what were once looked upon as exclusively Afrocentric issues to the front and center of Egyptological debate.

Yurco was pulled into the controversy almost by accident. In January 1989, the *Biblical Archaeology Review* (*BAR*, for short) ran an advertisement from a firm selling hand-painted porcelain dolls modeled after the bust of Queen Nefertiti. The peaches-and-cream complexion of the doll aroused the ire of Joan P. Wilson of Austell, Georgia. Convinced that the doll had been artificially whitened to cater to the tastes of white customers, Wilson angrily undertook to set the record straight. She wrote the editor, saying, "Queen Nefertiti was a beautiful black Egyptian queen. This doll has creamy white skin color. . . . It surprised me that a magazine of your standing would even print such an ad."[3]

Editor Hershel Shanks dutifully printed Wilson's letter. He probably would have given it little thought, after that, had it been the only letter he received on the subject. But, in the weeks ahead, the *BAR* was literally swamped with mail, most of it attacking Wilson. Among the comments were the following:

"There is an enormous body of evidence that Nefertiti and the Egyptian people as a whole were not blacks. . . . By general scientific agreement, the ancient Egyptians were Hamites."

"The quaint belief that the Egyptians were black is held only by some American blacks. It is not held by anyone who looks at the evidence."

"Mrs. Wilson's objections are based solely on ignorance of historical fact and perhaps a touch too much racial sensitivity."

"I am surprised that you printed the letter from Mrs. Joan P. Wilson . . . to publicly embarrass her for her ignorance."[4]

And so on. Shanks was astonished both by the number of letters and by the passion that seemed to drive them. In all his years as editor, he had never seen anything quite like it. Clearly, the race of the ancient Egyptians was an issue that people cared deeply about.

To his credit, Shanks did not simply acquiesce in the opinions of what appeared to be the overwhelming majority of his readers. Instead, he decided to explore the issue objectively by asking an Egyptologist to write an article on the subject of the Egyptians' racial identity.

Frank Yurco was already under contract with *BAR* to write a piece about his celebrated reinterpretation of the Israel Stela—an Egyptian inscription that includes the first historical mention of Israel. Shanks asked Yurco whether he would mind putting the Israel Stela on hold for the time being and devoting his attention to what had suddenly become the more pressing issue of Nefertiti's putative blackness.

Yurco was intrigued by the project. All his training in Egyptology had provided him with surprisingly little information on the question of Egypt's relationship to the rest of Africa. To write the article, Yurco would have to conduct a full search of the scholarly literature. In the process, he could finally satisfy the curiosity that had been building in his mind since that first day, in 1971, when he had walked down an Egyptian street, overwhelmed by the sheer Africanness of his surroundings.

Yurco's piece was published in the September 1989 issue. It contained no astounding revelations. In effect, Yurco had done little more than to summarize, for the lay reader, what, by then, had become standard Egyptological thinking. Even so, Yurco's article was a first. Never before had any Egyptologist sought to give such a straightforward, comprehensive answer to the question that formed the title of the piece: "Were the Ancient Egyptians Black or White?" Yurco wrote, "The mummies and skeletons of ancient Egyptians indicate they were Africans. . . . No doubt, many darker-colored Egyptians would be called black in our modern, race-conscious terminology. . . . Some modern Afro-Americans, particularly those with mixed racial ancestry, will find that they look like some ancient (and modern) Egyptians."[5]

Nevertheless, Yurco emphasized that there was no single physical type among the Egyptians. In both ancient and modern times, diversity was the rule. He wrote:

> Ancient and modern Egyptian hair ranges from straight to wavy to woolly: in color, it varies from reddish brown to dark brown to black. Lips range from thin to full. Many Egyptians possess a protrusive jaw. Noses vary from high-bridged—straight to arched or even hooked—to flat-bridged, with bulbous to broad nostrils. In short, ancient Egypt, like modern Egypt, consisted of a very heterogenous population.[6]

But what about Nefertiti? Yurco observed that she seemed to fit into the lighter and more Caucasoid end of the Egyptian spectrum. Her best-known (though not her only) portrait shows her with light skin, thin lips, and a narrow nose—features generally associated with Europeans.

Nefertiti was, in short, an Egyptian of the "light Mediterranean type," as Yurco put it.[7] The same could not be said, however, for many of Nefertiti's blood relatives. Yurco noted that the pharaoh Seqenen-Re Tao—who died about 1580 B.C. and is believed to be a distant ancestor of Nefertiti—possessed "tightly-curled, woolly hair . . . and strongly Nubian features."[8] The pharaoh Thutmose IV—another possible ancestor of Nefertiti—had "wavy" hair, but nevertheless "Egypto-Nubian" features.[9] However "white" Nefertiti may have looked on the surface, it seems likely that her ancestry was just as mixed as that of any other Egyptian.

According to the one-drop rule employed by most Afrocentrists, Nefertiti's complicated ancestry would probably have made her black, no matter how she looked. Yurco drew the line, however, at accepting such debatable racial definitions.

"In their ability to ignore race and absorb foreigners," Yurco wrote in the closing lines of his article, "ancient Egyptians outshine our own achievements and should serve as our model. . . . How then can we be so presumptuous as to assign our primitive racial labels onto so wonderful a culture?"[10]

Yurco's personal life appears to have played some role in his aversion to racial labeling. As the father of two "biracial" children, Yurco was acutely conscious of the peer pressure put on his children to identify themselves as black. He and his wife sought to balance such influences by teaching their children to take pride in *both* of their parents—rather than choosing one or the other.

While engrossed in the research for his article, Yurco had found himself identifying, in a highly personal way, with the ancient Egyptians. In a recent interview, he commented:

> I realized that it was incorrect to view this population, in its great diversity, through the American social lens of black versus white. ... There was no racial image in Egypt. The Egyptians were open to intermingling with Nubians. They were open to intermingling with people from the Levant and with others who came into their country. They intermarried with them and they became part of Egyptian culture. In a sense, that echoed what was going on in my own life. It certainly has shaped my views about the way things should go in this country.

Far from resolving the controversy over Egyptian blackness, as Hershel Shanks had hoped, Yurco's article only seemed to fan the flames higher. After it appeared, the volume of letters, both pro and con, grew so large—and their content so angry and insulting much of the time—that, after a few issues, Shanks finally decided to pull the plug on the whole affair and stop printing the letters altogether. Paradoxically, it turned out to be the Afrocentrists who were least happy with Yurco's article.

"It was like running into a buzzsaw," Yurco recalls. "They were all claiming that I was misrepresenting the evidence, claiming that Egypt is all black and not willing to accept that it's a North African culture with a variety and diversity of populations."

The rocky reception might have discouraged others. But, in the years since his article appeared, Yurco has gone on to become the most active Egyptologist in the country in terms of fulfilling Roth's vision of building bridges to Afrocentrism.

In the early 1990s, for example, Yurco helped organize a program in the Chicago school system called Extending the Great Conversation. Its purpose was to encourage schools to extend their curricula backward in time, to include more detailed study of the history and literature of Egypt and Mesopotamia.

"It was to make teachers aware of the fact that our historical tradition begins not with the Greeks," Yurco explains, "but rather begins in Egypt, on the one hand, and in Mesopotamia, on the other."

The project was largely the brainchild of Dr. Jacob Carruthers, a prominent Afrocentrist from the Center for Inner City Studies in Chicago. Yurco worked closely and productively with Carruthers, even though the two men did not always see eye to eye on many issues—among them the alleged blackness of Nefertiti.

Even more important was a project that unfolded in 1996—a major exhibit at the Indianapolis Museum of Art entitled "Egypt in Africa." Working with curator Theodore Celenko, Yurco helped assemble a massive collection of artifacts, borrowed from leading museums throughout the world, all of which served to emphasize Egypt's African connection.

The catalogue for the show featured papers by well-known Afrocentrists, such as Asa G. Hilliard III and Molefi Kete Asante, alongside those of leading Egyptologists, anthropologists, classicists, and Africanists. Much of the artwork on display showed Egyptians with Negroid-looking features—such as a carved head of the pharaoh Narmer dating from 3100 B.C. and a face of Pharaoh Senwosret III from the Twelfth Dynasty. In the catalogue for the exhibit, Afrocentrist Asa Hilliard praised the organizers for their unusual choices: "This exhibit is one of the first to select items that show more typical African phenotypes, rather than the atypical and sometimes foreign images that Europeans like to see, e.g. Nefertiti, the Sheik el Bilad, or Kai the scribe, those ambiguous enough to be regarded as 'white.'"[11]

Yurco and Celenko had proved that it was possible to work with Afrocentrists and to incorporate their views in a way that enhanced, rather than compromised, the scholarly integrity of a project. For Yurco, at least, this was no great revelation. He had long since learned that Afrocentrism is nothing like the monolith that many conventional scholars imagine it to be. Yurco comments:

> As I became more deeply involved in it, I saw that you have a variety of individuals involved in Afrocentrism, who argue in different ways. Some of the Afrocentric books are just utter trash. They have one misrepresentation after another. On the other hand, there are people like Molefi Kete Asante at Temple University who is a very solidly based academic. Asante I can respect, as a scholar. At the same time, I think the more academic Afrocentrists have been awakened to the fact that there isn't a monolithic viewpoint standing in opposition to them. In fact, some people have been more openminded.

Yurco has tried very hard to be one of those openminded people. In the process, he has re-created himself as a new breed of Egyptologist, willing not only to concede Egypt's strong connections with Africa, but even to revel in them.

In the often highly politicized battle over Egypt's African identity, Yurco cuts an enigmatic figure. His beliefs and background make him almost the polar opposite of Martin Bernal. Where Bernal was a child of wealth and privilege, Yurco was a working-class kid from Manhattan's Upper East Side whose father was a cabinetmaker. Where Bernal was a "red-diaper baby," reared from childhood in the doctrines of socialism, Yurco was the son of Czechoslovakian emigrés, for whom hatred of Communism was a deeply personal affair.

During the 1960s, Bernal mastered Vietnamese so that he could pursue his anti-war activism more effectively. Yurco learned the language for a different reason—to interrogate Viet Cong prisoners. He served proudly as an intelligence specialist in Vietnam from 1970 to 1971. In Yurco's view, the American cause was just. Antiwar protesters—such as Bernal—he looked upon as dupes or worse.

"As a college student in the late 1960s, I simply didn't see eye to eye with what many of the hippies were pushing," Yurco recalls. "I had a very anti-Communist upbringing. We still had family back there in Czechoslovakia who lived under the Communist system. We knew what Communism was and which way it cut. There was a real Communist threat of expansionism at that time, and Vietnam was part of that."

As young men, Bernal and Yurco found themselves fighting on what amounted to opposite sides of the Vietnam War. But in the battle over Afrocentrism, they have become allies. The two scholars disagree on many points. Yurco, for example—like most Egyptologists—rejects Bernal's theory of Egyptian colonies in Greece. But, when it comes to the bitterly disputed question of Egypt's African identity, both find themselves conspicuously—albeit not always comfortably—in the same academic corner.

When the first volume of *Black Athena* appeared in the United States, Bernal noticed a curious phenomenon. In his native England, the book's reception had been sharply divided along ideological lines. "In general," Bernal later wrote, "the left and liberals liked the book, but from the *Independent* rightwards it was ignored."[12] In

America, by contrast, the "liberal establishment"—as exemplified, in Bernal's view, by *Time, Newsweek,* and the *New York Times*—ignored the book for years, while certain conservative publications, such as *Insight Magazine,* weighed in with what he called "scrupulously fair" reviews.

Whatever the reason for this difference in treatment, Bernal's experience combines with that of Frank Yurco to illustrate that, in the raging controversy over Afrocentrism, traditional divisions between left, right, black, and white seem to matter less and less all the time. Today, Afrocentrism's most outspoken critics include blacks such as Frank Snowden and liberals such as Arthur M. Schlesinger, Jr. Its most effective defenders, on the other hand—as personified by Bernal and Yurco—span the gap between left-wing peaceniks and defiant Cold Warriors.

It is probably best left to future historians to figure out why Afrocentrism in America cuts so jagged a path across racial and political lines. But if Frank Yurco and his "bridge-building" crusade are any indication, there would seem strong grounds for hoping that we, as a people, have begun, at last, to cherish truth over ideology.

CHAPTER 80

THE MYTH OF THE
PURE RACE

*No matter how low (in a socioeconomic sense) an American white may
be, his ancestors built the civilizations of Europe; and no matter how
high (again in a socioeconomic sense) a Negro may be, his ancestors
were (and his kinsmen still are) savages in an African jungle.*

— PROFESSOR HENRY E. GARRETT, 1962,
Former chairman, Department of Psychology, Columbia University

IN THE WINTER OF 1994, I WAS INVITED BY A FRIEND IN NEW YORK
City to give a presentation to his monthly debate group based
on the research I was doing for *Black Spark, White Fire*. We all
looked forward to a provocative evening together. None of us, however, realized quite how provocative it was going to be.

A squadron of neo-Nazis somehow got wind of the event and
showed up en masse. I later learned from a reliable source that
many of our unexpected visitors were members of the National Alliance, a white supremacist group led by William Pierce, author of
The Turner Diaries—the novel that allegedly inspired the Okla-
homa City bombing. Fortunately, their goal seemed to be to participate in the event, rather than disrupt it. Although their sheer
numbers created a certain pandemonium, Pierce's followers turned
out, in general, to be well behaved.

The talk, as usual, was structured as an open debate. After my
initial remarks, the floor was opened to anyone in the audience who
wished to make a response. The neo-Nazis all waited patiently for

their turn to mount the podium. They followed the rules of the debate. Several even proved to be articulate speakers. Their message, however, raised more than a few eyebrows around the room.

Each one took a slightly different approach. But their arguments tended to fall within five basic categories: (1) that black people constituted a separate species from whites, (2) that it was unnatural and disgusting for two different species or races to commingle sexually, (3) that the proof of white superiority was the long history of great civilizations built by whites, (4) that blacks had built neither the Egyptian civilization, nor any other worth mentioning, and (5) that the recent massacre of white commuters on the Long Island Railroad by a crazed black gunman named Colin Ferguson served as eloquent proof of all the above.

To anyone familiar with the doctrines of white supremacy, there was nothing especially new in these arguments. Far more intriguing was a photocopied article that the Pierce followers distributed around the room just before the debate began. It was a piece from the November 1977 *National Geographic*, written by British archaeologist Colin Renfrew.

Entitled "Ancient Europe Is Older Than We Thought," it argued that the standard radiocarbon dates used by archaeologists have been found to be inaccurate by several centuries. The new, readjusted dates, according to Renfrew, prove that Europe has been civilized longer than anyone ever suspected.

Stonehenge, for example, now appears to have been built around 2100 B.C., rather than 400 years later, as previously thought. The mysterious stone temples on the island of Malta, formerly dated to around 2400 B.C., now appear to be 700 years older, which would mean that they predate the pyramids. "And in just the past few years," writes Renfrew, "it has become clear that the great stone tombs dotting Western Europe are even older. Some, built around 4000 B.C., are quite simply the oldest buildings in existence."[1]

What does all this mean? Renfrew seems to imply that it makes Europe, rather than Egypt or Mesopotamia, the true cradle of civilization. He writes, "All this contradicts long-accepted theories which held that the earliest stone tombs and temples and the practice of metallurgy began in the great cultures of ancient Egypt and Mesopotamia, the traditional 'cradle of civilization.' "[2]

Yet, despite this new evidence, Renfrew complains, the textbooks still portray Europe as having been "something of a barbarian fringe" during the third and fourth millennia B.C. He seems to expect that this will change, though. Renfrew implies that there is a new thinking in the air about prehistoric Europe. He writes, "What really matters is that we no longer seek to explain European prehistory by reference to the early civilizations of the eastern Mediterranean. In the right conditions, prehistoric men anywhere in the world were capable of ingenious inventions and impressive achievements."[3]

In other words, according to Renfrew, Europe did not need any cultural inspiration from abroad. It was perfectly capable, on its own, of ingenious and impressive feats. And who knows? Perhaps he is right. Nevertheless, twenty years after Renfrew wrote this article, experts seem no closer than they were in 1977 to moving the "cradle of civilization" to western Europe. And it seems a safe bet that they never will.

The new radiocarbon dates remain in considerable dispute. Indeed, they have lost most of their supporters over the last 20 years. But even should Stonehenge really turn out to be a few centuries older than we thought, it is hard to accept Renfrew's implication that Europe's primitive Copper Age cultures are somehow comparable, either in age or grandeur, to the civilizations of Egypt and the Near East.

The earliest level of the walled city of Jericho, for example, located in Israel, has been dated to 8300 B.C.—making it some 4,300 years older than the European tombs that Renfrew calls "the oldest buildings in existence." Moreover, a team of Swiss and American scholars concluded in 1987 that faulty radiocarbon readings may have dated the pyramids 374 years too late. Martin Bernal suggests a more modest adjustment of about 300 years.[4] This would still place Djoser's Step Pyramid in the neighborhood of 3000 B.C.—a full thousand years before Stonehenge, even by Renfrew's reckoning.

Had any truly high civilization existed in western Europe during prehistoric times, it would surely have left a few traces for Julius Caesar to find when he marched through Gaul and Germany in the first century B.C. But as any second-year Latin student who has ever slogged through the *Commentaries* knows, the Gauls and Germans Caesar encountered were far from urban sophisticates.

Renfrew's theory is clearly fraught with problems. Nevertheless, it is easy to see why the National Alliance would wish to promote it. Renfrew's article speaks directly to the one issue that has always proved the greatest stumbling block to white supremacists through the ages—the fact that Europe, the homeland of the white race, was the very last continent in the Mediterranean region to acquire civilization.

"We really should do our best to keep quiet about this past," Adolf Hitler once urged, concerning the primitive origins of the Germans.[5] Today's racial theorists, it would seem, are no less haunted by a past they would like to forget but cannot.

In 1961, a man named Carleton Putnam published a book entitled *Race and Reason*. In it, he argued that integration of blacks and whites would lead quickly to interracial marriage, degradation of the white race, and, finally, the collapse of American civilization.

Putnam did not represent the lunatic fringe. He was an influential corporate leader, who had recently retired from his position as chairman of the board of Delta Airlines. Putnam's book was warmly praised by geneticists, psychologists, anthropologists, and journalists. In many respects, Putnam was simply enunciating what others were thinking but dared not say aloud.

The crux of his argument was the same as Adolf Hitler's, the same as Elliot Smith's, the same, in fact, as that of virtually every other proponent of the Master Race theory who ever lived: Putnam argued that it was the biological purity of the white race that enabled it to build and maintain great civilizations. Once that purity was destroyed—specifically through intermarriage with blacks—civilization itself would soon follow.

"What great civilization," Putnam asked rhetorically, "ever arose after an admixture of Negro genes?"[6]

One answer, of course, would be Egypt. But Putnam never knew that. He was not even sufficiently informed of Egypt's African roots to bother trying to deny them. In Putnam's view, the white man's monopoly on civilization was beyond dispute. Equally obvious, in his opinion, was the role of "pure" white genes in maintaining that monopoly.

A French nobleman named Count Joseph-Arthur de Gobineau (1816–1882) is widely credited with having been the first to propose that racial purity—or the lack of it—lay behind the rise and fall of civilizations. Gobineau espoused this theory in a work called *The Inequality of the Human Races*, published in several volumes between 1853 and 1855. In it, he wrote: "Everything great, noble and fruitful in the works of man on this earth, in science, art, and civilization, derives from a single starting point, is the development of a single germ and the result of a single thought; it belongs to one family alone, the different branches of which have reigned in all the civilized countries of the universe."[7]

That one family, of course, was the white, or Aryan, race. Gobineau traced its origins all the way back to the biblical patriarch Noah. According to Gobineau's fanciful interpretation of the Bible, Ham was the first of Noah's sons to leave home after the ark ran aground on Mount Ararat. Ham traveled south and founded many nations. Unfortunately, his pure white blood was "mongrelized" by intermarriage with blacks, giving rise to "Hamitic," or mulatto, civilizations, such as Egypt.

The next of Noah's sons to leave was Shem. The "Semites" too became contaminated with black blood, mainly by consorting with the mulatto Hamites; and consequently the Semitic civilizations also failed to live up to their potential. In the end, only the sons of Japheth managed to keep their bloodline pure, wrote Gobineau. They became the Aryans—the Master Race, whose destiny it was to rule the world.[8]

For Gobineau, blood was everything. He believed "that the racial question overshadows all other problems of history, that it holds the key to them all, and that the inequality of the races from whose fusion a people is formed is enough to explain the whole course of its destiny."[9]

In Gobineau's view, nations rose or fell, succeeded or failed, according to their ability to keep their blood pure. Once they succumbed to intermarriage with inferior races, "degeneration" set in, and the nation was doomed. "The word degenerate," Gobineau explained, "when applied to a people, means . . . that the people has no longer the same blood in its veins, continual adulteration having gradually affected the quality of that blood."[10]

Of all the different types of "blood" in the world, the worst, in Gobineau's view, was African. He wrote, "The black variety is the lowest and lies at the bottom of the ladder. The animal character lent to its basic form imposes its destiny from the moment of conception."[11]

Not surprisingly, Gobineau's book was warmly greeted by advocates of black slavery when it was published in America in 1856.[12] It attained its greatest popularity, however, in the 1930s, when *The Inequality of Human Races* was adopted as a standard text in the schools of Nazi Germany. Many of Gobineau's ideas proved influential in the formation of Nazi doctrine. Among these was Gobineau's view that both Jews ("Semites") and Phoenicians ("Hamites") were part black.

This notion, in particular, appears to have contributed to a new style of anti-Semitism that arose in the late nineteenth century. For hundreds of years, Jews had been persecuted mainly on religious grounds. If they converted to Christianity, they were, more or less, left alone. By the dawn of the twentieth century, however, religious conversion no longer helped. Under the influence of Gobineau and other writers, the new breed of anti-Semite focused now on the Jew's "racial impurity"—a fault that no amount of baptismal water could cure. "Racial" anti-Semitism had been born.

Speculation on the alleged African ancestry of the Jews reached a crescendo in Nazi Germany during the 1930s. Edgar Schultz, for example—a leading medical expert for Germany's Office of Racial Policy—opined in 1935 that Jews suffered from higher rates of mental illness as a direct result of "tensions and contradictions" caused by their alleged mixture of "Negro" and "Oriental" blood.[13] It was "scientific" opinions such as these that led directly, in 1935, to the passage of laws forbidding Jews to marry or have sexual relations with Germans.[14]

The new racial anti-Semitism had repercussions in classical scholarship as well. It was precisely during the period when anti-Semites began to take up the cry of "racial impurity" that a major turnaround occurred in the interpretation of Greek history. Martin Bernal observes that it was during this period—roughly from 1880 to 1945—that scholars suddenly decided that it was no longer "scientific" to believe the old stories about Kadmos and his Phoenicians colonizing Greece.[15]

Bernal sees a clear connection between the two events. Whether the Phoenicians were seen as black Hamites or as "mongrelized" Semites, the consensus, by the turn of the century, was that they—like their Hebrew cousins—were racially impure. For that reason, says Bernal, the Phoenicians were no longer welcome in the pages of Greek history.[16]

The accusation that Jews are mulattoes remains, to this day, a pillar of anti-Semitic propaganda. As recently as 1966, a British anthropologist named Roger Pearson argued that blood group research showed the Jews to have been partly African.[17] Pearson warned against the consequences of Nordic peoples becoming similarly mongrelized. In a 1959 paper, he called on fellow Nordics to "develop a worldwide bond between our own kind" whose purpose would be to preserve racial purity, so as "not to be annihilated as a species."[18]

Pearson has the distinction of having formulated what is perhaps the most honest and succinct encapsulation of the doctrine of racial purity to appear in recent times. In 1966, he wrote, "If a nation with a more advanced, more specialized, or in any way superior set of genes mingles with, instead of exterminating, an inferior tribe, then it commits racial suicide."[19]

Here, in a nutshell, is the reason that so many educated and influential people to this day continue to oppose race mixing. At its root, the fear of interracial marriage is nothing less than the fear of "race suicide"—of the wholesale collapse of white civilization.

In view of this fact, it is easy to see why proponents of William Pierce's National Alliance would have felt obligated, back in 1994, to invade my little talk on Egypt's role in history. It is easier still to see why they felt it necessary to ply the audience with copies of Colin Renfrew's article from *National Geographic.*

The crux of the matter is this: *If Egyptian explorers really civilized ancient Europe—and if the Egyptians really were black, or even partly black—then the pure race theory cannot be correct.*

Even if we were to accept, for the sake of argument, the "whitest" of all possible Egypts—say, the Egypt of the Hamitic hypothesis, which portrays the Egyptians as whites, mongrelized with black blood—we are still left with a perplexing question. How did these mongrelized Egyptians manage to build a high civilization, while their allegedly pure counterparts back in Europe languished in barbarism? And why is it that the "purest" of all white people, the Nordics, took longer than almost anyone else in Europe to shed their primitive ways?

Proponents of the pure race theory have never provided a good explanation for these phenomena. The fact is that entire legions of Colin Renfrews could never successfully ascribe to Bronze or Copper Age Europe any civilization even remotely comparable to those that emerged in Egypt and the Near East during the same time period. Nor could they ever change the fact that, when Caesar marched into Germany, the people he found there, in the embarrassed words of Adolf Hitler, were "still throwing stone hatchets and crouching around open fires."[20]

Only the intervention of "mongrelized" peoples, such as the Egyptians and Phoenicians, appears to have tipped the balance, launching Europe on its trajectory toward future glory. "What great civilization," asked Carleton Putnam, "ever arose after an admixture of Negro genes?"[21] The answer, it would seem, is Western civilization.

The doctrine of racial purity obviously violates the evidence of history. It is perhaps worth noting that it also violates one of the core principles of modern genetics. "In general," says Stanford University geneticist Luigi Luca Cavalli-Sforza, "mixed marriages, including those between people of very different origins, create a more robust line of descendants."[22]

Cavalli-Sforza is here referring to the phenomenon known as heterosis, or "hybrid vigor." When widely different gene pools are crossed—whether among people, plants, or animals—the hybrid offspring often turn out to be healthier, stronger, larger, or otherwise better developed than either parent. Gene pools that are kept "pure," on the other hand, usually stagnate after a few generations of inbreeding into weaker and sicklier forms. This, of course, is exactly the opposite of what proponents of the pure race theory teach. To them, the largest, strongest, and healthiest people are those that breed only within a certain gene pool.

In fact, purity works best for the amoeba, which reproduces by splitting in half and making two copies of itself. Each new amoeba is genetically "pure," having no contamination from outside genes. But higher life forms seem to need diversity to thrive. The very reason that sexual coupling seems to exist among higher organisms is to ensure the maximum amount of mixing among different gene pools. The more mixing, it seems, the healthier the species.

After identifying what he believed were Egyptian skulls in Mycenaean Greece—as discussed in chapter 75—anthropologist Larry Angel proposed a rather unusual theory for the rise of Greek civilization. He suggested that the peculiarly diverse mixture of peoples in Greece had induced a nationwide heterosis. It was this invigorating impulse, he believed, that led directly to Hellenic greatness.[23]

A serious problem with Angel's theory is that it presumes that civilizations arise from biological causes—a dubious proposition, as I hope this book has helped to establish. In one respect, however, Angel appears to have been on the right track.

The Mediterranean Sea is, after all, the only place on earth where three continents are joined by a small and easily navigable body of water. Thor Heyerdahl assures us that even the great ocean "was a conveyor of early contact among civilizations and not an element of their isolation."[24] How much more, then, would a small pond like the Mediterranean have acted as a highway, joining the peoples of Europe, Africa, and Asia in a melting pot of unusual size and richness. Can it really be an accident that so many of the world's earliest and greatest civilizations took form around its shores?

It does not seem likely that any biological process of heterosis gave rise to these civilizations, as Angel speculates. But a different kind of heterosis—a heterosis of the mind, if you will—may well have come into play. Even more than they mingled their genes, the peoples of the Mediterranean traded cultures, religions, and ideas. This phenomenon—what Cyrus Gordon called "international stimulation"—appears to have played the greatest role in seeding the Mediterranean with such a fabulous overflow of civilizations. As Gordon put it, "All high, technologically developed civilizations are the result of international stimulation so that all of them are connected by what they have learned from each other."[25]

If Heyerdahl and Gordon are correct, then it is no accident that Europe's Mediterranean shoreline developed faster and earlier than its primitive interior. In this regard, Africa seems to mirror Europe exactly, for it too spawned its oldest and greatest civilization— Egypt—along the Mediterranean littoral. In Europe and Africa alike, the Mediterranean coastlines were the very regions where international stimulation would have been strongest.

But did it really happen? Did this "international stimulation" occur exactly as the legends of the ancients told it? Did Kadmos and Danaos really cross the sea? Did mighty Sesostris march through Russia? Did the Egyptians build pyramids in Greece? In the end, dear reader, only you can decide. The heroes of old have finished their work. They lived and fought bravely, but now they are gone. Likewise the poets did their part, recording the deeds of the Bronze Age explorers in song. Diligent scribes copied and recopied those verses through the ages so that no one would forget. But now all are dead, and only we remain to preserve the legacy.

It is we, the living, who must now decide what to do with the legends. Only we can judge whether the Bronze Age explorers really lived. Think long on the question, dear reader, and choose your words carefully. For, in Hades, where the souls of the dead whirl "clangorously . . . like wild birds this way and that," someone who knows the answer may, even now, be listening.

NOTES

INTRODUCTION

1. Mary Lefkowitz, *Not Out of Africa: How Afrocentrism Became an Excuse to Teach Myth as History,* Basic Books/HarperCollins, New York, 1996, p. 5.
2. Saul K. Padover, *Thomas Jefferson on Democracy,* Mentor, New York (first edition, 1939), p. 42.

CHAPTER 1

1. Julius Caesar, *The Gallic War,* VI, 28 (H. J. Edwards, trans.), Harvard University Press, Cambridge, Mass., 1917.
2. Ibid.
3. Ibid.
4. Thomas Cahill, *How the Irish Saved Civilization: The Untold Story of Ireland's Heroic Role from the Fall of Rome to the Rise of Medieval Europe,* Anchor Books/Doubleday, New York, 1995, p. 12.
5. Douglas Jehl, "Under Beirut's Rubble, Remnants of 5,000 Years of Civilization," *New York Times,* February 23, 1997, p. 15.
6. Nicolas Grimal, *A History of Ancient Egypt* (Ian Shaw, trans.), Blackwell, Oxford, England, 1992, p. 389; and Walter B. Emery, *Archaic Egypt,* Penguin Books, Baltimore, 1961, p. 192.
7. Mary Settegast, *Plato Prehistorian: 10,000 to 5,000 B.C. Myth, Religion, Archaeology,* Lindisfarne Press, Hudson, N.Y., 1990, p. 45.
8. J. Lesley Fitton, *The Discovery of the Greek Bronze Age,* Harvard University Press, Cambridge, Mass., 1996, p. 70.
9. Herodotus, *The History,* IV, 45 (George Rawlinson, trans.), Encyclopedia Britannica, Chicago, 1952.
10. Ibid., VII, 126.
11. John Pollard, *Wolves and Werewolves,* Robert Hale, London, 1964, p. 25.
12. Ibid., p. 136.
13. Ward Rutherford, *The Druids: Magicians of the West,* Sterling Publishing Company, New York, 1990, pp. 31 and 39; Caesar, VI, 16; Diodoros, V, 28; and Cahill (1995), p. 136.
14. Diodoros Siculus, V.26.3 (C. H. Oldfather trans.). Harvard University Press, Cambridge, MA, 1933.
15. Diodoros, V.28.5–6.
16. Cahill (1995). p. 135.
17. Caesar, VI, 16.
18. Herodotus, *The Histories,* IV, 46 (Aubrey de Sélincourt, trans.), Penguin Books, New York, 1954.

19. Herodotus, IV, 64 (Rawlinson, trans.).
20. Ibid.
21. Herodotus, IV, 65 (de Sélincourt, trans.).

CHAPTER 2

1. Herodotus, VI, 55 (de Sélincourt, trans.).
2. Ibid., V, 58.
3. Caroline Alexander, "Troy's Prodigious Ruin," *Natural History,* April 1996, p. 49.

CHAPTER 3

1. Marija Gimbutas, *The Civilization of the Goddess: The World of Old Europe,* HarperSanFrancisco, 1991, p. 352.
2. Ibid., p. 348.
3. Ibid., p. 352.
4. Ibid., p. 361.
5. Ibid., p. 352.
6. Ibid., p. 364.
7. Herodotus, IV, 26, 106.
8. Strabo, IV, 5.4; *The Geography* (Horace Leonard Jones, trans.), Harvard University Press, Cambridge, MA, 1988 (first edition, 1927).
9. Pollard (1964), p. 132.
10. Patrick Tierney, *The Highest Altar,* Viking, 1989, pp. 10.; also Pausanias VIII, 2.6.
11. Tierney (1989), p. 10, 443; also Pausanias Viii. 2.6, 38.7.
12. Pausanias, VIII, 36.7. *Description of Greece* (W. H. S Jones Trans.), Harvard University Press, Cambridge, MA, 1995 (first edition 1935).
13. Tim Severin, *The Ulysses Voyage: Sea Search for the Odyssey,* E. P. Dutton, New York, 1987, p. 134.
14. Frank J. Yurco, "Black Athena: An Egyptological Review," *Black Athena Revisited* (Mary Lefkowitz and Guy MacLean Rogers, eds.), The University of North Carolina Press, Chapel Hill, NC, 1996, p. 74; Martin Bernal, *Black Athena,* vol. II, Rutgers University Press, New Brunswick, New Jersey, 1991, pp. 145, 480; *Oxford Classical Dictionary,* p. 212.
15. Pseudo-Aristotle, *On Marvelous Things Heard* (quoted in James D. Muhly, "Phoenicia and the Phoenicians," *Biblical Archeology Today,* Jerusalem, April 1984, pp. 185–186.
16. Geoffrey Bibby, *Four Thousand Years Ago,* Alfred A. Knopf, New York, 1961, p. 224.
17. Bibby (1961), p. 216.
18. Gimbutas (1991), p. 195; Editors of Time-Life Books, *Lost Civilizations: Early Europe,* Time-Life Books, Alexandria, VA, 1995, p. 94.
19. Bibby (1961), pp. 216, 225.
20. Fitton (1996), p. 11.

CHAPTER 4

1. "The Enlightenment," *Encyclopedia Britannica Online* (1996).
2. M. C-F. Volney, *Travels Through Syria and Egypt in the Years 1783, 1784, and 1785,* G. G. J. and J. Robinson, London, 1787, p. ii.
3. Ibid., p. ii.
4. Herodotus, II, 148 (de Sélincourt, trans.).
5. Volney (1787), p. 80.

6. Ibid., p. 81.
7. Ann Macy Roth, "Building Bridges to Afrocentrism: A Letter to My Egyptological Colleagues, Part II," *American Research Center in Egypt Newsletter*, no. 168, December 1995, p. 14; and Graham Hancock and Robert Bauval, *The Message of the Sphinx: A Quest for the Hidden Legacy of Mankind*, Crown, New York, 1996, pp. 3–4.
8. Volney (1787), p. 81.
9. Ibid., p. 81.
10. "Volney, Constantin-François de Chasseboeuf, Count (Comte) de," *Encyclopedia Britannica Online* (1996).
11. Robin Blackburn, *The Making of New World Slavery*, Verso, New York, 1997, p. 384.
12. Volney (1787), pp. 82–83.
13. "Volney, Constantin-François de Chasseboeuf, Count (Comte) de," *Encyclopedia Britannica Online* (1996).
14. Count Constantin de Volney, *The Ruins: or a Survey of the Revolution of Empires*, 1791 (cited in Cheikh Anta Diop, *Civilization or Barbarism: An Authentic Anthropology*, trans. Yaa-Lengi Meeme Ngemi, Lawrence Hill Books, New York, 1991; first published in French, 1981, p. xx).

CHAPTER 5

1. Richard Noll, *The Jung Cult: Origins of a Charismatic Movement*, Princeton University Press, Princeton, NJ, 1994, pp. 96–97.
2. Cheikh Anta Diop, *Civilization or Barbarism: An Authentic Anthropology* (Yaa-Lengi Meema Ngemi, trans.), Lawrence Hill Books, New York, 1991, p. 66.
3. Cheikh Anta Diop, *The African Origin of Civilization: Myth or Reality* (Mercer Cook, trans.), Lawrence Hill Books, Chicago, 1974, p. 17.
4. Ibid., p. 15.
5. Ibid., p. 34.
6. Adolf Erman, *Life in Ancient Egypt*, Dover Publications, New York, 1971 (originally published in German 1886, in English 1894), p. 29.
7. Gaston Maspero, *Histoire ancienne des peuples de l'Orien,.* Hachette, Paris, 1917, pp. 17–18, 12th ed. (cited in Diop, 1974, p. 73; translated as *The Dawn of Civilization*, London, 1894; reprinted, Frederick Ungar, New York, 1968).
8. D. O'Connor, "Ancient Egypt and Black Africa—Early Contacts," *Expedition: The Magazine of Archaeology/Anthropology*, 14, 1971, p. 2.
9. Frank J. Yurco, "Were the Ancient Egyptians Black or White?" *Biblical Archaeology Review*, September/October 1989, vol. 15, no. 5, pp. 25, 58.
10. Jaques Joseph Champollion-Figeac, *Egypte ancienne*, Collection l'Univers, Paris, 1839, pp. 30–31 (cited in Diop, 1974).
11. Diop (1974), p. 53.

CHAPTER 6

1. Selim Hassan, *The Sphinx: Its History in the Light of Recent Excavations*, Government Press, Cairo, 1949, p. 91 (cited in Hancock and Bauval, 1996, p. 13).
2. Zahi Hawass and Mark Lehner, "The Sphinx: Who Built It and Why," *Archaeology*, September–October 1994, p. 34 (cited in Hancock and Bauval, 1996, p. 8).
3. Frank Domingo, taped interview, April 6, 1997.
4. John Anthony West, "The Case of the Missing Pharaoh," *New York Times*, June 27, 1992, Section 1., p. 23.
5. Hancock and Bauval (1996), p. 9.
6. Ibid., p. 18.

Frank Domingo, taped interview, September 18, 1996.

CHAPTER 7

1. Neal Ascherson, *Black Sea*, Hill and Wang/Farrar, Straus and Giroux, New York, 1995, p. 52.
2. Frank M. Snowden, Jr., "Bernal's 'Blacks,' Herodotus, and Other Classical Evidence," *Arethusa*, Fall 1989, pp. 84–88.

CHAPTER 8

1. Herodotus, IV, 114 (Rawlinson, trans.).
2. Ibid., 116–117.
3. Ibid., 105.
4. Herodotus, II, 123 (cited in Fitton, 1996, p. 20).
5. Herodotus, II, 148 (Rawlinson, trans.).

CHAPTER 9

1. O. Kimball Armayor, "Did Herodotus Ever Go to the Black Sea?" *Harvard Studies in Classical Philology*, vol. 82, Harvard University Press, Cambridge, Mass., 1978, pp. 60–61.
2. O. Kimball Armayor, "Sesostris and Herodotus' Autopsy of Thrace, Colchis, Inland Asia Minor, and the Levant," *Harvard Studies in Classical Philology*, vol. 82, Harvard University Press, Cambridge, Mass., 1980, p. 64.
3. Hippocrates, *Airs, Waters, Places*, 15 (cited in David Braund, *Georgia in Antiquity*, Oxford University Press, New York, 1994, p. 49).
4. Armayor (1978), p. 61.
5. Ibid., p. 46.
6. Ibid., pp. 51–52.
7. Ibid., p. 62.
8. Ascherson (1995), p. 112.
9. Jeannine Davis-Kimball, "Warrior Women of the Eurasian Steppes," *Archaeology*, January/February 1997, pp. 47–48.
10. Ibid., p. 45.
11. Herodotus, IV, 71 (Rawlinson, trans.).
12. Herodotus, IV, 74 (de Sélincourt, trans.).
13. Ascherson (1995), pp. 78–79.
14. Martin Bernal, *Black Athena*, vol. I, Rutgers University Press, New Brunswick, New Jersey, 1987, pp. 118, 218, 377–378.
15. James Norman, *Ancestral Voices: Decoding Ancient Languages*, Barnes & Noble, New York, 1975, p. 137.
16. C. W. Ceram, *Gods, Graves, and Scholars* (E. B. Garside, trans.), Alfred A. Knopf, New York, 1951, p. 50.

CHAPTER 10

1. Herodotus, II, 104 (de Sélincourt, trans.).
2. David Braund, *Georgia in Antiquity*, Oxford University Press, New York, 1994, p. 71.
3. Herodotus, II, 103–104 (Rawlinson, trans.).
4. Herodotus, II, 99 (de Sélincourt, trans.).
5. Ibid., II, 104.

6. Allison Blakely, *Russia and the Negro: Blacks in Russian History and Thought*, Howard University Press, Washington, DC, 1986, p. 78.
7. Ibid., p. 9.
8. Pindar, *Pythian Odes*, 4.11 (cited in Bernal (1991), p. 249).
9. Patrick T. English, "Cushites, Colchians, and Khazars," *Journal of Near Eastern Studies*, vol. 18, January–October 1959, p. 53.
10. Slava Tynes, "When Did Africans Get to Soviet Union?" *The Afro-American*, February 3, 1973, p. 6.
11. H. Hoetink, *The Two Variants in Caribbean Race Relations: A Contribution to the Sociology of Segmented Societies* (E. M. Hooykaas, trans.), London and New York, 1967, p. 186; and *Slavery and Race Relations in the Americas: Comparative Notes on Their Nature and Nexus*, New York and London, 1973, pp. 187–188 (both cited in Frank M. Snowden, Jr., *Before Color Prejudice*, Harvard University Press, Cambridge, Mass., 1983, pp. 96–97).
12. C. Stern, "The Biology of the Negro," *Scientific American*, 191, 4 (1957), p. 85 (cited in Frank M. Snowden, Jr., *Blacks in Antiquity*, Harvard University Press, Cambridge, Mass., 1970, pp. 195, 329–330).
13. Dmitri I. Gulia, *Istoria Abkhazii*, Narkompros Abkhazii, Tbilisi, 1925 (cited in *Dmitri Gulia: Stikhotvorenniya I Poemi*, Izdatelstvo "Sovyetskii Pisatel," 1974, p. 25).

CHAPTER 11

1. Manetho, *Aegyptiaca* (W. G. Waddell, ed. and trans.), Frs 32, 34–6, Loeb Classical Library, London, 1940, pp. 64–73 (cited in Bernal, 1991, p. 197).
2. Ibid.
3. Ian Shaw and Paul Nicholson, *The British Museum Dictionary of Ancient Egypt*, British Museum Press, London, 1995, p. 260.
4. Grimal (1992), p. 166.
5. Bernal (1991), p. 189; also Grimal (1992), p. 168.
6. Emily T. Vermeuhle, "The World Turned Upside Down," *Black Athena Revisited* (Mary R. Lefkowitz and Guy Maclean Rogers, eds.), University of North Carolina Press, Chapel Hill, NC, 1996, pp. 269–279.
7. Sir Alan Gardiner, *Egypt of the Pharaohs*, Oxford University Press, Oxford, England, 1961, p. 126.
8. Frank J. Yurco, "Were the Egyptians Black or White?" *Biblical Archaeology Review*, September/October 1989, vol. 15, no. 5, p. 27.
9. Gardiner (1961), p. 126.
10. Grimal (1992), p. 138.
11. Ibid.
12. Yurco (1989), p. 27.

CHAPTER 12

1. Gardiner (1961), p. 125.
2. David M. Rohl, *Pharaohs and Kings: A Biblical Quest*, Crown, New York, p. 335.
3. Grimal (1992), p. 181.
4. Yurco (1996), p.73.
5. Bernal (1991), p. 225.

6. J. E. Dayton, "Geology, Archaeology and Trade," in *Interaction and Acculturation in the Mediterranean: Proceedings of the Second Congress of Mediterranean Pre- and Protohistory* (J. G. P. Best and N. M. W. de Vries, eds.), Amsterdam 19–23 November 1980, vol. 2, Amsterdam: Fruner, p. 155 (cited in Bernal, 1991, p. 227).
7. Grimal (1992), p. 165.
8. Yurco (1996), p. 74.
9. Bernal (1991), pp. 224–225.
10. Yurco (1996), p. 74.
11. William Y. Adams, "The First Colonial Empire: Egypt in Nubia, 3200–1200 B.C.," *Comparative Studies in Society and History*, vol. 26, Cambridge University Press, Cambridge, 1984, p. 44.
12. William Y. Adams, *Nubia: Corridor to Africa*. London: Allen Lane & Unwin; Princeton, NJ: Princeton University Press, 1984, pp. 176–181 (cited in Bernal, 1991, p. 206).
13. Bernal (1991), p. 206.
14. Gardiner (1961), p. 132.
15. Ibid., p. 190.
16. Miriam Lichtheim, *Ancient Egyptian Literature*, vol. 1, University of California Press, Berkeley, CA, 1975, p. 223.
17. Frank J. Yurco, "Black Athena: An Egyptological Review," *Black Athena Revisited* (Mary R. Lefkowitz and Guy MacLean Rogers, eds.), The University of North Carolina Press, Chapel Hill, NC, 1996, p. 73.
18. Bernal (1991), p. 191.
19. Grimal (1992), p. 166.
20. Bernal (1991), p. 191.
21. Grimal (1992), pp. 168–169.
22. Shaw and Nicholson (1995), p. 260.
23. William Foxwell Albright, *The Archaeology of Palestine*, rev. ed., Penguin, London, 1960, p. 85 (cited in Bernal, 1991, p. 191).

CHAPTER 13

1. Bernal (1991), p. 235.
2. Yurco (1996), p. 73.
3. Bernal (1991), pp. 188–189.
4. Yurco (1996), p. 73.
5. Bernal (1991), pp. 233–234.
6. Ibid., p. 232.
7. Ibid., p. 231.
8. Genesis 4:22.
9. David Marshall Lang, *The Georgians*, Thames and Hudson, Bristol, England, 1966, p. 49; and Bernal (1991), p. 231.
10. Ibid.
11. Grimal (1992), pp. 165–166.
12. Braund (1994), p. 10.
13. Lang (1966), p. 49.
14. Ibid.

CHAPTER 14

1. Michael Grant, *Cleopatra*, Barnes & Noble, New York, 1972, p. 8.
2. Bernal (1991), p. 219.

3. D. M. Lang, *Armenia: Cradle of Civilization*, 2nd ed., Allen & Unwin, London, 1978, p. 76 (cited in Bernal, 1991, p. 229).
4. Ibid., p. 242.
5. J. Mellaart, "The End of the Early Bronze Age in Anatolia and the Aegean," *American Journal of Archaeology* 62, p. 10, 1958 (cited in Bernal, 1991, p. 222).
6. Bernal (1991), p. 227.
7. Ibid., pp. 240–241.
8. Diodorus I.28 (C. H. Oldfather, trans.).
9. Bernal (1991), p. 120.
10. Herodotus, II, 100–110 (de Sélincourt, trans.).
11. D. Wildung, *Sesostris und Amenemhet: Agypten im Mittleren Reich*. Freibourg: Office du Livre; Munich: Hirmer Verlag, 1984, pp. 175–176, plates 150–151 (cited in Bernal, 1991, p. 242); and Armayor (1980), pp. 68–69.
12. Armayor (1980), pp. 68–69.
13. Bernal (1991), p. 242.
14. Ibid., p. 202.
15. Ibid., p. 227.
16. Ibid.
17. Ibid., p. 230.
18. Ibid.
19. Ibid., p. 229.
20. C. F. A. Schaeffer, *Stratigraphie Comparée et Chronologie de l'Asie Occidentale*, Oxford University Press, Oxford, England, 1948, pp. 544–545 (cited in Bernal, 1991, p. 229).
21. Bernal (1991), pp. 229–230.
22. Ibid., p. 273.

CHAPTER 15

1. Peter Sagal, "Thriller: Me and Michael Jackson," *The New Republic*, March 30, 1992, vol. 206, no. 13, p. 12.
2. Diop (1974), p. 51.
3. Lefkowitz (1996), p. 127.
4. Ibid.
5. George G. M. James, *Stolen Legacy*, United Brothers Communications Systems, Newport News, Va., 1989 (originally published in 1954), pp. 1, 7.
6. Ibid., p. 154.
7. Ibid., p. 31.
8. Lefkowitz (1996), p. 94.
9. Roger G. Kennedy, *Hidden Cities: The Discovery and Loss of Ancient North American Civilization*, The Free Press, New York, 1994, pp. 228–231.
10. Ibid., p. 12.
11. Ibid., p. 19.
12. Margaret S. Drower, *Flinders Petrie: A Life in Archaeology*, The University of Wisconsin, Madison, Wis., 1985, pp. 28–31, 70.
13. Hancock and Bauval (1996), pp. 88–91, 94–95.
14. Abraham Pais, *Subtle Is the Lord, The Science and Life of Albert Einstein*, Oxford University Press, New York, 1982, p. 131.
15. Win Wenger and Richard Poe, *The Einstein Factor*, Prima Publishing, Rocklin, CA, 1996, pp. 11–12.

CHAPTER 16

1. Evan Hadingham, "A Nova Crew Strains and Chants to Solve the Obelisk Mystery," *Smithsonian*, January 1997, p. 25.
2. Martin Short, *Inside the Brotherhood: Further Secrets of the Freemasons*, Dorset Press, New York, 1989, p. 85.
3. Ibid., p. 86.
4. Ibid.
5. Michael Baigent and Richard Leigh, *The Temple and the Lodge*, Arcade Publishing/Little, Brown, New York, 1989, p. 262.
6. Short (1989), p. 86.
7. Ibid., p. 261.
8. Robert Hieronimus, *America's Secret Destiny: Spiritual Vision and the Founding of a Nation*, Destiny Books, Rochester, VT, 1989, p. 53.
9. Ibid., p. 58.
10. John J. Robinson, *Born in Blood: The Lost Secrets of Freemasonry*, M. Evans, New York, 1989, p. 281.
11. Short (1989), pp. 33–34.
12. Manetho Fr. 11 (Waddell, pp. 41–42).
13. Shaw and Nicholson (1995), pp. 139–140.
14. Geraldine Pinch, *Magic in Ancient Egypt*, British Museum Press, London, 1994, p. 166.
15. Garth Fowden, *The Egyptian Hermes*, Princeton University Press, Princeton, New Jersey, 1986, pp. 32, 50.

CHAPTER 17

1. Ascherson (1995), pp. 68–73.
2. Edith Hamilton, *The Greek Way*, Mentor Books, New York, 1963 (first edition, 1930), p. 29.
3. *The Pythagorean Sourcebook and Library* (Kenneth Sylvan Guthrie, trans., David Fideler, ed.), Phanes Press, Grand Rapids, Mich., 1987, p. 59.
4. Fowden (1986), p. 53.
5. Shaw and Nicholson (1995), p. 174; and Robert Palter, "Black Athena, Afrocentrism, and the History of Science," *Black Athena Revisited* (Mary R. Lefkowitz and Guy Maclean Rogers, eds.), University of North Carolina Press, Chapel Hill, NC, 1996, p. 230.
6. Ibid., p. 248.
7. Barbara Mertz, *Red Land, Black Land: Daily Life in Ancient Egypt*, Peter Bedrick Books, New York, 1990, p. 211.
8. Herodotus, II, 3–4 (Rawlinson, trans.).
9. Herodotus, II, 4, 50 (de Sélincourt, trans.).
10. Herodotus, II, 52 (Rawlinson, trans.).
11. Herodotus, II, 57 (de Sélincourt, trans.).
12. Bernal (1987), p. 104.
13. *Bousiris* 16–23, 28 (cited in Bernal, 1987, p. 104).
14. Aristotle (Metaph. I) (cited in Bernal, 1987, p. 295).

CHAPTER 18

1. *The Pythagorean Sourcebook and Library*, p. 61.
2. Fowden (1986), pp. 58–59.

NOTES

3. Shaw and Nicholson (1995), p. 229.
4. Ibid., p. 286.
5. A. R. David and E. Tapp, eds., *The Mummy's Tale: The Scientific and Medical Investigation of Natsef-Amun, Priest in the Temple at Karnak*, St. Martin's Press, New York, 1992, p. 77.
6. Ibid., p. 74.
7. Mary Lefkowitz, "Lefkowitz on Bernal on Lefkowitz," *Bryn Mawr Classical Review* (Internet edition), June 19, 1994.
8. Pinch (1994), p. 62.
9. Sir E. A. Wallis Budge, *Egyptian Magic*, Wings Books, New York, 1991, pp. 136–141.
10. Shaw and Nicholson (1995), p. 32.
11. Raymond Faulkner, trans., *The Egyptian Book of the Dead*, Chronicle Books, San Francisco, 1994, plate 30.
12. Ibid., p. 153.
13. Ibid., p. 119.
14. Ibid., p. 153.
15. Martin Bernal, "The Afrocentric Interpretation of History: Bernal Replies to Lefkowitz," *Journal of Blacks in Higher Education*, March 31, 1996, p. 86.

CHAPTER 19

1. *The Pythagorean Sourcebook and Library*, p. 19.
2. Ibid., p. 63.
3. A. R. Burn, *The Pelican History of Greece*, Penguin Books, Baltimore, MD, 1974 (first edition 1966), p. 140.
4. *The Pythagorean Sourcebook and Library*, pp. 70, 97.
5. Homer, *The Odyssey* (T. E. Lawrence, trans.), Oxford University Press, Oxford, England, 1991, p. 168.
6. Ibid., pp. 164–165.
7. A. R. Burn (1966), p. 75.
8. Jeremy Black and Anthony Green, *Gods, Demons and Symbols of Ancient Mesopotamia: An Illustrated Dictionary*, University of Texas Press, Austin, 1992, p. 28.
9. Bernal (1987), p. 107.
10. Clement of Alexandria, *Stromateis*, I.15.66(3) (trans. John Ferguson), The Catholic University of America Press, Washington, DC, 1991.
11. Clement, I.15.69(1) (Ferguson, trans.).
12. Strabo, 17.1.29 (G. P. Goold, trans.).
13. Plato, *Phaedrus*, 274C–D (Harold North Fowler, trans.).
14. Guthrie (1987), p. 34.
15. Bernal (1987), p. 106.
16. Herodotus, II, 123 (Rawlinson, trans.).
17. Gay Robins, *Women in Ancient Egypt*, British Museum Press, London, 1993, p. 56.
18. E. A. Wallis Budge, *Osiris and the Egyptian Resurrection*, vol. II, Dover Publications, New York, 1973 (first published in 1911), p. 139.
19. *Book of the Dead* (Faulkner, trans.), plate 27, chapters 82–83, 87–88.
20. Faulkner (1994), p. 153.

CHAPTER 20

1. Diodorus, I, 96, 98.
2. Herodotus, II, 180 (Rawlinson, trans.).

3. James (1954), p. 35.
4. Herodotus, II, 178 (de Sélincourt, trans.).
5. *The Pythagorean Sourcebook and Library*, p. 124.
6. Diodorus, I, 28–29.
7. Ibid., I, 29.
8. Ibid.
9. Ibid.
10. Ibid.

CHAPTER 21

1. Martin Bernal, taped interviews, July 26–27, 1994.
2. Plato, *Timaeus* 21E (R. G. Bury, trans.).
3. Shaw and Nicholson (1995), p. 250.
4. Herodotus, II, 182 (de Sélincourt, trans.).
5. Bernal (1987), pp. 51–53.
6. Ibid., pp. 51–52.
7. Ibid., pp. 51–53.
8. J. D. Ray, "An Egyptian Perspective," *Journal of Mediterranean Archaeology*, June 1990, vol. 3, no. 1, pp. 77–81.
9. Bernal (1991), p. 303.

CHAPTER 22

1. Diodorus, I, 29.
2. Bernal (1991), p. 478.
3. Ibid., pp. 486–487.
4. Ibid., p. 480.
5. Ibid., p. 483.
6. Ibid., p. 482.
7. Ibid., p. 451.
8. Ibid.
9. James B. Pritchard, ed., *The Ancient Near East: An Anthology of Texts and Pictures*, Princeton University Press, Princeton, NJ, 1958, pp. 275–276 (cited in Orlando Patterson, *Freedom: Volume I: Freedom in the Making of Western Culture*, BasicBooks/HarperCollins, New York, 1991, p. 41).
10. Bernal (1991), p. 420.
11. Ibid., p. 426.
12. Ibid., p. 416.
13. David O'Connor, "Egypt and Greece: The Bronze Age Evidence," *Black Athena Revisited* (Mary Lefkowitz and Guy MacLean Rogers, eds.), The University of North Carolina Press, Chapel Hill, NC, 1996, p. 55.
14. Bernal (1991), p. 427.
15. Ibid., p. 435.
16. Ibid., p. 476.
17. Ibid., pp. 477–478.
18. Ibid., p. 418.
19. Ibid., p. 433.
20. O'Connor (1996), p. 59.
21. Grimal (1992), p. 216.
22. Bernal (1991), p. 451.

Chapter 23

1. Werner Keller, *The Bible as History* (William Neil, trans.), Barnes & Noble, New York, 1956, p. 176.
2. Bernal (1987), p. 446.
3. David Rohl, *Pharaohs and Kings: A Biblical Quest*, Crown, New York, 1995, p. 156.
4. Rohl (1995), p. 160.
5. Bibby (1961), pp. 338–339; Bernal (1991), p. 516; Shaw and Nicholson (1995), p. 255.
6. Keller (1956), p. 177.
7. Ibid., p. 176.
8. Steve Vinson, *Egyptian Boats and Ships*, Shire Publications, Buckinghamshire, England, 1994, pp. 35–36; also, Shaw and Nicholson (1995), p. 86
9. Ibid., pp. 20, 25.
10. Lionel Casson, *The Ancient Mariners*, Princeton University Press, Princeton, NJ, 1991, p. 30.
11. Casson (1991), pp. 30–31.
12. Ibid., p. 44.
13. Miriam Lichtheim, *Ancient Egyptian Literature, Vol. II: The New Kingdom*, University of California Press, Berkeley, 1976, p. 14.
14. Shaw and Nicholson (1995), p. 268.
15. George A. Christopoulos and John C. Bastias, editors, *Prehistory and Protohistory*, Ekdotike Athenon, Athens, 1974, pp. 151–152.
16. Ibid., p. 152.
17. Ibid., p. 241.

Chapter 24

1. Miriam Lichtheim, *Ancient Egyptian Literature—Vol. I: The Old and Middle Kingdoms*, University of California Press, Berkeley, 1973, p. 211.
2. Margaret Alice Murray, *The Splendour That Was Egypt*, Philosophical Library, New York, 1949, p. 309.
3. K. A. Kitchen, "The Land of Punt," *The Archaeology of Africa: Food, Metals and Towns* (Thurstan Shaw, Paul Sinclair, Bassey Andah, Alex Okpoko, eds.), Routledge, London, 1993, p. 591.
4. K. A. Kitchen, "Punt and How to Get There," *Orientalia*, vol. 40, 1971, p. 184
5. Kitchen (1993), p. 592.
6. Kitchen (1971), p. 192.
7. Kitchen (1993), p. 591.
8. Ibid., p. 601.
9. Ibid., p. 591.
10. Ibid., p. 587.
11. Ibid., p. 603.
12. Kitchen (1971), p. 188.
13. Kitchen (1993), p. 605.
14. Ibid., pp. 590, 591.
15. Grimal (1992), p. 77.
16. Kitchen (1971), pp. 189–190; Kitchen (1993), p. 608.
17. Kitchen (1993), pp. 602, 604.
18. Rodolfo Fattovich, "The Problem of Punt in the Light of Recent Fieldwork in the Eastern Sudan," *Akten Munchen* 1985 IV (S. Schoske, ed.), Hamburg, 1991, p. 260.
19. Graham Hancock, *The Sign and the Seal*, Crown Publishers, Inc., New York, 1992, p. 141.

20. Kitchen (1971), p. 196.
21. Ibid., p. 195.
22. Lichtheim (1973), p. 152.
23. Bernal (1991), p. 427; Casson (1991), p. 6.
24. Thor Heyerdahl, faxed interview, November, 11 1997.

CHAPTER 25

1. Kitchen (1993), pp. 590–591.
2. Vinson (1994), p. 8.
3. Grimal (1992), p. 360.
4. Herodotus, II, 158 (de Sélincourt, trans.).
5. Ibid., IV, 42.
6. Ibid.

CHAPTER 26

1. James D. Muhly, "Homer and the Phoenicians," *Berytus Archaeological Studies*, vol. 19, 1970, p. 30.
2. Emery (1961) p. 204.
3. Bernal (1991), p. 413.
4. Vinson (1994), p. 15.
5. Gerhard Herm, *The Phoenicians* (Caroline Hillier, trans.), William Morrow, New York, 1975, p. 34.
6. *The Eerdmans Bible Dictionary* (Allen C. Myers, ed.), William B. Eerdmans Publishing Company, Grand Rapids, MI, 1987, p. 405.
7. Lichtheim (1976), p. 226.
8. Michael C. Astour, *Hellenosemitica*, E. J. Brill, Leiden, Netherlands, 1965, p. 106.
9. Ibid., p. 348.
10. 2 Chronicles 8:18 (New International Version).
11. 1 Kings 10:11–12 (New International Version).
12. Rhys Carpenter, "Phoenicians in the West," *American Journal of Archaeology*, vol. 62, 1958, p. 35.
13. Ibid., p. 36.
14. Sarah P. Morris, *Daidalos and the Origins of Greek Art*, Princeton University Press, Princeton, NJ, 1992, pp. 204–205.
15. Ibid.
16. Herodotus, III, 115 (de Sélincourt, trans.).
17. Ian Cameron, "Early Quests," *Into the Unknown: The Story of Exploration*, National Geographic Society, Washington, DC, 1987, p. 26.
18. B. H. Warmington, *Carthage: A History*, Barnes & Noble, New York, 1993 (first edition 1960), p. 75.
19. Robert F. Marx and Jennifer G. Marx, *In Quest of the Great White Gods*, Crown Publishers, New York, 1992, p. 41.
20. Diodorus, V, 20.
21. Cyrus H. Gordon, *Before Columbus*, Crown, New York, 1971, p. 114.
22. Marx and Marx (1992), pp. 46, 314.
23. Gordon (1971), pp. 120–127.

CHAPTER 27

1. Herm (1975), pp. 27–29.
2. O'Connor (1996), p. 54.

3. Manetho, Fr. 43, p. 91.
4. Grimal (1992), p. 186.
5. Herm (1975), p. 42.
6. Diop (1981), p. 90.
7. Diodorus, I, 23.
8. Bernal (1987), p. 112.
9. Ibid., p. 83.
10. Bernal (1991), p. 474.
11. Ibid., p. 475.
12. Muhly (1970), p. 38.
13. Fitton (1996), p. 21.

CHAPTER 28

1. Diodorus, XX.14.2 (Oldfather, trans.).
2. Bernal (1991), p. 420.
3. Diop (1981), p. 86.
4. Herm (1975), p. 148.
5. Herodotus, III, 19 (de Sélincourt, trans.).
6. Morris (1992), p. 373.
7. Letter K. 137, Baikie, *The Amarna Age* (1926 ed.), p. 366 (cited in Savitri Devi, *Son of the Sun*, Supreme Grand Lodge of A.M.O.R.C., San Jose, CA, 1956, p. 227).
8. Casson (1991), p. 32.
9. Letter CLXV (W.84), Sir Flinders Petrie, *History of Egypt* (ed. 1899), vol. II, p. 292 (cited in Devi, 1956, p. 223).
10. Bernal (1991), p. 427.
11. Ibid., p. 426.
12. Herm (1975), p. 146.
13. Ibid.
14. A. B. C. Whipple, *To the Shores of Tripoli*, William Morrow, New York, 1991, pp. 46–47.
15. Ibid., pp. 56–57.
16. Stanley M. Burstein, "Greek Contact with Egypt and the Levant: Ca. 1600–500 B.C. An Overview," *The Ancient World* 27.1 (1996).

CHAPTER 29

1. Lefkowitz (1996), p. 145.
2. James (1989), pp. 83, 89.
3. Plato, *Euthyphro*, 11c–d (Harold North Fowler, trans.), Harvard University Press, Cambridge, MA, 1914, p. 41.
4. Diodorus, IV, 76.
5. Morris (1992), p. 259.
6. Diodorus, I, 97.
7. Ibid.
8. Ibid.
9. Herodotus, II, 148 (de Sélincourt, trans.).
10. Grimal (1992), p. 179.
11. Morris (1992), pp. 246–247.
12. Ibid., p. 248.
13. Diodorus, I, 97.

14. Ibid., I, 98.
15. Morris (1992), p. 242.
16. Dimitri Meeks and Christine Favard-Meeks, *Daily Life of the Egyptian Gods*, Cornell University Press, Ithaca and London, 1996, p. 125.
17. John Boardman, *Greek Art*, Praeger, New York, 1973, pp. 65–66.
18. Donald E. Strong, *The Classical World*, McGraw-Hill, New York, 1965, p. 37.
19. Morris (1992), p. 195.
20. Ibid., pp. 258–259.
21. Ibid., p. 257.
22. Ibid., pp. 257–259.

CHAPTER 30

1. Stephen Knight, *The Brotherhood*, Dorset Press, Newton Lower Falls, MA, 1984, p. 18.
2. Baigent and Leigh (1989), p. 155.
3. Ibid., p. 18.
4. Short (1989), p. 32.
5. Baigent and Leigh (1989), p. 118.
6. Ibid.
7. Robinson (1989), p. 179.
8. Ibid.
9. Baigent and Leigh (1989), p. 175.
10. Ibid., figs. 23–24.
11. Nigel Pennick, *The Ancient Science of Geomancy*, Thames and Hudson, London, 1979, p. 105.
12. John Michell, *The New View Over Atlantis*, Harper & Row, San Francisco, 1986, p. 51.
13. *The Quest of the Holy Grail* (P. M. Matarasso, trans.), Penguin Books, New York, 1969, p. 9.
14. Pennick (1979), p. 130.
15. Ibid., pp. 127–128.
16. Ibid., p. 136.
17. Ibid., p. 137.
18. Michell (1986), p. 174.
19. Ibid., p. 189.
20. Baigent and Leigh (1989), p. 133.
21. *The Pythagorean Sourcebook and Library*, p. 34.
22. Baigent and Leigh (1989), p. 133.
23. Ibid.
24. *The Pythagorean Sourcebook and Library*, p. 34.
25. Ibid.
26. Ibid.
27. Ibid.
28. Baigent and Leigh (1989), p. 138.
29. Plato, *Timaeus*, 69 C (R. G. Bury, trans.), Harvard University Press, Cambridge, MA, 1929, p. 179.
30. Ibid., 28 C, p. 51.

CHAPTER 31

1. Sir E. A. Wallis Budge, *The Gods of the Egyptians*, Vol. 1, Dover Publications, New York, 1969 (originally 1904), pp. 500–501.
2. Shaw and Nicholson (1995), pp. 230, 140.
3. Ibid., p. 230.

4. Herodotus, II, 99 (de Sélincourt, trans.).
5. Ibid.
6. Morris (1992), pp. 93–94; also Michael Wood, *In Search of the Trojan War*, Facts on File Publications, New York, 1985, p. 177.
7. Herodotus, II, 35 (de Sélincourt, trans.).
8. Ibid., II, 109.
9. Palter (1996), p. 231.
10. Shaw and Nicholson (1995), p. 174; also Palter (1996), p. 232.
11. Ibid., p. 229.
12. Ibid., pp. 232–233.
13. Ibid., p. 232.
14. Diodorus, I, 96 (Oldfather, trans.).
15. Palter (1996), p. 229.
16. Henri Frankfort, *Kingship and the Gods*, The University of Chicago Press, Chicago, 1948, p. 90.
17. Fowden (1986), p. 57.
18. Ibid., p. 58.
19. Shaw and Nicholson (1995), p. 12.
20. Ibid., p. 42.
21. Boardman (1973), pp. 60–61.
22. Lichtheim (1973), p. 51.
23. Ibid., pp. 54–55.

CHAPTER 32

1. Robinson (1989), pp. 218–222.
2. Baigent and Leigh (1989), pp. 129, 278.
3. 2 Samuel 5:11 (New International Version).
4. Eilat Mazar, "Excavate King David's Palace!" *Biblical Archaeology Review*, January/February 1997, vol. 23, no. 1, p. 57.
5. 1 Kings 5:6 (New International Version).
6. 1 Kings 6:7 (New International Version).
7. 2 Chronicles 2:1, 3, 7, 12–13 (New International Version).
8. 2 Chronicles 3:17, 4:11–12 (New International Version).
9. Robert Macoy, *A Dictionary of Freemasonry*, Bell Publishing, New York, 1989, pp. 350–351.
10. Carpenter (1958), p. 36.
11. Lichtheim (1976), p. 224.
12. Ibid., p. 227.
13. Ibid.
14. Ibid.
15. Palter (1996), pp. 247–248.

CHAPTER 33

1. Josephus, *Contra Apionem* I.28, cited in Bernal (1991), p. 6.
2. Keller (1956), p. 264.
3. Warmington (1960), p. 238.
4. Keller (1956), p. 265.
5. Aharon Kempinski, "From Death to Resurrection," *Biblical Archaeology Review*, September/October 1995, p. 59.

6. Morris (1992), p. 130.
7. Judges 2:11–13 (New International Version).
8. Morris (1992), p. 84.
9. Ibid., p. 85.
10. Ibid., p. 87.
11. Ibid., p. 83.
12. Ibid., pp. 79–80.
13. Ibid., p. 80.
14. Ibid., pp. 87, 96.
15. Sarah P. Morris, "The Legacy of Black Athena," *Black Athena Revisited* (Lefkowitz and Rogers, eds.), The University of North Carolina Press, Chapel Hill, NC, 1996, p. 170.
16. Morris (1992), p. 93.
17. Ibid., pp. 93–94.
18. Herodotus, II, 99 (de Sélincourt, trans.).
19. Morris (1992), p. 360.
20. Simon Hornblower and Antony Strawforth, eds., *The Oxford Classical Dictionary*, Oxford University Press, Oxford, England, 1996, p. 682.
21. Morris (1992), pp. 77–78.
22. Martin Bernal, taped interview, October 29, 1997.
23. Ibid., p. 76.
24. Ibid., p. 47.
25. Ibid., p. 80.
26. Ibid., p. 99.
27. George Hart, *Egyptian Myths*, British Museum Press, London, 1990, p. 62.
28. Diodorus, I, 97.

CHAPTER 34

1. Robinson (1989), p. 66.
2. Baigent and Leigh (1989), pp. 10–11.
3. Graham Hancock, *The Sign and the Seal*, Crown Publishers, New York, 1992, p. 100.
4. Ibid., pp. 94–95.
5. Baigent and Leigh (1989), p. 43.
6. Ibid., p. 46.
7. Ibid., p. 48.
8. Pennick (1979), p. 122.
9. Hancock (1992), p. 100.
10. Ibid., p. 102.
11. Ibid.
12. Ibid., pp. 99–102.
13. Baigent and Leigh (1989), p. 136.
14. Jean Markale, *King Arthur: King of Kings* (Christine Hauch, trans.), Gordon and Cremonesi, London, 1977, p. 150.
15. Markale (1977), p. 150.
16. Taichi Sakaiya (George Fields and William Marsh, trans.), *The Knowledge-Value Revolution*, Kodansha International, New York, 1985, p. 188.
17. Baigent and Leigh (1989), p. 80.
18. Ibid., p. 78.
19. Ibid.

CHAPTER 35

1. Baigent and Leigh (1989), figs. 18–19.
2. Ibid., p. 112.
3. Ibid.
4. Timothy Gantz, *Early Greek Myth*, vol. I, The Johns Hopkins University Press, Baltimore, MD, 1993, p. 262.
5. Morris (1992), p. 260.
6. Baigent and Leigh (1989), p. 5.
7. Ibid., p. 9.
8. Ibid., p. 65.
9. Ibid., pp. 29–30.
10. Ibid., pp. 34–37.
11. Ibid., p. 116.
12. Ibid., p. 115.
13. Ibid.
14. Morris (1992), p. 196.
15. Hornblower and Strawforth (1996), p. 425.
16. Morris (1992), pp. 195–196, figs. 8a, b.
17. Meeks and Favard-Meeks (1996), p. 125.
18. Diodorus, III.4.1 (Oldfather, trans.).

CHAPTER 36

1. Genesis 4:10–12 (New International Version).
2. Ibid., 4:17–22.
3. Patrick Tierney, *The Highest Altar: The Story of Human Sacrifice*, Viking Penguin, New York, 1989, p. 410.
4. Ibid., p. 11.
5. Ibid., pp. 410–412.
6. Genesis 4:15 (New International Version).
7. Mircea Eliade, *Patterns in Comparative Religion*, Meridien/World Publishing, New York, 1963, p. 246.
8. Genesis 11:5–8 (New International Version).
9. *The Eerdmans Bible Dictionary* (1987), p. 337.
10. Hancock (1992), pp. 183–187.
11. Ibid., p. 182.
12. Ibid., p. 181.
13. *The Book of Enoch the Prophet*, VIII:1–2 (Richard Laurence, trans. 1883), Wizard's Bookshelf, San Diego, 1983, pp. 7–8.

CHAPTER 37

1. Manetho, *Aegyptiaca* I, Fr. 1, pp. 3, 17.
2. Diodorus, I.15.4–5.
3. Ibid., I.14.1.
4. Shaw and Nicholson (1995), p. 134.
5. Lichtheim (1973), pp. 37–38.
6. Hugh Thomas, *Conquest: Montezuma, Cortés, and the Fall of Old Mexico*, Simon & Schuster, New York, 1993, p. 25.
7. Tierney (1989), p. 10.

8. Emery (1961), p. 139.
9. Shaw and Nicholson (1995), p. 266.
10. Ibid., p. 103.
11. Tierney (1989), p. 21.
12. A. Haas, *Rugensche Sagen und Marchen*, Johs. Burmeister's Buchhandlung, Stettin, 1903, no. 195, p. 173. Also, Karl Bartsch, *Sagen, Marchen und Gebrauche aus Mecklenburg*, Wilhelm Braumuller, Wein 1879, vol. 1, no. 372, no. 283. And J. W. Wolf, *Hessische Sagen*, Gottingen, Dieterichsche Buchhandlung, 1853, no. 218, pp. 136–137 (trans. D. L. Ashliman, 1997, "Human Sacrifice in Legends and Myths," Internet, http://www.pitt.edu/~sacrifice.html).
13. Tierney (1989), p. 201.
14. 1 Kings 16:34 (New International Version).
15. *The Eerdmans Bible Dictionary*, p. 486.
16. Tierney (1995), p. 372.
17. Hugh Thomas, *Conquest*, Simon & Schuster, New York, 1993, p. 318.
18. Thomas (1993), pp. 318, 328–329.
19. Diodorus, I, 17.
20. Ibid., I, 18–20.
21. Bernal (1991), p. 238.

CHAPTER 38

1. Diodorus, 20, 14.4–5.
2. Tierney (1989), p. 384.
3. Ibid., pp. 394–396.
4. 2 Chronicles 4:11 (New International Version).
5. R. J. Stewart, ed., *The Book of Merlin*, Blandford Press, London, 1987, pp. 21–22.
6. Tierney (1989), p. 173.
7. Robinson (1989), p. 221.
8. 1 Kings 7:13–14 (New International Version).
9. James (1989), p. 92.

CHAPTER 39

1. Thor Heyerdahl, *The Ra Expeditions* (Patricia Crampton, trans.), Doubleday, Garden City, NY, 1971, p. 5.
2. Ibid., p. 99.
3. Lichtheim (1973), p. 212.
4. Ibid., p. 99.
5. Lichtheim (1973), p. 212.
6. Isaiah 18:1–2 (New International Version).
7. Heyerdahl (1971), p. 247.
8. Ibid., p. 5.
9. Marx and Marx (1992), p. 238.
10. Ibid., pp. 187, 235.
11. Kitchen (1971), p. 196.
12. Marx and Marx (1992), p. 239.
13. Vinson (1994), p. 41.
14. Tim Severin, *The Jason Voyage*, F. A. Thorpe, Leicestershire, England, 1985, pp. 13–14.
15. Severin (1985), pp. 206–214.
16. Heyerdahl (1971), p. 239.

17. John Noble Wilford, "In Australia, Signs of Artists Who Predate Homo Sapiens," *New York Times*, September 21, 1996, p. 1.
18. Astour (1965), p. 348.
19. Marx (1992), p. 37.

CHAPTER 40

1. Fitton (1996), pp. 31–32.
2. Leonard Cottrell, *The Bull of Minos*, Holt, Rinehart and Winston, New York, 1953, pp. 14–15.
3. Homer, *The Odyssey* (T. E. Lawrence, trans.), p. 46.
4. Cottrell (1953), p. 33.
5. Ibid., p. 49.
6. Homer, *The Iliad*, IX, 362–435 (Richard Lattimore, trans.), p. 208.
7. Homer, *The Odyssey*, 4, 83–85 (T. E. Lawrence, trans.), p. 46.
8. Burstein (1996), p. 20.

CHAPTER 41

1. Joseph Alsop, *From the Silent Earth*, Harper & Row, New York, 1964 (first edition 1962), p. 87.
2. Geoffrey Bibby, *The Testimony of the Spade*, Alfred A. Knopf, New York, 1956, p. 263.
3. Ibid., p. 263.
4. Ibid., p. 264.
5. Ibid.
6. Ibid., p. 266.
7. Ibid., p. 371.
8. Ibid., p. 266.
9. Heyerdahl (1971), p. 111.

CHAPTER 42

1. Steve Connor, "Were Pharaohs Drug Runners?" *Sunday Times*, London, September 1, 1996.
2. S. Balabanova, F. Parsche, and W. Pirsig, "First Identification of Drugs in Egyptian Mummies," *Naturwissenschaften* 79, 358 (1992).
3. Connor (1996).
4. Ibid.
5. Thomas Moore, "Thor Heyerdahl: Sailing Against the Current," *U.S. News & World Report*, April 2, 1990, vol. 108, no. 13, pp. 55–58.
6. Barry Fell, *America B.C.: Ancient Settlers in the New World*, Pocket Books/Simon & Schuster, New York, 1976, p. 85.
7. Ivan Van Sertima, *They Came Before Columbus: The African Presence in Ancient America*, Random House, New York, 1976, p. 21.
8. Van Sertima (1976), p. 22.
9. Ibid., pp. 262–263.
10. Ibid., pp. 31, 269.
11. Ibid., p. 324.
12. Helge Ingstad, *The Norse Discovery of America, Vol. II*, Norwegian University Press, Oslo, Norway, 1985; and Anne-Stine Ingstad, *The Norse Discovery of America, Vol. I*, Norwegian University Press, Oslo, Norway, 1985.

CHAPTER 43

1. Strabo, *Geography* 1.3.2, cited in Gordon (1971), p. 41.
2. Kitchen (1971), p. 193.
3. Bibby (1956), p. 265.
4. Ibid., p. 266.
5. Dwight Lee, "The Perpetual Assault on Progress," *St. Croix Review* (October 1991), p. 13.
6. Theodore A. Wertime, "The Furnace Versus the Goat: The Pyrotechnologic Industries and Mediterranean Deforestation in Antiquity, *Journal of Field Archaeology*, vol. 10, 1983, p. 449.
7. Jane C. Waldbaum, *From Bronze to Iron, Studies in Mediterranean Archaeology* (SIMA), Vol. 54, Coronet Books, Goteborg, 1978, p. 67.
8. Ibid., p. 71.
9. Warmington (1960), p. 77.
10. Plato, *Timaeus*, 24 E–25 A.
11. Herodotus, III, 115 (de Sélincourt, trans.).
12. Gunnar Thompson, *American Discovery*, Argonauts Misty Isles Press, Seattle, 1994, p. 159.
13. Diodorus, V, 20 (Oldfather, trans.).
14. Gordon (1971), p. 38.
15. Diodorus, V, 20 (Oldfather, trans.).
16. Gordon (1971), p. 38.
17. Bibby (1956), p. 266.

CHAPTER 44

1. Cottrell (1953), p. 82.
2. Morris (1992), p. 165.
3. Thucydides, *The Peloponnesian War*, I.6 (Richard Crawley and R. Feetham, trans.); *Great Books of the Western World*, vol. 6. (Mortimer J. Adler, ed.), Encyclopedia Britannica, Inc. Chicago, 1952.
4. Ibid., I.4, 8.
5. Hans Georg Wunderlich, *The Secret of Crete* (Richard Winston, trans.), Macmillan, New York, 1974.
6. Cottrell (1953), p. 179.
7. Morris (1992), pp. 195–196, figs. 8a, b.
8. Ibid., p. 75.
9. Ibid., p. 170.
10. Bernal (1991), p. 76.
11. Cottrell (1953), p. 184.
12. Ibid.
13. Diodorus, I, 28 (Oldfather, trans.).
14. Ibid.
15. Cottrell (1953), p. 184.
16. Bernal (1991), p. 172.
17. Budge (1904), vol. 2, p. 346.
18. Shaw and Nicholson (1995), p. 35.
19. Budge (1904), vol. 2, p. 348.
20. Ibid., pp. 347–348.
21. Bernal (1991), p. 172.
22. Cottrell (1953), p. 185.

23. Bernal (1991), p. 185.
24. Diodorus, I, 61 (Oldfather, trans.).
25. Morris (1992), p. 187.

CHAPTER 45

1. Gordon (1971), p. 16.
2. Astour (1965), p. 344.
3. Ibid., p. 329.
4. Ibid., p. 328.
5. Cyrus H. Gordon, *The Ancient Near East*, W. W. Norton, New York, 1965, p. 21.
6. Astour (1965), pp. 346–347.
7. Cyrus Gordon, "The Decipherment of Minoan," *Natural History*, November 1963, pp. 22–31.
8. Bernal (1987), p. 419.
9. Gordon (1970), pp. 68–69.
10. Ibid., pp. 120–127.
11. Ibid., p. 179.
12. Ibid., pp. 89–92.
13. Ibid., pp. 135–138.
14. Ibid., p. 26.
15. Ibid., p. 22.
16. Ibid., pp. 22, 128–129.
17. Ibid., p. 29.
18. Ibid., pp. 128–129.

CHAPTER 46

1. Peter Throckmorton, "Oldest Known Shipwreck Yields Bronze Age Cargo," *National Geographic*, May 1962, p. 707.
2. Bernal (1991), p. 466.
3. Ibid.
4. George F. Bass, "Oldest Known Shipwreck Reveals Splendors of the Bronze Age," *National Geographic*, vol. 172, no. 6, December 1987, p. 709.
5. Ibid., p. 714.
6. Ibid., pp. 719–720.
7. Ibid., p. 726.
8. Bibby (1956), p. 263.
9. Bass (1987), pp. 723–726.

CHAPTER 47

1. Baigent and Leigh (1989), p. 55.
2. Ibid.
3. Ibid., pp. 55–56.
4. Morris (1992), p. 92.
5. Ibid., p. 96.
6. Ibid., p. 193.
7. Ibid., pp. 142–144.
8. Diodorus, V, 48 (Oldfather, trans.).

9. Morris (1992), p. 142.
10. Herodotus, III, 37 (de Sélincourt, trans.).
11. Gordon (1970), p. 46.
12. Ibid., p. 106.
13. Ibid., p. 46.
14. Morris (1992), pp. 143–144.
15. Ibid., p. 144.
16. Bass (1987), p. 699.
17. Diop (1981), p. 90.
18. Bernal (1991), pp. 427, 420.
19. Ibid., pp. 415–416.
20. Ibid., p. 427.
21. Lionel Casson, *The Ancient Mariners*, Princeton University Press, Princeton, NJ, 1991 (first edition 1959), 1991, p. 6.
22. Hinrich B. Semann, "Thor Heyerdahl Goes in Search of the Phoenicians in Morocco," *Deutsche Presse-Agentur*, May 1, 1996.

CHAPTER 48

1. Herodotus, IV, 45 (de Sélincourt, trans.).
2. Morris (1992), pp. 98, 176.
3. Astour (1965), p. 128.
4. Bernal (1991), p. 93
5. Astour (1965), p. 130.
6. Ibid., p. 129.
7. Ibid., p. 135.
8. Ibid., p. 132.
9. Ibid., p. 153.
10. Ibid., p. 137.
11. Emily Vermeule, *Aspects of Death in Early Greek Art and Poetry*, Berkeley, 1979, 69–82 (cited in Stanley Burstein, "The Debate Over Black Athena," *Scholia*, 5, 1996).
12. Homer, *The Odyssey* (T. E. Lawrence, trans.), pp. 164–165.
13. Diodorus, I, 29 (Oldfather, trans.).
14. C. Kerényi, *Eleusis* (Ralph Manheim, trans.), Schocken Books, New York, 1977, p. 14.
15. William Foxwell Albright, *From the Stone Age to Christianity*, Doubleday, New York, 1957, pp. 216–217.
16. V. Bérard, *Les Phéniciens et L'Odyssée*, 2 vols., Librairie Armand Colin, Paris, 1902–1903 (cited in Bernal, 1987, p. 381). Also, Astour (1965), p. xiv.
17. Sarah Morris, "Greece and the Levant," *Journal of Mediterranean Archaeology*, vol. 3, no. 1, June 1990, p. 62; also Morris (1992), p. 141.

CHAPTER 49

1. Apollodoros, *The Library*, 2.1.4 (Sir James George Frazer, trans.).
2. Pausanias, *Description of Greece*, II, 38.4 (W. H. S. Jones, trans.), Harvard University Press, Cambridge, MA, 1918.
3. Bernal (1991), pp. 500–501.
4. Pausanias, IV, 35.2 (Levi. vol. II, p. 187, trans.), cited in Bernal (1991), p. 112.
5. Apollodoros, 2.1.4.

6. Herodotus, II, 171 (de Sélincourt, trans.).
7. Euripides, *Archelaos* (lost) fragment, quoted in Strabo, V, 2.4., quoted in Bernal (1987), p. 79.
8. Bernal (1991), pp. 418–423, 433.
9. Manetho, *Aegyptiaca*, Fr. 50 (Waddell, trans.).
10. Ibid., p. 148.
11. Ibid.
12. Lefkowitz (1996), pp. 18–19.
13. Apollodoros, 2.1.3–4.
14. Apollodoros, 2.1.5.
15. Apollodoros, 2.1.3.
16. Herodotus, II, 41 (de Sélincourt, trans.).
17. Herodotus, VI, 53 (de Sélincourt, trans.).
18. Ibid., 55.
19. Snowden (1970), p. 157.
20. Plato, *Menexenos* 245d (Jowett, trans.), quoted in Morris (1992), p. 362.

CHAPTER 50

1. Manetho, Fr. 50, p. 105.
2. Diodorus, I, 28. 1–4.
3. Cottrell (1953), p. 184.
4. Christopoulos and Bastias (1974), p. 118.
5. Cottrell (1953), p. 184.
6. Michael A. Hoffman, *Egypt Before the Pharaohs*, Dorset Press, New York, 1979, pp. 295–298.
7. Thucydides, *The Peloponnesian War* I, 8 (Crawley and Feetham, trans.).
8. Christopoulos and Bastias (1974), pp. 107–108.

CHAPTER 51

1. Severin (1985), pp. 202–203.
2. Apollonius Rhodius, *The Voyage of Argo* [*Argonautica* I, 229–230] (E. V. Rieu, trans.), Penguin Books, New York, 1959, p. 41.
3. Pausanias, IX, 36, 4 (Jones, trans.).
4. Severin (1985), p. 385.
5. Ibid., pp. 353–354.
6. Christopoulos and Bastias (1974), pp. 218, 384.
7. Pausanias, 9.38.6–8 (Jones, trans.).
8. Christopoulos and Bastias (1974), pp. 319–322.
9. Strabo, 9.2.18 (Jones, trans.).
10. Bernal (1991), p. 134.
11. Ibid., p. 145.
12. Tom Weber, "Kon-Tiki Author Thor Heyerdahl Speaks at UM," *Bangor Daily News*, April 14, 1997.
13. Herodotus, II, 149 (de Sélincourt, trans.).
14. Ibid., 108.
15. Hoffman (1979), p. 314.
16. Ibid., p. 312.

CHAPTER 52

1. Bernal (1991), p. 106.
2. Herodotus, II, 43 (de Sélincourt, trans.).
3. Diodorus, I, 24.5.

4. Ibid., I, 24.3.
5. Bernal (1991), p. 111.
6. Herm (1975), p. 175.
7. Herodotus, II, 43 (de Sélincourt, trans.).
8. Apollodoros, 2.4.3.
9. Snowden (1970), pp. 153–154.
10. Snowden (1983), p. 77.
11. Apollodoros, 2.5.5.
12. Gantz (1993), vol. I, p. 409; and Bernal (1991), p. 117.
13. Apollodoros, 2.1.4.
14. Homer, *Iliad*, IV, 171 (Lattimore, trans.).
15. Theodore Spyropoulos, *Ampheion: Examination and Study of the Ampheion Monument of Thebes* (private translation by Yanni Simonides and Zoe A. Pappas, 1997), Sparta, Greece, 1981, p. 137.
16. Bernal (1987), p. 86.
17. Apollodoros, 2.1.4.
18. Bernal (1987), p. 96.

CHAPTER 53

1. Pausanias, 9.12.2 (Jones, trans.).
2. Homer, *Odyssey* (T. E. Lawrence, trans.), p. 159.
3. Pausanias, 9.5.8 (Jones, trans.); and Bernal (1991), p. 129.
4. Bernal (1991), p. 129.
5. Hekataios (fragment), Jacoby (1923–1929, I. Fr. 119), cited in Bernal (1991), p. 129.
6. Pausanias, 9.5.1 (Jones, trans.).
7. Ibid., 9.17.4–5.
8. Bernal (1991), p. 130.
9. Ibid., pp. 22–32.
10. Theodore Spyropoulos, "Egyptian Influence Over Prehistoric Greece," unpublished, 1996, p. 3.
11. Theodore Spyropoulos Sparta; (1981), p. 118.
12. Bernal (1991), p. 132.

CHAPTER 54

1. Spyropoulos (1997), pp. 72ff, 90.
2. Ibid., p. 110.
3. Ibid., p. 106.
4. Ibid., p. 132.
5. Pausanias, 9.25.7 (Jones, trans.).
6. Spyropoulos (1996), p. 6.
7. Bernal (1991), p. 134.
8. Ibid.
9. Spyropoulos (1996), p. 5.
10. Spyropoulos (1981), pp. 133–134; also, Spyropoulos (1996), p. 5.
11. Spyropoulos (1996), p. 5.
12. Bernal (1991), pp. 138–139.
13. Bernal (1991), pp. 135–137.
14. Ibid., p. 6; also Spyropoulos (1996), p. 6.
15. Spyropoulos (1996), p. 6.

16. Emily Vermeule, *Greece in the Bronze Age*, The University of Chicago Press, Chicago, 1972, pp. 26–27.
17. Spyropoulos (1981), p. 136.
18. Spyropoulos (1996), p. 7.

CHAPTER 55

1. Alsop (1962), p. 150.
2. Abbé Barthélemy, *The Voyage of the Young Anarchasis*, 1789, p. 62 (cited in Bernal, 1987, p. 186).
3. Connop Thirlwall, *A History of Greece*, 8 vols., London, 1835–1844 (cited in Bernal, 1987, p. 326).
4. Gaston Maspero, *Études de mythologie et d'archéologie égyptiennes*, Paris, 1893 (cited in Bernal, 1987, p. 260).
5. Bernal (1987), p. 8.
6. Ibid., p. 402.
7. Ibid., p. xiv.
8. John E. Rexine, "Was Athena Really Black?" *The Mediterranean*, Winter–Spring 1992, p. 58.
9. Morris (1996), p. 174.
10. Edith Hall, "When Is Myth Not a Myth?: Bernal's 'Ancient Model,'" in *Black Athena Revisited* (Lefkowitz and Rogers, eds.), p. 333.

CHAPTER 56

1. Robert B. Edgerton, *Like Lions They Fought*, The Free Press, New York, 1988, p. 14.
2. Ibid., p. 18.
3. Ibid., pp. 180–181.
4. Ibid., pp. 44, 116a (photo caption).
5. Edgerton (1988), p. 4.
6. Vitruvius, *On Architecture*, VI, I, 3–4 (Frank Granger, trans.), Harvard University Press, Cambridge, MA, 1934.
7. Ibid., VI, I, 9.
8. Ibid.
9. Ibid., VI, I, 10.
10. Ibid., VI, I, 10–11.
11. Aristotle, *Politics*, VII, 7 (Sinclair, trans.), 1962, p. 269 (cited in Bernal, 1987, p. 202).

CHAPTER 57

1. Herodotus, III, 21–22 (de Sélincourt, trans.).
2. Diodorus, III, 2.4 (Oldfather, trans.).
3. Frank M. Snowden, Jr., "The Physical Characteristics of Egyptians and Their Southern Neighbors: The Classical Evidence," *Egypt in Africa* (Theodore Celenko, ed.), Indianapolis Museum of Art/Indianapolis University Press, Indianapolis, 1996, p. 106.

4. Diodorus, III, 8.2 (Oldfather, trans.).
5. Frank M. Snowden, Jr., "Misconceptions About African Blacks in the Ancient Mediterranean World: Specialists and Afrocentrists," *Arion*, vol. 4, no. 1, December 10, 1996, p. 29.
6. Snowden (1983), p. 80.
7. Herodotus, III, 20 (de Sélincourt, trans.).
8. Snowden (1983), p. 77.
9. Snowden (1970), pp. 178–179.
10. Snowden (1996), p. 32.
11. Snowden (1970), pp. 4, 179.
12. Cahill, (1995), p. 23.
13. Snowden (1970), p. 179.
14. Snowden (1983), pp. 93, 99, 184.
15. Ibid., p. 55.
16. Ibid., p. 27.
17. Ibid., pp. 45, 54.
18. Ibid., p. 52.
19. Isaiah 18:2 (cited in Snowden, 1983, p. 45).
20. Strabo, 17.1.54 (Jones, trans.).
21. Snowden (1970), p. 30.
22. Snowden (1983), p. 31.
23. Diodorus, III, 2.4 (Oldfather, trans.).
24. Homer, *Iliad*, 1.423–424 (cited in Snowden, 1970, p. 144).
25. Diodorus, III, 2.2–3 (Oldfather, trans.).
26. Cited in Strabo, 1.2.24 (Jones, trans.).

CHAPTER 58

1. Herodotus, II, 104 (de Sélincourt, trans.).
2. Burkhard Bilger, "The Last Black Classicist," *The Sciences*, March/April 1997, vol. 37, no. 2, p. 17.
3. Frank M. Snowden Jr., "Bernal's 'Blacks,' Herodotus, and Other Classical Evidence," *Arethusa*, Fall 1989, pp. 84–86.
4. Diodorus, III, 2.1, 3.3–4 (Oldfather, trans.).
5. Snowden (1983), p. 52.
6. Herodotus, II, 104 (de Sélincourt, trans.).
7. Aeschylus, *Suppliant Maidens* 720, 743, Perseus Project, Tufts University (Internet), http://hydra.perseus.tufts.edu/cgi-bin/test?lookup-aesch.-supp.
8. Snowden (1983), p. 83.
9. Snowden (1970), p. 157.
10. Snowden (1989), pp. 84–85.
11. Frank J. Yurco, "Two Tomb-Wall Painted Reliefs of Ramesses III and Sety I and Ancient Nile Population Diversity," *Egypt in Africa* (ed. Theodore Celenko), 1996, p. 109.
12. Theodore Celenko and Frank J. Yurco, "Depiction of Humans in African Art," *Egypt in Africa* (ed. Theodore Celenko), 1996, p. 51.
13 Snowden (1989), p. 92.
14. Ibid., p. 90.

Chapter 59

1. Dinesh D'Souza, *The End of Racism*, The Free Press, New York, 1995, p. 38.
2. Ibid., p. 32.
3. Ibid.
4. Benson Bobrick, *Fearful Majesty: The Life and Reign of Ivan the Terrible*, Paragon House, New York, 1987, pp. 110–111.
5. "Gunpowder," *Hutchinson's Encyclopedia Online* (1997).
6. D'Souza (1995), p. 28.
7. Robert Wright, "Quest for the Mother Tongue," *The Atlantic*, April 1991, p. 44.
8. Steven Pinker, *The Language Instinct*, HarperPerennial, New York, 1994, p. 251.
9. D'Souza (1995), pp. 30–31.
10. Giuseppe Sergi, *The Mediterranean Race*, Charles Scribner's Sons, New York, 1901, p. 3.
11. Bernal (1987), p. 227.
12. Sergi (1901), p. 5.
13. Ibid., p. 9.
14. Ibid., pp. 8–9.

Chapter 60

1. Albert Speer, *Inside the Third Reich*, Avon Books, New York, 1970, p. 144.
2. Ibid., p. 144.
3. Adolf Hitler, *Mein Kampf* (Ralph Manheim, trans.), Houghton Mifflin, Boston, 1943 (first edition 1925), p. 408.
4. Speer (1970), p. 144.
5. Sergi (1901), p. 21.
6. Ibid., p. 20.
7. Ibid., pp. 19–20.
8. Lefkowitz (1996), p. 13.
9. "The Week," *National Review*, March 5, 1990, p. 14.
10. D'Souza (1995), p. 28.
11. V. Gordon Childe, *The Aryans*, Barnes & Noble, New York, 1993 (originally 1926), p. 207.
12. Thucydides, I, 12 (Crawley and Feetham, trans.).
13. Alsop (1962), p. 129.
14. Sarah P. Morris, "Daidalos and Kadmos: Classicism and 'Orientalism,'" *Arethusa*, Fall 1989, p. 49.
15. Herodotus, I, 56–57 (de Sélincourt, trans.); Diodorus, IV.37.3–4, 58.6 (Oldfather, trans.).
16. Hitler (1925), p. 393.
17. Speer (1970), p. 141.

Chapter 61

1. Genesis 9:18, 10:6 (New International Version).
2. Sergi (1901), p. 154.
3. Edith R. Sanders, "The Hamitic Hypothesis: Its Origin and Functions in Time Perspective," *The Journal of African History*, Cambridge University Press, vol. 10, no. 4, 1969, p. 522.
4. Ibid.

5. Genesis 9:25–27 (New International Version).
6. Sergi (1901), pp. 154–155.
7. Cyrus H. Gordon, *The Ancient Near East*, W. W. Norton, New York, 1958, p. 41.

CHAPTER 62

1. Ivan Hannaford, *Race: The History of an Idea in the West*, The Johns Hopkins University Press, Baltimore, 1996, p. 207.
2. Stephen Jay Gould, *The Mismeasure of Man*, W. W. Norton, New York, 1996 (first edition, 1981), p. 407.
3. Ibid., pp. 83–86.
4. Ibid., pp. 85–86.
5. Ibid., p. 101.
6. Ibid., p. 86.
7. Ibid., pp. 88–92.
8. Ibid., p. 99.
9. Ibid., p. 96.
10. Ibid., p. 85.
11. S. O. Y. Keita, "Studies and Comments on Ancient Egyptian Biological Relationships," *History in Africa* (ed. David Henige), vol. 20, 1993, p. 133.
12. Ibid., pp. 132–133.
13. Ibid., p. 133.
14. Gould (1996), p. 101.
15. Milford Wolpoff and Rachel Caspari, *Race and Human Evolution*, Simon & Schuster, New York, pp. 91–92.
16. Ibid., p. 91.
17. Keita (1993), p. 133.

CHAPTER 63

1. D. E. Derry, "The Dynastic Race in Egypt," *The Journal of Egyptian Archaeology*, vol. 42, 1956, p. 81.
2. G. Elliot Smith, "The Influence of Racial Admixture in Egypt," *The Eugenics Review*, vol. 7, April 1915–January 1916, p. 174.
3. Ibid., p. 179.
4. Ibid., pp. 177–178.
5. Ibid., pp. 179–180.
6. Derry (1956), p. 81.
7. Keita (1993), p. 29.
8. Smith (1915–1916), p. 168.
9. Ibid., p. 181.
10. Ibid., pp. 181–182.
11. Ibid., p. 182.
12. Ibid.
13. Ibid., p. 183.
14. Josiah C. Nott and George Gliddon, *Types of Mankind*, J. B. Lippincott & Co., Philadelphia, 1865, p. 214.

CHAPTER 64

1. Morris Dees and Steve Fiffer, *Hate on Trial*, Villard Books, Random House, New York, 1993, p. 187.
2. Dees and Fiffer (1993), p. 187; Lauren Tarshis, "The Ugly American," *Scholastic Update*, April 13, 1992, vol. 124, n. 14, p. 2.
3. Dees and Fiffer (1993), p. 206.
4. Seligman (1930), p. 97.
5. Ibid., pp. 97–98.
6. Sir Richard F. Burton, *First Footsteps in East Africa*, Dover Publications, New York, 1987 (first edition, 1856), pp. 75–76.
7. Sanders (1969), p. 528.
8. Seligman (1930), p. 97.
9. Ibid., pp. 157–160.
10. Ibid., p. 161.
11. Ibid., p. 53.
12. Ibid., pp. 19, 96.

CHAPTER 65

1. Arthur M. Schlesinger, Jr., *The Disuniting of America*, Whittle Direct Books, 1991, p. 66.
2. Ibid., p. 41.
3. Ibid., p. 42.
4. Ibid., p. 44.
5. Arthur M. Schlesinger, Jr., private letter to Shomarka O. Y. Keita, July 30, 1992.
6. Schlesinger (1991), p. 76.
7. Ibid., p. 44.
8. Shomarka O. Y. Keita, private letter to Arthur M. Schlesinger, Jr., September 26, 1992.
9. Diodorus, III, 8.2 (Oldfather, trans.).
10. Snowden (1970), p. 8.
11. Warmington (1960), pp. 73–74.
12. Serge Lancel, *Carthage: A History* (Antonia Nevill, trans.), Blackwell Publishers Limited, Oxford, England, 1995, pp. 103–104; Warmington (1960), p. 73.
13. Snowden (1970), p. 112.
14. Diodorus, III, 2.1, 3.3–4 (Oldfather, trans.).

CHAPTER 66

1. Seligman (1930), p. 154.
2. Joseph H. Greenberg, "Languages of Africa," *International Journal of American Linguistics, Part II*, vol. 29, no. 1, January 1963, p. 30.
3. Greenberg (1963), p. 49.
4. Joseph H. Greenberg, taped interview, September 6, 1996.
5. Christopher Ehret, "Ancient Egyptian as an African Language, Egypt as an African Culture," in *Egypt in Africa* (ed. Theodore Celenko), 1996, p. 25.

CHAPTER 67

1. Diodorus, III, 2.1, 3.3–4 (Oldfather, trans.).
2. Ibid., III, 11.

3. Ehret (1996), p. 25.
4. Henri Frankfort, *Kingship and the Gods*, University of Chicago Press, Chicago, 1948, pp. 162–163.
5. Ibid.
6. Ibid., pp. 164–165.
7. Ibid.
8. Ibid., p. 167.
9. Ibid., p. 165.
10. Ehert (1996), p. 25.
11. Mohamed Sahnouni, "Saharan Rock Art," *Egypt in Africa* (ed. Theodore Celenko), 1996, p. 29.
12. Ehert (1996), pp. 25–26.
13. Diodorus, III, 3.4 (Oldfather, trans.).
14. Charles G. Seligman, *Egypt and Negro Africa*, George Routledge and Sons, London, 1934, p. 5.
15. Ammianus Marcellinus, xxviii.5, 14, cited in James G. Frazer, *The Golden Bough: The Roots of Religion and Folklore*, Gramercy Books, New York, 1981 (first edition 1890).
16. Frankfort (1948), p. 57.
17. Seligman (1934), p. 31.
18. Ibid., p. 30.
19. Ibid., p. 52.
20. Frankfort (1948), pp. 82–88.
21. Seligman (1934), pp. 15, 59.
22. E. A. Wallis Budge, *Osiris and the Egyptian Resurrection*, Vol. II, Dover Publications, New York, 1973 (first edition, 1911), p. 104.
23. Budge (1911), vol. II, p. 264.
24. Frankfort (1948), p. 70.
25. Ibid., p. 114.
26. Ibid., p. 89.
27. Lanny Bell, "Ancestor Worship and Divine Kingship in the Ancient Nile Valley," *Egypt in Africa* (ed. Theodore Celenko), 1996, p. 57.
28. Budge (1911), vol. I, p. 211.
29. Bell (1996), p. 58.
30. Chapurukha M. Kusimba, "Animal Deities and Symbols in Africa," in *Egypt in Africa* (ed. Theodore Celenko), 1996, pp. 62–65.
31. Arlene Wolinski, "The Case for Ceremonial Masking in Ancient Egypt," in *Egypt in Africa* (ed. Theodore Celenko), 1996, pp. 71–74; also Lefkowitz (1996), p. 135; Herodotus, II, 60 (de Sélincourt, trans.); Budge (1911), pp. 206–209; Frankfort (1948), p. 85.
32. Shaw and Nicholson (1995), p. 65.
33. Theodore Celenko, "Depiction of Humans in African Art," in *Egypt in Africa* (ed. Theodore Celenko), 1996, pp. 50–54.
34. Diodorus, III, 3.4–5 (Oldfather, trans.).

CHAPTER 68

1. Herodotus, II, 29 (Rawlinson, trans.).
2. Herodotus, II, 29 (de Sélincourt, trans.).

3. Timothy Kendall, "Kingdom of Kush," *National Geographic,* vol. 178, no. 5, November 1990, p. 103.
4. William Y. Adams, "The First Colonial Empire: Egypt in Nubia, 3200–1200 BC," *Comparative Studies in Society and History,* Cambridge University Press, vol. 26, 1984, p. 48.
5. Ibid., pp. 55, 61.
6. Ibid., p. 55.
7. Ibid., p. 57.
8. Ibid., pp. 57, 62.
9. Ibid., p. 36.
10. Ibid., p. 40.
11. Ibid., p. 39.
12. Emily Vermeuhle, "The World Turned Upside Down," *The New York Review of Books,* March 26, 1992, p. 41.

CHAPTER 69

1. Bruce Williams, "The Lost Pharaohs of Nubia," *Archaeology,* September/October 1980, pp. 19–20.
2. Ibid., p. 14. Also, David Roberts, "Out of Africa," *Smithsonian,* June 1993, p. 93.
3. Williams (1980), p. 15.
4. Ibid., p. 14.
5. Ibid., p. 18.

CHAPTER 70

1. Bruce Williams, taped interview, September 7, 1996. All quotations from Williams not otherwise identified are from this interview, or from others conducted August 21 and 27, 1997.
2. Wolpoff and Caspari (1997), p. 91.
3. Bruce Williams, "Forebears of Menes in Nubia," *Journal of Near Eastern Studies,* vol. 46, 1987, p. 21.
4. Ibid.
5. Williams (1980), p. 19.
6. Ibid., p. 21.
7. Boyce Rensberger, "Ancient Nubian Artifacts Yield Evidence of Earliest Monarchy," *New York Times,* March 1, 1979, p. 1.
8. Williams (1987), p. 23.
9. Joseph W. Wegner, "Interaction Between the Nubian A-Group and Predynastic Egypt: The Significance of the Qustul Incense Burner," in *Egypt in Africa* (ed. Theodore Celenko), 1996, p. 98.
10. Lacovara *Egypt in Africa* (ed. Theodore Celenko), 1996, p. 92.

CHAPTER 71

1. Bruce G. Trigger, "Nubian, Negro, Black, Nilotic?" *Africa in Antiquity,* The Brooklyn Museum, 1978, pp. 31–35.
2. David and Tapp (1992), p. 65.
3. Ibid., p. 78.
4. Ibid., p. 166.
5. Richard Neave, taped interview, September 11, 1997.
6. "Two Brothers" exhibit, display plaque, Manchester Museum, Manchester, England, 1996.

7. David and Tapp (1992), p. 164.

CHAPTER 72

1. Walter White, *A Man Called White*, The University of Georgia Press, Athens, GA, 1995 (first edition, 1948), p. 3.
2. Ibid., p. 4.
3. Ibid., p. 3.
4. Lise Funderburg, *Black, White, Other*, William Morrow, New York, 1994, p. 13.
5. Molefi Kete Asante, *Afrocentricity*, Africa World Press, Inc., Trenton, NJ, 1992 (first printing, 1988), p. 97.
6. Paul Starick, "Pols Mold That Tiger to Fit Their Opinions in Race Debate," *New York Post*, April 24, 1997, p. 6.
7. Funderburg (1994), p. 16.
8. Ken Wells, "'Coloreds' Struggle to Find Their Place in a Free South Africa," *Wall Street Journal*, December 6, 1995, p. 1.
9. Bernal (1987), p. 242.

CHAPTER 73

1. C. Loring Brace, with David P. Tracer, Lucia Allen Yaroch, John Robb, Kari Brandt, and A. Russell Nelson, "Clines and Clusters Versus 'Race': A Test in Ancient Egypt and the Case of a Death on the Nile," *Black Athena Revisited* (ed. Lefkowitz and Rogers), 1996, p. 156.
2. Brace et al. (1996), p. 156.
3. Ibid., p. 134.

CHAPTER 74

1. Phillip Bonner, "Were the Pharaohs Blond?" *The Barnes Review*, November 1995, p. 8.
2. Ibid., p. 3.
3. Ibid., p. 7.
4. Ibid.
5. Brace et al. (1996), p. 162.
6. Peggy Anderson, *Great Quotes from Great Leaders*, Great Quotations Publishing Company, Lombard, IL, 1990, p. 39.
7. Brace et al. (1996), p. 131.
8. Ibid., p. 131.
9. Ibid., p. 153.
10. Ibid., p. 140.
11. Ibid., pp. 142–143.
12. Ibid., p. 140.
13. Ibid., p. 158.
14. Ibid., p. 156.

CHAPTER 75

1. Brace et al. (1996), pp. 144–145.
2. Bruce G. Trigger, "Nubian, Negro, Black, Nilotic?" *Africa in Antiquity*, The Brooklyn Museum, 1978, p. 28.
3. Adams (1977), p8 (cited in St. Clair Drake, *Black Folk from Here and There*, Vol. 1, University of California, Los Angeles, 1987, pp. 217–218).

4. Adams (1977), p. 8.
5. S. O. Y. Keita and Rick A. Kittles, "The Persistence of Racial Thinking and the Myth of Racial Divergence," *American Anthropologist,* vol. 99, no. 3, September 1997, p. 534.
6. Shomarka O. Y. Keita, taped interview, August 30, 1993. Unless otherwise indicated, all other remarks of Keita are taken from this or numerous other interviews conducted between 1993 and 1997.
7. J. Lawrence Angel, "Health As a Crucial Factor in the changes from Hunting to Developed Farming in the Eastern Mediterranean," *Paleopathology at the Origins of Agriculture* (eds. Mark Nathan Cohen and George J. Armelagos) Academic Press. Inc., New York, 1984, pp. 66–67.

CHAPTER 76

1. Brace et al. (1996), pp. 158–159.
2. Ibid., p. 147.
3. Ibid.
4. Ibid., p. 156.
5. Ibid., p. 147.
6. Van Sertima (1976), pp. 111–112.
7. Brace et al. (1996), p. 141.
8. Ibid. pp. 142–143.
9. S. O. Y. Keita (1993), p. 145.
10. Brace et al. (1996), p. 145.
11. J. Michael Crichton, "A Multiple Discriminant Analysis of Egyptian and African Negro Crania," *Papers of the Peabody Museum of Archaeology and Ethnology* 57: 45–67 (1966).
12. Crichton (1966), p. 62.

CHAPTER 77

1. S. O. Y. Keita, "Studies and Comments on Ancient Egyptian Biological Relationships," *History in Africa* 20 (1993), p. 130.
2. Keita and Kittles (1997), p. 538: also, Luigi Luca Cavalli-Sforza and Francesco Cavalli-Sforza, *The Great Human Diasporas,* Addison-Wesley, New York, 1995, p. 119.
3. Keita (1993), p. 140.
4. Ibid., p. 134.
5. Ibid., p. 140.
6. Crichton (1966), p. 62.
7. Richard Neave, taped interview, September 11, 1997.
8. David and Tapp (1993), p. 166.
9. Keita and Kittles (1997), p. 536.
10. S. O. Y. Keita, "The Diversity of Indigenous Africans," *Egypt in Africa* (1996), p. 104.
11. S. O. Y. Keita and A. J. Boyce, "The Geographical Origins and Population Relationships of Early Ancient Egyptians," *Egypt in Africa* (1996), p. 23. Also, Keita and Kittles (1997), p. 6.

CHAPTER 78

1. Ann Macy Roth, "Building Bridges to Afrocentrism: A Letter to My Egyptological Colleagues, Part I," *American Research Center in Egypt Newsletter,* no. 167, September 1995, 14.
2. Ibid., pp. 14, 17.

3. Ibid., p. 1.
4. Ibid., p. 16.
5. Ibid., p. 15.
6. "Egypt Says Ramses II Wasn't Black" (Associated Press), *The Washington Post*, March 23, 1989, p. d08.
7. "Black 'White' Man Challenges Federal Race Identity Law," *Jet*, January 1, 1991, p. 8.
8. Soheir A. Morsy, "Beyond Honorary 'White' Classification of Egyptians," *Race* (eds. Steven Gregory and Roger Sanjek), Rutgers University Press, New Brunswick, NJ, 1994, pp. 175–176.
9. John E. Rexine, "Was Athena Really Black?: The Current Attack on the Western Tradition," *The Mediterranean*, Winter–Spring, p. 59.
10. Judith Miller, "Upset by 'Sadat,' Egypt Bars Columbia Films," *New York Times*, February 2, 1984, p. 1.
11. Roth (September 1995), p. 15.
12. Ibid.
13. Roth (December 1995), p. 15.
14. Ibid., p. 15.
15. Ibid.
16. Ibid., p. 14.
17. Roth (September 1995), p. 1.

CHAPTER 79

1. Frank J. Yurco, taped interview, August 8, 1996. All other quotations from Yurco, unless otherwise indicated, are taken from this or other interviews, conducted in 1993–1996.
2. Roth (September 1995), p. 15.
3. Joan P. Wilson, "Objects to a White Nefertiti" (letter), *Biblical Archaeology Review*, May/June 1989, vol. XV, no. 3.
4. "Were the Ancient Egyptians of the Black Race?" (letters), *Biblical Archaeology Review*, September/October 1989, vol. XV, no. 5, pp. 8–12.
5. Frank J. Yurco, "Were the Ancient Egyptians Black or White?" *Biblical Archaeology Review*, September/October 1989, vol. XV, no. 5, pp. 25, 58.
6. Ibid., p. 25.
7. Ibid., p. 24.
8. Ibid., p. 25.
9. Ibid.
10. Ibid., p. 58.
11. Asa G. Hilliard III, "Are Africans African?" in *Egypt in Africa* (ed. Theodore Celenko), 1996, p. 112.
12. Bernal (1991), p. xvii.

CHAPTER 80

1. Colin Renfrew, "Ancient Europe Is Older Than We Thought," *National Geographic*, November 1977, pp. 615, 617.
2. Ibid., p. 615.
3. Ibid., p. 622.
4. Bernal (1991), pp. 209–210.
5. Speer (1970), p. 141.
6. Carleton Putnam, *Race and Reason*, Howard Allen, Cape Canaveral, FL., 1980 (first edition, 1961), p. 37.
7. Hannaford (1996), p. 265.

8. Bernal (1987), p. 344.
9. Hannaford (1996), p. 265.
10. Ibid., p. 266.
11. J. A. Gobineau, *Oeuvres*, vol. I, Pleiades, Paris, 1983, pp. 340–341, cited in Bernal (1987), p. 241.
12. Gould (1996), pp. 380–381.
13. Robert N. Proctor, *Racial Hygiene: Medicine Under the Nazis*, Harvard University Press, Cambridge, MA., 1988, p. 197.
14. Andrew S. Winston, "The Context of Correctness: A Comment on Rushton," *Psychology Publications Online* (Internet), 1996, p. 9. http://www.css.uoguelph.ca/psy/papers/winston/rushton.html
15. Bernal (1987), p. 34.
16. Ibid., pp. 33–35.
17. Winston (1996), p. 9.
18. Ibid.
19. Ibid.
20. Speer (1970), p. 141.
21. Putnam (1961), p. 37.
22. Cavalli-Sforza and Cavalli-Sforza (1995), p. 238.
23. Angel (1984), pp. 66–67.
24. Weber (1997).
25. Gordon (1970), p. 16.

INDEX

A

Aachen, cathedral at, 178
Aakheperkare. *See* Thutmose I
Abdi-Ashirta, 163
Abel, 218, 235
Abimilki of Tyre, 157, 163
Abiram, 227
Abkhazians, black, 55–56, 57–58
Aboul-Ela, Abdel Latif, 478–479
Abraham, Isaac and, 232
Abu, 413
Abu Simbel, temple at, 188
Abydos, 308, 428
Achilles, 17, 96, 293, 362–363
  Agamemnon's bribe, refusal of, 249–250
  Hephaistos and, 201
Achilles Tatius, 354
Acrisios, 303, 327
Adam and Eve, 218, 444
Adams, William Y., 66, 416, 417, 418, 455
Adaptive/non-adaptive traits, 450–451
Aegean islands, 129–130
  Thutmose III, tribute to, 162
Aegean language, 275
Aegyptiaca (Manetho), 59–60
Aelian, 270
Afroasiatic language, 404–405, 458
  cattle-herding, 409
  earliest speakers of, 408
  pottery-making and, 409
Afrocentrism, 393–394
  Brace, C. Loring and, 453
  Egyptologists and, 476–482

Nefertiti, blackness of, 489–490
  one-drop rule and, 441
  as opportunity, 481
  and "true Negroes," 461–462
Agamemnon, 11, 96
  Achilles refusing bribe of, 249–250
  Iphigenia, sacrifice of, 231
Agatharchides of Cnidus, 407
Agathokles, 250
Agenor, 158, 303
Age of Exploration, 17
Agiorgitika, 329
A-Group, 421
  incense burner and, 426
  rock drawings and, 426–427
Aha, 414
Ahab, 227
Ahhotep, 130
Ahmose I, 130, 136
Ahmose II. *See* Amasis
Aigyptos, 299, 303, 304, 352
  forces of, 300
  Memphis, founding of, 306–307
  naming of Egypt, 305–306
Airs, Waters, Places (Hippokrates), 47–48
Aischylos, 57, 303–304
  on Egyptians, 352
Aithiopes, 345, 350, 398, 413
Aithiopika (Heliodoros), 97
Akedah, 232
Akhnaton, 129
  Amarna Letters, 163
Akkadians, 292
Al-Aqsa Mosque, 206

Alasia, 71
Albright, William Foxwell, 68
Al-Dahr, Mohammed Sa'im, 24–25, 34
Alexander the Great, 162
  Lake Kopais and, 313
Alexandria, library at, 22
Algonkian, 403
Alkmene, 317
Al-Mansur, Abu Jaafer Abdullah, 146
Alpheios River, 318
Altai Mountains, 50
Amarna Letters, 163
Amarna period, 165–166
Amasis
  Athena/Neit, use of, 121
  Delphic oracle and, 114–115, 122
  Greece, friendship to, 115–116
  Phoenician mercenaries, 163
  Rhodes, temple of, 299–300
Amazons, 44–45
  Bobrinskoy, Count on, 49
  Davis-Kimball, Jeannine on, 49–50
Amber, 15–16
Amber Route, 16
Amenemes I, 60
Amenemes II, 60
Amenemhat I, 62, 63, 410
Amenemhat II, 65, 70, 141
Amenemhat III, 64
Amenhotep III, 130
America B.C. (Fell), 258
American Anthropologist, 457
American Indians, 27–28
  brain size of, 375

Balboa, Vasco Nuñez
de, 259
Bannockburn, battle
of, 214
Bantu peoples, 389
languages of, 403
Barbarism, 274
The Barnes Review,
448–449, 453
Barthélemy, Abbé,
333–334
Basques, 13
Bass, George, 280–281,
283, 288
Bastias, John C., 137
Bat Creek Inscrip-
tion, 277
Battle of Megiddo, 129
Batumi, 55–56
Bauval, Robert, 35
Baxter, Anne, 84
Beardsley, Grace H.,
346
Bedwyr, 208
Before Color Prejudice
(Snowden), 346
*Before Columbus: Links
Between the Old
World and Ancient
America* (Gordon),
273–274, 277
Beirut, 5
Belos, 303
Belsk, 50
Benin, 463, 464
Bennett, Emmett, 274–275
Bérard, Victor, 294
Berber, 403
Bering Strait hypothe-
sis, 479
Bernal, Martin Gardiner,
56, 61, 63, 66, 71,
75–76, 78, 79,
118–123, 128, 130,
132, 158, 260, 269,
271, 307, 316–317,
319, 333–334,
335–337, 417,
440–441, 443, 460,
491–492, 495, 498
Ancient Model, 337
blond Greeks, 363
on Osiris, 228–229
on Tubal, 71–72
Bernard of Clairvaux (Saint
Bernard), 207–208
Besserwissen, 50–52, 94
Bible, 369
Gobineau, Count
Joseph-Arthur de
on, 496
on Hiram, 193
polygenism, 444–445
race and, 444–445

*Biblical Archaeology Re-
view (BAR)*, 486
Biliotti, Alfred, 247–248
Biological Africans,
470–471
Biracial people, 439
Bissula, 347
Black Athena, Volume I
(Bernal), 333–334,
335, 337–338, 363,
417, 440–442,
460–461, 479,
491–492
Blacks
brains of, 375
definition of race,
373–374
in Greek and Roman
civilization, 346–347
in the Indies, 259
meaning of "Black,"
442–447
racial prejudice, 341
Black Sea, 41
Herodotos' measure-
ments of, 48
Jason and the Argonauts
to, 244
Blacks in Antiquity
(Snowden), 346, 458
Blacology Speaking Com-
mittee, 479
Blegen, Carl, 333, 364
Blemyes, 348
Blue Nile, 414
Blumenbach, Johann Fried-
rich, 373–374, 447
Blyden, Edward Wilmot, 85
Bobba Mustapha, 165
Bobrinskoy, Count, 49
Boiotia, 158, 327
dome-shaped buildings
in, 328–329
Bonner, Phillip,
448–449, 450
Book of Chronicles, 193
Book of Enoch, 220–221
Book of Kings, 192
Book of Samuel, 192
*The Book of the Coming
Forth by Day*,
103–104, 111
Book of the Dead,
103–104, 111
*Book of the Plan of the
Temple*, 187
*Book of the Plan of the
Temple* (Books of
Thoth), 187
Bosphorus Straits, 244, 310
Bos primigenus, 4
Boswell, John, 176
Boyz N the Hood, 84

Brace, C. Loring, 442–447,
449–453, 454, 455,
456, 460–461,
462–463, 464–465,
467, 468, 470
Brails, 244
Brandt, Kari, 442
Braund, David, 54
Brazil
discovery of, 255
Paraíba Stone, 277
Roman amphorae
near, 260
Brendan of Ireland, Saint, 9
Britain
empire of, 339
Phoenicians in, 152, 153
Zulu War, 339–341
Brøgger, A. W., 253–254,
260, 262, 265, 277
Bronze
invention of, 252–253
Rhodes, discovery in,
247–248
Bronze Age, 12–17. *See
also Pax Aegyptiaca*
Athena in, 122–123
collapse of industry, 262
Crete in, 266–267
Dark Age after, 262
Europe in, 499–500
explorers of, 501
gold in, 249
in Greece, 248–249
Ialysos tombs, 247–248
island strongholds
in, 288
Phoenicians in, 158,
163–164
sculpture in, 173
seafaring in, 137,
253–255
Sesostris initiating, 78
shipwrecks from, 280
Turkey, shipwrecks off,
279–280
Brown Race, 383–384, 385
Bruce, James, 220–221
Budge, Sir E. A. Wallis, 111
"Building Bridges to Afro-
centrism: A Letter
to My Egyptologi-
cal Colleagues"
(Roth), 476
Bulgaria, 75
Bulls, 6
Bunyan, Paul, 318
Burchard of Worms,
Bishop, 209
Burkert, Walter, 219
on Herakles, 315
Burn, A. R., 107
Burstein, Stanley, 250

Burton, Richard, 388–389
Bushman aborigines, 390
Byblites, 289
Byblos, 66–67, 199
Cyprus, trade with, 150
Egyptianization of, 156
excavations of, 155–156
in First Intermediate Period, 150
Jebeil, 155
Rib-Addi of, 157, 163, 289
sailing to, 143–144
Wenamun and, 195

C

Cabral, Pedro Álvares, 255
Caesar, Julius, 3, 6
on Druids, 7
Cain, 218–222, 235
Caligula, 352
Cambyses, 162, 344–345
Cameron, John, 434
Cameroons, 389, 398
Chadic languages, 404
Canaan, 369–370
curse on, 370–371
languages of, 335
Pharaoh, homage to, 129
Ulu Burun artifacts, 282
Canary Islands, 265
Cannabis sativa, 50
Cannibalism, 14, 224–225, 236
Cape Gelidonya shipwreck, 280–281
copper and bronze at, 282, 286
Cape Verde Islands, 153, 265
Carchemish, 133
Carians, 308
Caribbean, 36
Caricatures, 431
Carnegie, Andrew, 450
Carruthers, Jacob, 490
Carthage, 152, 161–162
Agathokles and, 230
emigration from, 264–265
library of, 198–199
seafaring knowledge and collapse of, 263
Carto, Willis, 448
Cassiopeia, 317
Cassiterides, 152–153
Casson, Lionel, 136
Castillo, Bernal Diaz del, 51
Cathedrals, 178–179
altars of, 179
layout of, 179–180
Cattle, significance of, 408–409

Caucasians, 443
Caucasoid features, 374
Caucasus region, 11, 55
metalworkers from, 78–79
Mount Elbrus, 39
Cavalli-Sforza, Luigi Luca, 499
Cayce, Edgar, 87–88
Cedars of Lebanon, 149
Cedarwood galleys, 243–244
Cedrus Libani, 149
Celenko, Theodore, 489
Celtic Ogam, 258
Celts, 6
in Bronze Age, 12
cannibalism of, 14
language of, 358
Cemetery L, 421
Williams, Bruce and, 421–423
Cenobites, 105
Censer. See Qustul censer
Central America
blacks in, 259
sculptures of, 277
Cepheus, 317
Cerne, 398
Cerny, 118
Ceryces, 116–117
Ceylon, papyrus ships to, 242
Chadic, 403, 404
Champagne, Count of, 210
Champollion-Figeac, Jacques Joseph, 29, 85
Charax of Pergamon, 122
Charlemagne, 178
Chartres Cathedral, 179
Chelmsford, Frederick, 339–340
Chephren. See Khafre
Childe, V. Gordon, 72, 363–364
Chivalry, 208
Christ, crucifixion of, 233
Christopoulos, George A., 137
Chronicle of the Pharaohs, 449
Churches, orientation of, 179–180
Church of the Holy Sepulchre, 207
Cicero, 46, 317
Cinnamon Country, 261
Circe, 294
Circumcision, male/female, 412
The Civilization of the Goddess (Gimbutas), 364

Civil rights, 438
Clement of Alexandria, 101–102, 109, 187
Cleopatra's Needle, New York City, 89–90
Clines, 444, 446, 449, 461
"Clines and Clusters v. 'Race': A Test in Ancient Egypt and the Case of a Death on the Nile" (Brace et al.), 449
Clusters, 443, 447, 461
craniometry and, 451–452
European clusters, 463
pure races and, 446
"true Negroes," 462–463
Cocaine, 256–260
Cocaine Mummies, 256–260
Colchis, 39–42
Armayor, O. Kimball on, 47–48
Besserwissen and, 52
Egyptian colonists in, 54–58, 350–351
Herodotos in, 40–42
hints of Black Colchis, 56
Hippokrates on, 48
linen of, 53–54
physical appearance of Colchians, 42
Sesostris and, 54–58
Tubal and, 72
Collegia, Roman, 216–217
Columbus, Christopher, 9, 17, 151, 245, 246, 285
Composite portraits, 33
Comyn, John, 214
Concerning Marvelous Things Heard (Aristotle), 264–265
Congo, 389
race in, 446
Conrad, Joseph, 416
Cooke Manuscript, 191–192
Coon, Carleton, 445, 448–449
Copper, 15
weapons, 253
Copper Age, 498–499
Coptic Christian church, 119
Coptic Etymological Dictionary (Cerny), 118–119
Coptic language
etymology, 118–123
Greek and, 336
Cortés, 51, 228, 306

PAUL RAPACIOLI

GOOD
SWEDEN
BAD
SWEDEN

The Use and Abuse
of Swedish Values in
a Post-Truth World

VOLANTE

Contents

A sinister tale

There is a country in the north, they say, where collapse is imminent. Criminal gangs have seized control of dozens of residential areas. Charred skeletons of cars line the streets and the police dare not enter. Rape is out of control and the women fear to leave their homes after sunset. There is talk that this northern land will be the epicentre of a European civil war, overrun by migrants and undermined by locals who are too blind or foolish to resist the erosion of their culture. They've even banned Christmas lights. Christmas lights!

Introduction

Most people don't know much about Sweden. But what they think they know is extraordinarily positive. This one-dimensional 'Good Sweden' reputation, constructed around qualities such as technological prowess, democratic design and concern for the environment has been a great help to Swedish trade and tourism and diplomacy in the last fifty years.

Now that reputation is being challenged by an alternative story about Sweden. It is a negative tale of collapse and crisis rooted in Sweden's decision to allow large numbers of immigrants to settle in the country in recent years. The 'Bad Sweden' story is based on the undeniable fact of challenges in a fast-changing Swedish society but it only works when it is stripped of context or injected with a serum of falsehood and exaggeration.

However far north Sweden may be geographically and however much an outlier the country is by many significant measures, it is not insulated from the unsettling winds howling through the West's established democratic processes: disinformation, fake news, filter bubbles, the collapse of trust in experts and the establishment, or, as all this has been neatly summed up, post-truth.

The alternative narrative is partly enabled by these disturbing developments. Disinformation is as old as information itself and Sweden is no stranger to it. But those who seek to discredit Sweden today have an arsenal of new and powerful weapons in the form of news web sites (real and fake) and social media, while widespread loss of trust in media, the psychology of news sharing and the economics of the news industry combine to create battlefield conditions strongly in their favour.

There's more to it, though, because for an alternative narrative to work there needs to be an established narrative for it to play off. The bigger the contrast between the two, the greater the dramatic effect and the greater the impact. If you stomp through a grubby, messy house with muddy boots, nobody notices; if you tramp across finely polished parquet floors – well, it looks pretty bad. And it gets people talking.

The established narrative about Sweden is one of unbelievable success. This Apple of countries has become so used to topping the various league tables measuring human development that any kind of slump, such as a fall in the OECD's PISA education rankings, is regarded as a national embarrassment.[1] Globally-known Swedish companies such as Ikea, Volvo and Spotify are associated with positive values such as innovation, design, value and sustainability. Perhaps the most famous Swedish brand of them all, ABBA (the band, not the fish company, for those readers fond of Swedish herring), still dominates people's associations with the country, along with other positive notions such as 'clean', 'forests', 'environment' and 'beautiful'.

As we shall see, the characteristics of the established narrative and how closely related it is to the alternative are key to the appeal of the Bad Sweden story. When we look at this distorted version of Sweden we see burning cars, police in riot gear and immigrant youths on the rampage. This is very different from most people's stereotypical image of Sweden – water, red cottages, elks – and that is what makes it so immediately forceful.

And yet the 'plot points' of the Bad Sweden narrative are usually based on something true – there *are* burning cars in Sweden and police in riot gear and marginalised angry youths who don't have blond hair and blue eyes. This is what gives the story its credibility. But while philosophers may argue over the nature of truth, when it comes to news, truth is context. A lack of context doesn't make a story false but it greatly reduces the truth of it.

There are a number of factors at play here and three relate directly to Sweden. The first is that many people in the international media still throw about the lazy myth that Sweden is, or thinks it is, some kind of paradise rather than a many-layered country of ten million people. Secondly, while it is no utopia, Sweden is by most international measures very successful indeed. The third factor is that Sweden vividly represents highly progressive values which make it a target for those who oppose those values. The combination of these three factors and the way they impact upon the image of the country abroad is unique to Sweden.

The fourth factor to consider is that today's conditions for the spread of information – social media, the psychology of news and the economics of the media business – greatly benefit those who want to undermine the values that Sweden represents.

The news company I founded in 2004 with James Savage, The Local, has published 40,000 articles about Sweden. These have been read by over 75 million readers around the world. We have reported on the bad stuff as it happens – that, after all, is news – but I believe we have presented a fair and balanced image of Sweden over the years, always providing a context. Our job is to report on Swedish affairs as we see them, not to promote or defend the country's image abroad. That is the job of others: people working in government, diplomacy, tourism and in Sweden's many international businesses.

But in recent years we have witnessed a surge of negative news about Sweden in certain quarters of the international media, painting a picture of the country that we do not recognise. Let me be clear: we do recognise Sweden's problems, as we recognise the problems in all the countries we cover. The Local has reported on Sweden's riots, gang violence, murders, rapes, corruption scandals and political crises more than anyone else in English. But when you paint a picture of a country you do it dot by dot, where every dot is one story among millions that combine to provide a complex, complete understanding of the place. We have seen how just a few of our Swedish 'dots' have been hijacked and magnified to paint a picture of Sweden that is crude, simplistic and misleading. Pull up a picture on your computer, zoom in twenty times until your screen is filled with different coloured squares and you'll see what I mean.

There is of course more than one perspective of a country. A country's reputation is woven from the many different threads of information about the place and that's the way it should be, so that stories can be cross-checked and balanced and so that the level of detail and understanding only increases.

But the active spread of negative news about Sweden in the international media *without the context* is something different altogether. The alternative narrative is not intended to help people to understand the country better and it is not even an attack on the country *per se.* It is about using Sweden as a weapon in a far wider battle of values, where Sweden is the embodiment of one set of values. Sweden's international reputation will be collateral damage in that battle and if the narrative is left unchecked, the cost to the country will be significant. It will be bad for Swedish business, bad for Swedish tourism, bad for Swedish cities and regions seeking to attract international talent or investment and bad for Sweden's efforts to build international relationships.

There is a widespread notion that holding progressive values is a sign of wide-eyed weakness in a wicked world and two words frequently attached to Sweden – not just abroad but by Swedes themselves – are 'innocent' and 'naïve'.

The murder of prime minister Olof Palme on a central Stockholm street in 1986 has often been described as the moment Sweden lost its innocence. He was on his way home from the cinema with his wife – but no bodyguards – when he was shot by an unknown assailant. In 2003 the country's similarly unprotected foreign minister, Anna Lindh, was stabbed to death in Stockholm's most prestigious department store, NK. This too was described as a loss of innocence for Sweden, as was the 2010 suicide bombing (which only killed the bomber) close to where Palme was shot and the terror attack in April 2017, in which a truck was driven down one of Stockholm's busiest shopping streets, killing five people.

As one commentator wrote in The Guardian after this latest attack, 'there are few countries in the world that have "lost their innocence" as many times as Sweden'.[2] But Sweden is no innocent and never has been. No 'innocent' or 'naïve' country could have kept itself largely unscathed during the Second World War and then danced on the razor's edge of the Cold

War as successfully as Sweden did. By declaring itself neutral and balancing its west-leaning instincts with its geographic proximity to the Soviet Union, Sweden demonstrated its guile, not its innocence. By building up the fourth largest air force in the world by 1957[3] and running a nuclear weapons programme for more than 15 years up to 1968,[4] Sweden showed that it had no intention of rolling over if the worst should happen.

Sweden is not innocent, but it has been complacent. In terms of defence, this complacency resulted in huge cuts to the country's military capacity in the last decade.[5] A worsening security situation in the Baltic was a wake-up call that has seen a sudden and rapid reinvestment in the armed forces, with the reinstatement of conscription and troops being permanently stationed on the strategically-significant island of Gotland.[6]

Sweden has been complacent about its reputation too. *Good Sweden, Bad Sweden* is a warning to those in Swedish business and public service who have come to take Sweden's stellar reputation for granted: there are powers out there working to take it away from you. I hope this book will help you to understand that the rules of the reputation game have changed – and not in your favour. You cannot keep playing *innebandy* while the world is playing ice hockey. You'll get hurt.

CHAPTER 1:

Christmas lights, riots and the fall of utopia

November may only have thirty days but it's by far the longest
month of the year in Sweden. The only way to get through
the dark, drizzly days is to focus on the candlelit traditions
of Lucia and Christmas that brighten up distant December.
With this in mind, I was intrigued by an email I received one
day in November 2016.

> Is it true Sweden has banned Christmas lights in public for
> fear of offending Muslims?

That was it. Anyone who works in the news business will be
quite used to receiving such emails. We become hardened to
the personal abuse, accusations of being a fascist or a communist (sometimes both in the same email) and vast number of
story suggestions, but occasionally an email will leap out of the
crowd and demand attention.

I replied to the man in Northamptonshire, England, who
sent me the above message and assured him that from where
I was sitting in Stockholm's Södermalm district I could see a
street already full of Christmas lights, sparkling in the November
gloom.

He thanked me for my response. But where had he got
this idea from? In contrast to a lot of the trolling emails

we receive it sounded like a genuine enquiry – and worth investigating.

We didn't have to look far. On October 23rd, Sweden's public TV news network SVT reported on its Jönköping region page that 'advent is a month away, and many local communities will be decorating the streets with Christmas lights. But in a number of small towns it will remain dark. The Swedish Transport Administration (Trafikverket) will no longer allow its lamp posts to be used for decorations'.[7]

The reason for this was straightforward. Local councils which want to hang their Christmas lights on roads owned by the state, rather than by the councils themselves, must apply to Trafikverket for permission. With rising traffic on the main roads through small towns leading to increased focus on safety, Trafikverket has been showing less Christmas spirit in recent years. After all, nobody wants to be responsible for a lamp post collapsing under the weight of Christmas. This, plus the fact that under Swedish law the transport administration is not allowed to give or sell electricity from its installations, meant that a few towns would have to find somewhere else to hang their lights. Trees, for example.

So far, so very bureaucratic and boring – and not the sort of news story that The Local's Sweden editor would consider of interest to our international audience.

But then a little-known news-based web site called Speisa covered the story.[8] Apart from the fact that its domain name is registered in the United States, there is not much information available about who runs the web site. However, Speisa's Twitter account declares that 'Speisa report [sic] on world events, with a special interest in Scandinavia – and especially the escalating mass-migration-related situation in Sweden'.[9]

The person who wrote the article about the Christmas lights appeared to know Swedish. Although it is just a simple rewrite, the report cites the original SVT article accurately – except for one sentence:

> The change is a victory for those who want to tone down the reminder of the country's Christian traditions, but according to the Swedish Transport Administration, the decision for the drastic change is 'security'.

Wait – what? There was certainly nothing in the original article about Sweden's 'Christian traditions' being toned down, but given Speisa's own Twitter description it is not a surprising angle for the site to layer into its story. Nor was there anything aggressive about the way the article was written. But that line was the first mutation that led to a rapid evolution of the story. What happened next demonstrates a pattern that we will see again and again, as Swedish news stories are dragged away from their sources, stripped of context and beaten into an entirely different shape.

The following day, the US web site Infowars published an article using Speisa as the source – and ramped up the rhetoric several notches:

> Towns across Sweden have banned Christmas street lights in the name of 'security,' but the real reason is almost certainly because the country has completely capitulated to Islam after importing countless Muslim migrants over the last two years...
>
> Despite there being no safety issue with the street lights for decades, this new rule has been instituted right after re-

cord numbers of Muslim migrants flooded into the country
– just a coincidence I'm sure.

In reality, the Christmas lights ban is almost certainly an
effort to avoid offending Muslim migrants who are causing
chaos in cities like Malmo, where the firebombing of cars and
businesses in or near Muslim ghetto 'no-go areas' is becoming
a routine occurrence.[10]

On October 26th, three days after the original article appeared on SVT, controversial British right wing commentator
Milo Yiannopoulos published his own interpretation of the
story. Yiannopoulos was a columnist for the American news
site Breitbart – of which more later – but he cited Speisa's
article on his popular blog:

> So what changed? The weight of these holiday lights? The
> durability of street poles? Or maybe it was the massive influx
> of Muslim migrants that dramatically altered the demo-
> graphic landscape of Sweden over the past two years…
>
> Indeed, it seems the only real 'security' concern is
> offending Muslim migrants—the same ones responsible
> for destroying local businesses.
>
> Progressivism? Cultural enrichment? More like capitula-
> tion to an invading army.[11]

According to a social media widget on the blog (now removed), his short piece was shared 45,000 times on Facebook
– not surprising considering the fact that Yiannopoulos
himself has 2.3 million followers on the social network.[12] By
comparison, SVT Nyheter, Sweden's public television news
channel, has 135,000 followers. Yiannopoulos's Facebook feed

may have been where another news web site, called Morning News USA but based in Australia, came across the story. Citing Infowars, Morning News USA began its October 27th piece as follows:

> Sweden has banned Christmas lights in the name of 'security' as immigrants continue to pour into the Scandinavian country. The country has seen a huge influx of refugees from Middle Eastern countries over the past two years and the Swedish government has tried its best to accommodate them, sometimes at the expense of its own citizens.[13]

On the same day, the notion that this was a 'war on Christmas' was debunked by fact-checking site Snopes.[14] But that did not stop the story from spreading further and given the number of people following Yiannopoulos and Infowars on Facebook, it is safe to say that millions of people were exposed to the idea that Trafikverket's decision was based on religious sensitivity.

In the week following this fuss, a unit within the Swedish newspaper Metro called Viralgranskaren (Viral Investigator) produced an inspired video that used the Christmas lights story to highlight the importance of checking the facts behind the news stories you read and share online. The English version of this film has been viewed 3.4 million times. But how many of the millions who saw the conspiracy version of the story were among them? My guess is not many.

Later in the month, when the festive period was in full swing, we asked our readers to send in pictures of the Christmas lights in their local towns and published a selection on December 1st. At the time of writing[15] if you Google 'christmas lights sweden' the top result is The Local's article, boldly declaring 'No, Sweden has not banned Christmas lights. Here's proof'.

Articles on SVT Nyheter's Jönköping news section are typically shared between fifty and a hundred times on Facebook. At the other end of the scale, SVT's lead article about the truck attack in central Stockholm in April 2017 – without a doubt, the biggest Swedish news story of the last twelve months – was shared 9,172 times.[16] Looking at the original Christmas lights article today, I see that it has been shared 6,717 times. That's a lot of shares for any kind of news story – but it's a fraction of the reach achieved by Milo Yiannopoulos. For an article about a minor administrative decision by a transport agency it's nothing short of ridiculous. The attention has evidently not been all positive, because there is now a note at the bottom of the article – in English:

> This article has unfortunately appeared on websites outside Sweden where it has been placed in a totally incorrect context. The decision to not allow Christmas decorative lights on poles belonging to the National Roads Authorities, is a question of technical and legal issues, and has nothing to do with religion or immigration. There will still be a [sic] lots of Christmas lights in the main parts of Swedish cities. The lights are not banned in any way.

In telling the original story, journalist Kristin Renulf spoke to a local politician who was annoyed about the decision.

'I think this is a waste of time,' said local council chair Marie Johansson.

In the end, a lot more time was wasted on the story than Johansson anticipated.

∗∗∗

At 6pm on May 13th 2013, Stockholm police received a report that a man in the north-west suburb of Husby was threatening neighbours with a large knife. The police unit dispatched to the scene was no doubt prepared for the unexpected – but they could not have anticipated the enormous domestic and international consequences of their actions in the coming hours.

When the officers arrived at the scene, they learned that the man, a 69-year old pensioner, was in his apartment with his wife and after a lengthy stand-off they decided to storm the home. The police unit smashed the door down and used a flash grenade to stun the man, but as he took a step towards them, two officers opened fire.

The man was shot in the head and died at the scene.[17]

Husby is just 22 minutes by subway from the centre of Stockholm, but it is a world away from the whirlwind of finance, technology and fashion at the heart of the self-proclaimed 'Capital of Scandinavia'. The district sits on a gentle hill and mostly consists of multistorey apartment blocks built in the late 1960s as part of Sweden's 'Million Programme' housing project. A pedestrian walkway links several squares which are dotted with fountains, small park areas and, in springtime, cherry blossoms. In 2015 it was named as one of fifteen 'particularly vulnerable' areas in Sweden, a label it retains two years later.

Six days after the 69-year old was shot, a group of youths set fire to cars in Husby. When police arrived at the scene they were met by a barrage of stones and by the time they managed to restore calm, at least 100 vehicles had been set alight.[18] The local shopping centre was vandalised and police estimated that up to 60 youths had been involved in the fracas. The following day, a social justice organisation in Stockholm's northern suburbs[19] claimed that the riot started 'as a reaction to police brutality against citizens, our neighbours' and it is widely accepted that while social tension had been simmering for years, the death of the 69-year old was the catalyst. But this was just the start.

For five nights, there was unrest in the Swedish capital's suburbs. Cars were torched in Rinkeby, Tensta, Kista and Edsberg in the north of the city, and Skarpnäck, Norsborg, Fittja, Bredäng and Flemingsberg in the south.[20] While the following nights were not as severe as the first, another fifty cars were set alight, along with part of a school. The windows of the police station in Jakobsberg were smashed and a nearby shopping centre was damaged. Each night, between fifty and a hundred rioters were estimated to be on the streets but calm was restored before dawn.

In total, police dealt with 400 incident reports and arrested 29 people. One man was jailed for burning two cars, while two others were fined for weapons- and drug-related offences. The total cost of the damage was put at 63 million SEK.[21]

Along with the rest of the Swedish media, The Local followed the riots' development closely. This was by no means the first time that Sweden had experienced rioting but it was nevertheless a very big news story and the ongoing violence and vandalism attracted the attention of the world's media. Our office in Stockholm was overwhelmed with calls from journalists from all around the world – to a far greater extent than for any other news story we had covered in Sweden. Our phones did not stop ringing for three days, as reporters who had never been to Scandinavia struggled to comprehend a development that simply didn't fit with their view of Sweden. This confounding of perceptions, of course, was what made it such a compelling story for the world's news desks. It is also why so many international journalists could not resist drawing definitive conclusions, with many claiming that the riots had left 'Sweden's dreams of perfect society up in smoke'.[22]

Great dollops of *schadenfreude* dripped from every headline as journalist after journalist caught the scent of this 'how-the-mighty-have-fallen' story from the north: at last, the curtain of perfection was being pulled back to reveal the same kind of dysfunctionality that every country grapples with; at last, those smug Swedes with their safe cars and bouncy pop music were getting a dose of reality; you see, even the Swedes are not immune to the civil unrest that has afflicted France and Britain in recent years.

The causes of the riots have been pored over in great detail in Sweden and abroad, and the reasons, such as rising inequality, failure to integrate immigrants into society and falling public spending, are of course deep and complex. But the media drew instant comparisons with the riots in Paris in 2005 and Britain in 2011; the Stockholm riots were the next chapter in that story but with the twist that nobody (in the international media) saw it coming.

'The intensity of the unrest in Stockholm has shocked the world,' wrote the Financial Times, continuing, 'France and Britain have experienced riots in recent years but Sweden was meant to be different.'[23] Under the headline 'Paradise Lost' the New Statesman explained that what made the Stockholm riots different to those in Paris and England was that Sweden is viewed as a social democratic paradise.[24]

This, then, was the reason for the massive global media scrutiny. It wasn't the scale of the riots themselves but the context, the location of the unrest: Sweden, a place whose reputation is so positive that, as the New Statesman put it, 'discontent with the country is unthinkable to many outsiders'.

In numerical terms, the Stockholm riots were no more than a little bit of local trouble compared to Paris and England. In Paris, almost 9,000 vehicles were destroyed, 3,000 people were arrested, well over a hundred police officers were injured and the cost was estimated at €200 million.[25] The riots in England were on a similar scale, although with many more police officers injured, widespread looting across the country and the added tragedy of five deaths.[26]

Remember, in Stockholm there were 150 cars destroyed and 29 arrests; any journalists reporting on the riots knew that. But it didn't stop them from laying on the hyperbole in thick slabs. 'Sweden in flames', ran the headline of Mail Online, which explained that 'as gangs of migrants riot for five nights running… the utopian boasts of a multicultural success story turn to ashes'.[27] CNBC linked the riots to 'the Nordic Welfare Myth'[28] while Reuters argued that the riots 'challenge the image of happy, generous state'.[29] 'Stockholm is burning', wrote The Week,[30] echoed shortly afterwards by the Independent's 'Fire and fury in Sweden'.[31] In these stories we glimpsed an early preview of the visual identity of the alternative narrative about Sweden.

The Economist expressed 'surprise' that '[a] Scandinavian idyll is disrupted by arson and unrest'.[32] Journalists who called The Local's office that week knew the true scale of the riots but it didn't stop them from asking if we would be able to get home after work or if we still had internet access. They were caught up in their own hyperbole.

Writing in Britain's left-leaning Guardian, Aditya Chakrabortty asked, 'If instability can happen here, what might unfold elsewhere?':

> Don't surveys repeatedly show Sweden as one of the happiest countries (certainly a damn sight cheerier than Britain)? Isn't it famous for its equality, its warm welcome to immigrants? Whatever happened to Stockholm, capital of progressivism, the Mecca towards which Guardianistas face for their daily five minutes of mindfulness?[33]

Chakrabortty hoped to draw lessons for the UK from the riots, but his angle on the story demonstrated that their impact was not because of the actual scale of the disturbances – but because of the world's preconceptions about Sweden as some sort of paradise.

If Paris and England were societal domestic violence on a grand scale, the Stockholm riots were the revelation that the street's most perfect couple was having marriage counselling. For more than half a century Sweden had been held up as representing the success of progressive values, championed by the left and apparently too prosperous, happy and strong for the right to knock the country off its pedestal. But the riots were a turning point adopted by the left as a warning of what can happen if a country turns its back on its socialist principles, and by the right as evidence that the progressive values that Sweden represented were themselves flawed.

For those who opposed these principles, the riots were the perfect starting point for an alternative narrative about Sweden and, by association, progressive values. Not, as I have empha-sised, because they were actually a critical point in Swedish social history, but because a combination of factors made this narrative irresistible. Sweden's unusually positive interna-tional reputation had set the protagonist up for a mighty fall. Widespread ignorance about Sweden created a vacuum that could be filled by distortion and untruth. The shock value of the images of the riots added a dangerous, scary frisson to the story. And finally, timing: powerful forces in the world were gathering against the progressive values that Sweden represents, providing the resources to keep feeding an alternative narrative.

Four years later, Husby is still one of many similarly trou-bled areas in Sweden that have become the Achilles heel of the country's reputation.

At the beginning of 2017 business owners in Husby were told that the local council would arrange for private security guards to patrol the shopping centre from April. By August the guards were still not in place and local newspaper Mitt i Stockholm reported that the bidding company, Securitas, was asking for more money than the council was prepared to pay.[34] 'Nobody dares to patrol Husby,' said the chairman of Husby's business association.

Two weeks after Mitt i Stockholm's report, the story found its way into the American right-wing news site Breitbart under the headline 'Swedish Businesses Helpless as Security Firms Refuse to Work in No-Go Zone'.[35] The report described Husby, Rinkeby and Tensta as 'some of the most notorious no-go zones in Sweden where police are often attacked, cars set on fire, and local shops smashed and looted during riots'. It was shared almost 2,500 times on Facebook and prompted well over 1,000 comments.

The day after Breitbart's article, Norway's Migration and Integration Minister, the nationalist Progress Party's Sylvi Listhaug, flew to Stockholm. She planned to visit Rinkeby and had a meeting scheduled with Sweden's Migration Minister Heléne Fritzon. But after reading an interview with Listhaug in Norwegian newspaper Verdens Gang, Fritzon abruptly cancelled the meeting.[36] In the paper, Listhaug claimed that 'parallel societies have developed in more than 60 places in Sweden', calling them 'no-go zones' and insisting that there are 'conditions of lawlessness and criminals in control' in places with 'a large quantity of people with immigrant backgrounds'.

It later emerged that the Norwegian government had warned their Swedish counterparts that the visit 'maybe had a misleading purpose'. Sylvi Listhaug is one of many in Norway to have talked about 'The Swedish Conditions' as a warning to Norwegians about the effects of liberal immigration policies.[37] Her trip happened to be scheduled two weeks before Norway's general election.

In the years since Stockholm's suburban riots exploded onto the world's front pages, stories like this have become commonplace in the international media. Soon we will explore this alternative narrative in more detail but before we talk about the muddy boots, we need to peer into the polished parquet floor of Sweden's international reputation.

CHAPTER 2:

Trump, Eisenhower and the values of success

On the morning of February 19th 2017 Sweden awoke to the sound of frenzied tweeting – and it wasn't the early return of migrating birds. Leading the dawn chorus was a tweet from Sweden's former prime minister, and more recently foreign minister, Carl Bildt: 'Sweden? Terror attack? What has he been smoking? Questions abound.'[38] It accompanied a picture of the US president, Donald Trump, and a link to an article suggesting that he had referred to a non-existent terror attack in Sweden the previous night.

Speaking at a rally in Florida about his plans to implement stricter immigration rules in the US, President Trump had rattled off a series of examples from Europe:

> You look at what's happening in Germany, you look at what's happening last night in Sweden. Sweden. Who would believe this? Sweden. They took in large numbers. They're having problems like they never thought possible. You look at what's happening in Brussels. You look at what's happening all over the world. Take a look at Nice. Take a look at Paris.[39]

With the Sweden reference sitting pertly in the middle of a passage about places where terror attacks had recently taken place, people assumed that Trump was imagining a similar incident in Sweden and were baffled.

But Sweden's ambassador to the United States at the time was not surprised by Trump's statement. Two weeks earlier, Björn Lyrvall had attended the annual Red Cross Ball at the president's exclusive Mar-a-Lago club in Palm Beach, Florida.

'We were in a VIP area with a few other ambassadors on the way into the event and I was introduced to President Trump and Melania,' Lyrvall told me.

'The very first thing Trump said to me was, "Sweden – you have your problems with immigration, don't you?" This immediate connection with immigration problems was obviously in his mind, even then.'

Back in Sweden, Trump's comments led to a rather amusing surge of responses on social media in which people not only pointed out that nothing sinister had happened in Sweden the previous night but also speculated about what he could have meant. A major meatball heist? The opening of a can of fermented herring? Snow?

The Swedish embassy in Washington played it by the book. The ambassador declined many requests to appear on American news shows and instead submitted a formal request to the US State Department to clarify Trump's statement.

Shortly afterwards – and perhaps surprised by the rolling wave of humour emanating from Sweden – Trump clarified that he was in fact referring to an interview with an American documentary maker called Ami Horowitz that he had seen on Fox TV the previous evening. In his 2016 documentary, 'Stockholm Syndrome', Horowitz argued that Sweden was covering up immigration-related problems and the Fox News show 'Tucker Carlson Tonight' gave Horowitz plenty of space to describe the '…absolute surge in both gun violence and rape in Sweden…rapes at music festivals…no-go zones cops won't enter because it's too dangerous… There's no assimilation at all… social unrest… terrorism…'[40]

As Horowitz spoke, the show's host, Tucker Carlson, shook his head in despair at the folly of the Swedes. 'Right,' he said. 'Because the most important thing is to feel virtuous, I guess.'

But many of the claims in the broadcast and in Horowitz's 10-minute documentary were promptly disputed by Swedish experts.[41] For example, the 'absolute surge in gun violence' meant that the overall rate of deadly violence in Sweden is still about 1 per 100,000 inhabitants, compared to 5 per 100,000 in the US[42] – hardly something for Fox News hosts to worry about. And contrary to the film's claim that the police avoid certain 'vulnerable areas', these are the places where the police have strengthened their presence most, however challenging it may be to conduct their work there.[43] Two Swedish police officers who participated in the film described the filmmaker as 'a madman' who took their general statements about crime in Sweden out of context and completely misrepresented their views.[44] Horowitz rejected the criticism and was probably grateful for the unexpected publicity boost.

The Swedish embassy's only public response was a terse tweet in response to Trump's own clarification: 'We look forward to informing the US administration about Swedish immigration and integration policies.'[45]

That tweet was retweeted over 70,000 times and liked 150,000 times. By the summer of 2017 it had been seen by 12.5 million people.[46] That's just as well, because when a sitting US president makes a casual comment about Sweden, the fallout can last a long, long time.

Sweden and suicide

You probably know that Sweden has a reputation for its high suicide rate. What you may not know is that Sweden doesn't have a high suicide rate and that this particular myth originated from another American president.

The story was recorded by academic Frederick Hale in his 2003 article for the Swedish-American Historical Quarterly.* In July 1960, as Hale explained, Dwight D Eisenhower was nearing the end of his eight-year Republican presidency and attempted to use his broad popularity to bolster the presidential campaign of his vice president, Richard Nixon. Nixon's opponent was John F. Kennedy and the election had been billed as the choice between freedom and state socialism. Convinced that his policies supporting the former path had led to unprecedented American wealth, Eisenhower was keen to discredit the opposing ideology. His method was to verbally attack a certain small European nation which for the previous twenty years had been celebrated as a socialist utopia, a successful middle way between the capitalism of the west and the communism of the Soviet bloc.[47]

In fact, 'Sweden: The Middle Way' was the name of the book that sparked these reputational good times. Written in 1936 by an American journalist called Marquis Childs, it described how the country had discovered an economic model that blended a cooperative approach to labour relations with effective state intervention to create a buoyant economy that delivered the means to tackle social problems. The book influenced the thinking of an earlier American president, Franklin Roosevelt, who declared himself '...a good deal interested in

---

* This section is indebted to Hale's paper, which is well worth reading in its entirety for a more detailed historical perspective on the way Sweden is being treated today.

31

the cooperative development in countries abroad, especially Sweden. In Sweden, for example, you have a royal family and a Socialist Government and a capitalist system, all working happily side by side.'[48]

Speaking at Columbia University in 2006, the Swedish journalist Per T. Ohlsson noted that Sweden's reputation 'got something of an international breakthrough with Childs' book':

> Decades later Allan Kastrup, who for many years worked as a Swedish information officer in the United States, remembered the impact of Sweden: The Middle Way: 'With regard to importance and effects, Marquis Childs' book weighs more heavily than any other book about Sweden published in America, and it is not likely that it ever will have any real competitors.'
>
> The public interest and publicity that surrounded Childs' book was, of course, noticed in Sweden, and was seen as a sort of confirmation of Swedish methods and Swedish solutions.[49]

This was precisely the opposite of the message Eisenhower wanted to give to the American people twenty-four years later. Sweden's economic reputation had certainly not gone unchallenged in that time, and by the end of Eisenhower's presidency conservative commentators had added a moral element into their criticism of the country. The fuel for this was a high profile 1955 article in Time magazine headlined 'Sin and Sweden' in which writer Joe David Brown made the case that the country was a nest of depravity.[50] 'Whatever the cause, sexual moral standards in Sweden today are jolting to an outsider,' he wrote. Brown was appalled to discover that in

1950s Sweden unwed mothers were not stigmatised by society and noted that one such slattern was recently a candidate for the role of Lucia, part of the traditional Swedish Christmas celebrations in which a young woman leads a dawn candlelit procession.

'The sex education given in public schools would make even the most modern, broad-minded American parent blanch', reported Brown. Speaking to a Catholic priest, he expressed his shock 'that parents and teachers condone promiscuity, do not even try to tell the young people that such things are wrong.' The priest told the fearless reporter that the Swedish mentality was to accept that things such as unwed mothers, birth control and abortions exist and to try to do something constructive about them.

The article, which coincided with the release of several Swedish films pushing against the boundaries of sexuality in cinema, sparked an international debate and embedded the notion of Swedish sexual liberty in the world's consciousness.

All of which gave President Eisenhower plenty to work with when he stood up on the morning of July 27th 1960 at a breakfast for 600 Republicans in Chicago and declared that welfare excess was the path to ruin:

> Only in the last few weeks, I have been reading quite an article on the experiment of almost complete paternalism in a friendly European country. This country has a tremendous record for socialistic operation… and the record shows that their rate of suicide has gone up almost unbelievably and I think they were almost the lowest nation in the world for that. Now, they have more than twice our rate. Drunkenness has gone up. Lack of ambition is discernible on all sides.[51]

He didn't mention Sweden by name but everyone present knew which country he was talking about – as did the Swedish politicians who learned of the president's off-the-cuff remarks the following day. Frederick Hale noted that Eisenhower got his facts wrong and his comments were largely dismissed as 'uninformed and springing from ideological considerations.' The suicide rate in Sweden had been high long before the Social Democrats came to power and had in fact fallen since the 1930s. So if anything, the safety net of socialism had reduced the number of suicides in Sweden.

In a remarkable precursor to the social media reaction to President Trump's comments more than five decades later, Swedish politicians and commentators deployed wry humour in response Eisenhower's statement. As Hale wrote, prime minister Tage Erlander pointed out that 'juvenile delinquency, misuse of alcohol, and the other difficulties cited are international problems – and the United States itself is a relevant example of this.' Meanwhile, Defence Minister Sven Andersson told the Swedish daily newspaper Dagens Nyheter that 'Sweden's consolation lay in the fact that the American president's term in the White House was nearly finished.' And an editor in rival publication Svenska Dagbladet wrote that '…Swedes must be forgiven if we entertain a quiet hope that he consult a reference book appropriate for heads of state in very large countries.'

Anyone who doubts that a false statement from an American president can live long in international mythology should note that even in 2017 the notion persists that Sweden has a high suicide rate.[52] This is despite the fact that, at 12.7 deaths per 100,000 people, it is significantly below the European average of 14.1 deaths per 100,000 people and barely above the US rate of 12.6.[53]

Two years after his comments to the Republican gathering, Eisenhower visited Sweden and graciously apologised for his misrepresentation of the nation:

> Before anyone gets the chance to ask, I want to make clear that the remark I made about Sweden in Chicago some years ago was based on what I had then recently read in an American magazine. Since then, I have had many friends who have returned from Sweden and who have told me that I was wrong. I apologise for my error.[54]

***

Neither Trump nor Eisenhower had any interest in harming Sweden or the Swedes, but they were both perfectly happy to sacrifice a chunk of goodwill from a small Nordic country on the altar of domestic politics. In 1960 and then again in 2017 Sweden was used by the most powerful man in the world as a vivid symbol of a particular way of life, a set of values that ran contrary to his own. When Eisenhower made his comments Sweden was a paragon of functioning socialism and had enjoyed uninterrupted growth since the war. It would have been tricky for the president to use the economic facts to argue that the Swedish model was failing, but by implying that 'even Sweden' was beset by drunkenness, lack of ambition and loose morals, he had a convenient emotional tool for associating that model with failure.

Today, what Sweden represents is more complex. In many people's minds the notion of a socialist paradise remains but this is no longer the pre-eminent association. This is partly down to the decline of socialism: since 1993 government spending as a percentage of Sweden's GDP has declined from 70% to 50%,[55] while the country has aggressively opened up traditionally public sectors such as healthcare and education to private organisations. But it is also because Sweden in 2017 stands for much more than an economic model.

Nothing so provocative as success

Compared to the 1950s we have a lot more data for comparing countries and barely a month goes by without some new international ranking capturing the media's attention. Gender equality, gay rights, happiness, language skills, openness, transparency, democracy – when it comes to progressive values, Sweden is a world champion. But there are harder qualities too where Sweden is considered to excel, such as IT connectedness, financial technology, biotechnology, safety and healthcare. These rankings, ranging from rigorous economic indicators to vague surveys, matter because they get people talking and as such they are building blocks of a country's reputation. Indeed, if any country's reputation could be said to have benefited from the ranking frenzy of recent years, then it is Sweden's.

As if to lay to rest once and for all the notion of Sweden as a socialist paradise, the American business magazine Forbes ranked Sweden the number one country in the world for business in 2017.[56] With 139 countries in its index, Forbes gave Sweden particularly high marks for personal freedom, monetary freedom, corruption (lack of, naturally) and technology.

The European Commission's rigorous regional 'Innovation Scoreboard' for 2017 backed up the Forbes ranking. With scores for a wide range of variables, such as lifelong learning, international scientific co-publications, research and development expenditures, trademark applications and sales of new-to-market/firm innovations, Sweden came top for the second year in a row while Stockholm was rated the most innovative region in the European Union.[57]

In the 2016 Corruption Perceptions Index produced by Transparency International, Sweden came fourth,[58] where countries nearer the top of the table exhibit 'higher degrees of press freedom, access to information about public expenditure, stronger standards of integrity for public officials, and independent judicial systems'. Sweden also took fourth place – for the eighth year running – on the World Economic Forum's Global Gender Gap Report.[59] This ranking measures the gap between the genders in areas such as public sector roles, educational attainment and political empowerment.

And so it continues. The Swedish passport is ranked second most powerful in the world,[60] based on the number of countries that holders can enter without requiring a visa. Sweden is the best country for immigrants,[61] quality of life for old people is third best globally[62] and Swedes generally are tenth happiest in the world.[63] When it comes to the ability of non-English speakers to speak English, Swedes are ranked third in the world.[64]

In 2015 the Financial Times reported that Stockholm is second only to Silicon Valley for the per capita number of billion-dollar tech companies – 'unicorns' – that have been born in the city, a measure that led the city to be dubbed 'the Unicorn Factory'.[65] Meanwhile, as a percentage of gross national income, Sweden is the world's most generous provider of overseas development assistance, committing 1.41% of its gross national income[66] – double the United Nations' stated target for developed countries.[67]

In January 2017 the World Economic Forum conveniently summed up Sweden's performance in these national league tables with an article entitled 'Why Sweden beats other countries at just about everything'.[68] For anyone engaged in the promotion of Sweden abroad, in tourism, business or politics, it was as if Midsummer, Christmas and a couple of crayfish parties had all come at once.

Such consistent high performance must contribute to a generally positive international reputation. Luckily, there's an index for that, and indeed Sweden's reputation is strong. In an annual survey of country reputations produced by the Reputation Institute – an international consultancy – Sweden has been in the top three since the research began in 2012, peaking at number one in 2016.[69] The 2017 study ranked 55 countries and interviewed 39,000 consumers.

According to the Reputation Institute, we live in a 'reputation economy' in which country reputations can be measured in a similar way to those of people or companies. The 'overall reputation of a country is an emotional perception constructed through experience, communication, third parties' perspectives and generally accepted stereotypes.'

What's interesting about the Reputation Institute's survey is that while Sweden is in the top three for reputation, the country is only 19th out of the 55 countries surveyed when it comes to familiarity. This point is significant, as we shall see later, since a low level of familiarity with a country creates an opportunity for anyone wishing to spread a distorted picture of the place.

A similar index produced by a consultancy called Future-Brand is based on the hypothesis that 'countries can usefully be understood as the sum of their identity and reputation'. FutureBrand makes the point that the strength of perception of a country influences people's decisions about visiting, living or investing there. A strong positive 'country brand' is a competitive advantage, to the extent that consumer choice is affected by the country of origin.

> This is not least because strong brands associated with a country make a significant contribution to perceptions of it, but also because people actively prefer products and services when they are from specific countries. Which means every time they buy a car, eat a type of food or wear a clothing brand, they can be consciously consuming an aspect of the country that made them. Countries that do not benefit from these 'Made In' associations are at a measurable disadvantage to their peers.[70]

In other words, strong consumer brands improve the perception of a country, while a better perception of a country supports its consumer brands. Sweden has clearly spun this virtuous circle to maximum effect, with global companies in sectors as diverse as furniture, clothing, home appliances and gaming going from strength to strength.

One man who knows more about the value of Sweden's reputation than most people is Olle Wästberg. In his long career, Wästberg has been the editor of one of Sweden's most popular newspapers, a member of parliament and the Consul-General of Sweden in New York. In February 2017 he told The Local that 'Sweden is a small country which relies on foreign trade. We are dependent on having a good reputation, [so] that investors dare to invest in Sweden because they know that there is some kind of continuity.'[71]

Sweden's strong and positive reputation is good for business, which is why organisations like the Swedish Institute and many regional marketing offices invest so much in cultivating this image. It means that when Swedish companies do business abroad, many of the important boxes – innovative, trustworthy, efficient – are already ticked.

Of the six 'dimensions' incorporated in the FutureBrand rankings (value system, quality of life, good for business, tourism, heritage and culture, made in), Sweden comes top of the pile for one – its value system. This takes us to the findings of one of the more interesting of all these global surveys, the World Values Survey.

With its headquarters in Stockholm, the World Values Survey has been running since 1981 in almost 100 countries. Unlike many of the surveys mentioned above, it is non-commercial and claims to be 'the largest cross-national, time series investigation of human beliefs and values ever executed, currently including interviews with almost 400,000 respondents'.

The data garnered from the survey is used by social scientists and economists all over the world to help policy makers to understand beliefs and values around the world and the role they play in areas such as economic development, democratisation and gender equality. But it is the interpretation of the data by two political scientists, Ronald Inglehart and Christian Welzel (who is also the director of research at the World Values Survey Association), that has attracted most attention to the survey, at least in Sweden. Inglehart and Welzel believe that cultural variation in the world – the differences in countries' values – can be distilled to four kinds of values.[72]

Traditional values emphasise the importance of religion, parent-child ties, deference to authority and traditional family

Secular-Rational

● JAPAN

● SWEDEN

● CHINA

● FINLAND
● GERMANY ● HOLLAND

● DENMARK

● RUSSIA ● HUNGARY

● SWITZERLAND
● FRANCE

Survival

● SPAIN

● MOLDOVIA

● ITALY

● GREAT BRITAIN

Self-Expression

● UNITED STATES

● ROMANIA

● CHILE

● CANADA

● IRELAND

● TUNISIA ● IRAQ

● BRAZIL

● JORDAN

● COLOMBIA

● QATAR

Traditional

Figure 1 – Inglehart and Welzel's interpretation of the World Values Survey data, selected countries, 2014. Author's adaption.

values. People who embrace these values also reject divorce, abortion, euthanasia and suicide. These societies have high levels of national pride and a nationalistic outlook.

Secular-rational values have the opposite preferences to the traditional values. These societies place less emphasis on religion, traditional family values and authority. Divorce, abortion, euthanasia and suicide are seen as relatively acceptable. (Suicide is not necessarily more common.)

Survival values place emphasis on economic and physical security. It is linked with a relatively ethnocentric outlook and low levels of trust and tolerance.

Self-expression values give high priority to environmental protection, growing tolerance of foreigners, gays and lesbians and gender equality, and rising demands for participation in decision-making in economic and political life.

To illustrate this, they produced a chart with two axes. The vertical axis represented a scale from traditional values at the bottom to secular rational values at the top. The horizontal axis represented a scale from survival values on the left to self-expression values on the right.[73]

As we have seen, the values that Sweden stands for are progressive values such as gender equality. And sure enough, Sweden is in the top right corner, an outlier among nations for its secular-rational, self-expression values. There it sits on its own, more secular-rational than self-expressionist Denmark, more self-expressionist than secular-rational Japan.

Sweden is proudly, provocatively unique. But having anchored its destiny to these values, what if they go out of fashion? Or what if those values themselves are in opposition to the interests of powerful forces and, say, an unapologetic US president and his media associates start spreading myths about Sweden in an attempt to undermine them? Is Sweden's positive and valuable reputation resilient enough to withstand such an attack?

That depends to a large extent on how much people know about Sweden. Regardless of his apology two years later, Eisenhower knew full well that he could make a statement about Sweden and it would stick in the minds of his intended audience – because while they may have had a strong *sense* of what Sweden was all about, they actually knew very little about the place. Certainly not enough to be able to place his comments in context and evaluate them from an informed perspective.

So how much do people know about Sweden today? Anybody reading this probably knows rather more than the average global citizen, so let's turn the question around: how much do *you* know about Portugal?

The Portugal Problem

I shall now tell you everything I know about Portugal. I am not going to use Google. I am simply going to rely on my own experience, perceptions and stereotypes – and my ability to remember everything I've ever learned about Portugal in my life. Here goes.

Portugal is the country to the left (or 'west', as the experts say) of Spain. It has an Atlantic coastline with lots of holiday resorts. One of these areas is called the Algarve. Portugal has a warm southern European climate and I imagine it gets a bit windy on the Atlantic coast.

Approximately 10 million people live in Portugal. I assume that Catholicism is the dominant religion. Portugal is a member of the European Union. The country's currency is the Euro. The capital of Portugal is Lisbon, which is probably somewhere in the middle of the country – I guess by the coast.

Portugal used to be a great maritime power and did a fair bit of colonizing. Angola springs to mind. That got nasty.

Cristiano Ronaldo. CR7. Portugal won the European Championship in 2016. While I'm on football there's José Mourinho too. And Eusebio. Benfica is the best-known football team in Portugal. Another is Porto, which is presumably a city and not just a football team.

The official language of Portugal is Brazilian.

***

OK, I *do* know the language, but I don't know anything about the politics of Portugal. I don't know what kind of parliamentary system they have or which party is in power or the name of the prime minister. Or president, if they have one of those instead. I don't know what the big societal issues are for the Portuguese, I don't know anything about the state of their healthcare system or their roads or their technology infrastructure. I can't name any Portuguese companies and, apart from tourism, I don't know what the main industries are in the country.

I expect Portugal has great composers, artists and writers but I can't name one. Who is the country's most loved pop star? Who is the country's most watched celebrity? No idea.

By the way, is Portugal in Nato?

I don't know anything at all about Portugal's stance on immigration or whether integration has been a challenge for the country. I wonder if unemployment is rising or falling? What kind of an army does Portugal have and do they have conscription? Is the murder rate above or below the EU average? Gender equality? Rape? Suicide? Are there far right or far left parties in Portugal and if so, are they gaining in popularity?

Portugal is a modern European country with a great history (I guess). But I know shamefully little about the place. So if someone tells me something about Portugal, I have almost no context – other than a sense of what's 'normal' for a modern European state – for parsing that information. In my busy life, with information coming at me from all angles, a flash of news about Portugal will slip past the gates of my consciousness with no interrogation, no searching and no background checks.

And that's how most people deal with information about Sweden.

It's an old cliché that people mix up Sweden and Switzerland but it's true. It's the countries' own faults, of course, both beginning with 'Sw' and both being neutral, but it became such a problem for Swedish and Swiss officials in China (where the names are even more similar) that the Swedish consulate in Shanghai produced a humorous poster to explain the differences.[74] The cartoon, which stuck to the safest of stereotypes (a viking, a moose, a blonde in a bikini, Pippi and gay marriage for Sweden; chocolate, a watch, banks, snow-covered mountains and Roger Federer for Switzerland) went viral in China but whether it helped to separate the two countries in the minds of the Chinese is unclear. A quick search on Google for 'Sweden Switzerland confusion' shows that the problem is by no means limited to China.

This is not an issue that France or Germany needs to deal with.

***

It is clear that Sweden has a very positive reputation, which is valuable and is vital for the country's commercial and political influence around the world. Part of Sweden's reputation stems from uncontroversial and not particularly unique skill sets such as technology and innovation. But what *really* differentiates Sweden's reputation from that of other countries is the country's relatively extreme progressive values. These values are certainly not universal, even in the West (and if you think they are, you need to step out of your bubble). This makes Sweden's reputation a tempting target. Meanwhile, the general ignorance about Sweden and its limited reach as a small nation make it vulnerable in the event of an attack.

That wouldn't be a problem if there weren't people out there who would seek to use Sweden as a tool to attack those progressive values. Unfortunately, as we saw with Eisenhower, there have been such people out there in the past and there are today. Trump's statement made him the most visible but there are many others. They are not necessarily formally connected but they are all pulling in the same direction. Most importantly, they have all understood that to undermine the values that Sweden represents they need to show that Sweden is failing.

CHAPTER 3:

Refugees and the alternative media

When Last-Night-In-Sweden-Gate was raging on social media, there was a sense that Swedes saw the whole thing as a bit of fun, a crazy way to brighten up a cold, dark February Sunday morning. Hey, check this out, The Donald is talking about us! Not Norway, not Denmark – us! It was obvious from Trump's remarks and speedy clarification that he was not referring to an imagined terror attack, but commentators and politicians stretched the story as far as they could. Swedish newspapers began publishing articles in English on the subject, everyone scrambled to interview the documentary maker and Swedes collectively joked their way back to normality.

It turned out to be the right approach and provides one model for dealing with similar situations in future. Not only did it prompt that clarification from the US president, but it may also have had a positive commercial effect.

A couple of weeks after the incident I called the Boston office of Cheapflights, an online flight booking service. I asked them if they had observed any significant changes in the number of searches for flights from the US to Sweden following Trump's remarks. What they told me was astonishing. The weekend after Trump referred to 'what happened last night in Sweden', flight searches from the US to Sweden dropped by 13% compared to average weekend volumes. The remarks inflicted immediate damage on Sweden's economy – small, perhaps, but remember, these are just figures from one company. But the following weekend, after five days of sustained positive media coverage about Sweden in the States, searches for flights from the US to Sweden were 30% *above* the levels that Cheapflights usually experiences.

That's good news. But President Trump's impromptu comment was just the smoke. It will be a lot harder to put out the fire.

***

Sweden, as we saw in the previous chapter, is the world's most self-expressionist, secular-rational society. Such a society, you will remember, is broadly characterised by a positive attitude towards gender equality, concern for the environment, an emphasis on democracy and a tolerance of foreigners.

So if you happen to favour Inglehart's and Welzel's traditional, survival values (with greater emphasis on the roles of religion and family in a more authoritarian, nationalistic, ethnocentric society) and you want to spread your philosophy, you need to convince your audience that Sweden is failing. This is tough because Sweden, by most economic and social indicators, is one of the most prosperous and well-functioning societies the world has ever seen. You therefore need to focus aggressively on the problems in Sweden and be deceptively selective about what you present from the country.

Now, your job would be made a lot easier if Sweden were to commit a high-profile policy action that epitomises its famous values and to which the Swedes themselves would quickly attach the word 'crisis'.

The refugee crisis

On September 7th 2015 an unprecedented number of people began to arrive at Malmö central station, flowing north by train in the following days and weeks to Gothenburg and Stockholm. The largest group were fleeing the war in Syria but there were almost as many people arriving from Afghanistan and a significant number from Iraq. Between September and December of 2015, some 114,000 people made the hellish, perilous journey across land and sea to find sanctuary in Sweden. This surge took the total number of asylum seekers for 2015 to 163,000, double the number who arrived the previous year and more than five times the average since 2000.[75]

Of those who arrived in the autumn of 2015, 70,000 were children. Along with local authorities, many other central government agencies were involved in organizing different aspects of the refugees' needs. The police handled border control while social, health and educational matters were handled by the National Board of Health and Welfare, the Health and Social Care Inspectorate, the Public Health Agency of Sweden, the National Agency for Education, the Swedish Schools Inspectorate, the National Board of Institutional Care and the Swedish Agency for Youth and Civil Society.[76] The Swedish public played their part too, with volunteers donating cash, collecting food, clothing, toys and other supplies for the refugees, opening up their homes, supervising the temporary accommodation in community centres and acting as legal guardians for the children who arrived alone.

But the agency that bore the brunt of the pressure was the Swedish Migration Agency. The official inquiry into the handling of the situation noted that the government was unprepared for such a large number of arrivals and was forced to activate its crisis management procedures. According to the official report, 'the situation for the Swedish Migration Agency was extremely intense during the autumn of 2015. The Migration Agency prioritised the acquisition of accommodation, and it succeeded in living up to its ambition of organizing a roof over the heads of everyone who came, apart from on one single night'.[77]

For two extraordinary months, Sweden seemed to be living up to its claim to be a 'humanitarian superpower', a rather immodest label applied in the calmer times of February 2013 by the then foreign minister Carl Bildt[78] and echoed two years later by his successor Margot Wallström.[79] The government hoped that by standing alongside Germany and leading by example, other countries would be pressured to bear their share of the refugee burden.

On November 4th, prime minister Stefan Löfven issued a stark call for support from the rest of the European Union, arguing that Sweden had taken an unreasonably large responsibility in comparison with other countries.[80]

'Now we are in a very tight position. It is time that other countries now take responsibility and therefore the government requests the redistribution of refugees from Sweden,' he said.

The plea was met with deaf ears, and the number of refugees arriving in Sweden continued rising. The following week, the Swedish authorities took the unprecedented measure of introducing stringent controls in the south of the country. In a radical reversal of the long-established Schengen open borders agreement, the policy shift allowed police to begin checking the identification documents of people arriving at the border. The number of refugees entering Sweden fell abruptly.

Inevitably, the 'humanitarian superpower' tag was thrown back at Sweden. 'Even Europe's humanitarian superpower is turning its back on refugees,' wrote the Washington Post, noting that 'the new policies have triggered intense soul-searching'.[81] Carl Bildt recognized later that the U-turn had cast doubt upon Sweden's own values.[82]

'We had been on very high moral horses against the rest of the world for some time and then we turned around completely. That raised a number of questions about stability,' he said.

The enormous costs of taking in so many refugees will be borne for many years to come,[83] but the crisis period for Sweden, although intense, was short. In 2016 the country had 29,000 asylum applications, the lowest number since 2009.[84]

But for detractors of the values that Sweden represents, the refugee crisis was very useful indeed. It continued a narrative thread from the Husby riots in 2013 and provided an emotionally-charged wealth of stories and images with which they could claim that the decision to let in 'the migrant hordes' was leading to the collapse and ruin of the country that 'beats other countries at just about everything'. And the message was clear: the logical conclusion of these progressive values was self-destruction. You must reject these values, or your world will also collapse. Look at Sweden. *Even* Sweden.

And given today's image-driven media, it was an extra bonus that Sweden also happens to be home to globally-ingrained and aesthetically-appealing motifs as fine-looking blondes, red cottages by pristine lakes and ABBA. Against such a backdrop, images of burning cars and rioting immigrant youths would have a much more powerful effect on the visual cortex.

The necessary elements of the Bad Sweden narrative were falling into place.

***

As far as the various international rankings and mainstream news outlets are concerned, Sweden's high-tech cities are dominated by creativity and innovation and civic harmony. It is a place of low crime and top quality care for children and the elderly. The country is a leader in gender equality and provides better opportunities for girls than anywhere else in the world.[85]

But if you restrict your consumption to a certain subsection of the media, what has become known as the 'alternative media', a loosely connected network of news web sites, television channels and radio stations whose content ranges from strongly conservative, populist news reporting to the unabashed promotion of far-right conspiracies, you will have a very different view of Sweden.

As far as you are concerned, Sweden is ground zero for Europe's impending 'multicultural civil war', a state overrun by immigrants and on the verge of collapse. You will be convinced that Swedish streets are riddled with the charred skeletons of Volvos burned in youth riots. And you will be well aware that Malmö, Sweden's third largest city, is now 'the rape capital of Europe' due to the sky-high number of rapes since the country's spineless politicians opened the doors to all those migrants.

Sweden's international 'audience'

Who is being told the Good Sweden story and who is being told the Bad Sweden story? Does it matter if the alternative media is painting a different picture of Sweden? To answer that question, let's start by dividing Sweden's 'target audience' for its reputation communication into three categories of 'users'.

Informed Users

Informed Users are a small group with an above average knowledge of Sweden. They have lived in the country, perhaps for work or studies, or visited more than once. They maintain a connection to Sweden by keeping in touch with friends and colleagues in the country and by following the news. They know a lot of Swedes well and probably have some command of the language. They can put any information they receive about Sweden into context and they have a framework for assessing its credibility. Their perceptions about Sweden are shaped by their personal experience of the country. They are unlikely to be influenced by distorted or false reports about Sweden and if they are doubtful about certain information they are able to check it out with original sources. They often see themselves as informal ambassadors for Sweden and are more likely to share positive information about the country than negative information.

Neutral Users

The vast majority of people out there are Neutral Users – not just about Sweden but about every country in the world apart from their own. I am a Neutral User when it comes to Portugal. These people have no personal connections to Sweden although they may have visited once. Their work and studies have not given them any special insights into Sweden and Swedish society, but they have almost certainly been exposed to Sweden's cultural and commercial exports, and to occasional coverage of Sweden in the media they consume, which is domestic and mainstream. Their immediate associations with the country are likely to include well-known Swedish brands such as Ikea, cultural icons such as ABBA and Pippi Longstocking and Wallander, and broadly positive abstract qualities such as beautiful, welfare and clean. Unlike Informed Users, Neutral Users do not have a framework for assessing the credibility of information they receive about Sweden. Anything that confounds their perceptions of Sweden is likely to make a bigger impact on them than information that confirms their perceptions. Since they do not particularly care about Sweden's fortunes either way, they are therefore more likely than Informed Users to share negative information about Sweden with their peers.

Resistant Users

Resistant Users have a similar level of awareness about Sweden to Neutral Users: no personal connections to Sweden and no special insights to the workings of Swedish society but almost certainly some exposure to Swedish commercial and cultural exports. What distinguishes them from Neutral Users is the strength of their value system, which places them in the traditional-survival quadrant of the Ingelhart-Welzel chart – the opposite quadrant to Sweden. They are far more likely than Neutral Users to consume alternative media. Resistant Users adhere to an aesthetic notion of Sweden and Swedishness which they feel is being eroded by the secular-rational values and politically correct policies now being practised in the country. They are highly susceptible to negative information about Sweden that confirms their view and actively distrustful of information which contradicts it. They will share negative information about Sweden and attack positive or neutral information.

The two different stories about Sweden are targeted at the opposite ends of this short spectrum but the audience that really matters, just by weight of numbers, is the Neutral Users in the middle. Among them are the tourists who Sweden wants to attract, the buyers of Swedish products and the international talent whose skills are in demand by Swedish start-ups. The risk for those whose work depends on a strong reputation for Sweden abroad is that the unbalanced, decontextualized version of Swedish news being told to Resistant Users starts filtering into the enormous community of Neutral Users. And that is exactly what has been happening.

It happens partly because of social media and people's tendency to share negative news. Despite all the recent analysis of filter bubbles and our tendency only to share news that confirms our world view, news travels between individuals in these groups. But what is more significant is the way that certain mainstream media brands, particularly in the UK, now approach news about Sweden with the same kind of hyper-partisan stance as the more fringe US outlets, repackaging negative news about the country for an audience that would consider itself to be among the Neutral Users.

Bad Sweden in the US

The most prominent news outlet trumpeting the negative view of Sweden is Breitbart. The site was set up in 2007 by a conservative American commentator called Andrew Breitbart, who felt that the US media was too left-leaning and biased against Israel.[86] Andrew Breitbart died in 2012 and the media company was taken over by Steve Bannon – who went on to become Donald Trump's campaign director and chief strategist in the White House before returning to Breitbart in August 2017. In Bannon's own words, Breitbart during his tenure became 'the platform for the alt-right',[87] an informal term that has become shorthand for groups such as nationalists, populists, men's rights activists, nihilists, conspiracy theorists and white supremacists.[88]

If such a collection of standpoints can be united by a single philosophy, it is characterised by ultraconservative values and a fierce rejection of political correctness. There is no better issue for the alt-right to get its teeth into than multiculturalism as epitomised by the European refugee crisis – and no better distillation of the issue than Sweden. While the alt-right has so far been primarily an American movement, Sweden has been called 'the most alt-right country in Europe', with its own network of alternative news sites feeding a steady flow of stories into outlets such as Breitbart.[89]

Stories such as 'Wear A Headscarf Or Be Raped, Swedish Women Warned',[90] 'Sweden So Violent, Migrants Consider Moving Back To War-Zone Homelands',[91] 'Scared Sweden: Almost Half Of Women Afraid To Be Out After Dark In Europe's Rape Capital'[92] and 'Sweden Facing Collapse Thanks To Migrant Influx, Foreign Minister Warns'[93] are standard fare when Breitbart covers Sweden. In the first six months of 2017, the site produced well over 100 such articles about the country and the havoc being wrought by immigration. As with the bizarre Christmas lights story, Breitbart's articles tend to be based on accurate local news reports but the basic facts are stripped of context and regurgitated in lurid and exaggerated form, while tropes such as 'migrant rape crisis' and 'no go zones' are bandied about as if they are incontrovertible descriptions of the status quo.

(Actually, these were not the only stories written about Sweden; a handful of others addressed issues such as 'Swedish PM Wants to Force Priests To Marry Same Sex Couples',[94] 'Christian Preschoolers Banned from Saying "Amen", Talking About The Bible',[95] and 'Number of Swedish Children Wanting to Change Gender Doubling Each Year'.[96])

For its sheer volume of Bad Sweden content, Breitbart is ahead of the rest of the alternative media pack. Indeed, the site, which is still a relatively small news operation, produces significantly more content about Sweden than major news outlets such as Le Monde in France and La Repubblica in Italy.

Breitbart is part-owned by the family of an American technology and hedge fund billionaire called Robert Mercer,[97] who, it was widely reported, invested $10 million in the media company in 2011.[98] With somewhere between 20 million and 45 million users per month,[99] Breitbart is the largest of the news and comment sites specifically targeting an alt-right audience. But it is not the only one with a predilection for news about Sweden.

Infowars, a site run by a radio host and conspiracy theorist called Alex Jones, takes a similar line to Breitbart. I mentioned Infowars' spin on the Christmas lights story in the first chapter and this is complemented by articles such as 'What They're Not Telling You About Sweden'[100] and 'Suicide Of Sweden: Only One In Five Foreign Rapists Are Deported'.[101] And then there are activists and bloggers such as Pamela Geller, whose January 2016 post entitled 'Europe's Civil War Breaks Out:

The Battle For Stockholm's Train Station, Overrun, Occupied by Muslim Migrants' was hyperbolic to say the least: 'Swedish towns have become terror hubs. Lawlessness is rampant, violent crimes skyrocket. There is this now constant state of violence, terror and fear.'[102]

Does it matter what commentators such as Alex Jones and Pamela Geller write about Sweden? It does, because a lot of people follow what they say. President Trump is said to follow Infowars and appeared on Jones's radio show in 2015.[103] The show is syndicated to 160 other stations and Jones has accumulated over a billion views on YouTube. After Trump won the election, he apparently called Alex Jones to thank him for his support and said that his influence was 'second to none'.[104] Infowars has over 800,000 followers on Facebook.[105] Pamela Geller has over a million followers on Facebook.[106] Twenty-five years ago, activists with the same kind of fervour and persuasiveness would have attracted a small audience in their own backyards through local radio, cable TV or printing leaflets. Today these commentators are influential nodes in an infinitely connected world.

They boast follower numbers that most news organisations would be very happy with. For the sake of comparison, the Swedish broadsheet Dagens Nyheter has fewer than 200,000 Facebook followers[107] and the most popular newspaper in Sweden, Aftonbladet, has just under 400,000.[108] But so what if Breitbart and Infowars are pumping out negative information about Sweden? There's no law that says they must provide balance or context. What they write and how they write it is their prerogative, however inconvenient, and surely their audience isn't a top priority for Sweden when it comes to cultivating its reputation abroad? Clearly, when it comes to Sweden, Breitbart & co are talking to Resistant Users, a group which is always going to be outside of Sweden's sphere of influence. The problem is that there is no clear dividing line between these groups, no firebreak to stop the flames of the Bad Sweden narrative spreading from Resistant Users to Neutral Users. And of course Breitbart has millions of the latter among their readers too.

Bad Sweden in the UK
The Daily Express and the Daily Mail have occupied the middle ground of British news media for decades. Sitting between the red-top tabloids such as the Sun and the Mirror and the venerable broadsheets such as the Daily Telegraph and the Guardian, they serve middle class, middle England with a diet of news and sport, showbiz gossip and fiercely partisan opinion.

The Express hit a circulation peak in the middle of the last century, shipping over four million copies per day.[109] Today, the paper edition only reaches 400,000 daily readers but its web site claims 9.2 million users per month.[110] With the exception of a few articles about Sweden's princesses and football stars, the picture of the country painted by the Express is similar to Breitbart's. Here are some recent examples:

SWEDEN CRUMBLING: Demands For Military Intervention As Thugs Turn Malmo Into 'No-Go Zone'[111]

Battlefield Sweden: Police Admit Malmo Isn't Safe As Thugs Send Fireworks Into Crowds[112]

Nigel Farage Warns Sweden's Crisis Is Being 'COVERED UP' By 'POLITICALLY CORRECT' Media[113]

SWEDEN MAYHEM: Police find HAND GRENADE
in crisis-hit 'no-go zone' after deadly shooting[114]

SWEDEN AT BREAKING POINT: Police make urgent
plea for help as violent crime spirals[115]

LAWLESS SWEDEN: Violent migrant youths turn
shopping centre into 'NO-GO ZONE' – officials[116]

Mayhem, crumbling, a battlefield, politically correct, no-go
zones, at breaking point, lawless – for the readers of the Daily
Express, this is modern Sweden. To anyone familiar with the
history of the publication, this will come as no surprise. As
far back as 1948 the paper's owner, Lord Beaverbrook, told a
Royal Commission on the Press that he saw the paper 'purely
as a propagandist project'.[117] In the late 1960s the Express was
the loudest media voice against Britain joining the European
Economic Community and in 2000 the paper was bought by
billionaire publisher Richard Desmond, a generous donor to
the UK Independence Party.[118]

Given the focus on the city of Malmö in the Express's content, the paper did publish a surprising article in May 2017 that
provided evidence not so much of balance but of how insincere
their editorial stance on Sweden really is. In a travel piece
entitled 'Discovering Sweden's Trendy City Malmö by Kayak',
the writer enjoyed the 'Swedish tradition of coffee and cake,
which is religiously adhered to by locals' and concluded that
'whatever angle you witness it from, Malmö is a true treasure,
crammed with Scandi charm.'[119]

The journalist may have gone wildly off-message with her
enthusiastic travel piece but the comments under the article

were true to form. 'Yeah sure…let's all go and get our daughters r@-p-ed,' said one, followed by another in the same vein: 'Better take pepper spray and knuckledusters with you if you go to Sweden or get robbed and raped. Your choice.' Let's hope nobody in the Swedish tourist industry paid for the journalist to visit Malmö.

The long-standing rival of the Express, the Daily Mail, has a daily print circulation of almost 1.5 million. But online, the Mail is a global powerhouse. With more than 15 million unique browsers per day (a measure of the number of devices accessing the site, not readers) and over 220 million per month, Mail Online is one of the biggest news websites in the world.[120] Turbocharged by its legendary 'sidebar of shame', a never-ending column of celebrities in (and out of) bikinis and lingerie, the site produces a vast amount of content every day, including stories about Sweden on the time-honoured themes of offbeat news, royalty and amusing wildlife. But the Mail also aggressively pursues its traditionalist, anti-European Union, anti-immigration agenda – and inevitably, Sweden gets caught in the crosshairs:

How Europe's Most Liberal Nation Gagged Its Own People On Migration Attacks: The Swedish Conspiracy To Hide The Truth About The Refugee Influx[121]

Women Are Warned Not To Go Out Alone At Night In Swedish Town After Multiple Sex Attacks By 'Foreigners'[122]

EXCLUSIVE – The Lawless Asylum Centre Where Migrants Rule: Inside Squalid Swedish Shelter That Police Will Not Enter, Where 10-Year-Old Boy Was Raped And That Has Just TWO Staff On Duty For 600 Refugees[123]

Was Trump Right About Sweden? As The President Is Mocked For His Remarks On Swedish Crime And Immigration, ANDREW MALONE Provides A Disturbing Dispatch From One Of The World's Most PC Nations[124]

Where Females Fear To Tread: KATIE HOPKINS Reports From Sweden, The Scandi-Lib Paradise Where Terrified Women Have Vanished From The Streets And A Conspiracy Of Silence And Self-Censorship On Immigration Buries The Truth[125]

The Mail's coverage of Sweden did not go unnoticed by the Swedish embassy in London. In a report to the Foreign Ministry in Stockholm in 2016, officials wrote that the Daily Mail had 'launched a campaign against Swedish migration policy'. They said that Sweden was being used as an argument against allowing more refugees into the UK. More pointedly, the embassy report found that The Daily Mail was characterizing Sweden as 'naïve and an example of the negative consequences of a liberal migration policy'.[126]

If the Mail was transmitting this message, who was receiving it? Mail Online's own traffic statistics from 2014 show that around 73% of their readers are in the US, the UK, Canada and Australia. But they also show that the site has over 800,000 monthly readers in Sweden. That's more than most Swedish news sites have. What effect will the Mail's content have on the next Swedish election? This is new territory for Sweden's political parties but they need to be aware that at least some of the battles in the next election will be fought in the international media.

CHAPTER 4:

Mutation

The commentator responsible for the last article mentioned in the previous section, Katie Hopkins, was also a presenter on LBC, a British radio station which attracts two million listeners each week.[127] As well as being popular, LBC is influential, entirely mainstream and well-respected for its journalism. But LBC's format – discussion driven by listeners calling in to air their views – relies upon employing provocative presenters such as Hopkins among their more balanced journalists. In 2017 they appointed another, in the form of Nigel Farage, the member of the European Parliament whose persistent anti-EU activism through his UK Independence Party (UKIP) helped to force the referendum on Britain's membership of the European Union.

Sweden's rape numbers
After Britain voted narrowly to leave the EU in June 2016, Farage resigned as the leader of UKIP. He became a political pundit, speaking in the US at Republican Party events, contributing to Fox News and joining LBC to present their evening phone-in show.

It didn't take him long to turn his sights on Sweden. A couple of days after Donald Trump talked about 'last night in Sweden', Farage was discussing the statement on his show. He noted that Trump was not referring to a specific incident but went on to make a more explicit point to his audience:

> In terms of direction of travel, what [Trump] was saying was very valid… Sweden has taken in more young male migrants than any other country in Europe and there has been a dramatic rise in sexual crime in Sweden. So much so, that Malmo is now the rape capital of Europe, and some argue that perhaps it is the rape capital of the world. And there is a Swedish media who frankly just don't report it.[128]

Farage's comment was widely reported in British and international media and his tweet containing a video clip from the radio show has been liked over 13,000 times.[129] To clarify his point further, Farage wrote in the tweet that 'Malmo [sic] in Sweden is the rape capital of Europe due to EU migrant policies. Anyone who says there isn't a problem is lying to you.'

The notion of Sweden and Malmö as a 'rape capital' is vividly arresting as it coarsely shatters the two common associations of 'Swedish women' and a 'safe Sweden' with a single shot. The term wasn't coined by Farage; it has been familiar currency in anti-immigration circles – including Breitbart – since an article[130] published in February 2015 by the Gatestone Institute, a right wing think tank that describes itself as 'dedicated to educating the public about what the mainstream media fails to report' in various policy areas.[131]

But Farage's comments led to a massive spike in Google searches for 'Sweden rape'[132] and a wave of debate in the international media about whether or not he spoke the truth. The Swedish National Council for Crime Prevention (Brå) makes a vast amount of crime-related data available to the public and a selective analysis of the headline figures can make it look as though Farage has a point. But many Swedish analysts and commentators took issue with his statement, arguing that any rise in the numbers was for different reasons.[133] The problem is that while it is easy to make a claim like Farage's, refuting it is much more complicated. But since the notion that rape has exploded in Sweden has made such an international impact and is likely to stick around like the suicide myth, it is worth looking at those arguments more closely.

Evidence for the 'rape capital' claim usually comes in the form of comparative international statistics suggesting that Sweden has a significantly higher number of reported rape incidents per 100,000 citizens than most other countries. But comparing the number of reported rapes – or indeed any crimes – from one country to another is a process vulnerable to inaccuracies because there are no international standards for how crime statistics are collected.

In some countries, a series of similar offences by one perpetrator against one victim will count as one crime. In Sweden, however, each incident will be tallied separately. Swedish data on reported crimes also includes incidents that are later found not to have constituted criminal offences, as well as attempted offences.[134]

But even if it is unwise to compare rape numbers between countries, can we look at Sweden's own figures and see a 'dramatic rise', as Farage put it, caused by the large intake of refugees since the autumn of 2015? Of course, we can't draw any conclusions about causality from one year of headline data but we can at least see how the number for 2016 compares to previous years.

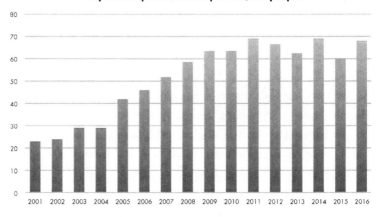

Reported rapes in Sweden per 100,000 people

Figure 2: Data from Brå 2017

Figure 2 shows that the number of reported rapes per 100,000 people in 2016 was indeed higher than in 2015, although lower than in 2014 and 2011. But that's not what's striking about the chart. What's most striking is the rapid rise in the numbers from 2005 to 2011. In 2005, Sweden significantly broadened its definition of rape, which means the word is used to record acts which would be called sexual assault or bodily harm in other countries. Eight years later the legislation was expanded further to cover cases where the victim, perhaps asleep, unconscious, drunk or under the influence of another drug, is unable to give consent. Unsurprisingly, that led to an increase in the number of rapes reported in the country in the years following the two law changes.

The numbers for the city of Malmö broadly reflect the national pattern, with a steep rise to 2010 and then a flattening-off. It is interesting to note that while the average number of reported rapes per 100,000 people in the city was higher

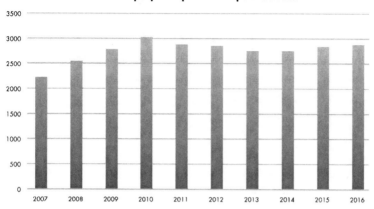

Number of people suspected of rape in Sweden

Figure 3: Data from Brå 2017

than the Swedish average up to 2011, there has been a change in recent years. From 2012 to 2016, the average annual number of rapes per 100,000 people in Malmö was 61, compared to the national average of 65.

Brå also presents data on the number of people suspected of crimes in Sweden from 2007. The number of individuals suspected of rape[135] has been quite consistent since 2009, as shown in Figure 3.

In its commentary on crime trends in Sweden in 2015, Brå also noted that 'data from the healthcare system shows no increase in the number of individuals who sought medical care as a result of sexual assaults'.[136]

Another way to try comparing the rate of sexual crimes in different countries is by consulting crime victim surveys rather than the number of reported crimes. One such study looking into violence against women in Europe was published by the European Union Agency for Fundamental Rights (FRA) in

2014. It showed that 18% of Swedish women consulted said they had been the victim of sexual violence since the age of 15, the same percentage as in the Netherlands, slightly less than Denmark (19%) and one percentage point above Finland. These countries showed the highest rates in Europe.[137] But one of the conclusions of the study is that different values in different countries could lead to different levels of women's willingness to report sexual violence. The authors wrote that 'gender equality could lead to higher levels of disclosure about violence against women. Incidents of violence against women are more likely to be openly addressed and challenged in societies with greater equality.'[138]

As we know, Sweden is an outlier for the value of gender equality and it is therefore likely that Swedish women feel less stigmatised when reporting sexual violence than women in other countries. The fact that the Netherlands, Denmark and Finland, countries with similar attitudes towards gender equality as Sweden*, show similar numbers, would appear to support that notion.

One piece of crime data that Brå does not record is the country of origin of the attacker or some similar categorisation. Whether or not they should is the subject of debate in Sweden[139] but if the information is not collected, then any claim about the nationality of attackers is only speculation.

Nigel Farage's claim that there was a 'dramatic rise' in sexual crime in Sweden due to the country's immigration policy got enormous international exposure. It was compelling, raising a dramatic question about Swedish values. And as with Eisenhower's suicide statement, the audience didn't stick around for answers. Realistically, only the Informed

---

* ...although quite different attitudes towards immigration.

Users I described above care enough about Sweden to bother checking the details. If you are a Resistant User, then the burst of coverage at the beginning of 2017 would have been an 'I *knew* it' moment, hardening the notion of Sweden or Malmö as a 'rape capital' in your mind. The triumvirate of facts that logically lead to higher numbers presented by Swedish and international experts – a wider definition of rape, multiple incidences classified as individual rapes and a higher tendency in a gender-equal society to report sexual violence – would be irrelevant to you, a minor technicality or evidence of the Swedish government trying to cover up the truth.

If you are a Neutral User, you may have encountered this claim for the first time thanks to Nigel Farage and the ensuing exposure. You will probably have found it surprising and it may have made you angry but since you aren't particularly interested in Sweden, it would have been a fleeting moment of reflection before you moved on to other things. But some residue would remain.

How news stories mutate

Whether the subject is riots by 'migrant youths', 'no-go zones' abandoned by the authorities, rape statistics or the banning of Christmas lights, it should be becoming clear by now that there is a process by which real stories mutate into damaging and tenacious myths with a broad reach.

The starting point is always a *legitimate and verifiable story*. This will have been reported in Sweden, in Swedish, according to accepted journalistic standards by a respected news source. One such article, headlined 'Brottsplats Nordstan – så ser vardagen ut' (which translates to 'Nordstan – an everyday crime scene'), appeared in the tabloid Expressen on January 14th 2017. It told of increasing problems with youth gangs gathering at Sweden's biggest shopping mall, Nordstan in Gothenburg as shops closed their doors each day.[140] Journalist Claes Petersson spoke to shop owners, police, social workers and the youths themselves to paint a balanced portrait of an inner city shopping centre suffering inner city troubles, with plenty of vivid examples of drugs, assaults, theft and intimidation. As Petersson noted, many of the youths were from Gothenburg's suburbs but others were recently arrived immigrant children from Afghanistan and Syria.

While the article demonstrated that there are some serious social problems to be dealt with in Gothenburg, it wasn't all bad news. In fact, the police statistics cited in the article showed that in 2016 the number of reported crimes was 5.5% lower than in 2015, leading police analyst Thomas Pettersson to comment that overall there was no dramatic change for the worse in the mall. Violent crime had actually fallen three years running and in 2016 the number of reported violent crimes was down 30% compared to its peak in 2013, two years *before* the large number of asylum seekers arrived in the city.

The next day, we saw the first mutation when the Expressen article was used as the basis for an article in Avpixlat,[141] a news site with links to the far right Sweden Democrats. In September 2017 Avpixlat changed its name to 'Samhällsnytt' (Society News) and expanded its editorial team to include one former Sweden Democrat politician and one SD staffer.[142] Before its makeover, Avpixlat said it 'provides uncomfortable truths and opinions about Swedish immigration policies and the underlying cultural relativism behind the political decisions and the journalists' pens'.[143]

Avpixlat's version of the article, 'Laglöst land på galleria i Göteborg' ('Lawlessness at Gothenburg mall'), focused on the immigrant aspect of the Expressen story. It was up to Avpixlat to *angle* the story according to its editorial objectives and the damage to Sweden's reputation at this stage is *limited and local*. The site was in Swedish, as is its new incarnation, and anyone reading it knows – and probably supports – its stance.

A few hours after Avpixlat's article, the story found its way onto the Russia Today web site, RT.com. With Russia Today we step into a whole other world of news choices where, rather than alt-right ideology, it is geopolitical issues such as the tension between Russia and the European Union and Sweden's relationship with Nato which are the driving force. But the upshot is the same: a lot of content about Sweden's imminent collapse under the weight of its immigrants.

RT's interpretation of the story ran with the headline 'Leading Swedish mall turned into 'no-go zone' by migrant teen gangs – report' and like Avpixlat's it was based entirely on Expressen's report.[144] But there were extra dashes of colour, such as the claim that 'sales are reported to have taken a massive hit'. There was no mention of sales in the original report and since the trouble was starting after the shops closed it's unlikely that sales were affected. The article concluded:

As a result, the shopping mall becomes a place of almost total lawlessness after 8pm, joining other spots in Sweden now labelled as no-go zones, according to the local media report. To be considered a no-go zone, the area usually has to be marked by a dangerous incidence of muggings, robberies, harassment, and sexual assault. In September 2016, the number reportedly rose to 55 areas.

Expressen's piece did not mention 'no-go zones' and Nordstan certainly was not on the police's list of 'vulnerable areas' published in June 2017.

RT claims 3 million unique visitors per day and 50 million per month,[145] so when it *decontextualises* Swedish news in this way, the impact is felt far and wide. As far, in fact, as the offices of Mail Online and the Daily Express in the UK, both of which covered the story shortly afterwards.

Two linked references to RT show that Mail Online's version was simply a rewrite of Russia Today's piece, now headlined 'Sweden's leading shopping mall is deemed a no-go zone, with police blaming gangs of unaccompanied minors who have arrived in the country for spate of attacks'.[146]

And in this third retelling of the story the truth is blurred further, with claims that Nordstan 'has seen a spike in sinister behaviour' and that 'the troubles have seen the mall labelled a no-go zone, according to Expressen'.

As we know, neither of those statements were accurate. But when the world's biggest news web site describes it as such, the message is *amplified* and causes widespread reputational damage.

The final stage in the mutation of the story is *embedding* and it happens when the angled, decontextualized version is more prevalent on Google than the original balanced reporting (obviously the use of English gives disproportionate weight to the latter versions). At the time of writing – that is, more than six months after the articles were published – the sixth result from a Google search for 'Nordstan Gothenburg' is the Mail's article.[147] If you were the owner of an international retail brand and you were considering putting a boutique in one of Sweden's largest shopping centres, this might just make you think again.

1. Reporting	2. Angling	3. Decontextualising	4. Amplifying	5. Embedding
Local mainstream news provider	Local hyper-partisan news site in local language	International hyper-partisan news site in English	International mainstream news site in English	Google and Facebook
Legitimate verifiable story	Limited local damage to reputation	Limited international damage	Widespread international damage	Permanent international damage

Figure 4: The mutation of a news story

The youth gangs may not be hitting sales at Nordstan but content like this, distributed globally, probably will.

A *legitimate and verifiable* report is picked up by a local hyper-partisan site which *angles* the story to support its own agenda. The damage is still limited and local. But then an international news site will *decontextualise* the story further, before it is *amplified* by one of the giants and *embedded* in Google and Facebook, causing permanent international damage to Sweden's reputation.

But it does not stop there. Once the stories are posted on Facebook they can rapidly spread the headline message to an audience many times higher than the audience for the original article. Milo Yiannopoulos's Facebook post about how Sweden had banned Christmas lights 'in an effort to avoid offending Muslim migrants' was shared 45,000 times. The number of people who ended up seeing the post depends on how many 'friends' those sharing the post had. On average, Facebook users are connected to 338 friends,[148] which suggests that the Christmas lights post would have shown up in the Facebook feed of 15.2 million people on top of the two million people following Yiannopoulos. Recent research suggests that only 6.5% of Facebook posts are viewed, but that still means the post was likely to have been seen by over 1.1 million people.[149] The article by Katie Hopkins in the Mail, which itself has 12 million followers, was shared 17,500 times, suggesting it would have been seen by 1.2 million people. The mutated versions of the Nordstan story published by RT, the Mail and the Express were shared 15,600 times, meaning exposure to a similar size of audience.

As we shall see in the next chapter, the odds are all stacked in favour of the people who want to spread the Bad Sweden narrative: negative news travels faster and further, regular journalists are under pressure to churn out high volumes of articles without the resources to fact-check them, social media users are quite happy to share posts without checking the origin and once the story is out there, most people don't care enough about Sweden to listen to a complex correction.

We haven't even mentioned fake news yet.

***

We have identified plenty of examples of Swedish news reaching the world through various channels, from local hyper-partisan news sites right up to the President of the United States himself. But are these sources connected? Most news travels from one outlet to another without any formal content-sharing agreement and journalists routinely monitor the sites that give them the right kinds of stories for their audience. And given that social media clusters form around values – so-called filter bubbles – it's not surprising that we see the same news brands and bloggers echoing each other's views about Sweden.

But there are some very obvious and open links that allow us to map the dimensions of the alternative narrative about Sweden. If we take it from the top, it has been widely reported that the billionaire hedge-fund manager Robert Mercer helped to finance not only Donald Trump's campaign but also a range of political activities that helped to propel Trump to the White House.[150] As I mentioned earlier, the Mercer family is also the part-owner of Breitbart. The chairman of Breitbart, Steve Bannon, joined Trump's campaign a few months before the election but already had a well-established relationship with the Mercers.[151] Despite not having a role in the British government, one of the first foreign politicians to meet Donald Trump after he was elected president in November 2016 was Nigel Farage.[152] When Farage was the leader of the UK Independence Party (UKIP), it received a £1 million donation from Richard Desmond, the owner of the Daily Express newspaper.[153] Nigel Farage's chief of staff in 2015 went on to become Breitbart's UK managing editor when the company set up its London office.[154] UKIP is part of the Europe of Freedom and Direct Democracy group in the European parliament, alongside the Swedish nationalist party, the Sweden Democrats.[155]

Not that the Sweden Democrats need anyone on the international stage to do their talking for them. Three days after Trump's 'last night in Sweden' statement the party was given stunning exposure in Rupert Murdoch's prestigious Wall Street Journal newspaper. In an opinion piece entitled 'Trump Is Right: Sweden's Embrace of Refugees Isn't Working', party leader Jimmie Åkesson and parliamentary group leader Mattias Karlsson argued that 'Mr. Trump did not exagger- ate Sweden's current problems. If anything, he understated them.'[156] The pair emphasised the number of asylum seekers who had arrived in Sweden since 2014, noting that 'riots and social unrest have become part of everyday life'. Their article wove the familiar tropes – a failed suicide attack in 2010, the Husby riots of 2013, rising gun and gang violence, rising anti-Semitism, rising sex crime, high immigrant unemployment and assaults on Swedish culture – into a bleak tapestry, a dark image of a lawless, broken country for a high-level, influential, international audience.

In an echo of Donald Trump's 'Make America Great Again' campaign slogan, Åkesson and Karlsson promised that they would not rest 'until we have made Sweden safe again'.

It's fair to say that this homegrown attack on Sweden's international reputation did not go down well with the Swedish government back home.

The minister for enterprise and innovation, Mikael Damberg, told Aftonbladet that such an article could hit inward investment and end up costing Sweden jobs. 'While I'm travelling abroad as enterprise minister to attract more investment to Sweden, the Sweden Democrats are writing articles in the international press to smear Sweden,' he said.[157]

Meanwhile, justice minister Morgan Johansson told The Local that the Sweden Democrats were 'intentionally harming Sweden by lying about how things are'.[158]

'We can't let that go unchallenged. They're painting a picture of a country characterized by violence, when it's the exact opposite,' he said, adding that the risk of being the victim of deadly violence in the US is four times higher than in Sweden.

Johansson combatively promised that the government would respond to Åkesson's implicit claim to be the voice of Sweden with its own opinion article in the Wall Street Journal within a few days. A week later, he did get the opportunity to refute the Sweden Democrats' piece. But while the party Johansson described as 'extreme right-wing, racist... with Nazi roots' was given a high-profile spot in the Journal's opinion pages, the government minister's words were relegated to the letters page under the lame heading 'Sweden and Immigrants Mostly Get On Well'.[159]

While the Sweden Democrats were given 614 words to make their case, Johansson was given 281. The Sweden Democrats' piece was shared more than 35,000 times on Facebook – one of the sharers was Pamela Geller, with her million followers[160] – and was written up on Breitbart[161] and many other similar sites. It attracted 1,131 comments; Johansson's attracted 31. And to complete the humiliation, Johansson's letter wasn't even the last word on the subject on the Journal's web site. Directly under his letter was one from another reader, a Margaret Pfister from Naples, Florida. It read: 'Regarding the Akesson-Karlsson piece: Amen.'

CHAPTER 5:

The psychology and economics of news

Trump and Bannon and Farage and the rest of them are not sitting around together dreaming up new ways to discredit Sweden. They have bigger domestic targets but the use of Sweden by these values warriors in their arguments against immigration, for example, is an instinctive reaction to what works. They've all seen the impact on an audience when they talk about Sweden and the speed at which their words spread. They have discovered that Bad Sweden is a highly resilient 'meme'.

Take a chance on meme

The notion of memes was proposed by the evolutionary biologist Richard Dawkins in his 1976 masterpiece, *The Selfish Gene*.[162] A meme, he said, is 'a unit of cultural transmission, or a unit of imitation' analogous to the biological version, the gene. Dawkins explained that 'just as genes propagate themselves in the gene pool by leaping from body to body via sperms or eggs, so memes propagate themselves in the meme pool by leaping from brain to brain via a process which, in the broad sense, can be called imitation'.

These days the word is most commonly applied to humorous images or phrases that spread quickly through social media, Dawkins gave as examples 'tunes, ideas, catch-phrases, clothes

78

fashions, ways of making pots or of building arches'. Just like genes, some memes are more successful than others. Some never manage to replicate at all, while some replicate quickly, spread fast and then die out. Other memes display great survival value, dominating the meme pool for centuries or millennia. In a pre-internet world, Dawkins wrote that if the meme is a scientific idea then its survival value could be measured by the number of citations in scientific journals. Today we have an instant measure by looking at the number of times articles or posts are shared on social media.

The longevity and penetration of a meme depends on its psychological appeal and the environment in which it exists. The Bad Sweden meme has been around since 1960 in the form of the suicide myth. For fifty years or more it proved itself to be resilient and fertile but not particularly potent in comparison to the more dominant Good Sweden meme. But the environment has changed. We are now in a world where social media monopolises information flows, traditional news companies are on the defensive and trust is plummeting. The Bad Sweden meme has adapted faster and is better suited to the new conditions.

If you are reliant upon, or in some way partly responsible for, Sweden's international reputation, your natural response when confronted by a false or exaggerated story about the country will be to respond rationally, using well-sourced and verifiable facts to present a clear explanation about why that information was wrong. As well as correcting a misunderstanding you will be demonstrating Swedish values of calmness and transparency. Unfortunately, considering what you are dealing with, you might as well bring a butter knife to a gunfight.

The psychology of news

Clearly there is something extraordinarily potent about the Bad Sweden meme, the alternative narrative that is being told about Sweden. If we are to understand why these articles gain such traction among people who are not remotely connected to Sweden – and work out how to respond – then we need to look at what makes negative news in general so compelling.

The first question that many people ask when they encounter a journalist is why is there so much bad news? The quick answer is that people don't read good news – at least not to the same extent. In 2014 a local news site in the city of Rostov-on-Don in south-west Russia tested the old newsroom cliché, 'If it bleeds, it leads'. For one day, the City Reporter published only good news, chirpily proclaiming, for example, that a new underpass would be ready in time for Victory Day.[163] Readership on that day dropped by two thirds. 'We tried to find a positive in the daily flow of news,' rued the site's deputy editor. 'It turned out that this is practically unnecessary for anyone.'

The key word is practically. Because news is not just about entertainment; news performs a vital social function as a binding agent. News is the glue of society, telling us who we are, what we care about and what we *practically* need to know as a community. It is not practically useful to know that something you expect to happen is going to happen as expected. Knowing that an underpass will open when it was supposed to open does not move you from a position of ignorance to a position of knowledge; this new information does not require you to adapt your behaviour in any way and it would not enhance your community status if you were to pass it on to your friends.

The relevance of any piece of news is defined by its relationship to the community for which it is produced. We are all members of many different communities and every day we consume news generated by and for each of them. You care about what happens in the block where you live, so you read the free weekly local papers that drop through your door. You care about what's happening in the greater city area, so you read the city's big news brands. And you care about what happens elsewhere in your country too, so you listen to national radio and (sometimes) watch the national TV news.

Each of these community strata will generate different kinds of news, ranging from low *impact information but immediately practical* information in the local papers to *high impact information over which you have no influence* in national or global news outlets.

What they have in common is that they will tend to focus on the negative, the stories that arouse indignation, anger or astonishment. This is not cynical journalists transferring their world-weary disillusionment onto their readers (although writing this stuff day after day certainly takes its toll); rather, this is journalists feeding a demand created by the wiring of our brains.

What do you say when someone asks you 'do you want the good news or the bad news'? Studies have shown that 8 out of 10 people will ask for the bad news first; maybe they justify their choice by saying they want to 'get it out of the way' but they feel compelled to process the negative information immediately.[164]

In 2001 a team of psychologists from the Case Western Reserve University in Ohio and the University of Amsterdam surveyed decades of research on the relative impacts of bad events and good events on psychological behaviour.[165] Their conclusion was that bad is stronger than good, with 'hardly any exceptions'.

Studies of brain activity show that more cognitive energy gets channelled into processing bad information than good information as we rush to seek meaning, trying to make sense of the bad news. Our brains instantly begin analysing and justifying the causes of the bad event, worrying about the consequences, calculating a reaction. And all this activity leads to higher likelihood that the bad stuff will be remembered. If the bad news is also unexpected, that too will induce more cognitive activity.

This greater initial imprint on the mind of bad events or bad information has the consequence that, while the effect of both good events and bad events will wear off over time, it takes longer for the psychological effects of bad events to wear off.

The evolutionary benefits of applying greater brain time to bad news are well-established. Our ability to recognise, adapt and respond to negative cues is key to our survival – positive events might make you feel good, but negative events can kill you, so spotting them and remembering them is important. If you quickly forget the bad things that happen to you, you will repeat your mistakes.

For millennia storytellers have played with character shifts for increased dramatic effect and a protagonist who behaves against type is compelling (the obvious comic-book examples are when Superman or Spiderman 'turn bad'). The fact that information about bad behaviour is more alluring is one thing, but a 1999 study showed that the character of the person committing the behaviour also plays a role. Scientists at the University of North Carolina demonstrated that neural activity increased when participants in the study read accounts of good people doing bad things (compared to bad/good, bad/

bad or good/good combinations of character and behaviour),[166] which perhaps explains the attraction of stories such as Tiger Woods' fall from grace or why tales of punished hubris are so engaging.

Real and immediate threats to our personal safety don't usually present themselves in writing, but our response to visual signals is almost instant. One of the things that is striking about the articles about Sweden published by Breitbart or Mail Online is the aggressive images that accompany the text. Flaming cars, police in riot gear and angry-looking youths are the visual theme of the alternative narrative about Sweden, which is all the more powerful when it is contrasted with the gentle, pleasing aesthetics of the accepted narrative. Even the blog post falsely claiming that Swedish authorities were banning Christmas lights for religious reasons was accompanied by a picture of an angry-looking bearded young man apparently yelling with all his might.

These kinds of images talk directly to the amygdala, the part of the brain that processes threats, without needing the cumbersome activity of 'thinking'.[167] In the last thirty years a number of experiments have demonstrated that we identify angry faces more efficiently and more quickly than happy faces.[168] The difference is just as significant when the faces are buried in a crowd of other faces; thanks to what is known as an 'anger superiority effect', threatening faces in a crowd of happy faces are perceived more efficiently than the opposite.[169]

So negative information gets priority over positive information in the brain; it uses up more processing power, it gets through more quickly and it contributes more to the overall impression of an event or an individual. This asymmetry between negative and positive information explains beautifully why a good reputation is hard to acquire but easy to lose, while a bad reputation is easy to acquire and hard to shake off.

There is no way around this; in this time of ubiquitous social media the only way to fight a wave of bad news is to put out more good news – a lot more. Because bad news not only has a greater impact on an individual level; it is also more shareable and more likely to get the sharers engaged in a community issue.

When we think about 'viral content' we tend to focus on the quirky and amusing but ultimately meaningless stories or images that dominate social media for a few hours and then disappear. Indeed, we are not averse to such mood-lightening stories at The Local; when a picture of a drunk elk stuck in an apple tree[170] gets viewed over a million times in 24 hours, who's going to complain?

But as occasional snippets of entertainment, these kinds of stories are outliers – partly because what makes them shareable is their scarcity (if we ran a daily animal-stuck-in-tree story it would soon lose its appeal) and partly because a news brand does not build its credibility on such content.

Still, every modern newsroom dedicates considerable resources to figuring out what content gets shared the most, and there is a wide range of factors that contribute to 'shareability'. The news focus of the publisher itself, the construction of the audience, the time an article is published, its prominence on the site, the practical application of the news, the reputation of the writer, the choice of headline and luck all play a role.

To answer the question 'what makes online content viral?', Wharton professors Jonah Berger and Katherine Milkman analysed 7,000 articles published in a three-month period by the New York Times.[171] After controlling for various factors outside of the quality of the content itself, they found that while positive content is generally more viral than negative content (we may be irresistibly attracted to bad news, but most of us at least have the self-awareness to limit our own distribution of gloom and misery among our friends), what matters is the emotional punch that a story packs.

If a story evokes what the researchers called a 'high-arousal emotion', stimulating a stronger physiological response, then it will be more viral. A high-arousal emotion can be positive (such as awe) or negative (anger or anxiety) but turning up the anger quotient on a story increases its shareability more than boosting any other emotional value. An article that prompts a low-arousal emotion such as sadness, on the other hand, decreases its likelihood of being shared.

A few years after his initial study, Berger removed the emotion from the equation altogether and tested the idea that it is simply the state of physiological arousal that increases sharing.[172] Forty university students were split into two groups. One group was told to sit still for a minute while another group jogged on the spot for a minute. Then both groups were given a mood-neutral news article to read and were told that they could mail it to anyone they wanted afterwards. Remarkably, 75% of the joggers shared the article compared to only 33% of the sitters. The state of being physically aroused more than doubled the participants' tendency to share the content.

Again, this suggests an evolutionary imperative – if you're running away from something dangerous, you're going to warn your friends about it. Similarly, negative content that makes you feel threatened or angry will drill straight into your brain, your heart will thump and your blood will pump, and you will feel compelled to share that information.

When it comes to news, you can forget the old notion that 'a trouble shared is a trouble halved'. In fact, the opposite is true. By sharing a piece of content on Facebook you become part of the news distribution mechanism. You may not be the original source of the information but by being the first to 'break' the story to your contacts you will be viewed as a source by your network, and you will enjoy the associated psychological benefits of status and credibility. If you've ever had an article published in a newspaper or a tweet that generates thousands of retweets, you'll know the feeling of that rush that comes from seeing your name in print or from knowing that many thousands of people are experiencing some intellectual reaction because of you. By asserting your identity as well-informed and connected, this semi-editorial role increases your sense of relevance and empowerment in your community. You are becoming an opinion leader and the affirmation you get, in the form of comments and questions on your posts, increases your sense of expertise and ownership over the story. And this is not only true of the extreme sharers; experiments have shown that even on a small scale, sharing news on Facebook will increase your sense of involvement in the story.[173]

But you also become locked into what you share, because it has now defined you and created an expectation among your contacts, which prompts you to go looking for more evidence, other articles or video clips, to support your initial post.

So the greater the emotion that a piece of bad news arouses, the more likely it is to be shared. The more it is shared, the more people it reaches, stimulating more physiological responses, making a greater and longer-lasting mental impact. Ultimately this increases the likelihood that it becomes part of a community's beliefs.[174] The shared emotional reaction to the news becomes a defining characteristic of the community, mobilizing members to behave in the same way in response to the information.[175]

Thinking more about a story is a step on the path to real world involvement. The most high profile writers become participants in the story rather than external observers. They are no longer commentators but activists for whom the story has become a civic engagement.

If we compare the content of the competing narratives about Sweden from the perspective of shareability, there is a clear winner. Traditional stories about technology, innovation, business success and quality of life will continue to win real estate on the screens of Informed Users, and sometimes there will be overspill when there's a quirky or surprising element to a story. But the Bad Sweden meme has all the best lines: themes such as fire, rape and invasion are far more potent, triggering the most primal instincts of survival. A detailed explanation of the data-collection methodology that leads to higher rape figures may be rigorous and comprehensive, but as a shareable narrative it is weak. Facts are just the foundation; if a balanced narrative is to compete for mindspace, it needs to be more widespread, more surprising, more awe-inspiring, funnier and better-told than the alternative narrative.

The economics of news

It's hard to think of another industry that has been so thrillingly boosted and yet so brutally damaged by the internet as the old newspaper business. Yet, considering the role of the press as society's so-called Fourth Estate (or third, in Sweden, after the government and parliament) this is not just a tale of massive industry disruption. The internet and its effect on the business of news has changed the role of news in society. It has changed the ability of newspapers to hold power to account and – more relevant to us – it has dispersed 'centres of trust' from a few newspapers to hundreds of news sites, thousands of commentators and millions of social media users.

For journalists and executives conditioned to think in terms of audience numbers, the advent of the internet promised a global readership and global influence. But it also destroyed the very barriers to entry – the need for printing presses, distribution networks and large editorial and sales operations – that had allowed the business to thrive for so long.

In the rush to grab their share of the online audience and desperate to remain in the game, media companies made their expensive content freely available. Before long, news had become a commodity. However much content they produced, there was always infinitely more out there competing for banner advertisements and the new currency of online advertising, the click. Which brings us to Google and Facebook.

The best way to describe the relationship between the news industry and these two digital giants is like that between a victim and an abuser.* For more than a decade the two companies have alternately battered and flattered the news industry. They have reduced publishers to panic with their domination of searches for news but kept them begging like puppies for more traffic. They sparked desperate fury among news executives as they captured the digital advertising market but still they supply the platforms that drive the publishers' own advertising businesses.

---

* Like many other new, digital-native news companies, The Local has benefited enormously from the changes brought about by digital technology in general and by Google in particular. Indeed, it is these very changes that allowed us to start our business and expand year after year. But for most of the established media companies with their print legacy the upside is still a long way off, despite a massive shift in working practices.

Advertising revenue in the American news industry has fallen from $49.4 billion in 2005 to just $18.3 billion in 2016.[176] Here in Sweden, the Institute for Media Studies (Institutet för mediestudier) reckons that since 2008 news media has lost a third of its advertising revenue.[177] Just since 2014 that equates to almost a billion kronor.

Meanwhile, anyone with an internet connection and a lot to say can now set up a news site. With a few hours of design work and a traditional-sounding name, it can look quite credible and can become a vehicle for any kind of message, positive or negative, rational or crazy, worthy or worthless. Because it looks like news it gets treated like news. I'm not complaining about this state of affairs – this is how we started The Local, after all. But it's radically different from how it was and society's relationship with news has been shaken hard.

Of course, the biggest news brands such as Mail Online and the New York Times still reach vast audiences, as do established news brands on all continents. But faced with Google and Facebook, all that the old industry could do was cut costs and chase clicks. Despite soaring demand for instant and constant news, the number of people employed in America's newsrooms dropped from 68,610 in 2006 to 41,400 in 2015 – and the slashing isn't over yet.[178] In 2017 the owner of Mail Online cut 400 jobs and at the other end of the news spectrum the Guardian ditched 250 people, while the New York Times warns of further cuts to come.[179]

Fewer journalists are being pushed to produce more content, more quickly – and obviously, something's got to give. As a news publisher, you will be forced to rely more heavily on news agencies, but the problem with that is that you end up with the same content as everyone else. So your remaining journalists will be put to work rehashing articles from other sites, especially on international news, angling them for your own audience, grabbing comments from Twitter and racing to get a quote from a local journalist closer to the action (since your paper cut its foreign correspondents in the first wave of redundancies).

The other solution to the economic pressures of news is to replace costly reporting with cheap opinion. And if you're going to pay writers to churn out opinions then you will expect them to be more alarmist, more outrageous and more populist than your competitors. You need to get people talking, you need to get them commenting on your stories and above all you need to get them sharing your content on social media because shares mean clicks and clicks mean cash. So your writers will focus relentlessly on stories that stoke anger and indignation among your audience. But your competitors will do the same and you will race each other to the extremes, stuffing your pages with increasingly visceral images and increasingly enraging headlines.

It is true that it has taken the traditional news industry a lot longer than anyone expected to adapt to the new market conditions imposed by the internet. But news is not broken.

Undeterred by the challenges of the industry, the smartest young graduates are willing to invest years of their lives in honing their craft, answering an irresistible call. They understand instinctively that it is their duty to inform their community, provide balance and hold power to account – even if the economic imperative forces them to write fluff or to churn. In the face of cuts and uncertainty journalists remain committed, professional and courageous. And they need to be. In 2016, 74 journalists were killed in connection with their work as reporters.[180] Week after week, the president of the United States decries the mainstream media as 'fake' or 'failing'. Here in Sweden, 30% of reporters say they have been threatened because of their work.[181] The risks for journalists in war zones are part of the job, but our own local journalists in Paris, Berlin and Stockholm have shown their true mettle when faced with local terror attacks, putting their emotions to one side and fulfilling their responsibility to keep our readers informed.

Every day, all around the world, brave, innovative and entertaining reporting sheds a light on what's going on, not only in traditional newsrooms but also by freelancers, bloggers and start-up news sites. Commercially, as lean new digital news brands emerge, the old industry will never again see the riches of the previous century but it is gradually recalibrating itself for the new conditions. This adjustment is largely built on a return to getting people to pay for the content they read. In contrast to fifteen or even five years ago, the payment technology is now widely available and cheap enough even for the smallest publishers. Readers who have become accustomed to e-commerce are far more willing to submit their credit card details to news sites. And crucially, people once again value journalism as they struggle to make sense of this uncertain world.

That's good news for good news, so to speak, but not necessarily for society as a whole. Because if fair and balanced and analytical reporting now starts disappearing behind paywalls, it becomes harder to access and harder to share. It becomes a smaller part of the global conversation which will be increasingly dominated by content from the news sites that choose to stay freely-available. And since the only viable way to stay free is to attract a massive audience, the free sites will be the most aggressively populist, such as Mail Online, or those funded by people or organisations with a specific agenda and for whom the commercial aspect is a secondary consideration, such as Breitbart or Russia Today. We'll be left, in other words, with the sort of free news providers for which Bad Sweden is the only Sweden.

CHAPTER 6:

Entering the arena of post-truth

The Bad Sweden narrative is being pushed by powerful, connected forces. Human psychology makes this narrative highly compelling. The disruption of the news industry makes journalists less likely to analyse, question or provide context for the narrative. But there is one more challenge to Sweden's international reputation and it is perhaps the most significant challenge we all face today: a post-truth world, in which facts are no longer anchors for debate but pieces of debris bobbing around at the mercy of the waves. For a thorough analysis of the phenomenon I suggest you read one of many books released in 2017 called 'Post Truth'.[182] But before you do, let's look at how fake news – the sharp edge of post-truth – is yet another weapon for those who wish to discredit Sweden.

It's tempting to draw up an 'authenticity spectrum' for news, with purely true at one end and purely false at the other. In between we would see 'skewed left or right' and 'hyper-partisan' and we could place news sources in the appropriate position as a helpful guide to readers. In fact, that's more or less what an American lawyer called Vanessa Otero posted to her Facebook page in December 2016.[183] On her chart, Breitbart and Infowars were classified as 'Conservative Utter Garbage/Conspiracy Theories'. A few days later Infowars responded with a chart of its own 'depicting how most leftist mainstream media sites promote tyranny, while the conservative 'garbage' sites on the previous map actually promote liberty and freedom'.[184] I don't think the debate needs another chart.

Most of the news examples that we've looked at so far have not been 'fake news' – that is, stories deliberately fabricated from start to finish. They have been exaggerations or distortions of truths, or they have been reported fairly accurately but with a total absence of context. But a study published in January 2017 argued that Russia was deploying fake news and counterfeit documents in an attempt to influence Swedish decision-making.[185] The authors, Martin Kragh and Sebastian Åsberg, pointed to the use of so-called 'troll armies' on Twitter in Swedish as well as ten forged documents relating to Swedish affairs.[186]

One, a letter relating to the sale of weapons to Ukraine, was apparently signed by Sweden's minister of defence Peter Hultqvist and appeared on social media through the Twitter identity of a well-known Swedish military affairs journalist. Another letter, apparently signed by Tora Holst, head of the International Public Prosecution Office in Stockholm, concerned an attempt to quash prosecution of a Swedish citizen for war crimes committed in Ukraine. It was uploaded to a CNN website and later broadcast on Russian state television. In a third example, a letter to foreign minister Margot Wallström purporting to be from a female IS leader related to a conspiracy to send weapons to Islamic State via Turkey.[187]

According to Kragh and Åsberg, there were enough factual errors in the letters to make it obvious that they were all forgeries – but they continued to resurface in other media as evidence for the conspiracy theories. The researchers argued that the objective of this disinformation campaign 'is to preserve the geostrategic status quo, which is identified with a security order minimising NATO presence in the region'.

Russia denied Sweden's claims,[188] dismissing them as 'James Bond theories'[189] and Russophobia.[190]

But the Swedish public is waking up to the idea that all may not be as it seems. A survey commissioned by the Swedish Media Publishers' Association (TU) in March 2017 found that eight out of ten Swedes think fake news is having an impact on their perception of basic facts, while six out of ten said that they see news articles 'they don't believe to be entirely true' on a weekly basis.[191]

At the same time, Sweden's prime minister, Stefan Löfven, warned of 'attempts from another country to influence a government, a population or specially identified groups, to further its own interest'. Writing in Dagens Nyheter, Löfven said that such attempts could consist of 'the spread of false documents, created by fictitious people in social media or planted news'.[192]

Löfven outlined some security and political measures that the Swedish government was taking and in August 2017 the Finance Department proposed to scrap an advertising tax paid by print publications.[193] 'In the time we now live in of online rumours and fake news we think our daily press in Sweden is incredibly important,' said finance minister Magdalena Andersson. 'One way of supporting it is to remove this tax.' Two days later, Sweden's defence minister Peter Hultqvist and his Danish counterpart announced that the two countries would increase their military cooperation to counter the threats posed by 'Russian fake news'.[194]

A threat that is coming from many different directions and for many different reasons needs a range of responses. While the Swedish government appears to be acting on one level, eight out of ten Swedes think the main responsibility for preventing the spread of fake news lies with the media.[195]

The following example, not from Sweden but from Switzerland (whatever!), proves their point.

The winner fakes it all

One Sunday morning in July 2017 the news desk at The Local received an email from the sports editor at Al Jazeera's English language television channel. She asked about an article that had appeared during the night on our Swiss edition, in which the president of FIFA, Gianni Infantino, threatened to withdraw the 2022 World Cup from Qatar. Apparently Infantino had told The Local that Saudi Arabia and five other countries had asked FIFA to replace Qatar as host since 'the country is a supporter of terrorism'. And now, the journalist said, the article had disappeared.

We didn't know what she was talking about. To put the incident in context, this was an extremely sensitive time for Qatar. Several neighbours had cut economic and diplomatic ties with the small but exceedingly wealthy Gulf state and imposed sanctions. Saudi Arabia had closed its border with Qatar and the country's airline was forced to reroute to avoid its neighbours' airspace while other regional airlines suspended flights to the capital, Doha. The dispute was part of an ongoing regional power quarrel in which Saudi Arabia, Egypt, the United Arab Emirates and Bahrain accused Qatar of financing militants and siding with their local foe Iran. For its part, Qatar alleged that its Gulf neighbours had hacked government web sites to plant inflammatory false quotes attributed to the Qatari emir. FIFA's decision to award the 2022 World Cup to Qatar was controversial enough in the first place. But given the

Some Arab nations calls FIFA to replace
Qatar as 2022 World Cup host

AFP
news@thelocal.ch

15 July 2017
08:41 CEST+02:00

qatar

fifa

Share this article

Figure 5: Screenshot of the faked version of The Local's Swiss edition

regional tensions, a story about replacing the country as hosts
risked being explosive.

James Savage, who oversees our news operation, confirmed
immediately that we had not interviewed Gianni Infantino
and we had not written, published or removed the article. And
yet reputable news organisations such as Reuters and the Daily
Telegraph in the UK were already running the story, citing
The Local as a source. The BBC's sports news correspond-
ent, Richard Conway, tweeted to his 63,000 followers that
the story had appeared on The Local but had now been removed.[196] He even posted a link to the article and screenshots
of what looked very much indeed like an article on our site.
And searches on Google for 'Qatar 2022 boycott' were already
returning top stories based on 'our article'. What the hell was
going on? Had we been hacked?

It took our head of technology, James Pearn, about thirty
seconds to prove that nobody had tried to access our systems
and that no such article had been published on our Swiss site

during the night. And then he told us to look closely at the URL, the web address of the article, that Richard Conway had posted. Here is the link:

http://www.thelocal.com/20170715/some-arab-nations-calls-fifa-to-replace-qatar-as-2022-world-cup-host/

Did you spot what James had spotted? Did you see the dot under the 'h' of thelocal? Well done if you did, because I certainly didn't. Immediately it became clear what had happened. Someone had created a web page that looked identical to The Local, using the Turkish letter ḥ in the web site address instead of the h. All the links on the page directed to our real site and at first glance the article looked genuine, topped by a photo of the former president of FIFA, Sepp Blatter, opening the envelope that declared Qatar would be the host country in 2022.

There were some clues and inaccuracies indicating that the article was not genuine. It was attributed to the news agency AFP, and yet the text claimed that Infantino 'told The Local that Saudi Arabia and 5 other Arab courtiers in a letter asked FIFA to cancel the Qatar 2022 FIFA World Cup bid as the country is the 'supporter of terrorism'. The headline – 'Some Arab nations calls FIFA to replace Qatar as 2022 World Cup host' – was obviously written by someone whose English was less than perfect and the text was scarred with grammatical and stylistic errors.

But as with Nigel Farage's claims about Sweden's rape numbers, the weight of the story's potential significance gathered a momentum of its own, leaving reason and analysis choking in the dust. I don't know how Reuters ended up running the story – we asked but received no response – but they started a news cascade and soon the story was appearing on the Daily Telegraph in the UK, Huffington Post in America, the Times of India, the Sydney Morning Herald and the pan-Arab daily Asharq Al-Awsat along with many other news sites using Reuters' content feed.[197] The 'news' was also picked up in the sports press on sites like the Bleacher Report, ESPN and Sports Illustrated.

If it hadn't been for Al Jazeera's diligent sports editor, whose fact-checking email allowed us to quash the story, it could have gone a lot further. But the article is still firmly embedded in the digital records. Almost two months after the incident, Google returned hundreds of results linking to the fake story, which remained available on news sites all over the world.[198] Reuters removed the original article from their main page and issued a correction – but at the time of writing it is still appearing on their Africa page and the Thompson Reuters Foundation news page whose web address, ironically enough, is 'trust.org'.[199] The Sydney Morning Herald and many others still state that 'Swiss website The Local reported that Saudi Arabia, Yemen, Mauritania, the United Arab Emirates, Bahrain and Egypt had collectively written to FIFA asking it to remove Qatar as hosts under Article 85 of the FIFA Code'.[200] We didn't and they hadn't.

The web address for the faked site was registered to an address in Hawaii that didn't exist. We will never know who was behind the story but, really, it doesn't matter. What matters is that this sort of thing is becoming more prevalent and more professional.

A month after The Local was copied, Buzzfeed reported on a similar incident in which the Guardian was mimicked to host a fake article headlined 'Former MI6 Chief Admits

Defeat to Putin on the Russia Fragmentation Strategic Plan'. Just like on the bogus version of The Local, the web address of this story looked almost identical to the Guardian's but used a Turkish dotless i, to give 'theguardıan.com'. Other sites copied in the same way include Le Soir, Al Jazeera, Haaretz and The Atlantic.[201]

But faked web sites – quickly revealed – are nothing compared to what we've got to look forward to. When audio and video technology allows us to convincingly change what a president or a prime minister says in a speech, then we really have problems. And that time is not far away.

In 2015, computer scientists at the University of Alabama showed how vulnerable the human ear and automated voice verification systems are to faked recordings of people's voices.[202] They demonstrated that 'with just a few minutes of audio samples', it is possible to build a model of the speaker's speech patterns using voice-morphing software and to clone 'the victim's voice itself'. Once cloned, the voice can be used to say anything – so far, convincingly enough to trick around half of human listeners.[203]

The researchers suggested other ways in which voice-cloning software could be used, such as posting morphed samples on the internet, creating 'fake audio evidence in court and even impersonating the victim in real-time phone conversations'. They concluded that 'the possibilities are endless'.[204]

That's the audio; what about the video? A paper published in 2017 by computer scientists at the University of Washington showed how they had altered a video of President Barack Obama to make it look as though he was saying something completely different. Supasorn Suwajanakorn, Steven M. Seitz and Ira Kemelmacher-Shlizerman took a video of one of

Obama's weekly presidential addresses and 'reanimated' his face and lips to match the audio from an entirely different speech.[205]

The adjusted video of Obama is frighteningly realistic, at least on a small screen. In the context of fake news, the implications are obvious: we will need to find new ways to authenticate video footage of our politicians and influencers because seeing will soon no longer be believing.

It's not hard to imagine the public reaction the first time a newspaper gets duped by a fake video of a country leader making a speech. We saw with the FIFA-Qatar example how quick newspapers can be to run fairly obviously false stories in article format; when a news organisation receives an actual video of a president or prime minister saying something sensational the pressure to publish first will be enormous – and must be resisted until the source has been verified beyond all doubt.

Trust me, I'm a journalist

Most fake news out there is not so much intended to sell a false story as to undermine trust in the media and create uncertainty. Stories can be removed from news sites and replaced with long-winded demonstrations of their inaccuracy. But every time it happens the public is left with an increasing sense of doubt about an industry it doesn't really trust,[206] in a world where trust in general is collapsing.

An international study conducted by Edelman Insights, a global research firm, in 2017 shows how fragile the public's relationship now is with governments, non-governmental organisations, business and the media.[207] Trust in all four of these institutions fell compared to 2016 but the trust in governments and the media was far lower than in business and NGOs. Media was distrusted in 23 out of the 28 countries surveyed and in 17 of these countries the trust level hit an all-time low. The Edelman study also revealed that 59% of people felt they were more likely to get the truth from a search engine, while only 41% favoured a human editor. And given that people were found to be almost four times more likely to ignore information that supports a point they did not agree with, it is suddenly not so hard to see how we've arrived at a place where false, twisted or exaggerated news about Sweden's 'migrant crisis' or 'rape crisis' can pervade the information channels of the Neutral Users out there in the world.[208]

I say 'out there in the world' because interpersonal trust in Sweden, as in other Nordic countries, remains high for now. An annual study of a wide range of Swedish social trends conducted by Gothenburg University's SOM Institute shows remarkably consistent levels of trust since measurements began in the mid-1990s. On the basis of how much people say they trust others, respondents are divided into three groups: high trustfulness, medium trustfulness and low trustfulness. In the latest study (2016), 59% of respondents were classified as highly trustful, somewhat above the average for the last twenty years.[209] This gives the country an enormous advantage over countries with low levels of interpersonal trust. As Sören Holmberg and Bo Rothstein write in their analysis of the annual results, trust works as a lubricant in a well-functioning society. But they also warn about the risks of declining trust in a more fragmented society:

> For many smaller but welfare-dependent groups, such as the unemployed, people in bad health and those born outside of Sweden, the level of social trust clearly tends to the lower end of the scale... We see a picture of a more fragmented society

emerging – reinforced by a political group which is also characterised by a clearly lower level of interpersonal trust. This
group is those who sympathise with the Sweden Democrats.[210]

The study also measures how worried Swedes are about
certain issues facing society. Since 2013 Swedes have become
increasingly concerned about terrorism, the rising number of
refugees, increasing xenophobia and the situation in Russia.
There are real-world reasons for these concerns, but they also
reflect most of the news stories that we've looked at.

***

Whether fake news is being produced to generate cash from
clicks, to make people believe something untrue or to stop
them from believing anything at all, the phenomenon has
become a daily menace.

The decisions we make, whether everyday choices or important democratic actions such as votes in elections or referen-
dums, are based on what we know. We are used to critically
processing obvious advertising or what we hear coming out of
politicians' mouths but we are evidently not yet equipped to
reject information that is dressed up as real news. Dot by dot,
fake news reduces our ability to act in our own interests, cleverly
polarising us and turning us against people we once trusted.

Call it propaganda, disinformation, hoaxes, conspiracy
theories or scams, the lie is as old as the truth. It's tempting
to wander down the path of the history of propaganda but for
the purposes of this book let's just note that there is nothing
new about fake news.

But we do need to be careful about how we use the term.

Indeed, in the first year of his presidency, Donald Trump's almost constant cries of 'fake news' whenever he talks about mainstream news organisations such as CNN, the 'failing New York Times' and the 'Amazon Washington Post'[211] (the Washington Post is owned by Amazon founder Jeff Bezos) have rendered the expression almost meaningless.

Yes, there are genuinely faked stories such as the FIFA-Qatar article or the so-called Pizzagate conspiracy theory – in which members of America's Democratic Party were said to be involved in a paedophile ring run from some Washington, DC restaurants – at the height of the 2016 US election campaigning.[212] But these are exposed as fakes by news sites which the most powerful man in the world slams as fake news. And crying 'fake news' has increasingly become the first line of defence for politicians who are being challenged by journalists. Putting Russia's contribution to one side, it's impossible to say how many of the fake news merchants, from Trump down, genuinely want to bring down western democracy. Yet that is what they risk doing. Because if we are all to feast at the *smörgåsbord* of democracy, we must be able to agree on the most basic ingredients. Whether a herring is pickled, fried in breadcrumbs or fermented until it smells like the sewers of hell, we must all be able to agree that it is actually a herring. If memes are the cultural equivalent of genes, then facts are their DNA and when we mess with them we are messing with the very building blocks of modern life.

In recent years a small sub-industry has emerged in order to separate the herrings from – well, fake herrings: the fact-checkers. Since 1995, Snopes.com has been the go-to site for anyone who wanted to check whether a story they had heard was true or just an urban legend, myth, rumour or propaganda. The site clearly states the claim and then gives a rating based on how true or false the claim is.

One of the many Sweden-related rumours that the site has investigated was the notion that the country was officially moving to a 6-hour workday, a story that started spreading in September 2015.[213] Snopes noted that the idea got lift-off from an article in business magazine Fast Company, entitled 'Why Sweden is Shifting to a 6-Hour Workday'.[214] The basis for the story was that a handful of organisations in Sweden had introduced a shorter working day. For a weary journalist, this story must have seemed like a great opportunity to send a hint to management and, sure enough, it spread all over the world – with the implication that this was some kind of official policy. Only in Sweden, right?

The story was rated as 'Mostly False' by Snopes, which cited a debunking article by The Local as proof. But the mere fact that 'Sweden' was *not* conducting a 6-hour workday experiment didn't stop dozens of news sites from reporting a year later that the experiment had failed. 'Sweden abandons six-hour workday scheme because it's just too expensive', declared the UK's Daily Telegraph,[215] while Bloomberg wrote that 'Swedes looking forward to a six-hour workday just got some bad news: the costs outweigh the benefits'.[216]

In the early 2000s, more politically-focused fact-checking organisations emerged in the United States with a focus on testing claims made by politicians. According to a report by the Reuters Institute for the Study of Journalism, there are now more than a hundred fact-checking groups in fifty countries.[217] Almost half of these were set up since 2014. Some are run by news companies, such as the Les Décodeurs unit at Le Monde,[218] Viralgranskaren at Metro Sweden[219] and Reality

Check at the BBC[220]. Others are projects funded and driven by non-governmental organisations whose mission is to spread and strengthen democratic institutions. Their intentions are noble and their work is painstaking, but it takes more than small pins of truth to pierce the thick hide of a lie.

Indeed, as day follows night, the appearance of a fellowship of fact-checkers has had an unintended consequence: fake fact-checkers. At the beginning of 2017 a Swedish-language Facebook page called Mediekollen started making its own assessment of articles in the Swedish media, stamping them as true or false in the style of Metro's own fact-checkers, Viralgranskaren. Mediekollen gave a big green 'true' stamp to a claim – later retracted – made by author Katerina Janouch that Sweden had more than fifty no-go zones. When Viralgranskaren wrote an article about Mediekollen, Mediekollen responded by giving it a red 'false' stamp – before being removed from Facebook.[221]

This is the arena in which the battle for Sweden's reputation must be fought.

In 1961 the Swedish government distributed an information pamphlet called 'Om kriget kommer' ('In the event of war') to every household in the country.[222] It was packed with instructions about what the public should do in a war situation and included a section about the threat of psychological warfare. The document explained that the best way to be resistant to hostile propaganda is through information and knowledge, and it urged Swedes to be on their guard against fake radio broadcasts: 'Remember that even well known voices on the air can be imitated. Listen critically!'

More than fifty years later, this is still sound advice.

CHAPTER 7

Fighting back, the Swedish way

A country's reputation is not a single unit; rather, it is the sum of opinions about the place. Every Swede travelling abroad on holiday contributes a little bit to the country's reputation. Sweden's cities present a narrative of technical prowess and quality of life to attract investment and talent to the phenomenal start-up scene. Businesses infuse their brands with the very Swedish qualities of sustainability, innovation and design. The tourist industry focuses on Sweden's nature-inspired architecture, an ongoing culinary revolution and the country's unique environment. For those in Sweden's international aid sector, the emphasis is on the progressive values that have made Sweden one of the world's most prosperous and happy nations. And the culture crowd tells an incredible story of cheerful musical success balanced by a gloomy literary movement that has claimed the word 'noir' as its own. So who wants to get their hands dirty by wrestling with the Bad Sweden narrative?

Nobody does, of course, but everybody must. Perhaps you own a café in Malmö that depends on the summer tourism trade. Perhaps you work in the Swedish news industry and are concerned about how your reports could be weaponised by the alt-right media. Maybe you work at one of many global companies where your Swedish brand has always been a passport to success, or you work in national or local government and your goal is to get talented programmers to move here, or your job is to distribute Swedish money to projects supporting women's rights in Africa. In any of these situations and many more it is in your interests to help ensure that the image of Sweden out there in the world is balanced and fair. Considering Sweden's table-topping performance in so many different independent global rankings, a balanced and fair image of the country will still be an enormous competitive advantage over just about anywhere else.

But as I hope I have made clear by now, balanced and fair is no longer the default. The rules of the game have changed and Sweden's reputation is being hijacked by groups who oppose the values the country represents. As we saw with the example of President Eisenhower's suicide statement, the idea of challenging Sweden's reputation as part of a battle of values is not new. What's different today is the battlefield itself. While the impetus comes from those who are opposed to the values Sweden represents, it is the post-truth, social media-driven environment that makes Bad Sweden so compelling. In this context, we all bear some responsibility, because very few of us can claim to share with care. As a member of the news-consuming public, you may say that you don't trust journalists or the media but how often do you check the facts and sources of an article before you share it among your friends on Facebook? The answer is almost certainly 'never'. In 2016, researchers at Columbia University and the French National Institute (Inria) found that 59% of links shared in social media have not been clicked. In other words, six times out of ten, social media users are sharing information that they have not even read themselves.[223]

We have become unthinking nodes in the global news distribution system, tools of the fake news merchants. It is time to recover our consciousness and become self-appointed firebreaks in this system. However frequently the media is slammed as 'fake news', serious journalists are rigorous about checking their facts and sources. Now that we have all become distributors of content, we must also act with restraint and consider the consequences of our sharing. In a post-truth world, the last line of defence is, as my colleague James Savage put it, 'the scepticism of the crowd'.[224]

This is a matter of education and it is extremely encouraging that schools in Sweden are beginning to teach children to think critically about the news they read.[225] Just prompting children to ask questions like 'What is the publication's objective?', 'Is the source real?' and 'Can you check the facts?' will help them to calibrate their brains to the rules of the world they are entering – and it will put them several steps ahead of older generations. Even Sweden's favourite honey-gobbling superhero bear, Bamse, has joined the fight, with an edition of the comic in 2017 dedicated to the theme of questioning sources.[226]

As far as the news industry is concerned, the real issue is not that false stories are created but, as the FIFA-Qatar example showed, that they can spread to trusted news outlets so easily. A firebreak is needed here too, perhaps in the form of a news authentication system that securely logs participating news companies' articles as they are published. When journalists want to base a story on another news outlet's article, they would be able to check that it is authentic by searching for it in the system. Let's say Dagens Nyheter is a participant. All of their articles would be registered, along with metadata such as author and publication time. If another publication wanted to base an article on a DN story, then the journalist would be able to verify that it is a real DN article by checking in the system. If that story is not in the system, then it is not an authentic DN article. When a journalist publishes a new article based on the first, it also enters the system and references the original piece. Enlightened readers would be able to check the system to find out whether the article they are reading – or sharing – is authentic. Commercial publishers must find ways to control their own output and protect their brand credibility. An authentication system such as this would be a start. Meanwhile, the news industry's pivot towards reader subscriptions seems to have sparked a revival for quality, long-form, analytical content.

How this post-truth world unfolds will depend on players outside of Sweden – the technology companies which control the flow of global information, the media giants and the politicians engaged in the clash of values. But Sweden's place in that world will hinge on how responsive the country's communicators are to the new environment. Here are some thoughts on how they might act.

Disarm the Bad Sweden narrative with success stories
In 2017 the Swedish police identified some 61 areas that they described as 'vulnerable'.[227] Of these, 23 merited the label 'especially vulnerable', with 'generally high crime and poverty rates, where police regularly adapt their methods and equipment to the volatile situation, where there may be violent religious extremism and where residents often do not report crimes to the police, either out of fear of retaliation or because they think it will not lead to anything'.[228]

The Swedish police reject the idea that these areas are no-go zones. On the contrary, police resources are prioritised to these areas, with extra personnel, increased cooperation with local housing companies, religious organisations and community groups, and more engagement with parents and residents' associations.[229]

For as long as these problem areas remain 'vulnerable', they will be used as examples in the Bad Sweden narrative. Obviously, the most important reason to work to solve these problems is for the residents themselves, so that the children growing up in these places have the same opportunities as Swedish children anywhere else in the country. But there are pockets of hope and improvement, and these positive stories need to be told with passion and conviction and intelligence. Local heroes must be celebrated and achievements must be shouted from the rooftops. Remember the qualities that make stories shareable. Bad news may spread faster than good news but people share awesome, inspiring and funny stories too. Tales of 'triumph over adversity' are irresistible.

Take the Malmö area of Södra Sofielund, for example, neighbour to the better-known Rosengård and one of the 23 'especially vulnerable' areas listed by the Swedish police in 2017. When The Local's editor, Emma Löfgren, visited Södra Sofielund in June 2017 she found cautious optimism among residents.[230] Improvements in housing, community initiatives such as volunteer litter patrols and the success of the area's youth football club formed in 2014 – combined with a police crackdown on the local crime network – have resulted in a turnaround that Hjalmar Falck, the council official leading the city's efforts in the district, described as 'like day and night'.

For years Södra Sofielund was notorious for its drug dealers and burning cars but the improvements in recent years prompted Falck to talk about the area's potential as 'a new destination in Malmö':

We want to turn it into a business area. Could we get restaurants that can attract people with micro breweries, culture and art... who knows? Because if people want to stay here, if businesses want to stay in the area, the area will become more stable, everyone takes responsibility and that's the win-win situation.

Nobody in the area pretends that Södra Sofielund's problems have been solved. But with the criminal influence gradually being replaced by a community spirit, the seeds of recovery have been planted. Positive publicity can contribute to that recovery by helping to keep the wheel spinning: small improvements generate positive publicity, which attracts more investment for more improvements, and gradually the small wins become big wins which generate another wave of positive publicity – and so on.

To leap from one end of Sweden's reputation spectrum to the other, an understanding of this cycle has been key to Stockholm's rise to prominence over the last five years as the 'start-up capital of Europe'. The raw material was certainly there in the form of early start-up successes and a lot of hard work from city officials. But what set Stockholm apart from other European cities with successful tech start-ups was the coordinated and passionate communication of these successes and the benefits of being in the city. The buzz inspired more activity and brought more investors to the city. The bigger the investor, the greater the expectation of success. The story became more compelling, attracting more money, ideas and talent to the city. Today, the Stockholm region is second only to Silicon Valley for technology start-ups, from billion-dollar 'unicorns' like Spotify, Mojang, Klarna and King to early-stage ventures run by a couple of founders with a vision. Swedish tech companies have attracted almost 25 billion SEK in investment in the last three years.[231]

The communications expertise exists in Sweden's cities but the question is, which story do you want to tell? The billion dollar stories have been well told; if the same skills and principles were applied to telling the stories of smaller successes in the country's most vulnerable areas, the effect would be just as significant – and perhaps even more so if they can inspire greater investment and commitment to change.

Own the plot points of the Bad Sweden story

People working with Sweden's international reputation often tell me that they share the positive articles that we publish on The Local. This is quite natural. Proactive public relations has always been about accentuating the positive stories, while reactive public relations, or crisis control, is about how to contain the negative stories.

But that approach is out of date. It ignores the power of social media to spread negative stories and it ignores the fact that there is a section of the international media dedicated to amplifying these negative stories, not to provide a balanced view of Sweden but to discredit the country's values. You can no longer contain negative stories and if you care about Sweden's reputation you shouldn't even want to. That may sound counter-intuitive but as I mentioned earlier, Good Sweden's finely-polished, one-dimensional, picture-perfect image makes it disproportionately vulnerable to negative news. Larger countries, such as Germany, the UK or the US have such stratified reputations, with complex, overlapping layers of good and bad, that it is almost impossible for one domestic story to make a significant impact on their reputations in the short term. It takes something on the scale of Brexit or the Trump Presidency, both seismic international events, to damage the reputations of the UK and the US significantly. But stories from the UK or US equivalent to those in the Bad Sweden narrative wouldn't have any effect at all on those countries' reputations. A single stain is more noticeable on Sweden's clean reputation. That's why Jimmie Åkesson's article in the Wall Street Journal was so infuriating to Michael Damberg, Sweden's minister for enterprise and innovation and effectively the country's chief salesman: it ruined his pitch.

Remember, the stories which become part of the Bad Sweden narrative generally start as news reports in Sweden before they spread to the international alternative media in a mutated or decontextualised form. The themes are limited, which means that once you've spent some time on Breitbart, it is fairly easy to see which stories are likely to end up there. This provides an opportunity to act before they do. When bad things happen that *might* end up in the international press, get out there early on with a comment and an explanation. When the spotlight is on an issue in Sweden, react quickly to own the issue.

In September 2017 the Sweden Democrats revealed on their Facebook page that Nacka municipality had 'bought three apartments for 13,950,000 SEK for a man with three wives'.[232] This story ticked all the boxes: the money, the special treatment of an immigrant in an extremely tight housing market, the effect on prices in that market when the municipality is buying up properties and, of course, the not uncontroversial matter of a polygamous family in a country where polygamy is illegal and more or less the polar opposite of its feminist values. It would trigger the anger emotion of most people who encountered it and spread like wildfire through social media.

The story took the usual path through Sweden's alternative media outlets[233] and ended up on the Russian news site Sputnik a couple of days later. But by then the mayor of Nacka, Mats Gerdau, had put out his own statement explaining that the man had not been 'given' the apartments. The municipality owned them and the family paid rent. Perhaps most importantly, Gerdau spoke frankly about the matter:

> I am as frustrated as everyone else. We're doing it because we have to. Some say we should ignore the law. Maybe I'm old-fashioned, but I think you should obey existing laws.[234]

This gave Swedish news sites, including my colleagues at The Local, the opportunity to explain the story in a more balanced way: it's the law, nobody was being gifted millions of kronor worth of property, and the politicians involved not only understood but also shared the concerns of the public. By responding personally, Gerdau gave the story nuance and took the sting out of its tail. It was viewed over 12,000 times on Sputnik, but the story didn't make it to any of the big alternative news sites.

Nuance is the enemy of the Bad Sweden narrative, so my suggestion to people who say they share The Local's positive stories in social media is that they should also share the negative stories that we and other news organisations publish.

Politicians: speak to the world

In the days following Donald Trump's 'last night in Sweden' statement, Jimmie Åkesson spoke to the world through the

Wall Street Journal. Not only did he take ownership of one of Sweden's problems on the international stage; he also projected that problem through his own party's lens and put his domestic political opponents on the defensive.

The Swedish government's response to that article hinted at a lack of understanding about the ways of the international media. Why would a newspaper owned by Rupert Murdoch – the proprietor of Fox News, and good friend and weekly advisor to President Trump[235] – tell the Good Sweden story on behalf of the government? Why wait a week to respond? This inward-looking attitude is not unique to Swedes; politicians everywhere tend only to communicate to their own constituency of voters. But Swedish politicians need to start directing more of their communication to the outside world. They need to understand that there's a global discussion taking place in big news sites and in social media and for the sake of Sweden's reputation they need to be a part of it. Not just selling a positive image of the country – leave that to the enterprise minister – but engaging in debate and discussing problems and solutions in an honest and open way. The fact is, Swedes consume international media like never before. Facebook and Reddit (an American news sharing site) are the fourth and fifth most popular web sites in the country,[236] while Omni, a news app used by hundreds of thousands of Swedes, is as likely to link to international news sites as Swedish sites. On the limited number of issues in the Bad Sweden narrative, if politicians want to talk to Swedes they should talk to the world.

But if they are going to do so, they need to learn how and where to tell a story. They need to learn that facts are not enough: the narrative is everything. And I'm not talking about retelling the Good Sweden story. I assume that will continue to be told. No, there needs to be a new response to the alternative narrative. It needs to be anchored in facts, of course, but the 'alternative alternative' must be compelling, surprising and inspiring. It must pack an emotional punch and it must salvage the themes of the Bad Sweden narrative and weave them into a nuanced picture of an increasingly nuanced country. Against this more mature multidimensional backdrop, Sweden's outstanding achievements in all those international rankings will be even more impressive.

But don't be surprised if the Wall Street Journal doesn't run a story from a politician it's never heard of telling a story it doesn't support. Swedish politicians need to work on their personal international brands and build up their followings outside the country. Who wants to become the world media's go-to politician for comment on Scandinavian affairs? Because the role is up for grabs. And it might not be easy but having a recognisable profile will make it a lot easier for politicians to get their voices heard next time the Bad Sweden story starts taking off.

Let the people speak – and amplify their words

Sweden's decision in 2011 to allow a different member of the public to run the country's official Twitter account, @sweden, each week was radical and quite brilliant.[237] The campaign, called 'Curators of Sweden', perfectly encapsulated Swedish democratic values, showcasing everything from the nation's flat society to its openness, trust and the many kinds of people and attitudes here, all in one go. After the initial burst of global press attention – and some controversy from the occasional rogue curator – the account settled into a routine of mundane insights into life in Sweden, pleasant chitchat and misogynistic or racist abuse.* The @sweden account got another shot in the arm thanks to Donald Trump's 'last night in Sweden' comment. To have a member of the public fielding questions from all around the world prompted by the US president was quite unique and no doubt contributed to the generally positive reaction that followed his statement.

Clever and brave though the @sweden concept is, it is nevertheless presented by the Swedish government and this fact in itself reduces the credibility of each curator's voice. Completely independent individuals with a powerful story to tell are more credible. In August 2017 a Croatian sports journalist called Slobodan Mufić used his Facebook page to post an account of his experience registering his 11-year-old daughter in a Swedish school, one year after his family moved to Skövde.

Mufić asked the head of the school what his daughter needed to bring with her. The head said she didn't need to bring anything – she would be provided with books, notebooks, pencils, erasers, rulers and so on. All she had to do was make sure that the battery on her iPad was charged.[238]

Parents: So we have to buy her an iPad?

Head: No, she'll get an iPad at school, to make it easier to translate and study. But she needs to check the battery.

Parents: Do we need to arrange for her to bring food to school?

Head: No need, breakfast is from 7.30, and lunch is at 12.00. Each day we have two menus, meat and vegetarian.

---

* One of the curators was a scientist and writer called Emma Frans. After her week tweeting on behalf of Sweden, she wrote that she was overwhelmed by hateful comments emanating from the far right: 'But this hatred was not directed at me personally. The hatred was targeting Sweden.' (Min vecka i trollskogen, 23 September 2016)

Parents: Do you think we should speak Swedish at home with [our daughter]?

Head: You should talk Croatian at home. And it would be good for her to learn Croatian as native language education.

Parents: Do you have someone who teaches Croatian?

Head: Not in our school, but the Croatian class is held on Thursdays from 16:00 in Eriksdal School.

Parents: That's on the opposite side of town...

Head: No problem, we'll order a cab.

The original post was shared over 2,000 times and attracted more than 11,000 likes, prompting coverage about the Swedish school not only in all the major Croatian media channels but also in Slovenia and other parts of the Balkans.[239] Slobodan told me he was surprised by the way the post spread, but it was completely authentic and independent, just like the tweets and Facebook posts of the thousands of Swedes who responded to Donald Trump's statement.

Another example is the image of a dozen residents of Tensta, one of the areas labelled a no-go zone in Breitbart[240], helping to push a fire engine which had become stuck in a muddy field when dealing with a blaze. The photographer, Erica Heikenborn, posted her image in social media and this too went viral, appearing on many of Sweden's news sites.[241]

We have seen how the emotional reward mechanism of Facebook can turn a regular user into a civic activist and how effective this is for the spread of the Bad Sweden meme. But the same methods can be used to propagate a positive narrative. People like Slobodan and Erica are the new opinion leaders, popping up spontaneously with an authentic story in the right place at the right time. A future 'Curators of Sweden' project should focus on identifying these authentic stories and turbocharging their spread using all the tools that Facebook and other social media platforms offer.

The response to Trump in February 2017 demonstrated that in this connected world, everyone can be an ambassador without even leaving home. This kind of communication will be a major part of Sweden's reputation in future: hundreds of thousands of people equipped with cameras in their mobiles and social media accounts pushing out stories about the country in dozens of languages to friends and family all over the world. When aggregated, these messages will be fair and balanced, a multitude of 'dots' that paint the true picture of the country. As more of these stories reach the world, Sweden's reputation resilience will be strengthened from the ground up.

Bad things will continue to happen in Sweden. Mainstream news outlets will report on these things as they see them. Hyper-partisan news outlets will continue to use them as a stick with which to beat Sweden's reputation. But if there is already a body of nuanced debate and discussion spreading through international news sites and social media, that stick will be brittle.

Conclusion

There will of course be no outright winner in the battle for Sweden's reputation. Instead, the effects will be felt by degrees: it will be easier or harder for Swedish companies to do business abroad, Swedish diplomats will have more or less international influence. And while a person's reputation can collapse overnight with a single sordid revelation, country reputations change slowly, dependent as they are upon many millions of cultural, historical, economic, political and personal touch-points.

The Good Sweden story will continue to be told. As the billions invested in new companies in the last few years starts bearing fruit, more will be invested, attracting more talent to Sweden, creating more momentum and more success. Swedish design and innovation will continue to inspire the world through global consumer brands. And with Swedish authors and musicians as popular as ever, the world will still be fascinated by this country in the north.

On the other hand, the Bad Sweden story is not going to go away, because the forces behind it are committed to their cause, extremely well-financed, well-connected and highly influential. For the foreseeable future, they have no shortage of dots to magnify and no qualms about eliminating the context from their coverage.

This is not a debate in which two sides are arguing over a set of facts. For now, the spheres in which these two narratives are told barely touch each other. Good Sweden is told to Informed Users with their personal knowledge and positive perceptions of Sweden. Bad Sweden targets Resistant Users, whose aesthetic, idealised and shallow notion of Sweden means they are angered by the negative images of this new narrative.

The real struggle is to capture the imagination of the far larger group of Neutral Users and in this, Bad Sweden has the advantage. The themes of the narrative are limited but in their negativity and their contrast to the established image of Sweden they are potent. The Bad Sweden meme effectively exploits the interaction between our psychology and social media, compelling us to share what angers and surprises us and usually without checking whether it's actually true. Meanwhile, the economic trajectory of the traditional news industry means that we get less balanced analysis and more polarising commentary, less locally-sourced news from informed foreign correspondents and more rewrites of other news outlets' interpretations.

In such an environment, local news stories quickly mutate into fuel for the Bad Sweden fire. Balanced local reporting becomes angled by local hyper-partisan news sites and is then fed into their international equivalents. From here, the decontextualised version of the story becomes amplified by more mainstream news organisations and embedded in the digital record by Google and Facebook.

With the menace of fake news and a general breakdown of trust in society added to the mix, it starts to look like Bad Sweden's time has come. I think there are methods of weakening the meme and significantly reducing its viral potential, but the key to these methods is understanding *why* the Bad Sweden narrative has emerged in recent years.

Until 2013, the mainstream international media had been happy to maintain the idea of a Swedish utopia, where highly progressive values combined with economic wisdom to produce a paradise up there in the north. Anyone living here knew that the reality was far more nuanced, but it suited Sweden to push this narrative – which it did, very successfully and with a very Swedish humility. But after a while, success makes humility look like smugness – and smugness will always be attacked. With the gloating coverage of the Husby riots in 2013, perhaps Sweden was paying the price for breaking the law of Jante.*

In the introduction, I said that truth is context. Individual stories in the alternative narrative about Sweden can be factually accurate but without context they portray a false image of the country. This works both ways. If Sweden had been more outwardly communicative about its social problems before 2013 and had woven them into a more nuanced country narrative, then the Husby riots would not have been half the story they were. The riots were shocking because they blew a hole in the world's *idea* of Sweden as a socialist paradise. The fact that there was no socialist paradise was irrelevant.

In the week of the riots we went to Husby, and along with many other Swedish journalists we spoke to residents about the troubles there. We reported that Stockholm was not burning.[242] But as the US and UK issued travel warnings for the city, it was clear that the Bad Sweden meme had already begun to spread.

Soon after that, my colleagues and I first started talking about what appeared to be a campaign to discredit Sweden's

---

* For readers outside of Scandinavia, this is not a real law. Jantelagen is a fictitious set of rules which punish ambition and the notion that anyone is better than anyone else.

reputation in parts of the international media. We saw our own articles being referenced and used to build up this image of a failing Sweden but until President Trump's 'last night in Sweden' comment it was hard to convince people that something was going on without appearing to be conspiracy theorists ourselves.

While the Swedish military and some politicians and civil servants have long been aware of disinformation campaigns targeting the country, Trump's comments suddenly brought the issue to the attention of the public. And a common question following the initial excitement was: why? Why would anyone want to discredit Sweden?

The simple answer is that this country of ten million people matters. Sweden matters because its economy is among the most successful in the world. Sweden matters because of geopolitics. Sweden matters because it is one of the biggest aid donors in the world. Sweden matters because it produces corporate giants in industries as diverse as packaging, music streaming, home furnishings, clothing, telecommunications, home appliances, construction and forestry. And most importantly, Sweden matters because its values are among the most progressive, and therefore the most provocative and controversial, in the world. I say 'most importantly' because it is not just Sweden's reputation that is at stake – the very values that Sweden represents and promotes around the world are under threat.

Husby, Tensta and Rinkeby in Stockholm, along with Rosengård in Malmö and Biskopsgården in Gothenburg are not just 'vulnerable areas' with low socio-economic status and high levels of criminal influence on the community. Like it or not, they have become a symbol of something much bigger.

They have become weapons in a global clash of values. When the relevant Swedish authorities are deciding how much public money to invest in solving the social problems in these areas, their equation should include the damage to Sweden's reputation that will be caused by *not* solving the problem. And they should think about the billions of kronor that are spent on spreading Sweden's progressive values abroad through international aid, and reflect that the greatest threat to the spread of those values could be what's going on just 15 kilometres from the Government Offices in Stockholm.

The name of the game

Decades without challenge enabled Sweden to build a reputation that became its greatest international asset, smoothing the way for its companies and underpinning a formidable diplomatic strength for such a small nation. But the world in which Sweden built its reputation was very different to the one in which it must defend its reputation. It is more complex, more cynical and more unpredictable.

When Sweden was building its spectacular reputation, the name of the game was competitive advantage. But the essence of Sweden's reputation is not its technology or design or unicorns or furniture or pop music: it is its highly progressive values. Now, with aggressive efforts around the world to reverse the spread of those values, Sweden finds itself on the front line. Indeed, the values themselves are being tested, not just by critics abroad but also by severe social challenges at home. That test must be regarded as an opportunity to prove the strength of these values. If the progressive values which Sweden represents really are the best way to run a society, then now is the time to prove it.

One of those values is transparency, which is something to be cherished in an increasingly opaque and untrusting world. When major influencers in the world's media promote a distorted image of Sweden, when a nearby country is said to be behind forged documents fed into the Swedish news flow, when the most powerful man in the world makes misleading statements about Sweden and when reasonable people everywhere know so little about the country that they believe the myths, one thing is clear: we have begun a new chapter in the story of Sweden.

Acknowledgement

Thanks to the journalists of The Local whose work has informed this book. Thanks to our commercial colleagues and investors who understand the value of news. And thanks to our millions of knowledgeable readers, whose deep interest in the countries of Europe is inspiring.

References

(Endnotes)

1   OECD Pisa Results by Country: http://www.oecd.org/pisa/ retrieved 5 July 2017

2   Why rightwingers are desperate for Sweden to fail: https://www.theguardian.com/commentisfree/2017/apr/14/rightwingers-sweden-fail-terrorists retrieved 10 September 2017

3   https://en.wikipedia.org/wiki/Swedish_Air_Force retrieved 10 September 2017

4   Den svenska atombomben: https://www.nyteknik.se/energi/den-svenska-atombomben-6421374 retrieved 10 September 2017

5   Swedish Armed Forces cuts troops and bases: https://www.thelocal.se/20100306/25378 retrieved 10 September 2017

6   Sweden stations permanent troops on Baltic Sea island: https://www.thelocal.se/20160914/sweden-stations-permanent-troops-on-baltic-sea-island retrieved 10 September 2017

7   Ingen julbelysning I småorter till advent: https://www.svt.se/nyheter/lokalt/jonkoping/ingen-julbelysning-i-smaorter-till-advent retrieved 10 July 2017

8   Sweden bans Christmas lights on state-owned poles: http://speisa.com/modules/articles/index.php/item.3272/sweden-bans-christmas-lights-on-state-owned-poles.html retrieved 11 July 2017

9   https://twitter.com/speisatweets retrieved 11 July 2017

10   Sweden Bans Christmas Street Lights; To Avoid Offending Muslim Migrants?: https://www.infowars.com/sweden-bans-christmas-street-lights-to-avoid-offending-muslim-migrants/ retrieved 11 July 2017

11   Sweden Bans Christmas Lights In Public To Avoid Angering Muslim Refugees?: https://milo.yiannopoulos.net/2016/10/sweden-ban-christmas-lights/ retrieved 11 July 2017

12   https://www.facebook.com/myiannopoulos/ retrieved 11 September 2017

13   Sweden No Longer Celebrating Christmas: Bans Holiday For Fear Of Offending Muslim Migrants https://www.morningnewsusa.com/sweden-no-longer-celebrating-christmas-bans-holiday-fear-offending-muslim-migrants-23116514.html retrieved 11 July 2017

14   Lights Öff!: http://www.snopes.com/sweden-bans-christmas-lights/ retrieved 11 July 2017

15   July 2017

16   Polisen: tre döda i misstänkt terrordåd: https://www.svt.se/nyheter/lokalt/stockholm/uppgifter-fordon-pa-drottninggatan-personer-skadade retrieved 11 July 2017

17   Stockholm man shot dead by police: https://www.thelocal.se/20130514/47872 retrieved 26 July 2017

18   Youths burn 100 cars in north Stockholm riots: https://www.thelocal.se/20130520/48006 retrieved 26 July 2017

19   Youths burn 100 cars in north Stockholm riots: https://www.thelocal.se/20130520/48006 retrieved 26 July 2017

20   Thirty fires in third night of Stockholm riots: https://www.thelocal.se/20130522/48050 retrieved 26 July 2017

21   https://en.wikipedia.org/wiki/2013_Stockholm_riots retrieved 26 July 2017

22   Stockholm riots leave Sweden's dreams of perfect society up in smoke: http://www.telegraph.co.uk/news/worldnews/europe/sweden/10080320/Stockholm-riots-leave-Swedens-dreams-of-perfect-society-up-in-smoke.html retrieved 26 July 2017

23   Riots in Sweden: Fire in the people's home: https://www.ft.com/
content/ddbcd180-c44c-11e2-bc94-00144feab7de retrieved 26 July 2017

24   The Swedish riots: what really happened: http://www.newstatesman.
com/economics/2013/06/swedish-riots-what-really-happened retrieved 26
July 2017

25   https://en.wikipedia.org/wiki/2005_French_riots retrieved 26 July
2017

26   https://en.wikipedia.org/wiki/2011_England_riots retrieved 26 July
2017

27   Sweden in flames: As gangs of migrants riot for five nights running...
the Utopian boats of a multicultural success story turn to ashes: http://
www.dailymail.co.uk/news/article-2330247/Sweden-flames-As-gangs-
migrants-riot-nights-running--Utopian-boats-multicultural-success-
story-turn-ashes.html retrieved 26 July 2017

28   Riots Erupt in Sweden: the Nordic Welfare Myth?: http://www.cnbc.
com/id/100757907 retrieved 26 July 2017

29   Stockholm riots challenge image of happy, generous state: http://
www.reuters.com/article/us-sweden-riots/stockholm-riots-challenge-
image-of-happy-generous-state-idUSBRE94L1BW20130522 26 July 2017

30   Stockholm is burning: why the Swedish riots bode ill for Europe:
http://theweek.com/articles/463981/stockholm-burning-why-swedish-
riots-bode-ill-europe retrieved 26 July 2017

31   Fire and fury in Sweden as riots spread: http://www.independent.
co.uk/news/world/europe/fire-and-fury-in-sweden-as-riots-
spread-8632374.html retrieved 26 July 2017

32   A blazing surprise: http://www.economist.com/news/
europe/21578725-scandinavian-idyll-disrupted-arson-and-unrest-blazing-
surprise retrieved 26 July 2017

33   Swedish riots: if instability can happen here, what might unfold
elsewhere?: http://www.guardian.co.uk/commentisfree/2013/may/27/
swedish-riots-inequality-stockholm retrieved 26 July 2017

34   Vaktbolag ratar Husby – upphandling försenas: https://mitti.se/
nyheter/vagar-vakta-husby/ retrieved 10 September 2017

35   Swedish Businesses Helpless as Security Firms Refuse to Work in
No-Go Zone: http://www.breitbart.com/london/2017/08/28/swedish-
businesses-helpless-security-firms-refuse-work-no-go-zone/ retrieved 10
September 2017

36   Meeting between Swedish and Norwegian ministers scrapped
following 'no-go zone' claims: https://www.thelocal.no/20170829/meeting-
between-swedish-and-norwegian-ministers-scrapped-following-no-go-
zone-claims retrieved 10 September 2017

37   Listhaug bekymret for Oslo, men avviser «svenske tilstander»: https://
www.dn.no/nyheter/2017/08/30/1616/Politikk/listhaug-bekymret-for-oslo-
men-avviser-svenske-tilstander retrieved 10 September 2017

38   https://twitter.com/carlbildt/status/833219648044855296 retrieved 11
September 2017

39   'Sweden, who would believe this?': Trump cites non-existent terror
attack: https://www.theguardian.com/us-news/2017/feb/19/sweden-trump-
cites-non-existent-terror-attack retrieved 11 September 2017

40   What the US could learn from Sweden's refugee crisis: http://video.
foxnews.com/v/5327830979001/ retrieved 11 September 2017

41   Six claims and facts about Sweden: a closer look at Ami Horowitz'
report: https://www.thelocal.se/20170220/sweden-facts-a-closer-look-at-
filmmaker-ami-horowitz-claims retrieved 26 July 2017

42   https://en.wikipedia.org/wiki/List_of_countries_by_intentional_
homicide_rate retrieved 8 October 2017

43   So… are they no-go zones? What you need to know about Sweden's
vulnerable areas: https://www.thelocal.se/20170621/no-go-zones-what-
you-need-to-know-about-swedens-vulnerable-aeas / Police: There
are no 'no-go zones' in Sweden: http://sverigesradio.se/sida/artikel.
aspx?programid=2054&artikel=6630452 retrieved 26 July 2017

44   Swedish police featured in Fox News segment: Filmmaker is a
madman: http://www.dn.se/kultur-noje/nyheter/swedish-police-featured-
in-fox-news-segment-filmmaker-is-a-madman/ retrieved 26 July 2017

45   https://twitter.com/SwedeninUSA/status/833462568257732612
retrieved 24 September 2017

46   Data from Twitter, according to the embassy.

47   'Challenging the Swedish Social State: the case of Dwight David Eisenhower' – Fredrick Hale, Swedish-American Historical Quarterly, 2003 (North Park University)

48   https://en.wikipedia.org/wiki/Sweden:_the_Middle_Way retrieved 26 July 2017

49   Sweden: Still The Middle Way? Talk given by Per T Ohlsson: http://www.columbia.edu/cu/swedish/events/fall06/PTOChilds92806Web.doc retrieved 3 September 2017

50   Sin & Sweden: https://content.time.com/time/magazine/article/0,9171,861357,00.html retrieved 26 July 2017

51   Challenging the Swedish Social State: the case of Dwight David Eisenhower – Fredrick Hale, Swedish-American Historical Quarterly, 2003 (North Park University)

52   10 Swedish Myths Uncovered: https://sweden.se/culture-traditions/10-swedish-myths-uncovered/ retrieved 27 July 2017

53   https://en.wikipedia.org/wiki/List_of_countries_by_suicide_rate retrieved 27 July 2017

54   Challenging the Swedish Social State: the case of Dwight David Eisenhower – Fredrick Hale, Swedish-American Historical Quarterly, 2003 (North Park University)

55   Data: https://tradingeconomics.com/sweden/government-spending-to-gdp retrieved 11 September 2017

56   Forbes Best Countries for Business: https://www.forbes.com/places/sweden/ retrieved 27 July 2017

57   European Innovation Scoreboard 2017: https://ec.europa.eu/growth/industry/innovation/facts-figures/scoreboards_en retrieved 27 July 2017

58   Transparency International Corruption Perceptions Index 2016: https://www.transparency.org/news/feature/corruption_perceptions_index_2016 retrieved 27 July 2017

59   World Economic Forum Global Gender Gap Report 2016: http://reports.weforum.org/global-gender-gap-report-2016/ economies/#economy=SWE retrieved 27 July 2017

60   Henley & Partners Visa Rstrictions Index: http://visaindex.com/ retrieved 27 July 2017

61   https://www.usnews.com/news/best-countries/immigrants-full-list retrieved 9 September 2017

62   Global AgeWatch: http://www.helpage.org/global-agewatch/ population-ageing-data/global-rankings-table/ retrieved 27 July 2017

63   World Happiness Report 2017: http://worldhappiness.report/wp-content/uploads/sites/2/2017/03/HR17.pdf retrieved 27 July 2017

64   EF English Proficiency Index: http://media2.ef.com/__/~/media/ centralefcom/epi/downloads/full-reports/v6/ef-epi-2016-english.pdf retrieved 27 July 2017

65   Stockholm: the Unicorn Factory: https://www.ft.com/content/ e3c15066-cd77-11e4-9144-00144feab7de retrieved 9 September 2017

66   Foreign Aid: These countries are the most generous: https://www. weforum.org/agenda/2016/08/foreign-aid-these-countries-are-the-most-generous/ retrieved 9 September 2017

67   Data: https://data.oecd.org/oda/net-oda.htm#indicator-chart recovered 9 September 2017

68   Why Sweden beats other countries at just about everything: https:// www.weforum.org/agenda/2017/01/why-sweden-beats-most-other-countries-at-just-about-everything/ retrieved 11 September 2017

69   2017 Country Reptrak® – Most Reputable Countries: https://www. reputationinstitute.com/Resources/Registered/PDF-Resources/2017-Country-RepTrak-Most-Reputable-Countries.aspx retrieved 25 August 2017

70   Country Brand Index 2014-2015: http://www.futurebrand.com/ uploads/CBI2014-5.pdf retrieved 27 July 2017

71 Analysis: Why Trump's false claims are bad news for Sweden: https://
www.thelocal.se/20170220/analysis-why-trumps-false-claims-are-bad-
news-for-sweden retrieved 29 July 2017

72 World Values Survey: http://www.worldvaluessurvey.org/
WVSContents.jsp retrieved 27 July 2017

73 Chart recreated by author based on Inglehart and Welzel's original
chart.

74 Swedes tell Chinese: 'We are not Swiss': https://www.thelocal.
se/20131101/swedes-tell-chinese-we-are-not-swiss retrieved 27 July 2017

75 Data: https://www.migrationsverket.se/
download/18.585fa5be158ee6bf362fd5/1485556063080/
Application+for+asylum+received+2000-2016.pdf retrieved 28 July 2017

76 Att ta emot människor på flykt: http://www.regeringen.se/493c42/
contentassets/e8c195d35dea4c05a1c952f9b0b45f38/att-ta-emot-manniskor-
pa-flykt-sou-201712-hela retrieved 28 July 2017

77 Att ta emot människor på flykt: http://www.regeringen.se/493c42/
contentassets/e8c195d35dea4c05a1c952f9b0b45f38/att-ta-emot-manniskor-
pa-flykt-sou-201712-hela retrieved 28 July 2017

78 'Sverige är en humanitär stormakt.'
Utrikesdeklaration 2013 http://www.regeringen.se/49b753/
contentassets/3f435e49030a4954a799aa5d8e044c9a/regeringens-
deklaration-vid-2013-ars-utrikespolitiska-debatt-i-riksdagen-onsdagen-
den-13-februari-2013

79 Interview with Radio Sweden 18 February 2015 http://sverigesradio.
se/sida/artikel.aspx?programid=2054&artikel=6091340

80 Sweden steps up push for EU refugee sharing: https://www.thelocal.
se/20151104/sweden-steps-up-push-for-eu-refugee-help retrieved 11
September 2017

81 Even Europe's humanitarian superpower is turning its back on
refugees: https://www.washingtonpost.com/world/europe/even-sweden-
is-turning-its-back-on-refugees/2015/12/30/6d7e8454-a405-11e5-8318-
bd8caed8c588_story.html?utm_term=.278ff495fb5a retrieved 10 September
2017

82   'There's great respect for the Swedish model': https://www.thelocal. se/20170118/theres-great-respect-for-the-swedish-model retrieved 10 September 2017

83   Flyktinginvandring och kommunal kostnadsutjämning, Statskontoret 2016

84   Data: https://www.migrationsverket.se/download/ 18.585fa5be158ee6bf362fd5/1485556063080/ Application+for+asylum+received+2000-2016.pdf retrieved 28 July 2017

85   Every Last Girl, 2016, Save The Children http://www.savethechildren. org/atf/cf/%7B9def2ebe-10ae-432c-9bd0-df91d2eba74a%7D/EVERY%20 LAST%20GIRL%20REPORT%20FINAL.PDF

86   Breitbart News Network: Born In The USA, Conceived In Israel: http://www.breitbart.com/big-journalism/2015/11/17/breitbart-news-network-born-in-the-usa-conceived-in-israel/ retrieved 26 July 2017

87   How Donald Trump's New Campaign Chief Created an Online Haven for White Nationalists: http://www.motherjones.com/ politics/2016/08/stephen-bannon-donald-trump-alt-right-breitbart-news/ retrieved 28 July 2017

88   https://en.wikipedia.org/wiki/Alt-right retrieved 30 September 2017

89   How Sweden Became 'The Most Alt-Right' Country In Europe: https://www.buzzfeed.com/lesterfeder/how-sweden-became-the-most-alt-right-country-in-europe?utm_term=.axYP61P24#.xrEnYMnv9 retrieved 28 July 2017

90   Wear a Headscarf Or Be Raped, Swedish Women Warned: http:// www.breitbart.com/london/2016/07/14/wear-headscarf-or-be-raped-swedish-women-warned/ retrieved 28 July 2017

91   Sweden So Violent, Migrants Consider Moving Back To War-Zone Homelands: http://www.breitbart.com/london/2016/09/23/sweden-violent-somali-moving-back/ retrieved 28 July 2017

92   Scared Sweden: Almost Half Of Women 'Afraid' To Be Out After Dark In Europe's Rape Capital: http://www.breitbart.com/ london/2016/03/04/scared-sweden-almost-half-of-women-afraid-to-be-out-after-dark-in-europes-rape-capital/ retrieved 28 July 2017

93   Sweden 'Facing Collapse' Thanks To Migrant Influx, Foreign Minister Warns: http://www.breitbart.com/london/2015/10/31/sweden-facing-collapse-thanks-migrant-influx-foreign-minister-warns/ retrieved 28 July 2017

94   Swedish PM to Force Priests to Conduct Gay Marriages, Compares them With Abortions: http://www.breitbart.com/london/2017/06/24/swedish-pm-wants-force-priests-marry-sex-couples/ retrieved 11 September 2017

95   Christian Preschoolers Banned from Saying 'Amen', Talking About the Bible: http://www.breitbart.com/london/2017/06/26/christian-preschool-banned-saying-amen/ retrieved 11 September 2017

96   Number of Swedish Children Wanting to Change Gender Doubling Each Year: http://www.breitbart.com/london/2017/03/15/swedish-children-gender-double-year/ retrieved 11 September 2017

97   Breitbart reveals owners: CEO Larry Solov, the Mercer family and Susie Breitbart: http://www.politico.com/blogs/on-media/2017/02/breitbart-reveals-owners-ceo-larry-solov-mercer-family-and-susie-breitrbart-235358 retrieved 28 July 2017

98   What Kind of Man Spends Millions to Elect Ted Cruz?: https://www.bloomberg.com/news/features/2016-01-20/what-kind-of-man-spends-millions-to-elect-ted-cruz- retrieved 28 July 2017

99   Breitbart News #45 Most Trafficked U.S. Website, Beats HuffPo, WaPo, FoxNews; 2 Billion Pageviews in 2016: http://www.breitbart.com/big-journalism/2017/01/09/breitbart-news-45-trafficked-u-s-website-beats-huffpo-wapo-foxnews-2-billion-pageviews-2016/ retrieved 11 September 2017

100   What They're Not Telling You About Sweden: https://www.infowars.com/what-theyre-not-telling-you-about-sweden/ retrieved 11 September 2017

101   Suicide Of Sweden: Only One In Five Foreign Rapists Are Deported: https://www.infowars.com/suicide-of-sweden-only-one-in-five-foreign-rapists-are-deported/ retrieved 11 September 2017

102   Europe's Civil War Breaks Out: The Battle for Stockholm's Train Station — Overrun, Occupied by Muslim Migrants: https://pamelageller.com/2016/01/europes-civil-war-breaks.html/ retrieved 11 September 2017

103   Donald Trump Praises Leading Conspiracy Theorist Alex Jones And His 'Amazing' Reputation: https://www.mediamatters.org/blog/2015/12/02/donald-trump-praises-leading-conspiracy-theoris/207181 retrieved 28 July 2017

104   Conspiracy Theorist Alex Jones Says President-Elect Trump Called To 'Thank' His Audience: https://www.mediamatters.org/blog/2016/11/14/conspiracy-theorist-alex-jones-says-president-elect-trump-called-thank-his-audience/214424 retrieved 28 July 2017

105   https://www.facebook.com/InfoWars-80256732576/ retrieved 11 September 2017

106   https://www.facebook.com/pamelageller/ retrieved 11 September 2017

107   https://www.facebook.com/dn.se/ retrieved 11 September 2017

108   https://www.facebook.com/aftonbladet/ retrieved 11 September 2017

109   https://en.wikipedia.org/wiki/Daily_Express retrieved 29 July 2017

110   Daily Express Media Pack: http://www.northernandshell.co.uk.s3.amazonaws.com/media/static-files/nsplus/Daily-Express-Media-Pack-2015.pdf retrieved 30 September 2017

111   SWEDEN CRUMBLING: Demands For Military Intervention As Thugs Turn Malmo Into 'No-Go Zone': http://www.express.co.uk/news/world/755997/Sweden-Malmo-military-intervention-no-go-zone-crime-surge retrieved 11 September 2017

112   Battlefield Sweden: Police Admit Malmo Isn't Safe As Thugs Send Fireworks Into Crowds: http://www.express.co.uk/news/world/749735/Sweden-police-malmo-not-safe-NYE-thugs-grenade-attack retrieved 11 September 2017

113   Nigel Farage Warns Sweden's Crisis Is Being 'COVERED UP' By 'POLITICALLY CORRECT' Media: http://www.express.co.uk/news/world/771303/Nigel-Farage-Sweden-crisis-covered-up-politically-correct-media retrieved 11 September 2017

114   SWEDEN MAYHEM: Police find HAND GRENADE in crisis-hit 'no-go zone' after deadly shooting: http://www.express.co.uk/news/world/771405/Malmo-Sweden-hand-grenade-migrant-Kronobord-shooting retrieved 11 September 2017

115   SWEDEN AT BREAKING POINT: Police make urgent plea for help as violent crime spirals: http://www.express.co.uk/news/world/759946/Swedish-violence-crime-police-urgent-plea-malm-Rosengard retrieved 11 September 2017

116   LAWLESS SWEDEN: Violent migrant youths turn shopping centre into 'NO-GO ZONE' – officials: http://www.express.co.uk/news/world/754126/Violent-migrant-gangs-Swedish-shopping-centre-no-go-zone-Gothenburg retrieved 11 September 2017

117   https://en.wikipedia.org/wiki/Daily_Express retrieved 11 September 2017

118   Daily Express owner Richard Desmond hands Ukip £1m: https://www.theguardian.com/politics/2015/apr/16/daily-express-owner-richard-desmond-ukip-donation retrieved 11 September 2017

119   Discovering Sweden's trendy city Malmö by kayak: http://www.express.co.uk/travel/shortbreaks/804074/Sweden-Malmo-travel-trendy-holiday-kayak retrieved 29 July 2017

120   Data: https://www.abc.org.uk/Certificates/4841286I.pdf retrieved 29 July 2017

121   How Europe's Most Liberal Nation Gagged Its Own People On Migration Attacks: The Swedish Conspiracy To Hide The Truth About The Refugee Influx: http://www.dailymail.co.uk/news/article-3477510/Migrant-attacks-conspiracy-hide-truth-Europe-s-liberal-country-Sweden-stopped-citizens-discussing-refugee-influx.html retrieved 29 July 2017

122   Women Are Warned Not To Go Out Alone At Night In Swedish Town After Multiple Sex Attacks By 'Foreigners': http://www.dailymail.co.uk/news/article-3481882/Women-warned-not-night-Swedish-town-multiple-sex-attacks-foreigners retrieved 29 July 2017

123   EXCLUSIVE – The Lawless Asylum Centre Where Migrants Rule: Inside Squalid Swedish Shelter That Police Will Not Enter, Where 10-Year-Old Boy Was Raped And That Has Just TWO Staff On Duty For 600 Refugees: http://www.dailymail.co.uk/news/article-3425640/The-lawless-asylum-centre-migrants-rule-Inside-squalid-shelter-ten-year-old-boy-raped-police-not-enter-just-TWO-staff-duty-600-refugees.html retrieved 29 July 2017

124   Was Trump Right About Sweden? As The President Is Mocked For His Remarks On Swedish Crime And Immigration, ANDREW MALONE Provides A Disturbing Dispatch From One Of The World's Most PC Nations: http://www.dailymail.co.uk/news/article-4258014/Was-Trump-right-Sweden.html retrieved 29 July 2017

125   Where Females Fear To Tread: KATIE HOPKINS Reports From Sweden, The Scandi-Lib Paradise Where Terrified Women Have Vanished From The Streets And A Conspiracy Of Silence And Self-Censorship On Immigration Buries The Truth: http://www.dailymail.co.uk/news/article-4269576/KATIE-HOPKINS-reports-Scandi-lib-paradise-Sweden.html retrieved 29 July 2017

126   'Daily Mail running migrant campaign against Sweden': https://www.thelocal.se/20160227/daily-mail-runs-campaign-against-sweden retrieved 29 July 2017

127   LBC boosts national audience by 18 per cent to over 2m – full breakdown of UK radio station audience figures: http://www.pressgazette.co.uk/lbc-boosts-national-audience-by-18-per-cent-to-over-2m-full-breakdown-of-uk-radio-station-audience-figures/ retrieved 5 August 2017

128   Nigel Farage: 'Malmo Is Now The Rape Capital Of Europe': http://www.lbc.co.uk/radio/presenters/nigel-farage/nigel-farage-malmo-sweden-rape-capital-of-europe/ retrieved 5 August 2017

129   https://twitter.com/nigel_farage/status/833793147729756161?lang=en retrieved 11 September 2017

130   Sweden: Rape Capital of the West: https://www.gatestoneinstitute.org/5195/sweden-rape retrieved 31 July 2017

131   https://www.gatestoneinstitute.org/about/ retrieved 31 July 2017

132   https://trends.google.com/trends/explore?date=today%20
5-y&q=sweden%20rape retrieved 31 July 2017

133   Why Sweden is NOT 'the rape capital of the world': https://www.
thelocal.se/20170221/why-sweden-is-not-the-rape-capital-of-the-world
retrieved 2 September 2017

134   Crime in Sweden – the difficulties in making international
comparisons: http://www.bra.se/bra-in-english/home/crime-and-
statistics/international-comparisons.html retrieved 2 September 2017

135   Personer misstänkta för brott, ålder och
brottstyp, år 2007-2016: http://www.bra.se/
download/18.5484e1ab15ad731149e3a85a/1505211890381/10La_mp_fr2007.xlsx

136   Crime trends in Sweden until 2015: http://www.bra.se/
download/18.1588ea4815b8a06a27c3826/1493811737077/Crime_trends_in_
Sweden_until_2015_-_In_brief.pdf

137   Violence against women survey: http://fra.europa.eu/en/
publications-and-resources/data-and-maps/survey-data-explorer-violence-
against-women-survey retrieved 31 July 2017

138   Violence against women survey: http://fra.europa.eu/sites/default/
files/fra-2014-vaw-survey-at-a-glance-oct14_en.pdf retrieved 2 September
2017

139   'Lögner sprids om våldtäkter och invandring': https://www.svd.se/
logner-sprids-om-valdtakter-och-invandring ; Heberlein: Vi behöver
veta mer om våldtäktsmännen: https://www.svd.se/heberlein-vi-behover-
veta-mer-om-valdtaktsmannen ; 'Varför bortse från allt vi redan vet om
våldtäkter?': https://www.svd.se/varfor-bortse-fran-allt-vi-redan-vet-om-
valdtakter retrieved 16 October 2017;

140   Brottsplats Nordstan – så ser vardagen ut: http://www.expressen.se/
gt/droger-och-valdsbrott--ny-vardag-i-nordstan/ retrieved 2 August 2017

141   Laglöst land på galleria I Göteborg: http://avpixlat.info/2017/01/15/
laglost-land-pa-galleria-i-goteborg/ retrieved 2 August 2017

142   Avpixlat blir Samhällsnytt: http://sverigesradio.se/sida/artikel.
aspx?programid=101&artikel=6770202 retrieved 10 September 2017

143   http://avpixlat.info/om-avpixlat/ retrieved 2 August 2017

144   Leading Swedish mall turned into 'no-go zone' by migrant teen gangs – report: https://www.rt.com/news/373853-sweden-no-go-zones-gangs/ retrieved 2 August 2017

145   https://www.rt.com/about-us/ retrieved 11 September 2017

146   Sweden's leading shopping mall is deemed a no-go zone, with police blaming gangs of unaccompanied minors who have arrived in the country for spate of attacks: http://www.dailymail.co.uk/news/article-4125726/Sweden-s-leading-shopping-mall-deemed-no-zone.html retrieved 2 August 2017

147   https://www.google.com/search?q=gothenburg+nordstan searched July 2017

148   Marketing: 47 Facebook Statistics for 2016: https://www.brandwatch.com/blog/47-facebook-statistics-2016/ retrieved 3 August 2017

149   The Decline of Organic Facebook Reach & How to Outsmart the Algorithm: https://blog.hubspot.com/marketing/facebook-declining-organic-reach retrieved 23 August 2017

150   The Reclusive Hedge-Fund Tycoon Behind the Trump Presidency: http://www.newyorker.com/magazine/2017/03/27/the-reclusive-hedge-fund-tycoon-behind-the-trump-presidency retrieved 2 September 2017

151   The Mercers and Stephen Bannon: How a populist power base was funded and built: https://www.washingtonpost.com/graphics/politics/mercer-bannon/ retrieved 2 September 2017

152   Nigel Farage: President Trump and I Are 'Probably the Two Most Vilified People in the West': http://time.com/4697883/nigel-farage-donald-trump-bbc/ retrieved 2 September 2017

153   Express owner Richard Desmond gives UKIP £1m http://www.bbc.com/news/election-2015-32340976 retrieved 2 September 2017

154   Meet The Right-Wing Ex-Muslim Who Wants To Save UKIP: https://www.buzzfeed.com/jimwaterson/raheem-kassam-ukip?utm_term=.xnpwq4wd6#.dexa4RaAq retrieved 2 September 2017

155   http://www.efddgroup.eu/ retrieved 2 September 2017

156   Trump Is Right: Sweden's Embrace of Refugees Isn't Working: https://www.wsj.com/articles/trump-is-right-swedens-embrace-of-refugees-isnt-working-1487807010 retrieved 9 September 2017

157   Justitieministern: Sverigedemokraterna ljuger i debattartikeln: http://www.aftonbladet.se/a/9a3wp retrieved 9 September 2017

158   Minister blasts Sweden Democrats' Wall Street Journal op-ed: 'They're lying about Sweden': https://www.thelocal.se/20170223/minister-morgan-johansson-blasts-sweden-democrats-wall-street-journal-op-ed-theyre-lying-about-sweden retrieved 9 September 2017

159   Sweden and Immigrants Mostly Get On Well: https://www.wsj.com/articles/sweden-and-immigrants-mostly-get-on-well-1488404814 retrieved 9 September 2017

160   Sweden Politicians: Trump was right: https://pamelageller.com/2017/02/trump-is-right-sweden.html/

161   Sweden's Anti-Mass Migration Leader in Wall Street Journal: 'Trump Is Right': http://www.breitbart.com/london/2017/02/23/swedens-anti-mass-migration-leader-in-wall-street-journal-trump-is-right/ retrieved 9 September 2017

162   The Selfish Gene, 1976 – Richard Dawkins

163   Russia: 'Good news day' decimates website's readership: http://www.bbc.com/news/blogs-news-from-elsewhere-30318261 retrieved 9 August 2017

164   Do You Want the Good News or the Bad News First? The Nature and Consequences of News Order Preferences (Angela Legg & Kate Sweeny, Personality and Social Psychology Bulletin, 2013)

165   Bad is Stronger Than Good (Baumeister, Bratslavsky, Finkenauer & Vohs, Review of General Psychology 2001)

166   A Psychophysiological Examination of Cognitive Processing of and Affective Responses

to Social Expectancy Violations (Bruce Bartholow, Monica Fabiani, Gabriele Gratton, B. Ann Bettencourt, Psychological Science Vol. 12 No. 3, 2001)

167   As explained in fascinating detail by Daniel Kahneman in Thinking, Fast and Slow, 2011

168   Elaine Fox, Victoria Lester, Riccardo Russo, R.J. Bowles, Alessio Pichler & Kevin Dutton (2000): Facial Expressions of Emotion: Are Angry Faces Detected More Efficiently?, Cognition & Emotion, 14:1, 61-92

169   Finding the Face in the Crowd: An Anger Superiority Effect Christine H. Hansen and Ranald D. Hansen (Journal of Personal and Social Psychology, 1988)

170   Drunken elk rescued from Swede's apple tree: https://www.thelocal.se/20110907/36002 retrieved 11 September 2017

171   What Makes Online Content Viral? Jonah Berger and Katherine Milkman (Journal of Marketing Research, Vol XLIX 2012)

172   Arousal Increases Social Transmission of Information, Jonah Berger (Psychological Science, 2011)

173   Posting, commenting and tagging: Effects of sharing news stories on Facebook (Anne Oeldorf-Hirsch, S. Shyam Sundar, Computers in Human Behaviour, 2014)

174   Talking about others: Emotionality and the dissemination of social information (Peters, Kashima & Clark, European Journal of Social Psychology, 2009)

175   Emotion in Social Relations: Cultural, group and interpersonal processes (Parkinson, Fischer, Manstead, 2005)

176   Pew Research Center Newspapers Factsheet: http://www.journalism.org/fact-sheet/newspapers/ retrieved 17 August 2017

177   Institutet för Mediestudiers årliga mätning av reklamintäkterna till samhällsjournalistik, 2017

178   Pew Research Center using Bureau of Labor Statistics' Occupational Employment Statistics: http://www.journalism.org/fact-sheet/newspapers/

179   Plummeting Newspaper Ad Revenue Sparks New Wave of Changes: https://www.wsj.com/articles/plummeting-newspaper-ad-revenue-sparks-new-wave-of-changes-1476955801 retrieved 17 August 2017

180   2016 Round-Up: 74 journalists killed worldwide: https://rsf.org/en/
news/2016-round-74-journalists-killed-worldwide retrieved 18 August 2017

181   Ledarskribenter mest utsatta för hot: https://www.sjf.se/
nyheter/201606/ledarskribenter-mest-utsatta-for-hot retrieved 18 August
2017

182   In particular I recommend 'Post Truth: the new war on truth and
how to fight back' by Matthew D'Ancona (2017) and Post-Truth: How
bullshit conquered the world' by James Ball (2017). For a Swedish take on
the subject, see 'Alternativa Fakta: om kunskapen och dess fiender' by Åsa
Wikforss (2017)

183   https://www.facebook.com/photo.php?fbid=10155015975956062
retrieved 16 September 2017

184   Alternate Reality: Viral Propaganda Chart Demonizes Independent
Media: https://www.infowars.com/alternate-reality-viral-propaganda-
chart-demonizes-independent-media/ retrieved 16 September 2017

185   Russia's strategy for influence through public diplomacy and active
measures: the Swedish case, Martin Kragh and Sebastian Åsberg, Journal
of Strategic Studies, Volume 40, 2017

186   Crime trends in Sweden until 2015: http://www.bra.se/
download/18.1588ea4815b8a06a27c3826/1493811737077/Crime_trends_in_
Sweden_until_2015_-_In_brief.pdf

187   Russia spreading fake news and forged docs in Sweden: report:
https://www.thelocal.se/20170107/swedish-think-tank-details-russian-
disinformation-in-new-study retrieved 17 September 2017

188   'We need to make sure Sweden-Russia relationship is not based on
lies': https://www.thelocal.se/20170221/we-need-to-make-sure-sweden-
and-russias-relationship-is-not-based-on-lies retrieved 17 September 2017

189   Russia mocks Sweden over 'James Bond' conspiracies: https://www.
thelocal.se/20160520/russia-mocks-sweden-over-james-bond-conspiracy-
theory retrieved 17 September 2017

190   'All homosexuals in Sweden may freely come to Russia': https://
www.thelocal.se/20160509/all-homosexuals-in-sweden-may-freely-come-
to-russia retrieved 17 September 2017

191   Åtta av tio svenskar anser att fejknyheter påverkar synen på fakta: http://tu.se/pressmeddelanden/atta-av-tio-svenskar-anser-att-fejknyheter-paverkar-synen-pa-fakta/

192   Så ska vi skydda valrörelsen från andra staters påverkan': http://www.dn.se/debatt/sa-ska-vi-skydda-valrorelsen-fran-andra-staters-paverkan/ retrieved 16 September 2017

193   Sweden's government wants newspapers to pay less tax in an effort to combat fake news: https://www.thelocal.se/20170829/swedens-government-wants-newspapers-to-pay-less-tax-in-an-effort-to-combat-fake-news retrieved 16 September 2017

194   Ryska 'fake news' – en fara för våra länder: http://www.aftonbladet.se/debatt/a/wWv45/ryska-fake-news-en-fara-for-vara-lander retrieved 16 September 2017

195   Åtta av tio svenskar anser att fejknyheter påverkar synen på fakta: http://tu.se/pressmeddelanden/atta-av-tio-svenskar-anser-att-fejknyheter-paverkar-synen-pa-fakta/ retrieved 16 September 2017

196   https://twitter.com/richard_conway/status/886509430283567104 retrieved 11 September 2017

197   6 Boycotting Countries Demand FIFA Strip Qatar of World Cup 2022: https://english.aawsat.com/theaawsat/news-middle-east/6-boycotting-countries-demand-fifa-strip-qatar-world-cup-2022 retrieved 3 September 2017

198   https://www.google.se/search?q=fifa+qatar+boycott+%22The+Local%22 search conducted 3 September 2017

199   Soccer-Boycott nations demand FIFA strips Qatar of 2022 World Cup – report: http://news.trust.org/item/20170715234007-bf8oj retrieved 11 September 2017

200   Boycott nations demand FIFA strips Qatar of 2022 World Cup: report: http://www.smh.com.au/sport/soccer/boycott-nations-demand-fifa-strips-qatar-of-2022-world-cup-report-20170716-gxc46a.html retrieved 11 September 2017

201 How A Hoax Made To Look Like A Guardian Article Made Its Way To Russian Media: https://www.buzzfeed.com/craigsilverman/how-a-hoax-made-to-look-like-a-guardian-article-made-its retrieved 3 September 2017

202 UAB research finds automated voice imitation can fool humans and machines: https://www.uab.edu/news/innovation/item/6532-uab-research-finds-automated-voice-imitation-can-fool-humans-and-machines retrieved 3 September 2017

203 All Your Voices are Belong to Us: http://spies.cs.uab.edu/all-your-voice-are-belong-to-us/ retrieved 3 September 2017

204 Crime trends in Sweden until 2015: http://www.bra.se/download/18.1588ea4815b8a06a27c3826/1493811737077/Crime_trends_in_Sweden_until_2015_-_In_brief.pdf

205 Synthesizing Obama: Learning Lip Sync from Audio (Suwajanakorn, Seitz and Kemelmacher-Shlizerman, ACM Transactions on Graphics, Vol. 36, No. 4, Article 95, 2017): http://grail.cs.washington.edu/projects/AudioToObama/siggraph17_obama.pdf

206 The most and least trusted professions: https://www.aol.co.uk/money/2017/07/17/the-most-and-least-trusted-professions/ retrieved 18 August 2017

207 2017 Edelman Trust Barometer: http://www.edelman.com/global-results/ retrieved 20 August 2017

208 Crime trends in Sweden until 2015: http://www.bra.se/download/18.1588ea4815b8a06a27c3826/1493811737077/Crime_trends_in_Sweden_until_2015_-_In_brief.pdf

209 Svenska Trender 1986-2016, Henrik Ekengren Oscarsson & Annika Bergström (red.) SOM-Institutet, Göteborgs Universitet

210   Mellanmänsklig tillit bygger goda samhällen, Sören Holmberg och
Bo Rothstein, SOM-Institutet, Göteborgs Universitet, 2016: 'För flera
mindre men välfärdspolitiskt utsatta grupper som arbetslösa, personer med
dålig hälsa och utrikes födda, skiljer sig i graden av social tillit klart åt det
lägre hållet. I några fall ökar dessutom skillnaden över tid. Vi tyckte oss
se bilden av ett mer fragmentiserat samhälle träda fram – förstärkt av att
en politisk gruppering också utmärker sig med en klart lägre nivå på den
mellanmänskliga tilliten. Den grupperingen är de som sympatiserar med
Sverigedemokraterna.'

211   This column brought to you by the 'Amazon Washington Post':
https://www.washingtonpost.com/opinions/this-column-brought-to-you-
by-the-amazon-washington-post/2017/07/25/0189b49c-716f-11e7-8839-
ec48ec4cae25_story.html?utm_term=.826cac651dbf retrieved 17 October
2017

212   What to Know About Pizzagate, the Fake News Story With Real
Consequences: http://time.com/4590255/pizzagate-fake-news-what-to-
know/ retrieved 9 September 2017

213   How Swede It Is: http://www.snopes.com/sweden-6-hour-workday/
retrieved 9 September 2017

214   Why Sweden Is Shifting To A 6-Hour Workday: https://www.
fastcompany.com/3051448/why-sweden-is-shifting-to-a-6-hour-work-day
retrieved 9 September 2017

215   Sweden abandons six-hour workday scheme because it's just too
expensive: http://www.telegraph.co.uk/business/2017/01/04/sweden-
abandons-six-hour-workday-scheme-expensive/ retrieved 9 September
2017

216   Swedish Six-Hour Workday Runs Into Trouble: It's Too Costly:
https://www.bloomberg.com/news/articles/2017-01-03/swedish-six-hour-
workday-trial-runs-into-trouble-too-expensive retrieved 9 September 2017

217   The Rise of Fact Checking Sites in Europe (Graves &Cherubini,
2016) http://reutersinstitute.politics.ox.ac.uk/sites/default/files/The%20
Rise%20of%20Fact-Checking%20Sites%20in%20Europe.pdf

218   http://www.lemonde.fr/les-decodeurs/ retrieved 30 September 2017

219   https://www.metro.se/viralgranskaren retrieved 30 September 2017

220   http://www.bbc.com/news/topics/267ada11-b730-4344-b404-63067c032c65/reality-check retrieved 30 September 2017

221   Swedish fake fact-checker page pulled from Facebook: https://www.thelocal.se/20170122/facebook-deleted-swedish-fake-fact-checker-page retrieved 10 Sepetember 2017

222   Om kriget kommer, 1961. Viewed at http://www.skymningslage.se/om-kriget-kommer-1961/

223   New Study Highlights Power of Crowd to Transmit News on Twitter: http://datascience.columbia.edu/new-study-highlights-power-crowd-transmit-news-twitter retrieved 24 September 2017

224   Opinion: The fakers' little lies are eating our brains: https://www.thelocal.se/20170804/opinion-the-fakers-little-lies-are-eating-our-brains retrieved 23 September 2017

225   Skolverket Guide för källkritik: https://www.skolverket.se/skolutveckling/resurser-for-larande/kollakallan/kallkritik/guide-for-kallkritik-1.251678 retrieved 24 September 2017

226   Why this Swedish comic hero is going to teach kids about fake news: https://www.thelocal.se/20170116/why-this-swedish-comic-hero-is-going-to-teach-kids-about-fake-news-bamse retrieved 24 September 2017

227   Utsatta områden – Social ordning, kriminell struktur och utmaningar för polisen, 2017: https://polisen.se/Global/www%20och%20Intrapolis/Ovriga%20rapporter/Utsatta%20omr%C3%A5den%20-%20social%20ordning,%20kriminell%20struktur%20och%20outmaningar%20f%C3%B6r%20polisen.pdf

228   'Especially vulnerable areas' increase in Sweden: report: https://www.thelocal.se/20170612/especially-vulnerable-areas-increase-in-sweden-report retrieved 4 October 2017

229   Polisens rapport om utsatta områden: https://polisen.se/Aktuellt/Nyheter/Gemensam-2017/Juni/Polisens-rapport-om-utsatta-omraden/ retrieved 4 October 2017

230   No-go zone? Here's how one of Sweden's roughest areas edged out its drug gangs: https://www.thelocal.se/20170607/heres-how-one-of-swedens-roughest-areas-edged-out-its-drug-gangs-seved-malmo-crime retrieved 4 October 2017

231   Turning $100M exits into $100B exits: The challenges and opportunities facing Sweden as a tech hub: https://medium.com/startup-grind/turning-100m-exits-into-100b-exits-the-challenges-and-opportunities-facing-sweden-as-a-tech-hub-a3fa6cb20efe retrieved 21 September 2017

232   https://www.facebook.com/SDNacka/photos/a.429788143801075.1073741831.363986787047878/1426409937472219/ retrieved 21 October 2017

233   Kommun köpte tre bostäder för 14 miljoner till nyanländ man med tre fruar: https://samnytt.se/kommun-kopte-tre-bostader-for-14-miljoner-till-nyanland-man-med-tre-fruar/ retrieved 21 October 2017

234   Did a Swedish council buy apartments for a man and his three wives?: https://www.thelocal.se/20170919/did-a-swedish-council-buy-apartments-for-a-man-and-his-three-wives-nacka retrieved 21 October 2017

235   Trump Reaches Beyond West Wing for Counsel: https://www.nytimes.com/2017/04/22/us/politics/donald-trump-white-house.html retrieved 23 September 2017

236   https://www.alexa.com/topsites/countries/SE retrieved 23 September 2017

237   https://twitter.com/sweden retrieved 23 September 2017

238   Croatian family's unexpected Swedish school encounter goes viral: https://www.thelocal.se/20170906/croatian-familys-unexpected-swedish-school-encounter-goes-viral retrieved 23 September 2017

239   Slobodans skolhyllning blev viral – på Balkan: http://www.expressen.se/gt/slobodans-skolhyllning-blev-viral-pa-balkan/ retrieved 23 September 2017

240   WATCH: Journalist Stoned While Trying To Film In Swedish No
Go Zone: http://www.breitbart.com/london/2015/10/27/journalist-stoned-
in-swede-no-go-zone/ retrieved 23 September 2017

241   Viral photo of locals helping firefighters 'shows positive side' of
Stockholm suburb: https://www.thelocal.se/20170320/viral-photo-shows-
locals-helping-firefighters-in-vulnerable-stockholm-suburb-tensta
retrieved 23 September 2017

242   Stockholm's not burning: https://www.thelocal.se/20130524/48126
retrieved 17 September 2017

© Paul Rapacioli and Volante 2018

Volante
Stora Nygatan 7
SE-111 27 Stockholm
Sweden

www.volante.se

Book design: Jonas Lindén
First edition

ISBN 978-91-88659-23-1

CPSIA information can be obtained
at www.ICGtesting.com
Printed in the USA
LVOW08s1432230118
563689LV00001BA/182/P